To Arturo

all the best &
don't forget that
only you could do your
life

Nov. 20 - 2002

PRODUCTION AND OPERATIONS MANAGEMENT

Total Quality and Responsiveness

McGRAW-HILL SERIES IN MANAGEMENT
CONSULTING EDITORS
Fred Luthans
Keith Davis

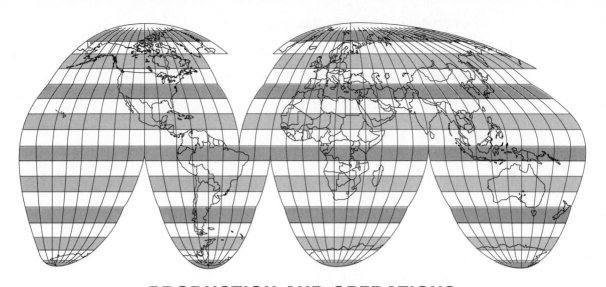

PRODUCTION AND OPERATIONS
MANAGEMENT
Total Quality and Responsiveness

Hamid Noori
Laurier Business School
Wilfrid Laurier University

Russell Radford
Faculty of Management
University of Manitoba

McGRAW-HILL, INC.
New York • St. Louis • San Francisco • Auckland • Bogotá • Caracas
Lisbon • London • Madrid • Mexico City • Milan • Montreal • New Delhi
San Juan • Singapore • Sydney • Tokyo • Toronto

PRODUCTION AND OPERATIONS MANAGEMENT
Total Quality and Responsiveness

 This book is printed on recycled, acid-free paper containing 10% postconsumer waste.

1 2 3 4 5 6 7 8 9 0   DOC   DOC   9 0 9 8 7 6 5 4

P/N 046923-7
PART OF
ISBN 0-07-912037-7

This book was set in Sabon by Ruttle, Shaw & Wetherill, Inc.
The editors were Lynn Richardson and Dan Alpert;
the designer was Joseph A. Piliero;
the production supervisor was Elizabeth J. Strange.
R. R. Donnelley & Sons Company was printer and binder.

Library of Congress Cataloging-in-Publication Data

Noori, Hamid.
    Production and operations management: total quality and
responsiveness / Hamid Noori, Russell Radford.
        p.   cm.
    Includes bibliographical references and index.
    ISBN 0-07-912037-7 (set)
    1. Production management.   2. Total quality management.
I. Radford, Russell W.   II. Title.
TS155.N57   1995
658.5—dc20   94-33821

ABOUT THE AUTHORS

Hamid Noori is Director of the Research Center for Management of Advanced Technology (REMAT) and a Professor of Operations Management at Wilfrid Laurier University in Waterloo, Ontario, Canada. He is also an adjunct professor at the Department of Management Sciences, University of Waterloo. He obtained his Ph.D. in operations research from the University of Western Ontario. His industrial experience includes three years with Nippon Electric Company (NEC) of Japan.

Professor Noori has conducted research for the Natural Sciences and Engineering Research Council of Canada, the National Research Council of Canada, the Social Sciences and Humanities Research Council of Canada, the Manufacturing Research Corporation of Ontario, the Department of Regional Industrial Expansion, and the National Center for Management Research and Development. His research interests include global manufacturing, management of technology, enterprise integration, operations strategy, and materials management. He is the author/co-author of two books and one collection of conference proceedings, several monographs, over 60 papers, and three commercial software packages. He has taught in the United States, Europe, the Middle East, and Southeast Asia and was the recipient of the University Research Professor Award at Wilfrid Laurier University in 1994. He currently serves on the editorial board of several journals.

Professor Noori has been a consultant for public and private organizations and has conducted numerous workshops and seminars for industry in Canada and abroad. He has served as a technology adviser to the government of Canada and has close ties with industry.

Russell Radford teaches operations management in the Faculty of Management at the University of Manitoba. He received his DBA from Harvard Business School. He has worked in the private and public sectors in New Zealand and teaches and consults in Canada and Europe. Dr. Radford has authored/co-authored several publications and teaching cases in the areas of management of technology, operations strategy, and quality management. With Hamid Noori he has one previous book on the management of technology. He teaches operations strategy in executive programs across Canada. His research interests include global operations, fast-response operations, operations strategy, and quality management.

To Annie, Arshia, and Keian
and
To Barbara, Michelle, and Simon

CONTENTS IN BRIEF

CONTENTS

CONTENTS

CONTENTS

CONTENTS

PREFACE

The Batamindo Industrial Park on the Indonesian island of Batam contains only one Indonesian firm. The remainder come from outside the region. Labor and utilities are the only local resources; all raw materials are imported from around the world, and the manufactured products are shipped anywhere in the world. Most products from the park's tenants are used as components for more complex products. An observer would therefore have a hard time distinguishing what would be the country of origin for a product containing components manufactured at Batamindo. Twenty years ago this phenomenon of the "world product" was rare; North American manufacturers were concerned with their major competition, from North America, and foreign products fought for niche markets. Now foreign parts, components, and products are commonplace, and increasing numbers of "local" producers find themselves competing against "global" manufacturers or global products. The local firm now competes against the best in the world and must be responsive to the needs and expectations of customers.

The Batamindo example highlights the impact of operations management within the firm and across its boundaries. Local operations decisions within a firm will have an impact on corporate operations and performance; they will also have an impact on Batamindo Park operations. Thus, operations managers must think globally and act locally, always aware of their impact on corporate effectiveness and competitiveness. This is fundamentally different from the recent philosophy of operations managers being focused internally and letting others manage relationships with the outside world.

OUR FOCUS: THE FAST-RESPONSE ORGANIZATION AND THE NEW MANAGER

This book is designed to prepare students for dealing successfully with challenges posed by an increasingly competitive and time-responsive marketplace. This requires students to understand and accept that competing against the world's best requires a firm to use *all* its resources at their most effective. These resources must therefore be integrated and focused on how best to support the firm's competitive strategy.

We have therefore taken the viewpoint of the operating manager, not merely that of the technician, in developing this book. The operating manager in both manufacturing and service organizations must be capable of conducting and managing complex design, planning, and control activities. In addition, however, operating managers must be capable of making decisions, and that requires an ability to think strategically and to understand *why* and *when* to do something, not just *how*. Every manager should understand the impact of operations on corporate strategy and other elements in the value chain and how to integrate operations effectively into the corporation at all levels. Every manager should also have command of available quantitative tools and techniques. This book has been written and organized to reflect and integrate these two important trends.

We emphasize the context of the leading-edge firm we call the fast-response organization (FRO). An FRO is organized around six dimensions of competition, or competitive drivers:

- Product quality
- Total service support for products and for suppliers and customers
- Product and process flexibility
- The strategic use of time, especially as a value-adding concept
- Costs, primarily in a customer-oriented, net value sense
- Dependability in honoring commitments in the marketplace

These drivers are an integral part of the philosophy underlying *total quality management* (TQM). The strategic implication of the TQM philosophy is that FROs must use all their resources to the fullest, including the capabilities of all employees. This departure from traditional operations management approaches is a distinctive aspect of the book.

ORGANIZATION

The book is organized to meet the needs of the operating manager in the FRO (or in any operating organization). Its five parts correspond to the logical sequence of decisions an operating manager must make when planning and operating a new operating site, line, or piece of equipment; the sequence also applies to evaluating current operations. The book's organization also accommodates the elements of its subtitle—total quality and responsiveness—which are integrated as ongoing themes. The sequence of chapters and topics (many of them not covered in other introductory texts) thus follows a conscious stream of integrated quality decisions that managers must make for effective response to customer needs and expectations.

Part I is dedicated to strategic concerns. As a prelude to this coverage, the Startup Chapter visits six very different but highly successful firms—benchmarks against which the student can test personal concepts of strategy. Chapter 1 offers an analysis of the increasingly competitive environment of the 1990s and a history of the development of the practical and competitive field of operations.

Chapter 2 is in many ways the philosophical center of the book, for the model of the FRO is developed here. This provides the generic context within which the operations strategy can be developed, and Chapter 3 is devoted to a discussion of models for crafting an operations strategy. Chapter 3 emphasizes the true measures of the value of an operations strategy: how effectively it supports the corporate strategy and also how the strategy contributes to attainment of the firm's longer-term goals. The supplement to Chapter 3 deals with the important topic of benchmarking, again from a managerial point of view.

Part II—Chapters 4 to 6—is concerned with that essential component of the corporate and operations strategies, the products to be provided by the firm. Chapter

4 focuses on demand management and forecasting, without which the firm can rarely be effective and can never be efficient.

Chapter 5 treats a topic rarely covered in introductory operations texts, organizing for product design and product quality. The philosophy is one of thinking-in product quality, rather than inspecting-out defective products before they are used by customers. Responsiveness is an important strategic aspect of the new design philosophy, and students will be exposed to tools such as concurrent engineering and the use of advanced technologies in new design processes.

Chapter 6, a discussion of product design, emphasizes the obligation to understand and incorporate customer needs and expectations into the design of the product or service. While concepts of design for manufacture and whole life design are covered, the chapter's main feature is quality function deployment (QFD), a powerful tool for ensuring that critical requirements of the product are included. The treatment of QFD and new approaches to experimental design are dealt with more extensively in the chapter supplement.

Part III—Chapters 7 to 11—covers locating and designing processes that will manufacture the products and deliver the services customers want. Chapter 7 deals with capacity strategies. Once managers are satisfied that the overall capacity strategies are appropriate, they turn to detailed consideration of all the operating facilities the firm will need. These details include how many facilities to have, where to locate them, and what each facility will do. Facility strategies are complex, and the chapter examines the principal qualitative and quantitative factors involved in developing an effective facilities plan.

Once the facilities have been determined, it is necessary to site them and to look inside the facility at the operating layout. Several models for location and layout are presented in Chapter 8. Internal layouts or operations organization are strategically important, and the strong quantitative treatments are couched inside a strategic framework.

The design of processes, the subject of Chapter 9, should be done in conjunction with design of the product. In this iterative process, though, it is important that the product concept be developed in advance of the start of process design, and this book follows that practice. Interestingly, the treatment of QFD in Chapter 6 and its supplement makes it clear that the two design processes are integrated. The supplement to Chapter 9 is devoted exclusively to an extended discussion of new technology.

Chapter 10 is concerned with the integration of people and processes through job design, with a focus on quality of worklife. The extensive quantitative and qualitative treatment is based on the philosophy that processes support people, rather than the reverse. This philosophy is extended in Chapter 11, where the focus is improving process capability. Process improvement is discovered to be the responsibility of operators and managers; the former cannot play an effective part in this process if they are mere servants to the process. The supplement to Chapter 11 deals with acceptance sampling, still an important activity in processes not yet in control.

The theme of Part IV—Chapters 12 to 19—is the effective planning and control of operations. In Chapter 12 the focus is on project management. Because of the importance of projects and project management in both manufacturing and service organizations of all sizes, the treatment is extensive. Both qualitative and quantitative aspects of project management are discussed. One important aspect of project management rarely discussed is the formation and management of project teams; this is the subject of the chapter supplement.

Chapters 13 through 15 cover demand management. The essential question for the operating manager is how much of a product to make at what time in order to satisfy customers most effectively. Independent, or market, demand is the subject of Chapter 13, while the demand for components of end items—dependent demand—is the subject of Chapter 15. Between these two chapters is a discussion on aggregate and capacity planning, two essential and integrated elements in the management of the flow of components through a complex process organization. The sequencing of the chapters is deliberate, following as it does the flow process of *material requirements planning* (MRP). The very extensive treatment of MRP in Chapter 15 includes recent extensions to the technique.

In Chapter 16 the management of dependent demand is extended by an in-depth examination of newer process control philosophies. These philosophies—*just-in-time* (JIT) and *synchronous operations*—are also shown to be related to market requirements and process organization.

Chapter 17 is devoted to a discussion of the last act before manufacturing or service performance actually starts—the scheduling of individual jobs on individual machines or to individual operators. The treatment is mostly quantitative, discussing several techniques for scheduling job shops and repetitive manufacturing operations. This activity is essentially internally focused and is not normally carried out without all elements being in place. Because of the pace of leading-edge operations, however, managers are being called upon to schedule operations without having all the necessary components in place. Chapter 18 therefore deals with a very critical aspect of operations planning and control—managing suppliers and managing the distribution of finished products. The theme of the chapter is integration throughout the value chain, a philosophy mentioned frequently in earlier chapters.

Chapter 19 treats the effective measurement of performance. If we cannot measure we cannot evaluate, and if we cannot evaluate we cannot improve. Thus the theme of continuous improvement introduced in Chapter 2 is revisited with a discussion of total performance measurement. The chapter introduces a comprehensive model for performance measurement, arguing that the measurement of performance must be carried out despite its complexity. Integration is the theme of the Chapter 19 Supplement, which deals with cost accounting from an operations point of view. The treatment also includes a discussion of *activity-based costing,* a key strategic development in strategic cost and operations control.

Part V contains only one chapter, Chapter 20, in which the book is reviewed in an attempt to integrate the important concepts discussed throughout and to take a look forward at where the world of operations management is headed. The basic message is that what distinguishes leading-edge organizations today will become essential parts of all operating entities. One key element of the chapter is a revisiting of total quality management and the recognition that quality is, or will be, an entry-level condition and not a principal competitive discriminant or differentiator.

PEDAGOGY

This book makes extensive use of both quantitative and qualitative discussion—quantitative, because many of the available tools and techniques are quantitative and must be understood; and qualitative, because effective managers take the results of quantitative analysis as the starting point of decision making and not as a substitute. The extensive treatment has been incorporated in a pedagogical framework that includes the following major elements:

Learning Focus. At the beginning of each chapter, its principal aspects are discussed and its learning objectives are outlined. This boxed feature provides a brief roadmap for the reader; more important, it provides a marker against which students can check their broad grasp of the material and its significance.

FRO Profiles. At the beginning of Chapter 3 and subsequent chapters, real situations in one service and one manufacturing organization are described. These profiles highlight aspects of the chapter topic and provide a real linkage to the chapter material.

Managerial Orientation. This brief section at the start of each chapter is intended to help the student develop a managerial focus of the subjects discussed.

Examples. The extensive quantitative treatment is supported by worked examples, many derived from actual operations. These examples are extended to show some qualitative techniques in action.

Managerial Implications. This boxed section, preceding each chapter summary, focuses on the critical managerial implications of the chapter material.

Chapter Summary. This comprehensive summary of chapter material reinforces the substantive knowledge the student should have gained.

Discussion Questions and Problems. Each chapter ends with a series of discussion questions and problems to reinforce the chapter material from a managerial point of view and test the student's mastery of that material. The extensive problems have been designed to be supported by problem-solving software, although this is not essential in any but the most difficult problems; these have been highlighted by a special computer icon in color.

Group Exercises. A unique feature of this book is the set of comprehensive group exercises included in Chapters 3 through 19. These require extensive research and discussion among group members.

Chapter Supplements. Many chapters have optional supplements devoted to topics only briefly treated in the chapter. This organization is intended to separate out material that requires extended treatment but does not require a chapter of its own.

ADDITIONAL STUDENT SUPPORT

OM-Expert. Although a variety of software packages can be used with this text, we developed a graphic-based software, OM-Expert, to deal specifically with the complete range of tools and techniques discussed. This new package is available separately from McGraw-Hill. Please contact your local McGraw-Hill representative for more information.

OM-Companion. *OM-Companion,* a combined workbook and study guide accompanying this textbook, has some important and exclusive features. First, it contains detailed treatments of several quantitative tools (including computer modelling) used extensively in operations. Second, it provides an integrated treatment of service operations by consolidating the services aspects of individual chapters of the textbook.

OM-Companion also provides further discussion of chapter highlights. In addition, the book includes what has been entitled "P/OM Storyteller," a series of examples drawn from business and nonbusiness settings that reflect the chapter material in use in established organizations. Finally, *OM-Companion* contains self-study pages that can be detached and submitted for evaluation and feedback by the instructor. These self-assessment guides can be used effectively in courses in which individual and group self-assessment forms an integral part of the learning process.

ACKNOWLEDGMENTS

This book has been written to indicate what works and, where applicable, what doesn't work. More importantly, it has been written to show what is appropriate and how to decide what is appropriate. We have tried to use plain, understandable language. To this end, we used early drafts of chapters with our students, and we thank them for taking the time to express their opinions. Their concerns and their discussions among themselves and with practising managers have shaped both the chapter material and the end-of-chapter discussion questions, problems, and group exercises.

We would also like to thank our many reviewers for their thoughtful and incisive suggestions: Reza Agahi; Peter Billington, University of Southern Colorado; Elizabeth Booth, Louisiana State University; Yih-Long Chang, Georgia Institute of Technology; Burton V. Dean, San Jose State University; Douglas A. Elvers, University of North Carolina at Chapel Hill; Suan Tong Foo, Marquette University; Richard Gunther, California State University at Northridge; Ray Haynes, California State Polytechnic University at San Luis Obispo; Joseph Mosca, Monmouth College; William Newman, Miami University; James H. Perry, George Washington University; Fred Rafaat, San Diego State University; Gary D. Scudder, Vanderbilt University; Timothy Urban, University of Tulsa; and Emre A. Veral, SUNY Baruch. Without them, some gaffes might easily have slipped through, and some key trends might have received limited attention. Integrating the needs and expectations of this diverse, expert group of potential customers has been an interesting challenge.

Our friends and supporters at McGraw-Hill—Lynn, Josh, Frank, Linda, Anne, Dan, and Laura—have cheerfully borne our criticisms and frustrations. They have had their own frustrations, not the least of which has been the disappearance of both authors to different inaccessible parts of the world at a critical stage in the book's own production process. They have each and all given us valuable insight into aspects of textbooks we would never have dreamed existed. Without their long-suffering help the outcome would have been very different.

Our special thanks, though, go to those who struggled with us, conducting library research, testing problems and discussion questions, using new software packages, expertly interpreting our handwriting and typing drafts of chapters. The manuscript owes its existence to Liz Ruby, our invaluable research assistant, and Carole Litwiller, the former being engaged in another birth process at the time. The natural process was, we think, shorter and less painful.

Finally, we thank our families for their patience and understanding during our deep involvement with this project. We dedicate this book to them, in the hope that their world will be populated by well-managed businesses and enterprises.

Hamid Noori
Russell Radford

PRODUCTION AND OPERATIONS MANAGEMENT
Total Quality and Responsiveness

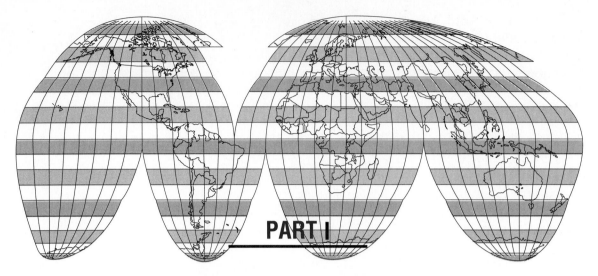

PART I

SETTING THE STAGE:

POSITIONING FOR QUALITY

Setting the Stage

Operations managers control over half of all the capital assets and personnel in most firms, and so it is essential for firms to understand the operations function and its management in all competitive situations. This book endeavors to provide that understanding as well as a toolbox, the tools, and an instruction manual for using tools that enable managers to exploit the competitive weapons their operations represent.

Part I develops a dynamic framework that describes how firms succeed in today's marketplace. This is offered as a collective framework for strategic and tactical decision making in operations management.

The Startup Chapter introduces six operating entities. Chapter 1 and its supplement present a formal definition of operations and discuss the evolution of the field. Chapter 2 presents an outline of what customers want from "leading-edge" operations in both manufacturing and service firms and introduces a new framework for organizing operations. This framework relates the dimensions of competition that firms must achieve to the four structural prerequisites that every operating organization must meet to succeed in the new competitive environment.

Chapter 3 discusses how to develop an effective operations strategy, which can be thought of as the driving force that allows firms to make decisions about their focus along each of the dimensions of competition. The Chapter 3 Supplement is devoted entirely to benchmarking, since effective benchmarking is essential for proper planning and decision making.

By the end of Part I you will appreciate what makes today's environment fundamentally different from earlier competitive environments; understand the importance of the competitive drivers from an operations perspective; and understand and be able to use the structural prerequisites in a strategic context. You will learn how to develop an operations strategy and to outline the characteristics of a competitive firm—a fast-response organization.

Few things happen instantaneously. Few people in the 1970s questioned the ways in which North American firms were organized and operated, yet those organizational forms had developed over a long period. A historical imperative is outlined in the Chapter 1 Supplement, but the essential story is one of change. Some firms took the lead, and others followed until a new organizational paradigm was universally accepted and enacted.

The new operating environment brings an opportunity and need to develop new solutions to new problems. Old problems have not disappeared, though, nor will new solutions automatically and totally replace old solutions and tools. Newtonian physics was not displaced by Einstein's theory of relativity, but became an important subset of relativity physics, useful for modeling and understanding many new discoveries. Visualize a matrix:

		Challenges/Problems	
		Existing	New
Tools	Old	Old tools applied to existing problems	Old tools applied to new problems
	New	New tools applied to existing problems	New tools applied to new problems

This book describes both old and new tools needed by today's and tomorrow's managers to be effective in a rapidly changing world. Understanding *how* to use a particular tool is not sufficient, though. A skilled carpenter knows how to use all the tools in the toolbox but also knows *when* to use a particular tool and how to choose from among a number of tools. Further, a carpenter knows how to use a combination of tools and knows when the toolbox is deficient. Managers need the same decision-making abilities. Understanding the implications of using a managerial tool in a particular context is more important than knowing how to use that tool. This book provides a limited operational tool kit for generalist managers and an understanding of when, where, and why each tool is relevant and appropriate.

Technology still plays an important role in determining industry structure and the ways in which firms compete. This book will focus on the role of technology in determining the limits of existing operations and corporate strategies and in defining the limits of a firm's tactical response.

It is not only the awareness of an advanced technology which is of vital importance. Equally important are the knowledge and courage to implement the necessary changes in an organization's structure and behavior. It is these factors, their importance, and their management that permeate this book.

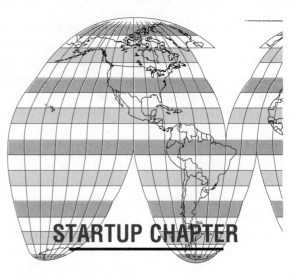

STARTUP CHAPTER

FOCUSING ON THE CUSTOMER: A LOOK AT RESPONSIVE COMPANIES

Many managers are asking themselves how they can make their companies competitive in the rapidly changing global environment, just as many are asking how they can focus their competitive strategy.

This introductory chapter provides snapshots of six companies. They are different in many respects, but they all have survived the transition to a global competitive environment. The chapter will also look at the competitive characteristics shared by these firms, themes that will be followed throughout the book. All these themes are "manageable," and no organization can succeed without every person with a stake in the organization working constantly to improve the firm's effectiveness in these areas.

The term for the philosophy underlying the enactment of these themes is *fast responsiveness*. This implies a customer-focused organization and an operation fully committed to *total quality management (TQM)*.

The need to understand and adopt these new competitive precepts underlies the establishment of quality awards at a national and lower level. These awards now play an important role in shaping the actions and philosophies of managers. This chapter will therefore spend some time discussing three of the major quality awards.

By the end of this chapter you will have been exposed to living examples of firms that have successfully adopted new competitive philosophies and practices and to the awards many believe will help encourage all firms to make the transition. With this background you will be ready to embark on a quality journey through this book.

Why do some businesses fail while others survive? That question is uppermost in the minds of business executives and business students. Managers are responsible to owners, suppliers, employees, and society at large for the survival and growth of their organizations. And survival requires that a firm attract enough customers to generate a positive cash flow and thus make a profit. The profit must be great enough to allow the firm to make the investments necessary for growth.

Firms fail for many reasons. Fifty percent of new firms fail within the first two years, primarily because they cannot attract enough customers to purchase a sufficient volume of their products. Others fail because they are undercapitalized and cannot cover the inevitable startup cash drain. A smaller percentage fail because large competitors use their market power to deny a firm access to customers or to suppliers through the usual market channels.

If a firm can get through the first two years, however, it should survive. Why, then, do established firms fail? Some do not react to competitor initiatives, changes in taste, and advances in product or process technology. Governments and regulatory bodies change the rules of competition, forcing legislated monopolies or otherwise protected firms to compete with new, usually innovative firms that entice customers away. Other firms fail because the suppliers fail, robbing a firm of the ability to produce a good or provide a service. Still others fail because disgruntled employees leave to set up more innovative firms. Many family firms fail because management loses the desire to compete.

In many instances firms survive in good times only to fail when economic conditions deteriorate. This is due in part to undercapitalization and a lack of cash to weather the storm and in part to increased levels of competition. Increased competition means a heightened awareness of, and more intense efforts to satisfy, the customer. In the long run a firm needs satisfied customers to survive.

Everyone is aware of instances in which organizations have dissatisfied customers and knows that the notion of service seems to be missing when one deals with a wide range of firms and public agencies. What does it mean, though, to *satisfy* a customer? Customers are satisfied when they receive the total product they desire (including ancillary and support goods and services) at a price they can afford and accept. If organizations fail to do this and customers have other ways of satisfying their needs, the customers will migrate and the firm will fail. This type of attrition happens more rapidly in turbulent times, when customers are prepared to search for alternatives to firms they can tolerate in good times.

It is important therefore for every organization to recognize the central position occupied by its customers and the need to have as its primary aim their satisfaction. This recognition is widely accepted, although there is still confusion about what it implies operationally.

The need to satisfy customers is being recognized by nonbusiness organizations as well. An increasing number of governments, government departments, and government-supported groups have developed awards that highlight and promote the need to satisfy customers.[1] Underlying most of these awards is the recognition that the profitable survival of for-profit businesses is an essential ingredient in the survival of the local, regional, and national economy. These awards are one way in which governments can encourage firms to act individually in their own interests and collectively in the interests of the greater economic unit.[2]

As was said above, it is easy to agree on the importance of satisfying the customer; however, it is another matter to agree on the definition of **customer satisfaction.** Each quality award has its own measure of what satisfying the customer means and how that satisfaction should be achieved. Let us look at three of these awards and see how each defines and measures a firm's ability to satisfy the customer. These awards come from different countries but, despite some national differences, there are striking similarities. All the awards define quality in common customer-centered terms. In these instances, quality management has as its aim, and as its measure of effectiveness, customer satisfaction. All three awards require evidence that qualifying firms actively practice **total quality management (TQM).**

> **DEFINITION:** Total quality management is a philosophy advocating four basic principles: (1) intense focus on customer satisfaction, (2) accurate measurement of activities, (3) continuous improvement of products and processes, and (4) empowerment of people.

This implies that the underlying philosophies and principles of satisfying the customer hold true across national and cultural boundaries.

BUSINESS EXCELLENCE AWARDS

Malcolm Baldrige National Quality Awards

The Baldrige Award, instituted in 1987 in honor of the late U.S. Secretary of Commerce Malcolm Baldrige, is without doubt the premier quality award in the United States. Its scope goes beyond product or service excellence alone; it stresses

---

[1] An American Society for Quality Control (ASQC) survey of U.S. states in early 1993 showed, for example, that 21 states had quality awards, 15 were developing quality awards, and 4 were considering developing them.

[2] Interestingly, there are very few quality awards for not-for-profit organizations. There is no reason why such awards should not exist, and one hopes more will appear soon.

customer-focused quality management systems and processes. The award provides a comprehensive framework for assessing a firm's progress in achieving its quality management goals. The criteria used to judge applicants are based on the following key concepts, which will be discussed throughout the book:

- Quality is defined by the customer.
- The senior leadership of business needs to create clear quality values and build those values into the way the company operates.
- Quality excellence results from well-designed and well-executed systems and processes.
- Continuous improvement must be part of the management of all systems and processes.
- Companies have to develop goals as well as strategic and operational plans to achieve quality leadership.
- Shortening the response time of all the operations and processes of the company must be part of the quality improvement effort.
- Operations and decisions need to be based on facts and data.
- All employees must be suitably trained and developed and involved in quality activities.
- Design quality and error prevention should be major elements of the quality system.
- Companies have to communicate quality requirements to suppliers and work to elevate the suppliers' quality performance.

Companies applying for the award are evaluated by a team of examinators and assigned scores in seven examination categories (see Exhibit 1). Each candidate must not only demonstrate that its approach to quality management has been successful; it must also demonstrate that its approach could be replicated or adapted by other firms.

Only a few companies requesting the application forms and guidelines in a single year actually apply for the award. Instead, many firms use the award criteria to evaluate their operations and develop comprehensive, long-term quality improvement strategies. This, too, satisfies the objectives of the award: quality awareness and information transfer.

Canada Awards for Business Excellence

The Canada Awards for Business Excellence (CABE) were created in 1984 by the Canadian government to honor businesses in all industry sectors for outstanding achievements. The awards are given in eight categories, one of which is **customer-based quality.**

The CABE quality award is "given in recognition of outstanding achievement in overall business quality through a commitment to continuous quality improvement. Emphasis is placed upon the total involvement of the company, including all business functions and all employees; on the competitiveness of the products or services in the marketplace; and on the high level of customer satisfaction."[3] Applicants are evaluated on the following criteria:

- Quality improvement policy and plan (10 percent)
- Implementation and operation of the plan (40 percent)

[3] *Canada Awards For Business Excellence* (1993), p. 19.

EXHIBIT 1 THE MALCOLM BALDRIGE AWARD

Malcolm Baldrige Awards are granted annually to individual companies or divisions of larger companies. There are three categories—manufacturing companies, service companies, and small businesses—and up to two awards may be granted in each category in any year.

Applicants for the award must submit a 75-page written report (50 pages for the small business category) which is examined and given scores under seven categories:

1. Leadership	100
2. Information and analysis	70
3. Strategic quality planning	60
4. Human resource utilization	150
5. Quality assurance of products and services	140
6. Quality results	180
7. Customer satisfaction	300
Total points	1,000

Let us take a closer look at the most heavily weighted category and the one many examiners turn to first: customer satisfaction. In general, the examiners are looking for evidence of customer understanding and commitment as well as impressive results. Specifically, the firm is evaluated on the following eight criteria:

1. Determining customer requirements and expectations (30 points)
   Examines (a) how the firm has divided its market into segments and its customers in groups and (b) the data collection and interpretation process.

2. Customer relations management (50 points)
   Examines the effectiveness of the firm in managing relationships with its customers and in making responsive product improvements.

3. Customer service standards (20 points)
   Examines how service standards are initiated, set, deployed, supported, tracked, evaluated, and improved.

4. Commitment to customers (15 points)
   Examines the firm's ability to meet customers' concerns and how the firm translates product improvements into a stronger commitment to the customers.

5. Complaint resolution for quality improvement (25 points)
   Examines the effectiveness of the process used to capture customer feedback, resolve complaints, and translate feedback into product improvements.

6. Determining customer satisfaction (20 points)
   Examines how the firm analyzes customer satisfaction data by market segment and by customer groups and evaluates and improves this process.

7. Customer satisfaction results (70 points)
   Examines the level of customer satisfaction as well as trends in customer satisfaction.

8. Customer satisfaction comparison (70 points)
   Compares the firm's customer satisfaction results with those of its competitors.

- Results achieved (40 percent)
- Future planning (10 percent)

As with the Baldrige Award, the number of firms that use the award criteria to gauge their progress is a key indicator of the significance of the CABE award.

The Deming Application Prize

The Deming Application Prize is the oldest quality award, established in 1951 by the Union of Japanese Scientists and Engineers (JUSE). Named in honor of an American, the late W. Edwards Deming, and his achievements in statistical quality control, the prize recognizes successful efforts in instituting quality control company-wide.

The Deming Application Prize is awarded to companies that have successfully applied quality control by using statistical quality control.[4] Firms also need to show that they are likely to maintain and improve their position. Applicants are expected to detail their procedures and achievements closely and are encouraged to work with previous winners and judges.

After winning the Deming Prize, companies that have demonstrated ongoing improvement for at least five more years are eligible for an even more prestigious award, the Nippon Quality Award.

SNAPSHOTS OF EXCELLENCE

The broad scope of the criteria for the awards described above should make everyone realize that satisfying the customer is a multidimensional problem. What does it take to satisfy the criteria and win one of the awards? Does winning an award signify that a firm *is* satisfying its customers? This section includes visits to six firms, each of which is recognized as satisfying its customers at levels that exceed most customers' expectations. Not all these organizations have won one of the three awards; those which have not won have simply not applied. Across the six organizations, though, all three awards have been won.

Each site visit concentrates on the operating elements of one firm. No firm could exist for long solely as an operations entity, though. Keep in mind the fact that no business function is any more or less important than any other in achieving a firm's objectives.

Notice that each firm is organized differently. Questions to keep in mind, then, are:

- What are the similarities in the operations function across these firms?
- Should all firms involved in the same business as one of these firms be organized in the same way?
- Are there any general organizing principles or practices for operations?
- If so, what are they?

Answers to these questions are important, for an understanding of organizing principles provides insight into the pressures on management and the workforce in any situation. This enables a firm to design its operation to support the people in the system.

Tour 1: Fujima International

Fujima International makes metal dies that shape sheets of metal in large stamping presses. The company is a joint venture between Fuji of Japan and Magna International, one of North America's largest and most diverse suppliers of components and systems to the automotive industry. Located in Brampton, Ontario, the firm can manufacture dies for Magna subsidiaries, major automobile manufacturers, and third-party suppliers to the automobile industry.

Manufacturing operations such as Fujima's provide the most challenging test for an operations manager. A wide variety of products can be made, each one is unique, and each may be made from different materials or by a different sequence and

---

[4] *Statistical quality control* refers to the use of statistical techniques such as control charts, experimental design, and statistical process control to support a firm's efforts to monitor and improve quality. Several statistical quality control techniques are discussed in Chapter 11.

combination of processes. Because the rate at which orders arrive changes constantly, the pressures to complete specific jobs may change from day to day.

One test or challenge for management is deciding which equipment to buy and how to set it out in the plant. Where no dominant flow exists and no logical sequence of processes is evident, managers traditionally decide to place all machines of the same type together.

In general, therefore, job shops, as these types of operations are called, are characterized by general-purpose, flexible equipment and highly technically skilled operators. Most of these operators have served or will serve a long apprenticeship while acquiring trade skills. The diversity of work means that most operators need to be skilled at running a number of machines.

Production lead times are generally long in a job shop because the general-purpose equipment is arranged in a process layout; that is, similar pieces of equipment are placed together in a work center. Jobs travel from work center to work center, spending a great deal of time waiting in queues. Large time gaps between processing stages make finding the cause of poor product quality and estimating the finishing date for a particular job difficult. And high work-in-process (WIP) inventories inflate working capital requirements. Thus, reducing production lead times is a major challenge in a job shop.

One way to reduce the lead time is to minimize the time jobs spend waiting in queues in front of machines. Fujima has done this by centralizing its scheduling system and creating teams of workers. Each job is assigned to a particular team, and that team is responsible for planning and executing the job.

A team consists of a team leader who is an experienced machinist, other operators, material handlers, setup specialists, designers, and engineers. The team "designs" the product and the manufacturing process for each job, blocking out the time requirements for each operation. The team leader then negotiates (with other team leaders) a specific date and time when each machine required will be made available for a particular job. This means that the queues in front of machines are centrally managed and are shorter than they would be if every queue were independent. Often, a machine is left idle to wait for a particular job, something unheard of in a traditional job shop in normal circumstances.

There is a tendency to be conservative in estimating the time required on a particular machine for a given job. These small time buffers are, however, known and integrated into the overall production plan. A customer can be confident about the completion time given for a die and can therefore plan with certainty the operations for which that die will be used.

The firm's design office designs the product so that it can be used and can be successfully manufactured. This is an important element of the firm's quality concept; not designing for manufacturability increases manufacturing costs and may not allow an acceptable product to be produced at all.

All design is done on computer-aided design (CAD) systems, with operator input to ensure that the die is built in the most cost-effective manner. A computer model of the tool is sent to the customer for approval and quickly returned. After approval, computer instructions for each machine involved in making the die are produced and automatically downloaded from the central computer to the computer controls on the relevant machine.

By getting the design right before the die is built, Fujima eliminates design changes during manufacture—a major source of delay, increased cost, and customer frustration. More important, time in manufacturing is reduced. Traditionally, die and mold makers would bid for a job and hope that changes would have to be made; all changes would be charged for at rates higher than those used in the quotation. Although this practice created higher margins on some jobs, the lengthy delays caused by the need to have the customer approve changes made planning almost impossible. In contrast, few (if any) changes in Fujima's designs are required. Production lead times are accurately known, making tight planning possible and reducing the lead time. Responsiveness is measured across the whole manufacturing cycle, from design to delivery; quality in and of design therefore improves responsiveness.

Fujima's guaranteed price is attractive to customers who are used to seeing prices increase over the course of a job because of extras. This guarantee puts pressure on the firm to estimate properly and eliminate operating errors which increase the time spent on a job. Team design and knowledge of processing times ensure that quality and accuracy in estimation are designed into the product.

The team concept, along with the need to identify to the day when a particular job will undergo a particular process, means that capacity is not totally utilized. If the machinists were committed by schedules for 100 percent of their working time, stoppages and time overruns would interfere with the plan. As a consequence, schedules would not be met and customers would receive products later than promised. This means that machinists are not fully loaded and can use the nonoperating time they have for value-added activities such as meetings, planning sessions, and training. If a job does have a problem, some of the unplanned time can be used for catching up while keeping all the other jobs on schedule. One consequence of this capacity underutilization has been a move to pay everybody a salary.

Responsiveness to critical customer concerns and the elimination of waste time and effort everywhere are competitively important. Eliminating waste time directly affects product quality and the profitability of a firm. In this instance, the responsiveness or sensitivity to customer issues is not usually related to time pressure. Rather, it is a matter of guaranteeing the accuracy and workability of the die and the reliability of the promised delivery date.

Tour 2: Mayo Clinic

The Mayo Clinic complex in Rochester, Minnesota, is the largest medical complex in the world. With satellite facilities in Jacksonville, Florida, and Scottsdale, Arizona, the clinic employs more than 1,200 physicians and scientists among a staff of over 18,000. Each day physicians, surgeons, and other health care professionals see more than 4,000 patients. Annual operating revenues (in the nonmedical sense of the word) are approximately $900 million in a nation which spent about $940 billion on health care in 1993.

Why is the Mayo Clinic so well known and well regarded internationally? The answer undoubtedly involves quality of the treatment patients receive and the short time between arrival at the clinic and the formal diagnosis and beginning of treatment. The clinic attracts leading clinicians, people who are interested in developing new knowledge in their fields. As a consequence, the clinicians seek, and have referred to them, cases that other practitioners cannot resolve. Unusual cases become the norm, and the clinicians thus become adept at diagnosing extraordinary forms of medical conditions. New and improved treatments that prove successful quickly become accepted techniques.

Unlike nearly all other medical facilities, all members of the medical and nonmedical staff are salaried. No doctor has to pay rent for office space; none has secretaries to pay or files to keep. Doctors work in teams and practice medicine in a noncompetitive atmosphere. Coordination is relatively simple, with medical specialists and a range of technologies located in the same facility. This combination of a deliberate absence of competition and high degrees of coordination of medical service is difficult to achieve in any other form of practice. The result is cost-effective, patient-centered health care.

The Mayo Clinic is a very vertically integrated yet diverse medical center. In addition to the physicians' and surgeons' consulting rooms and the two hospitals, there are extensive state-of-the-art laboratories, diagnostic facilities, and research centers. Determination to keep the facilities at the leading edge is reflected in the clinic's expansion program; $750 million is expected to be spent over five years to expand and improve patient care, education, and research facilities.

The clinic's integrated nature gives it another unique advantage: the speed with which most diagnoses are done regardless of the complexity of the tests involved. Most tests and examinations for outpatients are completed within a seven-day period; an identical battery of tests would take a month or more to complete in most outpatient settings. It would be wrong, however, to attribute the rapidity of diagnosis solely to the structure of the clinic. Most of the credit must go to the management systems the clinic has pioneered.

A medical clinic is a complex organization, yet information flows and patient flows within the Mayo Clinic are rapid and accurate. Since 1907 a single file has been created for every patient the clinic has seen. Now electronically supported and updated, the single file provides each doctor with quick access to up-to-date information. It also allows the the doctor to be fully aware of his or her part in the whole examination and treatment program. This prevents the administration of potentially harmful drug combinations, for example.

The Mayo Clinic's decision to maintain capacity at levels greater than demand is another reason why patients can be seen and treated quickly. This is particularly true of the support facilities, where excess capacity is sold to outside agencies. The clinic's laboratories, for example, perform over 4,000 blood and urine tests daily for other medical facilities.

Some experts suggest that a service facility operating at more than 75 percent of capacity cannot provide good service; the challenge for management is to ensure that there are alternative, lower-priority yet high-value-added uses for the available time. At the Mayo Clinic this spare time is spent in doing research, upgrading knowledge, and coordinating meetings designed to improve overall patient care. Again, the payment of a salary removes the pressure to see value-added activities only in terms of revenue-generating contact with patients.

Because of the capital- and knowledge-intensive nature of medical practice, the costs of operating the Mayo Clinic are high. Management therefore has to be vigilant in controlling costs without compromising care and ensuring that the expectations of its customers—the patients—are met. Satisfying patients' expectations is not easy, for quality treatment involves patient management at least as much as medical diagnosis and intervention. The guiding principle is for all the staff members to put themselves in the patient's place and treat the patient exactly as they would want to be treated. This means courteous, efficient service and plenty of information about where to go, what will happen, and when each activity will take place.

Quality and responsiveness are the keys to the Mayo Clinic's success. Quality is measured in more ways than correctness of diagnosis; it is also measured by the determination of everyone in the clinic to treat the whole patient and the patient's immediate circle. This is a quality-of-life issue. Responsiveness is inextricably intertwined with quality in this environment, for it involves recognizing how best to improve quality of life and how quickly that improvement begins. This is not restricted to current cases; the medical and organizational research conducted at the Mayo Clinic is aimed at further improving quality and responsiveness.

Tour 3: Reimer Express Lines Limited

Reimer Express Lines Limited is the express freight subsidiary of Reimer Freight Lines Limited, a trucking company based in Winnipeg, Manitoba. In 1990 Reimer Express Lines became the only service firm to win a Canadian Award for Business Excellence (CABE) for quality.

Reimer is the largest privately owned transport firm in Canada, operating about 3,000 trucks, vans, tractors, and trailers and employing about 300 people. Annual operating revenue is on the order of $300 million. The company also has one of the oldest surviving management teams; the two brothers who founded the interprovincial freight business in 1952 were still at the helm in 1994.

The task of a trucking company is conceptually simple: to pick up product at one point and deliver it to another point. This is made considerably more complex, though, by the need to make a profit and by almost unlimited combinations of loads, time limitations, and pickup and delivery points. The deregulation of North American trucking has led to increased competition on attractive routes, with more choices and lower rates for customers. How have trucking firms adjusted to this dramatically different competitive environment?

One of the ways in which Reimer has responded to environmental changes is by offering a money-back delivery guarantee on regular LTL (less than truckload) shipments between major centers. Total transit times are guaranteed to be equal to or better than normal air cargo times. This means, for example, 48 hours between Winnipeg and Toronto, at considerably lower cost than the rate for air freight.

The driving time between Winnipeg and Toronto is about 26 hours; any trucking company could get one small load between those centers in 36 hours. Why, then, is Reimer unique in offering a service guarantee, and how important is that guarantee?

From a customer's point of view the guarantee is vitally important, for the timing of delivery influences a firm's scheduling and inventory decisions. High variability generally requires a customer to hold higher than desired levels of safety stock; the cost advantages of trucking can easily be offset by the higher costs of covering the uncertainty of delivery timing.

Reimer could easily offer longer delivery times and eliminate variability simply by holding goods at the receiving depot until the time promised. However, that would not be in the best interests of the customers, who would probably bear the costs of the increased pipeline inventory. And for each extra day of promised transit time, customers would have at least one extra day of inventory in their facilities. Speed, care, and certainty of delivery are therefore important quality measures for Reimer and its customers.

While the time to drive from one center to another is appreciably shorter than the guaranteed delivery time, it is only one element of the delivery time and delivery process. The overall process is illustrated in Exhibit 2. This is a complicated example, including local pickup and delivery. The process begins with a call for service from

EXHIBIT 2   REIMER'S HUB AND SPOKE DISTRIBUTION SYSTEM

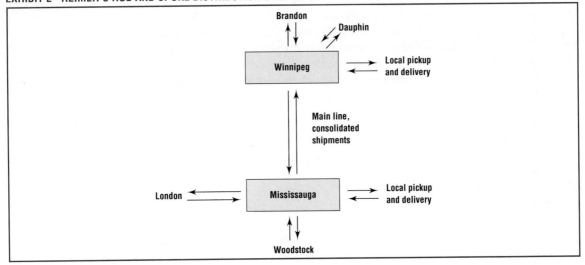

the customer. A vehicle is dispatched to pick up the load, which is then taken to Reimer's depot for consolidation. *Consolidation* is the process of stockpiling the cargo for a route in lots for each service center along the route. Once the loads are consolidated, the trailer can be loaded, the load documentation (manifest) given to the driver, and the vehicle dispatched.

Total delivery time can be reduced by increasing the driving speed between terminals, reducing the number of times goods have to be handled, reducing transit time in terminals by means of improved handling processes, and speeding up administrative processes that ensure delivery to the proper destination. Streamlining the handling, terminal, and administrative processes has been the key to improving the reliability of the total process, and this has become the cornerstone of the service quality provided by Reimer.

To streamline operations, Reimer uses a "hub and spoke" system for its transport fleet. Traffic from smaller centers or from smaller customers in major centers is brought by local delivery vehicles to a central terminal. There the loads are consolidated by destination, delivery date, and, if appropriate, special storage and handling category. The express highway trailers are then loaded, and the trucks are dispatched to their destinations. On arrival at the destination terminal, the vehicle is unloaded and the load is split up for dispatch by a local delivery vehicle to the customer or to a freight terminal in a smaller center.

Even with the multiple hub and spoke system it is possible for an item to be handled up to 18 times by Reimer employees. The potential for confusion and loss and the likelihood of delay increase with the amount of handling. To reduce the confusion, a good information system has to be developed.

No parcel travels by itself. Each is accompanied by its own transport or shipping documents, and each load is accompanied by the load manifest. In some instances the individual parcel is handled fewer times than is the documentation; the preparation and handling of the paperwork are very likely to delay the parcel. Thus the quality of the administrative processes directly influences the quality of the delivery process.

Another reliability issue that concerns management is the potential for vehicle delays on the road. Three time issues are associated with vehicle delays: how soon after the incident the vehicle can start on its journey again, how soon after the incident Reimer will know about the delay, and how quickly it will be able to notify the customers. The sooner notice is received and given, the more responsive Reimer and the customer can be. If notice is given soon enough, one response might even be to fly the goods. Although this is expensive, delaying a process or losing a sale may be more costly to the customer and thus to Reimer.

Quality is therefore related to safe, timely, reliable delivery. Responsiveness is measured by the ability to identify critical customer needs (in this instance the need for Reimer to achieve and accept responsibility for certainty of delivery) and the ability to overcome potential unplanned downtime. This last type of responsiveness is gained through time buffers (customers have to call or deliver goods by a certain time to ensure departure at a known later time) and planned responses to likely contingencies.

To this end, the service guarantee functions as a signal to the market that the worries associated with uncertainty will be borne by Reimer. The hidden costs associated with uncertainty also will be borne by Reimer. In an industry with margins driven ever lower by increased competition, the guarantee also acts as a signal internally to drive out inefficiency and excess costs.

Tour 4: Zytec Corporation

Zytec Corporation designs, manufactures, and repairs electronic power supplies for original equipment manufacturers (OEMs).[5] Zytec's customers use these power supplies in a variety of products, including computers, hard disk drives, telephone switching equipment, and medical and testing equipment. More than 400 firms worldwide compete in the North American market, which is worth more than $4 billion annually for power supplies in the range of 250 to 1,500 watts.

Zytec was formed in 1984 when three Control Data Corporation executives arranged a leveraged buyout of the power supplies operation of Magnetic Peripherals, a Control Data subsidiary. Zytec's head office and marketing, engineering, design, research and development (R&D), and purchasing functions are in Eden Prairie (a Minneapolis suburb), with the major manufacturing and repair facilities in Redwood Falls, Minnesota, about 100 miles to the southwest.

Zytec's product sales of about $50 million in 1990 made it the fifth largest U.S. manufacturer of AC to DC power supplies, and repair sales of approximately $6 million made it the largest power supply repair company in North America. With approximately 700 employees, Zytec is about one-third the size of its largest competitor.

Although there is a diverse range of potential customers, Zytec concentrates on high-volume power supplies for large electronics companies. Given its design capabilities, Zytec favors complex rather than simple power supplies. Zytec's 1993 product portfolio consisted of about 50 products, of which 2 accounted for about 40

---

[5] A power supply is a device that converts alternating current (AC) from domestic supply to the low direct current (DC) voltages required by electronic components such as integrated circuits.

percent of sales; the firm had about 15 customers, 2 of which were responsible for 60 percent of sales.

Although power supplies for different customers contain different components and are designed differently, the basic steps in manufacturing and assembly are the same. This similarity, combined with the relatively large volumes of a limited range of power supplies produced, has allowed Zytec to design a production process that logically follows the production steps. Such a layout is called a *product layout* and is used in batch manufacturing, where different members of a product family are sent through the process in batches, or lots. Because manufacturing and assembly details differ from one member of the family to the next, Zytec needs flexibility in its processes to cope with the differences among products going through the process.

To achieve this, Zytec has one line equipped with machines that can be adjusted so that all members of the family can be produced on that single line. The principal disadvantage of this line is the time lost in setting up for the next batch of product. The capital costs of this alternative are probably lower than those involved in having a number of lines dedicated to each product. The single line is also much less likely to sit idle than are the dedicated lines.

Zytec has organized production around the final assembly process. Components are manufactured in eight dedicated manufacturing cells in which the final stage of manufacturing has the finished component at the appropriate location in the assembly line. Each cell contains the equipment required for the manufacture of one family of components, such as transformers. The equipment is laid out to minimize the transport distance for the materials and to minimize wasted operator effort and time. Production is synchronized with the assembly process.

Zytec's single process poses some challenges to management. First, because the process is not dedicated to a single product, managers have to decide when to schedule a run of each product and how much to make in each lot or batch. One management challenge, therefore, is to change quickly from one product to the next and reduce the nonproductive time at each stage. Time lost in setting up to produce a particular product cannot be made up and is a cost to production. Any time lost through rework of low-quality product, slow changeovers between products, lack of materials, or slow production means increased product costs and reduced responsiveness to the market.

Responsiveness is a time- and customer-based concept. Given an understanding of a customer's requirements, Zytec can design a suitable product if one does not already exist. Poor quality in design or manufacture and/or an inability to respond to changes in market conditions will result in slow deliveries, lost sales, high material and finished goods inventories—and lost customers. With less time required to manufacture a product and the small batch sizes made possible by reduced setup or changeover times, customers do not have to accept long lead times. If one company cannot completely satisfy a customer's requirements, another firm will.

Disk drive manufacturers experienced this truth when Asian-designed and manufactured disk drives began appearing in North America in the mid-1980s. These drives were of better quality and lower cost than North American–built drives and nearly drove domestic manufacturers out of the market. This had a major impact on suppliers, including Zytec. Zytec's management realized that its own quality and cost problems were contributing to the disk drive makers' woes. Zytec was part of the problem, not an innocent victim.

These concerns were addressed in the total quality commitment program Zytec established in 1984 and extended in 1988. Zytec introduced new manufacturing concepts which included *just-in-time (JIT)* and *total quality control (TQC).*[6]

Inventories at Zytec fell from about $17 million to $6 million between 1985 and 1986 and cycle times fell about 78 percent in mid-1986, actions which generated the cash for survival. "Plug and play" performance (trouble-free operation on receipt by the customer) increased from around 90 percent to 99.5 percent; manufacturing yields increased over 50 percent from 1988 to 1991.

What has enabled the firm to progress so rapidly is a four-step strategic quality planning process. The first step is to collect data from customer feedback, formal and informal marketing research, and benchmarking, a process of ranking everything a firm does against the best in the world. This step ensures that no arbitrary strategic goals will be set. The second step is the development of a long-range strategic plan (LRSP). Six cross-functional teams, each under the guidance of senior executives, develop plans, which are then reviewed and critiqued by about 150 employees from all levels and functions in the firm. Suppliers and customers may also be invited to comment on the document, which is then refined and developed into a series of one-year corporate objectives.

The third step is the management by planning (MBP) process, in which each department sets its own annual improvement targets consistent with overall corporate objectives. The fourth step is turning the long-range strategic objectives into financial plans.

The results of this process have been impressive: a 26 percent reduction in manufacturing cycle time, a 50 percent reduction in design cycle time, a 30 to 40 percent reduction in product costs, double-digit annual productivity growth in the period 1988–1991, and an increase to an average of more than 1 million hours between failures in a power supply. This has been achieved by, among other things, more attention to the design process and to suppliers.

All these gains can be attributed in large part to the corporate culture, which aligns the human, technological, and informational elements of quality improvement with customer priorities. The TQC process also integrates the business functions with each other as well as integrating suppliers and customers into a "seamless" organization.

Tour 5: Milliken and Company

Milliken and Company is one of the largest textile companies in North America, with sales in excess of $1 billion annually. Established in 1885 and headquartered in Spartanburg, South Carolina, the privately owned firm is vertically integrated from yarn making through fabric finishing. It has over 14,000 associates (nobody is called a worker or operator) employed in 47 manufacturing facilities throughout the United States.

---

[6] As applied by Zytec and several other companies, JIT/TQC is a concept that focuses on eliminating all forms of waste from operating processes, particularly waste materials and waste time. The aim is to improve processes to the point where they are perfect, with no unplanned stoppages for breakdowns and lack of supply. This is the TQC aspect of the concept; perfection in all operations through the unceasing efforts of everyone involved. JIT requires that machines and processes supply their immediate customers (internal or external) only as required; given the single line and multiple products manufactured by Zytec, this requires small batches and very short setup times for each piece of equipment. More time will be spent looking at process quality in Chapter 11 and at the JIT philosophy in Chapter 16.

The principal products are apparel, furniture and automotive fabrics, floor coverings, and specialty chemicals; the firm has over 48,000 textile and chemical products in its product portfolio. Milliken won one of the two Malcolm Baldrige National Quality Awards presented in 1989.

Milliken's Decorative Fabrics Business Unit makes fabrics for furniture makers, among other customers. Fabrics can be formed in several ways, but fabric made from long lengths of yarn is usually either woven on looms or knitted on knitting machines. A fabric gets its distinctive characteristics from several elements: the yarn, the type of weave or knit, the color combinations and patterns, and the surface finishing. If the yarns are dyed before weaving, the weaving process determines the weave configuration and the color and pattern characteristics of the fabric.

Individual looms are quite small; one operator looks after several looms. Output from an individual loom in linear yards per hour is low, and high-volume output can be achieved only by having several looms operating at once. Large weaving sheds therefore have hundreds of looms arranged in rows, with a combined output measured in linear miles per hour.

A weaving operation is visually and managerially different from a paper mill or an automobile assembly line, where the machine or the line dominates the people. In those operations only one product can be run at a time. Managers plan daily operations and product changeovers to ensure minimal disruption to operations and the lowest possible levels of enforced labor idle time. The weaving operation, in contrast, offers the extreme possibility of having every loom used to produce a different fabric. Because of the control problems such an operation entails, large operations do not go to that extreme. Many, in fact, produce only one product at a time in an extremely long run, treating the looms as if they were one giant loom.

Machine operators are expected to keep the machines operating as close to capacity as possible by reducing the amount of unplanned downtime caused by stoppages. Many technological improvements have been based on automating the repair and maintenance functions to reduce the degree of dependence of the system on human operators.

Just as individual operators are judged on the basis of individual machine efficiency, managers are judged on the basis of mill efficiency. This is measured across all the operating machinery, and implicit in the measure is the ability to schedule the equipment. Different fabrics are produced at different rates by the same loom; it is management's task to ensure that the best combinations of loom and fabric are used to generate the greatest efficiency. And planners at the unit or head office level are judged on the decisions they make concerning the loading of each facility, or the assignment of specific jobs to specific mills. The better the overall assignment, the better the overall unit and corporate efficiency.

With the arrival of serious foreign competition in North America, the emphasis in operations has changed and, along with it, the ways in which employees are evaluated. The focus has been expanded to include effectiveness as well as efficiency. To become more effective, Milliken has had to adopt advanced technologies aggressively. For the mills in the Decorative Fabrics Business Unit, that has meant new looms that can operate at higher cyclic rates, increasing the number of linear feet of fabric woven per loom per hour. This means fewer loom hours to produces an order. Given other equipment that can reduce the changeover time between production runs, the minimum efficient length of a run can also be reduced.

Fewer loom hours, shorter changeover times between runs, and the ability to operate profitably on short runs create the potential for greater operational flexibility and responsiveness; a production run can be planned to be in production for a shorter period than was previously possible. Operational flexibility gained through technology purchases inevitably costs money, though, and other ways must be found to reduce costs if increased flexibility of this sort is to be cost-effective.

Milliken decided that the only way to reduce costs was to declare war on waste both operationally and strategically. Operationally, the firm has adopted a philosophy of making only what the customer wants, in the quantity needed, and at the time required. This was made possible through a commitment to hold excess manufacturing capacity which can be activated as the need arises. When this is done, production planning problems become less serious and few jobs have to be stopped to free up capacity for orders with a close due date.

Although the initial focus was inside mills (with the next process being defined as the immediate customer), the philosophy was extended to suppliers and customers as well. In the process of eliminating limited value-added activities, the firm discovered that the management structure could be flattened by eliminating management positions that essentially moved rather than transformed information. Seven hundred managers across the firm were affected, but none were fired. All were reassigned as process improvement specialists in manufacturing and support activities such as billing and customer service.

Production is only one aspect of operations, and focusing on waste in that area alone limits the improvements a firm can make. In the Decorator Fabrics Business Unit waste time has been reduced further by reducing the design cycle time, or the time from a customer's request for a new fabric through acceptance of a test swatch (small sample of woven fabric). This was made possible through the use of computer-aided design (CAD) tools which enable designers to modify existing designs quickly and easily. CAD tools also allow a new fabric specification to be transmitted electronically to the appropriate mill with no errors in translation.

The drive for improvement has led to the adoption of a continuous improvement philosophy at all levels of the firm. In 1988 this philosophy was evident in the formation of about 1,600 corrective-action teams that addressed specific internal issues identified by associates as impediments to continuous improvement in quality. These teams were made up mainly of lower-level associates, supported by process-improvement specialists and other management personnel. About 200 supplier action teams and 500 customer action teams were formed in that period; they led to reduced costs of doing business with suppliers and to new products and market opportunities through existing customers.

As a result of this change in philosophy, Milliken has experienced a 60 percent reduction in the cost of nonconformance to specifications, primarily through a reduction in the number of off-quality discounts given and the number of customer returns. In addition, on-time deliveries have gone from 75 percent to over 99 percent. Milliken now supplies Japanese and Korean automakers with fabric.

Although product quality is essential, it is quality in administrative and support processes that influences responsiveness and competitiveness. In a firm with many customers and an almost unlimited range of products, responsiveness is measured in two ways: the ability to provide a customer with a sample of the product quickly and the ability to get the fabric into production. Elimination of waste in all areas, a key focus of Milliken's improvement process, leads to less waste time and less confusion. Improved total quality means lower costs for everyone in the value chain.

Tour 6: Florida Power and Light Company

Florida Power and Light Company (FPL) is a private investor-owned electricity generation and distribution utility serving a 27,650-square-mile territory in northern Florida. In 1991 FPL was the fourth largest and fastest growing electric utility in the United States. At that time the firm had over 3 million customer accounts, 15,000 employees, more than 58,000 miles of distribution lines, and more than 13,600 megawatts (MW) of generating capacity from 13 operating plants. One of FPL's two nuclear generating plants, the Turkey Point facility, accounted for 1,332 MW of electricity, or approximately 10 percent of FPL's total capacity. In 1989 FPL was the first foreign firm to apply for and win Japan's oldest quality award, the Deming Application Prize.

Electric utilities are capital-intensive by nature; large, multi-million-dollar generating stations supply electricity through vast transmission and distribution networks. Included in the network are substations in which voltages are lowered from the thousands of volts in principal transmission lines to the 110 volts in domestic distribution systems. All the generating utilities in North America are linked into a continental grid; British Columbia Hydro in Canada may sell surplus power to FPL today, and FPL may sell surplus power to New Brunswick or Oregon or Louisiana tomorrow. This is an important safety net; not having the capacity to supply customers with the electricity they want when they want it can be embarrassing and costly.

Capital-intensive companies are very deeply concerned with demand forecasting and capacity planning. This is not surprising; adding capacity is expensive and time-consuming. In addition, the planning and approval process for environmentally sensitive projects has become increasingly complicated; it is common for the approval process to take five years or more. Capacity expansion projects also have to be considered alongside capacity replacement projects and pollution control projects; FPL budgeted $300 million to load fuel into Turkey Point in 1991 (this included the installation of a backup generator). In the case of a private utility, the funds to finance capital works have to be raised in the capital markets.

FPL has been very aggressive in adding capacity; seven facilities were added in the mid-1970s, creating an extra 6,800 MW of capacity. Aggressively adding capacity in anticipation of increased demand can be worrisome for a utility. If the expected growth is checked by a recession, the utility will have to live with the power it cannot sell to its consumers or to another utility. A utility would normally factor into the cost of a new or expanded power plant the anticipated underutilization of capacity. FPL, however, had a potentially worse problem: Demand for the 1990s was significantly underestimated by the Florida state authorities on which FPL relied for projections. As a consequence, FPL has budgeted $6.6 billion to add 5,400 MW of generating capacity by 1999. The cost per kilowatt of new capacity was anticipated to be more than 540 percent of the then average cost of installed capacity; this cost would have a significant impact on customers' bills.

Until this capacity comes on line there may be some anxious moments as demand comes close to available supply. A utility can rarely rely on having all its generating capacity available; maintenance and routine repair tasks take generators out of commission. Turkey Point, for example, was out of commission for 11 months in 1991, leaving FPL with only a 13 percent capacity cushion.

In addition to being capital-intensive, utilities have traditionally focused on being cost-effective. This attitude developed as a result of the regulation of prices to consumers. With the removal of regulation, entrepreneurs have been able to take away large customers from major utilities through imaginative possibilities such as cogeneration. Consequently, FPL and other utilities now have to be cost-competitive, not merely cost-effective. At the same time the nature of dependency on electricity has changed. The microchip/computer revolution means that very few consumers can be without power for even a fraction of a second without being affected; think of what happens to a digital bedside alarm clock when the voltage dips slightly. Utilities are now expected to supply uninterrupted power and highly reliable and customized services at a competitive price.

As FPL realized, utilities have to focus on quality in order to survive; they must understand all the costs and processes that enable them to satisfy their customers. Focusing on cost reduction alone cannot improve quality, but focusing on quality and the processes that influence quality can improve quality and productivity. Improving productivity automatically lowers costs. Since prices for power are established in a free market, FPL's rate of return results from the difference between price and the cost of operating efficiently. FPL therefore has had to concentrate on making its processes more reliable. This implies making the processes safe as well, for a regulator can shut down unsafe processes that are reliable and effective. Regulators are particularly sensitive to safety issues in nuclear generating stations.

As a result of several initiatives involving personnel from all functions, divisions, and levels of the company, FPL was able to document the following improvements that directly influenced productivity:

- A significant reduction in Nuclear Regulatory Commission violations from almost 60 in 1986 to fewer than 20 in 1990
- A reduction of automatic nuclear reactor trips from about 0.6 per 1,000 critical hours in 1986 to about 0.2 in 1990
- A reduction of outages from about 900 in 1986 to about 600 in 1990
- A reduction in the fossil equivalent forced outage rate (for nonnuclear generating capacity) from more than 14 percent in 1986 to 3.2 percent through May 1990
- A reduction in startup/shutdown defects per cycle in fossil fuel units from about 3.8 per cycle in 1986 to about 0.5 in 1990
- A reduction in meter reader errors from 1 in 2,000 to around 1 in 15,000

These improvements resulted in an equivalent capacity gain of 700 MW of capacity. This gain in capacity resulted in a cumulative net revenue requirement reduction of more than $300 million to customers. In addition, better and more flexible management of capacity enabled FPL to operate with a 15 percent reserve margin rather than the 30 percent the company had traditionally maintained.

Quality to FPL is more than an uninterrupted surge- and ripple-free power supply. Quality also applies to the administrative processes, for waste elimination reduces costs and appropriate contact improves a customer's perceptions of the utility. Responsiveness is also more than the emergency response to power outages, although that is important. It also means the ability to identify and overcome temporary power shortages and plan for longer-term capacity needs by planning to increase or replace generating capacity. Quality and responsiveness also apply to indirect concerns, particularly environmental concerns. Thus, the management of a nuclear generating facility has had to be changed to take into account emerging knowledge about nuclear generation.

LEARNING FROM THE TOURS

One can learn a number of lessons from these tours despite the differences among the six firms. This diversity of examples shows the universality of some of these lessons. What may differ are the ways in which these issues have to be addressed in each instance.

Responsiveness

Satisfying customers is in part a function of responding to real needs and expectations, which are constantly evolving and changing. This is perhaps the most critical management issue, and many firms are reluctant to alter a previously successful formula. **Responsiveness** is *not* a reaction; it is a planned state of preparedness to which these six firms aspire. This preparedness is both tactical and strategic, often dealing with issues about which customers may not yet be aware.

Because these firms have satisfied their customers, they have established standards below which they cannot slip. Indeed, customers expect more as time passes, and each company is continually responding and adjusting to these increased expectations.

Complexity

Satisfying the customer is becoming increasingly complex. Because of increasing knowledge and changing competitor actions, customers expect to be satisfied across a widening range of factors. Management of this increasingly complex sense of product requires an increasingly complex set of management skills. In most instances this complexity can best be exercised in a group rather than an individual decision-making setting.

Unity of Product

The traditional dichotomy between service and manufacturing operations must be questioned. There *is* a difference between tangible and intangible elements, and virtually *all* products have a mix of these elements. Thus firms may benefit by developing a new understanding of what a product actually is.

It must now be recognized that each product consists of a core concept, critical components, and facilitating goods and services. The **core product concept** defines the basic business (e.g., flexible transportation for automobile manufacturers). The **critical product components** involve the essential characteristics all competitive products must exhibit (e.g., independent power source, steering mechanism, wheels). **Facilitating goods and services** are discretionary product elements by which a firm differentiates its products from those of its competitors. For an automobile, examples might include antilock brakes and interest-free loans.

Integration and Value Added

Increasing complexity can lead to confusion and chaos. Firms therefore need to eliminate confusion through control devices that ensure that every person and function works with the same information and toward the same ends. This integration of functions, processes, and products must have a focus, and in all these companies the focus is the customer and satisfying the customer. In fact, each company has *institutionalized* the customer focus; that is, *everybody* in the firm accepts the customer's central position.

If the focus of the firm is the customer, everything the firm does should improve matters for the customers. This gives rise to the concept of **value added** and to thinking of processes and activities as being either value-added or non-value-added activities while enhancing the value they add to the customer at every step. This concept applies not only to essential manufacturing steps but to managerial, administrative, and service activities as well. An improved design process, for example, adds value.

Operations Excellence and Teamwork

To be responsive, the site visits suggest, a firm has to have excellent operations. Excellence in operations is not the only factor, of course. Operations must also be capable of effectively supporting what the firm wants to do. This means a couple of things: First, the operations must be well managed. Second, every manager must be aware of what the operations function is capable of supporting. The same can be said for marketing and sales, which, along with operations, are the value-added functions within a firm.

The quality awards reinforce this, for each one places a high priority on process excellence. Every activity within a firm can be thought of as a process or in process terms—people even speak of management process—and thus every activity the firm undertakes should be amenable to improvement. Every manager is in some sense an operations manager, and operations excellence should be observed in every facet of the firm.

Integration, responsiveness, and excellence all imply **teamwork,** and all six of these firms emphasize teams. These teams exist in the operating areas and markedly improve performance. These firms also use teams in other areas, starting with effective senior management teams. Most teams consist of people selected across functions. Teams that operate single process are called "gangs" (a time-honored name with no negative implications) or **work groups.** In all six firms teams reduce the need for formal communication, increase the effectiveness of coordination, and improve problem solving and decision making.

Difference and Commonality

Each of these organizations is different from the others and is unique in many ways. These differences are manifested in several ways: products, processes, markets, pressures on managers and other people, means of evaluation and control, and ways of organizing the enterprise.

There are, however, underlying characteristics that are common to all successful organizations:

- Close links between the organization and its customers
- Close links between the organization and its suppliers
- A commitment to continually improve the ability to compete simultaneously on cost, quality, flexibility, dependability, time, and service
- Effective use of technology for strategic advantage
- A less hierarchical, or compartmentalized, organization
- Policies that promote continuous learning, teamwork, and flexibility

WHERE DOES ALL THIS PLACE US?

Why is all this important? In a word, **competitiveness.** In most firms the function that has the greatest impact on profitability is operations, for the operations function by and large adds the most value to a firm's products. As the site visits show, though, no single function is more critical to the success of an enterprise than is any other. If a vehicle designer is asked what car parts are critical to the task of satisfying customers, the answer will be "All of them." If a carpenter is asked what tools are most important, the answer will be the same. Without excellence in *all* functional areas, firms cannot compete for long in free, competitive markets.

The role of operations is to support the objectives and strategy of the corporation as effectively and efficiently as possible. This requires that people in general management and other functional management positions understand how they affect, and are in turn affected by, operations decisions. Integration and responsiveness can come about only as a result of understanding and cooperation.

All managers must therefore have a good understanding of the principles that underlie the processes of designing and managing operating systems, integrating those systems with the rest of the firm and the external environment, and making the operating systems even more competitive as environments and resources change. That is what this book is about: *developing an understanding of and principles for the total management of operations.*

KEY TERMS

Fast responsiveness
Total quality management
Customer satisfaction
Customer-based quality
Malcolm Baldrige National Quality
  Awards

Canada Awards for Business
  Excellence
Deming Application Prize
Responsiveness
Core product concept
Critical product components

Facilitating goods
  and services
Value added
Teamwork
Work groups
Competitiveness

DISCUSSION QUESTIONS

1. What are the important factors in operations management that you want to learn about in this course? If you are not going to move into an operations position, what use will you make of that knowledge?

2. What role do quality awards play in shaping competitiveness? Does this vary from country to country? If so, why?

3. What are the differences among the Baldrige Award, the Deming Prize, and the Canada Awards for Business Excellence? Why do these differences exist?

4. The six site visits point out several common features in these firms. What are they, and how important are they?

5. How would you define quality after visiting these six operations? What does each organization emphasize about quality? Are there any common features in regard to the quality issue in these enterprises?

6. How important is teamwork to the six visited firms? Where have teams been used? Where have they not been used?

7. As Zytec shows, it is possible to recover well from a bad competitive position. How should this recovery process be managed? What should be done first?

8. After visits to the six firms—three manufacturing and three service operations—can you arrange these operations in some way? (This issue will be discussed later, but try to figure out what important dimension can be used to classify the operations.)

9. How important has changing the operating technologies been in achieving increased competitiveness? In what strategic ways is the technology used? (This will be discussed in later chapters.)

10. Knowledge has become an important competitive parameter. Where in the firm is this knowledge located, and how might it be used to the firm's strategic advantage?

11. Can you identify any businesses that are *not* under competitive threat from foreign competition? What characteristics do these firms have? Will they *ever* be exposed to increased competition? What should they do?

12. What is the role of the manager in charge of operations in today's world? What skills should such a person possess?

13. What does *value-added activities* mean? Can you identify any in these six companies or anywhere else? Can you identify non-value-added activities?

14. Why is the distinction between value-added activities and non-value-added activities important?

REFERENCES AND SELECTED BIBLIOGRAPHY

Bemowski, Karen [1993], "The State of the States," *Quality Progress,* vol. 26, no. 5, May, pp. 27–36.

Canada Awards for Business Excellence, Entry Guide 1993, Industry, Science and Technology Canada, Ottawa.

Cooper, Robin, and Peter B. Turney [1990], "Zytec Corporation (B)," Harvard Business School Case 190–066.

Garvin, David A. [1991], "How the Baldrige Award Really Works," *Harvard Business Review,* November–December, pp. 80–95.

Lopez, Charles E. [1991], "The Malcolm Baldrige National Quality Award: It's Really Not Whether You Win or Lose . . . ," *The Quality Observer,* November, pp. 1, 5, 13, 14, 20–23.

CHAPTER 1

OPERATIONS MANAGEMENT AND GLOBAL COMPETITION

Managers in progressive organizations ask two fundamental questions:

- How can we totally satisfy our customers?
- How can we do a better job than our competitors of satisfying customers?

These issues should not be addressed in a contemplative, philosophical fashion. They have to be dealt with urgently, exhaustively, and continually by all the managers in an organization. In an age of uncertainty and increased competitive pressures, fine-tuning is not enough. Most firms need to rethink their whole approach to competition.

This chapter will examine operations and the role of operating and operations managers within a firm. *All* managers are operating managers because they manage processes that employ and transform resources in the process of adding value. Thus, they need to apply the principles of operations management to their own jobs. Also, all managers in all functions must understand how operations man-

agement decisions affect other functions and in turn are affected by the decisions made by managers in other functions. These two interdependent foci are the lenses through which this book should be read and evaluated.

The changing competitive environment will be discussed, along with its impact on operations. The supplement traces the general history of operations and highlights the changing issues faced by operations managers. One fact will become clear: The issues facing operations managers have become more complex and more immediate as time has passed. You will also learn why and how this steady evolution has changed to a revolution in the last few years and why there is a need for a new way of thinking about operations in the new environment.

By the end of the chapter you will have been introduced to the new way of thinking and the new competitive form firms will have to adopt as they approach the twenty-first century: the fast-response organization.

1.1 MANAGERIAL ORIENTATION

Customers are demanding better quality, more variety, and increased responsiveness to their needs—all at lower prices. Revolutions in computer technology, telecommunications, logistics, and transportation are fueling this trend and intensifying competition.

Over the last few decades the North American share of the global market for manufactured goods has declined drastically. **Productivity** growth has also been relatively slow.

DEFINITION: Productivity is the ratio of outputs to inputs. At the national level, productivity is often measured by dividing the total economic output of a country by the total number of worker-hours expended.

As illustrated in Exhibit 1.1, in 1950 the gap between manufacturing productivity in the United States and that in other G-7 countries was quite large and favored the United States. Over the next 40 years, however, the gap was significantly narrowed as productivity growth in those countries outpaced that in the United States. At the same time, U.S. domination in the steel, automobile, consumer electronics, and other industries was severely eroded.[1] This trend has raised concern about the international competitiveness of North America and its future economic progress.

---

[1] Products such as VCRs, telephones, tape decks, machine tool centers, color televisions, semiconductors, and computers were invented in the United States, but American producers' share of the domestic market for these products declined significantly in the last decade. By the late 1980s the United States had become a net exporter of only wheat, soybeans, lumber, and aircraft.

EXHIBIT 1.1   MANUFACTURING PRODUCTIVITY LEVELS

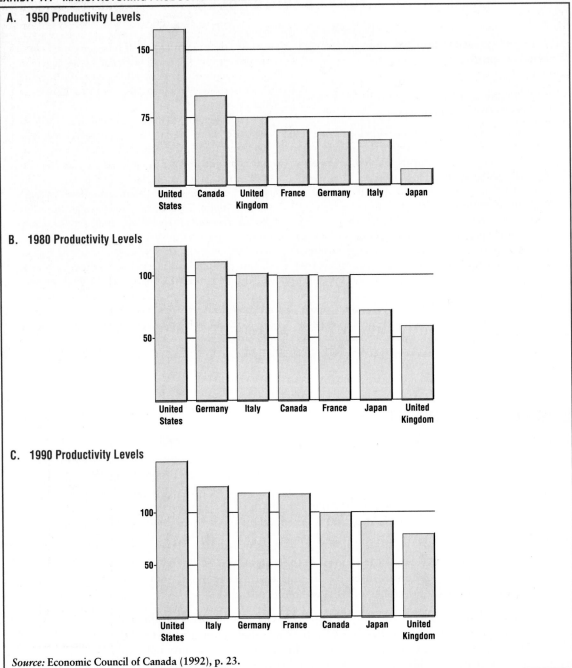

A.   1950 Productivity Levels

B.   1980 Productivity Levels

C.   1990 Productivity Levels

Source: Economic Council of Canada (1992), p. 23.

No market is completely safe; in order to survive, companies have to be responsive to changes in the marketplace. In almost every industry one can find companies like the ones described in the Startup Chapter. These companies have developed new and better ways of producing goods and services that meet customers' needs, and customers are responding enthusiastically. These companies have succeeded by recognizing that the world has changed and that the ways in which companies produce goods and services must change as well. Let us review these environmental changes and some of the new approaches. The aim here is to develop an understanding of what makes a company succeed.

1.2 THE NEW REALITIES OF THE MARKETPLACE

In the United States a strategy based on the "bigger is better" philosophy[2] worked extremely well in the years after World War II. Demand for consumer goods and services in that period was so strong that firms struggled just to keep up.

In an economy characterized by a seemingly unlimited supply of resources, ever-expanding markets, and consumer acceptance of standardized products, **mass production** makes sense. Today, however, customers are more discriminating and competition is much more sophisticated. Consider the following trends:

- Rapid advances in technology and in the biological and physical sciences are providing industries with new materials, new products, and new market needs. Over 90 percent of all recorded scientific advances have taken place in the last 30 years.
- Escalation of new product introductions is shortening the life span of most products. Electronic and other high-technology products now have life spans as short as several months.
- Continuous reductions in transportation and communication costs are increasing global competition. In a recent survey, over 70 percent of U.S. industries indicated that they were under a full-scale attack by foreign competitors [Albin (1992)].
- Global competition is intensifying as countries are moving to eliminate protectionism and create large free-trade zones.[3]
- Markets in general are fragmenting, not expanding. Competition is intense. Customers are demanding high-quality products, at a reasonable price, that meet their needs. Unsatisfied customers are switching from one product to another.
- Growing international concern about the environment is being translated into stricter legislation. Conventional energy supplies are not limitless, nor is the world's ability to absorb disposed of products and process by-products.

As illustrated in Exhibit 1.2, these trends have profound implications for operations. Large volumes of standardized products will not necessarily be absorbed by

---

[2] This philosophy is based partly on the concept of economies of scale. Economies of scale occur when total operating costs increase at a slower rate than does production volume. For example, it may cost $200,000 to produce 100,000 units of a particular product ($2 per unit) but only $350,000 to produce 200,000 units ($1.75 per unit).

[3] Trading blocs are being established in Europe and in the Pacific rim, for example. The North American Free Trade Agreement (NAFTA) has drawn Canada, the United States, and Mexico together into a trading bloc. African and Latin American countries (which account for roughly 20 percent of the world's population and a major share of its natural resources) are beginning to imitate the export-driven development strategies of South Korea, Taiwan, and other rapidly developing southeast Asian nations.

EXHIBIT 1.2 MARKET FORCES AND MASS PRODUCTION

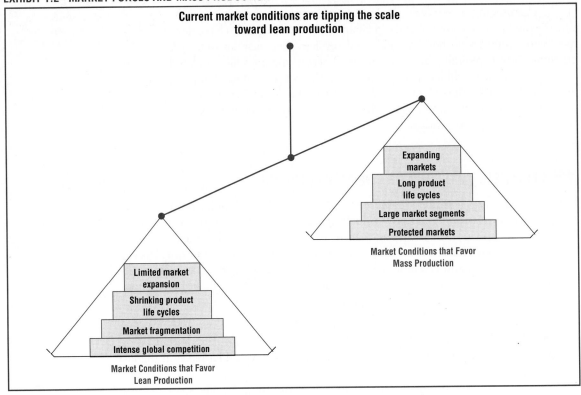

**Current market conditions are tipping the scale
toward lean production**

Expanding
markets

Long product
life cycles

Large market segments

Protected markets

Market Conditions that Favor
Mass Production

Limited market
expansion

Shrinking product
life cycles

Market fragmentation

Intense global competition

Market Conditions that Favor
Lean Production

the market. New and revised products must be developed quickly and brought to market in increasing numbers. The increased risk of inventory obsolescence and widening product lines means that holding large inventories is becoming prohibitively expensive. Another means will have to be found to protect firms from forecasting errors, manufacturing defects, and scheduling problems.

North American industry is moving away from using enormous facilities to house mass-production operations. Effective operation requires smaller facilities housing operating processes that can produce a variety of products in various volumes and for random orders. This flexibility allows a firm to be more responsive across a number of market segments and to different customers within each segment. Demand for a firm's products should increase while the firm maintains low inventory levels.

Operating costs are being reduced through process simplification and through the design of products that are easier to manufacture and assemble. This is how Northern Telecom, a North American manufacturer of telecommunications equipment, has reduced the cost of its electronic telephones while maintaining a high level of quality.

Computer-integrated operations help a firm quickly absorb, analyze, and disseminate the complex data associated with wide product ranges and evolving markets and processes. The number one U.S. retailer, Wal-Mart, attributes its success partly to the adoption of advanced communications technology and integrated computer systems.

These are some of the ways in which firms are meeting the challenges of a changing marketplace. There are two important messages to note here:

1. Underpinning corporate productivity and effectiveness is the need for functional areas to become closely linked among themselves and with the whole value chain.[4]
2. The operations function is important to these strategies, and operations plays a central role in the well-being of a firm.

Today's dynamic operating environment brings with it the opportunity and the necessity to develop new solutions to new and existing problems. This chapter will present many exciting new ideas, tools, and techniques that relate directly to operations. It will also describe tools and concepts that have been in use for decades and are still valuable. First, however, let us examine the basic terms relating to operations and operations management.

1.3 DEFINING OPERATIONS AND OPERATIONS MANAGEMENT

DEFINITION: Operations refers to the production of goods and services, the set of value-added activities that transform inputs into outputs.

A firm's products are combinations of various types of **inputs:** materials, labor, energy, information, and technology. When a firm uses a combination of tools, machines, techniques, and human skills, value is added to the inputs, transforming them into products that are sold (or provided) to a firm's customers (**outputs**). **Operations management** refers to the management of the transformation process.

DEFINITION: Operations management is concerned with the production of goods and services. In conjunction with other functional areas,[5] it also deals with the management of resources (inputs) and the distribution of finished goods and services to customers (outputs).

Since *operations* refers to all the activities along the value-added chain, it is a much broader term than **production** (see Exhibit 1.3). The specific responsibilities of operations may vary from one firm to the next, depending on the nature of the transformation process and the organizational structure chosen by the firm.

The transformation process can be as simple as getting a haircut or as large and complex as manufacturing an automobile. Automobile production involves thousands of people in several industries who produce hundreds of intermediate products which become inputs for the final assembly process.

Outputs of the transformation process range from **pure goods** to **pure services.**

DEFINITION: A **pure good** is a tangible product that can be stored, transported, and purchased for later use.

DEFINITION: A **pure service** is an intangible product which cannot be stored since it is consumed as it is produced.

---

[4] The *value chain* is the continuous thread running from initial suppliers through manufacturers to final customers.

[5] Marketing, finance/accounting, research and development, human resources, and data processing are examples of functional areas.

EXHIBIT 1.3 OPERATIONS VERSUS PRODUCTION SPAN OF CONTROL

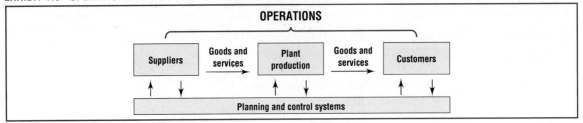

A university lecture is a pure service, while the pad of paper and the pencil with which a student takes notes are pure goods. In reality, most products are not pure goods or pure services but a combination of both.

Consider a stereo manufacturer. The stereo equipment makes up only part of the product the manufacturer is selling. The warranty, after-sales support, and financing options are also part of the package. The customer may be buying status and prestige as well. Within a firm, services such as maintenance, training, billing, payroll administration, and internal auditing must also be provided.[6]

General Motors' biggest supplier is the health care provider Blue Cross–Blue Shield. In terms of output, one of GM's biggest products is financial and insurance services, which, together with EDS (its computer services arm), account for a fifth of total revenue.

Consider the local McDonald's, a hospital operating room, or a custom home builder. None are strictly service or manufacturing operations; in each case a strong service element and a strong production element go hand in hand.

In the new world of business, a factory is a service operation and service is a factory operation. The time interval between production and consumption of the total product is decreasing; in some instances these two acts occur simultaneously. Intense competition is forcing firms to provide more and better service. The service potential of operations can no longer be ignored and *must* be exploited.

As demonstrated in Exhibit 1.4, in many situations operations managers in both the manufacturing[7] and service sectors have to make similar types of decisions. Whatever the firm, there is a wide range of issues for which the operations function must assume leadership. The concepts and methods examined throughout this text are therefore relevant to firms in both sectors. Note that the questions raised in Exhibit 1.4 are neither mutually exclusive nor exhaustive; many of them can be best answered by taking an integrative perspective and ensuring that every function is involved.

1.4 OPERATIONS MANAGEMENT IN THE SERVICE SECTOR

The service sector is now growing far more rapidly than is the manufacturing sector; over 75 percent of the North American workforce is now employed in the service sector. The motion picture industry employs more people in the United States than

---

[6] Between 65 and 75 percent of the people employed in manufacturing industries typically perform "service tasks" such as accounting, human resources, law, and marketing.

[7] In the operations management field, agriculture, mining, fishing, and construction are considered parts of the manufacturing sector. This convention is followed here.

does the auto parts industry. Health and Medicare now account for about one-eighth of total U.S. output. More people work in the computer industry than in the auto, auto parts, steel, mining, petroleum, and natural gas industries put together.

As was emphasized in Section 1.3, the majority of issues and concerns faced by managers in both the service sector and the manufacturing sector are the same. However, the special nature of services imposes additional constraints. The type and extent of these constraints depend on the kind of service provided. It is thus reasonable to assume that service operations depend in part on the type of service provided.

Classification of Service Operations

Because management issues differ with the type of service operation, it is important to find an appropriate way to classify and segment the service sector. One way of classifying services is on the basis of where the transformation process takes place. For some services (e.g., pest control) the firm must go to the customer, while for others (e.g., a movie theater) the customer goes to the firm. Some services (e.g., credit cards) can be performed without the firm and the customer meeting. Alternative bases for classification include:

- Extent of customer contact (e.g., hospital versus postal service)
- Extent of service customization (e.g., legal service versus public transportation)
- Extent to which customer contact personnel exercise judgment in meeting individual customer needs (e.g., medical practice versus movie theater)
- Extent of relationship between customer and firm: discrete versus continuous or formal, membership basis versus no formal relationship (e.g., car rental versus insurance, automobile club versus police protection)

EXHIBIT 1.4 ISSUES AND CONCERNS IN OPERATIONS MANAGEMENT

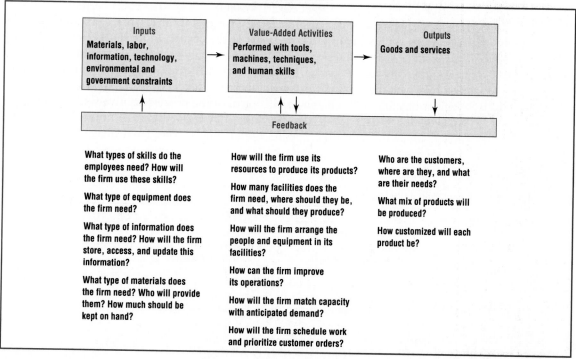

- Extent of labor intensity (e.g., law firm versus movie theater)
- Direct recipient of the service: people or things (e.g., restaurant versus janitorial service)
- Tangibility of service (e.g., haircut versus news broadcast)

Examples of services classified by both the degree to which customers are involved in the transformation process (extent of customer contact) and the tangibility of the service provided are included in Exhibit 1.5.

High-Contact and Low-Contact Services

Classifying services by the extent of customer contact is particularly helpful. As the time spent by customers in the transformation process increases, the difficulty of controlling the operation increases while the firm's freedom to design efficient procedures decreases. The relationship between the customer and the firm's employees who have direct contact with the customer becomes more important. It also becomes more difficult to match the supply of services to the demand for them.

High-contact services such as those provided by doctors, teachers, and taxi drivers are difficult to control. This is the case because the customer is in essence *always* involved in the production of the service. Consequently, the customer has a direct voice in the type and quality of the service as well as the time required to complete the service.

This raises two issues. First, unless an appointment system is used, customer demand varies from day to day (or even from hour to hour) and it is difficult for a firm to determine how many staff members to schedule. In these cases the effective management of waiting lines is important.

Second, the workforce's attitude affects the customer's view of the service. Any employee who interacts with the customer automatically becomes part of the product. Thus, the interpersonal attributes of the employee directly influence service effectiveness in a high-contact service system.

Low-contact services such as those provided by insurance companies and the post office do not require the presence of the customer during the transformation process. Physical contact with the customer occurs only at a service desk where the customer requests the service. Since the customer cannot strongly influence the process by which the service is provided, there is a tendency to standardize procedures. Standardization makes managerial control of the process relatively straightforward and enables managers to gauge efficiency. Low-contact service firms tend to have a systematic and predictable operation and can be considered quasi manufacturing service firms.

EXHIBIT 1.5   SERVICE CLASSIFICATION TABLE

	Extent of Customer Contact	
	Low	**High**
Low	● Financial institutions ● Entertainment ● Maintenance services	● Schools ● Travel agents ● Legal services
Tangibility of Service		
High	● Supermarkets ● Fast-food outlets	● Gourmet restaurants ● Specialty retail stores

In contrast to a high-contact system, customer demand in a low-contact system is relatively stable; therefore, matching capacity to demand is much easier. In such a system there is continually increasing freedom in designing efficient procedures. Rather than needing strong public and interpersonal skills, employees are evaluated more on the basis of their technical and analytic attributes.

1.5 TYPES OF OPERATING PROCESSES

Think back to the tours through six different types of companies in the Startup Chapter. In each case an effective operating process was essential to the company's continuing success. In general, the processes by which goods and services are produced can be categorized on the basis of the following classification system:

Job shop (jumbled flow). A wide variety of customized products are made by a highly skilled workforce using general-purpose equipment. These processes are referred to as jumbled-flow processes because there are many possible routings through the process.
Examples from the Startup Chapter: Mayo Clinic and Fujima International. Other examples: home renovating firm, stereo repair shop, gourmet restaurant.
Intermittent (batch) flow. A mixture of general-purpose and special-purpose equipment is used to produce small to large batches of products.
Examples from the Startup Chapter: Zytec Corporation and Reimer Express Lines. Other examples: clothing and book manufacturers, winery, caterer.
Repetitive flow (mass production). Several standardized products follow a predetermined flow through sequentially dependent work centers. Workers typically are assigned to a narrow range of tasks and work with highly specialized equipment.
Example from the Startup Chapter: Milliken's Decorator Fabrics Business Unit. Other examples: automobile and computer assembly lines, insurance home office.
Continuous flow (flow shop). Commoditylike products flow continuously through a linear process.
Example from the Startup Chapter: Florida Power and Light. Other examples: chemical, oil, and sugar refineries, cafeteria.

These four categories represent points on a continuum of process organizations. Processes that fall within a particular category share many characteristics that fundamentally influence how a process should be managed. Some of these characteristics are outlined in Exhibit 1.6 and will be discussed in detail throughout the book.

Frequently a firm has more than one type of operating process in its production system. For example, a firm such as Zytec may use a repetitive-flow process to produce high-volume parts but use an intermittent-flow process for lower-volume parts.

A link often exists between a firm's product line and its operating processes. Job-shop organizations are commonly utilized when a product or family of products is first introduced. As sales volumes increase and the product's design stabilizes, the process tends to move along the continuum toward a continuous-flow shop. Thus, as products evolve, the nature of the operating processes used to produce them evolves as well. The product-process life cycle matrix developed by Hayes and Wheelwright (1984) depicts this relationship well. This classic framework will be examined presently, but first let us briefly review the concept of the product life cycle.

EXHIBIT 1.6 CHARACTERISTICS OF DIFFERENT OPERATING PROCESSES

Characteristics	*Traditional Continuum of Process Organizations*			
	Job Shop	Intermittent Flow	Repetitive Flow	Continuous Flow
Type of products supported by process	Wide variety of customized products	Multiple products	Few, standardized products	Commoditylike products
Type of equipment used	General purpose	Mixture of general purpose and special purpose	Special purpose	
Process layout	Sets of similar-purpose equipment are grouped together		Equipment required for each product or product family is grouped together	
Routing of products through the process	Many possible routings		Predetermined flow through sequentially dependent work centers	Linear process
Production runs	Very small batches	Large batches	Larger batches	Continuous flow
Relative size and cost of permanent capacity increases	Small and inexpensive		Large, expensive, and difficult to justify	
Product changeovers	Quick		Time-consuming, may require plant closure	
Labor content of product	High		Low	
Size and type of workforce	Small, craft-trained, product-oriented, often required to perform a variety of changing tasks, problem solvers		Large, process-oriented, perform well-defined and specialized tasks, problem reporters	
Size of support staff	Small compared with workforce		Large compared with workforce	
Information flow between (1) workforce and management, (2) operations and its customers (e.g., marketing department)	Informal, product-focused Frequent interaction, close relationships		Formal, process-focused, distant Routine but distant; sales are frozen for long periods before production	
Industry examples from Startup Chapter	Fujima International, Mayo Clinic	Reimer Express Lines, Zytec	Milliken (DFB)	Florida Power and Light

The Product Life Cycle

Many students are introduced to the **product life cycle** in marketing courses.

DEFINITION: The pattern of changing rates of sales growth, product standardization, and competitive pressures exhibited by most products and product families is called the product life cycle.

The product life cycle (see Exhibit 1.7) comprises four stages: introduction, growth, maturity, and decline. In general, product forms (e.g., compact cars) follow this evolution more faithfully than do product classes (e.g., car) or specific product brands (e.g., Chevrolet). Let us examine this process:

- During a product's introduction to the market, prices are high and sales volumes are low. The few competitors in the market compete on the basis of product characteristics.

- As sales volumes grow and the product becomes more standardized, prices fall and many new competitors are attracted to the market. Product quality and availability are very important during this stage.
- Price and distribution pressures force many competitors either to consolidate or to leave the market. The few remaining competitors are large.
- As the product matures, a dominant design emerges and the focus shifts to price again. Sales volumes are high.
- Eventually consumer demand for the product erodes, and the product enters the decline stage. By this point, the product has been standardized and price is the basis of competition.

The Product-Process Life Cycle Matrix

Hayes and Wheelwright's **product-process life cycle matrix** illustrates the joint evolution of products and the process by which they are made (see Exhibit 1.8). The columns represent the product variety and volume associated with each of the four product life cycle stages: introduction, growth, maturation, and commodity/decline. Process organizations (job shop, intermittent flow, repetitive flow, and continuous flow) are represented by the rows in the matrix.

The matrix assumes that for a given product portfolio, there is a process organization that best fits the needs of the operation. The converse is more deterministic; for a given process organization, an operation is limited to a narrow range of product options.

A business such as Fujima International (see the Startup Chapter) can be placed in the upper left-hand corner. For Fujima, each job is unique and a job-shop process is effective in meeting product and market requirements. There is marked variety among orders and low volumes per order. The job-shop process permits the production of small lots, relying on flexibility of both the workforce and the equipment.

At the other extreme, operations such as Florida Power and Light produce standardized products through very expensive, capital-intensive continuous-flow operations; they can be placed in the bottom right-hand corner of the matrix. Here the focus is on operating efficiency and minimizing product costs.

Moving off the diagonal incurs costs. For example, moving to the right implies using a process more flexible than the product mix requires; therefore, the opportunity costs of maintaining a more flexible process are incurred. By contrast, moving off the diagonal to the left implies greater than necessary out-of-pocket expenses for

EXHIBIT 1.7 THE PRODUCT LIFE CYCLE CURVE

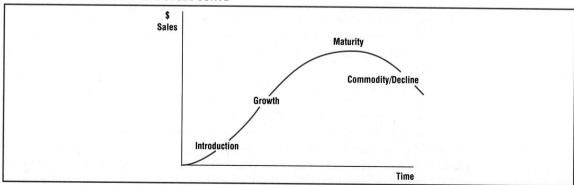

EXHIBIT 1.8 THE PRODUCT-PROCESS LIFE CYCLE MATRIX

Process Life Cycle Stage \ Product Life Cycle Stage	I. Introduction	II. Growth	III. Maturity	IV. Commodity/ Decline	PERFORMANCE MEASURES
I. Job Shop	Fujima International Mayo Clinic			Void (Insufficient Capacity and Excess Flexibility)	Labor Utilization Period Billings Average Days Late
II. Intermittent Flow		Reimer Express Lines Zytec			Throughput Time Setup Time Capacity Utilization Balance Loss Absenteeism
III. Repetitive Flow			Milliken		
IV. Continuous Flow	Void (Insufficient Flexibility and Excess Capacity)			Florida Power and Light	Capacity Utilization Unit Cost Waste
MANAGEMENT PRESSURES	Delivery Scheduling Bidding	Operator Motivation Volume/Product Mix Flexibility	Motivating Management Technological Change Cost Management		

investing in a more dedicated and capital-intensive process that is too rigid for the product characteristics.

The regions of the matrix marked "void" represent mismatches between the market requirements for the product and the facility's process capabilities. Consider the lower left-hand corner, for example. The market requires small quantities of customized products. A continuous-flow process would not have the necessary flexibility or be able to produce such small quantities efficiently.

For many years the product-process life cycle matrix has been a valuable tool in discussing the competitive placement of a firm. As companies move down the diagonal, high degrees of flexibility and quality are exchanged for lower unit costs and increased process dependability. Every position on the diagonal therefore entails a corresponding set of corporate strategies that the operation can support and a set of corresponding management concerns. Given the characteristics of the product and the industry, the choice of technology and operational facility becomes easier for the company.

When that positioning is complete, other important issues, such as the types of skills required, become easier to resolve. The matrix can help a firm recognize its distinctive competency (the distinguishing characteristics that fuel its success) and real competitors, focus its facilities, and identify the managerial implications of its positioning. In regard to this latter point, Exhibit 1.8 uses the categories "management pressures" and "performance measures" to reflect operations priorities that go from "flexibility" and "quality" at the upper left-hand end to "dependability" and "cost" at the bottom right-hand end of the diagonal. When deciding which operating process organization to use, the designers must consider the implications of particular types of organizations for both managers and operators. If managers and operators and those who support them do not act appropriately, the process will not meet its objectives. Selecting the appropriate people, skills, and knowledge is important, as is ensuring that they will act in ways consistent with the best interests of the firm. Evaluating and compensating operators and managers is a major issue for senior managers, since most employees attempt to improve their evaluations and thus increase their compensation.

The product-process life cycle matrix, however, reflects an operating environment in which few firms function today. The life cycle of many products and industries no longer follows the curve depicted in Exhibit 1.7. As was mentioned earlier, product life cycles are being shortened drastically. Products are more frequently being withdrawn before they reach the maturity stage, let alone the decline stage.

Changes in manufacturing technology are compounding this problem. Flexible manufacturing processes that can produce a variety of products in very small batch sizes are becoming more common. Many firms therefore are no longer moving down the diagonal of the matrix as their products mature. These firms are discovering that they *do not have to trade off high degrees of flexibility and quality for lower unit costs and increased process dependability*. In fact, as was stated at the beginning of this chapter, in many situations the marketplace no longer allows firms to make this traditional trade-off.

Chapter 2 will present a framework which describes how companies that try to satisfy their customers are simultaneously providing high-quality yet reasonably priced products by using flexible and dependable processes. These companies are **fast-response organizations**.

MANAGERIAL IMPLICATIONS

In analyzing a firm's operations, three facts become apparent:

- Operations are not homogeneous.
- Pressures on managers and workers differ across operations.
- Customer needs and expectations, and therefore competitive emphases, change with the type of operation.

Thus it is not realistic or strategically desirable to expect operations managers to focus primarily on cost reduction in all settings and under all sets of conditions. However, many firms, big and small, attempt to "downsize," "rightsize," or "rationalize" through capital elimination. Managers must understand the strategic role played by their operations before they can begin to make changes. Otherwise they run a grave risk of bringing about their own demise.

Traditionally, one way of segmenting operations was by identifying an operation as a "manufacturing" or a "service" operation. This distinction no longer makes sense, and one should think *operationally* in terms of the tangible and intangible elements of a product and the degree of direct customer participation in production. Once the balance of elements and the role of the customer have been established, the firm will be in a position to design the *total* operation.

CHAPTER SUMMARY

The competitive environment in which most firms operate is changing. Firms are competing globally but in markets that are fragmenting, not coalescing. Well-informed and value-conscious customers are buying goods and services that meet their individual needs regardless of the country of origin.

The mass-production approach that worked so well in the years after World War II is no longer viable in many markets. Firms that succeed in these new markets have developed flexible processes to produce a wide variety of high-quality but reasonably priced goods and services. Other trends include:

- Reducing operating costs through process simplification and by designing products with fewer parts that are easier to produce
- Using computer-integrated operations that enable a firm to quickly absorb, analyze, and disseminate data throughout the firm and along the entire value chain
- Building smaller plants close to the firm's customers
- Designing processes capable of producing successive generations of a family of products
- Encouraging closer ties between functional areas within the firm, between different levels in the firm's hierarchy, between the firm and its suppliers, and between the firm and its customers

All these trends are forcing firms to change the way they think about and manage operations.

Operations management is concerned with the production of both goods and services. Many of the issues faced by operations managers in the service sector are similar to those faced by managers in the manufacturing sector.

Classifying operating processes by their characteristics can provide valuable insights into how they should be managed. This chapter described a continuum of process organizations ranging from the job shop to the continuous-flow shop.

As demonstrated by the product-process life cycle matrix, there is often a close relationship between the product life cycle and the process organizations selected by a firm. The market trends discussed earlier, however, have disrupted the continuum of process organizations and weakened this relationship. Many firms cannot afford to trade off quality and flexibility for lower costs and increased process dependability. Chapter 2 will present a framework which describes how fast-response organizations are satisfying their customers by rejecting these traditional trade-offs.

KEY TERMS

Productivity	Operations management	Low-contact services	Product life cycle
Mass production	Production	Job shop	Product-process life cycle
Operations	Pure good	Intermittent flow	matrix
Inputs	Pure service	Repetitive flow	Fast-response
Outputs	High-contact services	Continuous flow	organizations

DISCUSSION QUESTIONS

1. You have seen, although only in outline, the new forces that are being unleashed on the global economy. Do you think there are firms that have a built-in advantage as they face the new competition? Who are they (if they exist), and what exactly is their advantage? Is it structural, technological, managerial, or workforce-centered?

2. What other inputs are used in the transformation process shown in Exhibit 1.5? Can you think of processes in which labor is not used at all?

3. What examples of pure services can you identify? What is being transformed in each of these service processes?

4. What examples can you give of less permanent manufactured goods and more tangible permanent services?

5. Can you identify processes in your house or apartment that are organized like a job shop? Like a batch process? Could you change these processes to another form and still be effective?

6. What are the differences among pure service, quasi manufacturing, and manufacturing operations from a customer's point of view? From the operation's point of view?

7. The Mayo Clinic is a complex system. Using the service classification table in Exhibit 1.5, which of the clinic's services can be used to fill the table?

8. Is McDonald's a service operation, a manufacturing operation, or both? Where would you place McDonald's on the product-process life cycle matrix?

9. Use the product-process matrix to position the following automobile manufacturers:

General Motors   Toyota
Volkswagen   BMW
Rolls Royce   Honda
Chrysler   Acura

What does the positon tell you about the likely competitive position of each company? Which companies are in the best position? Why? Do you see any limitations to the product-process matrix when used in this way? Could anything be done to overcome the deficiencies in this tool?

10. Where would you place the IBM personal computer on the product-process matrix? Where was it in 1980? Where will it be in the year 2000?

11. Can you think of any products that do (or did) not follow the product life cycle? What characteristics do (or did) these products have?

12. "History is bunk." Henry Ford is reputed to have said this when he was told that his new manufacturing process would not work because it had no precedent. What would Henry Ford say today?

13. One of the tasks of an operations manager is setting operating rules, operating procedures, and decision rules. What examples of these rules are established in your home? In the classroom? What say did you have when these rules and procedures were set?

14. As companies move from the mass-production era to the flexible-production era, will the role of operations management change? If so, how? Will increased automation have an impact? (See the supplement to this chapter to answer this question.)

15. Is process reengineering consistent with Taylor's teachings? Why or why not? (See the supplement to this chapter to answer this question.)

16. "The world has come full circle. In the last decade of the nineteenth century, F. W. Taylor expounded his Scientific Management theory, a theory that was debunked by 1930. Now, in the last decade of the twentieth century, North America is learning from the Japanese and others that Scientific Management lies at the heart of the Japanese miracle. It is time to get back to the basics and operate scientifically and efficiently." Is this statement correct? (See the supplement to this chapter to answer the question.)

REFERENCES AND SELECTED BIBLIOGRAPHY

Albin, John T. [1992], "Competing in a Global Market," *APICS,* January, pp. 29–32.

Belli, Pedro [1991], "Globalizing the Rest of the World," *Harvard Business Review,* July–August, pp. 50–55.

Dertouzos, M., R. Lester, and R. Solow [1988], *Interim Results of the MIT Commission on Industrial Productivity,* American Association for the Advancement of Science, Boston.

Dumaine, B. [1989], "What the Leaders of Tomorrow See," *Fortune,* July 3, pp. 48–62.

Economic Council of Canada [1992], "Productivity Growth," *World Business,* June 5, pp. 22–23.

Hara, R. [1990], "Current and Future Manufacturing Industry," *Management Japan,* vol. 23, no. 1, pp. 11–16.

Hayes, Robert H., and Steven C. Wheelwright [1984], *Restoring Our Competitive Edge: Competing through Manufacturing,* Wiley, New York.

Little, B. [1991], "Tilting at Smokestacks," *Globe & Mail,* July 20, p. B18.

Lovelock, C. H. [1983], "Classifying Services to Gain Strategic Marketing Insights," *Journal of Marketing,* vol. 47, Summer, pp. 9–20.

Tenner, Arthur R., and Irving J. DeTero [1992], *Total Quality Management: Three Steps to Continuous Improvement,* Addison-Wesley, Reading, Mass.

Thurow, Lester C. [1992], "Lessons for Success: Skilled Workers Are Tomorrow's Only Real Asset," *Challenges,* Winter, pp. 8–14.

SUPPLEMENT TO

CHAPTER 1

THE EVOLUTION OF

OPERATIONS MANAGEMENT

Operations management is not a new concept; people have been producing goods and services since the dawn of civilization. The way in which these goods and services are made, however, has evolved over time. Advances in technology, combined with political, social, and economic forces, have fueled this evolution. Not surprisingly, the focus of operations management and the role of operations within a firm have changed as well.

In this supplement we will describe the major milestones in the development of operations management. An overview is provided in Exhibit 1S.1.

S1.2 CRAFT-PRODUCTION ERA (UP TO APPROXIMATELY 1850)

The large-scale production of goods and services is a relatively recent phenomenon. Until the nineteenth century the western world was predominantly rural and agricultural. Most goods were made by highly skilled people who used simple but flexible tools one at a time. They were then sold in small stores or village markets by the people who had made them.

The Apprenticeship System

Under the **apprenticeship system,** an artisan closely supervised the work of several apprentices during a lengthy training period. Parts were manufactured individually by hand and customized for a specific product. In most cases the product was made from start to finish by the same person. Production management in this environment was often a matter of "management by walking around." The artisans or workers themselves largely determined how the work was to be done. Quality craftsmanship was essential; the artisan's name went on the product, and an excellent reputation was the key to business success.

The Cottage Industry System

In the eighteenth century most manufacturing in countries such as Italy and England was performed by rural families in their own homes under the domestic or **cottage industry system.** Merchants supplied families in small towns with raw materials and later found markets for the finished products. The family was an independent operating unit that set its own pace of work and often worked for more than one merchant.

Scheduling was difficult in this environment, as was quality control: standards did not yet exist, and the quality of workmanship varied from one family to the next. As merchants increased production to meet the demand of expanding markets, the limited labor pool drove costs up. Industry was ripe for change.

The Birth of the Factory System

The development of steam power and the introduction of labor-saving equipment[1] early in the eighteenth century led to the development of the **factory system** in England. The first factories were small and housed a series of craft operations. Inflexible equipment limited output to a narrow range of products.

Factory owners were technically competent and made all key decisions regarding the choice of equipment and process technology. Coordination and control were relatively simple and were delegated to factory foremen who also had complete control of the workforce.

The concept of **labor specialization** advocated by Adam Smith in *The Wealth of Nations* (1776) had a tremendous impact on the production process. The principle is simple: Assigning workers a small set of tasks that they repeat over and over increases their proficiency; it also reduces the time spent by workers in switching tasks and encourages the development of specialized tools. The net result is improved labor productivity and lower production costs.[2] In this system workers with little or no education can use machines to perform tasks that once required highly skilled artisans.

The factory system was quickly adopted in the United States and more slowly in the rest of Europe. At the end of the eighteenth century the American Eli Whitney paved the way for mass production by combining the concept of labor specialization with the notation of **interchangeable parts.** Specifications were established for each part, and parts were manufactured to meet those specifications. This was a radical departure from the practice of customizing parts to fit a specific assembly. Parts could be manufactured independently, and the manufacturing process could be subdivided and streamlined. Factories became more complex but were still simple enough to be managed by foremen.

---

[1] The first machines mechanized agricultural processing activities such as yarn production, followed by fabric formation and then clothing manufacturing.

[2] In the 1830s Charles Babbage noted that production costs could be lowered further by extending the labor specialization concept to wages. He suggested that rather than having everyone earn the same wage, workers should be paid according to their skills and expertise.

EXHIBIT 1S.1 A HISTORICAL PERSPECTIVE ON OPERATIONS MANAGEMENT

Environmental Factors	Consequential Impact on the Nature of:	
	Operations	Operations Management
Craft Production (Up to 1850)		
• Industrial revolution • Breakdown of agrarian economy and feudal system • Labor specialization • Interchangeability of parts	• Independent artisans and cottage industries replaced by factory system • Single-unit; single-product high-volume factories	• Factories controlled by technically competent owners and powerful foremen • Centralized operations increase ability to control processes • Workers become machine-paced
Mass Production (1850–1975)		
• Taylor and the scientific management movement • Rapid market expansion • Improved transportation • Human relations movement • Development of control techniques (EOQ, MRP, etc.) • Growth of computer applications	• Increase in factory size and output • Multiunit, multiproduct plants, multiple sites • Assembly lines, repetitive flow processes • Automated processes	• Establishment of staff specialists and middle management to handle increasingly complex operations • Adversarial labor-management relations; first attempts to motivate and develop workforce • Emphasis on cost reduction and process control
Flexible (or Lean) Production (1975 on)		
• Limited market growth • Fragmenting markets • Global competition • Rapid pace of new product and process introductions • Cost/quality trade-off no longer, acceptable • Service sector expansion	• Highly flexible processes to accommodate small volumes of a variety of products • Software-driven technology • Computer-integrated firms	• Information as a corporate resource • Operations viewed as a competitive weapon • Increased involvement of upper management in technological decisions • Workers viewed as "partners"

S1.3 MASS-PRODUCTION ERA (APPROXIMATELY 1850 TO 1975)

Technological breakthroughs in power, transportation, communications, and production processes in the second half of the nineteenth century transformed the factory system. Factories became larger as they produced huge volumes of identical products to serve growing markets. Manufacturing costs fell as processes were continually improved and economies of scale were achieved.

Responsibility for the day-to-day management of the production process was still assumed by foremen, who ran the factories using rules of thumb based on their own experience. However, as factories began to produce a wider range of products and to use multiple production processes, coordination and control became a problem. Industry was ready when Frederick Winslow Taylor introduced a more systematic approach to operations management at the turn of the century.

Taylor and the Scientific Management Movement

Taylor's study of work methods and views on the roles and responsibilities of workers and managers revolutionized operations management. Many of his ideas and techniques are still in use.

Taylor is considered the founder of the industrial engineering discipline and the father of the **scientific management** movement. His intent was to eliminate waste, especially wasted effort, in order to minimize total manufacturing costs.

Rather than have the worker decide how to do a job, Taylor advocated the use of **standardized work methods** developed by industrial engineering specialists. These methods could be used to create job standards and set wage rates. The responsibility of factory foremen was to select workers on the basis of their capabilities, train them, closely supervise their work, and ensure that no one was tempted to slacken the workpace. The responsibility of workers was simply to do what they were told.

Improving work methods did increase productivity (by up to 400 percent) and lower production costs, but in many cases it aggravated already poor labor-management relations. The "command and control" atmosphere discouraged workers from making suggestions for improvements and reduced their motivation.

Followers of Taylor such as Frank and Lillian Gilbreth extended his work. The Gilbreths applied the new technology of motion pictures to the study of work methods. The results of these time-and-motion studies were used to improve processes by achieving maximum economy of effort and to set reasonable, attainable work standards. Unlike Taylor, the Gilbreths focused on the elements of a job rather than the total job. They also recognized the need to consider psychological as well as physiological elements when designing jobs.

The Moving Assembly Line

Henry Ford combined the teachings of Taylor with the concepts of labor specialization and interchangeable parts to design the first **moving assembly line** in 1913. Direct labor productivity soared, and cars could be produced at a previously unthinkable rate. Assembly lines—composed of unskilled or semiskilled workers performing a narrow range of tasks using relatively expensive single-purpose machinery—became *the* way of implementing a strategy for **mass production.**

The Emergence of Middle Management

Although assembly lines and other efforts to improve labor productivity were successful, they also led to a proliferation of indirect workers: material handlers, quality control inspectors, engineers, schedulers, and so on. Factory foremen could no longer comprehend and manage all the information flowing to them; this led to the introduction of the staff function. Line management became responsible for supervising day-to-day operations, while specialist staffs provided all planning, training, and control support. As middle management grew, the power of line management diminished and top management's direct involvement in the operating process and process technology faded.

Typically, production managers were the custodians of 70 to 85 percent of firm's assets; their goal was to provide a satisfactory return on those assets. To achieve this, they tried to minimize production costs by stabilizing the production process.

The Human Relations Movement

Despite continued efforts by managers and scientists to improve their ability to design products and jobs, discrepancies between theoretical and actual job output remained high. A landmark series of studies were conducted at the Hawthorne Works of Western

Electric in the 1920s and 1930s by Elton Mayo and F. J. Roethlisberger. The results showed that psychological factors were as important in determining the pace at which work was performed as was scientific job design.

The Hawthorne Studies stimulated the development of the **human relations movement** by demonstrating that worker motivation is a crucial element in improving productivity. Job enrichment and other management concepts used today have their roots in this movement.

The Development of Control Techniques

New technologies, products, and markets were the legacy of both world wars. Factories became even larger and more complex, and so sophisticated decision-making tools were urgently needed. A new field was born—**operations research**—in which mathematical models were used to solve operational problems.

Many of the quantitative models and statistical techniques used by modern operations managers were developed during this era. Here are a few examples:

- Walter Shewhart's **statistical quality control (SQC)** techniques enable managers to control product quality by controlling the process by which products are made. This can be much more effective than randomly sampling finished goods.
- Ford Harris developed one of the first models designed to find the least-cost inventory position: the **economic order quantity (EOQ)**.
- Henry Gantt recognized that processes are a combination of operations. He developed tools such as the **Gantt chart** for sequencing operations.
- George Dantzig introduced **linear programming** as a management tool for resource allocation in 1947.

The drive to increase productivity led to another new field: **ergonomics**, or **human factors engineering.** Ergonomics stresses the need to design equipment to suit the needs and capabilities of the user.

The Impact of the Computer

The 1950s heralded the growth of the computer (first described by Babbage 100 years earlier) and was the beginning of the information technology era. The discovery by Shockley of the transistor, coming shortly after the invention of the digital computer, led to the ability to process data and information at continuously decreasing costs.

The vast increase in data processing capacity encouraged the development of tools and techniques such as **material requirements planning (MRP)** and the **critical path method (CPM)**. One can imagine the difficulty of monitoring inventories consisting of hundreds of parts, scheduling jobs through a complex process, or managing a large-scale project *without* a computerized system.

Operations Management as a Field of Study

In the late 1950s and early 1960s scholars began to write texts dealing specifically with the problems faced by operations managers and the application of quantitative models to operations management.

At about the same time, however, production capacity began to exceed consumer demand. Marketing rose in importance as firms tried to increase demand for their products. A desire to diversify and acquire other companies meant that the finance and legal areas of firms became more important as well. It was not until the energy crisis in the mid-1970s and the influx of foreign goods that operations moved back into the limelight.

S1.4 FLEXIBLE (OR LEAN) PRODUCTION ERA (1975 ON)

Unlike the United States, the competitive, social, and economic environment of post–World War II Japan and many parts of Europe was not conducive to the mass-production approach. Instead, the Japanese developed an alternative approach that involved using teams of multiskilled workers equipped with flexible automated tools to produce an enormous variety of products in small volumes. Continuous improvements in both product and process design meant that quality was high and prices were reasonable. Consumers in North America responded enthusiastically, and in many markets domestic firms were outclassed.

In response, North American firms have started to pay much more attention to their operations and have turned away from the mass-production approach. **Software-driven equipment** is allowing production processes to be more flexible than ever before. Changing from one product to another, or incorporating changes in product designs, entails changes to the equipment's software only. This is much faster and less expensive than physical changes to the equipment.

Smaller production runs combined with much wider product lines have increased the complexity of operations management, but the introduction of advanced information systems has not led to a corresponding increase in the number of middle managers and staff specialists. In many cases firms are reducing their numbers.

Process reengineering—rethinking and radically changing the way in which business processes are organized—is leading to dramatic improvements in productivity. During process reengineering a business process is redesigned from scratch. The process is streamlined, non-value-added activities are eliminated, each worker performs a much wider range of tasks, and functional areas work more closely with each other.[3]

The impact of flexible production processes and the need to run a "lean" system has been great on operations managers. Consider the following examples:

- Operations managers are moving from being "custodians" of a firm's assets to being active contributors to the development of the firm's competitive strategy.
- Operations managers are pressured to eliminate waste and improve the operating system. Average inventories are a fraction of their former levels, and manufacturing defects are beginning to be measured in parts per million.
- The relationship between operations managers and the workforce is changing as the workforce is becoming multiskilled and assuming more responsibility. The role of managers and supervisors is largely one of facilitating a team approach.
- Operations and other functional areas of a firm are more involved in all stages of the product development process. This is shortening that process and improving product quality.
- Operations managers are dealing with fewer suppliers and enjoying a much closer relationship with each one. Advances in communications technology which allow a firm's computers to "talk" to a supplier's computers are facilitating this relationship.
- Operations managers are getting much closer to the customers. Again, advances in information and communications technology are fueling this trend.
- These continually strengthening bonds along the above chain are leading to what is being called **enterprise integration,** a concept in which the value chain acts as a single, integrated entity.

Another major development in operations management is the rising importance of the service sector: over

---

[3] In many cases process reengineering represents a radical departure from Adam Smith's notion of labor specialization and the consequent fragmentation of work.

75 percent of the North American workforce is now employed in this sector. Many of the tools and concepts originally developed for the manufacturing sector are being adapted by the service sector. Of course, new tools and concepts specifically tailored to service sector firms are being developed as well.

Knowledge is becoming the most critical input into the transformation process for firms in both manufacturing and the service sector. In the future **intelligent manufacturing systems (IMSs)** may be used routinely to collect, store, and disseminate knowledge. An IMS is a blend of information technologies (such as expert systems), distributed data/information systems, and hu-

man decision makers. The computerized portion of the system can manage the transformation process within predetermined limits, and when those limits are exceeded, human decision makers intervene.

Operations management has changed and continues to change. This makes operations one of the most exciting areas of the firm.

KEY TERMS

Craft-production era	Standardized work methods	Economic order quantity (EOQ)	Critical path method (CPM)
Apprenticeship system	Moving assembly line	Gantt chart	Flexible (or lean) production
Cottage industry system	Mass production	Linear programming	Software-driven equipment
Factory system	Human relations movement	Ergonomics (human factors engineering)	Process reengineering
Labor specialization	Operations research		Enterprise integration
Interchangeable parts	Statistical quality control (SQC)	Material requirements planning (MRP)	Intelligent manufacturing systems (IMS)
Scientific management			

REFERENCES AND SELECTED BIBLIOGRAPHY

Abernathy, William J., Kim B. Clark, and Alan M. Kantrow [1983], *Industrial Renaissance,* Basic Books, New York.

Chase, Richard B., and Eric L. Prentice [1987], "Operations Management: A Field Rediscovered," *Journal of Management,* vol. 13, no. 2, pp. 351–356.

Hammer, Michael, and James Champey [1993], *Reengineering the Corporation: A Manifesto for Business Revolution,* HarperCollins, New York.

IIE Focus [1989], "Taylor and Gilbreth: A History of Industrial Engineering," *Industrial Engineering,* October, pp. 1 and 6.

IIE Focus [1990], "The Future of Industrial Engineers: From the Drawing Room to the Shop Floor," *Industrial Engineering,* February, pp. 1 and 6.

Niebel, Benjamin W. [1993], *Motion and Time Study,* 9th ed., Richard D. Irwin, Homewood, Ill.

Skinner, W. [1985], "The Taming of Lions: How Manufacturing Leadership Evolved, 1780–1984," in K. B. Clark, R. H. Hayes, and C. Lorenz (eds.), *The Uneasy Alliance,* Harvard Business School Press, Boston, pp. 63–110.

Wheelwright, Steven C. [1984], "Restoring the Competitive Edge in U.S. Manufacturing," *California Management Review,* vol. 27, no. 3, pp. 26–42.

Womack, James P., Daniel T. Jones, and Daniel Ross [1991], *The Machine That Changed the World,* Harper-Perennial, New York.

CHAPTER 2

ORGANIZING OPERATIONS
FOR COMPETITION

The competitive and social context in which companies compete is changing. As a result, managers must reevaluate their attitudes and approaches to competing.

This chapter will answer the following two questions:

- What makes a customer buy a product?
- How should managers manage operations in the new environment?

The chapter begins with a brief look at changes in the environment and their impact on operations. Then a framework is introduced that describes the characteristics of responsive and proactive organizations. The framework is general and robust, yet appropriate for today's complex and fast-moving environment, and by the end of the chapter you will be aware of its structure and its relationship to a firm's strategy.

2.1 MANAGERIAL ORIENTATION

Chapter 1 described the new realities of the marketplace. It is apparent that the nature of competition has changed and that this has affected the way successful firms must operate. The Startup Chapter provided examples of firms that have shaped their business practices to fit the new competitive environment. This chapter will further explore the characteristics of these and other successful firms and present a descriptive framework which synthesizes those characterisics. To clarify the presentation, the framework is outlined in Exhibit 2.1.

Go back to the Startup Chapter and look at the definition of total quality management (TQM) and the criteria for awarding each of the national quality awards described; it will become apparent that Exhibit 2.1 is a road map for implementing and institutionalizing TQM.

The strong implication here is that *only firms that actively implement TQM will prosper in the new competitive environment.* Understanding the framework is therefore important. Let us begin by examining the most important characteristic, a customer focus.

2.2 SATISFYING THE CUSTOMER: THE DIMENSIONS OF COMPETITION

Customer satisfaction leads to customer loyalty, which, according to recent studies, is crucial to long-term profitability. Loyal customers spend more, refer new clients to the firm, and are less costly to do business with. Attracting a new customer tends to be about six times as expensive as retaining an old one, and a recent survey of nine U.S. industries showed that companies can boost profit 25 to 85 percent by retaining just 5 percent more of their customers [Wood and Pitts (1992)]. Knowing what entices a customer to continue to prefer one product over another or deal with company A rather than company B is therefore of great concern to a firm.

Obviously, the specific factors that influence the buying decision vary from one type of product to the next and from one market to another. On the basis of observations in the Startup Chapter, however, it can be concluded that these factors can be grouped into at least six broad categories. As the following discussion will show, each category reflects a specific message customers are sending firms today.

EXHIBIT 2.1 THE ROADMAP TO RESPONSIVENESS

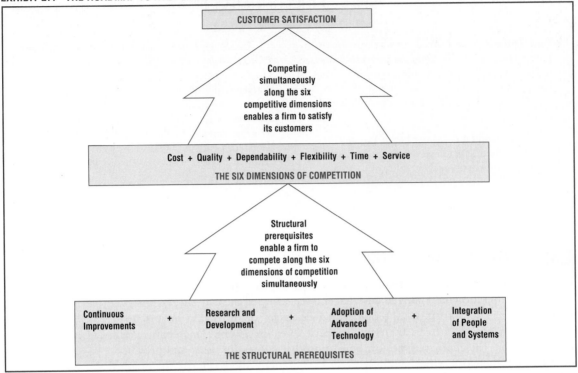

The implications of these messages are particularly important to operations management.

Selling Price (Product Cost)

Price is a function of a product's **cost**. A common practice in the past was simply to increase a product's unit cost by a certain percentage to arrive at its selling price. That is,

$$\text{Cost} + \text{Desired profit} = \text{Selling price}$$

If costs increased, the selling price would automatically increase as well, preserving the profit margin. Customers of these firms came to expect and accept annual price increases.

Today, however, many firms are operating in a buyers' rather than a sellers' market; customers are better informed, and competition is much more intense. People are buying not the cheapest products but the ones that give them the most value for their money. The challenge for a firm is to provide the best value while ensuring that total costs are lower than market-dictated prices. That is,

$$\text{Market-dictated price} - \text{Cost} = \text{Profit}$$

Consumers are also concerned with the total cost of owning a product, not just the initial purchase price. When buying an automobile, for example, consumers compare operating and maintenance costs as well as sticker prices.

Message 1. Most prices are market-driven, and customers are price-sensitive. Therefore, costs must be tightly controlled.

Quality

In recent years the Japanese have demonstrated that firms can continually increase the **quality** of their products without increasing the cost. Customers are becoming accustomed to high-quality but reasonably priced goods and services. Ten years ago only 4 of 10 Americans saw quality as being equal to or more important than price in their buying decisions; today this figure has increased to 8 of 10 [Ernst & Young Quality Improvement Consulting Group (1990), p. 50]. Poor quality is unacceptable in today's competitive marketplace.

The importance of preserving a firm's image of quality by keeping its customers satisfied is illustrated by Saturn's astounding offer in 1991 to *replace* over 1,800 cars that had been filled with a faulty radiator coolant.[1]

Message 2. Customers expect high-quality products.

As demonstrated in Exhibit 2.2, quality has more than one dimension, and the importance of each dimension varies with the type of product. For example, people judge the performance of a sports car differently from that of a minivan. They expect a luxury car to have more features than a subcompact. A firm needs to know exactly what customers in its targeted market perceive as "high quality."

---

[1] Saturn also named the supplier of the coolant, who may have to pay a portion of the cost of replacing the contaminated cars.

EXHIBIT 2.2   THE DIMENSIONS OF QUALITY

Quality Dimension	Description	Example: One customer's view of quality in an automobile
Tangible Elements		
Performance	Product's principal operating characteristics	"I do a lot of highway driving, so I need quick acceleration and good gas mileage."
Features	Characteristics that supplement the basic functioning of the product	"I like to drive in comfort; I want air-conditioning."
Reliability	Probability of product failure or malfunction within a specified period	"I'm a doctor. When I get into my car, I want to be sure it will start."
Conformance	Degree to which product meets its design specifications	"This car gets only 30 (not 35) miles to the gallon."
Durability	Product's economic life span	"I want a car that will last at least 10 years."
Intangible Elements		
Aesthetics	Product's look or feel	"I want a car that looks sleek, not boxy."
Empathy	Ability of supplier to understand and satisfy "human" needs of customer	"I want to deal with a salesperson who genuinely respects me and does not pressure me into buying."
Professionalism	Ability of supplier to provide whole-life product and customer support	"I want to deal with a distributor who can always properly service, maintain, and repair my car."

Dependability

Dependability can be defined as the ability of an organization to honor its commitments. The importance of dependability with respect to the professional services provided by doctors and lawyers is clear, but dependability is also critical to other firms. Consider a transport company such as Reimer Express Lines ("On time or free"). How well would it do if it could not meet its delivery promises? Although dependability may revolve around delivery, this is only one aspect. Another is honoring legal and moral contracts with customers as well as suppliers.

> **Message 3.** Customers want peace of mind and are wary of companies they cannot trust. They want dependable producers.

Flexibility

Flexibility is the ability to respond to or conform to new situations. Like quality, it means different things to different people. Exhibit 2.3 describes 10 different forms of flexibility. These overlapping types of flexibility are grouped into three broad categories: product, process, and infrastructure.

EXHIBIT 2.3   TYPES OF FLEXIBILITY

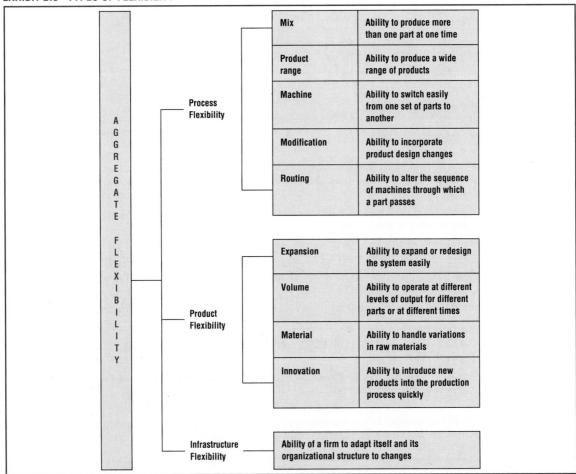

AGGREGATE FLEXIBILITY	**Process Flexibility**	**Mix** — Ability to produce more than one part at one time
		Product range — Ability to produce a wide range of products
		Machine — Ability to switch easily from one set of parts to another
		Modification — Ability to incorporate product design changes
		Routing — Ability to alter the sequence of machines through which a part passes
	Product Flexibility	**Expansion** — Ability to expand or redesign the system easily
		Volume — Ability to operate at different levels of output for different parts or at different times
		Material — Ability to handle variations in raw materials
		Innovation — Ability to introduce new products into the production process quickly
	Infrastructure Flexibility	Ability of a firm to adapt itself and its organizational structure to changes

- **Product flexibility** refers to a firm's ability to quickly develop new products and modify existing ones to meet changing market requirements.
- **Process flexibility** is the ability of a firm to produce a broad range of products, switch from one product to another quickly and easily, incorporate new or revised products, and handle variations in the raw materials used.
- **Infrastructure flexibility** is the ability of a firm to adapt itself and its organizational structure to changes.

Together, the three categories constitute the **aggregate flexibility** possessed by a firm that enables it to respond quickly to specific environmental uncertainties.

The exact nature of the flexibility required depends on the firm's competitive circumstances. Vehicle manufacturers, for example, must contend with regulatory requirements that vary by country and change over time. Therefore, at Cadillac's Detroit-Hamtramck assembly plant vehicles destined for the Middle East are given engines that run on leaded fuel, while special glass is installed for cars shipped to Europe.[2]

> **Message 4.** Customer needs and preferences are continually evolving. Hence, flexibility is important if a firm is to respond quickly to changes in the marketplace.

Time

Strategically, **time** is money. Consider the market for home computers, automobiles, and prescription eyeglasses. Consumers want up-to-date products and want those products delivered quickly.

Firms that can design, produce, and distribute their products faster than their competitors incur lower product development costs and production costs; this allows them to capture a greater market share, all other things being equal. Toyota, for example, can build and deliver customized cars within five working days.[3] Other companies that use time to create a strategic advantage include AT&T, GE, and Motorola (see Exhibit 2.4).

[2] This tailoring process is referred to as *homologation.*

[3] Buyers customize their cars by selecting from a set of modular options.

EXHIBIT 2.4 COMPRESSING THE TIME TO MARKET

Company	Product	Old Time	New Time
Research and Development			
AT&T	Telephones	2 years	1 year
Navistar	Trucks	5 years	$2\frac{1}{2}$ years
HP	Computers	$4\frac{1}{2}$ years	22 months
Manufacturing			
GE	Circuit breakers	3 weeks	3 days
Motorola	Pagers	3 weeks	2 hours
Brunswick	Fishing reels	3 weeks	1 week
HP	Test equipment	4 weeks	5 days

Source: Albin (1992), p. 32.

Message 5. Customers value time. Products must be designed, produced, and delivered quickly.

Service

Service is no longer incidental to the product but is an integral part of the total product. Today the notion of service includes developing a capacity for product variety, making a commitment to each customer as an industry entity, helping customers install their products, and providing after-sales support. The results of recent surveys indicate that service is highly correlated with market share.

As companies are becoming more customer-oriented, they are changing the market's perception of what good service means. General Motors Canada, for example, has followed Nissan's lead and has introduced a comprehensive roadside assistance program for its new vehicles. Infiniti may rebuild car seats if the owner of a vehicle finds the seat too hard, and Lexus may buy cars back from owners unhappy about polishing marks on the paint finish. Exhibit 2.5 describes how Lexus transformed a vehicle recall into an opportunity to provide a customer with excellent service.

Message 6. Customers appreciate the provision of service before and after the sale.

In summary, the messages derived from customer buying behavior can be translated into six **competitive dimensions:** cost, quality, dependability, flexibility, time, and service. These dimensions form the basis of the descriptive framework around which this book has been written [Noori and Radford (1993)].

It is important to remember that no single dimension of competition is universally more important than another; the importance of each depends on the product and its market and may vary over time. Quality may be the overriding concern in one situation, and flexibility in another.

The six competitive dimensions, however, are not inherently incompatible. This book has presented examples of firms that provide high-quality products at low prices and firms that are both very flexible and very dependable. This is a significant departure from the product-process life cycle matrix approach presented in Chapter 1 (see Exhibit 1.8), which assumes that a trade-off must be made between flexibility and quality and between dependability and cost.

EXHIBIT 2.5 THE POWER OF EXCELLENT SERVICE

A Philadelphia-based CEO decided on a whim to replace his traditional Mercedes sedan with a Japanese luxury vehicle. After he had driven the vehicle a month or so, the manager of the local Lexus dealership called to inform him that there was a company-initiated recall on the vehicle. The dealer asked which night the CEO would be at home and would not be using the vehicle.

On the appointed night a representative of the dealership called for the vehicle, told the CEO the vehicle would be returned in about two hours, and drove the car away. Less than two hours later the doorbell rang; it was the service representative saying that the vehicle was safely in the CEO's garage and that the minor adjustment had been made.

When the CEO went to the garage the following morning, he found his car—washed, polished, and groomed inside and out, with a full tank of gas and a box of Belgian chocolates on the front passenger seat.

As the CEO said, guess which vehicle he is going to lease the next time, and guess which vehicle and service he is going to tell his friends and acquaintances about?

Why Six Dimensions?

Some people will ask the obvious question: Why six dimensions? Why not concentrate on one or two dimensions as we did previously? The answer is that people need to manage as much of the real-time complexity of the competitive world as they can; if they do not, they tend to distort the information and therefore their responses. Ashby's (1952) **law of requisite variety** states that control can be obtained only if the variety of the controller is at least as great as the variety of the situation being controlled. This can be translated to mean that a manufacturer or service provider should take account of every competitive dimension a customer or market *might* consider in trying to decide whether to purchase the manufacturer's product or use the provider's service. If the market begins to use a larger set of criteria against which to judge suppliers, a firm must use all those factors when deciding how to satisfy its potential customers. Whether six dimensions is too few, time will tell. Certainly, the leading-edge firms are considering all six and looking for synergies among them rather than trading off against each other.

Admittedly, managing or considering all six dimensions simultaneously is difficult. A firm can, however, gain a definite advantage by considering more factors than do its competitors, especially if the extra dimensions or factors are perceived of as valuable by the customers. This advantage was gained by Japanese automobile manufacturers in the 1980s in North America, and it took several years before domestic automakers could convince the buying public that the local manufacturers had begun to use a greater number of competitive dimensions. And as the ability to recognize and manage greater complexity is realized, the first group to effectively expand (and satisfy) the set of decision-making criteria even further will gain a competitive advantage.

2.3 FAST-RESPONSE ORGANIZATIONS AND TOTAL QUALITY MANAGEMENT

Firms that can compete along all six dimensions are referred to as **fast-response organizations (FROs).**[4]

> **DEFINITION:** A fast-response organization is built around the six dimensions of competition: cost, quality, dependability, flexibility, time, and service. Such an organization is capable of using different combinations of these dimensions of competition to address the needs of its customers in different markets.

Linking the definition of an FRO with a statement made in Section 2.1, fast-response organizations actively embody the TQM philosophy. This linkage is important, for it makes it easy to differentiate firms living the TQM philosophy from those paying lip service to it. *FROs* must *have successfully implemented the TQM philosophy, and successful implementation of TQM* must *result in fast-response organization.* Although the two phenomena are different, they are inextricably connected.

---

[4] *Fast response* is a shorthand descriptor for an operating entity that approaches its dependencies in a manner fundamentally different from that of its traditional forebears and counterparts. The term does *not* imply a merely reactive firm; there is much more to fast response than quick reflexes. Other terms that might be used are *agile* and *world class.*

Developing the ability to compete simultaneously along the six dimensions of competition and becoming an FRO can be a challenging process. In most cases it calls for a radical departure from the traditional role of operations in a firm. Section 2.4 will show how firms are transforming themselves into FROs.

2.4 BUILDING BLOCKS OF FAST-RESPONSE ORGANIZATIONS

How can a firm develop and maintain an ability to compete along the six dimensions? To answer this question, one must look at studies of successful companies, including the ones discussed in the Startup Chapter. What became clear there is that successful companies invest heavily in certain structural prerequisites to enhance their operations. While the nature and extent of these investments may vary, that chapter identified four distinct **structural prerequisites:**

- An emphasis on continuous improvement throughout the organization
- Investment in research and development
- The adoption of advanced product, process, and organizational/managerial technology
- The integration and coordination of activities throughout the value chain

Note. As with the six dimensions of competition, *no one structural prerequisite is always more important than any other.* All four must be satisfied, but the emphasis placed on each varies from one firm to the next, from one industry to another, and over time.

Continuous Improvement

How can a company increase product quality and the speed with which goods and services are developed without increasing its prices? One of the keys is to identify and eliminate all **non-value-added activities.** In practice, 90 percent of the time customers spend waiting for their orders to be filled is taken up with steps and procedures that do not increase the usefulness or value of the product as perceived by the customer [Anderson (1991), p. 38].

Eliminating non-value-added activities decreases costs and increases the speed with which products can be developed and produced. Increased speed means that a company receives feedback on the quality of its products more quickly and has an opportunity to improve product quality more often.[5] Eliminating non-value-added activities as part of a firm's continuous improvement efforts therefore fuels further improvements.

Non-value-added activities can be found in all areas of a typical company. Examples include equipment setups, scrap and rework, and excess inventories. Poorly designed production equipment and process layouts that lead to worker injuries also contribute to waste. Time is wasted when managers and professionals attend meetings, write and then revise reports, and exchange memos. Waste can also be found in the way a firm designs, develops, and supports products.

A natural goal for an FRO is to eliminate all non-value-added activities. Xerox, for example, is implementing what it calls the "A-delta-T" program as part of its

---

[5] Suppose a company builds stereos. The time span between ordering components and delivering the stereo to its final customer is two months. Therefore, the company has six opportunities a year to receive feedback from its customers. If the total time span is only one week, the company has 52 opportunities a year to receive feedback and improve its operations.

continuous improvement efforts. The idea is to classify activities as value-added or non-value-added and then reduce the time spent on non-value-added activities [Equation (2.1)].

> **Xerox's A-delta-T program**
>
> $$A = \Delta + T \tag{2.1}$$
>
> where A = total actual time spent on all activities
> Δ = time spent on non-value-added activities
> T = theoretical time required for all value-added activities

Continuous improvement consists of a series of small, incremental, long-term, and (mostly) undramatic changes. Large capital outlays are not needed, but a great deal of continuous effort and the commitment of everyone in the firm are required. Continuous improvement is a departure from the "if it ain't broke, don't fix it" attitude prevalent in many traditional firms. This attitude overlooks the enormous long-term potential of incremental improvements.[6]

Consider a product that requires a modest number of operations, say, 30. Suppose that each operation is sequentially dependent and that the probability of making a mistake in any operation but not finding the mistake in subsequent operations is 0.01. The probability that the final product will be free of defects is $(1 - 0.01)^{30}$, which is less than 75 percent!

Let us go one step further. Suppose performance standards are universally set at 99 percent. This sounds fairly high, but a 99 percent defect-free rate still translates into at least 20,000 wrong drug prescriptions a year, unsafe drinking water almost one hour every month, and 10 defects per 1,000 solders on every IBM computer motherboard. It also means approximately 2.5 million unsatisfied customers a year for Federal Express.

Many firms that are no longer satisfied with even a 99.7 percent defect-free rate now measure defects in parts per million. Motorola, for example, is striving for just 3.4 defects per 1 million opportunities. Motorola compares the difference between this goal and a 99.7 percent defect-free rate to the difference in area between a small hardware store's floor and a typical diamond! More analogies are given in Exhibit 2.6.

It is clear that constantly improving all a firm's activities is an integral part of an FRO's philosophy of **dynamic evolution**. This book will discuss a number of techniques and concepts that can help a firm identify activities that are inefficient or unsafe or do not add value to the products. Many of these practices originated in North America but have been adapted by the Japanese and are referred to collectively as **kaizen**.

The underlying philosophy of kaizen is that everyone in the firm, both workers and managers, must be actively involved in ongoing improvement efforts. Many observers see kaizen as the key to Japan's competitive success.

How can a firm create an environment that fosters ongoing improvements? The

---

[6] Perhaps this attitude can be traced back to Taylor and his scientific management principles (discussed in the Chapter 1 Supplement). Engineers set standards that appear to optimize current performance, and those standards become cast in stone. Managers attempt to keep operations running smoothly by stabilizing activities, allowing an atmosphere of **static optimization** to set in. Thus, even though the firm gains a better understanding of its processes, adjustments are rarely made. Only radical technology or organizational changes result in upgrades in performance standards.

EXHIBIT 2.6 SIX-SIGMA QUALITY

Sigma (σ) refers to the number of standard deviations from the mean in any statistically measured process. In a normally distributed process about 95.44 percent of all values lie within $\pm 2\sigma$ of the mean, 99.73 percent lie within $\pm 3\sigma$, and 99.9999998 percent lie within $\pm 6\sigma$. A process with 0.0000002 percent defects is referred to as a six-sigma process. The chart below illustrates the vast difference between processes with high and low sigma values.

Sigma	Number of Defects per Million Opportunities†	Analogies*		
		Area	Spelling	Distance
$\pm 1\sigma$	317,400	Floor space of an average factory	170 misspelled words per page in a book	From here to the moon
$\pm 2\sigma$	45,600	Floor space of a large super-market	25 misspelled words per page in a book	1½ times around the world
$\pm 3\sigma$	2,700	Floor space of a small hardware store	1.5 misspelled words per page in a book	Coast-to-coast trip
$\pm 4\sigma$	63	Floor space of a typical living room	1 misspelled word per 30 pages in a book	45 minutes of freeway driving
$\pm 5\sigma$	0.57	Size of the bottom of a telephone	1 misspelled word in a set of encyclopedias	A trip to local gas station
$\pm 6\sigma$	0.002	Size of a typical diamond	1 misspelled word in all the books in a small library	4 steps in any direction
$\pm 7\sigma$	0.000003	Point of a sewing needle	1 misspelled word in all the books in several large libraries	⅛ inch

* These figures have been approximated on the basis of known proportions and average and/or best estimates. This table does not correct the number of defects per million opportunities for typical sources of variation.

† Unadjusted for typical shifts and drifts in the universal average.

Motorola's goal is six-sigma quality in all its activities. Compare this to the three-sigma quality long considered acceptable by many North American firms. Why such a challenging goal? Is there a competitive advantage to be gained by moving from 99.73 percent defect-free work (three-sigma) to 99.9999998 percent (six-sigma) or even just to 99.9937 percent (four-sigma)?

The answer is yes when one realizes that there is a second type of process variation. Not only does the output of a normally distributed process fluctuate around the process mean, the mean itself can shift as much as ± 1.5 standard deviations. When the shift in the process mean is considered as well, six-sigma translates into 3.4 defects per million, while four-sigma translates into 6,210 defects per million and three-sigma into 66,810 defects per million.

Source: Adapted from Denton (1991), p. 24.

full commitment and involvement of the firm's managers is essential, as is a sincere customer focus. There is also a need for a simple, consistent companywide program that motivates everyone to contribute. This means not only that the firm must invest in training programs but also that workers must be given more power and responsibility and that the adversarial relationship between workers and managers must become harmonious. Performance-measuring systems must be realigned to measure and support continuous improvement efforts. Once these elements are in place, the firm can begin to focus everyone's efforts on "doing the right things" and then on "doing these things right."

Research and Development (R&D)

Shrinking product life cycles and fragmenting markets mean that a firm must continually improve its ability to introduce new and revised products quickly and successfully. For example, Northern Telecom, the only manufacturer of telephones in North America, has put a replacement product for its latest residential telephone on the drawing board *before* launching the telephone into the marketplace. The firm anticipates a two-to-three-year product life before international competitors and improving component technology can make the "new" product obsolete.

Research efforts can be classified as basic or applied. **Basic research** is directed not toward solving a specific problem but toward expanding the frontiers of knowledge. Most basic research is performed in government and university laboratories[7] and by firms that are pursuing a strategy of technological leadership. **Applied research,** by contrast, focuses on solving general problems and generating inventions that have a high probability of being used within the firm. The boundary between basic and applied research is broad and indistinct.

Development efforts are required to transform inventions discovered during basic and applied research into commercially successful innovations. The focus is on meeting specific needs within the firm. This typical sequence of research, development, and commercialization is illustrated in Exhibit 2.7.

Note that traditionally there is generally a time lag between the stages in the sequence. Frequently, too, a long series of refinements is needed to turn an invention into products that meet marketplace needs. The economic impact of an invention therefore is often not known for quite a while. The invention of the facsimile (fax) machine, for example, goes back several decades, but its commercial success has been relatively recent. The fax machine's appeal is due to several crucial factors, not the least of which have been technical improvements that brought down costs and made the machine faster, more reliable, and easier to operate. In effect, fax manu-

---

[7] In 1991 the U.S. government spent $14.5 billion on basic science and $13.1 billion on nonmilitary applied research. In 1993, however, the Clinton administration was encouraging a change in emphasis from basic to applied research.

EXHIBIT 2.7 SEQUENCE OF RESEARCH AND DEVELOPMENT *Traditional R&D Pipeline*

Research	Development	Commercialization
Invention (Scientific discovery)	Innovation (Design)	Diffusion (Production and marketing)

facturers have routinely made their products obsolete in the search for the perfect match between current technology and users' needs.

A new approach, called a **system focus**, integrates the entire R&D process [Iansiti (1993)]. Rather than establish the traditional R&D pipeline shown in Exhibit 2.7, system-focused companies form an integration team. The team is composed of a core group of managers, scientists, and engineers who balance new research from the lab with the firm's existing manufacturing capabilities. That is, the team adapts new technologies to what the firm already knows how to do. The result is high-quality products produced relatively quickly and cost-effectively.

The innovations that come from R&D efforts can be revolutionary, resulting in major product or process breakthroughs that create new industries or significantly change existing ones. R&D innovations can also be evolutionary, resulting in incremental improvements to existing products and processes. Both evolutionary and revolutionary innovations differ from the changes and modifications that result from continuous improvement efforts in that they are shorter-term and more dramatic. They also involve fewer people but require larger capital investments.

Adoption of Advanced Technology

In broad terms, **technology** is the total body of knowledge brought to the transformation process. It is embodied in physical equipment and captured in manuals and in human memory. Zeleny (1986) divides technology into three components:

- **Hardware.** The physical structure and logical layout of the equipment used to carry out the required tasks
- **Software.** The set of rules, guidelines, and algorithms for using the hardware to carry out the tasks
- **Brainware.** The reason, purpose, and justification for using, expanding, and developing the technology in a particular way

These three components are interdependent and equally important. The hardware element, for example, is no more important than the software element, and vice versa. This concept is clearly illustrated when one considers a car as technology:

> A car consists of its own physical structure known as hardware. The car's software includes manuals setting out operating rules such as "press the brake pedal to stop," "turn the steering wheel to the left to go left," and "push this button to turn on the rear window defroster." The brainware is supplied by the driver as he or she decides when to use the car, where it would go, and how fast it should travel.

Similarly, one can look at computers in terms of these three dimensions. (Can you explain how?)

Naturally, to make the technology work a firm must have the requisite organizational, administrative, and cultural structures (work rules, task rules, required skills, and work content). This supportive sociotechnical environment is called the **technology support net (TSN)**. In the automobile example, the roads and bridges, and in the computer example, the electrical power and the facility to host the computer components, are some of the TSNs required.[8] Any technology that changes a

---

[8] One might point out, quite correctly, that roads, bridges, and traffic signals are hardware technology and that the rules of the road and the computer-controlled signal switching program are software technology. What exactly constitutes each element of technology depends on the situation and on where in the organization the observer sits.

firm's TSN will have a substantial impact on the way in which that firm produces goods and services.

Technology Development   Historically, technology was used in high-volume operations for the division of labor, for further specialization of tasks, and for the replacement of labor with machines—all in the name of efficiency or cost reduction in mass-market industries.

Today, however, technology plays a different role. The new emphasis is on *symbiotic* (mutually enhancing) relationships between operators and machines rather than on increasing the specialization of knowledge. Today's technology requires operators with a broader range of knowledge and skills, supported by specialists and managers who also possess such a set of skills and knowledge.

Advanced Operating Technologies   Firms in almost all industries are affected by emerging technologies ranging from speech recognition to remote sensing and from biotechnology to structural ceramics. The focus in this book, however, is on the operating technologies used in the production of goods and services.

Advances in automation have played a significant role in the development of **advanced operating technologies. Fixed,** or **hard automation** has been employed in mass-production and continuous-flow production processes for decades. Today microchip technology has led to the **soft automation** used extensively in **advanced manufacturing technologies (AMTs).**

Flexibility is a key benefit of software-driven technologies. Of course, the individual types (refer back to Exhibit 2.3) and degrees of flexibility provided depend on the advanced operating technologies acquired by a firm and the way in which they are used. Flexibility is not the only benefit of advanced operating technologies. Case studies of various companies suggest that the successful implementation of different forms of new technology results in considerable benefits, such as savings in direct manufacturing costs (up to 40 percent), lead time (up to 75 percent), work-in-process inventory (up to 60 percent), quality costs (over 50 percent), floor space (up to 60 percent), and design engineering costs (up to 20 percent).

Integration of People and Systems

The notion of integration separates an FRO from a traditional organization. To quickly produce higher-quality and lower-cost products, firms must integrate people and systems within and along the value chain. This type of integration is often referred to as **enterprise integration.** Of the four structural prerequisites, enterprise integration often is the most challenging to operationalize and institutionalize.

Internally, enterprise integration can be viewed in two forms: hierarchical and horizontal. **Hierarchical integration** joins together corporate and plant operations, thus encouraging a greater sense of coordination and a more efficient decision-making process. **Horizontal integration** tears down the barriers between a firm's functional areas, resulting in better and more efficient teamwork. *Externally,* integration of activities improves communication between operations and its suppliers and between operations and its customers.[9] The three forms of integration can be viewed as three sides of a pyramid (see Exhibit 2.8).

---

[9] This chapter views integration from an operations perspective. Marketing, finance, human resources, and other functional areas within the firm are also concerned with internal and external integration.

EXHIBIT 2.8 THE INTEGRATION PYRAMID

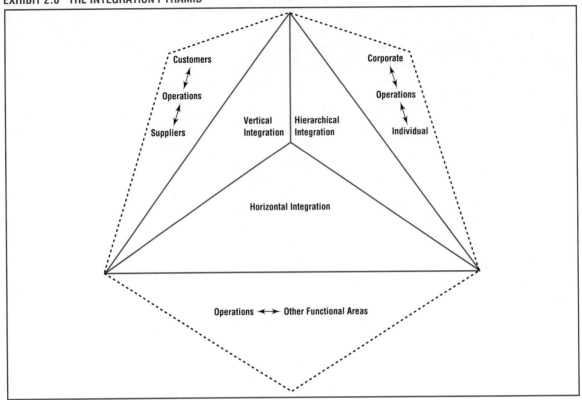

Hierarchical Integration Hierarchical integration of activities refers to the coordination between a firm's operations and its corporate goals and objectives. It involves bringing together the business strategy and the operations strategy. As will be discussed in Chapter 3, such coordination and congruence are essential to an FRO.

Hierarchical integration of activities provides other immediate and tangible benefits to a business. Current information from any or all local operations is coordinated and made available to other sites or to a centralized unit. Better information makes for better decisions, all other things being equal; better decisions make for better management.

Horizontal Integration The essence of an FRO lies in its synchronization of activities and its inclusion of all functional areas (production, marketing, finance and accounting, R&D, purchasing, etc.) in making coordinated decisions on the **five P's of operations:** people, plant, product, process, and production. Exhibit 2.9 lists some of the decisions that have to be made under each category. For example, plant-related decisions include selecting an appropriate location and choosing an effective facility layout.

Synchronization of functional activities allows a firm to concentrate on value-added activities and reengineer its business processes.[10] As a result, the firm can

---

[10] Process reengineering, discussed in the Chapter 1 Supplement, involves dramatic changes in the way processes are designed and challenges the commonly accepted benefits of labor specialization.

compete more successfully along the six dimensions of competition and better meet the challenges of the marketplace.

Unless functional areas work together, the strategic benefits offered by any of the areas cannot be fully exploited. Consider a firm whose processes can produce a wide variety of products. If R&D and engineering cannot provide a variety of product designs or if marketing and distribution cannot handle the greater variety of products and markets, the firm will not derive much benefit from its flexible processing capabilities.

The ability of functions to work together is influenced by the structure of the organization at all levels. This is particularly true for FROs, since their designers *must* ensure that all the characteristics of the FRO are in place. There are no hard and fast rules for when to use a particular organizational structure, but an understanding of the principles of organizational design and the firm's context will lead senior managers to favor a particular organizational form. This choice will then influence other elements of design for the firm.

The integration of product, process, and facility design is a good example of horizontal integration. By working together, design teams can strategically align their designs. Problems are identified quickly and solved more easily when information is shared and feedback is provided on an ongoing basis. The resultant designs are better

EXHIBIT 2.9   THE FIVE P'S OF OPERATIONS

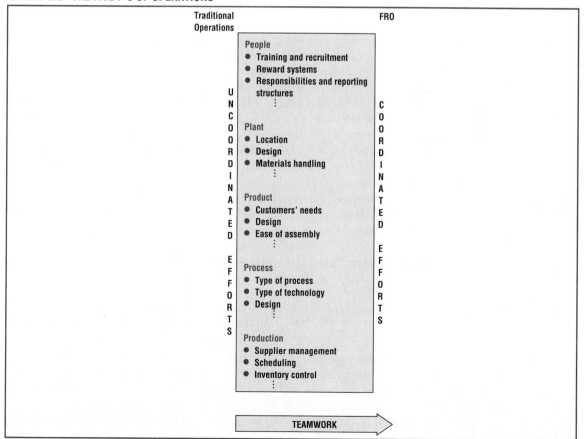

and the total design time is considerably shorter than is the case when design teams work independently. Product, process, and facility design processes are explored in depth in Chapters 5 to 9.

Vertical Integration   **Vertical integration** refers to the span of processes in the value chain over which a firm has influence or control. It covers both the linkage downstream between the firm and its customers and the linkage upstream between the firm and its suppliers. **Downstream integration** allows a company to better understand customer needs, produce the right product, and emphasize the service aspect of the operation. Integration enables a firm to anticipate customer wants and needs and effectively compete by bundling services with products in response to a wide variety of specific customer needs.

Upstream, or **backward, integration** focuses on the relationship between suppliers and the company. The experience of successful firms indicates that long-term contracts and relationships with suppliers can achieve significant benefits for the whole value chain. In an attempt to streamline outsourcing, companies are looking at retaining only a small number of reliable suppliers. This should improve the quality and delivery reliability of their purchased materials.

How to Integrate Operations   The degree to which total integration can be achieved in a firm is dependent on the firm's structure and organization, information system, and people. Of the three, it is the attitude of the employees that is crucial. When all is said and done, it is people who do the essential integrating within organizations.

Structurally, an FRO is a flatter organization than a traditional multilevel firm. This facilitates horizontal integration and allows an FRO to take advantage of many small but cumulatively significant improvements to its operations. In a multilevel firm departmental responsibilities are often clearly delineated. In this environment small improvements that affect more than one department are difficult to implement because information must flow up several management layers before it can be shared between functional areas. Since the success of each department is usually measured independently of the success of the firm, there is little motivation to work together.

Removing management levels means that more responsibility and authority must be pushed down through the organization. Empowering its employees enables a firm to tap its true potential but requires the company to make a sincere, long-term commitment to ongoing training and employee development. Job descriptions, career paths, reward systems, and department charters must be aligned with the FRO's new structure.

Consider the shop floor. The workers there are the ones most familiar with the firm's operating processes. If a firm invests in their personal development, it can improve its processes on a continuous basis. This investment may begin with a program to upgrade technical skills, followed by cross-training and the development of problem-solving skills. As the workers become more independent and accept more decision-making responsibility, it is no longer appropriate for first-line supervisors to dictate work methods and closely monitor performance. Self-regulation of processes by teams of workers striving to meet ambitious and dynamic performance standards becomes the norm. Supervisors become knowledge managers whose role is to facilitate the team approach. This evolution is depicted in Exhibit 2.10.

Once again it is important to stress that none of the four structural prerequisites

EXHIBIT 2.10 THE EVOLVING ROLE OF THE WORKFORCE IN AN FRO

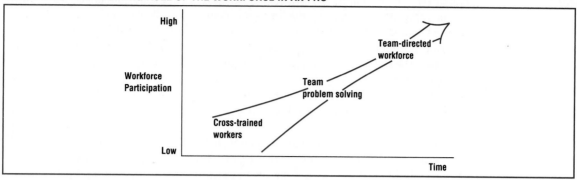

EXHIBIT 2.11 THE FRO DESCRIPTIVE FRAMEWORK

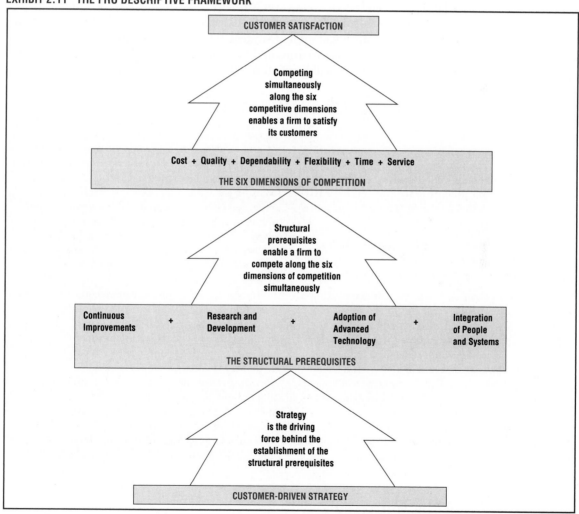

can be seen by itself as a "savior" for a firm. Simply purchasing advanced technology, for example, will not solve all the firm's problems. Consider the experience of General Motors. The company spent more on automation in the early 1980s than the gross national product of many countries. The intent was to maintain market share and beat back the tide of Asian imports. Unfortunately, GM focused solely on technology and ignored the other, equally serious prerequisites outlined above. In late 1992 the number one automaker conceded that its market had shrunk and that it had started to downsize. For GM, the productivity payoff from automation alone was highly negative.

Exhibit 2.1 introduced a framework which describes how firms succeed in today's marketplace. That framework, extended in Exhibit 2.11, can be viewed as a road map for an FRO to follow as it strives to reach its goal of delighting the customer.

The structural prerequisites discussed in this chapter enable a firm to satisfy its customers continually by competing simultaneously on cost, quality, dependability, flexibility, time, and service. However, **strategy** is the driving force behind the establishment of the structural prerequisites. The allocation of all of Chapter 3 to the formulation and implementation of strategy reflects its importance.

The framework applies to firms in the service sector as well as the manufacturing sector. In Chapter 3 this will be reinforced by a profile of an FRO from each sector.

MANAGERIAL IMPLICATIONS

The six competitive dimensions and management's attitudes toward them are fundamentally different from the "traditional" four dimensions of the Hayes and Wheelwright product-process life cycle matrix (see Exhibit 1.8 in Chapter 1). The differences are as follows:

- The six dimensions are *customer*-focused.
- Managers must be *positively* concerned with all six dimensions, not one or two as in the past.

This makes a manager's task more difficult because it forces managers to be critically aware of more factors. Managers are also required to integrate across functional areas because of the external, or customer, focus operations managers must now have. Integration with marketing personnel and with suppliers is especially important. The longer the supply chain, the more critical integration becomes for the operations function.

One reason for improved, effective integration is the elimination of waste or dead time. Rapid response to orders is only one element managers consider when using time as a competitive weapon. The time dimension requires managers to *anticipate* and *respond to* customer requirements rather than *react* to customers. True responsiveness involves product and process design, material and labor positioning, and *knowing* customers as well as order turnaround. Responsiveness is based on two important elements: delegation of authority to the lowest possible level and effectively integrated information systems.

If there is a single phenomenon that has had the greatest impact on operations and operations management, it is new technology. Advanced automation has given new meaning to customer-driven issues such as flexibility and quality. Managers must remember, of course, that new technology is much more than hardware; changes in procedures and relationships are as much new technology as are changes in products and processes. A manager's positive attitude toward advanced technologies must include acceptance of all forms of technology: "hardware," "software," and "brainware."

CHAPTER SUMMARY

This chapter introduced a framework which describes how fast-response organizations (FROs) succeed by producing goods and services that satisfy their customers' needs. Important points to remember about this framework include:

- Satisfying the customer requires the firm to develop the ability to compete simultaneously on cost, quality, dependability, flexibility, time, and service.
- No single dimension of competition is universally more important than another; the importance of each depends on the product and its market and may vary over time. Therefore, the emphasis placed on each dimension differs from one company to the next.
- Achieving the ability to compete on the six dimensions calls for establishment of the four structural prerequisites: continuous improvements, research and development, adoption of advanced technology, and integration of people and systems.
- No single structural prerequisite is always more important than the others. All four must be satisfied, but the emphasis placed on each varies from company to company.

As the reader will see in Chapter 3, it is the firm's strategy that enables it to establish these prerequisites successfully.

KEY TERMS

Cost	Fast-response	Development	Advanced manufacturing
Quality	organization (FRO)	System focus	technologies (AMTs)
Dependability	Structural prerequisites	Technology	Enterprise integration
Product flexibility	Non-value-added	Hardware	Hierarchical integration
Process flexibility	activities	Software	Horizontal integration
Infrastructure flexibility	Continuous improvement	Brainware	5 P's of operations
Aggregate flexibility	Static optimization	Technology support net	Vertical integration
Time	Dynamic evolution	Advanced operating	Downstream integration
Service	Kaizen	technologies	Upstream (backward)
Competitive dimensions	Basic research	Fixed (hard) automation	integration
Law of requisite variety	Applied research	Soft automation	Strategy

DISCUSSION QUESTIONS

1. What is a fast-response organization? Can you think of a better term for this form of organization?

2. What is cost, and how does it differ from value?

3. What is flexibility? Is any type of flexibility more strategically important than any other? Or does it depend on the type of firm and the circumstances in which it finds itself? Is flexibility related to firm size? Is responsiveness the same as flexibility?

4. What examples can you provide of services for which any or all of the five dimensions of quality can be defined?

5. What is dependability? Where does it apply in an organization? How, if at all, does dependability differ from reliability?

6. Describe the four structural prerequisites for a fast-response organization. Which of these prerequisites is more important than the others? Why?

7. Research and development (R&D) is one of the structural prerequisites. Does it matter where the R&D is carried out and by whom, and does it matter what the focus of the R&D is?

8. Is continuous improvement *always* possible? Is there a point at which it is actually detrimental to a firm? Is there a point at which a firm could eliminate all waste?

9. Are continuous improvement programs significantly different from process reengineering? If so, are they compatible? Which is more important for an FRO? Do you see one leading to the other?

10. How would you define technology? Why is technology so important at the end of the twentieth century?

11. What is the difference between horizontal integration and hierarchical integration? Can these forms of integration occur independently?

12. What provides the "glue" of integration? How should a firm manage that glue?

13. Must all companies compete along all six dimensions of competition? Should all companies aspire to become fast-response organizations? Explain.

14. Is it possible to be a fast-response organization and still bear traces of a traditional organization? If it is, what elements can be left until later to be altered? What process of change from traditional to fast response would you adopt if you were tasked with transforming your small (single site, 100 employees) automotive parts machining company? Your small (seven employees) gas station maintenance company?

15. What are the implications for operations managers of product/divisional, functional/traditional, and matrix/project organizational structures? Which type is most likely to be most fast response and why? Which is least likely to be fast response? How does firm size influence your answer?

GROUP EXERCISES

Many of the tools and concepts discussed in this chapter are meant to be used in a team setting. The following problems are best solved by small groups of students. Ideally, each group should be composed of people with different backgrounds, interests, and areas of expertise.

1. Select an industry (e.g., consumer electronics, news media) and outline its evolution. What changes have taken place in the marketplace? How have firms responded to those changes? What types of products have been the most successful? What types of operations have been the most successful? Can you identify any fast-response organizations in this industry?

2. a. Identify a leading local company that is organized along product lines and determine how *operations management* is organized. Find out how operations managers are linked with managers from other functions and with senior management.

   b. Now discuss the impact a change to a functional or matrix organization form would have on the organization and functioning of operations managers and on the ability of the firm to be an FRO. Identify the major negative implications of this potential change and describe ways to overcome them.

REFERENCES AND SELECTED BIBLIOGRAPHY

Anderson, Duncan Maxwell [1991], "Time Warrior," *Success,* December, pp. 38–40.

Ashby, W. Ross [1952], *Design for a Brain,* Chapman & Hall, London.

Albin, John T. [1992], "Competing in a Global Market," *APICS,* January, pp. 29–32.

Chase, R. B., and D. A. Garvin [1989], "The Service Factory," *Harvard Business Review,* July–August, pp. 61–69.

Davidow, W. H., and B. Uttal [1989], *Total Customer Service: The Ultimate Weapon,* Harper & Row, New York.

Denton, D. Keith [1991], "Lessons on Competitiveness: Motorola's Approach," *Production and Inventory Management Journal,* Third Quarter, pp. 22–25.

Dertouzos, M., R. Lester, and R. Solow [1988], *Interim Results of the MIT Commission on Industrial Productivity,* American Association for the Advancement of Science, Boston.

Deutsch, C. H. [1990], "Pared-down AT&T Learns to Produce More with Less," *Globe and Mail,* Report on Business, June 7, p. B2.

Ernst & Young Quality Improvement Consulting Group [1990], *Total Quality: An Executive's Guide for the 1990s,* Richard D. Irwin, Homewood, Ill.

Hayes, R. H. [1993], "Production and Operations Management's New Requisite Variety," *Productions and Operations Management,* vol. 1, no. 3, pp. 249–253.

Iansiti, Marco [1993], "Real-World R&D: Jumping the Product Generation Gap," *Harvard Business Review,* May–June, pp. 138–147.

Imai, M. [1986], *Kaizen: The Key to Japan's Competitive Success,* Random House, New York.

McFadden, Fred R. [1993], "Six Sigma Quality Programs," *Quality Progress,* vol. 26, no. 6, pp. 37–44.

Noori, H. [1990], *Managing the Dynamics of New Technologies: Issues in Manufacturing Management,* Prentice-Hall, Englewood Cliffs, N.J.

——— and R. Radford [1993], "Modelling of a World-Class Operation," *Industrial Management,* vol. 35, no. 4, July–August, pp. 23–29.

"Production Lines: On the Road to Continuous Improvement" [1992], *Manufacturing Engineering,* September, pp. 80–82.

Rice, Faye [1992], "What Intelligent Consumers Want," *Fortune,* December 28, pp. 56–60.

Shycon, H. [1990], "A Study of Customer Service: Its Impact on Market Success," *Arthur D. Little Customer Service Bulletin 1,* Fall.

Stalk, G., and T. M. Hout [1990], *Competing against Time: How Time-Based Competition Is Reshaping Global Markets,* Free Press, New York.

Swamidass, P. [1985], "Manufacturing Flexibility: Strategic Issues," *Discussion Paper No. 305,* Graduate School of Business, Indiana University, Bloomington.

Thompson, Dick [1992], "America's Big Shift," *Time,* November 23, pp. 36–37.

Treece, J. B. [1991], "Greeting Mileage from a Recall," *Business Week,* May 27, pp. 38–39.

Wood, Murray, and Gordon Pitts [1992], "Zero Defections: Taking Care of Old Business Can Produce Bigger Payoffs Than Chasing New Accounts," *The Globe and Mail,* Toronto, October, 6, p. B28.

Zeleny, M. [1986], "High Technology Management," *Human System Management,* vol. 6, pp. 109–120.

CHAPTER 3

OPERATIONS STRATEGY

In an era in which change will be (or will seem to be) continuous, there may be pressure to adapt or change corporate strategy. For this to be practicable, the operations strategy must allow the operations function to support the attainment of the new corporate goals and objectives. Therefore, the elements of the operations strategy must be carefully designed to support a flexible corporate strategic framework. This raises the following important issues:

- What is an operations strategy? What are its elements? How are those elements related?

- How is an operations strategy developed?
- How can an operations strategy help a firm be more competitive?

By the end of this chapter and its supplement you will have been introduced to the major elements of corporate and operations strategies and the process by which they are developed. You will also be familiar with competitive benchmarking, in which firms compare themselves to the "best of the best" to improve their operations.

EXHIBIT 3.1   FRO MANUFACTURING PROFILE

A mass-production strategy worked wonders for the American textile industry until foreign competitors developed a new approach. Manufacturers in West Germany, Italy, Japan, and other countries lured customers away by slashing the time required to fulfill a customer order, keeping pace with rapidly changing customer requirements (and often providing design support), and offering high quality at very reasonable prices. In the first half of the 1980s over a quarter of a million textile jobs were lost in the United States.

Milliken, one of the companies visited in the Startup Chapter, responded by changing its focus from process efficiency to customer satisfaction. Its successful change of focus was a result of a comprehensive strategy that included:

- Aggressively adopting advanced technologies capable of providing a high degree of operational flexibility. Production runs are much smaller, and the design cycle time is considerably shorter.
- Channeling about 2 percent of sales revenue into R&D and focusing on innovations. The company is developing new products and its own machinery to protect proprietary technology.
- Declaring war on waste. Non-value-added activities were identified and eliminated.
- Recognizing that "good is the enemy of best and best is the enemy of better" and implementing a philosophy of continuous improvements at all levels.
- Tightening the links with its suppliers and customers by forming hundreds of action teams.

Milliken's new strategy is working very well; the firm can now compete *simultaneously* on cost, quality, time, dependability, flexibility, and service.

Source: Adapted from Dertouzos, Lester, and Solow (1989), pp. 288–302.

EXHIBIT 3.2   FRO SERVICE PROFILE

Wal-Mart is the largest and most profitable retailer in the world. What is the secret of its success? How can it consistently offer lower prices and better service than its competitors?

By utilizing a logistics technique known as *cross-docking* and running a full 85 percent of its goods through its warehouse system, Wal-Mart has reduced its cost of sales by 2 to 3 percent compared with the industry average. The high volume of goods enables Wal-Mart

(Exhibit 3.2 continues on next page)

EXHIBIT 3.2   *(continued)*

to achieve the economies that come with purchasing full truckloads of goods, while cross-docking substantially reduces inventory and handling costs.

With cross-docking, goods are continuously delivered to Wal-Mart's 19 distribution centers, where they are selected, repacked, and then shipped to the retail stores. Rather than sit in inventory, goods cross from one loading dock to another within 48 hours.

To make cross-docking work, Wal-Mart has had to make significant investments in interlocking support systems, including the following:

- A private satellite system that enables Wal-Mart to send point-of-sale data directly to 4,000 vendors daily.
- A company-owned fleet of nearly 2,000 trucks that permits Wal-Mart to replenish its store shelves about twice a week, compared with the industry norm of once every two weeks.
- Close relationships with suppliers. Wal-Mart has worked with suppliers to smooth production schedules. It also offers far better payment terms.

Since customers "pull" products from the warehouse to individual stores when they are needed, Wal-Mart has made fundamental changes in its approach to managerial control. Responsibility for merchandising, pricing, and promotion has been pushed down to the store level. Informal cooperation and communication takes place between store managers, headquarters, suppliers, and distribution centers.

Source: Adapted from Stalk, Evans, and Shulman (1992), pp. 57–61.

3.1 MANAGERIAL ORIENTATION

- A customer focus
- Competing simultaneously on cost, quality, flexibility, dependability, time, and service
- Investing in R&D and advanced technology
- Integrating systems and people
- Continuously improving the firm, its products, and its processes

These concepts, which were introduced in Chapter 2 as part of the fast-response organization (FRO) framework, drive the development of operations strategy.

The operations area is usually the custodian of the vast majority of a firm's capital investments, and the impact of operations on a firm's ability to compete simultaneously along the six competitive dimensions is great. However, the potential contribution of operations has frequently been overlooked. Operations can, and should, be used as a competitive weapon. An operations strategy that supports and enhances the corporate strategy is essential.

Milliken (Exhibit 3.1) is a firm that has fought off intense foreign competition by revitalizing its operations area and using operations as a competitive weapon. Strategic investments in advanced technologies, supplier relations, employee training, continuous improvements in operating procedures, and R&D have enabled Milliken to meet the changing needs of its customers.

Before looking in detail at the development of operations strategies, let us briefly discuss the development of corporate strategies. The corporate strategy must be known when one is developing all functional strategies.

3.2 THE CORPORATE MISSION AND STRATEGY

A firm's **corporate mission** and **corporate strategy** are about ends and means.

> **DEFINITION:** The corporate mission outlines a firm's corporate values, intended markets and product, broad goals and objectives, core competencies, and strategic capabilities.

> **DEFINITION:** The corporate strategy states how a firm will achieve its goals and objectives.

The process of corporate strategy formulation varies from firm to firm, but certain key elements are common to most successful firms. For example, strategy formulation is an iterative process that requires the involvement of all the firm's functional areas,[1] and the operations area can and should play a key role in this process. Overall, strategy formulation can be viewed as a dynamic learning process.

The strategy formulation process can be divided into three phases, beginning with an **assessment phase**.

The Assessment Phase

Assessing a firm's internal and external environments is one of the first steps in strategy formulation. Specifically, the following types of questions are addressed:

- Who are the customers? What are their needs? What emphasis do they place on each of the six competitive dimensions?
- Is the firm a domestic, multinational, or global company?[2] How integrated are its plants and divisions? What competitive advantage does each plant or division offer? How does each one contribute to the firm's core competencies?
- What is the current economic, political, and social climate in the firm's markets? Are there any projected changes? What trends have been identified?
- What is the structure of the industry? Who are the competitors? Are any new firms ready to enter the industry? What are the competitors' current and projected strengths and weaknesses? In what areas do they outperform the firm? How much better are they? What are their strategies?
- What are the rate and direction of technological changes in the industry? Do any new technologies have the potential to change the structure of the industry? What types of technology strategies are the competitors following, and how successful have they been?
- What are the firm's strengths and weaknesses? What are its core competencies and strategic capabilities? How sustainable are they? How can the firm nurture, protect, and exploit them? What are the firm's human, physical, financial, and technological resources? What new competencies and capabilities is the firm developing?
- In what type of alliances (e.g., joint ventures, licensing agreements) is the firm involved? How successful have these alliances been? What market advantages are they providing that the firm could not have obtained on its own?

---

[1] This chapter will refer to the corporate and functional levels of a firm. In practice, though, many firms have several more layers. The principles covered in this chapter can be applied to multilevel companies.

[2] What is the difference between a multinational company and a global company? A *multinational* company has plants and/or divisions in several countries, but each plant or division acts autonomously. In a *global* company plants and/or divisions are highly integrated for the overall benefit of the firm.

Answering these questions enables a firm to update the corporate mission and strategy. **Competitive benchmarking** can be a very useful tool at this stage. It can ensure that a firm's goals are realistic and provide insight into how those goals can be attained. Benchmarking is discussed in the supplement to this chapter.

At the same time the corporate strategy is formulated, each functional area develops its own **functional strategy.**

DEFINITION: A functional strategy details how a functional area will contribute to the achievement of the firm's corporate goals and objectives.

The strategy formulation process at the functional level reveals both opportunities and constraints. Therefore, communication must flow up from the bottom of the organization as well as from the top down. Communication between functional areas during the strategy formulation process also ensures that each functional strategy is mutually supporting and derives the greatest benefit from the **core competencies** developed by a particular functional area.

DEFINITION: Core competencies refer to the expertise found at specific points along the value chain. They can be translated into a wide range of products and thus can give a firm access to a variety of markets.

At the Mayo Clinic diagnostic expertise is one of the core competencies. Sony's core competency lies in miniaturization, while engine and power train expertise constitutes Honda's core competency.

Honda has used its expertise in engines and power trains to move from motorcycles into a wide range of businesses, including lawn mowers, outboard motors, and automobiles. However, this expertise is not solely responsible for Honda's success. The ways in which the company trains and supports its dealer network and develops new products are also key elements in Honda's success (see Exhibit 3.3).

Dealer management and product realization are two **strategic capabilities** consciously developed by Honda.

DEFINITION: Strategic capabilities are customer-focused business processes that support and leverage a firm's core competencies.

EXHIBIT 3.3   COMPETITIVE COMPETENCIES AND STRATEGIC CAPABILITIES AT HONDA

Honda's success in markets as diverse as motorcycles, lawn mowers, outboard motors, and automobiles reflects that firm's ability to design and manufacture innovative products. It is also a result of Honda's superior dealer management and product realization capabilities.

When Honda entered the motorcycle market, local dealers were typically motorcycle enthusiasts eager to support their hobby but possessing few business skills. In contrast to other companies, Honda actively trained and supported its dealers. The company provided operating procedures and policies for merchandising, selling, floor planning, and service management as well as a computerized dealer-management information system. Competing dealers were no match for the better-prepared and better-financed Honda dealers.

As Honda moved into new markets, it replicated the same dealer-management capability. This capability, combined with Honda's expertise in engines and power trains, gave the company a competitive edge.

Honda's skill at product realization—translating customer needs into new products—is also central to its success. By overlapping product development phases and involving marketing, production, and other functional areas from day one, Honda can produce high-quality products quickly and inexpensively. And since its factories are flexible, new products do not require new factories. This saves Honda time and money.

Source: Adapted from Stalk, Evans, and Shulman (1992), pp. 57–69.

Strategic capabilities tend to be business processes that cross functional boundaries and require investments far beyond what could be justified by conventional return on investment (ROI) criteria. Wal-Mart (Exhibit 3.2) provides an example of this. To support its rapid inventory replenishment system, Wal-Mart has invested in a private satellite system, a dedicated truck fleet, and supplier relations. Most Wal-Mart employees have contributed to this strategic capability.

Like core competencies, strategic capabilities must make a significant contribution to the perceived benefits of a firm's end products. At Wal-Mart, the 2 to 3 percent cost saving generated by the inventory replenishment system is translated into things that customers notice: everyday low prices, extra checkout lines, and "greeters" at store entrances.

Think back to the FRO model that was introduced at the end of Chapter 2. Wal-Mart *has* focused on the customer and has developed a strategic capability that allows it to compete simultaneously on cost, time, quality, dependability, flexibility, and service. To establish this strategic capability, the company has made a series of investments in structural prerequisites such as advanced technology and internal and external integration. Maintaining and enhancing this capability entails involving everyone in continuously improving the process and identifying areas in which important (although small) changes can be made.

The Implementation Phase

The resources and policies needed to enact a firm's strategy are identified, acquired, and put into place during the **implementation phase.** The greater the impact of these changes on a firm's current activities, the greater the need for that firm to address the following important issues:[3]

- In what sequence and at what times must the strategy be implemented? Which people will implement the strategy?
- How can the firm ensure that it is still satisfying the customers during the transition period?
- What moves by the competitors would be most harmful during implementation, and how can their effect be minimized?
- Which critical changes will be the most difficult to implement? What is the likelihood of not meeting those implementation goals? How can this likelihood be minimized, and what should be done if a shortfall occurs?

Once the firm has implemented its strategy, it moves on to the awareness phase.

The Awareness Phase

The **awareness phase** finishes the cycle and starts another as it asks, How successful has the strategy been? and Given the firm's resources and potential, is the current competitive advantage and strategy still appropriate?

The full potential of the new resources put in place to implement a firm's current strategy is often unknown at first. It becomes apparent as the firm develops new knowledge, particularly operating knowledge, during the implementation phase. During the awareness phase the firm investigates the capabilities of its available resources. For example, the potential to produce other products with recently acquired technology may be explored.

---

[3] For example, if the strategy requires investment in an advanced technology new to the firm, the transition period tends to be long and arduous.

Once the full potential of the firm's resources has been identified, new opportunities to take advantage of those resources are investigated. The new opportunities are considered as the firm updates its corporate strategy.

> **Remember:** Formulating a corporate strategy is an iterative process that requires the input of all functional areas. Functional strategies must support each other as well as the corporate strategy.

Long-Range Strategy versus Opportunism

There are two schools of thought about corporate strategy. One school, based on concepts developed at the Harvard Business School, suggests that formal planning over a multiyear horizon is beneficial in terms of gaining a competitive edge and that firms should therefore engage in regular long-range strategic planning and strategy-setting processes. The work of Andrews (1980) is an example of this type of strategic thinking. The second school acknowledges that long-range planning is beneficial but suggests that in practice most managers do not undertake disciplined long-range planning. This school is based on the empirical observations of Quinn (1980) and others. Quinn discovered that managers tend to make decisions based mainly on current conditions and needs rather than on a more distant objective. Often this short-range action is dictated by resource constraints, usually a lack of finances. Even if managers know what they "should" do, they do what they "can" do. However, a series of small strategic "corrections" will result in a major shift in strategic direction and emphasis.

An extreme example may help illustrate this phenomenon. *The Saturday Evening Post* was a respected magazine before World War II; initially the magazine was a publisher, relying on printers capable of working at the last minute to produce topical stories. This flexible, responsive strategy was placed in jeopardy by a decision to integrate backward into printing, a decision that moved deadlines farther and farther from the publishing date as management became concerned with cost reduction. Eventually the firm integrated back into forests and papermaking, a decision that influenced the number of pages in the magazine and the ratio of advertising to copy. The *Post* eventually failed, principally because the initial clear strategy was compromised by reactive decisions, each of which was logical in terms of the immediate issues facing the managers. Because the decisions were not checked to determine their impact on the firm's strategy, there was no indication that they were not in the best long-term interests of the magazine.

When a firm is small and there is only one decision maker or decision-making team, the gap between an espoused long-range strategy and the enacted, resource-constrained strategy usually is manageable. The difficulties arise when those who make the strategic plans are not aware of the reactive strategic decisions being made by other managers. Provided that there is free sharing of information within the firm and a generally agreed-on vision, the long-range plans should be based on valid assessments of resource constraints and local actions should be taken in accordance with generally understood and accepted longer-range objectives. If these conditions do not exist, it is easy for a firm to destroy its competitive advantage without realizing that it is doing so.

When the environment is relatively stable, the gap also remains small and manageable. When the environment is unstable, though, and more dramatic action rather than incremental adjustment is required, the gap may grow wide without being evident. It is at that point that a major reassessment of the basic strategy should be undertaken. This does *not* mean rearranging the deck chairs on the *Titanic*; it involves a fundamental analysis of what the firm is capable of doing and desires to do. Until that assessment is made, initiating major change is not advisable.

One practice that should *not* be carried out until a major strategic evaluation has been made is **business process reengineering** [see, for example, Hammer and Champy (1993)]. This reengineering is intended to streamline a firm's major business processes to better serve the customers; usually measures of performance improvement are based on notions of cost, time, and customer satisfaction. The real danger here is that managers who favor radical change will use each detected shift in customer needs to precipitate another cycle of major process realignment and reengineering. When this adjustment is made without reference to the firm's strategy or the impact on other functions, the result will almost inevitably be a loss of both integration and the ability of operations to support the corporate strategy.

Paradoxically, the firms that are best placed to take advantage of this activity are those that are agile and opportunistic in the first place, and those capabilities can be put in place only through solid strategic planning [see Stewart (1993)].

Thus, the desirable way may not be the actual way in most cases. However, the concern here is not the average but the ideal: the fast-response organization. FROs become agile because they plan to, and they act in ways that are consistent with their basic strategies and policies. If the strategies are consistent with the competitive environment and the firm's capabilities and if short-range decisions are judged in regard to their ability to contribute to attaining the long-range objectives, the undesirable outcomes of reactive decision making should not occur. Firms that plan for and respond quickly to customers' needs and expectations may seem opportunistic, but they need not be simply reactive. If they are FROs, they will be better organized to achieve a fast response.

3.3 DEVELOPING OPERATIONS STRATEGY

The Operations Audit

As part of its strategy formulation process, operations conducts an audit of its resources. An **operations audit** is an in-depth review of resources, capabilities, strengths, and weaknesses. Specifically, the following issues are examined:

- The range of goods and services that can be produced with current resources
- The location, age, capacity, and processes in each facility
- The location, age, and capacity of each process
- Existing technology, its current uses, and its potential
- Mastery of special technologies
- Patent protection
- The ability to develop products and processes
- Ownership of or access to natural resources
- Distribution channels or delivery systems
- Relationships with suppliers, their dependability, and the quality of suppliers' products and services
- Workforce skills and knowledge and labor relations
- Management's capabilities, attitude toward risk, and ability to cope with uncertainty

The results of the operations audit are used to help form both the operations strategy and the corporate strategy. (The corporate strategy also has a major impact on the operations strategy.)

Components of the Operations Strategy

The **operations strategy** translates the corporate strategy into an appropriate integration of bricks and mortar, equipment, people, and procedures.

> **DEFINITION: The operations strategy is a statement of how the operations function will contribute effectively to the attainment of corporate goals and objectives.**

The operations strategy addresses the following issues:

- Which goods and services will be produced internally and which will be purchased?
- What processes will be used to provide goods and services? How flexible will those processes be?
- How many facilities will be used? Where will they be located? What strategic role will each facility play?
- How will each facility be focused; that is, what products will be produced in each facility and what markets will each facility serve?[4] There are many ways in which a firm can focus its facilities: by customer, by product, by process, and so on (see Exhibit 3.4).
- What type of operating process will be housed in each facility? How much capacity will be provided by each process?
- Who will be the suppliers, and what type of relationship will be pursued with them? How will the firm monitor their performance? Will the firm transfer any design responsibility to them?
- What type of workforce will be needed? What will be its role? How many skill levels will there be? How will the wages and benefits be structured? What guidelines will be followed when people are hired or fired? How much training will be provided?
- What type of materials handling and other support systems will be used? How will tasks be divided between the workforce and the equipment?
- What organizational structure should be used? What are the roles of managers and the support staff?
- Will the firm develop its technologies or purchase them? Will the firm be a technology leader or follower? What technologies will be developed: product or process?

These and other strategic decisions made by operations managers are reviewed in detail throughout this book. As illustrated in Exhibit 3.5, long-term decisions are discussed first, followed by intermediate-term and then short-term decisions.

Operations Competency

Must a firm have operations competency? The answer is emphatically yes. An FRO must have competencies in all functional areas to compete in the global econ-

---

[4] Why should a facility be focused? Focusing reduces a facility's need for information and streamlines the collection, use, and dissemination of that information. Improving information flow and management increases the ability to plan, control, and organize work. A focused operating unit can do a limited number of things very well.

EXHIBIT 3.4   TYPES OF FOCUS

There are many different ways in which a facility can be focused. Each type of focus has different implications for management, offers advantages over the others, and takes time, effort, training, and money to develop and change.

Customer. Each facility makes a range of products for a specific customer group. For example, one of a pharmaceutical company's facilities may produce drugs for hospitals while another produces drugs for pharmacies.

Geographic. Each facility makes the full range of the firm's products for the local market. For example, a pharmaceutical company may make all 30 drugs sold in Canada in one facility and all 40 drugs sold in the United States in another facility.

Product. Each facility makes a limited set of the firm's products. For example, one of a pharmaceutical company's facilities may produce painkillers while another produces cough suppressants.

Process. Each facility concentrates on a specific set of operation processes. For example, one of a pharmaceutical company's facilities may produce liquid formulations while another produces tablets.

Market size. Each facility operates processes that can efficiently produce the volume demanded by the market. This is a hybrid option. For example, a pharmaceutical company may produce all small-volume drugs in one facility but dedicate another facility to only one high-volume drug.

Product life cycle focus. Some facilities focus on the introductory and growth phases (and perhaps the decline phase), while others focus on the mature phase of the product life cycle. A pharmaceutical company may produce a new AIDS drug in one facility and an analgesic drug in another.

GENERAL OBSERVATIONS

- Facilities with a geographic or customer focus may find it easier to keep in touch with their customers' needs. The more customers' needs vary by region and/or customer group, the more sense these types of focus make.

- A geographic focus overcomes some tariff and nontariff barriers to imports.

- The greater the number of products and/or processes is, the more difficult and expensive production planning will be. Inventories also tend to be larger. Responsiveness to market changes may be slower.

- Facilities that produce a limited range of products (product focus) enable managers and workers to know more about each product. Planning and control are simpler and less expensive, and inventories tend to be lower. However, these facilities are more vulnerable to shifts in market demand, labor strikes, and competitive attacks. Overspecialized processes can rapidly become obsolete.

- A facility's focus need not affect the firm's strategic capabilities but may alter the facility's core competency. The specific operating competency gained by a process-focused facility, for example, may be lost if the facility shifts to a product focus.

- Changing a facility's focus is usually expensive and time-consuming.

omy, and these competencies must be identified and understood. For an FRO, every function has to be part of the competitive arsenal. For other firms, this is not so clear; while the competencies exist, they do not have to be understood or exploited. Firms that do *not* understand or exploit their competencies are, however, like owners of vehicles that do not run on all cylinders; the vehicle can be operated, but it is underpowered, sluggish, noisy, and expensive to operate; also, the repairs will be extensive and expensive.

Is a firm limited to one operations competency? The answer is no; separate elements can have separate competencies. Thus the operations competency of a GE whiteware plant in Kentucky can be different from that of a GE jet engine plant in Massachusetts. However, it is difficult for a single plant to operate with two different and competing operations competencies. The reasons for this are logical: different competencies require different forms of equipment and different people, procedures, and processes. Managing this divergence can be difficult, but confusion can be

EXHIBIT 3.5 KEY DECISION AREAS IN OPERATIONS MANAGEMENT

Key Decision Areas	Reference Chapters
How can the firm become a fast-response organization?	1, 2, 20
How can operations support the corporate strategy? How are operation's goals and objectives developed?	3
How can uncertainty be measured? How can the firm forecast the expected demand for its goods and services?	4
How can the firm design the right products? How can quality be assured and costs be contained?	5 and 6
How should the firm design its facilities and processes? What technologies should it choose? How should jobs be designed?	7 to 11
How should projects be managed?	12
How should resources be allocated to meet general demand levels?	14
When, where, and how much inventory should be maintained?	13, 15, 16
How and when should specific goods and services be produced?	17
How should suppliers and distribution channels be created and maintained?	18
What is productivity, and how can employees be motivated?	19

avoided by keeping all operations in a production unit in one place on the product-process matrix.

The danger is particularly acute if the mix is not planned but occurs in a gradual fashion. An example helps illustrate this.

A machine shop specialized in high-precision machining of castings for small customers in the aircraft industry. Most of the jobs required some design and redesign inside the company and interpretive machining by the operators assigned to each job. This required engineering and design competency which included machining competency. Because each operator paced the work, the firm used piece rates to reward good operator performance.

A contract was signed with an automobile manufacturer for the supply of a machined casting to be installed in a new automobile. The contract called for a large volume of castings supplied at regular intervals at a low and falling cost. The company chose to machine the castings by setting up a line of machines in which the machines paced production. Not surprisingly, the workers felt that they could not influence their output, and therefore their pay, and disrupted the project. The company finished the contract (at a loss) only after paying a premium to the operators for working in the cell.

The firm might have been able to separate both systems within the factory. However, failing to recognize the need for two different competencies meant that management did not give the trial a chance.

Finally, does it matter what competency is developed? The answer is yes. The competency developed will be the integrative element around which the firm develops its operations strategy, and the operations strategy will have to support the corporate strategy. It does not matter whether a firm has an existing competency around which it develops its strategies or whether it develops its strategy and then decides what competency it needs. The firm must ensure that its strategies, competencies, and capabilities are integrated and mutually supporting.

When a firm decides to operate in several different countries, it adds another dimension to its strategic deliberations. Take another look at the operational issues introduced earlier in this chapter, this time from a global perspective.

- **Capacity.** What capacity will the firm need globally? What products are required in which markets? Can the product be transferred freely between countries?
- **Facilities.** Where should the facilities be located? What should the firm make where? Who should have world product mandates? In how many sites should products be duplicated? What restrictions will the firm face on changing or eliminating a specific facility? Where are the necessary skills located? What infrastructure exists?
- **Technology.** What technology strategies should the firm follow in different centers? What technology diffusion policy should it adopt? What product technologies can the local markets absorb?
- **Integration.** How will parts and components flow through the whole company? What transportation and distribution channels will the firm use and own? How integrated should the whole value chain be in each country?
- **Innovation.** Are the patent laws and the support for innovation more favorable in one country than in another? How should new knowledge be stored and disseminated? Are there barriers to knowledge and technology transfer?
- **Workforce.** Will the firm maintain the same global personnel policies, or will each unit or country be separate? How mobile should the managers and workforce be? What special circumstances exist in each country or region that the firm should be concerned with or take advantage of?
- **Procedures and planning.** Who will be responsible for planning for a particular facility and market? How will inventory be managed: globally, regionally, or locally? What special local circumstances will influence local or global decisions?
- **Management and organization.** From where should the managers come at each level of the organization? Should the firm keep managers locally, or should each site have managers from anywhere in the world? Should the firm undertake its own management development; if so, to what level, and where should management development be carried out? Should managers be evaluated globally using one evaluation process, or should specific processes and criteria be developed for each area? Should each operation be wholly owned, or should the firm be involved in joint ventures or alliances?

The assumption made in these questions is that an FRO is a single legal entity, an independent firm. This need not be true, though; remember from the Startup Chapter that Fujima International is a joint venture between two firms, one Canadian (Magna) and the other Japanese (Fujima). And Moscow McDonald's is a joint venture between McDonald's Restaurants of Canada and Moscow's city council. There are several ways in which an FRO can organize itself to improve its international operations and competitiveness other than establishing wholly owned facilities in other countries. These methods range from new legal entities (joint ventures), to cooperative alliances (international or domestic), to very unstructured and multifirm aggregations (networks).

Joint ventures are a traditional approach to expansion often undertaken by a firm to enter a market heavily protected by import restrictions or tariffs. Under these circumstances the external firm seeks a local partner to share the risks and rewards of entering the market, with the local partner providing labor and local management and the external partner providing product and process knowledge and often a source of specific materials and components for the product. If the impetus for the joint venture comes from the local firm, this usually represents a desire to obtain specific skills and gain access to particular expertise that is not available locally.

In a joint venture it is common for the knowledge-supplying parent company to supply critical operating technologies, operations managers, and supervisors and essential technical personnel while the local parent provides the rest of the management and the workforce. Blending the cultures may be difficult and may take time. However, the joint venture should have no impact on the parent companies apart from personnel transfers; the joint venture should be a source of otherwise unobtainable profits.

Another form of extension is the alliance, a cooperative rather than legal relationship. Cowhey and Aronson (1993, p. 7) define an international alliance as "an ongoing relationship between companies from two or more countries that involve significant markets, products, R&D, and other important process technologies that shape the strategy of market leaders." Krubasik and Lautenschlager (1993) state that there are four reasons for entering into an alliance: to swap products, to gain the right to produce a product, to gain access to technology, and to increase product and process development capability.

From an operations standpoint, alliances usually entail knowledge transfers, not the people integraton that can make joint ventures problematic. Of course, there is still the potential for problems; if a product is picked up to increase capacity utilization in a factory, there may be problems with processes, operator skills, and scheduling. It may take time to build the trust that allows proprietary knowledge to flow freely across boundaries and to build up the capabilities of the receiving company so that it can take advantage of the newly available knowledge. The alliance partners must jointly develop a strategy for transferring knowledge so that trust and strategic momentum are maintained.

A third means of extending the global competitiveness of a firm involves the use of networks, the essence of which is interfirm collaboration on the basis of complementarity. The nature of the collaboration in a network usually is carefully defined so that the independence and business interests of the individual firm are preserved. Networks provide leverage not available to the individual firm whether the network focus is purchasing, marketing, knowledge sharing, or technology sharing. Sematech, the technology development network for North American semiconductor manufacturers, is a network that allows all the members to gain leverage from coordinated R&D activities carried out across the member firms. Support networks can be created in which users share their experiences with a particular technology or approach and help one another work through difficulties. Members need not participate fully, however, and networks can disintegrate if some members feel that others are not giving as much as they are taking. Since it is composed of actual or potential competitors, a network is subject to political tensions as the competitive and economic climate changes.

Global competitiveness does not require developing operations in all major markets. Selective use of the different ways of extending a firm can provide greater advantages at less cost in both the short term and the long term. All three basic forms, though, require that the firm establish a level of trust with its partners that will lead to collaborative rather than merely legal integration.

The importance of ensuring that corporate and operations strategies support each other cannot be overstated. This is true for any organization, but especially for a fast-response organization. When the operations strategy and other strategies do not reinforce each other, the results will be counterproductive. It is the seamless interplay between and among functional strategies that produces the synergy managers seek; destroying the synergy will damage the firm.

A firm can ensure that strategies do support each other by developing strategic capabilities. Capabilities provide superior value to customers by effectively using the whole organization to lever key competencies. Key operations competencies have a major technological component. A key fact about technologies, especially new technologies, is that it takes a long time to understand their true potential.

For this reason, using a balanced approach to operations strategy development is important. This approach requires managers to acknowledge that strategy development and deployment is a continuous process, not an occasional task. An important aspect of the strategy is the organization's learning and knowledge development process, for determining the competitive "envelope" of technology is a matter of individual and group learning.

As with all strategies, the technology strategy requires a focus. A firm cannot be on the leading edge of all technologies, because the cost and resource constraints are too great even for large organizations. Consequently, a firm must decide specifically which technologies it is going to develop and in what ways that development will occur. Naturally, the technology strategy must fit with the corporate and other functional and specialist strategies, or the impact will not be predictable—or desirable.

CHAPTER SUMMARY

It is the strategy that keeps a firm together and drives that firm toward its goals and objectives. Important points to remember from this chapter include:

- A firm's corporate mission and strategy are about ends and means. The corporate mission outlines the firm's corporate values, intended markets and products, broad goals and objectives, core competencies, and strategic capabilities. The corporate strategy states how the firm will achieve its goals and objectives.
- Core competencies refer to the expertise found at specific points along the value chain. They can be translated into a wide range of products and thus can give a firm access to a variety of markets. An FRO must have competencies in all functional areas.
- Strategic capabilities are customer-focused business processes that support and leverage a firm's core competencies.
- Strategy formulation is an iterative process that requires the involvement of all the firm's functional areas.
- The strategy formulation process can be divided into three phases:
  1. During the assessment phase, the firm's internal and external environments are examined. Competitive benchmarking can be useful during this phase. Competitive benchmarking involves analyzing the performance and practices of best-in-class companies. Their performance becomes a benchmark to which a firm can compare its own performance, and their practices are used to improve a firm's own practices.
  2. The resources and policies needed to enact the firm's strategy are identified, acquired, and put into place during the implementation phase.

3. The awareness phase finishes the cycle and starts another as it asks, How successful has the strategy been? and Given the firm's resources and potential, is the current competitive advantage and strategy still appropriate?

- Functional strategies are often developed at the same time as the corporate strategy. Functional strategies must support each other as well as the corporate strategy.
- The operations strategy translates the corporate strategy into an appropriate integration of bricks and mortar, equipment, people, and procedures.
- As part of its strategy formulation process, operations conducts an audit of its resources. The operations audit involves an in-depth review of resources, capabilities, strengths, and weaknesses.
- When a firm decides to compete globally, it adds another dimension to its strategic deliberations.

KEY TERMS

Corporate mission	Competitive	Strategic capabilities	Business process
Corporate strategy	benchmarking	Implementation phase	reengineering
Assessment phase	Functional strategy	Awareness phase	Operations audit
	Core competencies		Operations strategy

DISCUSSION QUESTIONS

1. What is the relationship between the corporate strategy and the operations strategy of a firm? Which is developed first?

2. How would you focus a pharmaceutical plant by customer? By process? By market size? By product life cycle?

3. Can a firm have more than one focus at one time? If so, how? If not, why not?

4. Firms should organize around core competencies and strategic capabilities. What *are* core competencies and capabilities? How do they differ? How might they influence operations strategy?

5. Might two firms have similar core competencies but different operations strategies?

6. Is an operations strategy always evident? Why or why not?

7. What is the relationship between operational focus and strategic capabilities?

8. How will a "make or buy" decision for a furniture maker influence workforce decisions when the firm is formulating its operations strategy? What might this decision include for a group of medical specialists?

9. What examples can you think of for each of the five technology strategies?

10. In 1992 IBM, through restructuring, created nine wholly owned independent business units worldwide. One of these units is IBM Personal Computer Co. What do you propose as a core competency for this unit? What strategy will give the unit FRO status?

11. Why is an operation audit important?

12. Strategy formulation is an iterative and dynamic process. How can the formulation of an operations strategy benefit from such a process?

13. Why might a manufacturer of refrigerators use a supermarket for benchmarking? Why might a restaurant use an automobile manufacturer as a benchmark? Where would *you* look for benchmark operations for all four firms? (See the supplement to this chapter to answer this question.)

14. What should a general hospital benchmark? A paint manufacturer? A law firm? A semiconductor manufacturer? (See the supplement to this chapter to answer this question.)

15. How does a global operations strategy differ from

the operations strategy of a smaller, regional company? Why is thinking about global operations important?

16. American Express, General Motors, and Westinghouse all have gone through a shake-up to bring about a turnaround through reengineering their operations. How can the FRO framework help them (or any company) rethink and reformulate their business strategies?

GROUP EXERCISES

Many of the tools and concepts discussed in this chapter are meant to be used in a team setting. The following problems are best solved by small groups of students. Ideally, each group should be composed of people with different backgrounds, interests, or areas of expertise.

1. Take a simple operation, such as a take-out pizzeria or a copy center, with which you are familiar.
   a. Identify the competitive capabilities this operation must possess. Divide the operation into a set of activities or major tasks.
   b. Select two major tasks and document how you think they are performed.
   c. What types of companies would you target as potential benchmarking partners? Are there any companies in other industries that are candidates? How would you persuade candidates to participate?
   d. Prepare a benchmarking questionnaire.
   e. How would you use the benchmarking data? How would you implement an ongoing benchmarking program?
   (See the supplement to this chapter before attempting this exercise.)

2. According to Yves L. Doz (in "Managing Manufacturing Rationalization within Multinational Companies" in *Columbia Journal of World Business*):

   > Rationalization means shifting from a set of local-for-local plants, each serving its own national market with a broad product range, to an integrated network of large scale production-specialized plants serving the world market. Only a few products, or components, are made in each plant, but in very large numbers. Rationalization also involves the development of a single worldwide product line and the integrated management of product engineering activities to avoid duplications and to maintain production specialization.

   Do you agree that rationalization is a stepping-stone for a firm striving to become a fast-response organization?

REFERENCES AND SELECTED BIBLIOGRAPHY

Andrews, Kenneth R. [1980], *The Concept of Corporate Strategy*, Dow Jones–Irwin, Homewood, Ill.

Bleeke, Joel, and David Ernst (eds.) [1993], *Collaborating to Compete*, Wiley, New York.

Cowhey, Peter F., and Jonathan D. Aronson [1993], *Managing the World Economy*, Council on Foreign Relations Press, New York.

Cyert, Richard M., and James G. March [1963], *A Behavioral Theory of the Firm*, Prentice-Hall, Englewood Cliffs, N.J.

Davenport, Thomas H. [1993], *Process Innovation*, Harvard Business School Press, Boston.

Davis, Stanley M., and Paul R. Lawrence [1977], *Matrix*, Addison-Wesley, Reading, Mass.

Dertouzos, Michael L., Richard K. Lester, and Robert M. Solow [1989], *Made in America: Regaining the Productive Edge*, MIT Press, Cambridge, Mass.

Galbraith, Jay [1973], *Designing Complex Organizations*, Addison-Wesley, Reading, Mass.

Hammer, Michael, and James Champy [1993], *Reengineering the Corporation*, Harper Business, New York.

Krubasik, Edward, and Hartmut Lautenschlager [1993], "Forming Successful Strategic Alliances in High-Tech Businesses," chap. 4 in Joel Bleeke and David Ernst (eds.), *Collaborating to Compete*, Wiley, New York, pp. 55–65.

Martin, M. J. C. [1992], *Managing Technological Innovation and Entrepreneurship*, Reston, Reston, Va.

Ohmae, Kenichi [1990], *The Borderless World*, Harper Business, New York.

——— [1993], "The Global Logic of Corporate Alliances," chap. 3 in Joel Bleeke and David Ernst (eds.), *Collaborating to Compete*, Wiley, New York, pp. 35–54.

Porter, Michael E. [1985], *Competitive Advantage: Creating and Sustaining Superior Performance*, Free Press, New York.

Prahalad, C. K., and Gary Hamel [1990], "The Core Competence of the Corporation," *Harvard Business Review*, May–June, pp. 79–91.

Quinn, James Brian [1980], *Strategies for Change: Logical Incrementalism*, Richard D. Irwin, Homewood, Ill.

Saporito, B. [1991], "Is Wal-Mart Unstoppable?" *Fortune,* May 6, pp. 50–59.

Stalk, George, Philip Evans, and Lawrence E. Shulman [1992], "Competing on Capabilities: The New Rules of Corporate Strategy," *Harvard Business Review,* March–April, pp. 57–69.

Stewart, Thomas A. [1993], "Reengineering: The Hot, New Managing Tool," *Fortune,* August, pp. 41–48.

Twiss, B. C. [1986], *Managing Technological Innovation,* 3d ed., Pitman Publishing, London.

Wheelwright, Steven C., and Robert H. Hayes [1985], "Competing through Manufacturing," *Harvard Business Review,* January–February, pp. 99–109.

SUPPLEMENT TO
CHAPTER 3

COMPETITIVE
BENCHMARKING

S3.1 MANAGERIAL ORIENTATION

How can a firm ensure that its operational goals and objectives are realistic? How does it know how much improvement is needed in each of the six dimensions of competition to catch up with others or maintain its lead? **Competitive benchmarking** can help answer these questions.

> **DEFINITION:** A benchmark is a standard or point of reference by which something can be measured or judged.

> **DEFINITION:** Competitive benchmarking involves analyzing the performance and practices of best-in-class companies. Their performance becomes a benchmark to which a firm can compare its own performance, and their practices are used to improve that firm's practices.

In competitive benchmarking, the performance of other firms in an area of interest is measured and the best performance becomes the firm's benchmark. By studying the best, a firm hopes to discover how this performance is achieved and how the practices and performance of the benchmarked company differ from its own. The firm then uses this knowledge to improve its practices and thus its performance. Benchmarking is an essential element in a firm's efforts to improve its operations. However, it is *not* a process for exposing a company's weaknesses and punishing those "responsible." Instead, it should be used for finding areas to improve, for determining how to improve them, and ultimately for rewarding those who initiated the changes.

The potential benefits of competitive benchmarking are substantial. Not only is a firm able to recognize and adopt world-class standards, it learns how those standards can be met. Although the firm's new goals may be challenging, the people in the firm know that they are reasonable and achievable.

By examining the most successful practices, a firm can shed its inward orientation. This reduces the possibility of setting modest goals for improvement when there is an appreciable gap between the firm's performance and that of its competitors. Also, by emulating the practices of a company in another industry, a firm can catapult itself ahead of its competitors.

Suppose the Wilson Computer Company discovers that a competitor can produce better instruction manuals in less than one-quarter of the time. In this situation an annual improvement goal of 5 percent per year is inappropriate; the company will slip further behind. Wilson must reevaluate how it produces manuals and set much higher improvement goals that will enable it eventually to surpass the competitor.

In 1979 Xerox used a competitive benchmarking strategy to recover from and combat Japanese competition in the plain paper copier industry. After an intense examination of competing products and practices, Xerox adopted the much lower Japanese costs as its target. By applying what it had learned to its own operations, Xerox was able to meet and eventually surpass those targets. Competitive benchmarking has been built into Xerox's "Leadership through Quality" program and is now used in conjunction with employee involvement programs and problem-solving teams to establish quality and performance goals (see Exhibit 3S.1).

S3.2 EVALUATING INTERNAL OPERATIONS

The first step in benchmarking is to choose one or more areas in which the firm does not excel. The target can be a core functional area (e.g., production), a support area (e.g., finance), or a business process (e.g., product design) that crosses organizational boundaries. It can also be a subfunction (e.g., billing) or even a specific activity or task (e.g., receipt recording). If many areas require substantial improvement, areas in which improvement will have the greatest impact should be selected first.

Alternatively, the firm may choose to benchmark at a strategic level. That is, it may compare its business strategy and the areas in which it has competitive strength with those of its competitors.

Before the firm can compare its operations to those in another firm, it must examine the area of interest in great detail. The firm must understand exactly *how* it performs tasks and *how well* it performs them. This intensive internal analysis starts with quantifiable measures such as throughput, product quality, customer satisfaction, equipment setup times and availability, and the number of worker classifications. From there, the analysis moves on to a detailed study of how the area operates. Some of the questions that must be asked are:

- What is the exact nature of the work performed?
- Under what constraints are we operating?
- What do we see as our strengths and weaknesses?

Armed with this information, the firm can prepare a questionnaire that will be completed during visits to benchmarked companies. The purpose of this questionnaire is to uncover answers to the following questions:

One of Xerox's most valuable benchmarking experiences was carried out by its logistics and distribution (L&D) unit in the early 1980s. Industry price cuts had made the 3 to 5 percent annual productivity gains in the L&D unit insufficient to maintain profit margins. Warehousing and materials handling productivity had to be boosted, but how this could be done was not clear. The unit handled products so diverse in size, shape, and weight that automated storage and retrieval systems (AS\RS) were not suitable.

After combing through trade journals and speaking with professional associations and consultants, an L&D staff member identified companies with the best reputations in the distribution business. He then targeted the companies that handled the same types of products as his L&D unit: products that are diverse in size, shape, and weight. L.L. Bean, an outdoor sporting goods retailer and mail-order house, was singled out as the best candidate for benchmarking.

The headquarters operations manager and the field distribution center manager accompanied the L&D staff member on a visit to Bean's operations in Freeport, Maine. Xerox found that Bean could pick almost three times as many lines per worker-day. After studying Bean's system, Xerox decided that the labor-intensive system used by Bean could be adapted fairly easily for its own systems. Practices such as arranging materials by velocity and increasing computer involvement in the picking operations have been implemented. The L&D unit now strives for, and reaches, annual productivity gains of 10 percent.

Source: Adapted from Tucker, Zivan, and Camp (1987), pp. 14–16.

- How much better is the competition?
- Why are they better?
- What is the true source of their strength or competitive advantage?
- How are they handling or avoiding tasks or issues that are causing us problems?
- What can we learn from them?
- How can we apply what we have learned?

If more than one company is being benchmarked, the questionnaire can ensure that comparable information is collected from each company.

IBM Rochester developed a systematic method of evaluating its internal operations and the operations of benchmarked companies. As outlined in Exhibit 3S.2, this evaluation model ensures that comparable data are collected.

S3.3   SELECTING A BENCHMARKING PARTNER

For each area of interest, one or more companies must be targeted as benchmarks. Candidates can be found by reading journal articles, annual reports, and other company publications; attending industry seminars; and speaking with personal and professional contacts or with consultants. The International Benchmarking Clearinghouse (IBC) in Houston runs an electronic bulletin board that enables IBC members to share information or post appeals for benchmarking partners.

Benchmark companies should be ones that have achieved relative or total excellence in the chosen area, firms that can be used to develop standards that are significantly higher than a firm's current standards (but not impossible to achieve). They should also be similar enough to the firm to ensure that the comparisons made are valid.

Potential benchmarking partners include competitors, other divisions of the firm, subsidiaries, joint-venture partners, and suppliers. The company with the best practices is not necessarily a member of the same industry; nor does it have to serve the same market. Xerox compared its warehousing and materials handling activities with those of L.L. Bean (Exhibit 3S.1) and its billing practices with those of Federal Express. Texas Instruments targeted Eli Lilly, a drug manufacturer, as a benchmarking partner for analyzing receiving transactions on the loading dock. Henry Ford studied Sears-Roebuck's mail-order plant in detail before adapting it to the automobile industry.

Adopting technological advances utilized in another industry can also help a firm achieve a competitive advantage. For example, bar coding originated in the grocery industry but has been adopted by other industries.

Why would a benchmarked firm share information? Many firms participate in benchmarking exercises because they too can learn from the results of such a study. Functional specialists are often eager to compare notes. Some firms like to trade benchmarking information. Texas Instruments, for example, traded information about its award-winning internal newsletters with Wallace Co. for information on Wallace's excellent customer satisfaction index. Companies such as Canon and Britain's Lucas Industries encourage reciprocal visits from the companies they use as benchmarks.

The computer-integrated manufacturing (CIM) implementation team at IBM Rochester used competitive benchmarking to help the firm become the best CIM site in the world.

The team began its competitive benchmarking exercise by dividing its main goal into four subgoals and identifying the success factors required to reach those subgoals. Each success factor was then analyzed into a set of carefully defined requirements. These requirements gave the team a clearer idea of what had to be done to achieve its goals.

A cross-functional team was formed to rank the relative importance of each of the 30 requirements. A weight between 0 and 1 was then assigned to each requirement. The greater the requirement's relative importance, the higher its weight.

Next, a five-point maturity scale was developed for each requirement. A brief definition was created for each requirement in regard to each of the five points on the maturity scale. The definitions for the "flexible" requirement are shown below:

Maturity Index	Definition
1	No consideration
2	Starting to consider on an individual basis
3	Built into select processes
4	Built into all key processes
5	Built into all processes

The team then reevaluated IBM Rochester's performance on each requirement, using the maturity scale. The result was a baseline that could be used to compare IBM Rochester with other companies.

Source: Adapted from Eyrich (1991), pp. 40–47.

S3.4 VISITING THE BENCHMARK COMPANY

Once a benchmarking partner has been found, the firm usually visits the partner's operations. The questionnaire can often be completed and key personnel interviewed in one or two days.

Competitive benchmarking can be more successful if the firm goes beyond comparing results to discover different management approaches. Qualitative factors such as practices, processes, and methods must be discussed. The relationship the benchmark company has with its suppliers, for example, may be more responsible for its competitive edge than is the price it pays for raw materials. By collecting both qualitative and quantitative data, a firm can acquire a depth of understanding that shows how the benchmarked company is achieving its success.

S3.5 USING THE BENCHMARKING DATA

Once the visits have been made, the results must be compiled and analyzed. Key gaps between the benchmarked company and the firm can form the basis of aggressive goals for performance improvement. Ideas and practices used by the benchmarked firm can be adapted and used to create action plans to meet the performance goals.

Benchmarking provides insight into how the best in class performs *today*, not how it must perform tomorrow. Benchmarking therefore is an ongoing improvement exercise that must be done as part of the continual evaluation of the firm, its competitors, and the marketplace.

A study carried out by Ernst & Young and the American Quality Foundation indicates that benchmarking cannot improve performance unless a company already has a comprehensive quality program in place. Quality novices that try to match the techniques used by the "best of the best" may make things worse by trying to do too much, too soon.

KEY TERMS

Competitive benchmarking
Benchmark

REFERENCES AND SELECTED BIBLIOGRAPHY

Camp, Robert C. [1989], *Benchmarking*, ASQC Quality Press, White Plains, N.Y.

Eyrich, H. G. [1991], "Benchmarking to Become the Best of the Breed," *Manufacturing Systems,* April, pp. 40–47.

"First Find Your Bench," *The Economist,* May 11, 1991, p. 72.

Micklewright, Michael J. [1993], "Competitive Benchmarking: Large Gains for Small Companies," *Quality Progress,* vol. 26, no. 6, pp. 67–68.

Owen, Jean V. [1992], "Benchmarking World-Class Manufacturing," *Manufacturing Engineering,* March, pp. 29–34.

Port, O., J. Carey, and K. Kelly [1992], "Quality: Small and Midsize Companies Seize the Challenge—Not a Moment Too Soon," *Business Week,* Nov. 30, pp. 66–72.

———— and G. Smith [1992], "Beg, Borrow—and Benchmark," *Business Week,* Nov. 30, pp. 74–75.

Sprow, E. [1993], "Benchmarking: A Tool for Our Time?" *Manufacturing Engineering,* September, pp. 56–69.

Tucker, F. G., S. M. Zivan, and R. C. Camp [1987], "How to Measure Yourself against the Best," *Harvard Business Review,* January-February, pp. 14–16.

Zivan, S. M. [1990], "Benchmarking: The Effective Managers' Tool," *Boardroom Reports,* Nov. 15, pp. 3–4.

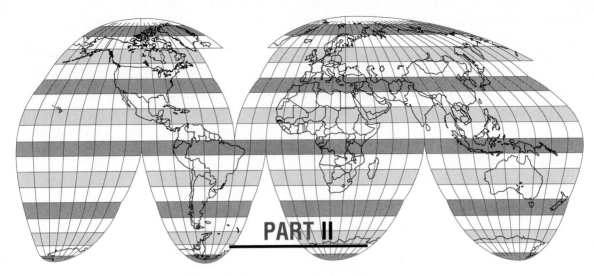

PART II

SATISFYING THE CUSTOMER

The first test of the effectiveness of a firm's operating system is the ability of that firm to supply customers with products and services they actually want, leaving enough of a margin to enable the firm to prosper in the long term. This means supplying the products and services needed in the quantities desired and at the time required. This practice is called *total product quality*. If a firm is not prepared to do this, another firm will oblige its customers.

Although the "who," "what," and "how much" questions asked by the firm in trying to develop the ability to satisfy customers are interrelated, the "who" and "how much" questions usually are asked first, particularly in the traditional model of demand management (see Chapter 4). In the traditional model, the focus is on the firm's operating system and the emphasis is on figuring out how to move enough products to the final customers to keep the operations running at a profitable capacity. One therefore sees manufacturers finding ways to load distributors with unwanted products and then managing demand through price incentives. U.S. automobile manufacturers have engaged in managing demand "outward" since the time of Henry Ford.

Managing demand outward does *not* involve listening to the customers. Managing demand "inward," however, places customers at the center of the process, and fast-response organizations must do this. It is for this reason that the following three chapters were placed at the front of this book.

The theme of Chapter 4 is demand management: identifying the potential sources of demand, figuring out the timing of that demand, and determining how the demand parameters may be influenced by the firm's actions. At this point management must make a strategic decision about which markets are going to be served and which customers are going to be satisfied if total demand exceeds the firm's ability to supply.

Demand is a reflection of the ability of products to provide value to customers. To stimulate the greatest demand, therefore, it is necessary to determine exactly what the customers require. This is not merely a matter of producing something and then finding a market-clearing price. Instead, it involves understanding what customers' needs and expectations are and meeting those needs and expectations profitably. Chapters 5 and 6 are therefore devoted to product quality: Chapter 5 to how to organize in order to design quality into products, Chapter 6 to the mechanics of the design process.

Getting the design elements right is an important step but not the only step toward ensuring that operations are effective. Getting these elements wrong, though, will significantly impair the ability of operations to help the firm attain its goals.

CHAPTER 4

DEMAND MANAGEMENT

To design and run an operating system that will satisfy customers, a firm must know how much demand it has to satisfy. That leads to three important questions:

- How does the firm know what to produce?
- How does the firm know how much to produce?
- How does the firm know when to produce?

Forecasting and demand management help answer these questions.

Demand management involves identifying all potential sources of demand as well as influencing the level and timing of demand. Attempts at gauging initial demand and the effects of demand management are called *forecasts*.

This chapter will show that forecasting is a complicated activity that involves several time frames and objectives. Nevertheless, there is a pattern to forecasting, and by the end of this chapter you will be able to judge which of several forecasting techniques is most appropriate for a given set of circumstances.

EXHIBIT 4.1   FRO MANUFACTURING PROFILE

After a few years of running a homegrown system, GE Silicones has learned that forecasting is not a black box with history going in and forecasts coming out. Forecasting is a process that must be managed.

One of the causes of the company's poor customer service and climbing inventory was its inaccurate and insufficiently monitored forecasts. Consider the following example:

- As a result of a successful promotion, the demand levels for a particular product increased to a record high in December.
- After noting this increase in demand, the forecasting system included a huge trend factor in its calculations. The forecast for January was therefore even higher than the actual demand in December.
- However, the actual demand in January was very low (because every customer stocked up at the December price). This increased the forecast error, which in turn caused the systems to recommend a higher safety stock.
- The resulting large inventory was expensive; it also meant that expensive capacity was tied up producing the wrong product.
- GE's problems were compounded when marketing product managers, in an effort to ensure that they would get some of the production for their customers, overforecasted their own products.

GE Silicones now has a new forecasting system that it regularly monitors and controls. Any forecast that falls outside its predetermined control limits is flagged for investigation. On the basis of its marketing intelligence, the forecasts for some items are amended. Once the actual demand figures are in, these changes are reviewed to determine whether they helped or hurt the forecast accuracy. In this way GE learns from its mistakes.

Inventory planners at GE Silicones now have confidence in their plans. Customer service has improved 40 percent, while the firm's investment in finished goods inventories has declined substantially.

Source: Adapted from Duncan (1992), pp. 18–21.

EXHIBIT 4.2   FRO SERVICE PROFILE

B.C. Hydro, the electric utility for the province of British Columbia, Canada, is being transformed into a more socially conscious organization, and demand management has been made a top priority by its new chairman, Marc Eliesen. The utility has been managing demand through its Power Smart program, which is now being used by other utilities in

(Exhibit 4.2 continues on next page)

EXHIBIT 4.2 *(continued)*

Canada, the United States, and Europe. Starting with the simple notion of saving power by encouraging customers to turn off lights, the program is saving enough power to light 110,000 homes. As new accounts have increased by that number since the program was started in 1989, the reduced rate of load increase has meant that no new dam has had to be planned. With the cost of a new dam estimated at $3 billion, or 6 to 8 cents per kilowatt-hour, the $600 million that will be spent over 10 years to delay or eliminate the need for a new dam becomes attractive.

B.C. Hydro relies not only on consumer action but also on manufacturers to produce more energy-efficient appliances. The rebates given to consumers to buy energy-efficient devices have encouraged manufacturers to concentrate on producing them, allowing the utility to slowly get out of the rebate business. Now the program is attracting more manufacturers of energy-efficient products to the country and the province.

Source: Adapted from Williamson (1993), p. B6.

4.1 MANAGERIAL ORIENTATION

A fast-response organization (FRO) focuses its strategic planning efforts on answering two questions: How can we totally satisfy the customers? How can we do this better than the competitors? An integral part of a firm's strategic planning involves identifying and analyzing current and potential sources of demand for its goods and services. The firm must then determine which sources of demand it will cultivate and how it will satisfy anticipated demand. As illustrated by GE Silicones (Exhibit 4.1), there is a direct link between **demand management** and customer satisfaction.

> **DEFINITION:** Demand management involves recognizing sources of demand for a firm's goods and services, forecasting demand, and determining how the firm will satisfy that demand.

Together, marketing and operations share the responsibility for demand management. Marketing usually provides market-related information and demand forecasts, while operations makes sure the firm's goods and services are provided when needed. Marketing also manages demand through pricing and promotion policies. For example, off-peak discounts may level out the demand for a product or service.

Although the information exchange between marketing and operations appears to be straightforward, it is often complicated by out-of-date, inconsistent, or inaccurate data flowing in both directions. The confusion is compounded by (1) large numbers of parts, finished goods, and services demanded, (2) multiple sources of demand, and (3) differences in the timing of demand by each source.

The obvious source of demand is the ultimate customer. However, a firm's immediate customers may be other manufacturers, distributors, wholesalers, or retailers. A firm may even own its immediate customer.

For many firms there are additional demands for end products, resources, and materials. For example, there may be (1) internal and external demands for service parts, (2) demands for spare units to be used as emergency replacements or demonstration units, (3) prototypes and mockups of the next generation of products, (4) demands to transfer parts among plants, and (5) demand for additional materials and products to cover breakage and unplanned shortages during production.

What should be produced? How much should be produced? Where should it be produced? When should it be produced? These questions are addressed by the firm throughout the planning horizon.

During long-range planning a firm makes decisions regarding its product line, the location of its facilities, the capacity of each facility, the technology utilized in its production processes, and its network of suppliers. Because the future is not known with certainty, the firm needs economic, technological, and demand forecasts to make these decisions.

> **DEFINITION:** Economic forecasts are predictions of what general business conditions will be several months or years in the future.

Economic forecasts are made by governments, banks, and econometric forecasting services.

The National Bureau of Economic Research (NBER) in the United States has identified 26 statistical indicators which reflect business conditions. *Leading indicators* such as new building permits, hiring rates, and new orders for durable goods provide advance warning of probable changes in economic activity. Gross national product, personal income, and the employment level are *coincident indicators,* or indicators that reflect the current performance of the economy. *Lagging indicators* confirm changes in the economy. Examples include long-term unemployment and the yield on mortgage loans.

Economic forecasts help a firm assess the general state of a country's economy and identify expanding, contracting, and fragmenting markets. The cost and availability of capital and other resources can also be estimated.

Apart from general economic conditions, the demand for a firm's goods and services is affected by that firm's competitors. As part of its analysis of the external environment, the firm must identify its competitors and predict what they will do in the future.

What technology will the firm's competitors incorporate into their products and processes? How will this affect demand for the firm's goods and services? Are there any technological advances with which the firm can create a competitive advantage? **Technological forecasts** can help answer these questions:

> **DEFINITION:** Technological forecasts predict the probability and significance of possible future developments. They indicate the expected direction of technology change and the expected rate of change.

The rapid development of technological advances means that many products and processes quickly become obsolete and that technological forecasts are extremely valuable. This is especially true of FROs, which often pursue a strategy of technological leadership.[1]

The results of economic forecasts, technological forecasts, and analyses of a firm's internal and external environments are combined with previous demand data to develop **demand forecasts.**

---

[1] Refer back to Chapter 3 for a description of various technology strategies, including technological leadership.

DEFINITION: Demand forecasts predict the quantity and timing of demand for a firm's goods and services.

The level of detail required in a demand forecast and the length of its time horizon depend on how it will be used. The demand forecasts used to support short-term production planning and scheduling, for example, must be much more detailed than the forecasts used to support staffing plans. The time horizon covered, however, is much longer in the latter case. The relationship between (1) the planning purpose and (2) the forecast time horizon and level of detail is illustrated in Exhibit 4.3.

For long-term planning, demand for a firm's goods and services is often grouped by product families or major product categories. The forecasts are usually for 3-to-12-month periods and cover the next few years. Demand forecasts are then used to develop **resource forecasts.**

DEFINITION: Resource forecasts predict the timing and quantity of demand for a firm's facilities, equipment, and workforce as well as for purchased parts and materials.

The relationships among economic, technological, demand, and resource forecasts are illustrated in Exhibit 4.4.

Since a firm's flexibility is greatest over the long run, the firm's demand management options are also greatest over the long run. For example, a firm can expand its product line in a fragmenting market, retire obsolete products, enter new markets, and cultivate new sources of demand. New goods or services that require resources similar to those required by existing products but that have different demand cycles can be introduced to take advantage of processes that often stand idle. Facilities can be relocated to serve anticipated sources of demand, new technology can be incorporated into the firm's products and processes, and distribution channels can be realigned.

In the intermediate term (the next 3 to 18 months) the firm must have more specific information about demand levels. Though more detailed than long-range forecasts, intermediate-range forecasts also aggregate data over several products or for a product family. The forecast period is often a month.

EXHIBIT 4.3 DEMAND FORECASTS AND PLANNING DECISIONS

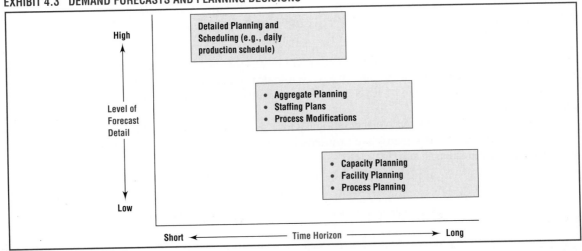

EXHIBIT 4.4   EXTERNAL AND INTERNAL FORECASTS

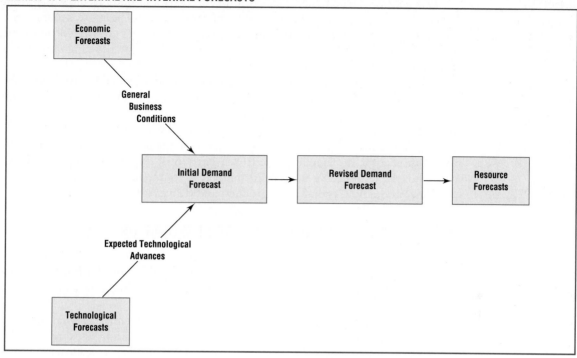

Intermediate-term, or medium-term, forecasts are used to develop aggregate production plans and staffing plans. An *aggregate plan* is a general schedule that specifies the quantity of each product family or product group that will be produced in each period.

As it moves from the long run to the short run, the firm has a decreased ability to manage demand. However, if demand requirements in the intermediate term do not coincide with available capacity, the firm still may be able to manipulate both the timing and the quantity of demand and available capacity. For example, the overall level of consumer demand can be increased by lowering the market price, expanding or contracting the geographic market, or improving the product or service. Discounts and promotions can shift demand from peak to off-peak periods.

Capacity can be increased in the intermediate term by subcontracting work, accumulating inventory during slow periods, asking employees to work overtime, hiring temporary employees, and so on. Shortening the workweek, asking employees to take vacations, and lending employees to other areas are ways in which capacity can be temporarily decreased.

In the short term the firm needs to know the exact mix of products and services that must be provided in each period. The aggregate plan is converted to a master production schedule. Parts and materials are then purchased, and resources are assigned to specific tasks or production orders. Short-term forecasts cover days or weeks, are updated frequently, and include firm customer orders.[2]

---

[2] Many companies are using point-of-sale data rather than short-term forecasts for short-term production planning.

It is generally true that (1) short-range forecasts are more accurate than long-range forecasts, (2) forecasts for groups of items tend to be more accurate than forecasts for smaller populations. Thus, a forecast of footwear sales in North America for next month should be more accurate than a forecast for the same month next year or one for boot sales in Georgia next month.

All firms want to have the most accurate forecasts available just before they "freeze" their production plans. The more accurate the forecast, the more efficiently and effectively a firm can use its resources to satisfy demand. Note that the forecast periods needed to support a production plan must be at least as long as the frozen portion of the plan. Therefore, a firm can increase the accuracy of supporting forecasts by reducing the length of the frozen portion of the production plan. This is accomplished by reducing the time it routinely takes the firm to purchase materials, schedule production, produce the product, and deliver it to the customer.

4.3 MANAGING DEMAND IN A FAST-RESPONSE ORGANIZATION

As was pointed out in the introductory text for Part II, the focus of demand in traditional organizations is the operating elements of the firm. If a firm switches to customer criteria demand management, what does it mean and how can the firm do it?

First, customer criteria demand management involves identifying what *customers* want (not what senior management decides has to be sold) and deciding how that demand should be met. This involves accurately identifying true demand, which means understanding current needs and expectations. The second part of this process consists of matching quantities and delivery envelopes with the attributes of the operating system. (These attributes are discussed in Part III.)

Second, the firm does this by truly understanding its customers. If a firm knows its customers well, including their needs and expectations, it can confidently predict when they will need new or replacement products. Predictions based on good knowledge are better than those based on speculation.

Sales personnel in Japanese automobile companies, for instance, spend much more time trying to understand existing and potential customers than they spend selling cars. This understanding of individuals is used to "drive" forecasts, for evaluations of individual consumer needs and timing are aggregated to provide total demand. These continually changing needs are also used to drive product improvements, and sales personnel test these changes on loyal customers.

These approaches take less time to implement and provide quicker feedback than do formal market research practices. Also, the feedback is more accurate because actual customers rather than "representative samples" are used. New concepts reach the market more quickly. The short time to market means that the buying public's needs will have changed only a little, if at all, between the time of asking and the time of product availability. This makes the manufacturer's product risk more reasonable than it is in the traditional forecasting model.

Three factors must be emphasized here. First, demand is forecast predominantly over the short to medium term, with little emphasis on the long term. Second, the operating system is assumed to be responsive so that actual demand can be quickly met. There is little point in accurate short-term forecasting if the operating system cannot respond in an appropriate fashion. (Operating system design is discussed in Part III.) Given the reduced risk, there is less need to hedge decisions by building up the finished goods inventory in case demand exceeds the forecast. Third, customers are more likely to pay a premium if their needs and expectations are closely met. Under these circumstances, a firm is less likely to have to discount products to clear the market. Incidentally, truly satisfying customers has another bottom-line benefit. As Reichheld and Sasser (1990) have shown, more profit comes from keeping customers than from replacing defecting customers.

This emphasis on building up detailed customer information is not really new, of course. Marketers of industrial products have always developed detailed customer profiles and used them for forecasting and product concept testing. FROs that make consumer products need to decide how to adopt this approach. As the Japanese have shown, it is possible to employ this approach with consumer durables. Real gains are made when consumable and nondurable products incorporate timely and real customer needs and expectations. This can occur only when unambiguous expectations can be satisfied quickly or, preferably, in advance.

When the planning horizon is unavoidably lengthy, however, a firm must fall back on traditional forecasting methods and models. An examination of these methods will constitute the remainder of this chapter, which looks at a variety of qualitative and quantitative forecasting techniques.

4.4 QUALITATIVE APPROACHES TO FORECASTING DEMAND

Qualitative forecasting techniques rely on educated guesses based on intuition and on experience with the firm and its external environment. They range in complexity from intuitive hunches about future events to expert panels and scientifically conducted opinion surveys. They all, however, are subjective in nature.

When historical data are insufficient, contradictory, expensive, or irrelevant, these techniques can be quite useful. For example, if a firm wants to develop a forecast for a radically new product or if there have been vast disruptions in the economy or the industry, a qualitative approach makes sense. These approaches are also used when developing and implementing a mathematical model is difficult or expensive. A qualitative approach is the most common forecasting approach among businesses and governments.

The four most common qualitative techniques are executive committee consensus, the Delphi method, the sales force composite, and consumer market surveys.

Executive Committee Consensus

Forecasts can be developed by asking a small group of knowledgeable executives to discuss their opinions regarding the future values of the items being forecast. The **executive committee consensus** technique allows the opinions of a cross section of functional experts to be amalgamated, but social factors or the presence of a powerful member may prevent the group from achieving a true consensus. This technique is relatively inexpensive and is the most commonly used long- and medium-range forecasting technique.

Delphi Method

The **Delphi method** also involves a group of experts who share information and eventually develop a consensus on a long-range forecast for future technologies or the future sales of a new product. Mitchell (1992), for example, reports on the implications of a Delphi method used to forecast the future of the financial market analysis industry, with concurrent forecasts of industry technologies and products.

In the Delphi method the panel members are usually located in different places and participate anonymously. This helps reduce the influence of powerful executives and the bandwagon effect of majority opinion. Although it may take longer to develop the forecast, the resultant forecast tends to be more accurate than those generated by means of the executive committee consensus approach.

Each member of the panel completes a prepared questionnaire and returns it to the firm's coordinator. The results are summarized by the coordinator and are employed to prepare a new questionnaire. The new questionnaire and the summarized results of the first one are sent to the panelists along with any information used by some panelists but not yet available to others. After reviewing the summarized results and any new information, panel members either defend or modify their original views. The process is repeated until a consensus forecast is reached or a predetermined number of iterations has been completed.

Sales Force Composite

In many companies the sales force deals directly with customers and is a good source of information regarding customer intentions in the short and intermediate terms. This knowledge can help a firm obtain a forecast quickly and inexpensively.

With the **sales force composite** technique, each sales representative is asked to estimate sales in his or her territory for the upcoming season. Individual sales estimates are then employed by the district manager to develop a district forecast. Managers may adjust the individual estimates to reduce optimistic biases (or pessimistic biases if the sales force receives bonuses for exceeding projections). District forecasts are then combined until an overall global forecast is developed.

Customer Surveys

A firm can also base forecasts on the stated future purchasing plans of its current and potential customers by using a **customer survey.** This information can be obtained directly through personal, telephone, or mail/fax surveys. Once all the information from individual firms has been combined, it normally is adjusted by an "experience" factor that takes into account the historical relationship between customers' stated requirements and actual purchases as well as the manufacturer's anticipated market share. This adjusted figure is used as the demand forecast.

The best information comes from asking all customers. For most firms, this is not practicable and asking a representative sample for their plans has to suffice. Introductory statistics and marketing courses teach that there are many ways of structuring samples; simple and stratified random samples, systematic samples, and cluster samples are among the most common structures. Remember that the validity and reliability of the survey results depend on the ability of the sample to reflect the intentions of the whole population. That in turn is a reflection of the time, money, and other resources available to the researchers.

4.5 QUANTITATIVE FORECASTING MODELS

Quantitative forecasting methods employ mathematical models and historical data to predict demand. Thus the past is used to predict the future.[3] There are two general types of quantitative methods: time series models and causal models. The following

---

[3] Many managers adjust forecasts by using quantitative methods to incorporate their knowledge of the firm's environment. If adjustments are made, a system (like GE Silicones') must be put in place to monitor the adjustments and ensure that they are improving, not hindering, forecast accuracy.

sections briefly describe some of these models, demonstrate how they work, and provide guidelines for their use.

Time Series Modeling

Time series modeling involves plotting demand data (or other types of data) on a time scale and studying the plots to discover consistent shapes or patterns. These patterns are then projected into the future.

> **DEFINITION:** A time series is a sequence of chronologically arranged observations taken at regular intervals for a particular variable.

Although the historical data reflect the combination of all the forces that act on the data and although the forecasts mirror the effects of the forces, these forces are not identified or directly measured. Time series are frequently analyzed, however, to identify any trends, seasonal factors, and/or cyclical factors that influence the demand data. Smoothing techniques such as moving averages and exponential smoothing can also be applied to time series data.

When short-range forecasts that support production scheduling, inventory control, product pricing, and the timing of special promotions are required, time series modeling techniques can be valuable.

Time series models require that data be collected regularly. However, they are easy to use, can be run quickly, and can be updated frequently.

Decomposition Models When one is analyzing a time series, any trend, seasonal, and/or cyclical factors that are influencing the variable under observation can often be identified. This enables forecasters to predict future values of the variable more accurately by projecting these patterns into the future.

Trends reflect changes in technology, living standards, population levels, and so on.

> **DEFINITION:** A trend is the gradual upward or downward movement of data over time.

Trends are monotonic (increasingly positive or negative) but not always linear. A trend can be logarithmic or exponential, for example (see Exhibit 4.5A).

Seasonal variations, or **seasonality,** can correspond to the seasons of the year, holidays, or different times of the day or week.

> **DEFINITION:** Seasonality is variation that repeats itself at fixed intervals. It can be as long as a year or as short as a few hours.

Seasonal patterns can be caused by many factors, including the weather (e.g., sales of air conditioners), working hours (e.g., traffic volume), and a firm's policies (e.g., the receipt of revenue for a firm may reflect its billing pattern).

The ups and downs of the economy or of a specific industry are represented by **cyclical variation.** The business cycle that repeats itself every 5 to 10 years is an example.

> **DEFINITION:** Cyclical variation has a duration of at least one year; the duration varies from cycle to cycle.

Random variations are variations in demand that cannot be explained by trends, seasonality, or cyclicality. An unpredictable event such as a war, strike, earthquake,

EXHIBIT 4.5 COMPONENTS OF A TIME SERIES

A. Three Examples of Positive Trends

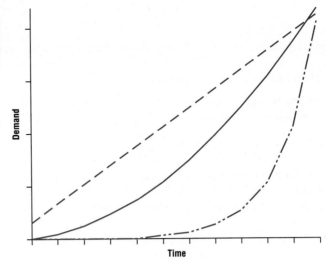

Legend
- — — Linear Trend
- —— Exponential Trend
- —·—· Logarithmic Trend

Demand

Time

B. A Time Series Exhibiting Trend, Seasonal, Cyclical, and Random Variation

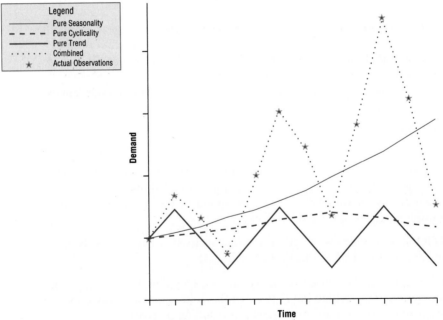

Legend
- —— Pure Seasonality
- — — Pure Cyclicality
- —— Pure Trend
- ····· Combined
- ★ Actual Observations

Demand

Time

Note that the actual observations fall randomly above or below the combined seasonality, cyclicality, and trend line.

or piece of legislation can cause large random variations. Unlike trend, cycle, and seasonal variations, random variation is always present.

Many mathematical relationships can be used to describe the interaction of the trend, cycle, and seasonal components of a time series. The relationship between these components in the time series illustrated in Exhibit 4.5B is multiplicative. The general mathematical representation for the **multiplicative form of a time series** is given in equation (4.1).

Multiplicative Form of a Time Series

$$A_t = T_t \times S_t \times C_t \times E_t \qquad (4.1)$$

where A_t = actual demand in period t
T_t = trend component for period t
S_t = seasonal component for period t
C_t = cyclical component for period t
E_t = random, or error, component for period t

Since the multiplicative form is straightforward and commonly used, it is the form that will be used throughout this chapter. The next section describes how trend and seasonal factors can be projected into the future.[4]

Trend Projections As was mentioned earlier, trends may or may not be linear. However, linear trends are fairly common, and most people find them easy to work with.

A time period, t, is selected as the base time period. The demand for a consecutive set of periods, starting with the base period, is plotted on a graph. The x axis usually represents the time periods, while the y axis represents the demand. The actual annual demand for Laslow Ltd., a small firm with one product group, is plotted in Exhibit 4.6.

These data are used to calculate a **trend line** or linear trend equation of the form shown in equation (4.2).

Linear Trend Line

$$F_t = a + bt \qquad (4.2)$$

where t = number of time periods following base time period
F_t = estimated demand for period t
a = demand for base period
b = slope of trend line

The trend line that best fits these data can be found by using the least-squares method or the linear regression analysis option of ©OM-Expert's forecasting module.[5] The trend line in this example is $F_t = 3,980 + 2,940t$. To find the forecasted demand for the next year (year 6), simply solve the equation for $t = 6$.

Seasonal Projections Laslow Ltd., like many firms, experiences seasonal demand, as can be seen in the first graph in Exhibit 4.7, which shows the quarterly demand

[4] The cyclical component of a time series can also be projected into the future, but techniques for doing this will not be described here.
[5] OM-Expert is computer software developed for use with this book or other OM books. Similar software packages are available and may be used.

EXHIBIT 4.6   TOOLBOX: A SIMPLE TREND PROJECTION

The annual demand over the last five years for Laslow Ltd.'s family of products is shown below:

Year	Annual Demand, units
1	6,600
2	10,450
3	12,700
4	15,450
5	18,800

The trend line that best fits the demand data over the five-year period can be found by using the least-squares method described below (or by using the linear regression analysis option of ©OM-Expert's forecasting module).

A. Calculating the Trend Line Using the Least-Squares Method

Regression analysis is used when a causal relationship exists between the variable to be forecast and at least one other variable. In simple linear regression, one variable (the dependent variable) is a linear function of a single independent variable.

GRAPH OF LASLOW LTD.'S ANNUAL DEMAND

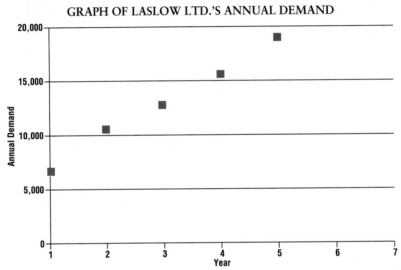

The objective of simple linear regression is to find a straight line which best "fits" the data. This is done by employing the principle of least squares: choose the line that minimizes the sum of the squares of the deviations of the observed values of y from those predicted. Mathematically, this can be expressed as follows:

$$\text{Minimize } SSE = \sum_{i=1}^{n} (y_i - \hat{y}_i)^2$$

where SSE = sum of forecast errors
  y_i = actual value of y
  F_t = predicted value of y

Since the predicted value of y_i corresponding with x_i is equal to $a + bx_i$, the objective is to

$$\text{Minimize } SSE = \sum_{i=1}^{n} [(y_i - (a + bx_i)]^2$$

The values of a and b that minimize SSE are given by the following formulas:

$$a = \bar{y} - b\bar{x} \qquad b = \frac{SS_{x,y}}{SS_x}$$

where

$$SS_{x,y} = \sum_{i=1}^{n} x_i y_i - \frac{\left(\sum_{i=1}^{n} x_i\right)\left(\sum_{i=1}^{n} y_i\right)}{n}$$

$$SS_x = \sum_{i=1}^{n} x_i^2 - \frac{\left(\sum_{i=1}^{n} x_i\right)^2}{n}$$

In this problem, the object is to find the trend line that best fits the demand data: $F_t = a + bt$. The following table simplifies the calculation of a and b.

y_i (or A_t)	x_i (or t)	$x_i y_i$ (or $A_t t$)	x_i^2 (or t^2)	y_i^2 (or A_t^2)
6,600	1	6,600	1	43,560,000
10,450	2	20,900	4	109,202,500
12,700	3	38,100	9	161,290,000
15,450	4	61,800	16	238,702,500
18,800	5	94,000	25	353,440,000
64,000	15	221,400	55	906,195,000

$$SS_x = 55 - \frac{15^2}{5} = 10$$

$$SS_{x,y} = 221,400 - \frac{(15)(64,000)}{5} = 29,400$$

$$b = \frac{29,400}{10} = 2,940 \qquad a = \frac{64,000}{5} - 2,940\left(\frac{15}{5}\right) = 3,980$$

Therefore, the trend line is $F_t = 3,980 + 2,940t$.

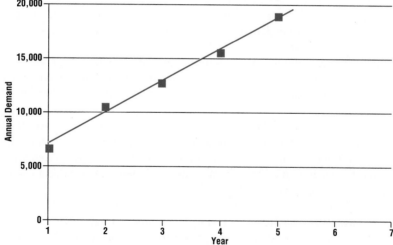

GRAPH OF LASLOW LTD.'S ANNUAL DEMAND, WITH TREND LINE

The strength of the *linear association* between y and x is indicated by the coefficient of correlation, r, and the coefficient of determination, r^2. Note that this association may or may not be a cause-and-effect relationship:

$$r = \frac{SS_{xy}}{\sqrt{SS_x SS_y}}$$

If $r = 0$, there is no evidence of a linear relationship between y and x. If there is a positive linear relationship between y and x, r will be between 0 and 1. The stronger the positive relationship, the closer r will be to 1. Conversely, the stronger the negative linear relationship between y and x, the closer r will be to -1.

(Exhibit 4.6 continues on next page)

EXHIBIT 4.6 *(continued)*

The value of r^2 is always between 0 and 1. It can be interpreted as the percent of variation in y that can be explained by the regression equation. For the Laslow example:

$$SS_y = 906,195,000 - \frac{64,000^2}{5} = 86,995,000$$

$$r = \frac{29,400}{\sqrt{(10)(86,995,000)}} = 0.997$$

$$r^2 = (0.997)^2 = 0.994$$

In this case, there is a very strong positive relationship between time and demand. The trend line explains almost all the variation in demand.

B. Using the Trend Line to Forecast Demand

The trend line can now be used to estimate demand in the future.

If $t = 6$, the forecasted demand is $F_6 = 3,980 + 2,940(6) = 21,620$ units.
If $t = 7$, the forecasted demand is $F_7 = 3,980 + 2,940(7) = 24,560$ units.

for the last three years. The demand in the second quarter of all three years, for example, is about 1.1 times higher than the quarterly average, while the demand in the last quarter is only about 0.8 times the quarterly average. The straight line on the graph represents the trend line that best fits these data. To be of value, Laslow's quarterly forecasts must include both a trend component and a seasonal component.

The seasonal influences on Laslow's quarterly demand have been removed by dividing the actual quarterly demand by its seasonal index, for example, 1.1 for the second quarter. The seasonally adjusted values are shown in the second graph in Exhibit 4.7. These demand values appear to be much more stable but still exhibit a noticeable trend.

After calculating the corresponding trend line, one can project this trend forward for one year. The quarterly forecasts must then be multiplied by their seasonal index. The resulting seasonally adjusted forecast is shown in the third graph in Exhibit 4.7.

Smoothing Models   When many short-term demand forecasts are required, developing a complex forecasting model for each item may be too expensive and time-consuming (e.g., inventory control of low-volume, low-cost items). Simple smoothing models such as moving averages and exponential smoothing often provide reasonably good forecasts quickly and inexpensively.

Simple Moving Average   A **simple moving average** calculates the average demand for the last n periods and uses it as a forecast for the next time period [see equation (4.3)]. Because they are combined in an average, individual highs and lows offset each other and the effect of random variation in the data is dampened.

Simple Moving Average

$$F_{t+1} = \frac{A_t + A_{t-1} + A_{t-2} + \cdots + A_{t-n+1}}{n} \tag{4.3}$$

where F_{t+1} = forecast for time period $t + 1$
A_t = actual demand for time period t
n = number of periods being averaged

The graph below illustrates the actual demand for Laslow's Ltd.'s products per quarter for years 3, 4, and 5. A strong seasonal variation is evident. Demand is quite high in quarters 2 and 3 and quite low in quarters 1 and 4. Assume that the time series is multiplicative.

GRAPH OF LASLOW LTD.'S QUARTERLY DEMAND, WITH TREND LINE

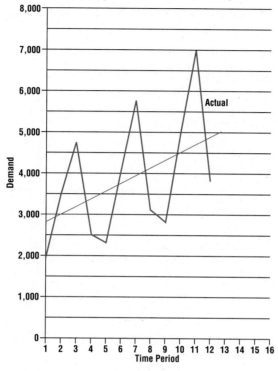

Before generating the trend line, it is necessary to identify the season variation and "deseasonalize" demand. One can then estimate demand in the future by using the trend line. The last step is to adjust these demand estimates by the seasonal variation.

Step 1: Identify the Seasonal Index

The seasonal index for each quarter has been calculated using the following formula:

$$SI_q = \frac{\sum_{j=1}^{m} \dfrac{D_{q,j}}{\overline{D}_j}}{m}$$

where SI_q = average seasonal factor for quarter q
   $D_{q,j}$ = actual demand for quarter q in year j
   $\overline{D}_j$ = average quarterly demand in year j
   m = number of years

	Actual Demand		
Quarter	Year 3	Year 4	Year 5
1	1,900	2,320	2,810
2	3,500	4,250	5,160
3	4,770	5,790	7,050
4	2,530	3,090	3,780
Average quarterly demand	3,175	3,862.5	4,700

(Exhibit 4.7 continues on next page)

EXHIBIT 4.7 *(continued)*

The seasonal index for quarter 1, for example, is 0.6:

$$SI_1 = \frac{\sum_{j=1}^{3} \dfrac{D_{1,j}}{\overline{D}_j}}{3} = \frac{\dfrac{1,900}{3,175} + \dfrac{2,320}{3,862.5} + \dfrac{2,810}{4,700}}{3} = 0.599$$

Similarly, the seasonal indexes for quarters 2, 3, and 4 are 1.1, 1.5, and 0.8, respectively.

Step 2: Deseasonalize Demand

The actual demand in each quarter can be deseasonalized by dividing it by the seasonal index for that quarter. For example, in year 3, quarter 1, demand was 1,900 units. The seasonal index for quarter 1 is 0.6; therefore, deseasonalized demand in quarter 1 is $1,900 \div 0.6 = 3,167$ units.

(1) Time Period	(2) Actual Demand	(3) Seasonal Index	(4) Deseasonalized Demand
1 (Yr3, Q1)	1,900	0.6	3,167
2 (Yr3, Q2)	3,500	1.1	3,182
3 (Yr3, Q3)	4,770	1.5	3,180
4 (Yr3, Q4)	2,530	0.8	3,163
5 (Yr4, Q1)	2,320	0.6	3,867
6 (Yr4, Q2)	4,250	1.1	3,864
7 (Yr4, Q3)	5,790	1.5	3,860
8 (Yr4, Q4)	3,090	0.8	3,863
9 (Yr5, Q1)	2,810	0.6	4,683
10 (Yr5, Q2)	5,160	1.1	4,691
11 (Yr5, Q3)	7,050	1.5	4,700
12 (Yr5, Q4)	3,780	0.8	4,725

Note: Column 4 = column 2 ÷ column 3 (rounded).

GRAPH OF LASLOW LTD.'S DESEASONALIZED QUARTERLY DEMAND

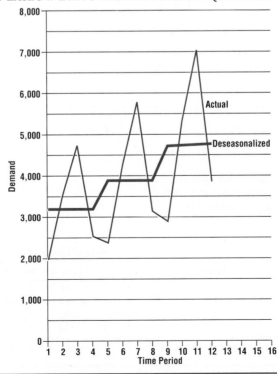

Step 3: Calculate the Trend Line

©OM-Expert's forecasting module was used to generate the trend line that best fits the data.

$$F_t = 2{,}799 + 171.2t$$

Step 4: Estimate Future Demand

It is now possible to estimate future demand by plugging in values for t in the trend line equation:

$$\text{Year 6, quarter 1: } F_{13} = 2{,}799 + 171.2(13) = 5{,}024.6$$

Similarly, one can estimate the demand in quarters 2 to 4 of year 6.

Quarter	Demand
1	5,025
2	5,196
3	5,367
4	5,538

Step 5: Adjust Future Demand Estimates Using the Seasonal Index

The demand estimates must now be multiplied by their corresponding seasonal indexes. For example, the quarter 1 demand estimates (5,025) must be multiplied by the quarter 1 seasonal index (0.6). The seasonally adjusted forecast for quarter 1 is therefore 5,025 × 0.6 = 3,015. The remaining forecasts are adjusted in the same way:

(1) Time Period	(2) Estimated Demand	(3) Seasonal Index	(4) Seasonally Adjusted Demand Estimate
13 (Yr6, Q1)	5,025	0.6	3,015
14 (Yr6, Q2)	5,196	1.1	5,715.6
15 (Yr6, Q3)	5,367	1.5	8,050.5
16 (Yr6, Q4)	5,538	0.8	4,430.4

Note: Column 4 = column 2 × column 3.

GRAPH OF LASLOW LTD.'S QUARTERLY DEMAND, WITH FORECAST

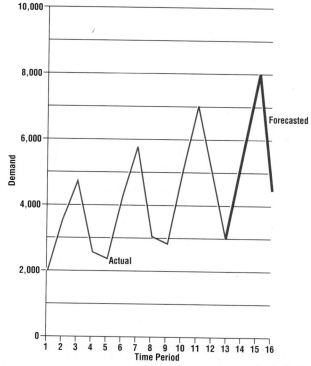

111

A two-month and a five-month moving average were used to predict the monthly demand at Laslow Ltd. For example, suppose it is now the end of February in year 5. The forecasts for March are calculated below:

Two-month moving average:

$$F_{Mar} = \frac{A_{Feb} + A_{Jan}}{2} = \frac{920 + 940}{2} = 930$$

Five-month moving average:

$$F_{Mar} = \frac{A_{Feb} + A_{Jan} + A_{Dec,yr4} + A_{Nov,yr4} + A_{Oct,yr4}}{5}$$

$$= \frac{920 + 940 + 1{,}020 + 1{,}030 + 1{,}040}{5} = 990$$

At the end of March one can forecast demand for April. The oldest demand value (October of year 4) is dropped, and a new one (March of year 5) is added. (This is why the technique is called a *moving* average). Note that the actual demand experienced in March (950 units) is used, not the demand forecast in the calculations.

EXHIBIT 4.8   TOOLBOX: SIMPLE MOVING AVERAGE

The graph below illustrates the actual monthly demand for Laslow's Ltd.'s products in year 5. It also shows the demand forecast using the two-month and five-month moving average techniques.

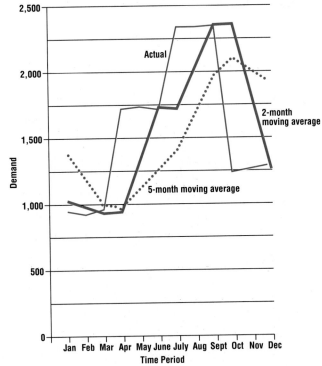

GRAPH OF LASLOW LTD.'S MONTH DEMAND IN YEAR 5

The two-month moving average forecast was calculated using the following equation:

$$F_{t+1} = \frac{A_t + A_{t-1}}{2}$$

The five-month moving average forecast was calculated using the following equation:

$$F_{t+1} = \frac{A_t + A_{t-1} + A_{t-2} + A_{t-3} + A_{t-4}}{5}$$

Time Period	Actual Demand	Forecast Demand	
		Two-Month Moving Average	Five-Month Moving Average
Year 4			
Aug.	1,920		
Sept.	1,940		
Oct.	1,040		
Nov.	1,030		
Dec.	1,020		
Year 5			
Jan.	940	1,025	1,390
Feb.	920	980	1,194
Mar.	950	930	990
Apr.	1,720	935	972
May	1,730	1,335	1,110
June	1,710	1,725	1,252
July	2,340	1,720	1,406
Aug.	2,360	2,025	1,690
Sept.	2,350	2,350	1,972
Oct.	1,240	2,355	2,098
Nov.	1,260	1,795	2,000
Dec.	1,280	1,250	1,910

Two-month moving average:

$$F_{Apr} = \frac{A_{Mar} + A_{Feb}}{2} = \frac{950 + 920}{2} = 935$$

Five-month moving average:

$$F_{Apr} = \frac{A_{Mar} + A_{Feb} + A_{Jan} + A_{Dec,yr4} + A_{Nov,yr4}}{5}$$

$$= \frac{950 + 920 + 940 + 1,020 + 1,030}{5} = 972$$

The forecasts for the remaining months in year 5 are shown in Exhibit 4.8, where the two-month moving average is much more responsive to the frequent shifts in demand.

What value should be used for n? Unfortunately, there is no value of n that always results in more accurate forecasts; there is no hard-and-fast rule for choosing a value of n. Usually a trial-and-error approach is employed.

In general, the higher the value of n is, the less responsive the average is to recent changes in demand. Therefore, if it appears that the underlying pattern is changing, it is best to use a small value for n. If n is too small, however, the average could be too responsive to variations in demand that are random rather than being true changes in trend or demand levels. If the underlying pattern is relatively stable or if there is substantial random variation, one increases the value of n. Remember, though, that as the value of n increases, the amount of data that needs to be stored increases as well.

Weighted Moving Average The simple moving average places the same weight on all demand periods included in the calculation. In many instances, though, the most recent observations have a greater impact on future observations than do older observations. A **weighted moving average** allows the user to assign a weight to each observation [see equation (4.4)].

Weighted Moving Average

$$F_{t+1} = w_t A_t + w_{t-1} A_{t-1} + w_{t-2} A_{t-2} + \cdots + w_{t-n+1} A_{t-n+1} \quad (4.4)$$

where F_{t+1} = forecast for time period $t + 1$
$\quad w_t$ = assigned weight to time period t, $\Sigma w_t = 1$
$\quad A_t$ = actual demand for time period t
$\quad n$ = number of periods being averaged

The two-month and five-month moving average forecasts for Laslow Ltd. are recalculated, placing the heaviest weights on the most recent observations. For example, March's forecasts are shown below:

Two-month moving average:

$$F_{\text{Mar}} = 0.8 A_{\text{Feb}} + 0.2 A_{\text{Jan}} = (0.8)(920) + (0.2)(940) = 924$$

Five-month moving average:

$$F_{\text{Mar}} = 0.5 A_{\text{Feb}} + 0.2 A_{\text{Jan}} + 0.1 A_{\text{Dec}} + 0.1 A_{\text{Nov}} + 0.1 A_{\text{Oct}}$$
$$= (0.5)(920) + (0.2)(940) + (0.1)(1,020)$$
$$+ (0.1)(1,030) + (0.1)(1,040) = 957$$

The forecasts for the remaining months in year 5 are shown in Exhibit 4.9, and the results are quite different from those obtained using the simple moving average technique.

Exponential Smoothing **Exponential smoothing** is an averaging technique that inherently assigns the highest weight to the most recent observation and assigns suc-

EXHIBIT 4.9   TOOLBOX: WEIGHTED MOVING AVERAGE

The monthly demand forecasts for Laslow Ltd. have been recalculated using the weighted moving average models shown below.

Two-month weighted moving average, with $w_1 = 0.8$ and $w_2 = 0.2$:
$$F_{t+1} = (0.8)A_t + (0.2)A_{t-1}$$

Five-month weighted moving average, with $w_1 = 0.5$, $w_2 = 0.2$, $w_3 = 0.1$, $w_4 = 0.1$, and $w_5 = 0.1$:
$$F_{t+1} = (0.5)A_t + (0.2)A_{t-1} + (0.1)A_{t-2} + (0.1)A_{t-3} + (0.1)A_{t-4}$$

MONTHLY DEMAND FORECASTS FOR LASLOW LTD.

Time Period	Actual Demand	Forecast Demand	
		Two-Month Weighted Moving Average	Five-Month Weighted Moving Average
Year 4			
Aug.	1,920		
Sept.	1,940		
Oct.	1,040		
Nov.	1,030		
Dec.	1,020		
Year 5			
Jan.	940	1,022	1,206
Feb.	920	956	1,075
Mar.	950	924	957
Apr.	1,720	944	958
May	1,730	1,566	1,338
June	1,710	1,728	1,490
July	2,340	1,714	1,560
Aug.	2,360	2,214	1,952
Sept.	2,350	2,356	2,164
Oct.	1,240	2,352	2,225
Nov.	1,260	1,462	1,731
Dec.	1,280	1,256	1,583

GRAPH OF LASLOW LTD.'S MONTHLY DEMAND, WITH FORECASTS

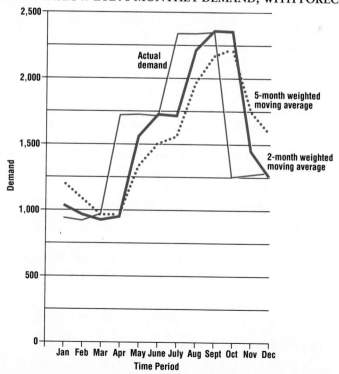

cessively lower weights to older observations. The value of the weights decreases exponentially.

The forecast for the next period is set equal to the forecast for the current period plus a percentage of the forecast error in the current period [see equation (4.5)]. The percentage is referred to as alpha (α) and is chosen by the model's user.

Exponential Smoothing

$$F_{t+1} = F_t + \alpha(A_t - F_t) \tag{4.5}$$

where F_{t+1} = forecast for time period $t + 1$
$\quad F_t$ = forecast for time period t
$\quad \alpha$ = selected value for alpha, $0 \leq \alpha \leq 1$
$\quad A_t$ = actual demand in time period t

Alpha lies between 0 and 1. An α value of 0.3 essentially relies on data for the last 3 time periods, while a value of 0.1 relies on data for the last 12 time periods. Theoretically, however, every past period influences the forecast value when exponential smoothing is used.

The monthly demand forecast at Laslow Ltd. has been recalculated using two exponential smoothing models (see Exhibit 4.10). The first model uses an α value of 0.2, and the second uses a value of 0.8.

The revised forecasts for March are shown below:

Alpha = 0.2

$$\begin{aligned} F_{\text{Mar}} &= F_{\text{Feb}} + (0.2)(A_{\text{Feb}} - F_{\text{Feb}}) \\ &= 1{,}004 + (0.2)(920 - 1{,}004) = 987.2 \end{aligned}$$

Alpha = 0.8

$$\begin{aligned} F_{\text{Mar}} &= F_{\text{Feb}} + (0.8)(A_{\text{Feb}} - F_{\text{Feb}}) \\ &= 956 + (0.8)(920 - 956) = 927.2 \end{aligned}$$

Notice how much more responsive the $\alpha = 0.8$ model is to seasonal fluctuations in the data. In general, the higher the value of alpha, the more responsive the model is to recent demand fluctuations. Just as increasing the value of n increases the smoothing effect in the moving average technique, descreasing the value of alpha increases the smoothing effect in the exponential smoothing technique.

Exponential Smoothing with a Trend Single exponential smoothing always lags a steadily rising or falling linear trend. However, the model can be extended to include a trend factor by using equations (4.6a) to (4.6c).

Exponential Smoothing with a Trend

The exponentially smoothed value:

$$\begin{aligned} SF_{t+1} &= \alpha(A_t) + (1 - \alpha)(SF_t + T_t) \\ &= \alpha(A_t) + (1 - \alpha)(TAF_t) \end{aligned} \tag{4.6a}$$

The trend estimate:

$$T_{t+1} = \beta(SF_{t+1} - SF_t) + (1 - \beta)(T_t) \tag{4.6b}$$

The trend-adjusted forecast:

$$TAF_{t+1} = SF_{t+1} + T_{t+1} \tag{4.6c}$$

EXHIBIT 4.10   TOOLBOX: EXPONENTIAL SMOOTHING

Once again, the year 5 monthly demand forecasts have been recalculated for Laslow Ltd. This time exponential smoothing models have been used, with alpha equal to 0.2 and 0.8.

MONTHLY DEMAND FORECASTS FOR LASLOW LTD.

Time Period	Actual Demand	Forecast Demand $\alpha = 0.2$	Forecast Demand $\alpha = 0.8$
Year 4			
Dec.	1,020		
Year 5			
Jan.	940	1,020	1,020
Feb.	920	1,004	956
Mar.	950	987	927
Apr.	1,720	980	945
May	1,730	1,128	1,565
June	1,710	1,248	1,697
July	2,340	1,341	1,707
Aug.	2,360	1,541	2,213
Sept.	2,350	1,704	2,331
Oct.	1,240	1,834	2,346
Nov.	1,260	1,715	1,461
Dec.	1,280	1,624	1,300

GRAPH OF LASLOW LTD.'S MONTHLY DEMAND, WITH FORECASTS

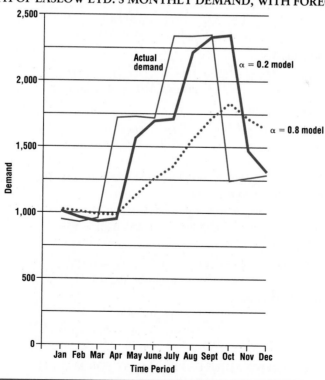

where SF_{t+1} = exponentially smoothed value for time period $t + 1$
  α = selected value for α
  A_t = actual demand in time period t
  T_t = trend estimate for time period t
  β = selected value for β
  TAF_t = trend-adjusted forecast for time period t

The trend-adjusted forecast is calculated in three steps. Exhibit 4.11 shows these steps for Laslow Ltd.

Step 1. Calculate the exponentially smoothed value for time period $t + 1$ using equation (4.6a).

The initial smoothed value (SF_t) is usually set to the most recent demand value or the average of the past few demand values. The initial trend value (T_t) can be estimated by calculating the slope of the trend equation using past data or can be set to zero. The value for alpha (α) is chosen by the modeler; in this case, $\alpha = 0.8$.

EXHIBIT 4.11 TOOLBOX: EXPONENTIAL SMOOTHING WITH A TREND

Let us recalculate the year 5 monthly demand forecasts for Laslow Ltd. using equations (4.6a) to (4.6c). Before beginning, it is necessary to find values for α, β, $SF_{\text{Dec, Yr 4}}$ and $T_{\text{Dec, Yr 4}}$. Let us choose $\alpha = 0.8$, $\beta = 0.5$. To keep the example simple, let us set $SF_{\text{Dec, Yr 4}} = A_{\text{Dec, Yr 4}} = 1,020$ and set $T_{\text{Dec, Yr 4}} = 0$.

TREND-ADJUSTED FORECAST FOR JANUARY, YEAR 5

Step 1: Calculate the exponentially smoothed value:

$$SF_{\text{Jan}} = (0.8)A_{\text{Dec}} + (1 - 0.8)TAF_{\text{Dec}}$$
$$= (0.8)(1,020) + (0.2)(1,020) = 1,020$$

Step 2: Calculate the trend estimate:

$$T_{\text{Jan}} = (0.5)(SF_{\text{Jan}} - SF_{\text{Dec}}) + (1 - 0.5)T_{\text{Dec}}$$
$$= (0.5)(1,020 - 1,020) + (0.5)(0) = 0$$

Step 3: Calculate the trend-adjusted forecast:

$$TAF_{\text{Jan}} = SF_{\text{Jan}} + T_{\text{Jan}}$$
$$= 1,020 + 0 = 1,020$$

TREND-ADJUSTED FORECAST FOR FEBRUARY

Step 1: Calculate the exponentially smoothed value:

$$SF_{\text{Feb}} = (0.8)A_{\text{Jan}} + (1 - 0.8)TAF_{\text{Jan}}$$
$$= (0.8)(940) + (0.2)(1,020) = 956$$

Step 2: Calculate the trend estimate:

$$T_{\text{Feb}} = (0.5)(SF_{\text{Feb}} - SF_{\text{Jan}}) + (1 - 0.5)T_{\text{Jan}}$$
$$= (0.5)(956 - 1,020) + (0.5)(0) = -32$$

Step 3: Calculate the trend-adjusted forecast:

$$TAF_{\text{Feb}} = SF_{\text{Feb}} + T_{\text{Feb}}$$
$$= 956 - 32 = 924$$

TREND-ADJUSTED FORECAST FOR MARCH

Step 1: Calculate the exponentially smoothed value:

$$SF_{\text{Mar}} = (0.8)A_{\text{Feb}} + (1 - 0.8)TAF_{\text{Feb}}$$
$$= (0.8)(920) + (0.2)(924) = 920.8$$

Step 2: Calculate the trend estimate:

$$T_{Mar} = (0.5)(SF_{Mar} - SF_{Feb}) + (1 - 0.5)T_{Feb}$$
$$= (0.5)(920.8 - 956) + (0.5)(-32) = -33.6$$

Step 3: Calculate the trend-adjusted forecast:

$$TAF_{Mar} = SF_{Mar} + T_{Mar}$$
$$= 920.8 - 33.6 = 887.2$$

The smoothed value, trend factor, and trend-adjusted forecast for each of the remaining months in year 5 are shown in the following chart:

MONTHLY DEMAND FORECASTS FOR LASLOW LTD.

Month	Actual Demand	Trend-Adjusted Forecast
Dec.	1,020	
Jan.	940	1,020
Feb.	920	924
Mar.	950	887
Apr.	1,720	929
May	1,730	1,870
June	1,710	2,010
July	2,340	1,902
Aug.	2,360	2,560
Sept.	2,350	2,627
Oct.	1,240	2,522
Nov.	1,260	1,100
Dec.	1,280	896

GRAPH OF LASLOW LTD.'S MONTHLY DEMAND, WITH FORECAST

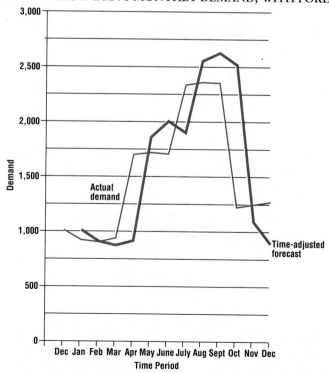

119

Step 2. Calculate the trend estimate for time period $t + 1$ using equation (4.6b).

Beta (β) is used to smooth the trend estimate. Like alpha, its value is chosen by the modeler. In this case, $\beta = 0.5$.

Step 3. Calculate the trend-adjusted forecast for time period $t + 1$ using equation (4.6c).

Since the trend factor is updated every period, the extended model has the ability to adjust to trends.

Focus Forecasting   Focus forecasting is an alternative to time series forecasting that was developed by Bernard Smith (1984), an inventory manager at the American Hardware Supply Company. Smith found that his 21 buyers used personal rules of thumb for purchasing many of the items for which they were responsible. Over 50 percent of the item forecasts generated by computer each month were ignored, and the local rules were used instead. With 100,000 items under control, Smith was worried by what he considered excessive purchases and levels of inventory resulting from the use of these rules, yet he was forced to agree that the local rule often was better than the computer-generated forecast.

After investigating the local rules, Smith chose seven rules as the basis for the new technique he called focus forecasting. The concept is simple; one uses the computer to see which of the seven rules would have produced the best forecast for the past three months for each of the 100,000 or so products in the firm's portfolio. The "best" forecast is the one with the smallest forecast error for the three-month period. That rule can be used to forecast the next month's demand for a particular product. The rules are:

- What was sold in the past three months is what probably will be sold in the next three months.
- What was sold in the same three-month period last year probably will be sold in the same three-month period this year.
- Ten percent more probably will be sold in the next three months than was sold in the last three months.
- Fifty percent more probably will be sold in the next three months than was sold in the last three months.
- The percentage change experienced over the past three months compared with the same three months this year probably will be the same for the next three months.
- A simple exponential smoothing model with $\alpha = 0.3$ is best.
- A double exponential smoothing model with $\alpha = 0.3$ and $\beta = 0.2$ is best.

The first five rules were actually used by purchasing agents, and the last two were added by Smith as a check. All the purchasing agents trust the system, and this is a very important consideration in all planning activities. Further, the system has resulted in sharply reduced inventories and costs. When Smith wrote his book on focus forecasting, he had been in his job for 10 years, during a period when the average life of an inventory manager was around two years.

What are the benefits of focus forecasting? First, all the users trust the process and the results. Now management and agents are dealing with the same numbers and talking with each other, not past each other. Second, the rules are simple and the computer time required for forecasting is short. When one is dealing with thousands of items, timeliness of results is important. Third, the impacts of underlying forces on demand are allowed to change each month and are allowed to be different for every item. Smith's agents are responsible for over 5,000 items each, and so checking the sensitivity of each item in the single model would leave no time for anything else.

The technique has limitations, though. It cannot be used for new products or when special, limited effects will occur or have occurred. It cannot be used for items that are rarely purchased by customers across the whole system, especially when the occasional purchase may be very large. It should not be used if the firm knows a great deal more about its customers, what they want, and when they want it than can be expected in a nationwide retailing chain. Finally, this is an aggregate technique and should not be used for time periods less than a month. The shorter the time period, the spikier the demand and the more problematic the selection of the appropriate forecasting model.

Causal Modeling

Unlike time series models, **causal models** directly identify and measure the effects of specific forces that influence demand. Therefore, they are more appropriate for predicting and evaluating the effects of decisions made by a firm (e.g., changes in advertising or prices) than are time series techniques. Time remains an important consideration, however, since demand is expected to lag behind the effects of the causal variables.

Many firms use economic indicators published by the government to predict demand for their goods and services. Housing starts, for example, may be useful in predicting carpeting and furniture sales. Other causal variables include a firm's advertising and promotional activities, a competitor's actions, the price and availability of substitute products, and weather patterns.

A **linear regression model** with one independent variable is a simple causal model. A **multiple regression model** is used when there is a linear relationship between demand and several independent variables. As demonstrated in Exhibit 4.12, **nonlinear models** can be used as well.

In general, adding variables increases the model's accuracy. However, it also increases the time and difficulty of developing, implementing, and monitoring the model.

EXHIBIT 4.12   TOOLBOX: CAUSAL MODELS

Suppose a hardware store wishes to predict the demand for snowblowers in a particular city. Several different types of causal models the store may use are given below:

Let y = annual demand, in units
x_1 = last year's snowfall, in inches
x_2 = last year's housing starts
x_3 = amount spent on advertising, in $

Simple Linear Regression Model:	$y = 50 + 4x_1$
Multiple Linear Regression Model:	$y = 45 + 3x_1 + 0.1x_2 + 0.02x_3$
Nonlinear Model:	$y = 55 + 4x_1 + 0.1x_2^3 + 0.02x_3^2$

4.6 **SELECTING AND MONITORING FORECASTING SYSTEMS**

There are many ways in which a forecast can be developed, and there is no best way; a forecasting model that works well under one set of circumstances may not work well under another set. When one is selecting a forecasting technique, the specific needs of the people using the forecast, the data available, and the characteristics of the items being forecast must all be considered. Therefore, before a demand forecast can be prepared, the firm must answer the following questions:

- For which goods and services is the firm attempting to forecast demand? What level of aggregation will be used? What is the time horizon of the forecast, and how long is each time period in the time horizon?
- Which sources of demand will be considered? How will the necessary data be obtained?
- Are there any cause-and-effect relationships in the data? Are there any trend, seasonal, or cyclical components?
- What is the purpose of the forecast? Is the firm trying to predict the effects of its actions? Project an existing demand pattern? Predict a turning point?
- Who will use the model? With what level of sophistication are the ultimate users of the forecast comfortable? (If the users do not understand the model, the chances are slim that the forecasts generated by the model will be used.[6])
- How accurate must the forecasts be? What is the cost of forecasting errors? What is more detrimental, underestimating or overestimating demand?
- How quickly must each forecast be prepared? How much time and money can be spent developing, implementing, and monitoring the model?

Once these questions have been answered, one or more forecasting techniques can be selected. Many firms use a mix of quantitative and qualitative techniques in their forecasting models.

Time series techniques such as trend projections, moving averages, and exponential smoothing are suitable for detailed short-term forecasts. Among these techniques, the moving average remains the most popular among manufacturing managers. Computer software packages are widely available and make forecasting quick, easy, and inexpensive.

Exponential smoothing models have relatively minimal data storage and computational requirements compared with other time series techniques. When forecasts for many items must be prepared frequently, data storage and computational time become very important. Other forecasting expenses include the costs of developing the model, gathering the data, interpreting the forecasts, and monitoring the model.

A major weakness with times series techniques is that they assume that the past is a good predictor of the future. In many cases this assumption is not valid.

Causal models such as single and multiple regression models provide insight into cause-and-effect relationships and allow a firm to play "what if" games. Developing and maintaining these models, however, is usually expensive and time-consuming. Data requirements are also large. Thus causal models are more suited to long-term forecasting. Regression analysis is the most popular long-range forecasting model.

Qualitative models also tend to be more effective for general long-range forecasts.

---

[6] This may explain why judgmental methods are used far more often than are quantitative methods.

Like causal models, they can provide predictions about what will happen as well as insights that help explain the predictions. When there are few or no relevant past data or when the data are too difficult to model mathematically, qualitative models are used.

Demand Management

Which techniques provide the most accurate forecasts? Often (but not always) increasing the accuracy of a model's forecasts means that the model will be more expensive to develop and maintain because it probably will contain more variables and have heavier data storage and computational requirements. In this case a trade-off has to be made between forecast accuracy and forecast costs and between the ease with which the forecast can be understood and the time needed to prepare the forecast.

How can a firm evaluate the accuracy of a particular set of forecasts? There are several ways in which this can be done.

Measuring and Using Forecast Errors

A **forecast error** is the difference between the actual demand observed for a period and the demand forecast for that period [equation (4.7)].

Forecast Error

$$E_t = A_t - F_t \tag{4.7}$$

where E_t = forecast error for time period t
$\quad\quad A_t$ = actual demand in time period t
$\quad\quad F_t$ = forecast for time period t

Measures of forecast errors are used to help judge the accuracy of a forecasting model. The **running sum of forecast error (RSFE)** is equal to the sum of the forecast errors for a consecutive set of demand periods [see equation (4.8)]. An unbiased forecasting model sometimes underestimates demand and sometimes overestimates it. Thus, its RSFE is about zero. If the RSFE is positive, the forecasting model tends to underestimate demand. A negative RSFE value indicates that the model has a tendency to overestimate demand.

MEASURES OF FORECAST ERRORS

Running sum of forecast error (RSFE)

$$\text{RSFE} = \sum_{t=1}^{n} E_t \tag{4.8}$$

Mean forecast error (MFE)

$$\text{MFE} = \frac{\sum_{t=1}^{n} E_t}{n} \tag{4.9}$$

Mean absolute deviation (MAD)

$$\text{MAD} = \frac{\sum_{t=1}^{n} |E_t|}{n} \tag{4.10}$$

Mean absolute percentage error (MAPE)

$$MAPE = \frac{\sum_{t=1}^{n} \left| \frac{E_t}{A_t} \times 100 \right|}{n} \qquad (4.11)$$

Mean square error (MSE)

$$MSE = \frac{\sum_{t=1}^{n} E_t^2}{n} \qquad (4.12)$$

where E_t = forecast error for time period t
n = number of time periods
A_t = actual demand in time period t

The **mean forecast error (MFE)**, or **bias**, indicates the magnitude of the model's bias as well as its direction. It is equal to the RSFE divided by the number of periods included in the RSFE [equation (4.9)].

The RSFE and MFE are useful if a firm wants the forecast to be consistently above or below actual demand. If a firm has an upper capacity constraint, for example, and needs to establish a capacity reserve for strategic purposes, it may want its forecasting model to consistently overpredict demand.

The **mean absolute deviation (MAD)** measures the overall accuracy of the forecasting model by considering the magnitudes of the errors [equation (4.10)]. Since error magnitude is so important, MAD is one of the most commonly used error measurements.[7]

[7] In using an exponential smoothing model, one can smooth the MAD by using the equation

$$MAD_t = \alpha |A_t - F_t| + (1 - \alpha)MAD_{t-1}$$

EXHIBIT 4.13 MEASURING FORECAST ERRORS

The monthly demand for Laslow Ltd. in year 5 was estimated using the simple moving average (with $n = 5$ periods). Let us now calculate the forecast errors by using equations (4.8) to (4.12).

The actual demand and forecast demand for each month are shown in the chart below. The forecasting error, the absolute value of the forecasting error, and the squared forecasting error have been added.

Five-Month Moving Average

Month	A_t	F_t	E_t	$|E_t|$	E_t^2	$|E_t \div A_t|$
Jan.	940	1,390	−450	450	202,500	0.479
Feb.	920	1,194	−274	274	75,076	0.230
Mar.	950	990	−40	40	1,600	0.042
Apr.	1,720	972	748	748	559,504	0.435
May	1,730	1,110	620	620	384,400	0.358
June	1,710	1,252	458	458	209,764	0.268
July	2,340	1,406	934	934	872,356	0.340
Aug.	2,360	1,690	670	670	448,900	0.284
Sept.	2,350	1,972	378	378	142,884	0.161
Oct.	1,240	2,098	−858	858	736,164	0.692
Nov.	1,260	2,000	−740	740	547,600	0.587
Dec.	1,280	1,910	−630	630	396,900	0.492
Totals			816	6,800	4,577,648	4.368

RUNNING SUM OF FORECAST ERROR (RSFE)

$$\text{RSFE} = \sum_{t=1}^{n} E_t = 816$$

MEAN FORECAST ERROR (MFE)

$$\text{MFE} = \frac{\sum_{t=1}^{n} E_t}{n} = \frac{816}{12} = 68$$

MEAN ABSOLUTE DEVIATION (MAD)

$$\text{MAD} = \frac{\sum_{t=1}^{n} |E_t|}{n} = \frac{6,800}{12} = 566.67$$

MEAN ABSOLUTE PERCENTAGE ERROR (MAPE)

$$\text{MAPE} = \frac{\sum_{t=1}^{n} \left| \frac{E_t}{A_t} \times 100 \right|}{n} = \frac{4.368 \times 100}{12} = 36.4$$

MEAN SQUARE ERROR (MSE)

$$\text{MSE} = \frac{\sum_{t=1}^{n} E_t^2}{n} = \frac{4,577,648}{12} = 381,470.67$$

The same error measures have been calculated for the remaining monthly demand forecasts. The results are shown below:

Forecasting Technique	RSFE	MFE	MAD	MAPE, %	MSE
2-month moving average	375	31.3	332.9	21.9	233,620.8
5-month moving average	816	68	566.7	36.4	381,470.7
2-month weighted moving average	306	25.5	268.2	19.7	191,876
5-month weighted moving average	561	46.8	411.3	27.1	247,572.8
Exponential smoothing, $\alpha = 0.2$	2,674	222.8	488.5	42.6	325,212.3
Exponential smoothing, $\alpha = 0.8$	334	27.83	268	17.6	193,210
Exponential smoothing with trend, $\alpha = 0.8$, $\beta = 0.5$	−447	−37.3	343.3	22.7	239,234.9

The **mean absolute percentage error (MAPE)** is a measure of the forecasting model's relative dispersion [equation (4.11)]. It is calculated in the same way as the MAD, but the forecasting error for each period is divided by the actual demand observed in that period and multiplied by 100 (so that it is expressed as a percentage).

The **mean square error (MSE)** penalizes large deviations more heavily than small deviations by squaring the errors [equation (4.12)]. When the cost of the error is exponentially related to its magnitude, this is reasonable.

The monthly demand forecasts generated for Laslow Ltd. have been evaluated using these measures of forecast errors; the results are shown in Exhibit 4.13. Overall, the exponential smoothing ($\alpha = 0.8$) model scores the highest. The forecasts derived from the simple and weighted two-month moving averages rate high as well. Note that the more the data were smoothed, the worse was the resultant forecast. The table in Exhibit 4.13 showing the actual demand in year 5 shows that this makes sense.

EXHIBIT 4.14 TOOLBOX: TRACKING SIGNALS

The tracking signal for the monthly demand forecasts generated for Laslow Ltd. has been calculated using exponential smoothing with a trend ($\alpha = 0.8$, $\beta = 0.5$) and the five-month moving average. The results are listed in the following chart. Note that the RSFE, MAD, and TS are all updated each month.

(1)	Simple Five-Month Moving Average				Exponential Smoothing with a Trend ($\alpha = 0.8$, $\beta = 0.5$)			
	(2)	(3)	(4)	(5)	(6)	(7)	(8)	(9)
Month	Error	RSFE	MAD	TS	Error	RSFE	MAD	TS
Jan.	−450	−450	450	−1	−80	−80	80	−1
Feb.	−274	−724	362	−2	−4	−84	42	−2
Mar.	−40	−764	254.7	−3	63	−21	49	−0.4
Apr.	748	−16	378	−0.04	791	770	234.5	3.3
May	620	604	426.4	1.4	−140	630	215.6	2.9
June	458	1,062	431.7	2.5	−300	330	229.7	1.4
July	934	1,996	503.4	4.0	438	768	259.4	3
Aug.	670	2,666	524.3	5.1	−200	568	252	2.3
Sept.	378	3,044	508	6.0	−277	291	254.8	1.1
Oct.	−858	2,186	543	4.0	−1,282	−991	357.5	−2.8
Nov.	−740	1,446	560.9	2.6	160	−831	339.5	−2.4
Dec.	−630	816	566.7	1.4	384	−447	343.3	−1.3

Column 5 = column 3 ÷ column 4. Column 9 = column 7 ÷ column 8.

The five-month moving average model has tracking signals ranging from −3 to 6. If the control limits are set to ±4 MADs, this model will "trip" a signal in August and September.

The tracking signal for the exponential smoothing with a trend model, however, has a much narrower range (−2.8 to 3.3). All values fall within the ±4 MAD control limits.

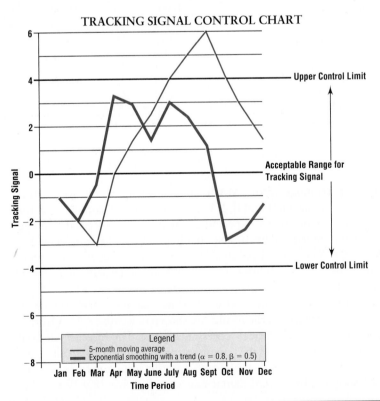

126

Tracking Signals

Managers must continually monitor a model's performance to make sure the model remains appropriate. The most common monitoring techniques are the **tracking signal** and **control charts.**

The tracking signal is given in equation (4.13). It is updated every period and indicates whether the forecast is keeping pace with nonrandom upward or downward changes in demand. The control chart in Exhibit 4.14 shows the tracking signal for the monthly demand forecasts generated for Laslow Ltd. using the exponential smoothing with a trend ($\alpha = 0.8$, $\beta = 0.5$) technique and the five-month moving average technique.

The Tracking Signal (TS)

$$TS = \frac{RSFE}{MAD} = \frac{n \sum\limits_{t=1}^{n} E_t}{\sum\limits_{t=1}^{n} |E_t|} \tag{4.13}$$

where n = number of time periods
E_t = forecast error for time period t

The upper and lower limits on the tracking signal control chart are often set at ± 4 MADs for high-volume products and at ± 8 MADs for low-volume products. The selection of the control limits is subjective. The tighter the control limits are, the less likely a problem is to be overlooked but the more often the control limits will be exceeded.

Control charts are also used to monitor forecast errors. "In control" forecasts generally fall within ± 2 or 3 standard deviations of the distribution of errors (a standard deviation is approximately equal to the square root of the model's MSE).

MANAGERIAL IMPLICATIONS

Demand management is one of the most important activities done by managers. It requires close coordination between marketing and operations, for it is the marketers who have the power to influence the amount and timing of demand and the operators who have the ability to satisfy the quantity and timing of demand. Without true integration, there is likely to be uncertainty, waste, and a loss of credibility with customers. One should not forget, though, that the patterns and timing of demand from the final customer are unlikely to be the patterns and timing around which the operations planners will work. Product must be marshaled through the delivery system, and demand for parts and spares must be factored into production plans.

All firms have to forecast, and forecasting forms the basis of all planning. Even for shop floor schedules, most firms cannot purchase all materials, build a product, and deliver it to a customer without lead times acceptable to the customer. Thus it makes sense to select the most appropriate forecast or portfolio of forecasts. At all levels it is the forecast of market demand made by the marketing function that is the driving force. All other forecasts for resources and materials are derived from the market demand forecast.

The most appropriate model is the one with the smallest forecast error, and there are a number of ways to measure error. Just as the form of the model has to be correct, so must the error-measuring technique. Firms are only as good as their measures, so if a firm measures inappropriately, it must assume that it will end up with an inappropriate forecasting model.

What happens when a control limit is exceeded? If the forecasting model is computerized like that of GE Silicones (see Exhibit 4.1), a flag will be tripped. Since control limits are occasionally exceeded by good models, the first flag is often ignored. If a second flag is tripped in the next five periods, an investigation is needed.

The investigation is intended to determine whether there have been significant changes in internal or external environmental factors. If there have been and they are not permanent, nothing has to be done. If major, permanent changes have occurred or if significant changes can be identified, the model should be reevaluated. Another model may now fit the data stream more closely.

CHAPTER SUMMARY

Managing the demand for goods and services is a fundamental activity for firms in the service sector as well as those in the manufacturing sector. Important points to remember about demand management include:

- Demand management involves recognizing sources of demand for a firm's goods and services, forecasting demand, and determining how the firm will provide for that demand. Together, marketing and operations share the responsibility for demand management.
- A firm's immediate customers (who may be manufacturers, distributors, wholesalers, retailers, or consumers) are its major sources of demand. The demand for service parts, spare parts, demonstration units, intrafirm transfers, and prototypes must be considered as well.
- Economic, technological, and demand forecasts are used by operations as it develops long-range plans for facility location, capacity, process technology, and supply networks.
- Economic forecasts are predictions of what the general business conditions will be several months or years in the future.
- Technological forecasts predict the probability and significance of various possible future developments. They indicate the expected direction of technology change and the expected rate of change.
- Demand forecasts predict the quantity and timing of demand for a firm's goods and services.
- The level of detail, as well as the length of the time horizon, required of a demand forecast depends on how it will be used. Shorter-term plans require very detailed demand forecasts that cover a relatively short time horizon.
- Demand forecasts are used to develop resource forecasts: the timing and quantity of demand for a firm's facilities, equipment, and workforce as well as for purchased parts and materials.
- Options for long-run demand management include cultivating new sources of demand, building new facilities, and investing in new process technologies. In the intermediate term, a firm can manipulate the timing and quantity of demand by expanding or contracting its markets. Capacity can be increased or decreased by hiring temporary employees, scheduling overtime, accumulating inventory during slow periods, and so on.
- The more accurate the forecast, the more efficiently and effectively a firm can use its resources to satisfy demand. Since shorter-term forecasts tend to be more accurate, managers should attempt to reduce the time needed to purchase materials, schedule production, produce a product, and deliver it to the customer.

- Forecasting techniques fall into two broad categories: those which are qualitative and those which are quantitative.
- Qualitative forecasting techniques rely on educated guesses based on intuition, expert opinions, and experience, given information about the firm and its external environments. They are used when historical data are insufficient, contradictory, expensive, or irrelevant.
- Executive committee consensus, the Delphi method, the sales force composite, and consumer market surveys are four commonly used qualitative techniques.
- Quantitative forecasting methods use mathematical models and historical data to predict demand. There are two general types of quantitative methods: time series models and causal models.
- Time series modeling involves plotting demand data (or other types of data) on a time scale and studying the plots to discover consistent shapes or patterns. These patterns are then projected into the future. Trend, seasonal and/or cyclical factors are often identified when one is analyzing time series data.
- Smoothing models such as the simple moving average and exponential smoothing can provide reasonably good short-term forecasts quickly and inexpensively.
- Unlike time series models, causal models directly identify and measure the effects of specific forces that influence demand. Therefore, they are more appropriate for predicting and evaluating the effects of decisions made by a firm and the effects of economic conditions than are time series techniques.
- In choosing a forecasting technique, the following factors must be considered: the purpose of the forecast, who will be using the forecast, the accuracy required, the nature and availability of the data, and the cost.
- There are many different ways in which the accuracy of a forecasting model can be evaluated, including the mean absolute deviation and the mean square error. Tracking signals and control charts are two common techniques for monitoring a model's performance.

KEY TERMS

Demand management	Time series	Exponential smoothing	Mean forecast error
Economic forecasts	Trend	Exponential smoothing	(MFE), or bias
Technological forecasts	Seasonal variation	with a trend	Mean absolute deviation
Demand forecasts	(seasonality)	Focus forecasting	(MAD)
Resource forecasts	Cyclical variation	Causal models	Mean absolute percentage
Executive committee	Random variation	Linear regression model	error (MAPE)
consensus	Multiplicative form of	Multiple regression model	Mean square error (MSE)
Delphi method	a time series	Nonlinear model	Tracking signals
Sales force composite	Trend line	Forecast error	Control charts
Consumer surveys	Simple moving average	Running sum of forecast	
Time series modeling	Weighted moving average	error (RSFE)	

DISCUSSION QUESTIONS

1. What is demand management? Which functional area of a firm is responsible for demand management?

2. How can firms manage demand?

3. What is the potential source of demand for goods or services produced by the following types of firms?
   - A battery-making plant for an automobile manufacturer

- A general hospital
- A manufacturer of computer power supplies
- A family restaurant in a suburban shopping center

4. Explain the difference between forecasting and planning.

5. What is the time frame of an economic forecast? A technology forecast? Find an example of each in a business magazine or newspaper.

6. How is the Delphi technique performed? Should experts or average citizens be canvassed? Why?

7. What is a time series? What are the components of a time series? Which components are present in all time series?

8. List several qualitative forecasting techniques. Over what time horizons are they used?

9. List several quantitative forecasting techniques. Over what time horizons are they used?

10. What is smoothing? Why is it used in forecasting?

In which quantitative forecasting techniques is smoothing used?

11. What is smoothed in single exponential smoothing? What is smoothed in the exponential smoothing with a trend technique? Why?

12. What is causal modeling? What are the differences between time series forecasting and causal model forecasting?

13. What factors should be considered in choosing a forecasting technique?

14. Should firms use a combination of qualitative and quantitative techniques in their forecasting activities? Explain. Who in the firm should do the forecasting?

15. Why do firms want to measure forecast errors? What measures of forecast errors are used?

16. What is a tracking signal? What actions should be taken when the tracking signal passes the predetermined control limits two periods in succession?

PROBLEMS

1. 💾 The historical demand for Mother Hubbard's fresh pies is, in thousands of dozens:

Month	Demand
January	14
February	12
March	12
April	11
May	17
June	16

a. Use a weighted moving average with weights of 0.6, 0.3, and 0.1 to find the July forecast.
b. Use a simple three-month moving average to find the July forecast.
c. Use single exponential smoothing with $\alpha = 0.1$ and a June forecast of 14 to find the July forecast.

2. 💾 The table below contains actual sales of barley (in thousands of metric tons) for six months and the forecast for January:

Month	Actual	Forecast
January	102	82
February	94	
March	105	
April	87	
May	70	
June	99	

a. Calculate forecasts for the remaining five months using single exponential smoothing with $\alpha = 0.3$.
b. Calculate the MAD and bias for the forecasts.

3. Mackinaw Accountants has recorded bookable hours (in thousands) for the past eight quarters:

Quarter	Quantity	Quarter	Quantity
1993		1994	
I	13	I	17
II	19	II	25
III	27	III	29
IV	17	IV	19

Forecast hours for 1995.

4. The results of using three different forecasting models are:

Period Sales	Forecast A	B	C	Actual
1	22	23	18	25
2	26	28	29	32
3	30	33	29	29
4	31	33	37	38
5	33	34	32	40

Which method do you prefer? Why?

5. 🔲 For the Dizzy Sales Co., the number of telephone inquiries is a good indicator of sales one week from now. Recent data are as follows:

Week	1	2	3	4	5	6	7	8
Calls	8	9	11	10	11	13	16	12

What is your forecast of calls for next week? Which model works best? Why?

6. 🔲 Demand for Acme Pumps' six-inch stock pumps in the nine months ended September 1992 was:

Month	Demand
January	114
February	126
March	151
April	167
May	161
June	183
July	138
August	133
September	140

Forecast March to September demand using a three-month moving average and simple exponential smoothing. How can you pick the better forecasting method? Calculate the figures.

7. 🔲 After using your forecasting model for nine months, you decide to test it using MAD and the tracking signal. Following are forecasted and actual demand for the product, a mountain bike:

Month	Forecast	Actual
January	445	505
February	490	555
March	550	408
April	600	510
Mary	650	680
June	700	610
July	750	750
August	800	823
September	850	789

Find the tracking signal and decide whether your forecasting model is appropriate.

8. 🔲 In the Minneapolis area the number of daily calls for repair of Bill's copy machines is:

Date	Calls
1	100
2	137
3	121
4	112
5	145
6	125
7	187
8	89
9	140

a. Calculate the three-period moving average forecast and the forecast error for each day.
b. Calculate a three-period weighted moving average forecast using weights of 0.5, 0.3, and 0.1. Which forecast is better? Why?

9. 🔲 Using the data in problem 8, prepare simple exponential smoothed forecasts when $\alpha = 0.1$ and the first day's forecast calls were 92 and when α is changed to 0.3 with a first period forecast of 92 calls. Which forecasting model is better?

10. 🔲 The Glitzy Auto House sold the following number of used cars in the last six months of 1992:

Month	Sales
July	88
August	60
September	68
October	47
November	92
December	99

a. Prepare a sales forecast for each month, starting with a forecast demand for July of 85 units and $\alpha = 0.2$.
b. Compute the MAD and tracking signal for the data in each period; use MAD for June = 0.
c. Are the MAD and tracking signal correct?
d. Redo the problem using $\alpha = 0.1$, 0.3, and 0.4. Which model gives the better forecast? Why?

11. 🔲 The weekly demand for chicken wings in the local roadhouse has been:

Week	Demand
1	650
2	543
3	580
4	742
5	504
6	612

a. Calculate demand for week 7 using a simple five-period moving average.
b. Calculate the demand for week 7 using a three-period weighted moving average with weights of 0.5, 0.3, and 0.2.
c. Calculate the demand for week 7 using simple exponential forecasting with $\alpha = 0.1$ and a week 6 forecast of 600 units.
d. Which is the better forecast? What assumptions did you make in each forecast?

12. The University Bookstore was flooded and lost some of its forecasting data. Recalculate the missing data from the remaining data:

Period	Demand	Forecast	Error	MAD	Tracking Signal
A_t	$F_t(\alpha = 0.3)$	$E_t = A_t - F_t$	$\alpha = 0.3$		
0	10				
1	120	100.0	20.0	Missing	1.5
2	140	106.0	34.0	19.3	Missing
3	160	Missing	Missing	Missing	Missing

13. 💾 Demand for hockey skates at a local sports store for the past eight weeks has been:

Week	1	2	3	4	5	6	7	8
Demand	122	130	98	121	96	152	113	124

a. Compute the forecast for the relevant periods using a three-period moving average.
b. Compute the forecast using a three-period weighted moving average with weights of 0.6, 0.3, and 0.1.
c. Use a simple exponential smoothing model with $\alpha = 0.6$. Assume the forecast for period 1 was 120.

Which is the best model? Calculate the bias and MAD for each model as a starting point.

14. 💾 A local soft drink bottler has the following sales (in thousands of dollars) over a five-year period:

			Year		
Quarter	1	2	3	4	5
1	346	361	381	401	408
2	468	483	494	515	520
3	375	390	392	416	436
4	279	300	296	355	420

a. Calculate the forecast sales for the first quarter of year 6 using a three-period moving average.
b. Calculate the forecast using a three-period weighted moving average with weights of 0.5, 0.3, and 0.2.
c. Use a simple exponential smoothing model with $\alpha = 0.2$. Assume the forecast for year 1, quarter 1 was 346.

Which of the models would you use? Why?

15. 💾 Gasoline prices for the past 10 months are as follows:

Month	Actual Price
1	1.20
2	1.23
3	1.27
4	1.29
5	1.27
6	1.29
7	1.30
8	1.31
9	1.29
10	1.30

Calculate the forecast for each period and the bias and MAD for each of the following models:

a. Three-period moving average.
b. Three-period weighted moving average with weights of 0.6, 0.3, and 0.1.
c. A simple exponential smoothing model using $\alpha = 0.1$. Assume the forecast for period 1 was 1.20.
d. A double exponential smoothing model using $\alpha = 0.2$ and $\beta = 0.3$. Assume the adjusted forecast in period 0 = 1.19, the actual price in period 0 = 1.19, the simple forecast for period 0 = 1.16, and the smoothed trend estimate for period 0 = 0.03.

For each model calculate the bias and MAD. Which is the most appropriate model? Why?

16. 💾 A retail chain of eyewear specialists has been experimenting with the sales price of contact lenses. The following data have been obtained:

Average Lenses per Day	Price per Lens, $
200	24
190	26
188	27
180	28
170	29
162	30
160	32

Conduct a regression analysis.

a. What is the 95 percent confidence interval for demand at a price of $28?
b. What is your estimate of demand at a price of $20 per lens?

17. 💾 Apple Security, a firm specializing in domestic security, has just completed an analysis of the demand for its services. Over the past 10 years the number of homes protected by Apple each year and the national rate of domestic break-ins per 1,000 homes have been:

Year	Homes	Break-ins
1	36	14.6
2	33	15.3
3	40	18.4
4	41	18.9
5	40	20.2
6	55	22.3
7	60	25.3
8	54	23.5
9	58	25.8
10	61	29.1

Using regression, what is your prediction for demand in years 11 and 12? How well does the model fit the data? What other information would you find useful?

18. Howard's Hardware is an independent hardware store in the local shopping mall. The store relocated to the mall when the mall opened in July two years ago; before that, Howard had operated from a strip mall across town. Howard is concerned that since the move to the mall sales have been erratic and the impact of the move on sales has been uncertain. Knowing that you have some familiarity with regression, Howard has asked you to conduct a regression analysis on his complete sales history and comment on your findings. What do you tell

Howard? The sales data, in dollars, are shown below:

	Year 1	Year 2	Year 3	Year 4	Year 5
Jan.	4,945.20	10,582.00	18,274.10	19,851.00	17,550.13
Feb.	5,980.39	8,268.07	15,518.39	23,959.10	25,201.35
Mar.	6,396.21	12,792.03	9,586.85	25,390.27	48,295.52
Apr.	6,630.26	10,465.78	19,189.85	18,219.75	18,232.93
May	9,363.12	13,520.14	14,821.21	20,436.23	24,050.47
June	12,350.77	12,838.46	15,236.60	22,295.87	25,041.33
July	10,208.19	11,791.34	16,628.18	23,270.05	32,300.79
Aug.	10,686.16	14,144.59	15,814.44	21,383.73	
Sept.	9,191.91	12,877.09	17,251.94	24,759.44	
Oct.	8,775.16	12,018.71	19,637.64	27,534.12	
Nov.	11,082.29	13,654.72	20,131.68	19,534.63	
Dec.	11,586.95	14,443.37	22,629.05	15,901.17	

GROUP EXERCISES

Many of the tools and concepts discussed in this chapter are meant to be used in a team setting. The following problem is best solved by small groups of students. Ideally, each group should be composed of people with different backgrounds, interests, or areas of expertise.

This exercise is based on focus forecasting. Go to the local library and build up a three-year time series of monthly sales for a product or product group; the *Wall Street Journal* regularly reports sales data for automobiles by company and by make (Chevrolet, Pontiac, Oldsmobile, Buick and Cadillac as well as General Motors as a whole). Alternatively, obtain detailed sales data from a company. In either case use the latest data available.

Using the seven rules in this chapter plus any other simple rule you might develop, create a forecast for the sixth, fifth, and fourth-to-last months for which you have actual sales data. Do not use (if possible, do not even *look* at) the last three months' data. Do this for as many products as you can find data; use the best fitting model to forecast the next month's sales.

Add the third-to-last month's sales to the time series and see how large the error was. Test all the models against the new time series and forecast the *next* month's sales. Repeat the process until you have used all the data and are forecasting for the month for which you have no data. When those data become available, check to see how large the error is.

If you can get sales data for shorter periods (the automobile industry reports sales in 10-day periods), try to use focus forecasting for these shorter periods. What differences do you notice when you shorten the forecasting period?

REFERENCES AND SELECTED BIBLIOGRAPHY

Chambers, J. C., S. K. Mullick, and D. D. Smith [1971], "How to Choose the Right Forecasting Technique," *Harvard Business Review,* July–August, pp. 45–74.

Duncan, Robert M. [1992], "Quality Forecasting Drives Quality Inventory at GE Silicones," *Industrial Engineering,* January, pp. 18–21.

Georgoff, D. M., and R. G. Murdick [1986], "Manager's Guide to Forecasting," *Harvard Business Review,* January–February, pp. 110–120.

Hanke, John E., and Arthur G. Reitsch [1989], *Business Forecasting,* 3d ed., Allyn & Bacon, Boston.

Mitchell, Vincent-Wayne [1992], "Using Delphi to Forecast in New Technology Industries," *Marketing Intelligence and Planning,* vol. 10, no. 2, pp. 4–9.

Reichheld, Frederick F., and W. Earl Sasser, Jr. [1990], "Zero Defections: Quality Comes to Services," *Harvard Business Review,* September–October, pp. 105–111.

Sanders, Nada R. [1992], "Corporate Forecasting Practices in the Manufacturing Industry," *Production and Inventory Management Journal,* third quarter, pp. 54–57.

Smith, Bernard T. [1984], *Focus Forecasting: Computer Techniques for Inventory Control,* CBI, Boston.

Wheelwright, Steven C., and Spyros Makridakis [1985], *Forecasting Methods for Management,* 4th ed., Wiley, New York.

Williamson, Robert [1993], "Power Smart Lightens the Load," *Globe and Mail Report on Business,* Aug. 5, p. B6.

Willis, R. E. [1987], *A Guide to Forecasting for Planners and Managers,* Prentice-Hall, Englewood Cliffs, N.J.

CHAPTER 5

MANAGING FOR PRODUCT QUALITY

Demand management decisions cannot be separated from decisions involving product quality and product design. As they focus on product issues, managers must ask themselves:

- How can the firm determine what customers want?
- How can the firm develop high-quality products that meet customers' needs?
- How can the firm develop these products quickly and cost-effectively?

This chapter addresses these questions and examines the role of operations in product design.

The focus will be on operational decisions concerning product design; an examination of specific design techniques appears in Chapter 6.

By the end of this chapter you will be able to describe a typical product design cycle from idea generation through the first use of the product. You will also appreciate new models of the design process and design activities, including concurrent engineering and design for manufacturing. These new ideas and concepts are important in their own right but also supply the background for the discussion of the product-process interface in Chapter 9.

EXHIBIT 5.1   FRO MANUFACTURING PROFILE

With product portfolios ranging from semiconductors, batteries, and recording tapes to computers and factory robots, Sony is the most consistently inventive consumer electronics enterprise in the world. Each year it introduces 1,000 new and improved products, an average of 4 every business day.

Not every product introduced by Sony is totally new. After working together to develop a basic product design, teams of design and manufacturing engineers create many variations on the basic design. Armed with a whole family of products, Sony can exploit differences in consumer preferences and uses.

Consider the Sony Walkman family of products. A series of incremental innovations, combined with significant technological advances, allow Sony to satisfy different customer needs and keep its product line fresh. Over 20 different versions of the original Walkman are available in the United States alone.

Since each model is a variation on the original, new models can be developed quickly and produced by Sony's flexible manufacturing processes. The "My First Sony" Walkman, a colorful version designed to appeal to children, for example, took less than a year from inception to market. Thus, despite intense competition in the personal stereo market, Sony has been able to sustain world leadership status from day one.

Source: Adapted from Schlender (1992), pp. 76–84.

EXHIBIT 5.2   FRO SERVICE PROFILE

After years of success, McDonald's Corporation is starting to feel the pressure of intense competition. New rivals such as the Olive Garden chain of Italian restaurants are luring customers away with a wider choice of more nutritious and tastier food at only slightly higher prices. Other chains, such as Taco Bell, are attracting customers with lower prices and faster service. Supermarkets, convenience stores, and gas stations offering microwavable food that is ready within 90 seconds are another source of competition.

With burger consumption down, McDonald's is using chicken fajitas, pizza, spaghetti, and other new products to attract people to its restaurants, especially during the dinnertime hours. While some products, such as the chicken fajitas, can be easily incorporated into the kitchen operations, others require revolutionary advances in technology. Take pizza,

(Exhibit 5.2 continues on next page)

EXHIBIT 5.2 *(continued)*

for example. Most pizzas take 10 to 20 minutes to bake, much too long for McDonald's customers. McDonald's engineers spent five years working with oven manufacturers to develop an oven that can bake a pizza in only 5-1/2 minutes. They also spent seven years developing a pizza crust that can be baked in that time. Spaghetti and meatballs is proving to be another major technological challenge.

McDonald's is facing its toughest food fight ever, and innovative new products may just give it the boost it needs.

Source: Adapted from Therrien (1991), pp. 114–122.

5.1 MANAGERIAL ORIENTATION

Fragmenting markets. Rapid technological advancement. Shortening product life spans. Intense global competition. Chapter 1 showed how these trends are rendering the mass-production approach infeasible in a growing number of markets. In these markets a **multiple-niche strategy**—producing a family of products, each of which responds to the needs of a specific customer or market segment—is much more successful.

Sony (see Exhibit 5.1) is a firm that uses a multiple-niche strategy. With product designers located throughout the world, Sony has been able to stay close to its customers. Sony's product families are updated frequently to take advantage of technological advances, keep the product lines fresh, and, most important, keep pace with changing customer needs and expectations. Radical as well as incremental changes in product design are made throughout the product life cycle.

Until recently product design was confined largely to the introductory and growth stages of the product life cycle. Once a product had matured and a dominant design[1] had emerged, firms standardized product design and began to pursue economies of scale. Specialized production equipment was put in place where possible, and few, if any, fundamental changes in the product design were made from then on. The most costly the effects of redesign, the less likely the redesign.

Now even firms, like McDonald's (see Exhibit 5.2), that are not following a pure multiple-niche strategy are finding that they must design and update the design of more products each year to stay competitive. And almost all firms are finding that they must increase the speed with which they design products as well as the quality of those products. There is no time to waste; a firm must develop products that satisfy customers' needs and expectations the first time and on time. Too many new products fail when companies overlook this important rule [*Business Week* (1993)].

The trend toward implementing advanced flexible technologies has also had an impact on the nature of product design. To fully realize the productivity improvements promised by these systems, product designers must be familiar with their capabilities and limitations. The product design must be carefully matched to the process by which the product will be made.

These new challenges call for a drastic change in the way in which products are designed and in the role of production in the development process.

---

[1] A *dominant design* is not necessarily the best design, but it is the one that becomes the industry standard. An internal combustion engine that runs on gasoline, for example, is the dominant design for an automobile engine. The layout of characters on a typewriter or computer keyboard is also a dominant design.

A new approach to product and service design—*concurrent engineering*—is enabling firms to meet these challenges. It represents a radical departure from the traditional sequential design process illustrated in Exhibit 5.3, in which operations is almost always on the receiving end of new designs. Both the new and the traditional approaches will be examined as part of this chapter's exploration of the design process from an operations perspective.

5.2 GENERATING AND SELECTING NEW PRODUCT CONCEPTS

A fast-response organization (FRO) constantly looks for new product concepts that meet market needs *and* exploit the full potential of its resources. Ideas for new or improved products come from a variety of sources. The firm's research and development department may generate many ideas. Feedback from customers, shop floor workers, and warranty claims may trigger other ideas. Competitors, research institutes, technical literature, and suppliers may also be the inspiration for new products.

Transforming an idea for a new good or service into an actual product is usually time-consuming and expensive. The costs associated with making major changes to a product concept or abandoning a product concept increase dramatically as the product development process progresses. Therefore, a rapid but effective process for identifying "winning" product concepts is essential for an FRO.

Product concepts usually are evaluated on the basis of many factors, both qualitative and quantitative. Here are some typical concerns:

- How familiar is the firm with the target market? Is it new to the firm? Will the firm be able to work closely with customers to ensure the product really meets their needs?
- If this is a substitute product, how satisfied are customers with the existing products? How willing are they to switch to a new product and/or supplier? How will this affect the sales of the current products?

EXHIBIT 5.3 THE SEQUENTIAL APPROACH TO PRODUCT DESIGN

Marketing or R&D is frequently the source of a new product concept. Product designers convert the concept into a set of functional specifications.

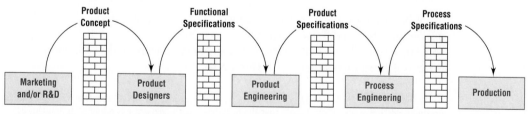

Functional specifications outline how the product should work, the features that should be included, its costs, and other details; functional specifications reflect market, legal, and internal product requirements. For example, a VCR's functional specifications may state that the user must be able to tape television programs that will be broadcast later in the day or week.

Functional specifications are translated into product specifications which detail how the product will work (e.g., how the VCR will be able to tape future broadcasts). This set of specifications includes a detailed drawing of the product and a description of the parts and materials used.

Manufacturing (or process) engineers then develop process specifications which indicate how the product should be made.

EXHIBIT 5.4   TOOLBOX: COMPARING PRODUCT CONCEPTS WITH THE WEIGHT SCORING MODEL

Samson Ltd. is evaluating two product concepts. The company has selected a set of criteria and has assigned a weight (between 0 and 1) to each criterion. Each product concept has been given a score (between 0 and 10) on each criterion.

(1) Factor	(2) Factor Weight	Concept A		Concept B	
		(3) Score	(4) Weighted Score	(5) Score	(6) Weighted Score
Present value of expected profit over entire life cycle	0.20	8	1.60	7	1.40
Fit with current product line	0.15	5	0.75	6	0.90
Technical difficulty	0.18	6	1.08	4	0.72
.	.	.	.	.	.
.	.	.	.	.	.
.	.	.	.	.	.
Total	1.00	40	6.86	36	7.02

Column 4 = column 2 × column 3.
Column 6 = column 2 × column 5.

Although product concept A has a higher score than concept B, its weighted score is lower. The difference, however, is not that great, and sensitivity analysis should be used; that is, the effect of changing the factor weights slightly should be examined.

- How well will the product fit in with the current product line? With other products being developed? What are its strategic implications? How will this product help the firm meet its goals?[2]
- Does the product exploit the firm's internal competencies? Does the firm have the necessary technical expertise? What resources does the firm have to acquire to develop the product? To produce the product? To distribute the product?
- How will the competitors react?
- How large is the target market? What is the product's expected life span? What is the expected cost of the product over the entire life cycle? Its initial investment? Its break-even quantity?[3] Its expected return on investment?
- How safe is the product? Is it environmentally friendly?

When various alternatives are judged against a set of criteria, the *weight scoring model* may be used.[4] Each criterion is assigned a weight, and then each product concept is scored on each criterion. The product concept with the highest total score is the preferred alternative (see Exhibit 5.4).

[2] Wheelwright and Clark (1992) expand on the need to consider the firm's strategic objectives during the product selection stage. They suggest that the firm develop an aggregate product plan that can be used to map out and manage a set of strategic development projects.

[3] The annual break-even quantity can be calculated using the following formula:

$$Q = \frac{F}{S - V}$$

where Q = annual break-even quantity, in units
F = annual fixed costs, in $
S = selling price, in $ per unit
V = variable costs, in $ per unit

[4] The weight scoring model is similar to the factor rating model used to solve facility location problems (see Chapter 8).

It was mentioned earlier that new product development is often a **sequential (over the wall) process** in which information flows predominantly downstream and the production area is on the receiving end of new product designs. For an FRO, this approach is too slow, expensive, and error-prone. Take a closer look at what happens when the "over the wall" approach is used.

Refer back to Exhibit 5.3. The product concept is transformed into **functional, product,** and **process specifications** and then turned over to production and purchasing. As the design evolves, decisions are made and the options available are usually dependent on earlier decisions. If problems are found, those choices are unraveled and the engineers redo much of their work. By the time production becomes involved with product and process designs, it is too late to make changes without setting in motion seemingly endless engineering changes. This leads to the **looping effect** (see Exhibit 5.5), which rapidly lengthens the product design process.

The high probability of engineering changes makes it difficult for a firm to accurately estimate when the product will be ready for market introduction. Lengthy delays can result in missed delivery dates and even missed windows of opportunity as the firm's competitors beat the new products to market. And delays for one project can trigger delays in subsequent projects.

In addition to lengthening the time needed to design the product, engineering changes increase product design costs, especially when the changes are made late in the product design cycle. As illustrated in Exhibit 5.6, the design becomes less flexible

EXHIBIT 5.5   THE LOOPING EFFECT

If a sequential approach to product design is taken, the product development cycle is shown below. Whenever a problem is found, work done during previous stages must be revised. This creates a looping effect which rapidly increases the length of the product development cycle.

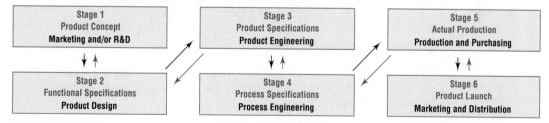

Suppose, for example, shop floor workers discover that the product cannot be produced per the process specifications. After modifying the process specifications several times, the process engineers then determine that the problem stems from the design of one of the product's components. After several iterations, a product design that is manufacturable is found. As shown below, repeated looping through stages 3, 4, and 5 drastically prolongs the development process.

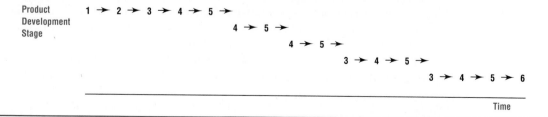

EXHIBIT 5.6 ENGINEERING CHANGES: THE ESCALATOR EFFECT

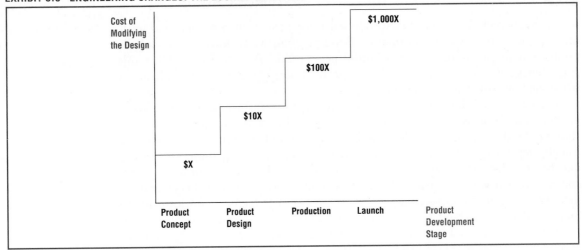

and the cost of incorporating engineering changes tends to increase by a factor of 10 as the product moves from the concept stage to the market launch.

Not only are the development costs associated with the "over the wall" approach high, the recurring costs of manufacturing the product tend to be high as well. Studies have shown that although the design of a product accounts for only about 5 percent of the total cost, its impact on costs (quality,[5] manufacturing, and equipment modification and technology acquisition) is so great that it influences at least 70 percent of the product's total costs.

An alternative to this approach has been very successful in today's competitive environment. This approach is called concurrent, or simultaneous, engineering. **Concurrent engineering (CE)** is a team approach that requires the operations area to take a much more proactive role in the product design process.

Concurrent Engineering

DEFINITION: Concurrent engineering brings together representatives from various functional areas to simultaneously design a product and the process by which it should be made.

Concurrent engineering is an organizational tool that facilitates integration. It breaks down the traditional barriers—organizational walls, time, and geography—separating product and process design. Instead, as illustrated in Exhibit 5.7, functional, product, and process specifications are developed concurrently.

Ideally, concurrent engineering involves a firm's customers and suppliers, along with representatives from a broad range of functional areas within the firm. Including customer representatives on the design team helps ensure that a product that really meets their needs will be developed the first time.

Since suppliers frequently have a great impact on product cost and quality, involving them from day 1 of the design process makes sense. Working closely with

---

[5] No more than 20 percent of quality defects can be traced to the production process. Poor product design, compounded by purchasing policies that emphasize cost over quality, are responsible for the remaining 80 percent.

suppliers is even more crucial when a firm transfers partial (gray box) or even full (black box) design responsibility for specific components to its suppliers. An overview of gray box and black box design is presented in Exhibit 5.8.

Representatives from marketing and production are typically included on concurrent engineering teams. Marketing can supply valuable information on the intended customer market; production can provide feedback on the manufacturability of product designs and the feasibility of process designs. It can also keep designers informed about the flexibility of its current resources. Purchasing, finance, R&D, and other functional areas also can contribute valuable information (see Exhibit 5.9) and may be represented on the design team.

Teamwork encourages design coownership and a commitment to making the product succeed; jobs are enriched, and creativity is unleashed. Because everyone is communicating with others throughout the design process, product quality tends to be higher while product costs are lower.[6] As illustrated in Exhibit 5.10, relatively

---

[6] Firms that implement concurrent engineering report that overall quality levels are 200 to 600 percent higher, white-collar productivity is 20 to 110 percent higher, and return on assets is 20 to 120 percent higher than before.

EXHIBIT 5.7   CONCURRENT ENGINEERING

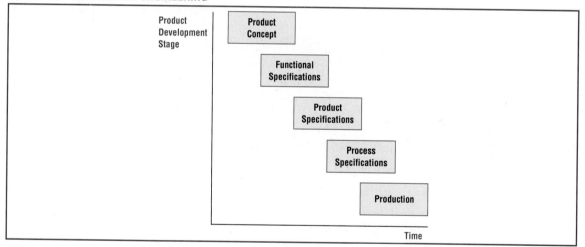

EXHIBIT 5.8   TRANSFERRING DESIGN RESPONSIBILITY TO SUPPLIERS

A firm can transfer different levels of design responsibility.

White Box Design. The firm completely designs the part and knows exactly how it should work. It has an arm's-length relationship with the supplier, who is judged solely on technical and financial performance.

Gray Box Design. The firm writes specifications for the part and may provide a prototype or sample. The supplier is judged on its design capability as well as its manufacturing capabilities. Gray box design tends to be used for complex components or subassemblies rather than for simple parts.

Black Box Design. The firm provides broad specifications but delegates complete design responsibility and liability to the supplier. Typical black box designs are seen in military hardware systems (e.g., aircraft). The firm has a close relationship with the supplier and judges the supplier on a broad set of criteria, including the supplier's managerial strength and responsiveness. The supplier may have suppliers of its own that provide it with gray or white box design capability.

EXHIBIT 5.9 THE CONTRIBUTIONS OF VARIOUS FUNCTIONAL AREAS TO THE PRODUCT DESIGN PROCESS

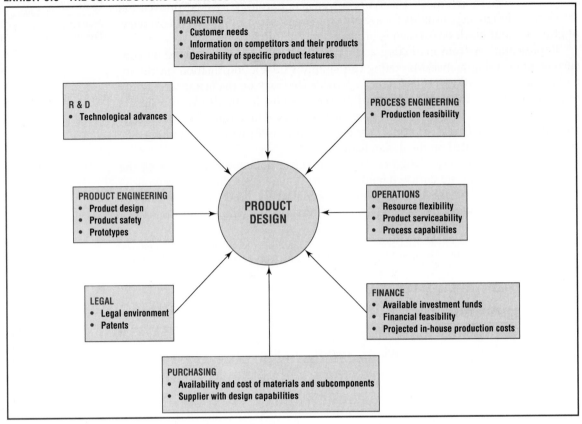

EXHIBIT 5.10 ENGINEERING CHANGES: SEQUENTIAL VERSUS CONCURRENT DESIGN

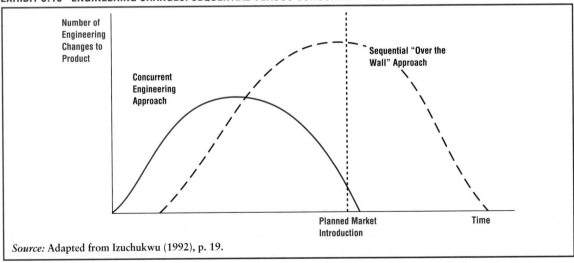

Source: Adapted from Izuchukwu (1992), p. 19.

few engineering changes are needed, and those which are needed are identified early in the product development process.

The speed with which products can be designed and introduced into the market is perhaps concurrent engineering's greatest contribution. Receiving input from the various functional areas early dampens the looping effect enormously, saving a significant amount of time. Time is also saved because work on functional, product, and process specifications is not performed in a strictly sequential manner; each area overlaps with adjacent activities. And because product quality is much higher, the firm's **break-even time** (measured from the day work begins on the product's functional specifications until the day cumulative profits for the product equal the total development investment)[7] is much shorter.

Concurrent engineering enabled Chrysler to bring the Viper Mania "muscle" car and the Ram truck to market in just three years; this is as fast as Honda and Toyota can develop a new car.[8] Chrysler estimates that the team approach is saving it $475 million a year. Allowing suppliers to engineer their own components is saving Chrysler even more money. (This is an example of the black box approach discussed in Exhibit 5.8.) Concurrent engineering is one of the key reasons why Intel, the number one American chip maker, has been able to cut its product development time from three to four years to only two years.

How can a firm move from an "over the wall" approach to a concurrent engineering approach to product and process design? This transition involves much more than creating cross-functional teams. Major changes in the way functional areas operate and communicate are essential. The following examples illustrate how traditional areas of responsibility, lines of authority, and reward systems have to be reformulated:

- Functional managers must delegate decision-making authority to their representative on the team so that the team can review, modify, and approve designs quickly. Lines of authority and reporting relationships must be reviewed and realigned. Increased efficiency reduces the need for much of the firm's entrenched bureaucracy; many individuals may feel threatened and reluctant to yield power.
- Any adversarial relationships that exist between functional areas must be overcome, and the status of each area must be equalized.
- The career paths of functional specialists are no longer well defined.
- Changes in the reward structure are needed to encourage teamwork rather than individual efforts as well as to minimize the possibility of inconsistent functional goals.

Functional specialists have to learn how to communicate effectively with specialists from other areas. Learning how to share their work before it is finished, how to criticize, and how to work with incomplete information is also necessary. Research indicates that communication between team members from different functional areas is easier if people are assigned to the team on a full-time rather than a part-time basis. Full-time membership improves the frequency and quality of idea exchange; it also prevents team members from being distracted or pressured by other matters.

[7] The break-even time measure was developed by Hewlett-Packard. Note how this measure distinguishes between rushing a product that still needs work to market and introducing a high-quality product that meets the users' needs.

[8] A study by Clark and Fujimoto (1989) suggests that overlapping phases in the product development cycle is one of the major reasons why Japanese companies produce cars faster than does the competition.

Quality Function Deployment   One of the most challenging aspects of product design is determining exactly what customers want and need and then ensuring that those needs and wants are the prime consideration in all design decisions. Using **quality function deployment (QFD)** is one way to meet this challenge.

> **DEFINITION:** Quality function deployment is a method by which cross-functional teams translate customer requirements into appropriate design requirements at each stage of the product development process.

This integrative approach to design is discussed in Chapter 6.

Design for Manufacture   This chapter has stressed the need for product and process designers to work together during the product development process. **Design for manufacture (DFM)** is both a process by which a product can be designed and a set of tools that help designers follow the DFM approach and meet its objectives.

> **DEFINITION:** The design for manufacture *process* provides a framework for designers to work together as they develop product and process designs concurrently.

> **DEFINITION:** Design for manufacture *methodologies and guidelines* embody product design approaches, techniques, and heuristics that have been developed over time.

At Cadillac, DFM is a formal written strategy that is an integral part of the business plan. Engineers, suppliers, and assemblers work together to reduce the time to market while improving quality and cutting costs. Ford, IBM, General Electric, and many other companies have also found that DFM can drastically reduce the length of the design cycle, improve product quality, and save millions of dollars.

The technical details of DFM are beyond the scope of this textbook. This chapter will quickly review several DFM guidelines and a few of the tools that can be used to ensure that those guidelines are followed.

DFM guidelines are codified statements of good design practices and appear in various forms. A few general DFM guidelines are listed below. All these guidelines can be broken down into a set of detailed guidelines; many companies have developed their own sets that apply specifically to their own businesses.

- **Design for a minimum number of parts.** Reducing the number of parts reduces the cost of assembling a product. This also means fewer parts to buy or purchase, fewer parts to monitor and control, and fewer parts to store, handle, and inspect. By cutting the number of parts required for the Seville's rear bumper in half, Cadillac reduced assembly time by 57 percent and saved over $450,000 in annual labor costs.
- **Develop a modular design.** By developing components that can be assembled in a variety of ways, a firm can offer a relatively wide range of products while keeping the number of parts it has to buy or produce to a minimum.

    Modular design at Hewlett-Packard (HP) has enabled that firm to release a steady stream of improved printers that cost less, do more, and perform better than anything else on the market. Modular design also allows HP to offer upgrade packages for its personal computers. These packages can be used to add many of the new features to the older models. Compaq Deskpro/M personal computers have placed all vital subsystems on separate boards so that customers can choose only the features they need. Upgrading and expanding take only about five minutes.

- **Minimize part variations ("commonization").** Keeping the number of part variations (e.g., type and size of screws) to a minimum saves time and money. Using standardized components keeps inventory levels, purchasing costs, and purchasing lead times down. The time required to prepare specifications for a unique component, find a supplier, and test the finished component is avoided. Standardization also makes products easier to repair and replacements easier to find.

  Automobile manufacturers are beginning to share parts among old and new models and even among different automakers. Sixty percent of the parts used in Honda's new Domani, for example, are also used in the company's other models. Previously, only 10 to 15 percent of other parts were shared between models.
- **Design parts for ease of fabrication.** The most suitable fabrication process should be chosen for each part, and the part should be designed for the selected fabrication process. The material used to make the part should result in the lowest overall production cost.

DFM tools include relatively new methodologies such as Taguchi methods and the Boothroyd-Dewhurst design for assembly (DFA) method as well as more traditional methodologies such as failure mode effects and criticality analysis and value engineering.

Design for Assembly (DFA)

DEFINITION: *Design for assembly (DFA)* enables a designer to evaluate the manufacturability of a product design quantitatively and helps ensure that the DFM guidelines are correctly applied.

The most widely used DFA method was developed by G. Boothroyd and P. Dewhurst at the University of Massachusetts. The intent of the **Boothroyd-Dewhurst DFA method** is to minimize the cost of assembly while observing the constraints imposed by other design requirements. Designers can use this methodology to determine the minimum number of parts for an assembled unit and estimate the relative ease or difficulty with which their designs can be assembled. Areas in which a design can be potentially improved are found by comparing that design to a theoretically ideal design (see Exhibit 5.11).

At the Ford Motor Co., more than 7,000 engineers have been trained to use the Boothroyd-Dewhurst DFA method; the resultant savings have been close to $1 billion. Xerox, IBM, Whirlpool, and many other North American companies have also adopted this method and have reported substantial savings.

Taguchi Methods   The intent of the **Taguchi methods** is to design a robust product of high quality despite fluctuations in materials, manufacturing, and environmental factors. Taguchi's approach to product and process design also leads to low production costs and relatively short design cycles. The Taguchi methods have been adopted successfully by many North American companies.

Failure Mode Effects and Criticality Analysis   **Failure mode effects and criticality analysis (FMECA)** is a system that provides designers with a methodical way of improving the design of a product. FMECA and Taguchi methods are discussed in detail in Chapter 6.

EXHIBIT 5.11   TOOLBOX: BOOTHROYD-DEWHURST DFA METHOD

The Boothroyd-Dewhurst DFA handbook is divided into three sections: choice of assembly method, design for manual assembly, and design for automatic assembly.

Should the product be assembled manually? With special-purpose equipment? With programmable automation? The first section of the handbook describes a procedure that helps the designer make this decision. The designer supplies information such as production volume per shift, number of parts in the assembly, and number of major changes expected during the product's life. The recommended assembly method is then found using this information and the color-coded chart in the handbook.

Suppose the handbook recommends manual assembly. The designer turns to the second section and then follows the procedure outlined below.

Step 1. Calculate the manual assembly efficiency rating for the original design.

- Determine the theoretical minimum number of parts (TMNP) by questioning the need for each part. A part is a good candidate for elimination if there is no need for (1) relative motion, (2) subsequent adjustment between parts, (3) service or repairability, and (4) materials to be different.
- Calculate the "ideal" assembly time:

$$\text{Ideal assembly time} = (\text{TMNP}) (3 \text{ seconds})$$

This ideal time assumes that each part i is easy to handle and insert and that about one-third of the parts are secured immediately on insertion with well-designed snap-fit elements.

- Calculate the actual assembly time:

$$\text{Actual assembly time} = \sum_{i=1}^{n} (\text{Handling}_i + \text{Insertion}_i)$$

The handbook provides time-study data in chart form. Using information such as part geometry, handling features, and method of attachment, the designer can use the charts to estimate the time needed to handle and insert a particular part.

- Calculate the manual efficiency ratio:

$$\text{Efficiency ratio} = \frac{\text{Ideal assembly time}}{\text{Actual assembly time}}$$

Step 2. Redesign the product.

- First eliminate and combine parts. Then design the remaining parts to reduce assembly time.

Step 3. Evaluate the new design by calculating its manual assembly efficiency ratio.

- Repeat steps 2 and 3 as many times as necessary.

Source: Adapted from Veilleux and Petro (1988), pp. 13–19.

DEFINITION: Failure mode effects and criticality analysis is a procedure in which the causes of potential failures are identified, their effects are assessed, and corrective measures are recommended.

Value Engineering

DEFINITION: During *value engineering* (*value analysis*[9]), (1) the product's attributes are assessed, (2) the costs of providing the specific attributes are calculated, and (3) lower-cost alternatives are identified.

Suppliers and customers may be involved in value engineering along with representatives from engineering, manufacturing, R&D, marketing, and accounting.

[9] The terminology differs with the nature of the product. *Value analysis* is performed on existing products, while new products are subjected to *value engineering.*

The goal is to reduce costs while maintaining a product's quality and functionality. For example, a material or subcomponent unique to the product may be substituted for one that is used in other products, eliminating the need to hold another item in inventory. A high-cost material may be replaced by a lower-cost material, or the product's design may be simplified. The weight of the product may be reduced, or the way it is packaged may be changed. Bells and whistles that customers do not want or that operations finds difficult or expensive to provide may be eliminated. More specific examples (provided by Toyota's chief engineer, Kiyokazu Seo) include attaching taillights with one connector instead of two, making a smaller plastic clip to anchor the body's weather stripping, and sealing only where needed instead of coating the entire underside with a sealing compound.

Design for Recycling

DEFINITION: *Design for recycling* focuses on designing products so that raw materials such as plastics can be retrieved once the product has finished its useful life.

At present, up to 30 percent of a typical car, for example, can be recycled. When a car is designed for ease of disassembly, however, this can increase up to 85 or 90 percent. Exhibit 5.12 describes BMW's design for recycling efforts.

Human Factors Engineering (Ergonomics)   Comfort, safety, and ease of use are becoming important dimensions of product quality for many consumers, especially in buying products for the workplace. Work-related injuries cost North American firms billions of dollars a year, and the majority of these injuries can be traced back to poorly designed products.

Although people are capable of a wide range of tasks and motions, certain consistently repeated activities are less tiring and easier than others. **Human factors engineering** attempts to increase the safety and comfort of a product as well as the effectiveness of the person using that product.

DEFINITION: Human factors engineering applies knowledge of human capabilities and limitations to the design of products and processes.

Decreasing the weight, noise, and vibration of handheld tools; decreasing the force needed to push buttons; placing displays at eye level; and making workstations height-adjustable are examples of how products can be made safer and easier to use. The way in which the product will be used and the frequency with which it will be used are also important design considerations. Human factors engineering is discussed in the context of process design in Chapter 6.

EXHIBIT 5.12   DESIGN FOR DISASSEMBLY: BMW'S AGENDA

For more than two years BMW has had a research team investigating the possibility of recycling plastics and raw materials from discarded automobiles. The team is also determining how to extract recyclable materials and how to design cars that are easier to disassemble. Today 75 to 80 percent of all the materials in a BMW are recyclable, and the company is striving to increase this to 100 percent by the year 2000.

The automaker plans to design a disassembly plant in Wackersdorf, Germany, and is considering running it as a joint venture with car makers elsewhere in Europe.

Source: Adapted from Johnson (1990), pp. 6 and 201.

Virtual Design At the beginning of this chapter Sony's versatility in design was mentioned: the company introduces an average of four new and improved products every business day. To maintain this pace, Sony overlaps the design work for the individual products in a product family. As illustrated in Exhibit 5.13, several teams work on the product family at one time. Note that the team assigned to each version of the product specifies its product requirements before the process design for the previous version has been completed.

Virtual designs are used to link the work done by each team.

DEFINITION: A virtual design is a high-level functional representation that is common to a product family.

Each product in the family represents a different physical realization of the virtual design. The virtual design enables designers to carry over the design of an existing product into the design of related products. This helps reduce waste by avoiding duplicated design efforts.

The Design Envelope

DEFINITION: The design envelope refers to the preset limitations on product characteristics that can be accommodated by a firm's production processes.

The **design envelope** concept assumes that production processes are designed to be very flexible with certain specified limits and can quickly and easily accommodate changes in the design of the product that fall within the envelope. Design changes outside the envelope are very difficult to implement.

The process used by Xerox to build its 1000 series of desktop copiers, for example, places limits on the product's dimensions, the weight of any component, and the minimum degree of accuracy required for inserting any component into the product as it is assembled. It also allows designers to build latent "add on" (or, more correctly, "switch on") features that fall within the design envelope into the copiers.

EXHIBIT 5.13 OVERLAPPING DESIGN OF A PRODUCT FAMILY

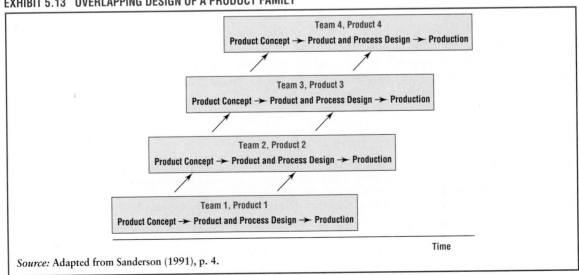

Source: Adapted from Sanderson (1991), p. 4.

Using Advanced Technology for Better Design

Designing products by hand is slow, cumbersome, and no longer necessary in many circumstances. **Computer-aided design (CAD)** tools that help designers quickly create and test high-quality products are now available. Fujima International, one of the companies visited in the Startup Chapter, uses CAD tools to design metal dies for its customers.

With computer-aided tools, a firm can create libraries of components which help designers standardize parts, implement modular design concepts, and enforce uniform parts numbering. Design libraries also enable design teams to review the decisions made by previous teams as well as the rationale behind those decisions. In this way, a firm avoids the pitfall of continually reinventing the wheel.

Computer-aided design tools are being integrated with computer-aided manufacturing[10] and other systems. One of the key benefits of such integrated systems is their ability to transfer data electronically to each other; data from one system do not have to be printed and then manually reentered into another system. (At Milliken, another firm toured in the Startup chapter, customer preferences and vendor data go directly into the CAD systems. Fabric specifications are transferred electronically to the appropriate mills.) Since designs can be passed from one system to another quickly and accurately, quality is improved and duplication of effort is eliminated. Some firms can now receive a customer order in the morning, custom design a product, produce it, and ship it out the door the same day.

Designing Products in Global Organizations

For single-market firms, the decision about how to organize for design is relatively straightforward. The issue becomes much more complex, however, when a firm moves to new markets, countries, and continents. There are no hard and fast rules beyond Ohmae's (1990) edict "think globally and act locally." In product strategy and product design this means developing products for local markets that fit into a coherent sectoral, regional, or global product portfolio. Often this means simply taking a *global* product concept and adapting it to local tastes or to meet local regulations. In other instances it means developing different products for different markets and then adapting these *lead* products as they are introduced into other regional markets.

Feedback from loyal customers gives a firm the best information for new products and product modifications. As a rule of thumb, when local needs and expectations should be reflected in the basic design, the principal design should be managed locally. When local needs can be accommodated through superficial modifications, the design does not need to be carried out locally. In *all* instances, however, the customer *must* be part of the design loop and the design center can *never* be farther distant than strategic response time and accuracy in information transfer allow.

5.4 PRODUCT TESTING

Many computer-aided design tools include **computer-aided engineering (CAE)** capabilities. Designers can use CAE to submit their designs to a series of mechanical, heat, stress, or other engineering tests without creating a physical model first. Once

---

[10] Computer-aided manufacturing (CAM) refers to the use of computers to control or monitor manufacturing operations directly.

again, time is saved and quality is improved. Intel estimates that its new technology for testing chips has shaved at least six months from the usual four-year design cycle.

Computer simulation is another way in which designs can be tested quickly and inexpensively. Simulation may take several forms, but the Boeing 777 aircraft provides a few important examples. The 777 is the first commercial aircraft designed entirely by computer. Every major component and assembly was rigorously tested, using computer simulations, before being approved and before the manufacturing process began. Most commercial 777 pilots will have their first taste of the controls in a flight simulator, as did the test pilots, who "flew" the simulator in normal and extreme conditions for many hours before exposing themselves to the potential danger of the first test flight.

Prototype models of a product are often built as well. In addition to testing, product models can be used to generate feedback from the customer before the general release of a product.

MANAGERIAL IMPLICATIONS

If the responsibility of the operating elements of a firm is to get products or provide services to customers, they must be the appropriate products or services. Consequently, designing products is a critical function. Organizing for design means organizing to identify appropriate products and getting those products to market in the shortest possible time.

It is now recognized that products should be designed to function effectively and efficiently for their *whole* life, not just until the warranty period is over. (While this may seem obvious, until recently few products were designed to be recycled.) By designing for repairability and serviceability, a manufacturer reduces a customer's in-service costs; that should weigh in the manufacturer's favor. It is interesting, though, that designing for repair and service *automatically* means designing the product for manufacture.

Product suggestions can come from anywhere, and a firm must have a good process by which concepts are filtered out to ensure that design work proceeds only on the concepts with the greatest potential. It is important to identify the better concepts and turn them into appropriate products in the shortest possible time. The organization for this invariably involves parallel development of product elements or even parallel development of competing product concepts. This is necessary to minimize design time while not committing the firm to a final design until the last possible minute. Reducing design cycle time allows the firm to capture what the market wants in a product before the mind of the market has changed. Product design takes time, but if a firm can design in half the time it takes the competitors, that firm should have more appropriate products on the market.

To give itself a better chance of having the "right" product, a firm needs to use all the design expertise it has available. This means involving design elements from the whole value chain. There is everything to gain by using suppliers and customers to help with design. If all the people in the chain have real influence on the product, then their concerns will have been met. And if everyone's concerns have been met in design, that will make building the appropriate product a lot easier.

CHAPTER SUMMARY

Fast-response organizations (FROs), are designing more new products every year and updating the design of those products throughout their product life cycles. The need to design high-quality but low-cost products quickly, combined with the trend toward more sophisticated and flexible operating processes, has changed the role of production in the product design process. Production must be involved early on and must take a much more proactive role than ever before.

The main concepts and points to remember in this chapter include:

- Product concepts usually are evaluated on the basis of many qualitative and quantitative factors. An FRO must choose new product concepts that meet market needs *and* exploit the full potential of its resources.
- Traditionally, the product development process has been a sequential "over the wall" process in which production is involved only during the later stages. This approach is too slow, expensive, and error-prone for FROs.
- Concurrent engineering (CE) is an alternative to the "over the wall" approach for both product and service design. It brings together representatives from various functional areas to simultaneously design a product and the process by which it should be made. North American companies have found that using a CE approach to product and process design has drastically reduced the time needed to introduce new products. Product quality is high, and costs are relatively low. CE is an excellent example of how integration can improve the competitiveness of a firm.
- The design for manufacture (DFM) process and guidelines provide a valuable framework and design tools for designers on CE teams. Other design concepts, such as design for recycling, virtual design, and human factors engineering, also support designers as they try to design products that meet customers' needs and can be produced efficiently.
- Advances in computer-aided design and computer-aided engineering have increased the speed with which high-quality products can be produced.

Chapter 6 will examine process design and the link between product and process design.

KEY TERMS

Multiple-niche strategy	Break-even time	Taguchi methods	Human factors
Sequential (over the wall) process	Quality function deployment (QFD)	Failure mode effects and criticality analysis (FMECA)	engineering (ergonomics)
Functional specifications	Design for manufacture (DFM)	Value engineering (value analysis)	Virtual designs
Product specifications	Design for assembly (DFA)	Design for recycling	Design envelope
Process specifications			Computer-aided design (CAD)
Looping effect	Boothroyd-Dewhurst DFA method		Computer-aided engineering (CAE)
Concurrent engineering (CE)			

DISCUSSION QUESTIONS

1. Product design is a very risky business. Why should a company bother?

2. What are the effects of globalization on product design strategies and processes?

3. Concurrent engineering has been adopted by many manufacturing firms. How might service firms use this idea?

4. Should a product be completely developed and tested before it is launched into the market? Or should managers expect changes and launch before development is finalized? What are the advantages and disadvantages of each approach?

5. Intel plans to introduce a new generation of chips every two years or sooner to keep cloners in a perpetual catch-up mode. Is this competitive design option available to a commercial bank? To a steel company? Why or why not?

6. There are several models showing *how* to evaluate new products. But *who* should do the evaluation? Will the choice of model influence who evaluates?

7. Value engineering and the design envelope are concepts used in manufacturing. Can these concepts be used in services? What examples can you cite?

8. What major potential problems can you see with the use of advanced technologies in product design?

9. Is it possible to apply human factors engineering principles to the design of a service? What characteristics might services amenable to ergonomic principles have?

10. At what stage in a product's life cycle should a firm be interested in design for assembly and design for manufacture?

11. The most obvious, yet the least recognized, of integrative devices in a firm is the product the firm makes. Do you agree? Why or why not?

12. What is the impact on the value chain of adopting the concept of design for recycling?

13. How might the use of black, white, and gray box design concepts help in the selection of suppliers and the allocation of work? Will the choice of concept influence the relationships in the value chain?

14. In traditional systems the design engineers "own" the design. How do the new design management concepts affect the question of ownership and accountability? What difficulties might this create?

15. How can a firm overcome functional stereotypes and status differences in its concurrent engineering efforts? How can people from different functional areas learn to communicate with each other and work together?

PROBLEMS

1. Product designers at Thirsty Lawns Ltd. are comparing three alternative types of hose nozzles. Each alternative has been assigned a score between 0 and 10 for each of five factors (higher is better).

Factor	Factor Weight	Scores		
		Concept A	Concept B	Concept C
Estimated development time	0.20	8	5	7
Ability to produce item with current production process	0.10	5	6	6
Present value of expected profit over entire life cycle	0.45	6	8	7
Availability of raw materials and purchased components	0.10	9	9	8
Fit with current product line	0.15	8	9	9

Which concept appears to be the most promising? How sensitive is it to the value of the factor weights used?

2. Do you feel that Thirsty Lawns Ltd. has developed a good set of factors on which to compare its hose nozzles? What factors would you add or delete? How would you weight those factors?

3. Given the following costs, what is the break-even quantity for each product?

Product	Annual Fixed Costs, $	Selling Price, $	Variable Costs, $
A	100,000	5	3
B	100,000	5	4
C	100,000	10	2
D	50,000	10	2

4. Microcircuits Inc. has decided to develop a new remote alarm system for automobiles. Two options have been looked at, and their attractiveness on several criteria is shown below. The factor scores are a maximum of 10 for each factor, with 10 being the best.

Factor	Factor Weight	Option A	Option B
Estimated development time	0.30	6	8
Fit with existing manufacturing processes	0.15	7	5
Profit over product life	0.35	9	8
Ease of installation (used cars)	0.15	7	6
Availability of materials	0.05	7	8

Which is the more attractive of the two options? Why?

5. Microcircuits Inc. had not begun to develop the alarm system in problem 4 when another factor was discovered. This factor, "false alarms," has been assessed a weight equal to "ease of installation" and has been given scores of 7 for option A and 8 for option B. Which option is now the more attractive?

6. Two alternative design approaches for a new jet engine have been developed by Aerosonics, a design studio. Both approaches will cost the same to set up, but there the similarities end. Major differences, their importance, and the ability of each approach to satisfy or take advantage of the factor are:

Factor	Factor Weight	Approach A	Approach B
Use of existing engineering skills	0.25	6	7
Development time	0.25	6	7
Flexibility in approach	0.15	7	4
Need for outside assistance	0.20	7	6
Concurrent development capability	0.15	6	8

Which approach would you choose? Why? What other information would you like to have?

7. Avstar, the manufacturer for which Aerosonics is designing the new jet engine, has been talking with potential customers for the engine. The two likeliest customers need a new engine. Each estimates a similar demand for the engine, but each favors a different design approach. What should Avstar do?

8. The Avignon Motor Company, an automobile manufacturer has assessed the time requirements for two different design approaches. For sequential design, the assessements are:

Concept development	6 months
Concept design	6 months
Prototype development	6 months
Detailed design	9 months
Process design	9 months
Process installation	12 months
Production testing	12 months

For concurrent design, the assessments are:

Concept development	9 months
Concept design	9 months; begins 3 months after concept development starts
Prototype development	12 months; begins 2 months after concept design starts
Detailed design	12 months; begins 6 months after prototype development starts
Process design	9 months; begins 5 months after detailed design starts
Process installation	10 months; begins 6 months after process design starts
Production testing	9 months; begins 6 months after process installation starts

Which design approach should Avignon use? Why? What other information would you like to have before making a decision?

9. Avignon has made the following personnel assessments for each of the two approaches used in problem 8:

Phase	Sequential	Concurrent
Concept development	7 engineers	7 engineers
Concept design	8 engineers	9 engineers
Prototype development	12 engineers	10 engineers
Detailed design	60 engineers	67 engineers
Process design	34 engineers	36 engineers
Process installation	17 engineers	17 engineers
Production testing	17 engineers	11 engineers

How would this information influence your design approach decision? What other information would you like to have before making a decision on the design approach?

10. Further assessment by Avignon shows that suppliers and customers can be brought into the concurrent design approach. Customers can be part of the team during concept development, prototype development, and production testing; suppliers can be part of the team during all phases. Four liaison engineers will be required if suppliers join the design team, and two liaison engineers will be required whenever customers are part of the team. During sequential design two liaison engineers will be required for working with suppliers, and they will be required only during the process design and process installation phases. The fully supported cost of an engineer is $175,000 per year. How does this influence your design approach decision?

11. Avignon, at your insistence, has conducted some financial and market assessments of the impact of concurrent development. To its surprise, Avignon has learned that concurrent engineering will probably *reduce* current profit margins of $1,150 by $250 per vehicle but will increase sales from 650,000 to 850,000 vehicles a year for each year during which competitors use sequential design. The profit loss is due to increased personnel costs

and materials improvements plus increased dealer support per vehicle. Once competitors come into the market with improved design processes, volumes will slip back to 750,000 vehicles per year. No competitor is expected to use concurrent engineering until the next design cycle starts in five years. What would you advise Avignon to do?

12. Bliss Brothers, one of Avignon's competitors, has just announced that it will use concurrent engineering on its next model and will have the model in full production in three years. As Avignon's trusted adviser, what is your advice? You can take some comfort in the fact that Bliss Brothers will have to bear the costs of missionary advertising of the new design approach, a $100 million cost Avignon factored into its fixed costs for first use of concurrent design. You know that Avignon's market share will be reduced by 200,000 vehicles per year until it, too, has a vehicle designed by the concurrent approach on the market.

13. The break-even volume for Avignon's cars designed using the sequential approach is 2,450,000 vehicles. The variable costs of production are $8,000. What are the fixed costs associated with a new model? How long will it take to achieve breakeven if no other manufacturer uses concurrent engineering? How long will it take to achieve breakeven if Avignon releases a new vehicle at the same time Bliss launches a concurrently designed vehicle?

14. The break-even volume for Avignon's cars designed using concurrent engineering is 3 million vehicles. The variable costs are $8,500. What are the fixed costs associated with this approach? How long will it take to reach breakeven if Bliss Brothers does not use concurrent engineering? How long will it take to reach breakeven if Bliss is the first to announce the use of concurrent engineering and Avignon can reduce its marketing costs by $100 million?

15. Assume that for each of the scenarios Avignon has calculated that fixed cost outlays occur in the following manner:

- Ten percent is committed at the beginning of the project; this increases steadily to 25 percent at the beginning of process design.
- At the beginning of process design the fixed cost commitment jumps to 35 percent; this increases steadily to 50 percent at the beginning of process installation.
- At the beginning of process installation the fixed cost commitment jumps to 80 percent; this increases steadily to 90 percent at the beginning of production testing.
- At the beginning of production testing the fixed cost commitment increases to 92 percent; this reaches 100 percent at the completion of production testing.

During this time Avignon is selling vehicles at a rate of 650,000 per year with a profit margin of $1,150 per vehicle. Breakeven for this vehicle occurs two years after the starting point of each scenario, and the current vehicle is withdrawn from the market at the time of launch of the new vehicle (that launch point coincides with the end of production testing). What are the major cash flow implications associated with each scenario?

GROUP EXERCISES

Many of the tools and concepts discussed in this chapter are meant to be used in a team setting. The following problems are best solved by small groups of students. Ideally, each group should be composed of people with different backgrounds, interests, or areas of expertise.

1. As a group, identify a company that has used the new design approaches discussed in this chapter and assess the impact of these approaches on the firm's products and competitiveness. This assessment should be prepared as a presentation for the class. As a suggestion, read the special issue of *Fortune* magazine "The Tough New Consumer," Autumn 1993–Winter 1994. For your presentation, use firms not mentioned in *Fortune*.

2. Find two similar products, one recent and one at least 20 years old, such as an old telephone and a new model. Compare these products along the following lines: design for manufacture, design for assembly, design for maintenance, and design for recycling. Present your findings to the class.

REFERENCES AND SELECTED BIBLIOGRAPHY

Blenkhorn, D., and H. Noori [1989], "Manufacturing-Marketing Interface for Product Design: The Era of Advanced Manufacturing Technologies," proceedings, *American Marketing Association,* Concordia University, Montreal, Quebec, Dec. 3–6, pp. 11–14.

Business Week [1993], "The Ram Can Go Head to Head with

Anyone," Aug. 23, p. 46, and "Flops," Aug. 16, pp. 76–82.

Clark, Kim B., and Takahiro Fujimoto [1989], "Overlapping Problem Solving in Product Development," in K. Ferdows (ed.), *Managing International Manufacturing,* Amsterdam, pp. 127–151.

Corbett, John, Mike Dooner, John Meleka, and Christopher Pym (eds.) [1991], *Design for Manufacture: Strategies, Principles and Techniques,* Addison-Wesley, Reading, Mass.

Desmond, Edward W. [1993], "Running on Empty," *Time,* Jan. 11, pp. 22–23.

Hayes, R. M., and T. E. Hendrick [1988], "New Product Introduction: Strategic Matching Problems," proceedings, Managing the High Technology Firm Conference, Graduate School of Business, University of Colorado at Boulder, Jan. 13–15, pp. 262–265.

Hof, Robert D. [1992], "Inside Intel: It's Moving at Double-Time to Head Off Competitors," *Business Week,* June 1, pp. 86–94.

Izuchukwu, John [1992], "Architecture and Process: The Role of Integrated Systems in Concurrent Engineering Introduction," *Industrial Management,* March–April, pp. 19–23.

Johnson, R. [1990], "Recycling Plant on BMW Agenda," *Automotive News,* Feb. 12, pp. 6, 201.

Mabert, Vincent A., John F. Muth, and Roger W. Schmenner [1991], "Collapsing New Product Development Times: Six Case Studies," School of Business, Indiana University, Oct. 31.

McElroy, J. [1991], "Fast, Faster, Fastest," *Automotive Industries,* September, pp. 45–49.

Mendelson, E. [1991], "HP's LaserJet IIIP Brings PCL5, Resolution Enhancement to Low-Price Laser Printing," *PC,* May 28, p. 38.

Miller, Karen Lowry, David Woodruff, and Thane Peterson [1992], "Overhaul in Japan," *Business Week,* Dec. 21, pp. 80–86.

Naderi, Babak, and Madina Baggerman [1992], "The Result of Ergonomics at the Forefront in Manufacturing: Quality," *Industrial Engineering,* April, pp. 42–46.

Ohmae, Kenichi [1990], *The Borderless World,* Harper Business, New York.

Port, O., Z. Schiller, and R. King [1990], "A Smarter Way to Manufacture," *Business Week,* Apr. 30.

Sanderson, Susan Walsh [1991], "Cost Models for Evaluating Virtual Design Strategies in Multicycle Product Families," Center for Science and Technology Policy and School of Management, Rensselaer Polytechnic Institute, Troy, N.Y.

—— and Vic Uzumeri [1991], "Industrial Design: The Leading Edge of Product Development for World Markets," Center for Science and Technology Policy and School of Management, Rensselaer Polytechnic Institute, Troy, N.Y.

Schlender, Brenton R. [1992], "How Sony Keeps the Magic Going," *Fortune,* Feb. 24, pp. 76–84.

Suárez, Fernando F., and James M. Utterback [1991], "Dominant Design and the Survival of Firms," working paper, International Center for Research on the Management of Technology, Massachusetts Institute of Technology, Cambridge, Mass.

Symonds, William C. [1991], "Pushing Design to Dizzying Speed," *Business Week,* Oct. 21, pp. 64–68.

Taguchi, Genichi, and Don Clausing [1990], "Robust Quality," *Harvard Business Review,* January–February, pp. 65–75.

Therrien, Lois [1991], "McRisky," *Business Week,* Oct. 21, pp. 114–122.

"The Tough New Customer," *Fortune,* special issue, Autumn–Winter 1993.

Veilleux, Raymond F., and Louis W. Petro (eds.) [1988], *Tool and Manufacturing Engineers Handbook,* 4th ed., vol. V, Manufacturing Management, Society of Manufacturing Engineers, Dearborn, Mich.

Wheelwright, Steven C., and Kim B. Clark [1992], "Creating Project Plans to Focus Product Development," *Harvard Business Review,* March–April, pp. 70–82.

Woodruff, David [1992], "Chrysler May Actually Be Turning the Corner," *Business Week,* Feb. 10, p. 32.

Woodruff, David, and Jonathan B. Levine [1991], "Miles Travelled, More to Go," *Business Week,* 1991 Bonus Issue on Quality, pp. 70–73.

CHAPTER 6

DESIGNING-IN PRODUCT QUALITY

Chapter 5 stated that success in today's market depends on how quickly companies identify their customers' needs and expectations and develop and introduce new products that satisfy those expectations. Continued success, even survival, hinges on the firm's ability to continue adapting products to changing market needs.

As they develop and control the product design process, managers need to ask these questions:

- How can the firm ensure that the "voice of the customer" is guiding its design efforts?

- What is the customer's perception of quality? How can the firm measure this?
- How can the firm estimate product costs and profitability early in the design process?
- How can the firm continually improve the product design process?

This chapter will introduce several new techniques from the strategic "tool kit" that can help managers make these microlevel decisions.

EXHIBIT 6.1   FRO MANUFACTURING PROFILE

In an attempt to become the first U.S. company in decades to make a profitable subcompact, Chrysler took a radically different approach to product design for its new Dodge/Plymouth Neon.

The goal was to develop the Neon in a speedy 42 months for a fraction of what any recent small car has cost. Here are a few of the ways in which Chrysler met this challenge:

- Quality function deployment was used to ensure that the "voice of the customer" guided the design process.
- The design team adopted a concurrent engineering approach to product design. Together, engineers, marketers, purchasers, and accountants designed the Neon and the process by which it was made.
- The cross-functional design team worked closely with suppliers as well as line workers. Workers proposed more than 4,000 changes in the car and the production process, many of which were implemented.
- The design team studied (and tore apart) the Honda Civic and the Ford Escort to generate ideas and set benchmarks for itself.

The Neon made its first public appearance at the Frankfurt auto show in September 1993. Automotive journalists and industry analysts involved in early testing were impressed. With a base price of $8,600, the Neon could just beat the Japanese at their game of selling well-equipped small cars at a profit.

Source: Adapted from Woodruff and Lowry Miller (1993), pp. 116–126.

EXHIBIT 6.2   FRO SERVICE PROFILE

In any 10-day period representatives of U.S. Surgical visit every one of the 5,000 American hospitals where surgery is performed. They gown up and enter operating rooms to coach surgeons in the use of the firm's complex instruments. They listen to what doctors like and dislike, need and do not need.

All sales representatives must take (and pass) U.S. Surgical's stringent six-week training course covering anatomy, scrub techniques, and the intricacies of the firm's products. And each year these representatives must pass a recertification exam.

A well-trained sales force and its close connection to customers means that U.S. Surgical can quickly recognize new product opportunities. In 1989, for example, a sales representative met a surgeon who was using a jury-rigged clip to remove gallbladders laparoscop-

(Exhibit 6.2 continues on next page)

EXHIBIT 6.2 *(continued)*

ically (i.e., by inserting a tiny television camera into the patient with slim, long-handled instruments; this is safer, cheaper, and less painful than open surgery). The sales representative reported this to U.S. Surgical, which was able to develop a laparoscopic stapler by early 1990. The result: a boom in laparoscopy, a market that analysts predict will grow to $3 billion by 1996. And U.S. Surgical has an 85 percent share!

Source: Adapted from Reese (1992), p. 26.

6.1 MANAGERIAL ORIENTATION

U.S. Surgical (Exhibit 6.2) illustrates the strategic advantages of being close to the customers and giving them exactly what they need. Determining what customers need and then designing goods and services to match those needs, however, is not easy. For example, how can product designers translate a customer requirement such as "a car should have comfortable seats" into technical product specifications? What about "nice to have" features such as cup holders built into the dashboard? How can the cost of incorporating these features be reconciled with their importance to the customer? How can the firm ensure that customer requirements will remain the focus of the entire product design process?

This chapter will discuss the tools, techniques, and tactics that many companies have employed to overcome these problems. Section 6.2 takes a look at quality and quality-related costs and examines their relationship to product design.

6.2 QUALITY AND QUALITY-RELATED COSTS

Quality was defined in Chapter 2 as "customers' perception of how well a product meets their total needs." It was acknowledged that quality has many aspects, including performance, features, reliability, durability, and aesthetic appeal. Naturally, the degree to which each aspect is emphasized varies from one product to another and from one market to another.

The service element of a product also contributes to its quality. For example, ensuring that everyone who deals with the customer is competent, approachable, and polite is an important aspect of quality.

In general, the higher the quality of a product is, the more consumers are willing to pay for it.[1] This makes sense because high-quality inputs and transformation processes often cost more than those of lower quality. The relationship between quality and cost, however, is not always an inverse one. Although some costs fall as quality deteriorates, others increase. This becomes evident when quality-related costs are divided into four categories:

1. **Prevention costs.** Costs incurred in an effort to minimize future quality costs and problems. Examples include quality planning and management, quality information systems, and process controls.
2. **Appraisal costs.** Costs incurred to determine the quality of a product. Testing and inspection costs account for the bulk of appraisal costs.

---

[1] People expect to pay more for a luxury car such as the Toyota Lexus, for example, than for a basic compact such as the Corolla. Womack, Jones, and Ross (1991) also point out that customers are prepared to pay more for a product that precisely satisfies all their needs than for one that partially satisfies some of their needs.

3. **Internal failure costs.** Costs incurred when substandard products are produced but are discovered before being shipped to the customer. Examples include the cost of scrap as well as that of reworking, repairing, and retesting defective products.

4. **External failure costs.** Costs incurred after a defective product has been shipped to the customer. These costs include the costs of answering complaints, returns, product liability charges, and warranty costs. The most significant cost of external failure is often the loss of future sales from this customer and others.

Prevention and appraisal costs are referred to as **costs of control,** while internal and external failure costs are considered **costs of failure to control.** Together, these costs constitute the total cost of quality.

Obviously, the costs of failure to control can be decreased by increasing the money spent on quality control. However, as illustrated in Exhibit 6.3A, conven-

EXHIBIT 6.3 THE COST OF QUALITY

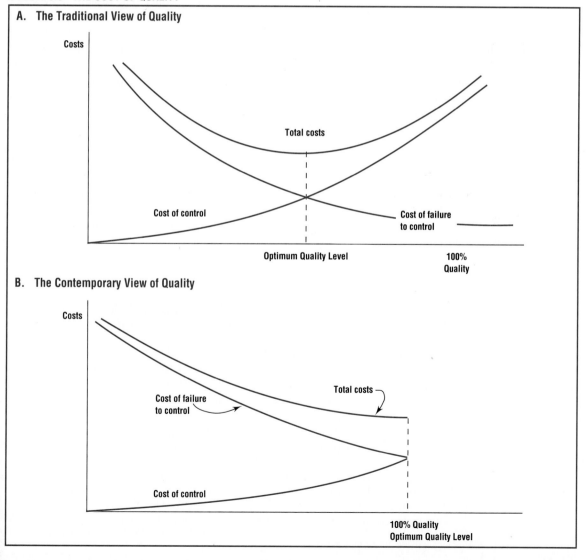

A. The Traditional View of Quality

Costs

Total costs

Cost of control

Cost of failure to control

Optimum Quality Level

100% Quality

B. The Contemporary View of Quality

Costs

Cost of failure to control

Total costs

Cost of control

100% Quality
Optimum Quality Level

tional wisdom argues that the lowest total cost of quality falls somewhat short of the cost of achieving 100 percent quality.

The experience of FROs indicates that this argument is flawed because the true cost of poor quality is so high that investing time, money, and effort to prevent quality problems almost always lowers direct and indirect product costs. Think back to Chapter 2 and six-sigma quality at Motorola. Even pushing quality levels up from 99 percent lowers the total costs for Motorola. As shown in Exhibit 6.3B, quality-related costs are lowest when product quality is perfect.

How can perfect (or nearly perfect) quality be achieved? Obviously, improving the production process can reduce many quality-related problems, but no process can transform a poorly designed good or service into a very high quality product. Studies show that 80 percent of quality-related problems are locked in at the design stage or are caused by the adoption of purchasing policies that emphasize cost over quality.

Firms need to think about total product cost. From the customer's point of view, this is the cost to the customer over the life of the product. The design process is a cost element to the customer, and it has to take into consideration the whole expected life of the product.

Product life here has two meanings: the life of the individual purchased product as perceived by the individual customer and the product life as perceived by the value chain and the market as a whole. Product cost in the latter sense also includes the consequential costs of the design for improvements to the product, improvements made necessary through experience in using the product. These improvements are likely to focus on reducing the cost of use to the customer by making the product easier, less costly, and less time-consuming to maintain and repair. As was pointed out in Chapter 5, firms that anticipate and meet changing customer needs and expectations before customers recognize those needs continue to delight their customers. Product redesign and improvement is therefore an ongoing activity.

How can a firm ensure that quality is built into the product at the design stage, that it is designing products that delight its customers by satisfying their needs? Section 6.3 will present a design tool—quality function deployment—that can vastly improve a firm's ability to produce the right new or improved product the first time and on time.

6.3 QUALITY FUNCTION DEPLOYMENT: TRANSFORMING CUSTOMER REQUIREMENTS INTO DESIGN SPECIFICATIONS

Even when products are designed by cross-functional teams, translating customer requirements into detailed technical product specifications can be very difficult. Customer requirements are often vague,[2] and it is not unusual for some of them to conflict. And since technical product specifications are expressed in a different "language" than are the needs of the customer, the voice of the customer is often lost. The end result is a product that does not fully meet customers' needs.[3]

Quality function deployment (QFD) is an excellent way for firms to capture the

---

[2] A survey conducted by Whirlpool revealed that people want clean refrigerators. After analyzing the data and asking more quesitons, Whirlpool discovered that this did not mean that people want fridges that are easy to clean. It meant that refrigerators should look clean with minimum fuss (e.g., hide fingerprints).

[3] A recent study indicates that fewer than 25 percent of American firms always or almost always develop new products that are based on customers' expectations. The Germans are twice as likely to do so, and the Japanese are three times as likely.

EXHIBIT 6.4 THE QFD PRODUCT PLANNING MATRIX

Customer Requirements	Chip density	Cookie thickness	Cookie size	Degree to which chips taste like chocolate	Calories per cookie	Biting force	Sweetness level	...
Lots of chocolate chips	●							
Chips taste like chocolate				●				
Sweet-tasting	○				○		●	
Chewy		○			○			
Size: about ¼ inch thick, 2½ inches in diameter		●	●					
Low calories	○							
Light brown color				△				
•								
•								
•								
	5 per inch³	¼ inch	2 inches³	9	100	0.3 ft-lb	6	...

Relationships
● Strong
○ Medium
△ Weak

"voice of the customer." QFD ensures that the customer is the focus of all design activities and "dictates" all design trade-offs.

DEFINITION: Quality function deployment is a method by which cross-functional teams translate customer requirements into appropriate design requirements at each stage of the product development process.

QFD originated as a formal concept at the Kobe shipyards of Mitsubishi Heavy Industries in 1972 and quickly spread to other Japanese industries, particularly the automobile industry. QFD is gradually gaining recognition in North America[4] and is being actively promoted by the American Supplier Institute. Xerox, Ford, and General Motors have been implementing QFD concepts since the mid-1980s, and over 200 American companies [including Chrysler (see Exhibit 6.1)] have followed their lead. Companies that use QFD claim that design cycle time can be cut in half, engineering changes can be reduced by two-thirds, and customer demands can be met better than ever before.

The QFD process consists of four phases. An overview of these phases follows, and a detailed discussion appears in the supplement to this chapter.

During the first phase—**product planning**—customer requirements are identified and then are translated into design requirements. Suppose a cookie company wants to add chocolate chip cookies to its product line. After extensive discussions with its customers, the company discovers that taste, size, and chewiness are important requirements. These requirements are shown in the left-hand column of the matrix in Exhibit 6.4.

A set of corresponding design requirements (chip density, cookie thickness, cookie size, etc.) is then generated and listed across the top of the matrix. The

---

[4] In North America QFD is also known as customer-driven engineering (CDE) and matrix product planning (MPP).

relationship between each customer requirement and each design requirement is shown in the body of the matrix. For example, there is a strong relationship between the "lots of chocolate chips" customer requirement and the "chip density" design requirement. Note that design requirements are measurable product characteristics and are *not* related to specific product concepts or designs. Preliminary target values for each design requirement are placed at the bottom of the matrix.[5]

On the basis of these design requirements, alternative design concepts are developed and compared during phase 2, **part deployment.** The best design is chosen, and the focus of analysis moves to the parts that constitute the product. Part characteristics that will enable the product to meet design requirements are identified and studied further. Target values are set for each critical part characteristic. In the cookie example, the margarine must be heated to room temperature. This ensures that the cookie dough will be soft enough to blend yet stiff enough to give the cookie its target thickness.

In phase 3—**process planning**—designers generate and compare alternative process designs. The best design is chosen, and critical process parameters are identified. These parameters have a strong influence on the firm's ability to ensure that each part will exhibit the mandatory characteristics identified in phase 2. In the cookie example, the power setting of the microwave used to heat the margarine and the length of time the margarine is heated are important parameters.

Production planning, the last phase, involves developing detailed shop floor instructions and controls for the process developed in phase 3. Possible shop floor instructions in the cookie example include "monitor the oven to ensure that it is heating evenly" and "cookie sheets must be cool before the dough is placed on them."

As illustrated in Exhibit 6.5, a wide range of tools can be used in conjunction with QFD. Design to cost concepts help designers balance the cost of incorporating product features and capabilities with their importance to the consumer. Failure mode effects and criticality analysis, product reliability tests, and product safety tests can be used to evaluate alternative product designs. Taguchi methods can be used to cost-effectively improve product quality at the design stage. The rest of this chapter will examine these tools.

6.4 DESIGN TO COST: MONITORING PRODUCT COSTS AT THE DESIGN STAGE

Although cost awareness and cost control are essential during the design stage, an estimate of a product's cost is typically deferred until the design is complete. Using standard labor, material, and equipment costs, an accountant calculates the product's cost and then the firm asks whether the product can be sold at a reasonable profit.

In a more progressive approach—the **design to cost** approach—the firm determines a target cost that will make the product attractive in the marketplace and then, working backward from the target cost, designs the product. The design to cost methodology is based on the **functional evaluation system** developed by Masayasu Tanaka (1989) and is an important adjunct to QFD.

---

[5] Other information (such as the results of evaluations of competing products, the relative importance of each customer requirement, and the difficulty of accomplishing each design requirement) is often added to the matrix (see Exhibit 6S.1 in the supplement to this chapter).

EXHIBIT 6.5   QFD PHASES AND SUPPORT TOOLS

QUALITY FUNCTION DEPLOYMENT (QFD) PHASE	TOOLS, TECHNIQUES, AND SOURCES OF INFORMATION
Phase 1: Product Planning • Determine customer requirements. • Translate customer requirements into design requirements.	• Customer surveys, interviews, focus groups, and other market research tools • Warranty records, customer complaint records • Regulatory requirements • Competitive benchmarking: ability of competing products to meet customer requirements • Cause-and-effect (fishbone) diagrams
Phase 2: Product Design • Develop alternative process design concepts. • Evaluate each concept; choose the best one. • Examine the relationship between each product part and the design requirements. • Identify the critical part characteristics, i.e., characteristics that must be evident if the part is to accomplish its intended purpose.	• Competitive benchmarking: engineering assessments of competitors' product designs • Tanaka's functional evaluation system • Fault tree analysis • Failure mode effects and criticality analysis • Taguchi methods: off-line quality control
Phase 3: Process Planning • Develop alternative process designs. • Evaluate each concept; choose the best one. • Examine the relationship between process parameters and critical part characteristics. • Identify critical process parameters, i.e., process parameters that have the greatest effect on critical part characteristics.	• Master flow diagram • Taguchi methods • Fault tree analysis • Failure mode effects and criticality analysis
Phase 4: Process Control Planning • Develop specific production process controls, training requirements, etc., to ensure that critical process parameters are met.	• Statistical process control (control charts) • Foolproof mechanisms (poka-yoke) • Operating instruction sheets • Preventive maintenance schedules

DEFINITION: Design to cost is a methodology in which designers work toward a target cost for the product and closely match the cost of providing each product feature with the cost of incorporating that feature.

The first step in Tanaka's functional evaluation system is to set a target price for the product. Next, the product is defined as a set of functions and each function is allocated a portion of the product's target cost. The more important the function is to the customer, the bigger is its allocated cost. The designer or design team then develops one or more alternative designs for the product. For each alternative, the designer does the following:

- Creates a parts list for the proposed design.
- Determines the relative importance of each part to each product function. In accordance with the part's importance, a portion of the product function's target cost is allocated to that part.
- Estimates the cost of each part.[6]
- Compares the estimated cost of each part with the target cost allocated to that part.

The closer the target cost for each part is to the estimated cost, the better the design is. The logic behind the design to cost approach, as well as its mechanics, becomes clearer when one examines the simple example shown in Exhibit 6.6.

---

[6] It may be difficult to accurately estimate the costs associated with incorporating a particular product feature when one uses traditional cost accounting systems. As will be discussed in Chapter 7, many firms are developing activity-based accounting systems that provide more accurate product cost data.

EXHIBIT 6.6   TOOLBOX: DESIGN TO COST

Adelaide Writing Instruments (AWI) Inc. is developing a new deluxe marker by using the functional evaluation system. Here is the eight-step procedure:

Step 1. Determine the target cost for the product.

Although cost ranges are generally used, for the sake of simplicity, assume that the target cost for AWI's new marker is $5.

Step 2. Define the product as a set of hard and soft functions.

A product's hard functions are its mechanical requirements. Marking, ink storage, and nib protection are all hard functions. Ease of handling, writing smoothness, and color quality are soft functions. A complete set of hard and soft functions appears below.

Hard Functions	Soft Functions
Marking	Writing feel
Ink maintenance	Nib's writing smoothness
Ink Guidance	Nib scratchiness
Nib attachment	Adequate ink supply
Ink storage	Nib balance
Marking air space in penholder	Design
Penholder ventilation	Shape and design
Leak prevention	Presentation
Protecting inside parts	Presentation of manufacturer's name
Maintaining inside parts	Presentation of product name
Pen ring attachment	Presentation of ink color
Cap attachment	Writing appearance
Preventing ink evaporation	Color quality
Connection between material soaking ink and	Uniformity of line width
the pen ring	Color consistency
Nib protection	Ink blotches
	Color evenness
	User convenience
	Cap and penholder fit
	Convenient size
	Attachment ease
	Staining fingers
	Ease of handling

Step 3. Allocate a portion of the target costs to the hard functions.

AWI believes that the marker's soft functions are very important; they are allocated 60 percent of the target cost ($3). This leaves 40 percent ($2) for the hard functions.

Step 4. On the basis of its relative importance to other hard functions in its set, assign a function importance value (FIV) to each hard function. Do the same for the soft functions.

Among the 15 hard functions, marking, ink maintenance, and ink guidance are the most important. They have been assigned FIVs of 16.2, 13.6, and 12.5, respectively.

The shape and design function is the most important soft function and has been assigned a value of 17.4.

Hard Functions	Function Importance Value
Marking	16.2
Ink maintenance	13.6
Ink guidance	12.5
Nib attachment	5.3
Ink storage	8.3
Marking air space in penholder	4.1
Penholder ventilation	5.3
Leak prevention	6.7
Protecting inside parts	3.9
Maintaining inside parts	3.9
Pen ring attachment	3.3
Cap attachment	3.0
Preventing ink evaporation	4.6
Connection between material soaking ink and the pen ring	6.0
Nib protection	3.3
Total	100.0

Soft Functions	Function Importance Value
Writing feel	
Nib's writing smoothness	5.5
Nib scratchiness	6.6
Adequate ink supply	5.9
Nib balance	5.8
Design	
Shape and design	17.4
Presentation	
Presentation of manufacturer's name	3.7
Presentation of product name	3.6
Presentation of ink color	6.1
Writing appearance	
Color quality	3.8
Uniformity of line width	4.9
Color consistency	4.6
Ink blotches	5.5
Color evenness	5.0
User convenience	
Cap and penholder fit	3.7
Convenient size	3.9
Attachment ease	3.5
Staining fingers	5.8
Ease of handling	4.7
Total	100.0

Note that each FIV value is between 0 and 100 and that the sum of FIV values assigned to the set of hard functions is 100. The same is true of the soft functions.

Step 5. Create a parts list for the proposed design. For each function, determine the relative importance of each part.

Suppose you have developed the product design illustrated below:

Sketch of the Prototype Marker

P_1 = Ink
P_2 = Nib
P_3 = Pen ring
P_4 = Material to soak ink
P_5 = Solid bar
P_6 = Penholder
P_7 = Tail cap
P_8 = Air hole
P_9 = Cap

(*Exhibit 6.6 continues on next page*)

EXHIBIT 6.6   *(continued)*

The ink guidance function, for example, is supported by seven of the nine parts. Each of these seven parts has been assigned a percentage (between 0 and 100) of the ink guidance FIV of 12.5. The percentage is based on that part's relative importance to ink guidance. These percentages have been placed in the part/function matrix shown below. For example, the ink and nib are the most important parts and have both been assigned values of 35 percent. The material to soak the ink is not as important and has been assigned a value of 6 percent.

Step 6. For each function/part combination, multiply the part importance percentage (PIP) assigned in step 5 by the function's importance value (FIV) to generate a joint importance value (JIV).

For example, the material to soak the ink has been assigned 6 percent of the ink guidance's FIV. Therefore, its joint importance value is 6% × 12.5 = 0.7. The JIVs have been placed in the part/function matrix shown below.

Soft Functions	FIV	Ink	Nib	Pen Ring	Material to Soak Ink	Solid Bar	Penholder	Tail Cap	Air Hole	Cap
					Joint Importance Values (JIVs)					
Nib's writing smoothness	5.9	40% 2.4	60% 3.5							
Nib scratchiness	6.2	15% 0.9	25% 1.6	8% 0.5	10% 0.6	14% 0.9	10% 0.6	4% 0.2	14% 0.9	
Adequate ink supply	5.9	15% 0.9	15% 0.9	10% 0.6	10% 0.6	18% 1.1	10% 0.6	4% 0.2	18% 1.0	
Nib balance	5.8	10% 0.6	50% 2.9	30% 1.7			10% 0.6			
Shape and design	17.4		11% 1.9	11% 1.9			37% 6.4	4% 0.8		37% 6.4
Presentation of manufacturer's name	3.7						100% 3.7			
Presentation of product name	3.6						100% 3.6			
Presentation of ink color	6.1						50% 3.0			50% 3.1
Color quality	3.8	95% 3.6	5% 0.2							
Uniformity of line width	4.9	10% 0.5	80% 3.9	10% 0.5						
Color consistency	4.6	95% 4.4	5% 0.2							
Ink blotches	5.5	95% 5.2	5% 0.3							
Color evenness	5.0	70% 3.5	30% 1.5							
Cap and penholder fit	3.7						50% 1.8			50% 1.9
Convenient size	3.9						50% 2.0			50% 1.9
Attachment ease	3.5						50% 1.8			50% 1.7
Staining fingers	5.8						53% 3.1	8% 0.5	5% 0.3	34% 1.9
Ease of handling	4.7						80% 3.8			20% 0.9
Total JIVs		22	16.9	5.2	1.2	2.0	31.0	1.7	2.2	17.8

Hard Functions	FIV	Ink	Nib	Pen Ring	Material to Soak Ink	Solid Bar	Penholder	Tail Cap	Air Hole	Cap
					Joint Importance Values (JIVs)					
Marking	16.2	35% 5.7	35% 5.7	10% 1.6			20% 3.2			
Ink maintenance	13.6	40% 5.4	60% 8.2							
Ink guidance	12.5	33% 4.1	33% 4.1	10% 1.3	6% 0.7	4% 0.5	10% 1.3		4% 0.5	
Nib attachment	5.3			100% 5.3						
Ink storage	8.3				100% 8.3					
Marking air space in penholder	4.1					50% 2.0	50% 2.1			
Penholder ventilation	5.3					32% 1.7	32% 1.7		36% 1.9	
Leak prevention	6.7	15% 1.0		10% 0.7	10% 0.7	10% 0.7	30% 2.0	5% 0.3	15% 1.0	5% 0.3
Protecting inside parts	3.9						90% 3.5	10% 0.4		
Maintaining inside part	3.9						90% 3.5	10% 0.4		
Pen ring attachment	3.3						100% 3.3			
Cap attachment	3.0						100% 3.0			
Preventing ink evaporation	4.6	20% 0.9	6% 0.3	4% 0.2			50% 2.2	10% 0.5		10% 0.5
Connection between material soaking ink and the pen ring	6.0			30% 1.8			50% 3.0	20% 1.2		
Nib protection	3.3	5% 0.2								95% 3.1
Total JIVs		17.3	18.3	10.9	9.7	4.9	28.8	2.8	3.4	3.9

Step 7. For each part, sum its joint importance values for all hard functions. Multiply the joint importance value by the target cost allocated to the hard functions. Repeat for the soft functions.

The material to soak the ink has three joint importance values for the hard functions: 0.7, 8.3, and 0.7. The sum of these values is 9.7. Therefore, the material to soak the ink should be assigned 9.7 percent of the $2 allocated to the hard functions, or about 19 cents.

| Part (1) | Soft Functions | | Hard Functions | | Total |
	Total JIV, % (2)	Target Cost, $ (3)	Total JIV, % (4)	Target Cost, $ (5)	Target Cost, $ (6)
Ink	22.0	0.66	17.3	0.34	1.00
Nib	16.9	0.51	18.3	0.36	0.87
Pen ring	5.2	0.15	10.9	0.22	0.37
Material to soak ink	1.2	0.04	9.7	0.19	0.23
Solid bar	2.0	0.06	4.9	0.10	0.16
Penholder	31.0	0.93	28.8	0.58	1.51
Tail cap	1.7	0.05	2.8	0.06	0.11
Air hole	2.2	0.07	3.4	0.07	0.14
Cap	17.8	0.53	3.9	0.08	0.61
Totals	*100.0*	*3.00*	*100.0*	*2.00*	*5.00*

Column 2 and column 4 have been taken from the FIV tables.
Column 3 = $2 × column 2.
Column 5 = $3 × column 4.
Column 6 = column 3 + column 5.

Step 8. Calculate the target cost assigned to each part. Calculate the value index for each part.

The total target cost assigned to a part is simply the sum of its hard function cost allocation and soft function cost allocation. The material to soak the ink, for example, has been assigned 23 cents.

The actual cost of the part should be as close to the target cost as possible. The table below compares the actual cost of each part used in the design to its target cost. The value index (shown in the far right-hand column) is equal to the target cost divided by the actual costs. The goal is to keep the value indexes as close to 1 as possible.

Part (1)	Target Cost, $ (2)	Actual Cost, $ (3)	Value Index (4)
Ink (P_1)	1.00	0.75	1.33
Nib (P_2)	0.87	1.20	0.73
Pen ring (P_3)	0.37	0.40	0.93
Material to soak ink (P_4)	0.23	0.25	0.92
Solid bar (P_5)	0.16	0.15	1.07
Penholder (P_6)	1.51	1.45	1.04
Tail cap (P_7)	0.11	0.10	1.10
Air hole (P_8)	0.14	0.15	0.93
Cap (P_9)	0.61	0.64	0.95
Totals	*5.00*	*5.09*	

Column 4 = column 2 ÷ column 3.

With the exception of the ink and the nib, most of the parts have value indexes near 1. The design calls for a nib that contributes more to the product's cost than to its value. The reverse can be said for the ink used.

The product design must be revised; steps 5 through 8 are then repeated for the new design. Once the value indexes are all reasonably close to 1, the projected cost will be close to the target cost and the design will be acceptable.

Source: Adapted from Tanaka (1989), pp. 61–65.

Matching the cost of product features with their importance to the customer, however, is only one concern of product designers. Section 6.5 looks at other criteria used to judge product designs.

6.5 EVALUATING THE PRODUCT DESIGN

Product designers evaluate and compare the quality of alternative product designs by examining the reliability, maintainability, and safety of each design.

Failure Mode Effects and Criticality Analysis

Products fail every day, and those failures result in a loss to consumers, manufacturers, and society in general. Reducing and ultimately eliminating these failures is therefore important.

DEFINITION: *Failure mode effects and criticality analysis (FMECA) is a procedure in which the causes of potential failures are identified, their effects are assessed, and corrective measures are recommended.*

FMECA can be applied to products or the processes by which they are made. For each product or process element, the following factors are considered:

- The most likely failure modes (i.e., the way in which the product element can fail)
- The cause or causes of failure
- The effect of the failure mode on the next higher assemblies, up to and including the end product
- The likelihood of a particular failure mode actually occurring in service
- The seriousness of a failure to the proper operation of the end product and thus to society
- Ways in which failure can be detected and/or prevented

Suppose a household lamp is being analyzed. Broken and/or frayed wiring from the lamp to the plug is a potential failure mode. Possible causes include fatigue, heat, and even the family dog biting the wire. A broken wire cannot conduct the electric current, and thus the light will not work. Excessive heat may be generated, breakers may blow, or someone may receive a shock. These effects are dangerous and thus quite serious. Possible corrective actions include using wire that has a long life in extreme environments and placing a warning label on the lamp.

How can failure modes and their effects be identified? People in the firm who are familiar with the product or similar products often have ideas. Brainstorming sessions by a multifunctional team in which a catalog of failure modes is generated and the potential causes of each failure mode are identified can be very helpful.[7] **Fault tree analysis (FTA)** is another useful tool.

Fault tree analysis is a procedure that begins with a failure mode and then works backward to uncover the causes of failure. A fault tree diagram (see Exhibit 6.7) shows the logical relationships between failures and causes.

Once failure modes and their effects have been identified, ways in which the failures can be minimized or eliminated are explored. The product and/or process

---

[7] Generally, it is not practical to analyze every potential failure mode. Failure modes that are most likely to occur, are relatively hard to detect, and have a significant impact on the final product should be the first priority.

EXHIBIT 6.7   FAULT TREE ANALYSIS

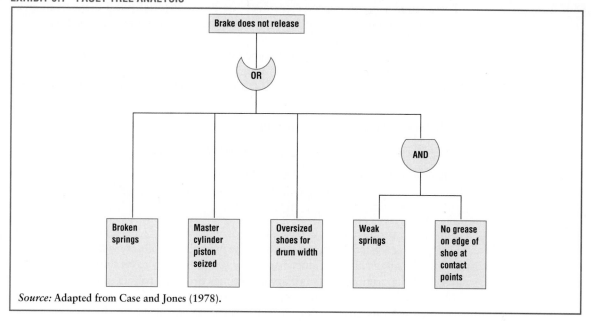

Source: Adapted from Case and Jones (1978).

may have to be redesigned, additional process control may have to be instituted, better user instructions may have to be issued, and so forth.

FMECA is gaining broad industry acceptance. U.S. automobile manufacturers are using it to eliminate safety problems that might have been ignored several years ago. FMECA is not limited to manufacturing industries but applies equally well to service industries. What is the impact on McDonald's if a clerk does not smile? If a customer must wait more than n minutes in line? If the drive-through speaker breaks?

Measuring Product Reliability, Availability, and Maintenance Requirements

DEFINITION: The *reliability* of a product under defined operating conditions is the probability of failure-free operation for a specified period.

Reliability figures can be compared to target values and used to estimate future warranty costs. If the failure rate is consistent, equation (6.1) gives the probability that the system will function for a given length of time. Note that it assumes that the expected product life can be described by the negative exponential distribution.[8]

Reliability over a Given Time Period

$$R = e^{-t/u} \qquad (6.1)$$

where R = probability of failure-free operation
for a time period equal to or exceeding t
e = natural logarithm = 2.7183 . . .
t = specified time period
u = mean time between failures

[8] The normal distribution is sometimes used as well.

For example, if the expected product life is exponential, with a mean of five years, the probability of failure-free operation for three or more years is $2.718^{-3/5}$, or about 55 percent.

The reliability of a product can also be expressed as the product of the reliability of the parts of which it is composed. Equation (6.2) gives the probability that the product will fail on any given trial. The assumption is that if one part fails, the entire product fails.

Reliability at a Specific Point in Time

$$R = R_1 \times R_2 \times R_3 \times \cdots \times R_n \qquad (6.2)$$

where R = probability that the product will not fail
R_i = 1 − (probability that part i will fail), i = 1 to n
n = number of parts in the product

Suppose a product has 10 parts, each of which has a 2 percent probability of failure; that is, each is 98 percent reliable. The product's reliability is therefore 0.98^{10}, or about 82 percent. If a product has many parts, backup parts that automatically switch on if the original parts fail are sometimes provided to increase reliability.

Maintainability tests can be used to compare the maintenance requirements of the product with its target values, previous generations of the product, or competitors' products. Typical maintainability measures include the **mean time to repair**, **mean preventive maintenance time**, and **mean downtime**.

DEFINITION: The mean time to repair is the time required to do repair work, assuming that parts are available.

DEFINITION: The mean preventive maintenance time is the time required to perform preventive maintenance.

DEFINITION: Mean downtime is the total downtime for any reason.

A product's **availability** can be calculated by using equations (6.3*a*) and (6.3*b*). Preventive maintenance and the time required to get any necessary parts (logistics) are included in equation (6.3*a*) but excluded from (6.3*b*). The latter formula is useful in cases where logistics are negligible or the actual repair time after failure is critical to the customer. However, maintainability is generally thought to have two components: *serviceability* (the ease of conducting scheduled inspections and servicing) and *repairability* (the ease of restoring service after failure).[9]

Product Availability

$$A = \frac{MTBF}{MTBF + MDT} = \frac{MTBF}{MTBF + MTTR + PM + L} \qquad (6.3a)$$

$$A = \frac{MTBF}{MTBF + MTTR} \qquad (6.3b)$$

where A = product availability
MTBF = mean time between failures
MDT = mean downtime
MTTR = mean time to repair
PM = preventive maintenance
L = logistics

---

[9] See Bemowski (1992), p. 25.

Product Safety Tests

DEFINITION: Product safety tests are conducted to ensure that consumers are exposed to as few hazards as possible.

Product safety tests begin at the design level and continue through all levels of product control. The general methodology is outlined below:

Step 1. Review the available historical data for similar products. Sources include records of complaints, claims, and lawsuits as well as the results of tests by independent laboratories.

Step 2. Using the information available, examine the ways in which the product was abused in the past. Brainstorm to think of more areas of possible abuse. Develop alternatives in product design to avoid those abuses.

Step 3. Assess the probability that an accident will occur. The probability of an accident or damage occurring should take into account product failure resulting in damage and misuse of the product resulting in damage.

Step 4. Quantify the time during which users are exposed to hazardous conditions.

Step 5. Determine the severity of the effects of hazards on both the product and the user.

Every possible hazard is considered when a product design is tested for safety. The safety level of a product can be calculated by using equations (6.4) and (6.5).

Product Safety

$$S = 1 - p \tag{6.4}$$

$$p = Kft \tag{6.5}$$

where S = product safety
p = probability of an unsafe event
K = severity of occurrence
  class I   = 0.0 (negligible effect)
  class II = 0.1 (marginal effect)
  class III = 0.5 (critical effect)
  class IV = 1.0 (catastrophic effect)
f = frequency of occurrence (probability)
t = time of operation in hours

If there were other independent probabilities of occurrence to take into account, the formula would be altered to

$$S = s_1 \times s_2 \times s_3 \times \cdots \times s_n \tag{6.6}$$

where s_i = product safety with respect to unsafe event i; calculated using equation (6.4)

Suppose that the frequency of gas furnace explosions is 8 in 100 million and that the severity of the accident falls under class IV, a catastrophic effect. At 100,000 operating hours, the probability of an explosion is $1.0 \times 0.000000008 \times 100{,}000 = 0.008$. The safety of the total system is therefore $(1 - 0.008) = 0.992$.

Product designers are interested not only in assessing and comparing the quality of alternative designs but also in improving the design of the product and the process by which it will be made. Section 6.6 looks at Taguchi methods for improving product and process designs.

6.6 TAGUCHI METHODS

Taguchi methods help product designers estimate the true cost of quality and then cost-effectively improve quality. This is done by improving the design of the product as well as the process by which it is made. Taguchi's off-line quality control methods are often an integral part of the QFD process.[10]

Taguchi's Quality Loss Function

Taguchi asserts that the quality of a product is a function of key product characteristics referred to as *performance characteristics*. The ideal value (or state) of a performance characteristic is its *target value*. A high-quality product performs near these target values consistently throughout its life span and under all operating conditions.

Taguchi's **quality loss function** [equation (6.7)] estimates the loss to society from the failure of a product to meet its target value for a particular performance characteristic.[11] This loss can be incurred by the consumer (e.g., short product life, increased maintenance and repair costs), by the company (e.g., increased scrap, rework and warranty costs, damage to the company's reputation, lost market share), or by society in general (e.g., pollution, safety).

Quality Loss Function

$$QLF = C(x - t)^2 \tag{6.7}$$

where QLF = loss to society
     C = a cost constant
     x = actual average value of parameter
     t = target value for parameter

Either exceeding or not reaching the target will result in a loss *even when the part falls within specifications* (see Exhibit 6.8).[12] The closer each part is to its target value, the better it fits with adjacent parts, the better it looks, and the better it performs its intended function.

Targets can also be of the form "more is better" or "less is better." For example, the target size of an automobile tire is a specific value, but the target life span is as long as possible. The targeted exhaust emissions of the engine are as low as possible.

The quality loss function enables a firm to quantify cost savings arising from product and process improvements that lead to reductions in variation from target values. When the auto parts maker Nippondenso recalculated the expected savings from three quality improvement programs, the savings grew from just over 8.5 million yen to over 85 million yen—almost a 10-fold increase.

Taguchi's Off-Line Quality Control Methods

How can variances from target values be minimized? One option is to use stringent process controls. A less expensive option is to use Taguchi's **off-line quality**

[10] Taguchi methods are used extensively outside the QFD framework as well.

[11] Although the loss function may take many forms, Taguchi has found that his simple function is often a good approximation. Of course, if a company has a more accurate method of calculating the loss to society, that method should be used.

[12] Consider Ford's recent experience. Mazda, which is partially owned by Ford, was building transmissions for one of Ford's cars. Even though Mazda and Ford were using the same design specifications, Mazda incurred lower production, scrap, rework, and warranty costs. An investigation revealed that the Ford parts were all within specifications but that the Mazda parts displayed little or no variability from the target values.

EXHIBIT 6.8 TAGUCHI'S QUALITY LOSS FUNCTION

Suppose the target value for the thickness of a steel plate is 1 inch. The following quality loss function has been developed for this key performance characteristic.

$$QLF = 100,000 \, (x - 1)^2$$

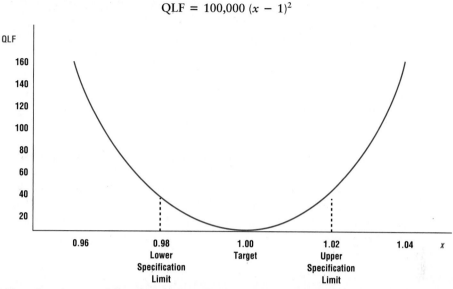

Note that although a part may fall within the specification interval of 1.00 ± 0.02 inches, unless it is exactly 1 inch in diameter, a loss will be incurred. Part of this loss may be attributed to a very serious (and costly) quality problem: tolerance stackup.

Tolerance stackup occurs when parts on the lower limit of their specification interval do not mate properly with adjacent parts which fall near their upper limit. Suppose the steel plate is placed beside a plastic plate in the product. If both plates are near their lower limits, the gap between them may be too large. If both plates are near their upper limits, they may not fit together. In both cases in-plant adjustments are required to achieve a proper fit.

In addition to in-plant adjustments, tolerance stackup may result in unacceptably high levels of friction or vibration which decrease the expected life of the product and inflate warranty costs.

control methods and focus on product and process design. The idea here is to design products and processes robust enough to achieve target values despite environmental fluctuations (e.g., humidity, temperature changes, vibration, manufacturing process fluctuations, improper use of the product by the customer).[13]

How can designers reduce the sensitivity of a product to environmental fluctuations? Taguchi prescribes the three-step approach outlined below and described in detail in the supplement to this chapter.

1. **System design.** An initial product design is developed. The design includes preliminary settings for parameters that affect the value of performance characteristics.

2. **Parameter design.** The factors that contribute most to variation in the end product are identified. A set of experiments is used to determine the settings that minimize the sensitivity of engineering designs to the sources of variation, that is, minimize the expected loss to society. Taguchi also uses these statistically

---

[13] Even very well designed products and processes will not eliminate all variation. Taguchi has also developed what he calls **on-line quality controls** to maintain quality during production.

designed experiments to identify design parameter settings that reduce costs without hurting quality.

3. **Tolerance design.** Acceptable tolerances around the target design parameter values set in step 2 are determined. Not all tolerances need to be tight, only those around design parameters whose variation results in significant variation in the product's performance characteristics.

The resultant product will have acceptably low levels of product variation despite fluctuations in materials, manufacturing (equipment, operators), and environmental conditions. One of Fuju Xerox's high-speed copiers, for example, had such a robust design that when people began using thicker recycled paper, no design modifications were necessary. By contrast, at least one competitor had to redesign its copier completely.

Since performance variation is minimized by *reducing the influence* of the sources of variation rather than by *controlling* them, Taguchi methods are cost-effective.

Taguchi methods, as well as QFD and the other tools presented in this chapter, are valuable not only at the design stage. These tools can also play an important role in a firm's efforts to continuously improve its products and the processes by which they are made.

MANAGERIAL IMPLICATIONS

Designing an appropriate product for the marketplace involves more than the basic product design. It is a process that starts with customer needs and expectations, which are turned into product requirements. From there a firm develops product and then process specifications and then produces the product. Product design does not take place in a vacuum: it starts and ends with the customer but also involves the ability to produce the desired product.

It should come as no surprise that the newer tools for product design work best in firms that are already noted for quality. That should not stop other firms from using these techniques; they merely have to accept the fact that their benefits will not be as great as those of better firms until they improve sufficiently to take full advantage of the techniques.

What does a firm try to achieve with the newer approaches? First, products that are better suited to their operating environments by being designed to operate effectively within understood environmental parameters. Second, better understanding of total product costs, including whole-life approaches to cost. Included in this are notions of strategic allocation of overhead to the principal component of variable product cost. A firm wants control systems that encourage managers to make decisions that fit in with the corporate strategy, and most cost allocation systems do not do that.

Third, the firm is trying to build in automatic processes for verifying product or process design. If the firm can identify in advance and then eliminate critical failure or cost-incurring characteristics, it can reduce the whole-life costs for its products.

Quality is what the customer wants at a price the customer is prepared to pay. This value-based notion of quality is becoming more widely accepted and should drive quality decisions. An important characteristic of this definition is that there can be too much quality in a product. If a product does more than the customer requires or costs a great deal more than a competing product that does not do as much, the firm is likely to lose sales. This upper limit to product quality is one that can be expected to increase as time goes by and customer needs and expectations increase.

The critical implication here is that firms should design products that meet customers' current needs and expectations and should keep improving products at a slightly faster rate than the rate at which expectations change. This will lead to customers who are continually delighted with the firm's products, and delighted customers are not likely to defect.

CHAPTER SUMMARY

Most firms must have new and improved products or they will lose out in the battle for market share and thus profitability. The product design concepts discussed in this chapter can help firms design the right product the first time and on time.

- The relationship between cost and quality is not always an inverse one. Although some costs fall as quality deteriorates, others increase. Total quality-related costs, however, are lowest when product quality is perfect.
- Quality function deployment (QFD) is an excellent way for firms to capture the "voice of the customer." QFD ensures that the customer is the focus of all design activities and "dictates" all design trade-offs. During the four phases of the QFD approach, customer requirements are translated into detailed product and process specifications.
- The design to cost concept is based on Tanaka's functional evaluation system and helps designers match the cost of incorporating a product feature with that feature's importance to the consumer.
- Failure mode effects and criticality analysis is a procedure in which the causes of potential failures are identified, their effects are assessed, and corrective measures are recommended.
- The reliability of a product under defined operating conditions is the probability of failure-free operation for a specified period.
- Typical maintainability measures includes mean time to repair, mean downtime, and mean preventive maintenance time.
- Product safety tests are typically conducted at several points throughout the product design process.
- Taguchi's quality loss function estimates the loss to society from the failure of a product to meet its target values. It can help a firm quantify the cost savings arising from product and process improvements that lead to reductions in variation from target values.
- Taguchi's off-line quality control methods can be used to design products and processes robust enough to achieve target values despite environmental fluctuations.

KEY TERMS

Quality	Part deployment	Fault tree analysis (FTA)	Product safety tests
Prevention costs	Process planning	Reliability	Taguchi methods
Appraisal costs	Production planning	Maintainability	Quality loss function
Internal failure costs	Design to cost	Mean time to repair	Off-line quality control
External failure costs	Functional evaluation	Mean preventive	On-line quality control
Costs of control	system	maintenance time	System design
Costs of failure to control	Failure mode effects and	Mean downtime	Parameter design
Quality function	criticality analysis	Availability	Tolerance design
deployment (QFD)	(FMECA)		
Product planning			

DISCUSSION QUESTIONS

1. What is the difference between product planning and production planning? Who is involved, and what are the outcomes of each activity? (Read the supplement to this chapter before answering this question.)

2. What is the relationship between product cost and product quality? What should a firm focus on in designing a product?

3. What is the most important principle in product design? Why?

4. What is QFD? How should a firm think about customer expectations and customer requirements? (Read the supplement to this chapter before answering this question.)

5. Who should be involved in QFD on a new product? On an existing product that a firm wants to improve? Why do these differences exist, if they do?

6. Can a firm carry out a QFD analysis in designing a service product? What if this service product is marking student reports?

7. What is the quality loss function? How does it compare with traditional loss approaches?

8. What is parameter design in the Taguchi system? What is tolerance design? Which takes precedence, and why? (Read the supplement to this chapter before answering this question.)

9. What is a robust product? How does this concept differ from traditional design concepts?

10. Design to cost is a functional evaluation system. What functions are evaluated, and why? How important is design to cost as a control mechanism?

11. If a firm cannot test every single product it makes, what options might it have? Why does a firm want to test products anyway?

12. What is FMECA? How might FMECA be used in the Mayo Clinic?

13. Why should a firm be concerned with maintenance and reliability issues?

14. The quality loss function indicates that there can be costs if there is *too much* quality in a product? Can you think of situations in which this might occur? Is there any factor common to the situations you depict?

15. In the first quarter of 1993 Toyota's U.S. sales shrank by 8.3 percent [Armstrong and Lowry Miller (1993), p. 28]. Part of the problem is that Toyota's new models may be overengineered. For example, the Corolla uses sophisticated soundproofing technology derived from the Lexus. Its base price has moved from less than $10,000 in 1992 to $11,198, and consumer sales have dropped 5.7 percent. Is there such a thing as too much quality? If so, what implications does this have for the quality loss function?

16. What is tolerance stackup? Why does it occur? In what ways can this problem be overcome?

PROBLEMS

1. It is the beginning of the term, and you have just been given a course handout. Marks will be awarded as follows:

Attendance	5%
Class participation	10%
Hand-in case	15%
Research paper	15%
Midterm exam	25%
Final exam	30%

The course consists of 24 ninety-minute classes spread over 12 weeks. Suppose you have allotted 100 hours to this course. Prepare a list of activities (e.g., read textbook, study for exam) you need to do for the course. Use the functional evaluation system to decide how many hours to spend on each activity. (*Hint:* the mark breakdowns correspond to product features, and the activities correspond to product parts.)

2. You have decided to purchase a new stereo system and see one you want on sale for $500. The salesperson tries to sell you a five-year warranty for $10 a year and claims that the average repair charge is about $100. If the stereo system's life expectancy is exponential with a mean of five years, should you buy the warranty?

3. Suppose the stereo system in problem 3 consists of four subsystems, each with a 2 percent probability of failure.
   a. What is the probability of the stereo system failing at a specific point in time?
   b. If two of the four subsystems have backup systems and the backup systems also have a 2 percent probability of failure, what is the probability of the stereo system failing at a specific point in time?

4. David owns an older car that seems to break down once a week. It usually takes David about three hours to fix it. He spends about an hour a week on preventive maintenance. What is the availability of his car?

5. The state is proposing that a nuclear power plant be built down the road from your house. If the frequency of a meltdown is 1 in 100 million, what is the probability of a meltdown after five years (43,800 hours)? How safe is the plant?

6. Your firm produces nuts and bolts. On a 25-mm-diameter nut the hole tolerance is ± 0.02 mm, the same as the tolerance for the shaft of the bolt. If the processes are centered at 25 mm, what is the probability that a randomly selected nut will not fit over a randomly selected bolt shaft?

7. Given a chance to think about how to specify dimensions, you decide to specify nuts as nominal dimension plus 0.02 mm and bolt shafts as nominal dimension minus 0.02 mm. You know, though, that you cannot tighten the nut properly if the hole in the nut is more than 0.035 mm greater than the diameter of the bolt shaft. Given that you can achieve process standard deviation of 0.005 mm, what is the probability that a randomly selected nut will not fit with a randomly selected bolt?

8. With the new specifications, to what dimensions will you have to set the machines to produce 25-mm nuts and 25-mm bolts?

9. One of the process engineers says that the tolerance stackup problem can be alleviated in one of two ways. The first is to inspect each nut and bolt and sell them as matched pairs. It will cost $5.30 per hour for a person who could inspect 1,000 nuts and bolts per hour. The second is to spend $12,000 on improving the processes and reduce process standard deviation to 0.002 mm. Which, if either, of the options would you choose given that each 6-mm nut you make costs $0.02 and each 6-mm bolt costs on average $0.10. (The 6-mm size is the reference unit you make.) Your firm makes 30,000 6-mm equivalent nuts and 25,000 6-mm equivalent bolts per day.

10. Anderson Inc. produces high-strength alloy rods for the aircraft industry. Each rod is 300 mm in length, with a tolerance of ± 3 mm. If a rod exceeds either limit, the rod is melted down and used again. The cost of being out of specification is $1 per rod. Using this information, construct a related quality loss function.

11. Endocon, a manufacturer of magnetic tapes, wants to reduce the variability of the thickness of the coating of the tape. It is estimated that the loss to the customer is $15 per reel if the thickness exceeds 0.007 ± 0.0005 mm. Each reel contains 200 meters of tape. A random sample of 10 tapes yielded the following thicknesses: 0.0078, 0.0072, 0.0068, 0.0071, 0.0069, 0.0066, 0.0072, 0.0074, 0.0068, and 0.0070. Find the average loss per reel.

12. Endocon is looking at a new process that will reduce coating thickness variability, but at an additional cost of $5 per reel. A random sample of 10 tapes taken from the new process gave the following thicknesses: 0.0071, 0.0069, 0.0069, 0.0068, 0.0072, 0.0071, 0.0070, 0.0069, 0.0071, and 0.0070. Is it cost-effective to use the new process? If Endocon makes 12,000 tapes a year, what is the annual saving?

13. A restaurant believes that two of the most important factors that help it attract business and retain customers are prices and service times. After reading a local survey, you estimate that the customer tolerance for price is $8, with an associated customer loss of $50. You find that the customer tolerance for service time is 10 minutes, with an associated loss of $40. A random sample yielded the following values of price: $6.50, $8.20, $7.00, $8.50, $5.50, $7.20, $6.40, $5.70, $7.40, $8.30. The sample service times were 5.2, 7.5, 4.8, 11.4, 9.8, 10.5, 8.2, 11.0, 12.0, and 8.5 minutes. Determine the expected loss per customer. If the restaurant expects to serve 2,000 customers monthly, what is the expected monthly loss?

14. The restaurant manager decided to add extra staff to reduce the service time. A random survey indicated the following service times: 8.4, 5.6, 7.8, 6.8, 8.5, 6.2, 6.5, 5.9, 6.4, and 7.5 minutes. The additional cost of serving customers increased by $0.75 per customer. Was it cost-effective to add the extra staff?

15. Analyze the following cost data. What do these data suggest to management?

	Product A	Product B	Product C
Total sales	550,700	245,000	400,000
External failure (%)	42	20	20
Internal failure (%)	45	25	45
Appraisal (%)	12	52	30
Prevention (%)	1	3	5

Note: Figures for cost represent the percentage of total quality cost for the particular product.

GROUP EXERCISES

Many of the tools and techniques discussed in this chapter are meant to be used in a team setting. The following problems are best solved by small groups of students. Ideally, each group should be composed of people with different backgrounds, interests, or areas of expertise.

1. Suppose your team has been commissioned to redesign the school's registration process (or a hamburger stand or shopping mall).
   a. Who is the customer? What does he or she want? Are there any other requirements that must be satisfied? Develop these "whats" into a set of "hows" and present this information in a product planning matrix.
   b. How would you use competitive benchmarking? (*Hint:* See supplement to Chapter 3.)
   c. Which items would you carry over from the product planning matrix to the part deployment matrix? Why?
   d. Develop a part deployment matrix.
   e. A good design is insensitive to a wide range of variables. Taguchi methods can be used to choose values of control factors which minimize the effect of noise factors.
      • Which key noise factors will you have to consider?
      • Which design parameters will these noise factors influence?

   • How many noise factors/design parameter combinations are there?
   • How could you use Taguchi methods to reduce the number of combinations that must be tested?

2. Select a simple product: an umbrella, knife, or briefcase.
   a. What hard and soft functions must this product serve? What is a competitive price for this product?
   b. Analyze an example of this product and create a parts list. Using Tanaka's functional evaluation system, calculate the target cost for each part.
   c. Estimate the approximate cost of each part. Are these costs close to their target costs? What does this imply? What improvements do you suggest?

3. Apply failure mode effects and criticality analysis to an overhead projector. Use your own judgment concerning the likelihood of particular failures. How serious are these failures? Make recommendations based on your analysis for improving the availability of overhead projectors in your institution.

REFERENCES AND SELECTED BIBLIOGRAPHY

Armstrong, Larry, and Karen Lowry Miller [1993], "While Toyota Loses its Hold . . . ," *Business Week,* Apr. 26, pp. 28–29.

Banker, R. D., S. M. Datar, S. Kekre, and T. Mukhopadhyay [1989], "Costs of Product and Process Complexity," working paper, Graduate School of Industrial Administration, Carnegie-Mellon University, May, pp. 1–17.

Bemowski, Karen [1992], "The Quality Glossary," *Quality Progress,* February, vol. 25, no. 2, pp. 18–29.

Case, K. E., and L. L. Jones [1978], *Profit through Quality: Quality Assurance Programs for Manufacturers,* QC & RE Monograph Series No. 2, Institute of Industrial Engineers, New York.

Ernst & Young and the American Quality Foundation [1991], *International Quality Study: Top Line Findings,* an Ernest & Young report, New York.

Ishikawa, K., and D. J. Lo (trans.) [1985], *What is Total Quality Control? The Japanese Way,* Prentice-Hall, Englewood Cliffs, N.J.

Noori, H. [1989], "The Taguchi Methods: Achieving Design and Output Quality," *Academy of Management Executive,* November, pp. 322–326.

Port, O. [1987], "How to Make It Right the First Time," *Business Week,* June 8, pp. 142–143.

Reese, Jennifer [1992], "Getting Hot Ideas from the Customers," *Fortune,* May 18, pp. 26–27.

Solo, Sally [1993], "How to Listen to Customers," *Fortune,* Jan. 11, pp. 77–78.

Taguchi, G., and D. Clausing [1990], "Robust Quality," *Harvard Business Review,* January–February, pp. 65–75.

Tanaka, Masayasu [1989], "Cost Planning and Control Systems in the Design Phase of a New Product," in Y. Mondon and M. Sakurai (eds.), *Japanese Management Accounting,* Productivity Press, Cambridge, Mass., pp. 49–71.

Womack, James P., Daniel T. Jones, and Daniel Ross [1991], *The Machine That Changed the World,* Harper-Perennial, New York.

Woodruff, David, and Karen Lowry Miller [1993], "Chrysler's Neon: Is This the Small Car Detroit Couldn't Build?," *Business Week,* May 3, pp. 116–126.

SUPPLEMENT TO

CHAPTER 6

QFD AND TAGUCHI
APPLICATIONS

S6.1 MANAGERIAL ORIENTATION

Quality function deployment (QFD) and Taguchi methods are often used in conjunction to design products and the processes by which they are made. The goal is to develop high-quality, low-cost products that meet customers' needs.

S6.2 QUALITY FUNCTION DEPLOYMENT

As was stressed in Chapter 6, product and process design teams must capture the "voice of the customer" and ensure that customers' needs dictate all design trade-offs. **Quality function deployment (QFD)** is an excellent way for a firm to meet these challenges. The next few sections will describe the four QFD phases outlined in Chapter 6, using the simple example of making chocolate chip cookies.

Phase 1: Product Planning

Phase 1: Product Planning: Customers' expectations are examined closely. These expectations become the WHATs of the product planning matrix. The WHATs are then converted into HOWs, that is, design requirements. The relationship between each HOW and each WHAT is determined. Preliminary target values are set for each HOW.

Product planning begins with the customer. What does the customer want and not want? How well do the firm's current products meet those requirements? How important is each requirement? How well do competing products satisfy customers' needs? A variety of market research techniques, including customer surveys, focus groups, and customer clinics, can be used to help the design team answer these questions.

Using customer feedback, the cross-functional design team develops a list of customers' requirements, that is, a list of WHATs that the firm wishes the product to exhibit. In this example, possible WHATs include "lots of chocolate chips," "sweet-tasting," and "chewy."

Not all requirements are directly expressed by customers. In the cookie example customers may not specify that the cookie should be baked all the way through

or should have a consistent texture; they may *assume* this. The design team may also have to supplement the customers' list to satisfy the requirements of internal or external agencies. For example, the health board may require that the cookies not contain certain chemicals or other undesirable materials.

Customers' requirements must eventually be translated into detailed design specifications. The first step toward this goal is to convert the WHATs into HOWs, or measurable product characteristics. In the cookie example, "lots of chocolate chips" can be measured by "chocolate chips per cubic inch" and "chewy" can be measured by "force needed to bite cookie." Note that the HOWs are not related to specific product concepts or product designs. They will be used, however, in the next stage to generate product concepts and evaluate product designs.

Determining the relationships between the WHATs and the HOWs is extremely important. Since each HOW can affect more than one customer requirement and since the HOW for one WHAT may have an adverse impact on another WHAT, these relationships are complex. For example, the number of chocolate chips per cubic inch affects both the "lots of chocolate chips" and the "sweet-tasting" customer requirements. The number of chocolate chips per cubic inch, however, can adversely affect a customer requirement such as "low calories." Because these relationships are so complex, failure to identify and understand the interaction between WHATs and HOWs can easily lead to product failure in the marketplace.

A preliminary target value must be set for each HOW. For example, the target value for the number of chocolate chips per cubic inch may be five, the target thickness may be $1/4$ inch, and the target force needed to bite the cookie may be 0.3 pound.

Target values provide specific, measurable objectives which guide product design and allow designs to be evaluated objectively. At this point, the results of competitive benchmarking are very helpful.[1] Engineering assessments of competing products and the firm's own products allow the firm to compare its performance with that of its competitors and set targets that reflect world-class performance.

The information generated during this phase is presented in a **product planning matrix** (see Exhibit 6S.1). This matrix illustrates the relationship between customer requirements and broad design requirements. When the HOWs, WHATs, and relationships are com-

---

[1] Refer back to the Chapter 3 Supplement for a general discussion of competitive benchmarking.

EXHIBIT 6S.1   THE BASIC PRODUCT PLANNING MATRIX: CHOCOLATE CHIP COOKIES

Customer Requirements	Chip density	Cookie thickness	Cookie size	Degree to which chips taste like chocolate	Calories per cookie	Biting force	Sweetness level	…
Lots of chocolate chips	●							
Chips taste like chocolate				●				
Sweet-tasting	○				○		●	
Chewy		○				○		
Size: about ¼ inch thick, 2½ inches in diameter		●	●					
Low calories	○							
Light brown color	Δ							
•								
•								
•								
	5 per inch³	¼ inch	2 inches³	9	100	0.3 ft-lb	6	…

Relationships
● Strong
○ Medium
Δ Weak

EXHIBIT 6S.2   EXTENDED VERSION OF THE PRODUCTION PLANNING MATRIX

		Correlation Matrix			
		Orientation Row			
		HOWS			
WHATS	Importance Rating	RELATIONSHIPS		Service Complaints	Customer Rating
		Organization Difficulty			
		Objective Target Values			
		Competitive Assessment Graphs			
		Service Repairs			
		Service Cost			
		Important Controls			

bined into one matrix, people with different backgrounds and from different areas of the company can easily read and understand them.

WHATs are listed on the left-hand side of the matrix, HOWs are shown at the top, and the strength of the relationship between each HOW and each WHAT is depicted by one of the symbols in the body of the matrix. If there is no relationship, the box is left blank.

A blank row in a product planning matrix indicates that a customer requirement, or WHAT, has no corresponding HOWs. At least one HOW must be added for each blank row to ensure that the corresponding WHAT will be fulfilled by the product design. A blank column, by contrast, indicates that a feature not listed as a customer requirement may creep into the product design. These HOWs are unnecessary and should be eliminated.   **181**

↟ max. ↡ min. • target		Chip Density	Cookie Thickness	Cookie Size	Degree to Which Chips Taste Like Chocolate	Calories per Cookie	Biting Force	Sweetness Level		Service Complaints	Customer Rating 1 2 3 4 5
Design Requirements		•	•	•	↟	↡	•	•	•		
Customer Requirements	Importance								•		
Lots of chocolate chips	8	●									A B
Chips taste like chocolate	8				●						B A
Sweet-tasting	6	○				○		●			B A
Chewy	5		○				●				A B
Size: about ¼" thick, 2½ inches diameter	3,3		●	●							A B B A
Low calories	2	○									A B
Light brown color	3		▶								B A
Organization Difficulty		1	3	3	5	4	3	5			
Objective Target Values		5 per inch³	¼ inch	2 inch³	9	100	0.3 ft lbs	6			
Engineering Competitive Assessment	Better 5 4 3 2 Worse 1	A,B	A B	A,B	A B	A,B	B A	A B			
Important Controls	Does not contain any unlisted ingredients										

Relationships
● Strong
○ Medium
▶ Weak

Correlations
• Strongly Positive
○ Positive
x Negative
Strongly Negative

A number of extensions can be made to the basic product planning matrix illustrated in Exhibit 6S.1. The general format of an extended product planning matrix is shown in Exhibit 6S.2. (This matrix is often called the **house of quality** because of the rooflike structure at its top.) Most of these extensions have been added to the revised chocolate chip cookie matrix as well (see Exhibit 6S.3). While going through this additional information, keep in mind that not all this information is always relevant. It is better to have a simple matrix that is easy to read than one cluttered with too many data.

- A *correlation matrix* which shows the relationship between each pair of HOWs can be added to the top of the matrix.

  If there is a strong positive relationship between two or more HOWs, it may be possible to eliminate a HOW.

  A strong negative relationship between two or more HOWs indicates that the design requirements are not compatible. R&D or innovation efforts designed to resolve these incompatibilities are therefore needed (and often lead to significant breakthroughs and new competitive advantages). If, however, incompatibilities cannot be resolved, trade-offs may be necessary.

- An *orientation row* can be added above the HOW section to indicate the direction in which each HOW should be optimized: as small as possible ($\downarrow$), as large as possible ($\uparrow$), or as close to the target as possible ($\bullet$).

  In the cookie example the firm wants to maximize the "degree to which chips taste like chocolate," minimize the "number of calories per cubic inch," and get as close as possible to the target for "thickness."

- *Competitive assessment graphs* illustrate how competitive products compare with the firm's current products. Customer ratings are used to compare competitors' performance on WHATs, a technical analysis carried out by engineers is employed to evaluate competitors' performance on HOWs, and the results of the technical analysis are frequently used to set "how much" values.

  Two other brands of chocolate chip cookies were analyzed by the cookie company. Neither one met all the customers' requirements.

- *Importance ratings* indicate the relative importance of each WHAT and each HOW and can be expressed using a scale of 1 to 10. When trade-offs have to be made, importance ratings can be valuable.

  The importance of each WHAT can be ascertained through market research. The importance of each HOW can be calculated by assigning weights to each relationship and then using equation (6S.1).

$$I - HOW_j = \sum_{k=1}^{n} RW_{j,k} I - WHAT_k \qquad (6S.1)$$

where $I - HOW_j$ = importance rating assigned to jth HOW
$RW_{j,k}$ = weight assigned to relationship between jth HOW and kth WHAT

Note that for each k,

$$0\% \leq RW_{j,k} \leq 100\% \qquad \sum_{j=1}^{n} RW_{j,k} = 1$$

$I - WHAT_k$ = importance rating assigned to kth WHAT

In the cookie example, the "chip density" HOW is related to two WHATs: "lots of chocolate chips" and "sweet-tasting." These WHATs have been assigned importance ratings of 8 and 6, respectively. The relationship weights shown below reflect the strength of the WHAT-HOW relationships.

What	How	Relationship Weight, %
Lots of chocolate chips	Chip density	100
Sweet-tasting	Chip density	20
	Calories per cookie	20
	Sweetness level	60

Therefore, the importance of "chip density" is equal to $(100\% \times 8) + (20\% \times 6) = 9.2$.

- The *service complaints* column helps designers identify problems with current products. Warranty information and reliability data are reflected in the *service repairs* and *service cost* rows.

  This information does not apply to the cookie example, because no cookies have been made yet.

- The relative difficulty of accomplishing each HOW is shown in the *organization difficulty* row.

  In this example, "sweetness level" and "degree to which chips taste like chocolate" represent the greatest degree of organization difficulty because it is very hard to measure these factors objectively. Conversely, "chip density" is simple to measure and control.

- *Important controls* are additional requirements demanded by the firm or by outside regulatory agencies. "Does not contain any unlisted ingredients," for example, may be a requirement demanded by the health board.

The product planning matrix is the best known of the QFD matrixes and is frequently the only one developed. If the firm really wants its product and process design efforts to focus on the voice of the customer, however, it must go beyond phase 1 and the product planning matrix.

Phase 2: Part Deployment

Phase 2: Part Deployment: The HOWs of the product planning matrix become the WHATs of the part deployment matrix. Alternative design concepts are developed and compared using these WHATs. Once the best design has been chosen, the parts that make up the product are studied. The characteristics essential to accomplishing the purpose of each part become the HOWs of the part deployment matrix and are studied further.

If a HOW is new, critical to the product's success, or difficult to accomplish, it is carried over to the **part deployment matrix**. The corresponding HOW MUCH values and importance ratings are transferred to this matrix as well.

The selected HOWs are expressed in more detail and form the WHATs of the part deployment matrix. The part deployment list of WHATs is supplemented by a list of functional requirements that are critical to the product's design but have not been identified by the customers. Product requirements meant to delight the customer with unexpected features that meet unexpressed needs may also be added by the team.

Continuing with the cookie example, the firm has decided to transfer the "thickness," "sweetness," and "chip density" HOWs to the part deployment list of WHATs. Extensive research has shown that a "subtle taste of rum" will delight the customers with something just a little different, and so it has been added as a WHAT.

Design teams must use extreme caution, however, when they add design requirements not specified by the customer. Cluttering up the product with features not wanted by the customer often backfires because these features make the product more complicated than it needs to be; the consumer is intimidated rather than delighted. Electronic equipment is an excellent example. The adage "If the clock on the VCR isn't flashing, a teenager must live here" is very often true. Mind you, we now have a VCR whose clock is automatically set!

The design requirements are used by the team members as they develop alternative product design concepts. A very detailed examination of competitors' products is often performed at this stage to help the team generate more alternatives and superior designs.

Once a design concept has been chosen, a list of parts [i.e., a bill of materials (BOM)] is examined. In the cookie example the design concept consists of the list of ingredients shown in Exhibit 6S.4A.

In the next step the characteristics essential to ac-

complishing the purpose of each part or ingredient and the product are identified. For example, the baking soda ensures that the cookie dough rises. Having the margarine and shortening at room temperature ensures that they are soft enough to blend but not so soft that the dough is too thin (and hence the cookie is too thin and burns). These part characteristics are referred to as critical part characteristics and become the HOWs of the part deployment matrix. Exhibit 6S.4B shows the part deployment matrix developed for the cookie example.

The relationship between each HOW and each WHAT is studied next, and target values for each HOW are established. Techniques such as design failure mode analysis, fault tree analysis, and Taguchi methods are helpful during this stage.

The critical part characteristics that are sensitive to manufacturing and/or environmental variations are carried over to the next QFD chart, the process planning matrix.

Phase 3: Process Planning

Phase 3: Process Planning: Selected critical part characteristics form the WHATs of the process planning matrix. During this QFD phase, the WHATs are translated into a set of critical process parameters. The goal of this phase is to design a process that can consistently produce products whose parts meet the targets that have been set.

Alternative process designs are analyzed and compared, and the best design is chosen. The basic process elements are identified, and a master flow diagram is used to illustrate the relationships between incoming materials and the basic process elements. The process chosen for the cookies is described in Exhibit 6S.5A and illustrated by the master flow diagram in Exhibit 6S.5B. Note that the master flow diagram reflects the constraints under which the process will operate.

The relationships depicted in the master flow diagram help the design teams identify process parameters critical to each operation. Again, techniques such as process fault trees and Taguchi methods can be used to identify process parameters and establish their target values.

The master flow diagram and the critical process parameters become the HOWs of the **process planning matrix** (Exhibit 6S.5C). The effect of controlling each critical parameter on each critical part characteristic is depicted in the relationship area.

Process parameters that are difficult to control or require new procedures or special control systems are carried over to the production planning matrix.

Phase 4: Production Planning: Selected process parameeters become the WHATs of the *production planning matrix.* The difficulty of controlling each WHAT, the frequency and severity of expected problems, and the ability to detect problems are then evaluated. Planning requirements and operating information corresponding to each WHAT, such as quality control charts and training requirements, are then examined and translated into shop floor instructions.

In the cookie example (see Exhibit 6S.6), possible shop floor instructions include "make sure all ingredients are mixed well," "monitor the oven to ensure it is heating evenly," "keep the batter between 50 and 60 degrees Fahrenheit as it waits to be placed in the oven," and "cookie sheets must be cool before the dough is placed on them."

Thus, the list of customer requirements has been

converted gradually into a product design, a process design, and a set of shop floor instructions.

Reminder. QFD is a flexible process. The QFD matrixes are tools for presenting information and should be adapted to the firm's needs. This flexibility makes QFD a useful design methodology for designers of goods and services.

Even in this straightforward example, QFD is a logical but painstaking and potentially confusing process. Most products for which QFD is used are more complex. To ensure its success, therefore, a comprehensive training program is essential before the design team begins to use QFD. And because the process can take several months and requires input from many functional areas, top and middle-level managers must be convinced of its value.

EXHIBIT 6S.4 THE PART DEPLOYMENT MATRIX: CHOCOLATE CHIP COOKIES

A. Bill of Materials

The list of design requirements has been used to develop a number of different recipes (i.e., product designs). The recipes were evaluated, and the best one was chosen. The bill of materials corresponding to the best recipe is shown below:

Item	Quantity	Item	Quantity
Baking soda	$1/2$ tsp	Rum flavoring	1 tbsp
Chocolate chips, semisweet	6 oz	Salt	$1/2$ tsp
Egg	1	Shortening	$1/3$ cup
Flour	$1 1/2$ cups	Sugar, brown	$1/2$ cup
Margarine	$1/3$ cup	Sugar, white	$1/2$ cup

B. Part Deployment Matrix

Design Requirements	Target Value	Importance	Quantity of Baking Soda	Temperature of Margarine	Temperature of Shortening	Quantity of Chocolate Chips	Quantity of Rum Flavoring	• • •
Thickness	$1/4$ inch	5	●	○	○			
Sweetness level	6	6				●		
Chip density	5 per cubic inch	9.2				●		
Rum taste level	1	5					●	
• • •								
Relationships ● Strong	Target Values		$1/4$ tsp	72°F	72°F	6 oz	1 tbsp	• • •
○ Medium ▷ Weak	Importance		4	5	5	7	6	• • •

A. Activity List and Network Diagrams for the Selected Process

Activity

A. Preheat oven to 375°

B. Mix wet ingredients
   B1: Measure and melt shortening to 72°
   B2: Add shortening to bowl
   B3: Measure and melt margarine to 72°
   B4: Add margarine to bowl
   B5: Measure brown sugar and add to bowl
   B6: Measure white sugar and add to bowl
   B7: Beat ingredients in bowl
   B8: Break egg and add to bowl
   B9: Measure rum and add to bowl
   B10: Stir ingredients in bowl

C. Mix dry ingredients
   C1: Measure flour and add to bowl

Activity

   C2: Measure baking soda and add to bowl
   C3: Measure salt and add to bowl
   C4: Stir ingredients in bowl

D. Add chocolate chips
   D1: Measure chocolate chips and add to bowl
   D2: Stir ingredients in bowl

E. Roll into balls
   E1: Shape batter into a set of balls, each ¾ inch
       in diameter
   E2: Place balls on baking sheets, 3 inches apart

F. Bake in oven for 10 minutes

G. Remove from oven; cool for 5 minutes

H. Remove from baking sheet and place in container

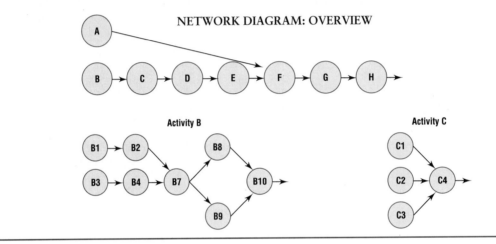

NETWORK DIAGRAM: OVERVIEW

S6.3 TAGUCHI'S OFF-LINE QUALITY CONTROL METHODS

The intent of Taguchi's off-line quality control methods is to improve product quality while reducing product costs. Taguchi's three-step procedure achieves this by focusing on product and process design. The aim is to produce a "robust" product whose quality holds despite uncontrollable environmental variation.

System Design

Step 1: System Design: Using customers' requirements and the firm's internal capabilities, an initial product design is developed. The de-

sign includes settings for parameters that affect the value of performance characteristics.

Suppose a firm is designing a new car and using the QFD methodology. The customer research done during the first QFD stage indicates that steering responsiveness is one of the key performance characteristics of a car. The team engineer establishes the fact that 13 critical design parameters affect steering responsiveness, including spring stiffness, shock absorber stiffness, and the dimensions of the steering mechanism. The firm sets preliminary target values for these and the other 10 design parameters and then develops an initial design for the steering system. This and all other systems are used in developing an initial design for the car itself.

B. Master Flow Diagram

Although many activities can be done concurrently, assume that only one person is available. Also assume that each batch is made separately and that the oven is large enough to accommodate several cookie sheets.

The master flow diagram below depicts the order in which the worker should perform the activities. The ▽ represents incoming material.

A → B1 → B2 → B3 → B4 → B5 → B6 → B7 → B8 → B9 → B10 → C1 → C2 → C3 → C4 → D1 → D2 → E1 → E2 → F → G → H

C. Process Planning Matrix

Master Flow Diagram					
O-- --O-- --O-- --O-- --O--					

Relationships ● Strong ○ Medium ▷ Weak			Activity A	Activity B1	Activity B2	Activity B3	● ● ●	Activity C2	● ● ●
Critical Parts and Part Characteristics	Target Value	Importance							
Quantity of baking soda	¼ tsp	4						●	
Temperature of shortening	72°F	5		●					
Temperature of margarine	72°F	4				●			
⋮									
Process capability			✓	✓	✓			✓	
Critical process parameter values				Heat at 70° for 80 seconds		Heat at 70° for 70 seconds		±5%	
Importance			2	6	5	6		4	

Parameter Design

Step 2: Parameter Design:[2] The factors that contribute most to variation in the end product are identified. A set of experiments is used to determine the settings that minimize the sensitivity of engineering designs to the sources of variation, that is, minimize the expected loss to society.

Once the system has been designed, the firm must establish which parameters have the greatest influence on the sensitivity of steering responsiveness. To determine this, it has to conduct experiments that involve all the factors influencing steering responsiveness. This supplement has identified 13 critical design parameters, but there are other factors whose settings are beyond the control of the designers. These variables, which include factors such as weather, road conditions, and tire pressure, are called *sources of noise* by Taguchi. What the designers want to do is identify design parameter settings that are the least influenced by noise and will make steering responsiveness least sensitive to noise.

A simple set of experiments would have the designers test their initial parameter settings against various combinations of noise levels and then repeat the experiments, varying the settings of each design parameter.

[2] Of Taguchi's three steps, U.S. companies have applied parameter design the most frequently.

Process Parameters	Critical Processes	Critical Process Parameter Values	Process Capability	Importance	Operation Evaluation					Planning Requirements			Operator Information	
					Difficulty	Frequency	Severity	Ability to Detect	Total Points	Quality Control Chart	Preventive Maintenance Standards	Education and Training Requirements	Job Instructions	Labor Time
A		Heat to 375°	✓	5	1	2	2	2	40	✓	✓	✓	✓	0.1
B	B1	Heat at 70° for 80 seconds	✓	5	2	1	1	1	10			✓	✓	1.5
		•												
		•												
		•												
C														
D														
E	E1 E2	• • • Place on cool cookie sheet	✓	6	2	1	2	1	24			✓	✓	0.4
F														
G														
H														

Legend for Operation Evaluation
1 = not critical
2 = critical
3 = very critical

Total points = Importance × difficulty × frequency × severity × ability to detect

Unfortunately, a classic full factorial set of experiments for the 13 design parameters in each of three settings (initial, lower, and higher) would require 3^{13}, or 1,594,323, separate experiments. If each experiment took 30 minutes, so that the firm was doing 80 experiments per week, it would take one team 19,929 weeks, or over 383 years, to complete the experiments. Needless to say, this form of experimental design is impractical for this number of variables.

Taguchi uses a partial factorial experimental procedure to dramatically reduce the number of experiments that have to be carried out without incurring a material loss of information from the experiments.[3] In Exhibit 6S.7 Taguchi's orthogonal arrays have reduced the experiments from over 1.5 million to 27.

> Caution. Once designers are more experienced with the product and the process by which it is produced, Taguchi's shortcut approach is no longer appropriate. A more comprehensive approach (i.e., testing all combinations of a particular set of variables) is needed to fine-tune the parameter settings.

These statistically designed experiments are also used to identify design parameter settings that reduce costs without hurting quality, do not have a detectable influence on other design parameters, or have a large influence on the mean value of the performance characteristic but have no effect on its variation.[4] Design parameters that fall into the last category can be used to adjust the mean value. Suppose, for example, using an expensive spring will result in steering responsiveness values very close to the target. A cheaper spring is also available, but it results in steering responsiveness values that are consistently 20 percent above the target. If another design parameter (say, suspension stiffness) can be used to lower the steering responsiveness values to the target, the firm can use the cheaper spring.

Tolerance Design

Step 3: Tolerance Design: Acceptable tolerances around the target design parameter values set in step 2 are determined.

Taguchi's methods have a significant effect on product cost by identifying which parameters need tight tolerances and therefore require relatively expensive manufacturing processes. The only design parameters in this category are those whose variation still results in sig-

---

[3] Taguchi's orthogonal arrays are not new; they were first used by the English statistician R. A. Fisher in his efforts to find quick methods of sorting through large quantities of data gathered during crop trials. Taguchi's developments are being extended and improved by North American researchers, and others will follow them.

[4] See Kackar (1985), p. 28.

EXHIBIT 6S.7 TOOLBOX: TAGUCHI METHODS

The steering responsiveness performance characteristic is influenced by 13 critical design parameters. Each column of the design parameter matrix below corresponds to one of these parameters. For example, the first column corresponds with spring stiffness. Each row of the array represents a different combination of the parameter settings.

Note that the three levels of each design parameter are exposed to the three levels of the other 12 factors an equal number of times.

Next, noise factors that significantly affect a car's steering responsiveness are identified and a noise factor matrix is developed. Each column of this matix corresponds to a noise factor, and each row corresponds to different combinations of noise levels. For example, the first row may represent a combination of high tire pressure, rough road, and high temperature.

Each experiment (row in the design parameter matrix) is run four times: once under each combination of noise factors. The value of the performance characteristic—steering responsiveness—is observed for each run. The results of these four runs are used to compute a signal (the desired value of the performance characteristic) to noise ratio.

STEERING RESPONSIVENESS: DESIGN PARAMETER MATRIX

Parameter Setting
 1 = initial setting
 2 = higher setting
 3 = lower setting

Experiment Combination Number	Parameter Setting												
	P_1	P_2	P_3	P_4	P_5	P_6	P_7	P_8	P_9	P_{10}	P_{11}	P_{12}	P_{13}
1	1	1	1	1	1	1	1	1	1	1	1	1	1
2	1	1	1	1	2	2	2	2	2	2	2	2	2
3	1	1	1	1	3	3	3	3	3	3	3	3	3
4	1	2	2	2	1	1	1	2	2	2	3	3	3
5	1	2	2	2	2	2	2	3	3	3	1	1	1
6	1	2	2	2	3	3	3	1	1	1	2	2	2
7	1	3	3	3	1	1	1	3	3	3	2	2	2
8	1	3	3	3	2	2	2	1	1	1	3	3	3
9	1	3	3	3	3	3	3	2	2	2	1	1	1
10	2	1	2	3	1	2	3	1	2	3	1	2	3
11	2	1	2	3	2	3	1	2	3	1	2	3	1
12	2	1	2	3	3	1	2	3	1	2	3	1	2
13	2	2	3	1	1	2	3	2	3	1	3	1	2
14	2	2	3	1	2	3	1	3	1	2	1	2	3
15	2	2	3	1	3	1	2	1	2	3	2	3	1
16	2	3	1	2	1	2	3	3	1	2	2	3	1
17	2	3	1	2	2	3	1	1	2	3	3	1	2
18	2	3	1	2	3	1	2	2	3	1	1	2	3
19	3	1	3	2	1	3	2	1	3	2	1	3	2
20	3	1	3	2	2	1	3	2	1	3	2	1	3
21	3	1	3	2	3	2	1	3	2	1	3	2	1
22	3	2	1	3	1	3	2	2	1	3	3	2	1
23	3	2	1	3	2	1	3	3	2	1	1	3	2
24	3	2	1	3	3	2	1	1	3	2	2	1	3
25	3	3	2	1	1	3	2	3	2	1	2	1	3
26	3	3	2	1	2	1	3	1	3	2	3	2	1
27	3	3	2	1	3	2	1	2	1	3	1	3	2

(Exhibit 6S.7 continues on next page)

NOISE FACTORS MATRIX					RESULTS MATRIX					
Combination Number	*Noise Factor*			Experiment	*Noise Combinations*				Signal to Noise Ratio
	NF$_1$	NF$_2$	NF$_3$		1	2	3	4	
1	1	1	1	1					32.7
2	1	2	2	2					33
3	2	1	2	3					31.5
4	2	2	1	•					•
				•					•
				•					•
				27					28.5

The formula used to calculate the signal-to-noise (S/N) ratio depends on the situation, but all the formulas are directly tied to Taguchi's QLF. In all cases the larger the S/N ratio, the better. Therefore, for each design parameter, the setting which results in the highest average S/N ratio is selected.

Suppose, for example, the average S/N ratio when the spring stiffness is at its initial setting is 32.4. A stiffer setting results in an average S/N ratio of 26.7, and the average ratio for a softer setting is 28.9. For steering responsiveness, the initial setting is the best setting.

Source: Adapted from Taguchi and Clausing (1990), pp. 65–75.

nificant variation in the product's performance characteristics. This is a significant departure from the very expensive but not uncommon strategy of tightening all tolerances to increase quality and thus increasing manufacturing costs. It is also a departure from the common practice of establishing tolerances by convention—that is, tolerances based on engineering judgment, general rule-based methods, or "the best we can hold" on a particular dimension—rather than scientifically.

The resultant product will have acceptably low levels of product variation despite fluctuations in materials, manufacturing (equipment, operators), and environmental conditions. Since performance variation is minimized by *reducing the influence of* the sources of variation rather than by *controlling* those sources, the Taguchi method is cost-effective.

Perspectives on Taguchi

Taguchi methods can be applied to both product and process design, but Taguchi indicates that product design is by far the more effective area in which to apply the technique.[5]

The lack of sophistication of Taguchi's experiments has been criticized, but American companies that use his methods are reporting substantial cost savings. ITT, for example, has saved over $35 million. The Taguchi method is even being incorporated into the computer-aided engineering (CAE) systems designers use to ensure that robustness is designed into products from the very beginning.

[5] See Ealey (1987), p. 23.

KEY TERMS

Quality function deployment (QFD)
Product planning matrix

House of quality
Part deployment matrix
Process planning matrix

Production planning matrix
System design

Parameter design
Tolerance design

REFERENCES AND SELECTED BIBLIOGRAPHY

American Supplier Institute, Inc. [1989], *Quality Function Deployment: Implementation Manual for Three-Day QFD Workshop, Version 3.4,* Dearborn, Mich.

Ealey, L. [1987], "Nipponsdenso: Hot Bed of Taguchi Methods," *Automotive Industries,* July, p. 23.

Kakar, Raghu N. [1985], "Off-Line Quality Control 'Parameter Design' and the Taguchi Method," *Journal of Quality Technology,* October, pp. 176–188.

—— [1986], "Taguchi's Quality Philosophy: Analysis and Commentary," *Quality Progress,* December, pp. 21–29.

Lowray, Miller, and Karen and David Woodruff [1991], "A Design Master's End Run around Trial and Error," *Business Week,* Oct. 25, p. 24.

Maddux, Gary A., Richard W. Amos, and Alan R. Wyskida [1991], "Organizations Can Apply Quality Function Deployment as Strategic Planning Tool," *Industrial Engineering,* September, pp. 33–37.

McElroy, John [1987], "For Whom Are We Building Cars?" *Automotive Industries,* June, pp. 63–70.

Noori, Hamid [1989], "The Taguchi Methods: Achieving Design and Output Quality," *The Academy of Management Executive,* November, pp. 322–326.

Port, O. [1987], "How to Make It Right the First Time," *Business Week,* June 8, pp. 142–143.

Port, Otis, and John Carrey [1991], "Quality: A Field with Roots That Go Back to the Farm," *Business Week,* Oct. 25, p. 15.

Reese, Jennifer [1992], "Getting Hot Ideas from the Customer," *Fortune,* May 18, pp. 26–27.

Sullivan, L. P. [1984], "Reducing Variability: A New Approach to Quality," *Quality Progress,* July, pp. 15–21.

——— [1986], "Quality Function Deployment," *Quality Progress,* June, pp. 39–50.

——— [1986], "The Seven Stages in Company Wide Quality Control," *Quality Progress,* May, pp. 77–83.

Sullivan, Lawrence P. [1987], "The Power of Taguchi Methods," *Quality Progress,* June, pp. 76–79.

Taguchi, G., and D. Clausing [1990], "Robust Quality," *Harvard Business Review,* January–February, pp. 65–75.

Verity, John W., and Jessie Nathans [1991], "I Can't Work This Thing!," *Business Week,* Apr. 29, pp. 58–59.

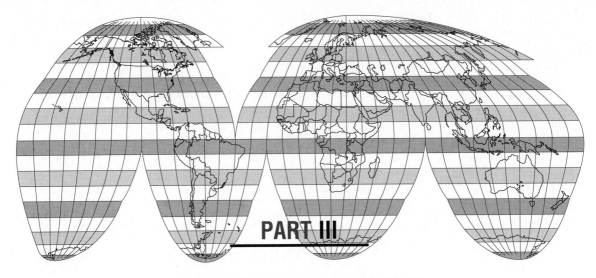

PART III

DESIGNING AND BUILDING
FAST-RESPONSE ORGANIZATIONS

Setting the Stage

The most visible aspects of a firm's operations strategy are the physical, structural elements. How much capacity is needed? Where should facilities be located? How should each facility be designed and What technology is required? are questions that must be answered once the needs and expectations of the customers are known. Because these elements are expensive to put in place and may be difficult, costly, and time-consuming to change, their design is critical. The best sequence for thinking about these issues is to start *big* and finish *small*. A good starting point is a proper understanding of market characteristics and future trends.

Chapter 7 is devoted to capacity strategy: a firm's long-range plan for satisfying the overall demand for its goods and services. The size of capacity increments, the timing of these increments, and the degree of vertical integration sought are all elements of a firm's capacity strategy. Chapter 8 discusses techniques for choosing the location of a new facility and arranging the operating elements within a facility.

Chapter 9 is the first of three chapters concerned with the operating process. This chapter looks first at the strategic relationship between products and processes and then at the relationship between technology and processes. Chapter 10 examines the relationship both between people and processes and between materials and processes.

Chapter 11 is devoted to process quality: how firms define, manage, and measure quality in processes. Note that there is an inherent relationship between the design of a product and the design of a process to produce the product in accordance with its specifications. Thus, Chapter 11 is related to Chapter 6.

Keep in mind that the transformation process aims at integrating machines, people, materials, and time in the provision of products or services that are of value to customers. These relationships are complex, and integrating them is difficult. It is particularly difficult as a firm continually refines or changes products to better suit the needs of its customers. Just as product quality underlay Part II, process quality underlies Part III. The absence of process quality will seriously jeopardize the ability of the operating elements to support a firm's strategy and help the firm attain its goals.

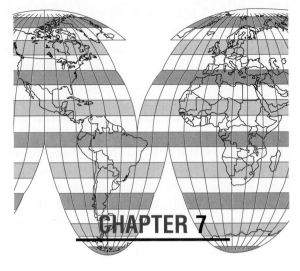

CHAPTER 7

CAPACITY STRATEGY

Chapter 4 described how a firm estimates when, where, and how much of its goods and services will be demanded in the future. The next important issue is how the firm can satisfy this expected demand. To address this issue, several important questions have to be discussed:

- How much capacity does the firm need to satisfy anticipated market demand? When is this capacity required?
- How much capacity does the firm have?
- If the current capacity is inadequate, how will the firm enhance or augment it? How should the firm deal with any additional capacity it may have?

These questions provide the starting point for capacity planning. This chapter will introduce capacity planning and underline its strategic importance. By the end of the chapter you will be able to describe the considerations that influence capacity and vertical integration strategies and be able to prescribe outline strategies for a number of competitive situations.

EXHIBIT 7.1   FRO MANUFACTURING PROFILE

While other companies reacted slowly to changes in the transformer market, Electronic Craftsmen Limited (ECL) of Waterloo, Ontario, repositioned itself as a specialist in the field of telecommunication magnetics. ECL soon established itself as a leader in innovative design techniques. Sales for its custom-designed products were growing at a steady rate of 25 percent per year. But when ECL learned that one of its customers was prepared to offer ECL a contract more than 10 times the size of a normal order as well as sole supplier status, ECL hesitated.

At the time ECL was operating at nearly full capacity and turning down orders. The plant was overcrowded, and attempts to add an extra shift would have been disastrous. If the new order was accepted, it would outstrip existing capacity and other customers and orders would suffer. But refusing the order would reduce ECL's credibility. Since requests for ECL to quote on larger production volumes were becoming more frequent, the capacity problem was becoming worse and worse.

EXHIBIT 7.2   FRO SERVICE PROFILE

When Naina Yeltsin, wife of Russian President Boris Yeltsin, officially opened the third McDonald's restaurant in Moscow on July 3, 1993, it was another milestone on the road to McDonald's planned 20 restaurants in the Russian capital. The joint venture between McDonald's Restaurants of Canada and the Moscow City Council, Moscow McDonald's, had its inception before the 1976 Olympics held in Montreal. Since 1988 McDonald's has spent over $65 million on the three restaurants (including the 700-seat restaurant off Gorki Square which opened in 1990), a 12-story office tower, and a modern food-processing plant for processing beef, buns, and dairy products. This latter facility, along with the vertical integration that is unique to the McDonald's system, was required, for nothing in Russia could meet McDonald's capacity needs or quality standards.

McDonald's also invested heavily in developing the staff, sending managers to North America for training before selecting and training local associates. This training was essential both to immerse people in the McDonald's philosophy and to ensure that they are able to maintain the product throughput and serve the customers at the planned rates. And the demand is high: the Gorki Square restaurant serves over 40,000 customers a day.

Source: Adapted from Canadian Press (1993) and Foster (1991), pp. 51–65.

195

7.1 MANAGERIAL ORIENTATION

Should the Mayo Clinic[1] build another satellite facility or enlarge its Rochester, Minnesota, operation? Should Milliken build another plant before its competitors do or wait a few more years? Should Milliken build one large plant or several smaller ones? These are the "brick and mortar" questions that need to be addressed by managers as they devise a firm's **capacity strategy.**

> **DEFINITION:** A capacity strategy is a long-range plan that details how a firm will satisfy the demand for its goods and services.

Investments in facilities, operating processes, and workforces are strategic in nature and tend to be made at the highest levels of the firm. This is the case because facilities and other resources tend to be expensive and take years to set in place and years to alter significantly. As Exhibit 7.1 demonstrates, capacity decisions significantly affect a firm's ability to compete. Electronic Craftsmen Limited (ECL) clearly did not have sufficient capacity to respond quickly to market needs and thus was in danger of losing its market niche. Earlier decisions regarding the size of its facility and location severely restricted ECL's current set of short-term and immediate-term options.

This chapter will look at several different capacity strategies firms can follow and the issues managers should consider as they decide which strategy to adopt. It will also review the issues firms such as McDonald's (Exhibit 7.2) consider when they make upstream (backward) integration decisions. First, let us discuss how firms can measure their available capacity. Once available capacity is measured, firms can make plans for bridging the gap between available capacity and the capacity needed to meet marketplace demands.

7.2 MEASURING CAPACITY

> **DEFINITION:** Capacity is the ability of a worker, machine, work center, process, plant, or organization to produce output per unit of time.[2]

The **capacity** of a process that produces a narrow range of products usually is expressed as a rate of output per unit of time. A brewery, for example, may measure its output in terms of cases of beer produced per day. A power-generating utility such as Florida Power and Light (see the Startup Chapter) may measure its output in terms of megawatts of electricity produced per year.

Expressing capacity as an output rate is difficult when a variety of products that require different resource levels are produced; the output rate will depend on the product mix and batch sizes. In these circumstances capacity can be measured by units of input available. For example, a hospital may measure its capacity by the number of available beds per day. An accounting firm or a manufacturer of custom-designed jewelry may use the number of labor hours available per month to measure its capacity.

When a process consists of a set series of operations, its capacity is determined by the slowest operation in the sequence. The capacity-limiting operation is called the **bottleneck operation.**

---

[1] The Mayo Clinic and Milliken were toured in the Startup Chapter.

[2] American Production and Inventory Control Society (APICS) definition.

DEFINITION: *Design capacity* is the maximum possible rate of output for a process given the current product designs, product mix, operating policies, workforce, facility, and equipment.

DEFINITION: *Effective capacity* is the highest reasonable output rate that can be achieved.

Effective capacity is generally lower than design capacity because time is needed to perform tasks such as doing preventive maintenance and making adjustments when a firm is changing from one product to another. At Earl's Custom Furniture Shop (see Exhibit 7.3) effective capacity is about 88 percent of design capacity,[3] and the shop's **actual capacity** is much lower than its design capacity.

DEFINITION: Actual capacity is the output rate achieved by the process.

Not only is the actual output rate achieved by a process usually lower than the effective capacity, actual capacity fluctuates over time. Machine breakdowns, scrap and rework, limited tooling, employee absenteeism, poor scheduling, and the like all contribute to lowering actual capacity rates. The lower the actual output of a process, the lower its **capacity utilization** [equation (7.1)] and **capacity efficiency** [equation (7.2)].

---

[3] As a rule of thumb, effective capacity is about 85 percent of design capacity.

EXHIBIT 7.3 TOOLBOX: CAPACITY, UTILIZATION, AND EFFICIENCY

Earl Rickman designs and manufactures wooden desks. He works five days a week, eight hours a day, and takes four weeks of vacation every year. On average, each desk takes Earl about 20 hours from start to finish. Earl also spends about three hours a week on preventive maintenance and two hours picking up supplies.

DESIGN CAPACITY

$$\frac{(5 \text{ days per week})(8 \text{ hours per day})(48 \text{ weeks per year})}{20 \text{ hours per desk}} = \frac{1{,}920 \text{ hours per year}}{20 \text{ hours per desk}} = 96 \text{ desks per year}$$

Therefore, the maximum possible rate of output for Earl's shop is 96 desks a year. The effective capacity, however, is much lower. Five hours a week, or 240 hours a year, is spent on preventive maintenance and picking up supplies.

EFFECTIVE CAPACITY

$$\frac{(1{,}920 - 240) \text{ hours per year}}{20 \text{ hours per desk}} = \frac{1{,}680 \text{ hours per year}}{20 \text{ hours per desk}} = 84 \text{ desks per year}$$

The actual capacity of Earl's shop is even lower than the effective capacity. Unexpected machine breakdowns, sick time, rework, and the like, account for about 200 hours per year.

ACTUAL CAPACITY

$$\frac{(1{,}680 - 200) \text{ hours per year}}{20 \text{ hours per desk}} = \frac{1{,}480 \text{ hours per year}}{20 \text{ hours per desk}} = 74 \text{ desks per year}$$

Using equations (7.1) and (7.2), it is possible to find the utilization and efficiency of the shop:

$$\text{Utilization} = \frac{74 \text{ desks per year}}{96 \text{ desks per year}} = 0.771, \text{ or } 77.1 \text{ percent}$$

$$\text{Efficiency} = \frac{74 \text{ desks per year}}{84 \text{ desks per year}} = 0.881, \text{ or } 88.1 \text{ percent}$$

Capacity Utilization and Efficiency

$$\text{Utilization} = \frac{\text{Actual capacity}}{\text{Design capacity}} \qquad (7.1)$$

$$\text{Efficiency} = \frac{\text{Actual capacity}}{\text{Effective capacity}} \qquad (7.2)$$

Once a realistic estimate of available capacity for a process has been developed, it can be compared with the capacity requirements for that process. Capacity requirements are generated from demand forecasts. The difference between available capacity and required capacity for a process is referred to as the **capacity gap** (insufficient capacity) or the **capacity slack** (excess capacity).

7.3 ADJUSTING CAPACITY LEVELS OVER THE PLANNING HORIZON

How should a firm adjust its capacity levels? In the short and intermediate terms a firm can build or run down inventory levels, work overtime or undertime, expand or contract the workforce, add or remove another complete shift, change the product mix, subcontract work, and so on. As was noted earlier, continuous improvements to the operating process, the facility, and product designs are other sources of increased capacity. (At Florida Power and Light, for example, quality improvements resulted in an equivalent capacity gain of 700 MW of electricity. See the Startup Chapter.)

Typically, providing the capacity to meet short-term and intermediate-term needs is achieved by means of aggregate planning and detailed scheduling systems; Chapters 14 and 17 will be devoted to each of these topics. The focus of this chapter is long-term capacity planning.

In the long run a firm has a wide range of options. It can build or lease one or more additional facilities, expand the existing facility, or relocate the existing facility to a larger one. Goods or services that were produced internally can be purchased. The firm can even buy another company. Developing new applications of advanced technology is another option. (This is one of the options chosen by Electronic Craftsmen Limited in Exhibit 7.1 to increase its capacity.) Alternatively, if the firm wishes to downsize, it can sell one or more facilities, relocate to a smaller facility, and so on.

7.4 CAPACITY STRATEGIES

How large should each capacity increment be? When should capacity increments be added? The answers to these interrelated questions form the foundation of a firm's capacity strategy.[4]

Economies and diseconomies of scale imply that there is an optimal operating level for a facility of a given size and an optimal size for a facility. Let us review these concepts.

---

[4] It is assumed that the firm wants to increase its capacity. However, as economic and other environmental conditions change, there are times when the firm may be interested in reducing its capacity. Consider, for example, the major downsizing decisions made by General Motors in early 1992. In practice, the economic considerations used in deciding which process or facility to close or downsize are similar to those used in deciding whether to expand.

EXHIBIT 7.4 TOOLBOX: OPTIMAL OPERATING LEVEL

The first graph illustrates the relationship between total costs for a period and various production levels. This relationship is expressed on a per unit basis in the second graph.

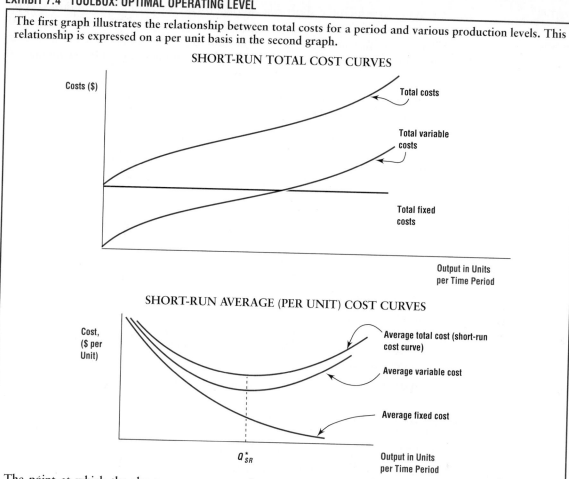

SHORT-RUN TOTAL COST CURVES

Costs ($)

Total costs

Total variable costs

Total fixed costs

Output in Units per Time Period

SHORT-RUN AVERAGE (PER UNIT) COST CURVES

Cost, ($ per Unit)

Average total cost (short-run cost curve)

Average variable cost

Average fixed cost

Q^*_{SR}

Output in Units per Time Period

The point at which the short-run average total cost is minimized, Q^*_{SR}, is the best operating level for a specific size of plant. Note that the quantity at which average variable cost is minimized is unlikely to be the same as Q^*_{SR}.

Determining Optimal Operating Levels

In the short run costs can be classified as fixed or variable. As illustrated in Exhibit 7.4, **fixed costs** are costs that are set for the period and are not influenced by production levels. Therefore, as production levels increase, the fixed costs per unit decrease. Management salaries, equipment leases, and facility rent are all costs that are fixed in the short run. In the long run, all costs are variable.

Variable costs are costs that change as the level of production changes. Initially, the short-run average variable cost per unit decreases as production levels increase. After a certain point, though, as a result of the **law of diminishing returns**,[5] the average variable cost per unit increases.

[5] The law of diminishing returns states that as successive units of a variable resource are added to a fixed resource, beyond some point the marginal product attributable to each additional unit of the variable resource declines.

The point at which the short-run average total cost per unit is minimized (Q_{SR}^* in Exhibit 7.4) is the optimal operating level for a facility of a given size.

What is the optimal size for a facility? Initially, as the size of a facility increases, its minimum average total cost decreases. This phenomenon is called **economies of scale.**[6]

> **DEFINITION:** Economies of scale occur when total operating costs increase at a rate slower than the rate of increase in production volume.

Economies of scale result from a variety of factors:

- As the production level increases, the amount of supplies and components purchased from other firms increases as well. Quantity discounts are often granted for larger purchase orders; this decreases per unit costs.
- As production levels increase, increases in cumulative production and the learning curve effect[7] lead to decreasing marginal production times. This results in a lowering of per unit production costs.
- When large volumes of a product are produced, firms often replace their general-purpose equipment with equipment dedicated to that product. This increases the efficiency of the process and lowers production costs.[8]

However, as illustrated in Exhibit 7.5, the optimal facility size (the size associated with the lowest average total cost) does not necessarily lead to the largest production volume. Once the size of a facility passes a certain level, **diseconomies of scale** set in and total per unit costs begin to increase.

> **DEFINITION:** Diseconomies of scale occur when total operating costs increase faster than does the rate of increase in production volume.

Diseconomies of scale occur for several reasons:

- As a facility's production volume increases, the area it serves also increases. Diseconomies of distribution may also be compounded by a reduced density of customers. The average travel time between customers increases, and so do delivery costs.
- If the facility's production volume is enlarged by increasing the number and type of products produced, diseconomies of coordination may set in. New layers of management are frequently added to deal with the complexity of handling dissimilar products and/or markets, increasing costs and decreasing responsiveness.
- As the facility grows larger, there is also a tendency for the workforce to unionize and for the firm to dominate the local economy. The political implications associated with management actions become even more important and may rule out some otherwise desirable alternatives.

The point at which the long-run average total cost per unit is minimized (Q_{LR}^* in Exhibit 7.5) is the **optimal economic facility size.** Economies of scale can be observed to the left of this point, and diseconomies of scale to the right.

[6] There does not seem to be a single unambiguous definition for the term *economies of scale*. This section will use the definition commonly employed in economic literature. See, for example, McConnell and associates (1990) and Pindyck and Rubinfeld (1989).

[7] The learning curve ("practice makes perfect") effect is discussed in Chapter 10.

[8] This increased efficiency is one reason why firms tend to move down the diagonal of the product-process life cycle matrix presented in Exhibit 1.8. Note that the savings accruing from process efficiency may be partially offset by corresponding increases in inventory-holding costs.

EXHIBIT 7.5 TOOLBOX: OPTIMAL FACILITY SIZE

The first graph below depicts the average total cost curves for facilities of varying capacities. In this case the optimal plant size is the size of plant C.

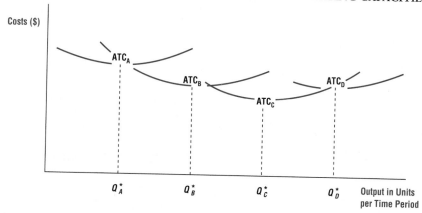

AVERAGE TOTAL COST CURVES FOR FACILITIES OF VARYING CAPACITIES

By connecting the optimal operating levels for facilities of varying capacities, one can develop the long-run average total cost curve shown below. Note that economies of scale are present to the left of the optimal long-run output level, Q_{LR}^*, but diseconomies of scale result once output exceeds Q_{LR}^*.

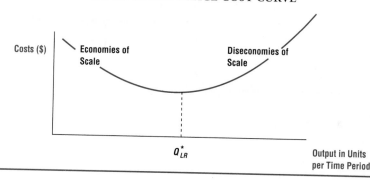

LONG-RUN AVERAGE COST CURVE

In summary, there is an **optimal operating level** for a facility of a given size as well as an optimal facility size. Whether a firm has the option of operating at the optimal level (or building a new facility of the optimal size) depends on the firm's competitors, the demand for its products, the availability of resources (people, equipment, raw materials), and so forth. As will be discussed in the next section, cost is only one of several factors considered by firms as they make decisions about the size of their facilities.

The Timing of Capacity Increments

Suppose Earl Rickman in Exhibit 7.3 wants to increase the size of his shop. The capacity of the shop is well below current demand, and as illustrated in Exhibit 7.6, Earl expects demand to continue growing. Should Earl make a series of small capacity increments or just a few large increments? Is one strategy generally better than the other?

Smaller increments are less risky for Earl because they can be implemented quickly, are a better mirror of demand changes, and are relatively inexpensive. In

EXHIBIT 7.6 TOOLBOX: CAPACITY EXPANSION

Every year Earl Rickman turns down more customer orders for his desks. On the basis of his past experience and some market research, Earl estimates that demand is growing about 20 percent per year. Last year's demand (year 0) was 100 units.

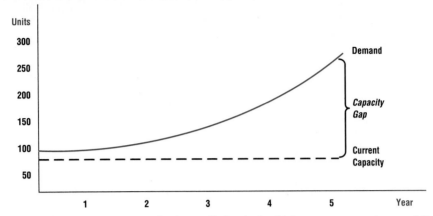

Earl is debating whether to increase capacity in small chunks by hiring a new part-time or full-time worker every year or to move to a new facility and expand more aggressively.

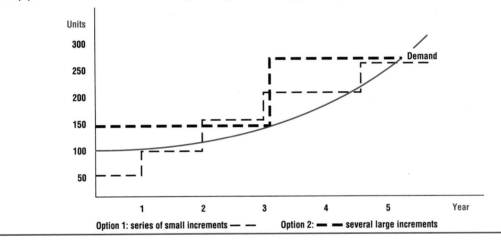

Option 1: series of small increments — —   Option 2: ▬ ▬ several large increments

general, the smaller the capacity increment, the shorter the interval between capacity additions.

Larger increments, by contrast, may be less expensive in the long run than the combined cost of several small increments. Because of economies of scale, annual operating costs may be lower as well. With larger increments, there is also less of a tendency to "shoehorn" new or expanded processes wherever there is room.

Now suppose Earl has decided to make a series of small capacity increments. When should he add them? Before he needs the additional capacity (the proactive approach)? After demand exceeds current capacity (the reactive approach)? Or should he match capacity as closely as possible to expected demand (the expected value approach)? These three strategies are depicted in Exhibit 7.7.

By building in advance of forecast capacity requirements, Earl can establish a **capacity cushion** for the shop; there will be enough capacity to meet expected and unexpected demand.

DEFINITION: A capacity cushion is the amount of capacity a firm holds in excess of its expected demand. If its capacity is less than its expected demand, the firm has a negative capacity cushion.

The Mayo Clinic, for example, maintains capacity at levels greater than demand. This **proactive capacity strategy** is commonly used in high-growth industries when the cost of stocking out is much higher than the cost of maintaining excess capacity. Firms with capacity cushions in these industries can potentially capture market share from capacity-constrained competitors. In addition to companies in high-growth industries, companies (such as Florida Power and Light) that provide essential utilities follow a proactive strategy.

Conversely, if the cost of maintaining excess capacity exceeds the cost of stocking out, a **reactive capacity strategy** is often followed. A company employing this strategy maintains a small or even negative capacity cushion. Capacity utilization is high, but the firm is in danger of eroding its market position (think back to Electronic Craftsmen Limited and its capacity problems in Exhibit 7.1). And if the firm's competitors

EXHIBIT 7.7 CAPACITY EXPANSION STRATEGIES

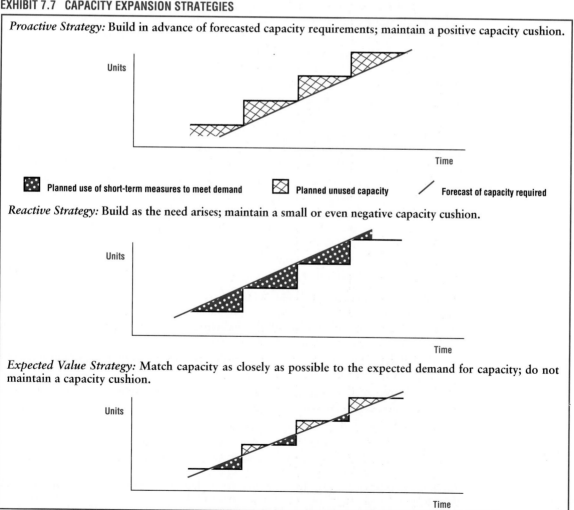

Proactive Strategy: Build in advance of forecasted capacity requirements; maintain a positive capacity cushion.

Units

Time

Planned use of short-term measures to meet demand   Planned unused capacity   Forecast of capacity required

Reactive Strategy: Build as the need arises; maintain a small or even negative capacity cushion.

Units

Time

Expected Value Strategy: Match capacity as closely as possible to the expected demand for capacity; do not maintain a capacity cushion.

Units

Time

are also following this strategy, they may all increase their capacity at the same time. This may result in overcapacity at the industry level and intensify competition.

Finally, the **expected value capacity strategy** is a middle ground approach. The intent is to match capacity as closely as possible to expected demand. The firm tries to make the likelihood of having excess capacity the same as the likelihood of not having enough capacity.

How does a firm decide which option to try? A potential method is to estimate the cost of excess capacity as well as the cost of stockout per unit and then look at the ratio of excess capacity to stockout costs, or the **capacity ratio** [equation (7.3)].

Capacity Ratio

$$CR = \frac{C_s - C_e}{C_s} \tag{7.3}$$

where CR = capacity ratio
 C_s = cost of stocking out per unit
 C_e = cost of excess capacity

As an operating rule of thumb and in the absence of other decision rules, managers should adopt an expected value approach when the ratio is between -0.5 and $+0.5$.[9] A reactive approach should be taken when the ratio is less than -0.5, and a proactive approach should be taken when it is greater than $+0.5$ (see Exhibit 7.8).

As Hayes and Wheelwright (1984) suggest, this decision rule is simplistic. In practice, it is very difficult to estimate the true costs of excess capacity and stocking out. However, the rule does yield rational results and can be useful.

Seasonality of demand further complicates the choice of capacity strategy. Should a firm provide enough capacity to meet peak requirements or average requirements? Banks, restaurants, public utility suppliers, and snowmobile manufacturers all face this problem. Again, the cost of excess capacity must be compared with the cost of stocking out. The higher the cost of excess capacity is, the more likely the firm is to provide enough basic capacity to meet average requirements and manipulate intermediate sources of capacity (e.g., overtime, accumulation inventories, subcontracting) to meet peak capacity requirements. These options are discussed in detail in Chapter 15.

In summary, decisions about the size and timing of capacity increments are intertwined. The factors that commonly influence these decisions are listed below:

- The predicted growth and variability of demand
- The cost and the time needed to build, staff, and equip the capacity increment
- The annual operating cost of the increment, the optimal operating level for existing facilities, and the optimal size for a new facility
- Anticipated reactions or behavior of current and potential competitors, both domestically and internationally
- Anticipated reactions and behavior of suppliers, workers, and other interested parties (local governments, for example)
- The rate and direction of anticipated technological changes

The quantifiable aspects of the firm's capacity alternatives can be evaluated by using financial tools such as the payback method, the net present value technique,

[9] In reality, what is being determined here is the point at which the expected value of stocking out equals the expected value of excess capacity. Given the probability distribution of demand in this case, capacity should be set at the point at which 50 percent of the cumulative demand can be satisfied.

EXHIBIT 7.8   TOOLBOX: SELECTING A CAPACITY STRATEGY

Suppose Micardo Inc. is evaluating a capacity expansion project. The firm estimates that the annual cost of excess capacity over the life of the project, C_e, will be $5 per unit. How much capacity should Micardo provide in each of the following situations?

Situation 1: The annual stockout cost, C_s, is $5.50.

$$\frac{C_s - C_e}{C_s} = \frac{\$5.50 - \$5.00}{\$5.50} = 0.09$$

Since the value of the ratio is greater than -0.5 but is still less than 0.5, the expected value approach should be taken. The cost of stocking out is relatively close to the cost of excess capacity, and Micardo Inc. should provide just enough capacity to meet the average forecast demand.

Situation 2: The annual stockout cost, C_s, is $20.

$$\frac{C_s - C_e}{C_s} = \frac{\$20 - \$5}{\$20} = 0.75$$

A positive capacity cushion should be maintained since the value of the ratio is greater than 0.5. That is, Micardo should take a proactive stance and build in advance of need. Given the high stockout cost (relative to the cost of excess capacity), the firm should provide enough capacity to satisfy more than the average forecast demand.

Situation 3: The annual stockout cost, C_s, is $50.

$$\frac{C_s - C_e}{C_s} = \frac{\$50 - \$5}{\$50} = 0.9$$

As in situation 2, a proactive approach should be taken. However, since the cost of stocking out is so high, an even larger capacity cushion should be kept in this case.

Situation 4: The annual stockout cost, C_s, is $2.

$$\frac{C_s - C_e}{C_s} = \frac{\$2 - \$5}{\$2} = -1.5$$

A reactive approach is appropriate in this situation. The cost of excess capacity is higher than the cost of stocking out; therefore, Micardo should ensure that its current capacity is fully utilized before it expands the facility. This may mean that Micardo will not be able to satisfy the average forecast demand.

and the internal rate of return.[10] Computer simulation is also an option. As relevant computer software packages become more user-friendly, simulation is gaining popularity.

Decision Trees

A quantitative tool that is frequently used in deciding on the size and timing of capital investments is the decision tree. The decision tree gets its name from its appearance, which is similar to that of a leafless tree on its side. Decision trees are logic pictures drawn to show the sequence of decisions that must be made to arrive at the solution with the greatest expected value. They are drawn from left to right (from base to top) and solved from right to left. Exhibit 7.9 provides a representation of this method and solves a capacity expansion problem for the Mother Goose Toy Company.

Several assumptions are required when one is using decision trees. First, the firm knows all the alternatives and all the states of nature. Second, the probabilities of all outcomes are known; the problem is deterministic. Third, the firm can assess the payoffs accurately. If these assumptions do not hold, the firm will have to use another

---

[10] Refer to the Chapter 9 Supplement for an illustration of the mechanics of these financial tools.

EXHIBIT 7.9 TOOLBOX: DECISION TREES

The Mother Goose Toy Company has developed a new educational video game for children. The results of the test market have been very favorable. The expected demand over the next five years and the probability of each demand level are shown below.

Annual Demand, units	Probability
150,000	0.4
100,000	0.5
50,000	0.1

To produce the new game, the company must expand its current plant or build another one. Of course, it can also choose to drop the product, that is, do nothing.

Expanding the current plant will cost about $0.8 million, but the maximum capacity will be only 100,000 units a year. Building a new plant is more expensive ($1.4 million), but the new plant will have an annual capacity of 150,000 units.

The chart below shows the annual revenue associated with each alternative at each of the three different demand levels. The game is expected to have a five-year life span.

(1) Alternative	If demand is 150,000 units		If demand is 100,000 units		If demand is 50,000 units	
	(2) Annual Revenue, $	(3) Total, Revenue, $	(4) Annual Revenue, $	(5) Total Revenue, $	(6) Annual Revenue, $	(7) Total Revenue, $
Build new plant	0.75M	3.75M	0.25M	1.25M	(0.25M)	(1.25M)
Expand existing plant	0.50M	1.50M	0.50M	1.50M	(0.10M)	(0.5M)
Do nothing	0.0	0.0	0.0	0.0	0.0	0.0

Column 3 = column 2 × 5 years.
Column 5 = column 4 × 5 years.
Column 7 = column 6 × 5 years.

The decision tree below depicts the problem facing Mother Goose.

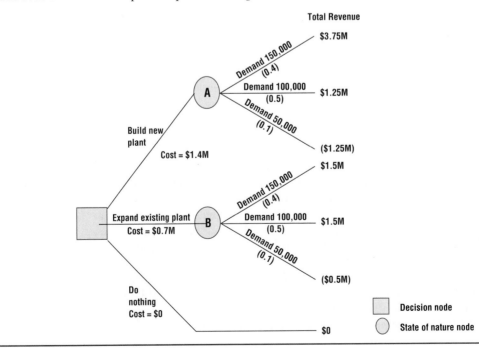

The first step is to calculate the expected value of each of the three alternatives. This is done by (1) multiplying the total revenue associated with each state of nature (i.e., demand level) by its probability, (2) summing the results, and then (3) subtracting the cost associated with the decision.

Expected Value of Alternative 1: Build a new plant.

(Total revenue @ demand = 150,000 units)(Probability of demand): ($3.75M)(0.4) =	$1.5M
(Total revenue @ demand = 100,000 units)(Probability of demand): ($1.25M)(0.5) =	$0.625M
(Total revenue @ demand = 50,000 units)(Probability of demand): (−$1.25M)(0.1) =	−$0.125M
Expected Return	$2M
Minus construction costs	(1.40M)
Expected value of this decision	$0.6M

Expected Value of Alternative 2: Expand existing plant.

(Total revenue @ demand = 150,000 units)(Probability of demand): ($1.5M)(0.4) =	$0.6M
(Total revenue @ demand = 100,000 units)(Probability of demand): ($1.5M)(0.5) =	$0.75M
(Total revenue @ demand = 50,000 units)(Probability of demand): (−$0.5M)(0.1) =	−$0.05M
Expected Return	$1.3M
Minus construction costs	(0.80M)
Expected value of this decision	$0.5M

Expected Value of Alternative 3: Do nothing.

If it is assumed that the status quo can continue without affecting the company, the expected value of the third alternative—doing nothing—is $0.

Since alternative 1 has the highest expected value, Mother Goose should choose this alternative.

Note: To keep this example simple, other variables (such as competitors' reactions) are not considered. In practice, decision trees tend to be much more complex than the one presented here. Sensitivity analysis (i.e., investigating the sensitivity of the solution to changes in the parameter values) shuld be done as well.

technique, probably a computer simulation. These assumptions are quite strong and usually invalid. Any decision maker should therefore take the "decision" that results from the analysis and temper it with judgment based on an assessment of factors that could not be quantified.

As was noted in Exhibit 7.9, Mother Goose's problem requires only a simple decision tree. If this were part of a more complex decision that involved manufacturing one or more of three potential video games, the firm would have to make several decisions at a number of levels.

7.5 UPSTREAM (BACKWARD) INTEGRATION

This chapter has described the timing and size of capacity increments and decrements. **Upstream (backward) integration** is another capacity-related issue.

Upstream integration refers to the span of processes that involve the production of goods and services supplied to a firm and controlled by that firm. It is not limited to the legal ownership of processes but includes legally independent suppliers with which the firm is integrated by joint knowledge generation. McDonald's, for example, makes its own milk shake mix, buns, and beef patties in its $40 million processing complex in Moscow. Although it may have no control over the production of beef, potatoes, and other farm produce, McDonald's is involved in their production. The fast-food giant worked with state-run farms to adopt new cattle-feeding programs, plant different strains of potatoes, and modify the milk pasteurization process.

Suppose that a firm wants to build a facility to produce components that were formerly purchased from outside suppliers. What should the firm do if the optimal economic size of that facility corresponds to an output level that exceeds the downstream requirements? This is a common problem, and there are two choices for a firm that finds itself in this situation. First, the upstream facility's output can be limited to the quantity the firm requires. Second, the firm can sell the facility's excess output on the open market. This second choice can be dangerous, however, because the pressures of managing the new business may cause the firm to lose its competitive focus. A series of poor vertical integration decisions effectively killed *The Saturday Evening Post* (see Exhibit 7.10).

What if the firm's requirements exceed the output of an upstream facility that is operating at the optimal economic size? **Tapered integration** is an option in this situation. Tapered integration is really partial integration. As shown in Exhibit 7.11, the firm's requirements are met by its in-house production and by outside sources of supply.

Tapered integration gives a firm the ability to remain up to date with technology and the product. It also provides a lens through which the firm can observe suppliers and does not commit the firm psychologically to overproducing components or systems if the demand for the final product falls. Tapered integration also reduces the firm's investment loss if the technology becomes obsolete. In the rapidly changing environment of the 1990s, the ability to shift quickly from the current process to a newer and better process is a decided strategic advantage, and a move from "legal" to "cooperative" upstream integration makes strategic sense.

Upstream integration decisions are often coupled with decisions about whether to place all processes on one site or spread them around a number of sites. Several options are illustrated in Exhibit 7.12. Products can flow from a central plant to a set of satellite plants, from satellite plants to a central plant, between sister plants, and so on.

Locating all processes on one site may place more (psychological) emphasis on balancing operations, or ensuring that the capacity of each successive process is roughly similar to that of the preceding process. (The Chrysler plant in Bramalea, Ontario, for example, makes all the body parts needed for its LH models.) Locating processes together may significantly increase the scale of processes if an upstream integration decision is made, and this may bring about all the problems described above.

EXHIBIT 7.10   VERTICAL INTEGRATION AT *THE SATURDAY EVENING POST*

Before World War II *the Saturday Evening Post* was a respected weekly publication that captured up-to-the-minute news stories by going to press very late in the week. A series of vertical integration decisions over a number of years saw the *Post* integrate backward into printing and then into papermaking. In both cases the upstream capacity was more than the immediate downstream operation could absorb, and financial pressures forced changes in the nature of the magazine. An inability to sell paper produced by the paper mill created pressure to increase the number of pages in the magazine. Cost containment pressures in the printing works created pressure to print the magazine earlier in the week. These actions forced up prices and drove away customers and advertisers. The magazine drowned in red ink in the 1960s but was effectively dead the moment the vertical integration decisions were made.

EXHIBIT 7.11 TAPERED INTEGRATION

The Altridge Company Ltd. assembles small appliances. Among other items, it produces the electronic circuits and plastic couplers used in these small appliances. The company is following a tapered integration strategy by producing fewer electronic circuits and plastic couplers than it needs.

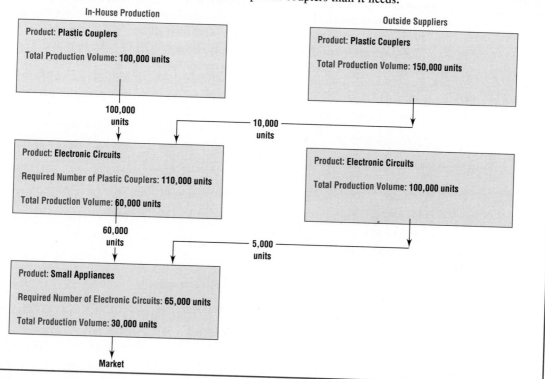

EXHIBIT 7.12 PRODUCT FLOWS BETWEEN PLANTS

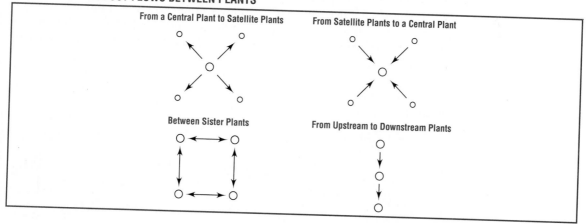

7.6 CAPITAL BUDGETING

One of the important considerations in capacity expansion is the ability of a firm to finance that expansion. Several techniques can determine the attractiveness of an investment and its cash flow implications. Cash flow is important; more firms have failed through not being able to satisfy working capital requirements than have failed for lack of customers.

In comparing investment alternatives, it is common practice to translate the benefits and drawbacks of each alternative into a set of cash inflows and outflows. The cash flows can be used to calculate financial measures which allow managers to easily compare alternatives to each other and to company standards.

The **payback period** for an investment is the length of time required to recover its initial cost, as shown in equations (7.4) and (7.5). In general, investments with shorter payback periods are preferred because they are considered less risky. Some firms have a maximum payback period; investments with a payback period longer than the maximum are rejected.

Payback Period

The payback period is the number of years, n, required for

$$\sum_{j=1}^{n} \text{NACF}_j = \text{IC} \tag{7.4}$$

where n = payback period, in years
 NACF_j = net annual cash flow for year j
  IC = initial cost of investment

If the net annual cash flows are positive and equal from one year to the next, the payback period is

$$n = \frac{\text{IC}}{\text{NACF}} \tag{7.5}$$

Note that the payback period does not take into account the time value of money (a dollar received today is worth more than a dollar received next year) and the cash flows generated after the payback period.

When investments that generate cash flows differently over a number of years are compared, the present value of all cash flows is often calculated and used as a basis of comparison. Future cash flows are frequently discounted in accordance with the firm's cost of capital.

An investment's **net present value** (**NPV**) is equal to the sum of its discounted net cash inflows minus the investment's initial cost [equation (7.6)]. If the NPV is greater than zero, the return on the investment exceeds the firm's cost of capital.

Net Present Value

$$\text{NPV} = \sum_{j=1}^{n} \text{PV}(\text{NACF}_j) - \text{IC} \tag{7.6}$$

where NPV = net present value
 n = number of years
$\text{PV}(\text{NACF}_j)$ = present value of net annual cash flow for year j
 IC = initial cost of investment

All cash flows are discounted at the firm's cost of capital.

A set of investments can also be compared by converting the cash flows associated with each investment into an **equivalent annual annuity value (EAAV)**. Cash flows are first discounted using the firm's cost of capital and then converted into an annuity value.

An investment's **internal rate of return (IRR)** is the interest rate that will equate the present value of its net cash inflows with the initial cost [equation (7.7)]. Investments with IRR values greater than the firm's cost of capital are usually deemed acceptable. The higher the IRR value, the better.

Internal Rate of Return (IRR)

IRR is the interest rate at which

$$\sum_{j=1}^{n} PV(NACF_j) = IC \qquad (7.7)$$

where n = number of years
$PV(NACF_j)$ = present value of net annual cash flow for year j
IC = initial cost of investment

Three investments are compared using the payback period, NPV, EAAV, and IRR criteria described in Exhibit 7.13.

While the information provided by this type of financial analysis can be valuable, it is dangerous to evaluate investment alternatives solely on the basis of this information. The Chapter 9 Supplement will examine several common errors that may be made when a firm uses financial analysis to evaluate investments in advanced technology.

Reminder. Capacity for an FRO will generally be more flexible than for other firms in the same industry. FROs will probably place a much higher cost on capacity shortfalls than the average firm in the industry and will therefore err on the side of excess capacity. One likely form for this excess capacity is deliberate underutilization of currently operating facilities rather than keeping plants in mothballs. Adding a shift or adding extra equipment to an existing plant is much easier than finding a new workforce and management. In fact, the most strategic capacity reserve for an FRO (or any firm) is likely to be management capacity. The strategic cost of excess managerial capacity, or other knowledge capability, will be offset by the ability to mobilize that capacity quickly as it is needed. Of course, capacity and capability need to be challenged and developed while being held in strategic reserve or else they will atrophy and be lost. No firm is without real challenges for improvement, though, and the challenges for "underemployed" managers will be easy to find.

EXHIBIT 7.13   TOOLBOX: FINANCIAL MEASURES

Adelaide Inc. can select one of three investments. The initial investment and the expected annual net cash flows associated with each investment are shown below.

	Investment		
	A	B	C
Initial investment ($)	100,000	50,000	200,000
Net annual cash flow ($)	62,000	16,000	35,400
Cash flow duration	2 years	5 years	10 years

The firm's cost of capital is 15 percent, and all cash flows take place at the end of the year.

PAYBACK PERIOD

The payback period for each investment is equal to its initial investment divided by its net annual cash flow [equation (7.4)].

$$\text{Investment A:} \quad \frac{\$100,000}{\$62,000} = 1.6 \text{ years}$$

$$\text{Investment B:} \quad \frac{\$50,000}{\$16,000} = 3.1 \text{ years}$$

$$\text{Investment C:} \quad \frac{\$200,000}{\$35,400} = 5.6 \text{ years}$$

NET PRESENT VALUE (NPV)

The NPV of investment A using equation (7.6) is equal to the present value of the net cash flows in year 1 and year 2 minus the initial investment of $100,000. But rather than calculating the present value of the annual cash flows separately, one can view the cash flows as a two-year annuity and use the present value interest factors for an annuity (PVIFA) table in Appendix C.

Investment A: $\$62,000 \times \text{PVIFA}_{15\%,2 \text{ yrs}} - \$100,000$

$$= \$62,000 \times 1.626 - \$100,000$$
$$= \$812.00$$

Investment B: $\$16,000 \times \text{PVIFA}_{15\%,5 \text{ yrs}} - \$50,000$

$$= \$16,000 \times 3.352 - \$50,000$$
$$= \$3,632.00$$

Investment C: $\$35,400 \times 2\text{PVIFA}_{15\%,10 \text{ yrs}} - \$200,000$

$$= \$35,400 \times 5.019 - \$200,000$$
$$= -\$22,327.40$$

EQUIVALENT ANNUAL ANNUITY VALUE (EAAV)

It is also possible to convert the initial investment required for each investment into an annuity equal in length to its cash flow duration.

$$\text{Investment A:} \quad i \times \text{PVIFA}_{15\%,2 \text{ yrs}} = \$100,000$$
$$1.626i = \$100,000$$
$$i = \$61,500.62$$

Therefore, the EAAV of investment A is $62,000 - $61,500.62 = $499.38

$$\text{Investment B:} \quad i \times \text{PVIFA}_{15\%,5 \text{ yrs}} = \$50,000$$
$$3.352i = \$50,000$$
$$i = \$14,916.47$$

Therefore, the EAAV of investment B = $16,000 - $14,916.47
$$= \$1,083.53$$

$$\text{Investment C:} \quad i \times \text{PVIFA}_{15\%,10 \text{ yrs}} = \$200,000$$
$$5.019i = \$200,000$$
$$i = \$39,848.58$$

Therefore, the EAAV of investment C = $35,400 - $39,848.58
$$= -\$4,448.58$$

INTERNAL RATE OF RETURN (IRR)

Using equation (7.7), the IRR for investment A occurs when

$$\$62,000 \times PVIFA_{IRR,2\ yrs} = \$100,000$$
$$PVIFA_{IRR,2\ yrs} = 1.6$$

The PVIFA table in Appendix C shows that the PVIFAs for two-year annuities with the closest value to 1.6 occur when the interest rate is 16 percent. Therefore, the IRR is 16 percent.

The IRR for investment B occurs when

$$\$16,000 \times PVIFA_{IRR,5\ yrs} = \$50,000$$
$$PVIFA_{IRR,5\ yrs} = 3.125$$
$$IRR = 18\ percent$$

The IRR for investment C occurs when

$$\$35,400 \times PVIFA_{IRR,10\ yrs} = \$200,000$$
$$PVIFA_{IRR,10\ yrs} = 5.65$$
$$IRR = 12\ percent$$

The table below summarizes the results. The best value for a particular measure is given in *italics*. Although it does not have the shortest payback period, overall investment B seems to be the best investment.

	Investment		
	A	B	C
Payback period	*1.6 years*	3.1 years	5.6 years
Net present value ($)	812.00	*3,632.00*	−22,327.40
Equivalent annual annuity value ($)	499.38	*1,083.53*	−4,448.58
Internal rate of return (%)	16	*18*	12

MANAGERIAL IMPLICATIONS

The first measure of effectiveness in an operating system is the ability of a firm to produce the volume of products required by the various markets the firm serves. *Sustained* inability to meet customers' needs will place the firm in jeopardy no matter what attributes the firm's products have. The operative word here is *sustained;* rushing to add capacity in a short-lived period of increased demand may be very costly in the long run. Having more capacity than is needed is a financial burden and will reduce operating profits. It may also be a strategic burden, for many managers feel compelled to use capacity to produce products even though they cannot foresee sales. No product is worth anything to the producer until it is sold.

More often than not firms think of adding capacity by investing in more or faster equipment, but that is not the only way to increase output. A firm can add capacity in three other ways: by adding more hours to the operating week (working extra shifts or working overtime), having other facilities help out (particularly subcontractors), and simply getting better at what the firm does.

Many operating facilities are balanced, with each process having the same capacity. The same may not be true of upstream or downstream facilities, especially when there are notions of minimum economic capacities. Vertical integraton decisions therefore may unwittingly force a change in capacity for the current processes. The simple message to managers is to check!

Remember also that the amount of capacity is influenced by how capacity is measured. Generally, one should measure capacity using the most critical resource; in a job shop, for example, labor hours may be the most appropriate measure. This is important, for using inappropriate measures will give a firm a false impression of capacity, rendering the organization ineffective, inefficient, or both.

CHAPTER SUMMARY

A capacity strategy is a long-range plan that details how a firm will satisfy the demand for its goods and services. This chapter discussed ways to measure capacity, options for increasing or decreasing capacity, and capacity strategies. The major concepts and points are as follows:

- Capacity is the ability of a worker, machine, work center, plant, or organization to produce output per unit of time.
- Capacity is usually expressed as a rate of output per unit of time (e.g., cases of beer produced per day). If a wide range of products that require different resource levels is produced, capacity is often expressed as the units of input available (e.g., number of labor hours available per month).
- Actual capacity is almost always lower than effective capacity and design capacity and tends to fluctuate over time.
- Capacity requirements are generated from demand forecasts. There is a capacity gap if the capacity required is lower than the capacity available. If available capacity exceeds required capacity, the firm has a capacity cushion (or capacity slack).
- Options for increasing capacity in the long run include building or leasing one or more additional facilities, expanding the existing facility, relocating the existing facility to a larger one, purchasing products formerly produced internally, buying another company, and developing new applications of advanced technology. If the firm wishes to downsize, it can sell one or more facilities, relocate to a smaller facility, and so on.
- Economies and diseconomies of scale imply that there is an optimal operating level for a facility of a given size and that there is an optimal size for a particular type of facility.
- Smaller capacity increments are less risky because they can be implemented quickly, can better mirror changes in demand, and are relatively inexpensive. In general, the smaller the capacity increment, the shorter the time interval between subsequent capacity additions.
- Larger increments may be less expensive in the long run than the combined cost of several small increments. All proposed capacity expansions should be subject to rigorous financial analysis.
- Capacity strategies include building in advance of forecast capacity requirements (proactive strategy), building only after demand exceeds current capacity (reactive strategy), and matching capacity as closely as possible to expected demand (expected value approach).
- In selecting a capacity strategy, a firm must consider future demand levels (and their variability), the probable reaction of its competitors, the cost of excess capacity in relation to the cost of stocking out, and its corporate strategy.
- Tapered integration is an option when a firm integrates downstream and acquires a facility whose output exceeds the firm's requirements.
- Rather than locate all operations at one site, a firm can use a set of plants. One plant may be the central site, with products flowing to and from satellite plants.
- Capacity strategies must fit with other strategies in order to support the corporate and business strategies of the firm. This is certainly true of FROs. The best flexibility will come as a result of accurate forecasts that extend beyond the time it will take to respond to real market change. The shorter this lead time, the better the forecasting and the response.

KEY TERMS

Capacity strategy
Capacity
Bottleneck operation
Design capacity
Effective capacity
Actual capacity
Capacity utilization
Capacity efficiency
Capacity gap

Capacity slack
Fixed costs
Variable costs
Law of diminishing
 returns
Economies of scale
Diseconomies of scale
Optimal economic facility
 size

Optimal operating level
Capacity cushion
Proactive capacity
 strategy
Reactive capacity strategy
Expected value capacity
 strategy
Capacity ratio

Upstream (backward)
 integration
Tapered integration
Payback period
Net present value (NPV)
Equivalent annual
 annuity value (EAAV)
Internal rate of return
 (IRR)

DISCUSSION QUESTIONS

1. What is capacity? How does design capacity differ from effective capacity?

2. How is capacity measured in a brewery? In an accounting firm? What impact does the measurement have?

3. How can a firm determine the capacity requirements for an individual process?

4. What is the difference between process utilization and process efficiency? Can either of these ratios be greater than 1?

5. What are diseconomies of scale? Give some examples.

6. Do you think facilities (like products) undergo a life cycle? Why or why not?

7. In what way can the following organizations adjust capacity in the short term?
   - Oil refinery
   - General hospital
   - Electricity utility
   - Take-out pizza restaurant

8. Which of the capacity strategies should the organizations in question 7 use? Why?

9. What strategy do you advise ECL's (Exhibit 7.1) management to adopt?

10. What is a capacity cushion?

11. What is the capacity ratio? How can managers use this ratio?

12. What is tapered integration? What are its benefits? Is this a viable strategy for fast-response organizations (FROs)?

13. A vegetable processor wants to increase its capacity to process peas. What capacity options does the processor have? What are the implications of each option?

14. People tend to think of vertical integration as a manufacturing phenomenon. Can you think of services that have vertically integrated? Did this integration move forward or backward in the value chain?

15. Many firms significantly underestimate the indirect costs of scheduling, coordinating, and controlling complex mixes of products and processes located in one facility. What effect would this have on the optimal operating level for a facility? On the optimal size of a facility?

16. Why do FROs tend to build small and very responsive facilities? What is the meaning of a focused strategy?

17. Should FROs evaluate capacity expansion proposals by using traditional financial techniques? What is your reasoning?

PROBLEMS

1. Spudfry Ltd., a newly established potato chip manufacturer, has an efficiency value of 90 percent on the only production line in its first plant. The utilization value is 80 percent. The line operates seven days a week and three eight-hour shifts per day. When operating at design capacity, it should produce 1,200 bags of chips per hour. What is the actual capacity of the line per week?

2. Devon Electronics Ltd. wants to expand its production capabilities for clone computers. The annual costs of excess capacity throughout the use of

the expanded facility, however, are expected to reach $8 per unit. How much expanded capacity should be added if the annual stockout cost is $4?

3. What expanded capacity should be added if in question 2, the stockout cost is $25? If it is $10?

4. What is the design capacity per week of a sump pump which actually pumps 1,000 gallons of water per day with an efficiency of 75 percent and a utilization of 80 percent?

5. Colloquist Systems produces computerized lecterns. The owner shuts down two weeks of the year, and production is maintained at eight hours per day. There are two people assembling and testing new lecterns. It takes approximately 40 labor hours to complete a single lectern. Each person, however, spends 10 hours per week servicing distributors. A further two hours a week, on average, is lost through component failures or hard disk crashes inside a lectern during assembly. The company produced and sold 50 units in the just completed fiscal year. What is the design capacity, effective capacity, and actual capacity of Colloquist Systems per week? What is the design capacity, effective capacity, and actual capacity of Colloquist Systems per year?

6. The coming economic year in El Paso, Texas, is receiving a favorable forecast from 60 percent of the economic pundits in the region and an unfavorable forecast from the remainder. The Holiday Inn in that city has three expansion alternatives on the table, and the economic forecasts are a factor in the decision-making process.

Profits/(Loss)

Alternative	Favorable Market	Unfavorable Market
Smallest	$50,000	($12,000)
Medium	$80,000	($45,000)
Largest	$100,000	($120,000)

Which alternative has the highest expected monetary value?

7. Pro-Blade is a skate manufacturer based in Buffalo. Pat Scoble, the manager of operations, is trying to determine whether the company should invest in a new production line to produce roller blades. The marketing staff has analyzed the potential success of a Pro-Blade roller-blade product in the current marketplace. The estimates indicate that there is a 20 percent likelihood that annual sales nationwide will reach 4,000 pairs, a 50 percent likelihood of ·

3,000 pairs, a 20 percent likelihood of 2,000 pairs, and a 10 percent likelihood of 1,000 pairs. Pro-Blade has three choices available:
a. Do nothing.
b. Invest $1 million in a production line with a capacity of 2,000 pairs per year.
c. Invest $1,400,000 in an alternative production line with a capacity of 4,000 pairs per year.

Alternative	Fixed Costs, $	Variable Costs, $
B	1,000,000	70/pair
C	1,400,000	60/pair

Each pair of Pro-Blades will be wholesaled at $150 per pair.

Investment in the production line has no residual or resale value. For simplicity's sake, assume that the net present values of future earnings and costs are 100 percent and that the expected life of either production line is 10 years. Also, excess capacity is worthless. Finally, assume that prices and achieved sales volumes will remain constant over the 10-year life of the production line.

Calculate the profitability of each possible outcome of this decision. Also, calculate the expected profitability of each decision. What should Scoble recommend?

8. The Ritzy Burger Joint (RBJ) is considering opening a drive-through. The fixed cost of the physical addition is $35,000. The additional cost of the people and the utilities required to service the drive-through is about $14,000 per year. Revenues from the drive-through are not as definite. There is a 25 percent expectation that the response to the added service will be poor and that earnings from the drive-through will be only $20,000 in the coming year. A good response is more likely (i.e., 55 percent) and will generate $50,000 in earnings. A great response could earn the restaurant $90,000.

If the market response is good, RBJ's owner anticipates that there is a 50 percent chance that the Burger Palace across the street will open its own drive-through. If RBJ's response is great, there is a 75 percent chance that the Burger Palace will open a drive-through. (If the response is poor, chances are 0 percent.) Also, if such a drive-through were opened by RBJ, it is expected to reduce RBJ drive-through earnings by half. Regardless of what happens across the street, opening the drive-through is expected to reduce RBJ's annual earnings from seated customers by $10,000. What is the expected return from this decision in the coming year? What would you recommend that RBJ do, given its goal of retrieving the cost of building the drive-through within three years. (Assume constant returns for three years.)

9. Determine the design capacity and the bottleneck department in the following system.

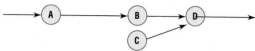

Procedure	Capacity Tons	Hour Tonnage Ratio
A	550	
B	275	
C	400	B:C = 1:2
D	625	

a. Which department is the bottleneck department?
b. If capacity in the bottleneck department could be increased, which department would become the new bottleneck?
c. How much capacity must be added to the bottleneck department so that it is no longer the bottleneck?

10. The Chocolate Chip Cookie Company produces cookies according to the following process:

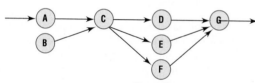

Step	Description	Pounds Per Hour	Mix Ratios
A	Premixed cookie mix	2,000	
B	Chocolate chips	800	A:B = 2:1
C	Bake cookies	3,000	
D	Stack cookies	4,000	D:E:F = 1:1:1
E	Cookie package	2,500	
F	Cellophane wrapping	2,500	
G	Bulk boxing	6,000	

a. What is the system capacity?
b. Which department is the bottleneck department?
c. What is the capacity cushion for department C?
d. What is the utilization rate for department C?

11. The Great Bicycle Company is considering whether to purchase or manufacture handlebars for its newest mountain bike model. The purchase price is $12 per unit. There are two alternatives available for producing them:

Alternative	Fixed Costs, $	Variable Costs, $
1	18,000	7/unit
2	8,000	9/unit

Which alternative should be selected if the firm plans to produce 2,000 bikes? 3,000 bikes? 6,000 bikes?

12. Joe Martin is about to open a hardware store. He has already leased 10,000 square feet of retail space but has an option to lease an additional adjacent 10,000 square feet.

Alternative	Fixed Costs, $
10,000	100,000
20,000	50,000

Anticipated Gross Profit, 10,000 sq ft/4 years, $	Probability
120,000	0.2
250,000	0.5
350,000	0.3

Anticipated Gross Profit, 20,000 sq ft/4 years, $	Probability
200,000	0.2
400,000	0.3
500,000	0.4
700,000	0.1

On the basis of the expected profit estimations, what should Joe do?

13. Phillips and Kleine Combining Service anticipates a busy harvest of Nebraskan grain this year. It faces a dilemma about whether it should add no, one, or two combines to the current fleet. Each combine costs $50,000 per year to maintain. The average combining contract takes three days to complete and incurs $500 per day in variable costs. Each machine day of combining, however, also provides $1,500 of revenue. The acquisition decision really depends on how many additional combining days over and above last year's contracts the company can contract this year.

Additional Days	Probability with Good Weather	Probability with Bad Weather
−20	0.0	0.1
0	0.0	0.2
20	0.1	0.3
40	0.2	0.2
60	0.2	0.2
80	0.3	0.0
100	0.2	0.0

Seven of ten years have favorable harvesting weather. What should the company do?

14. The Mother Goose Toy Company (see Exhibit 7.9) has the option of conducting a market survey. If the survey is conducted, the demand probabilities will change:

Annual Demand, units	Probabilities	
	Survey Favorable	Survey Unfavorable
150,000	0.70	0.10
100,000	0.25	0.70
50,000	0.05	0.20

The probability of favorable survey results is 0.4, and the probability of unfavorable results is 0.6. The cost of the survey is $300,000. What would you advise Mother Goose to do?

15. Baby Bouncer Inc., a manufacturer of children's furniture and accessories, is evaluating capacity expansion proposals. Two alternatives are being investigated: expanding the current plant and building a new plant in another part of the country. The local expansion will cost $1.8 million, and the new plant $3.4 million. For strategic reasons the proposals have an assessed life of 20 years, with a 25 percent residual value. The cash flow from each proposal in year 1 is $50,000 and $80,000, respectively, increasing in year 2 to $230,000 and $350,000 and reaching a steady-state contribution of $380,000 and $690,000 in year 3; these latter contribution figures hold through year 20. Given Big Brother's requirement for all investments to generate 14 percent before tax, what is the NPV of each proposal? Which is more attractive?

16. Given the information on Baby Bouncer Inc.'s alternatives in problem 15, what are the payback period, equivalent annual annuity value, and internal rate of return for each proposal?

GROUP EXERCISES

Many of the tools and concepts discussed in this chapter are meant to be used in a team setting. The following problems are best solved by small groups of students. Ideally, each group should be composed of people with different backgrounds, interests, or areas of expertise.

1. As a group, visit a fast-foot restaurant and try to determine what the capacity is, using several different measures of capacity. Who in the organization needs to be concerned with capacity and capacity utilization? What influences capacity? What is the limiting capacity? What is the capacity constraint or bottleneck? How could this bottleneck be removed? What would be the next constraint? Is it worth the effort of removing the bottleneck? Why or why not? You might want to talk with the manager and employees. Why?

2. This book has spent only a little time talking about downsizing—*reducing* the size of a company—but this is a very important aspect of management. Pick a medium- to large-sized company near you and find out whether it has a strategic plan for shedding assets. If it does, discuss how the plan was established with the managers involved in strategic planning. Then develop a strategic capacity plan of your own.

REFERENCES AND SELECTED BIBLIOGRAPHY

AIPCS Dictionary 6th ed. [1987], American Production and Inventory Control Society, Falls Church, Va.

Berlinger, C., and J. A. Brimson [1988], *Cost Management for Today's Advanced Manufacturing*, Harvard Business School Press, Boston.

Brigham, E. F., A. L. Kahl, and W. F. Rentz [1991], *Canadian Financial Management*, Holt, Rinehart & Winston, Toronto.

Canadian Press [1993], Wire Story, July 3, byline Moscow.

Farwell, P. [1985], "New Development in Technology Financing," *The Dynamics of Technology: A Symposium*, no. 28, pp. 249–276.

Foster, Peter [1991], "McDonald's Excellent Soviet Venture?" *Canadian Business*, May, pp. 51–65.

Hayes, R. H., and S. C. Wheelwright [1984], *Restoring Our Competitive Edge*, Wiley, New York.

McConnell, Campbell R., Stanley L. Brue, and William Henry Pope [1990], *Microeconomics*, 5th Canadian ed., McGraw-Hill Ryerson, Toronto.

Noori, H. [1990], *Managing the Dynamics of New Technology: Issues in Manufacturing Management*, Prentice Hall, Englewood Cliffs, N.J.

Pindyck, Robert, and Daniel L. Rubinfeld [1989], *Microeconomics*, Macmillan, New York.

CHAPTER 8

FACILITY LOCATION AND LAYOUT

THE LEARNING FOCUS

Chapter 7 examined capacity planning and focused on timing, size, and downstream integration. The focus in this chapter is on facilities, including the following particulars:

- Where should each facility be located?
- How should the departments and processes within a facility be arranged?

- How will facility location and facility design decisions affect the firm's ability to compete?

You will learn which factors to consider when choosing a new location for a facility and arranging items within that facility. You will also become familiar with quantitative models that help managers choose facility locations and designs.

EXHIBIT 8.1 FRO MANUFACTURING PROFILE

How have Northern Telecom (North America's second largest supplier of telecommunications equipment) and thousands of other firms reduced costs? By separating production activities that are knowledge- and capital-intensive from those which are labor-intensive. The labor-intensive activities are carried out in Mexico and other newly industrialized countries where the workforce is large and wage rates are low. This rapidly growing worldwide phenomenon is referred to as *global production sharing*.

In Mexico, Northern Telecom has subcontracted work to maquiladora assembly plants operated by more than 400 contract employees. More than 2,000 of these plants, employing almost half a million people, can be found along the northern border of Mexico.

Maquila means putting together a product with someone else's material. A maquiladora plant manufactures products with consigned raw materials from foreign companies and exports the finished or semifinished goods back to the country of origin or to a third country. The Mexican plant never takes legal possession of the raw materials, and the foreign firm pays no tariffs on them.

Low wages alone are not responsible for Northern Telecom's decision to locate in Mexico. Shortly after opening a full-fledged sales and marketing office in Mexico City in 1989, Northern Telecom won a contract to supply digital equipment for the first cellular telephone system in that capital. The company feels that the potential for future contracts is enormous: Mexico is the fastest growing cellular market in the world.

As North American nations join together into an economic bloc, more companies are moving to Mexico for its market opportunities as well as its abundant labor pool.

Source: Adapted from Laurier Trade Development Centre (1992), p. 59.

EXHIBIT 8.2 FRO SERVICE PROFILE

Calgary, followed by Vancouver and Ottawa, tops the list of Canada's best airports, according to experts in business travel. The three terminals excel in terms of accessibility, layout, and passenger handling.

The well-designed layout of Calgary's airport means that travelers do not have to walk far from the plane to the luggage retrieval area and from there to the parking lot. The terminal at Ottawa's international airport is V-shaped, and so passengers whose arrival gate is on one side but whose departure gate is on the other need walk only a short distance.

Unlike many other airports, Calgary's is easily reached from both suburbia and downtown. Another plus is the bus from the airport to downtown. The service is not only cheap—at $6.50 an economical alternative to cabs and limousines—but convenient. Vancouver's airport is also easily accessible from downtown. There is also a convenient helicopter service to nearby Whistler Mountain, a popular site for meetings and conferences.

The rent-a-car facilities at the Calgary airport also receive high marks. The pickup stands for cars are close to the counters.

Source: Adapted from Fine (1993), p. B24.

8.1 MANAGERIAL ORIENTATION

Almost every day there are announcements of new stores, plants, and offices opening up nearby or moving to another part of the country. Within the United States, companies are moving their plants from the Great Lakes and the mideastern states to the "sun belt" states. Internationally, there is a trend toward global production sharing and relocating production processes in Mexico and other newly industrialized countries (see Exhibit 8.1).

What influences a firm to select a particular site, city, or country for its new facilities? How should the people, equipment, and materials within the facility be arranged? And what impact do facility location and facility layout have on a firm's ability to compete? These are the questions that will be addressed in this chapter.

8.2 FACILITY LOCATION

Once a firm has decided to open a new facility or relocate an existing one, it must decide where that facility should be located.

DEFINITION: *Facility location* involves the evaluation of various sites for a new or relocated facility.

The proximity to the firm's markets; the cost and availability of labor, materials, water, and energy; and the local infrastructure all influence the facility location decision (see Exhibit 8.3).

The strategic role assigned to a facility influences and is influenced by its location. Ferdows (1989) has identified six strategic roles a facility can play (see Exhibit 8.4).

Although firms consider a wide range of factors, in practice one criterion is often dominant. Consider the following examples:

- Fast-food restaurants and other mass-service organizations often make the concentration of customers the principal location criterion.

EXHIBIT 8.3 FACTORS INFLUENCING FACILITY LOCATION DECISIONS

Factor	Considerations
Resources	
Labor	Availability, skills, attitudes, cost, unionization
Materials	Availability, quality, cost
Equipment	Availability, quality, cost, ability to maintain
Land	Availability, suitability, cost
Energy	Availability, cost
Water	Availability, quality, cost
Markets	Proximity, size, potential needs
Infrastructure	
Financial institutions	Availability, strength, attitude
Support	Construction costs, availability, specialist services
Government	Stability, taxes, attitude, import and export restrictions, tariffs
Community	Attitude, quality of life (schools etc.), language, cultural issues, local business and management practices
Environment	Regulations, disposal and prevention policies, cost
Transportation	Infrastructure, availability, cost
Competition	Size, strength, attitude

EXHIBIT 8.4 STRATEGIC ROLES FOR OPERATING FACILITIES

		Extent of Facility's Technical Activities	
		Low	High
Primary Strategic Reason for the Facility	Access to low-cost production input factors	**Offshore** Maquiladora operations in northern Mexico	**Source** Semiconductor manufacturing operations in Singapore and Hong Kong
	Use of local technological resources	**Outpost** Setting up a facility in Japan to make parts for Toyota so that the firm can learn enough to become a supplier to Toyota when it builds a plant in North America	**Lead** IBM's German and Japanese plants
	Proximity to market	**Server** Australian subsidiaries of U.S. firms	**Contributor** Exxon's Canadian subsidiary has a world mandate in lubricating oil development

Bata Limited, the world's largest shoe manufacturer, has established a balanced portfolio of facilities. Although operations in each country are market-independent, the product can be sourced for a market from any manufacturing facility anywhere in the world. This allows subsidiaries to reschedule operations cooperatively to suit current global conditions. In addition, the firm has a central research facility at Hellocourt in France, where researchers and ordinary operators continually develop new technologies for improving the responsiveness of individual factories to local market conditions. These innovations are broadcast widely throughout the firm, and it is up to local managers to adopt or reject technologies.

- Nonemergency professional service organizations—lawyers, dentists, accountants, doctors—tend to locate close to areas in which they spend a great deal of time. Doctors may therefore locate close to hospitals, lawyers close to courts, and lobbyists close to government offices. Individual professionals such as lawyers and doctors may locate with others to share fixed costs.
- Emergency services choose locations that minimize their response times.

In North America there has been a significant move away from city centers to the suburbs among both manufacturing firms and retailers. This movement has sparked the advent of the shopping mall and the industrial park. Because land is usually less expensive in industrial parks than in alternative sites downtown, firms are in a position to build single-story facilities. These buildings improve internal transportation efficiency and keep construction costs down. For many service industries, however, one-floor facilities offer no cost advantages. Many of these firms (especially those in information and professional services) are moving into rehabilitated facilities vacated by manufacturing operations downtown.

Managers making facility location decisions usually have several sites from which to choose. There are many analytic models geared toward the facility location problem. Let us discuss several simple but potentially powerful models that can be used for this purpose.

Factor Rating

Factor rating (or factor weighting) is a five-step scoring procedure for evaluating alternative sites on the basis of many different criteria. Mathematically, this procedure is summarized by equation (8.1).

Factor Rating

$$S_i = \sum_{i=1}^{n} w_j s_{i,j} \qquad j = 1, 2, 3, \ldots, m \tag{8.1}$$

where S_i = total score for location i
 w_j = weight for factor j
 $s_{i,j}$ = score for location i on factor j

Let us walk through the five-step procedure, using the example outlined in Exhibit 8.5.

Step 1. Identify the most important factors in evaluating alternative sites.

Samson Ltd. has identified three important factors: availability of skilled labor, availability of raw materials, and proximity to its markets.

Step 2. Assign a weight (w_j) between 0 and 100 percent to each factor. The weight should reflect the factor's relative importance; the higher its importance, the higher the weight. The sum of the weights should equal 1.

The goods produced by Samson Ltd. are handcrafted. Therefore, the availability of skilled labor is the most important selection criterion. It has been assigned a weight of 50 percent. The availability of raw materials has been assigned a weight of 30 percent, and the proximity to Samson's markets has a weight of 20 percent.

Step 3. Assign the first alternative a score between 0 and 100 for the first factor ($s_{1,1}$). A value of 0 implies that the site completely fails to satisfy that criterion, while a value of 100 implies that the location perfectly satisfies it. Repeat for the remaining factors. Repeat this step for the remaining alternatives.

Only three sites are being considered by Samson. Each site has been assigned a score on each of the three factors. The results are shown in Exhibit 8.5A.

Step 4. Convert each score ($s_{i,j}$) into a weighted score by multiplying it by the factor's relative weight (w_j).

The weighted scores for Samson's alternative sites are shown in Exhibit 8.5B.

Step 5. Sum the weighted scores for each alternative. The alternative with the highest total score (S_i) is the preferred location.

Since site A has the highest score, it appears to be the best alternative. Because the total weighted scores are so close, however, the sensitivity of the preferred solution to changes in factor weights and scores should be checked.[1] For example, what happens if the weight for availability of skilled labor is changed to 45 percent and the weight for proximity to market is changed to 25 percent? Does site A still have the highest weighted score? Samson Ltd. may want to include secondary considerations (i.e., factors other than the three listed here) in the analysis as well.

Keep in mind that the list of important factors, their weights, and their assigned scores are all subjective. It may be worthwhile for members of the firm to do the analysis alone or in small groups first and then pool the results.

---

[1] Even if there is a clear winner, remember that a model is a decision-making aid, not a decision maker in its own right. This is true of all the models, both quantitative and qualitative, presented in this book.

EXHIBIT 8.5 TOOLBOX: FACTOR RATING

Samson Ltd. is considering three alternative sites for its new facility. After evaluating the firm's needs, the managers have narrowed the list of important selection criteria down to three factors: availability of skilled labor, availability of raw materials, and proximity to Samson's markets. Weights that reflect the relative importance of each factor have been assigned:

Factor	Weight (w_j)
Availability of skilled labor	0.50
Availability of raw materials	0.30
Proximity to market	0.20
	1.00

The three sites have been studied, and each has been assigned a score between 0 and 100 on each factor.

A. Site Scores

Factor	Score ($s_{i,j}$)		
	Site A	Site B	Site C
Skilled labor	70	70	50
Raw materials	60	40	90
Market	70	95	60

Which is the best site? Since none of the three sites has scored the highest in all three factors, the best site is not obvious.

If each score is multiplied by its factor weight and the weighted scores are summed for each site, site A appears to be the best.

B. Weighted Site Scores

(1) Factor	(2) Factor Weight (w_j)	Site A		Site B		Site C	
		(3) Score ($s_{1,j}$)	(4) Weighted Score	(5) Score ($s_{2,j}$)	(6) Weighted Score	(7) Score ($s_{3,j}$)	(8) Weighted Score
Skilled labor	0.50	70	35	70	35	50	25
Raw materials	0.30	60	18	40	12	90	27
Market	0.20	70	14	95	19	60	12
Total weighted score (S_i)			67		66		64

Column 4 = column 2 × column 3.
Column 6 = column 2 × column 5.
Column 8 = column 2 × column 7.

Now the firm judges the sensitivity of the results by changing the factor weights. Suppose the factor weights are 0.45, 0.4, and 0.15, respectively. The revised weighted scores for each site are shown below. Now the best site appears to be site C.

C. Revised Weighted Site Scores

Factor	Factor Weight (w_j)	Site A		Site B		Site C	
		Score ($s_{1,j}$)	Weighted Score	Score ($s_{2,j}$)	Weighted Score	Score ($s_{3,j}$)	Weighted Score
Skilled labor	0.45	70	31.5	70	31.50	50	22.5
Raw materials	0.40	60	24	40	16	90	36
Market	0.15	70	10.5	95	14.25	60	9
Total weighted score (S_i)			66		61.75		67.5

Cost-Profit-Volume Analysis

When the fixed and variable costs for each site differ, **cost-profit-volume analysis** can be used to identify the location with the lowest per unit operating costs (profit). Consider the example outlined in Exhibit 8.6 in view of this two-step procedure.

> **Step 1.** Estimate the annual fixed operating costs and the per unit variable costs associated with each site. Develop an equation that relates total costs to the production volume.

Foster Paper Ltd. is considering three different sites. The fixed costs and variable costs associated with each site have been estimated and are shown in Exhibit 8.6. The variable costs are simply a linear function of the production volume.

> **Step 2.** Calculate the expected total costs associated with the expected output of the new facility. The preferred alternative is the location with the lowest total costs. If the sales price and/or expected output volume are not the same for all locations, compare the expected profit associated with each location.

The expected annual production volume of Foster Paper Ltd.'s new facility is 250,000 units. At this production volume, site B has the lowest costs.

Cost-profit-volume analysis can also be used to identify the range over which each location provides the lowest per unit operating costs (the highest profits). In this example site B is the lowest-cost location only if the annual production volume is between 150,000 and 350,000 units. If the expected production volume is higher, site C becomes the lowest-cost location.

Since the costs used to compare alternative sites are often estimates, the sensitivity of the solution to changes in these estimates should be checked.

Center of Gravity Method

The **center of gravity method** is used to find a location that minimizes the sum of the transportation costs to and from a new facility. Transportation costs are assumed to be a linear function of the number of units shipped and the shipping distance.

The location of the firm's existing shipping and receiving facilities are converted into x and y coordinates that represent their relative positions. The two center of gravity equations [equations (8.2) and (8.3)] are then used to find the most cost-effective location for the new facility.

Center of Gravity Coordinates

$$C_x = \frac{\sum_{i=1}^{n} x_i V_i}{\sum_{i=1}^{n} V_i} \qquad C_y = \frac{\sum_{i=1}^{n} y_i V_i}{\sum_{i=1}^{n} V_i} \qquad (8.2, 8.3)$$

where C_x = x coordinate of new location

C_y = y coordinate of new location

i = number of existing shipping and receiving locations

n = total number of existing shipping and receiving locations

x_i = x coordinate of location i

y_i = y coordinate of location i

V_i = number of units shipped to and from location i

EXHIBIT 8.6   TOOLBOX: COST-VOLUME-PROFIT ANALYSIS

Foster Paper Ltd. is considering three alternative sites for its new production facility. The annual product cost associated with each alternative is a linear function of the production volume: total production costs = [fixed costs + (variable costs per unit)(production volume)]. The expected production level will be approximately 250,000 units a year.

TOTAL ANNUAL PRODUCTION COSTS

Site A: $PC = 10,000,000 + 250x$
Site B: $PC = 25,000,000 + 150x$
Site C: $PC = 60,000,000 + 50x$

where PC = total annual production costs
x = annual production volume, in units

Which site has the lowest costs? At a production volume of 250,000 units a year, site B has the lowest costs.

Site A: $PC = 10,000,000 + (250)(250,000) = 72,500,000$
Site B: $PC = 25,000,000 + (150)(250,000) = 62,500,000$
Site C: $PC = 60,000,000 + (50)(250,000) = 72,500,000$

However, as illustrated by the graph below, site B is not always the lowest-cost site.

The exact range over which each alternative is superior can be found by determining the production volume at which sites A and B have the same total production costs and at which sites B and C also have the same total production costs.

GRAPH OF THE TOTAL PRODUCTION COSTS ASSOCIATED WITH EACH SITE

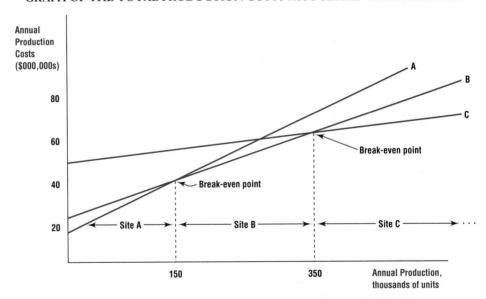

First, set the total cost equation for site A equal to the total cost equation for site B. Then solve for x:

Total cost equation, site A = Total cost equation, site B
$$10,000,000 + 250x = 25,000,000 + 150x$$
$$100x = 15,000,000$$
$$x = 150,000$$

Similarly, for sites B and C:

Total cost equation, site B = Total cost equation, site C
$$25,000,000 + 150x = 60,000,000 + 50x$$
$$100x = 35,000,000$$
$$x = 350,000$$

Therefore, the decision rules are:

- If the expected annual production volume is below 150,000 units a year, choose site A.
- If the expected annual production volume is between 150,000 and 350,000 units a year, choose site B.
- If the expected annual production volume is over 350,000, choose site C.

In Exhibit 8.7 these equations are used to locate a warehouse that will serve a set of distribution centers.

Transportation Model

A special form of linear programming, the **transportation model,** can be used to compare the total transportation costs associated with each of several potential sites. The underlying assumptions of the model are that (1) the items being shipped are homogeneous, (2) there is only one route and mode of transportation between each plant and each warehouse, and (3) the per unit shipping costs do not vary with the number of items being shipped.

For each location, the transportation model technique can be used to determine how many units should be shipped from each plant to each warehouse to minimize total transportation costs (maximize profits). The mechanics of this technique are tedious.[2] The transportation module of ©OM-Expert (the software that accompanies this text) was used to compare two potential sites for a manufacturer in Exhibit 8.8.

Simulation Models

Firms often consider many variables when choosing a facility location, and the values of the variables are difficult to estimate and prone to change. In these dynamic situations, simulation may be the best modeling technique. **Simulation models** allow managers to examine a range of scenarios and are well suited to open-ended problems such as emergency facility location. However, they require a considerable amount of data and may take a long time to run.[3]

8.3 FACILITY LAYOUT

Once a firm has decided where a facility will be located, the next important operational decision is the arrangement of people and equipment within the facility, or the **facility layout.**

> **DEFINITION:** Facility or plant layout involves the location of departments within the facility and the arrangement of people and equipment within each department.

Note that any layout decision affects, among other things, the flow of materials, handling and maintenance costs, equipment utilization, the productivity of the plant, and the effectiveness of employees and management. Facility layout can also directly affect customer satisfaction, as in an airport (see Exhibit 8.2).

---

[2] *OM-Companion,* a student workbook developed for use with this book, covers a broad range of issues. You will find, for example, a comprehensive review of the mechanics of some of the most popular quantitative tools, including the transportation model.

[3] Refer to the accompanying *OM-Companion* for a description of how simulation models are built and run.

EXHIBIT 8.7 TOOLBOX: CENTER OF GRAVITY METHOD

Aldrich Manufacturing Inc. plans to build a warehouse to serve its distribution centers in Columbus (Ohio), Frankfort (Ky.), Nashville (Tenn.), and Richmond (Va.) and its plant in Harrisburg (Pa.). These locations have been plotted on a grid map of the area.

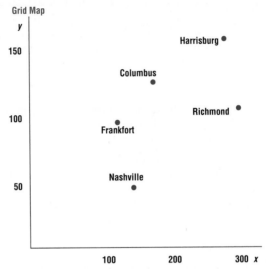

The numbers of units to be shipped monthly from Harrisburg to the distribution centers are shown in the following table.

SHIPPING VOLUMES AND GRID COORDINATES

	(2)	Grid Coordinates		Weighted Grid Coordinates	
		(3)	(4)	(5)	(6)
(1)	Annual Shipping	x axis	y axis	x axis	y axis
Location	Volume, in units				
Harrisburg	5,000	270	160	1,350,000	800,000
Columbus	750	170	130	127,500	97,500
Frankfort	1,250	120	90	150,000	112,500
Nashville	2,500	110	50	275,000	125,000
Richmond	500	275	100	137,500	50,000
Total	10,000			2,040,000	1,185,000

Column 5 = column 2 × column 3.
Column 6 = column 2 × column 4.

Using equation (8.2), the x coordinate of the new warehouse should be about equal to

$$C_x = \frac{\sum_{i=1}^{5} x_i V_i}{\sum_{i=1}^{5} V_i} = \frac{2,040,000}{10,000} = 204$$

Using equation (8.3), the y coordinate of the new warehouse should be about equal to

$$C_y = \frac{\sum_{i=1}^{5} y_i V_i}{\sum_{i=1}^{5} V_i} = \frac{1,185,000}{10,000} = 118.5$$

The nearest city to (204, 118.5) is Charleston, West Virginia.

EXHIBIT 8.8   TOOLBOX: TRANSPORTATION MODEL

The transportation model is an important quantitative tool in operations management; it is used to allocate product from *m* sources of supply to *n* destinations or users. Because of its importance, the transportation model is described more fully in the workbook accompanying this text. This exhibit describes how to set up the initial table, for this is important in ensuring that the correct data are correctly entered into any model, and then use ©OM Expert to solve a problem. Note that similar software can be used as well.

Straub Ltd. has three plants running at full capacity in Des Moines, Racine, and Gary. These plants supply four distribution warehouses in St. Paul, Milwaukee, Chicago, and Detroit. The expected demand next year is forecast to exceed current capacity by 10 percent, so Straub plans to build another plant. It has narrowed down the choice of sites to two possibilities: Kalamazoo and Duluth.

Using the transportation costs, warehouse demands, and plant capacities shown below, one can determine which site results in lower overall transportation costs.

PLANT CAPACITIES AND WAREHOUSE DEMANDS

Plant	Quantity Produced per Year, units	Warehouse	Quantity Demanded per Year, units
Des Moines	500	St. Paul	225
Racine	300	Milwaukee	175
Gary	200	Chicago	325
Kalamazoo	225	Detroit	350
Duluth	225		

SHIPMENT COSTS, $ PER UNIT

Plant	*Distribution Warehouses*			
	St. Paul	Milwaukee	Chicago	Detroit
Des Moines	15	20	20	30
Racine	20	3	5	20
Gary	25	8	3	13
Kalamazoo	28	11	6	6
Duluth	7	12	17	11

Straub Ltd. is very flexible: any plant can ship units to any distribution warehouse. Therefore, the first step is to find the optimal number of units to ship between each plant-warehouse combination, assuming that the new plant is in Kalamazoo. Then the assumption is that the new plant is in Duluth. Finally, the total shipping costs associated with each alternative are compared.

The data appear in the transportation table below. Note that the initial table is a matrix with a row for each plant and a column for each warehouse. An extra row is added to show demand at each warehouse, and an extra column shows the supply from each plant. Total supply and total demand must be equal for the model to work. Note also that the upper right-hand corner of each cell shows the shipping cost of sending one unit from the plant associated with the cell to the associated warehouse. Once the firm is confident that the details are correct and total supply and demand are in balance, it can enter the data into the computer program.

Plant	*Distribution Warehouses*				Plant Supply
	St. Paul	Milwaukee	Chicago	Detroit	
Des Moines	15	20	20	30	500
Racine	20	3	5	20	300
Gary	25	8	3	13	200
Kalamazoo	28	11	6	6	225
Warehouse demand	225	175	325	350	

(Exhibit 8.8 continues on next page)

EXHIBIT 8.8 *(continued)*

Using the transportation module of ©OM-Expert, the optimal number of units to ship between each plant and the proposed Kalamazoo distribution warehouse is as follows:

Plant	Distribution Warehouses				Plant Supply
	St. Paul	Milwaukee	Chicago	Detroit	
Des Moines	225 15	20	20	125 30	500
Racine	20	175 3	125 5	20	300
Gary	25	8	200 3	13	200
Kalamazoo	28	11	6	225 6	225
Warehouse demand	225	175	325	350	

The total transportation costs will be $10,225 if the new plant is built in Kalamazoo. (This can be calculated by hand simply by multiplying the shipment in each cell by its unit cost and summing the totals. ©OM-Expert does this automatically.)

Using ©OM-Expert again, the optimal number of units to ship between each plant and the proposed Duluth distribution warehouse was found:

Plant	Distribution Warehouses				Plant Supply
	St. Paul	Milwaukee	Chicago	Detroit	
Des Moines	15	20	20	250 30	500
Racine	20	175 3	125 5	20	300
Gary	25	8	200 3	13	200
Duluth	225 7	12	17	225 32	225
Warehouse demand	225	175	325	350	

The total transportation costs will be $13,825 if the new plant is build in Duluth. Therefore, the Kalamazoo plant will incur the lowest transportation costs.

Every plant layout must satisfy a specific objective or set of objectives. Usually the layout is planned to minimize a particular criterion: total travel time, cost, delays, or physical handling and processing. There are also situations in which the layout may be designed to maximize a criterion: quality, flexibility, or personal contact. Therefore, determining the objective is the first step in the facility layout process.

Layout Types

In practice, there are essentially four basic ways in which facilities are organized:

- **Process layout.** Similar pieces of equipment or functions are grouped together; for example, all drill presses are grouped together.
- **Product layout.** The pieces of equipment required to make a particular product are grouped together, as in an automobile assembly line.
- **Group technology layout.** The pieces of equipment required to make a set of products that have similar shapes or operational requirements are grouped together, as in the new accounts desk at a bank.

- **Fixed layout.** The equipment is brought to the object being processed, and the object does not move, as in house construction.

The desired layout type depends on the firm's operations strategy, the forecast volume of production, the physical characteristics of the product, the availability of resources, and the type of process technology that will be used. These layout types are examined in detail in Chapter 9.

From a facility design perspective, there is one major difference between process layouts and product layouts. A process layout begins with the building and places the departments inside, while a product layout begins with the process and establishes the building around the equipment. Once a product layout has been established, changing it can be expensive, and managers must closely examine the greenfield option each time a major refurbishing of a product layout is contemplated.

The greenfield approach to facility design is based on the idea that new facilities make it possible to start over in terms of facility layout. Rather than using a piecemeal approach to expanding or partially rearranging the existing layout, management makes the decision to start from scratch, by looking at the present machinery and seeing if any of it fits into future facility needs and then building from there. Toyota uses this approach with its engine plants in Nagoya. Each plant is dedicated to one engine model. The life of each plant is five years, after which it is pulled down and replaced by a new one. The new plant incorporates the latest engine-making technology, including improvements made by line operators who have used the previous generation of equipment.

Quantitative Models for Facility Layout Decisions

Arranging people and equipment in a facility can quickly become complex. If a firm has decided to group similar pieces of equipment or activities together in a process layout, there is usually a large number of alternative layouts from which to choose. The greater the variety of ways in which products are routed through the facility, the greater the number of potential layouts.

In most instances, however, there is an underlying sense of flow or relationship. Work may never flow directly from some departments or work centers to the others or may flow in one direction only. Conversely, work may almost always flow directly from one department or work center to another. Some work centers (such as a painting operation and a sanding operation) must be kept apart. Although these constraints partially limit the number of feasible layouts, many alternatives may still exist. When there are many alternatives to consider, the analytic models described in this section are helpful.

Minimizing Communication Costs   Departments or work centers are frequently arranged so that communications costs are minimized. For example, if there is considerable traffic between pairs of departments, a firm may want to minimize the cost of interdepartmental travel.

Consider the problem of Frontenac Ltd. illustrated in Exhibit 8.9. This part of the building will contain four departments arranged in a row. Frontenac has estimated the number of daily communications between departments and wishes to minimize the total daily interdepartmental distance traveled. Two possible configurations and the total interdepartmental distance traveled for each configuration are shown in the exhibit. The second configuration is better, but the firm has to consider all 24 possible configurations before it knows if this is the optimal configuration.

EXHIBIT 8.9   TOOLBOX: MINIMIZING INTERDEPARTMENTAL TRAFFIC

Frontenac Inc. wants to arrange four of its departments in a row so that the total distance traveled between departments is minimized. The number of daily communications between each pair of departments is shown below. Assume that adjacent departments are 20 feet apart.

NUMBER OF DAILY COMMUNICATIONS BETWEEN DEPARTMENTS

Pair of Departments	Number of Daily Communications
A and B	20
A and C	25
A and D	15
B and C	10
B and D	15
C and D	30

Configuration 1: | A | B | C | D |

(1) Pair of Departments	(2) Distance between Departments, feet	(3) Number of Daily Communications	(4) Total Daily Communication Distance, feet
A and B	20	20	400
A and C	40	25	1,000
A and D	60	15	900
B and C	20	10	200
B and D	40	15	600
C and D	20	30	600
Total			*3,700*

Column 4 = column 2 × column 3.

Configuration 2: | B | A | C | D |

(1) Pair of Departments	(2) Distance between Departments, feet	(3) Number of Daily Communications	(4) Total Daily Communication Distance, feet
A and B	20	20	400
A and C	20	25	500
A and D	40	15	600
B and C	40	10	400
B and D	60	15	900
C and D	20	30	600
Total			*3,400*

Column 4 = column 2 × column 3.

In terms of total daily communication distance, solution 2 is the preferred alternative.

This trial-and-error approach becomes time-consuming as the number of departments to be arranged increases and becomes complex when the nature and cost of communications vary between departments. For example, the communication between one pair of departments may consist of standard pieces of paper, while between another pair it may consist of large lots of manufactured components. Under these circumstances, costs are often assigned to the different types of communications and the objective is to minimize total communications costs.

Systematic Layout Planning   Systematic layout planning (SLP) is an organized approach to facility layout planning that was developed by Muther (1961). The heart of SLP is the activity relationship chart and diagrams that neatly summarize vast amounts of quantitative and qualitative information. SLP can be broken down into a seven-step procedure (see Exhibit 8.10).

Step 1. Collect and analyze information about the processes to be housed in the facility and the products to be produced. Select a process, product, or group technology layout.

The flow of work through Kendall, Stanford and Freeman (KSF), the accounting firm in Exhibit 8.10, varies from job to job. A process layout is the most suitable layout in this case.

Step 2. Analyze interactions between areas or departments to be arranged. Assess the desirability of placing areas or departments close together.

Interactions can take the form of materials movements, personal communications, and so forth. KSF has identified four different types of interactions between departments. The desirability of locating departments close together is based on the frequency and importance of these interactions.

Step 3. Construct an activity relationship chart that summarizes the information collected in step 2.

The activity relationship chart will contain an assessment code that reflects the desirability of placing two departments close together. For example, assessment code A means that it is absolutely essential that these two departments or functions be close together, while code X means that it is absolutely essential that these two departments or functions *not* be close together. KSF does not want the junior staff area to be near the reception area.

Reason codes may be added as well. As the name implies, these codes indicate why a pair of departments has been assigned a particular assessment code. The reason codes developed by KSF reflect the type of interactions identified in step 2.

Step 4. Construct an activity relationship diagram based on the activity relationship chart and information regarding the flow of communication, materials, and so forth.

The activity relationship diagram is essentially an illustration of the information contained in the activity relationship chart. All the departments in this diagram are represented by equal-sized boxes. This gives facility designers an overview of which departments should and should not be placed together.

Step 5. Estimate the space required for each department, keeping in mind the space available.

KSF has estimated the space, in square feet, that is required. Some firms want to specify the exact dimensions required for each area.

Step 6. Transform the activity relationship chart into a space relationship chart.

The size of each box should reflect the relative size of the department it represents in this chart.

Step 7. Keeping in mind practical limitations, develop and evaluate alternative layouts.

EXHIBIT 8.10   TOOLBOX: SYSTEMATIC LAYOUT PLANNING

Kendall, Stanford and Freeman, a small accounting firm, has just rented space in a new one-floor building. The firm has used a process layout and has allocated the 6,000 square feet (100 feet by 60 feet) to its seven departments as follows:

Departments	Allocated Space, square feet
1. Reception area	200
2. Offices for partners	1,200
3. Offices for managers	1,200
4. Junior staff area	2,500
5. Administration	500
6. Library	200
7. Meeting room	200

The firm has carefully analyzed its operations to determine the importance of locating specific areas close together. The results of this analysis are summarized in the planning chart below.

ACTIVITY RELATIONSHIP CHART

Departments	Department					
	1	2	3	4	5	6
1. Reception	—					
2. Partners	E, 2	—				
3. Managers	O, 1	O, 3	—			
4. Juniors	X, 2	U	I, 3	—		
5. Administration	X, 2	U	U	U	—	
6. Library	U	U	O, 1	O, 4	U	—
7. Meeting room	E, 2	E, 2, 4	O, 4	U	U	U

CLOSENESS AND REASON CODES

Closeness Code	Importance of Locating a Pair of Departments Next to Each Other	Reason Code	Meaning
A	Absolutely essential	1	Frequent personal communication
E	Essential	2	Frequent interaction with clients
I	Important	3	Ease of supervision
O	Ordinary importance	4	Frequent use of resources
U	Unimportant		
X	Undesirable		

The activity relationship diagram shown below illustrates the importance of locating departments close together (or far apart).

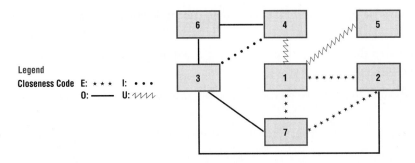

Legend
Closeness Code E: ★ ★ ★   I: • • •
                O: ———   U: ⋀⋀⋀

The next activity relationship diagram shows the relative size of each department. Note that in this case there are no restrictions on the length and width of each department.

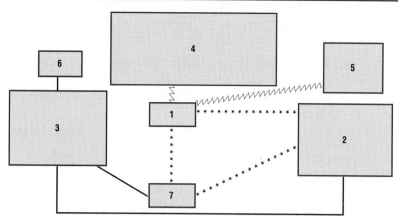

The facility has only one serious restriction: the reception area should be at the front entrance. If possible, the partners should be allocated offices along the outside wall of the building.

The floor plan shown below was developed as follows:

1. The reception area (department 1) was placed at the front entrance of the building.
2. It is considered essential that the offices for the partners (department 2), the meeting room (department 7), and the reception area be close to each other. Therefore, the partners' offices and the meeting room were placed around the reception area.
3. Since it is undesirable to have the junior staff area (department 4) and the administration area (department 5) near each other, these areas were placed in opposite corners of the building.
4. It is important that the juniors and the managers (department 3) be close together; the managers have been placed between the partners and the juniors.
5. The library (department 6) was placed in the only remaining spot.

INITIAL FLOOR PLAN

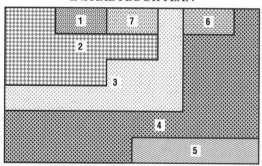

This floor plan will be revised until the firm is satisfied that the best layout has been found.

KSF has only one serious restriction: the reception area should be close to the front entrance. If possible, the partners should be allocated offices along the outside wall of the building.

Usually departments are positioned one by one, beginning with the department with the highest A ratings, followed by the department(s) with the highest X ratings. Once that is done, the other departments are usually located by taking the polar positions into account; it is typical to locate all A relationships first, then all E relationships, and so on.

SLP is essentially an organized trial-and-error approach. Therefore, unless all possible layouts are considered, there is no way to know if an optimal solution has been reached. In fact, it is difficult to find the optimal solution for any realistic layout problem. There are, however, a number of heuristics (rules of thumb) that can be used to generate good solutions quickly. Some examples of heuristics follow.

Application of Heuristics in Layout Planning   Layout planning heuristics are of two types: those which start with an initial layout and proceed to modify it (*improvement* heuristics) and those which start the layout analysis from scratch (*construction* heuristics).

> **Reminder.** When one uses heuristics, an optimal solution is not guaranteed.

Perhaps the most widely known algorithm requiring that an initial layout be developed by hand is the **computerized relative allocation of facilities technique (CRAFT)**. Since CRAFT was developed for situations in which materials handling costs were a major consideration, its goal is to minimize the total cost of moving items between departments. The initial CRAFT algorithm could handle single-story buildings with up to 40 departments. An extension of CRAFT called SPACECRAFT can handle multistory buildings with over 100 departments.

CRAFT attempts to improve an initial layout by switching the locations of pairs of departments. It begins with one department and, one by one, analyzes the effect on total travel costs of switching that department with each of the remaining ones. The switch that reduces travel costs the most is made. A second department is then selected, and the search for the greatest reduction in costs is made again. The process is repeated until total travel costs can be reduced no further.

The facility layout module of ©OM-Expert was used to apply the CRAFT algorithm to the problem described in Exhibit 8.11.

Computerized relationship layout planning (CORELAP) and **automated layout design program (ALDEP)** are two typical construction heuristics. Both start with an open floor area and proceed to fit departments into the area, using assessment codes (like those used in systematic layout planning) that reflect the desirability of placing departments close together. ALDEP and CORELAP are used when activity relationships are a major consideration.

ALDEP can be used to lay out up to 63 departments in a multistory building. The random-selection version of ALDEP begins by randomly selecting a department and placing it in the layout. Next, departments with the high assessment codes (e.g., SLP codes A and E) are placed next to the selected department. Then another unplaced department is randomly selected and placed in the layout. Unplaced departments with high assessment codes are then located close to this department. This process continues until all departments have been placed in the layout, and the layout is then scored. The program generates as many different layouts as the user desires.

CORELAP can lay out up to 70 departments in a single-story facility. Each assessment code is assigned a numerical value. A total closeness rating for each department is calculated by summing the assessment code values assigned to each pair of departments in which the code appears. The department with the highest total closeness rating is placed in the layout first. One by one, departments that have assessment codes A, E, and then O are selected and placed in the layout. The program then chooses the unplaced department with the highest total closeness rating until the last department has been placed in the layout. Only one layout is generated.

> **Reminder.** The physical facilities should be designed for replacement and obsolescence. Because technologies change rapidly and market needs and expectations shift rather quickly, facilities and technologies must be modified

EXHIBIT 8.11   TOOLBOX: DESIGNING OFFICE LAYOUTS WITH CRAFT

Kendall, Stanford and Freeman feels that a better floor plan exists and would like to improve its plan. A survey of traffic between all the areas has been conducted, and the results are shown in the tables below.

WEEKLY VOLUME OF TRAFFIC

| | Department | | | | | |
Department	1	2	3	4	5	6
1. Reception	—					
2. Partners	100	—				
3. Managers	50	200	—			
4. Juniors	25	50	300	—		
5. Administration	25	50	100	100	—	
6. Library	1	5	10	10	1	—
7. Meeting room	15	20	15	10	1	2

ESTIMATED COST OF EACH INTERACTION

| | Department | | | | | |
Department	1	2	3	4	5	6
1. Reception	—					
2. Partners	3	—				
3. Managers	2	3	—			
4. Juniors	1	2	3	—		
5. Administration	1	1	1	1	—	
6. Library	1	3	2	1	1	—
7. Meeting room	3	3	2	1	1	3

The facility layout module of ©OM-Expert was used to revise the initial layout. The revised layout below reduces communication costs from $163,691.33 to $154,471.33.

INITIAL LAYOUT (COST = $163,691.33)

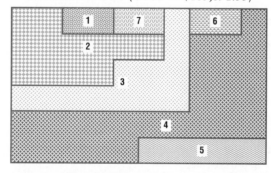

ITERATION ONE, ALSO THE FINAL LAYOUT (COST = $154,471.33)

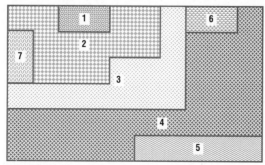

to suit the market. It is better to have greenfield sites than to modify existing structures; low-cost, expendable physical facilities can be torn down and replaced with more suitable structures designed for the life of the product or service. The same is true of the operating technologies installed within the plants. This requires, of course, managerial acceptance of the need for rapid replacement of structures as market requirements dictate. Managerial flexibility is therefore very critical.

Layout Planning for Distribution Centers

This chapter has described the design of operating layouts for production processes. Layouts also have to be designed for other operating environments, such as maintenance centers and distribution centers. This section will examine layout planning for two common types of distribution centers: warehouses and retail stores. Managers in these settings are concerned with both storage and movement of materials, the latter of which is less predictable than it is in most manufacturing environments. Self-service retail stores have the additional challenge of moving and managing crowds, adding another dimension to retail layout complexity (full-service retail shops—those with a counter past which customers cannot proceed—are laid out with regard to efficiency).

Retail Layouts   In self-service retail stores and shopping malls layouts must take into consideration the movement of materials and people, the location and allocation of space to particular merchandise, and the psychology of purchasing. This becomes complicated when the store has more than one entrance for customers and when shopping hours are extended beyond the "traditional" limits, for in this case replenishing displays must take place while customers are present.

The first issues to be decided are normally how to lay out the store and how to group merchandise. There are two basic layout patterns: *gridiron* (the typical rectangular display pattern favored by supermarkets) and *free flow* (the open, cellular pattern favored by department stores). Free flow formats are easy to change and often are altered periodically to reflect the season or give the store a new look. Heavy or special fixtures such as freezers and refrigerated displays, rarely if ever, are moved.

Once the product clusters and layout configurations have been chosen, floor space can be allocated. This critical management decision is normally based on sales history and sales expectations for the store, the firm, or the industry. Forecasts, of course, are never accurate, and managers must adjust displays periodically to reflect customer requirements.

Deciding *where* to place departments or products is also important, for it helps manage traffic flow and exposure to impulse purchasing. Perfumes and toiletries are usually placed near the busiest entrances in department stores, while staple items are placed farthest from the entrances to draw customers past other merchandise. The new social phenomenon of "swarming" is also influencing layouts, particularly the location of stores in malls.

For store managers and their suppliers of nondurable goods, the location of individual products is important, particularly in supermarkets. Items with the greatest turnover get the most shelf space and the most accessible shelf space. The amount of space also depends on the ability to restock without inconveniencing customers. Many stores or departments that sell durable goods get around the restocking problem by displaying stock only on the retail floor; purchased merchandise is delivered at the checkout or to the home from a separate storage area or warehouse.

Often forgotten in retail store layout are the location of checkouts and the attendant problems of checkout line management and the ability to provide information and assistance to customers. These issues will not be dealt with here, but remember that *every* aspect of operation must be consistent with the strategy and every other aspect.

Storage and Warehouse Layouts   While visibility may be very important in designing a self-service layout, ease of storage and retrieval is the most important criterion in a storage layout. Another important criterion is stock rotation, especially when items are perishable or prone to obsolescence.

Provided that ease of access has been achieved and stock is allowed to rotate, the denser the layout, the better. Aisles need to be little wider than the equipment for moving and handling stock, and equipment should be selected that allows the fullest use of the internal height of the building.

There are significant differences between automated and manually picked storehouses. In a storehouse using **automated storage and retrieval systems (AS/RS),** there need be no or little light, the aisles need be no wider than the largest dimension of the biggest stock item, buildings can be higher, and weight restrictions do not apply. Of more significance, however, is the need to store items at random.[4] Randomness is required to overcome the potential pitfall in an operating AS/RS: picking crane breakdown. A crane is dedicated to each aisle, picking from either side. If each product is stored in a unique location, a crane breakdown will mean no access to the affected stock until the equipment is repaired.

In a manual system, good lighting levels are required and all items of the same product should be in the same place or on the same pallet. Heavy items should be stored at knee level or lower, and the stored package sizes should be no heavier or bulkier than one person can comfortably handle.

It makes sense to reduce the travel time as much as possible, and high-turnover stocks should be kept close to the loading bays. Typical decision rules in a manually operated warehouse include:

- If all products require the same amount of storage space, the greater the rate of turnover, the closer to the loading bay.
- If each product requires a different amount of storage space, the greater the turnover per unit of storage area or volume, the closer to the loading bay.

If the products are seasonal, the warehouse manager should be concerned about changing the storage locations with the seasons. Relocating the entire stock in some cases, however, may be more expensive than the cost of leaving the stock as it is.

The assumption so far has been that the **out-and-back stockpicking** system is used. The stockpicker goes out, gets one item, comes back to the shipping area, and then goes back to get a second item. This system is often used in manually picked warehouses and is almost always used in warehouses with AS/RS systems. Other systems used in manually picked warehouses include:

- **Route collection system.** The stockpicker picks up a variety of products to be shipped to one customer, and the order is consolidated by the stockpicker in the consolidating/shipping area.

---

[4] The computer controlling the operation is capable of correctly recalling the location of every item in each cell.

- **Batch picking.** The stockpicker picks a quantity of a product for a group of customers who are shipped to by a common carrier. This system may be an aggregated out-and-back or an aggregated route system, depending on the amounts involved. In either case the goods are consolidated in customer lots before being placed on the vehicle.
- **Zone picking.** The stockpicker picks from a specific area of the warehouse and sends the goods to the shipping area, where the goods are consolidated by customer. The zone picker has no idea who the customer is or which carrier is being used.

The stockpicking system used influences how and where items are stored.

Office Layouts

Over 40 percent of the North American workforce is employed in offices, and some experts suggest that marked productivity improvements can be gained by improving office layout. Proximity and privacy are two key considerations in arranging an office.

People who need to work together should be close together so that they can interact. Although this may seem obvious, it often is *not* obvious at first glance. A national paper products company, for example, markedly improved its performance by moving its product cost accountants from the costing office in each plant to the office area of the managers responsible for manufacturing the products. Not only did the reduced distance increase the rate of communication, it allowed all managers to become conversant with manufacturing and accounting realities and conventions. The expanded management groups made better decisions and improved quality and output, both of which improved efficiency.

For many people privacy is related to personal importance and worth; to some it is an issue of personal space. To yet another group privacy is an issue of supervisory pressure and constant threatening observation.

Four basic types of office layouts—traditional, office landscaping, activity settings, and electronic cottages—offer different blends of privacy and proximity:

- **Traditional layout.** Managers have private offices, while clerical workers and perhaps first-line managers work in an open area. This may be an appropriate setting for specialized activities such as drafting stations in a large engineering shop and the workstations of people who are often out of the office, such as reporters or an outside sales force. One key requirement is that the work of each person in the room or space be independent from that of others. Another is that noise generated at any particular station should not distract others in the area.
- **Office landscaping.** Everyone is in one huge area; plants and low furniture are used to generate some privacy or screening. However, for most people the ability to hold private and sensitive conversations is severely limited.
- **Activity settings.** Each person has a very small private workstation as a firm base but is expected to work from a variety of workstations during the day as job needs dictate. Each public workstation allows electronic access to the private electronic files in the personal workstation. The activity settings include libraries, conference facilities, special shared graphics areas and terminal areas, and relaxation areas; the private workstations are grouped around sets of common-use settings. This setting is useful for people who work in official and unofficial groups and normally work in more than one group at a time. Advertising offices and accounting consultancies find this arrangement useful.

- **Electronic cottage.** People work from home without going into the office for extended periods. This option is suitable for managers who want to avoid commuting but stay in touch and for secretarial and clerical staffs. It allows traveling managers and sales force to keep in touch with the home base without physically returning. Where face-to-face contact is required, the electronic cottage is out of the question. In all situations, however, it seems necessary for the isolation to be brief and for physical, visual contact to be made with fellow workers at frequent intervals.

Whatever the layout chosen, compared to a manufacturing environment, it is relatively easy to rearrange people and equipment as the needs of the firm dictate.

MANAGERIAL IMPLICATIONS

Sometimes a firm has no choice when it locates a new facility or changes the location of an existing facility. When it does have a choice, though, it generally decides to locate facilities to produce the lowest overall cost of operation and coordination. Often, the lowest cost of coordination is associated with the greatest ease of coordination.

There are several techniques for deciding on the best combination of sites for a collection of operations. The best model to use is that which gives a firm the most *effective* combination of sites. Many managers use quantitative models, and these models focus on *efficiency*. In many situations efficiency and effectiveness are not synonymous; further, the only factors that can be used in quantitative models are factors that a firm can quantify. This is particularly difficult in considering people. How, for instance, can one quantify the work ethic of rural workers and their lack of skills compared with those of workers available in cities? Locating in rural settings worked well for Nucor but not for Babcock & Wilcox. Managers are much better off using a simple model that incorporates the factors that can

be quantified and then tempering the outcome with their analysis of the qualitative factors.

The same implications hold for facility layouts. Layout considerations must follow from the decision about what is to be located in the facility and what the facility is to focus on. Generally, if there is a dominant flow pattern, the firm will want to lay out the facility's elements in a manner similar to the process flow. If there are many jumbled flows, the layout should seek to minimize confusion and be as efficient as possible. Within elements the firm will repeat the analysis, working down ultimately to the smallest particle of operational organization: the work cell.

It is unlikely that facility location decisions would need to be made hastily, for market locations will not change rapidly except in dramatic cases. This is because populations are not highly mobile and population shifts within a country and across the world occur rather slowly. The key strategic decision for an FRO, then, is how large to make the facilities and what to put in them rather than where to put them.

CHAPTER SUMMARY

Once a firm has decided to open a new facility or relocate an existing one, it must decide where that facility should be located. Then it must decide how to arrange the people, equipment, and activities within the facility. This chapter has discussed the issues and concerns faced by managers as they make facility location and layout decisions. It also introduced several quantitative models that can be helpful in making these decisions. The major concepts and points are:

- The proximity to the firm's markets; the cost and availability of labor, materials, water, and energy; and the local infrastructure all influence the facility location decision. In practice, however, one criterion tends to dominate the others.

- In North America there has been a significant move away from city centers to the suburbs for both manufacturing firms and retailers. The move of firms to the fringes of cities has sparked the advent of the shopping mall and the industrial park. Many service sector firms, however, have been moving into rehabilitated facilities vacated by manufacturing operations downtown.
- The following quantitative models can be applied to facility location:
  1. Factor rating is used to evaluate alternative sites. Both quantitative and qualitative factors can be considered. Alternative sites are scored on each factor.
  2. Cost-volume-profit analysis is used to identify the site with the lowest per unit operating cost (profit).
  3. The center of gravity method is used to find the location that minimizes total transportation costs to and from a new facility.
  4. The transportaton model is used to compare total transportation costs for alternative sites.
  5. Simulation models are used to compare several sites. The effects of changing many variables are evaluated.
- Facility layout analysis can be done at two levels. At the higher level, the analysis concerns the location of departments or even whole plants within a facility. At the lowest level, the issue is one of laying out processes and individual items of equipment within a department.
- There are essentially four basic layout types: process, product, group technology, and fixed.
- Whenever there are many possible layouts, quantitative models can be helpful.
  1. Systematic layout planning (SLP) is a trial-and-error approach to facility layout. An activity relationship chart shows the desirability of placing two departments close together.
  2. CRAFT, CORELAP, and ALDEP are three heuristic-based algorithms that generate facility layouts.
- The emphasis in layout planning for retail stores is on arranging products to enhance sales. In storage facilities the emphasis is on efficient storage and retrieval.

KEY TERMS

Facility location	Product layout	Computerized	Out-and-back
Factor rating	Group technology layout	relationship layout	stockpicking
Cost-profit-volume	Fixed layout	planning (CORELAP)	Route collection system
analysis	Systematic layout	Automated layout design	Batch picking
Center of gravity method	planning (SLP)	program (ALDEP)	Zone picking
Transportation model	Computerized relative	Automated storage and	Traditional office layout
Simulation models	allocation of facilities	retrieval systems	Office landscaping
Facility layout	technique (CRAFT)	(AS/RS)	Activity settings
Process layout			Electronic cottage

DISCUSSION QUESTIONS

1. Which current trends are influencing facility location? What do *you* think will be a new or changed influence on facility location in the year 2001?

2. What are some of the critical factors influencing the location of an oil refinery, a general hospital, an electric utility, a take-out pizza restaurant, and a lawn care service?

3. Are the criteria used for locating a shopping mall different from the criteria used for locating a specialty store in a mall?

4. What models can be employed to make facility location decisions? What information is used in these models?

5. What are the advantages and disadvantages of relying on mathematical models in making facility location decisions?

6. What is facility layout?

7. What are the basic layout types? Which ones could be used for the facilities in question 2?

8. What are the two groups of techniques for designing a facility with a process layout? What computer algorithms are associated with each technique? How do the techniques differ?

9. How has the computer influenced the layout of warehouses? The layout of supermarkets?

10. What criteria are used for designing office layouts? How is their individual importance changing?

11. Is it possible to have different layout types at the plant level and the department level in a factory? Why or why not?

12. A friend comes to you and says, "Well, I've just built a brand-new factory with the best possible equipment and layout. I'll *never* have to worry about poor layouts again." What do you say to your friend?

13. What influences the layout of retail stores? Does the type of retail store make any difference in regard to the layouts available?

14. What influences lie behind the layout of your university or college? The layout of the building in which you take your operations management class? Do you think the layout is the best it can be? What changes would you make, and why?

15. Are there any differences in the layouts of the fast-food restaurants and full-service restaurants you visit? Why do these differences exist?

16. Why is the boss's office *always* called the "corner office"? Is this a layout issue?

17. What are the advantages and disadvantages of the greenfield approach to facility design?

18. What relationships exist among capacity, vertical integration, and facilities decisions? How should these decisions be made?

PROBLEMS

1. A new medical facility will be constructed in Detroit. City administrators are assessing the merits of a proposed location within the city limits. The table below indicates the location factors, weights, and scores (1 = poor, 5 = excellent) of that location. The weights total 100 percent. What is the weighted score for the proposed location?

Location Factor	Weight	Score
Capacity utilization	35	4
Average emergency response time	25	3
Total patient miles per month	15	3
Expressway accessibility	10	4
Construction and land costs	10	1
Employee preferences	5	5

2. Parsa, Inc., produces widgets at a plant in Boston for resale throughout the East Coast. The demand for the widgets at four distribution warehouses exceeds the Boston plant's capacity of 300 units per week. The estimated demand for the four warehouses is 150, 80, 300, and 220, respectively. Construction of another production plant with a capacity of 500 units per week has been planned, and Philadelphia is a possible location. Transportation costs per widget from Boston to the Parsa warehouses are $2.00, $4.00, $2.50, and $1.50. From Philadelphia the costs are $3.00, $3.00, $1.80, and $2.50. What will the minimum transportation costs for this company be if the second plant is built in Philadelphia?

3. Able Fasteners Ltd. is expanding by constructing a second plant. Four locations are in the running. An assessment of these sites based on six location factors is shown below (1 = poor, 5 = excellent). Calculate the weighted score of each location and recommend which location should be chosen.

Location Factor	Factor Weight	Weighted Score per Location			
		A	B	C	D
Labor supply	25	3	4	1	5
Materials sourcing	20	3	2	4	1
Proximity to markets	20	5	5	3	3
Transportation availability	15	2	4	4	3
Community's quality of life	10	5	2	3	4
Taxes	10	1	3	3	4

4. Jason Rolleman, manager of operations for Airtight Security Systems, has identified four possible sites for a new facility. He has calculated the fixed costs (land, taxes, insurance, equipment, etc.) and variable costs of each location (labor, materials, transportation, etc.) as follows:

Community	Fixed Cost, $ per year, thousands	Variable Cost, $ per 1,000 units
A	75	32
B	150	19
C	250	12
D	300	15

a. Calculate which of the four sites has the lowest annual costs for a production volume of 100,000 units.
b. Plot the total cost curves for each community on a graph. Using the graph, identify the approximate ranges over which each community provides the lowest cost.

5. Diane McFarlane is about to open an independent chain of gas stations. Initially, she will open five stations at the following xy coordinates.

Location	xy Coordinate, miles	Anticipated Sales per Month, gallons
A	(10, 50)	10,000
B	(30, 45)	25,000
C	(25, 10)	15,000
D	(40, 30)	30,000
E	(15, 35)	20,000

Using the center of gravity method, determine the optimal location for McFarlane to construct a fuel dump to supply all five stations.

6. Arrange six square departments in a two by three grid so that the nearness priorities shown in the matrix below are satisfied:

a = Absolutely necessary
e = Very important
i = Important
o = Ordinary importance
u = Unimportant
x = Undesirable

Departments

Department	1	2	3	4	5	6
1						
2	o					
3	x	o				
4	x	a	a			
5	a	a	a	o		
6	a	a	x	x	o	

7. Arrange nine square departments in a three by three grid so that the nearness priorities shown in the matrix below are satisfied.

Departments

Department	1	2	3	4	5	6	7	8	9
1									
2	u								
3	a	i							
4	x	a	i						
5	e	x	i	u					
6	i	a	a	i	a				
7	u	i	x	a	i	a			
8	x	a	a	x	u	i	u		
9	x	u	u	x	a	i	a	x	

8. Your task is to arrange five departments in a plant to minimize interdepartmental transportation costs. The number of trips between departments and the cost per unit of distance for a typical load are given below. Develop nearness priorities and an initial layout.

From	To	Expected No. Trips	Cost per Unit of Distance, $
A	B	100	0.20
A	C	150	0.20
A	D	100	0.20
A	E	75	0.20
B	A	50	0.36
B	C	40	0.36
B	D	30	0.36
B	E	45	0.36
C	A	50	0.22
C	B	10	0.22
C	D	40	0.22
C	E	75	0.22
D	A	25	0.24
D	B	40	0.24
D	C	150	0.24
D	E	50	0.24
E	A	100	0.32
E	B	25	0.32
E	C	45	0.32
E	D	50	0.32

9. Two departmental layouts, both 90 feet by 60 feet, are displayed below:

Layout 1

B	E	C
D	A	F

Layout 2

E	B	C
D	A	F

Using the information below, select the layout which minimizes the total distance traveled. Assume that all movements are between the centers of the specified departments, that all movements are made parallel to the walls of the building, and that all turns must be right angles (i.e., no diagonal aisles exist).

Departments	Loads per Year
A and B	2,600
A and C	2,200
A and D	5,000
A and E	8,400
B and C	6,400
B and D	7,200
B and E	9,200
C and E	8,600
C and D	4,200
D and E	3,200

10. 💾 Select a nearby food outlet. Develop a list of areas within the facility.
   a. Analyze the interactions among those areas. Assess the desirability of placing areas close together.
   b. Construct an activity relationship chart that summarizes the information collected in part *a*.
   c. Construct an activity relationship diagram based on the activity relationship chart and information regarding the flow of communication, materials, and so forth.
   d. Estimate the space required for each area.
   e. Transform the activity relationship chart into a space relationship chart.
   f. Develop an initial layout for the facility.

11. 💾 Atlantic Fisheries Ltd. has one cannery in Boston, Massachusetts, and another in Bangor, Maine. Trucks from both plants deliver processed fish to food terminals in Buffalo, Detroit, Washington, and Cleveland. Capacity and demand are given in truckloads per year. Costs are given in dollars per truckload.

	Buffalo	Detroit	Cleve.	Wash.	Capacity
Boston	320	380	270	440	590
Bangor	420	500	330	490	720
Demand	360	320	350	280	

   a. Determine from where the food terminals should source their fish so that transport costs are minimized.
   b. What happens to the sourcing plans if transportation costs from Bangor to Cleveland drop to $250 per truckload?

12. 💾 Re-Run Tire Co. has three retreading factories in Tijuana, Juarez, and Monterrey, Mexico. Tires retreaded in those plants are resold in five cities

on both sides of the Mexico–United States border: Mexico City, Dallas, Houston, Los Angeles, and El Paso. The transportation matrix is as follows:

	Distribution Outlets					
Plant	Mexico City	Dallas	Houston	Los Angeles	El Paso	Capacity
Tijuana	1.00	1.40	1.25	0.45	0.80	2,000
Juarez	0.80	0.70	0.60	0.90	0.25	1,000
Monterrey	0.50	0.80	0.75	1.35	0.70	1,500
Demand	7,500	10,000	7,500	12,500	4,000	

Where should each resale location source its tires to minimize transportation costs?

13. The Tijuana facility in question 12 needs a major injection of capital investment to replace aging equipment. Management intends instead to close the facility and expand capacity at the Juarez facility by 2,000 units. How much will transport costs rise annually as a result of this decision, assuming that regional demand remains constant?

14. In the new European Economic Community (EEC) the member states hope to eliminate identification checks of any kind for community citizens traveling anywhere within the community. Interpol, afraid that easing such movement restrictions will lead to an increase in terrorist acts, has decided to establish an antiterrorist squad capable of responding quickly to any situation within the EEC. It has been decided that the squad's base location should be one which allows the fastest overall response time to five prominent EEC cities: London, Berlin, Paris, Rome, and Madrid. Estimate the coordinates of the five cities on the map below and then calculate the ideal location for the squad's base. (Assume that the travel time per kilometer is constant.)

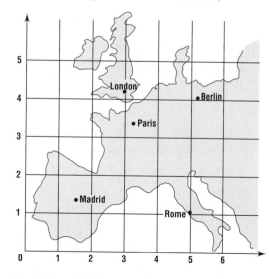

15. Everett Smyth is planning to open a factory to produce porcelain sinks and bathtubs in one of three locations: Denver, Salt Lake City, or Santa Fe. These are his estimates for fixed and variable costs:

Location	Fixed Costs, $	Variable Costs, $		
		Labor	Materials	Overhead
Denver	2,000,000	10	20	20
Salt Lake	1,800,000	15	40	30
Santa Fe	1,500,000	50	50	50

a. Graph the relationship between costs and units produced.
b. Calculate the intersection point of the Denver cost line and the Salt Lake City cost line. Do the same for Salt Lake City and Santa Fe.
c. Identify the range in which each facility has a competitive advantage over the others.

GROUP EXERCISES

Many of the tools and concepts discussed in this chapter are meant to be used in a team setting. The following problems are best solved by small groups of students. Ideally, each group should be composed of people with different backgrounds, interests, or areas of expertise.

1. People tend to shop close to home, a fact all professional service providers acknowledge. How far people are prepared to travel for professional services is debatable. As a group, devise a questionnaire and use it to determine how far people are prepared to go to seek professional services or advice from a doctor, an architect, or a lawyer. Then find out, from an operations perspective, what it would take to induce them to go farther. You will need to segment the survey so that a range of services are required, from minor to major.

2. Visit a manufacturer with more than one manufacturing site and find out why the facilities are located at their respective sites. Also find out what the *preferred* site would be, why the differences exist, and what it would take to make the necessary changes. (If that is not possible, develop and use a set of criteria for locating your faculty or school in the most appropriate place.)

REFERENCES AND SELECTED BIBLIOGRAPHY

Brown, E. [1988], "IBM Combines Rapid Modelling Technique and Simulation to Design PCB Factory-of-the-Future," *Industrial Engineering,* June, pp. 20–26, 90.

Buffa, E. S., G. C. Armour, and T. E. Vollman [1964], "Allocating Facilities with CRAFT," *Harvard Business Review,* March–April, pp. 136–159.

Ferdows, Kasra [1989], "Mapping International Factory Network," in K. Ferdows (ed.), *Managing International Manufacturing,* Elsevier, Amsterdam, pp. 3–21.

Fine, Phillip [1993], "These Airports Are Tops," *Toronto Globe and Mail,* Feb. 9, p. B24.

Francis, Richard L., and John A. White [1974], *Facility Layout and Location: An Analytical Approach,* Prentice-Hall, Englewood Cliffs, N.J.

Johnson, R. V. [1982], "SPACECRAFT for Multi-Floor Layout Planning," *Management Science,* April, pp. 407–417.

Lee, R. S., and J. M. Moore [1967], "CORELAP (Computerized Relationship Layout Planning)," *Journal of Industrial Engineering,* March, pp. 195–200.

Miller, F. W. [1988], "Three Luxury Cars Ride Same A-Line," *Manufacturing Systems,* March, pp. 36–38.

Muther, R. [1961], *Systematic Layout Planning,* Industrial Education Institute, Boston.

Stone, P. H., and R. Luchetti [1985], "Your Office Is Where You Are," *Harvard Business Review,* March–April, pp. 102–117.

CHAPTER 9

PROCESS DESIGN

Selecting the most appropriate process for producing a firm's goods and services is an important decision management must make. In the 1980s it was estimated that a typical company spent about one-quarter of its operating budget on finding and fixing mistakes on the production line. A significant percentage of direct laborers were not producing anything; they were just reworking products that had not been properly made the first time. To compete effectively, firms must develop efficient and responsive operating processes.

The following questions are addressed in this chapter:

- What is a process, and what are its key elements?

- How are operating processes designed?
- What is the relationship between process design and the corporate strategy? Between process design and product design?

By the end of the chapter and its supplement you will be able to describe the expanded product-process matrix and employ it to determine the most appropriate process to use in a given situation. You will be familiar with different forms of advanced operations technologies and will be able to assess the methods used to justify their acquisition.

EXHIBIT 9.1   FRO MANUFACTURING PROFILE

"To be global," says GFT's chairman, Marco Rivetti, "means to recognize difference and be flexible enough to adapt to it."

Based in Turin, Italy, Gruppo GFT is the world's largest manufacturer of designer clothing. It competes at the high end of the apparel business: "ready-to-wear" designer collections one step below made-to-order haute couture. GFT is the company behind well-known labels such as Giorgio Armani, Emanuel Ungaro, and Valentino. The 10,000 employees work in the 45 small companies and 18 manufacturing plants under the Gruppo GFT umbrella. Together they make, distribute, and market roughly 60 designer and brand collections in 70 countries.

After World War II GFT was the first European apparel company to introduce mass-production techniques. Throughout the 1950s and 1960s it established itself as a highly efficient producer of standardized men's clothing. By the early 1970s, however, the traditional wage advantage of Italian apparel manufacturers in foreign markets had been eliminated. The solution for GFT was to move upmarket and transform itself into a global company.

In the 1990s consumers of designer fashions are looking for high quality at a low price. The emphasis is on "value," and the fact that a designer label is on a product is not enough anymore. Consumers in the United States are looking for different fabrics, colors, and styles than are those in Germany, for example. In the words of a GFT manager in Turin, "The company may be global, but the consumer is not."

GFT's transformation to a global company has had a great impact on its operations. GFT's traditional focus on efficiency has not been dropped but combined with a new emphasis on flexibility and extremely high quality. At its facility in New Bedford, Massachusetts, for example, the specific retail customer for each piece of clothing is known before the garment is made. This allows workers to further customize clothes by sewing in the retailer's label in addition to that of the designer.

Source: Adapted from Howard (1991), pp. 28–44.

EXHIBIT 9.2   FRO SERVICE PROFILE

CHAPTER 9

Process Design

Every day more than 4,000 people turn to the Mayo Clinic for health care. Almost all these patients have been referred by competent physicians who have been unable to diagnose or treat their illnesses. Experience with a wide range of diseases, leading-edge treatments, and the speed with which most diagnoses are made have given the clinic a unique advantage and an excellent international reputation.

How has the Mayo Clinic become so successful? The design of its "operating" process is largely responsible. Consider the following key components:

- *The workforce.* The clinical attracts leading clinicians, people who are interested in developing new knowledge in their fields. Doctors work in teams and are paid a salary.
- *The equipment.* Substantial investments in R&D enable the clinic to provide state-of-the-art laboratory and diagnostic equipment.
- *The patient information system.* One computer file is maintained for every patient. This file is maintained by a central registry and can be easily accessed by every doctor involved in the patient's treatment. Information flows quickly and accurately.
- *The scheduling system.* The clinic can schedule health care professionals, support staff, and medical facilities centrally. This drastically reduces the time patients spend waiting to see specialists, take tests, and undergo treatments.

A well-designed process ensures that the Mayo Clinic can meet its goal of providing high-quality responsive health care.

9.1 MANAGERIAL ORIENTATION

American firms invest about two-thirds of their R&D spending in new products. Since a fast-response organization (FRO) must introduce a steady stream of new and improved products, this sounds reasonable. However, by itself, the ability to invent a new product will not give a firm a substantial competitive advantage. Consider the home video camera, the video recorder, and the fax machine. These very successful products were invented in the United States, but none are produced in this country today.

As was discussed in Chapter 8, involving production people in the product design process helps ensure that a firm can produce high-quality but low-cost products. Aligning the product design with current process capabilities is not enough, though; a firm must actively invest in its production processes to expand its capabilities and stay ahead of its competitors. As illustrated by GFT (Exhibit 9.1) and the Mayo Clinic (Exhibit 9.2), process design is directly related to customer satisfaction and is therefore of strategic significance.

It was mentioned earlier that the adoption of advanced technology is one of the four structural prerequisites of an FRO. Many different forms of advanced technologies are available today, and this chapter will discuss their impact on process design. First, however, turn to the supplement to this chapter for a brief description of advanced operating technologies.

9.2 PROCESS DESIGN: AN OVERVIEW

DEFINITION: A *process* transforms selected resources into defined end products. This involves a series of discrete tasks or activities performed by an integrated set of people and equipment.

DEFINITION: *Process design* is the task of selecting and arranging the equipment required for the transformation process and integrating the workforce and other resources with the equipment.

Each of the six firms toured in the Startup Chapter employs a different operating process. Florida Power and Light (see Exhibit 9.3) uses multi-million-dollar plants to generate electricity 24 hours a day every day. Conversely, Fujima (see Exhibit 9.4) custom-designs metal dies and then manufactures them with a set of small general-purpose machines run by highly skilled operators. The Mayo Clinic, Milliken, Reimer Express Lines, and Zytec have processes that fall between these extremes. Since all these companies are successful, the implication is that there is no one best way to produce a good or service.

What factors influence a firm's choice of process technology and organization? Of course, the cost and availability of suitable technology, resources, and workforces have a significant influence on the process. However, it is the characteristics of the goods or services to be produced by the process that make one type of process technology and organization more suitable than another. When one examines the product portfolio and designs the process, very specific information is required. Here is a sample set of questions:

- What goods and services make up the portfolio? What are the timing and level of expected demand? How frequently will changes be made to product designs?
- What tasks have to be performed for each product? How much do these tasks vary from one product to the next? In what order must they be performed? How long will each one take? How frequently will each task be performed?

EXHIBIT 9.3 OPERATIONAL SNAPSHOT: FLORIDA POWER AND LIGHT COMPANY

The Product:
- Electricity.

The Process:
- Thirteen multi-million-dollar plants generate more than 13,600 megawatts of electricity 24 hours a day every day of the year.
- The electricity travels over transmission lines to substations where its voltage is lowered and transferred to domestic distribution systems.
- The plants are linked to a continental grid which allows utilities to buy and sell power.

The Workforce:
- Fifteen thousand employees, including a large scientific and engineering support staff; operators are very well trained procedurally.

EXHIBIT 9.4 OPERATIONAL SNAPSHOT: FUJIMA INTERNATIONAL

The Product:
- Metal dies that are used in stamping presses to shape sheets of metal into automobile parts.
- Each die is custom designed by Fujima and weighs one or two tons.

The Process:
- CAD software is used by teams to design each die.
- General-purpose equipment controlled by a central computer is used to produce the dies.
- The materials and equipment used vary from one job to the next.

The Workforce:
- Highly technically skilled operators, along with material handlers, setup specialists, designers, and engineers, work in teams to design and manufacture the dies.

- What inputs are needed, how many are needed, where in the process are they needed, and how frequently will they be delivered?
- At which points should the customer be involved? How much influence will the customer have over the task performed?
- What are the target costs and acceptable quality levels for each type of product? How much flexibility should be built into the process?

Obviously, input from a variety of functional areas is needed to answer these questions. Assembly drawings and charts, process flow diagrams, and bills of materials are a few sources of detailed product information. CAD/CAM systems[1] allow production requirements to be generated automatically from design information.

Once decisions about the type of process technology and organization have been made, process designers determine how tasks will be performed and which tasks should be automated. Specific equipment must then be selected and arranged, tooling must be designed and built, workforce jobs must be conceived, and the appropriate support systems must be put in place.

The importance of job design and support systems should not be underestimated. A brief outline of some of the issues to be considered in designing jobs and support systems appears below. A detailed discussion is left to later chapters.

- **Job design** (Chapter 10). How should tasks be combined into jobs? What type of skills do particular groups of workers need? What type of relationship should exist between operators and the equipment they run? Between the workforce and management? How much responsibility should be delegated to the workforce?
- **Quality assurance** (Chapter 11). How will quality be measured and controlled? How will quality problems be detected, investigated, and solved? At what points in the process will items be inspected?
- **Maintenance** (Chapter 11). Who will perform preventive maintenance? How often will it be done? Who will make major repairs to the system? How will the effects of equipment downtime be minimized?
- **Inventory management** (Chapter 13). How large should raw material, work-in-process, and finished goods inventories be? How will the inventory be controlled? How will the firm determine when and how much is needed of each inventory item?
- **Materials handling** (Chapter 15). How will material be moved in and out of inventory storage areas? From one work center to another? How flexible must the materials handling system be?
- **Scheduling** (Chapter 17). What should be produced, and when should it be produced? How will production jobs be prioritized? Which workers should be assigned to which shifts? To which jobs?

9.3 PROCESS TECHNOLOGY AND ORGANIZATIONS

Section 9.2 mentioned that the choice of process organization is largely dependent on the goods and services produced. This section will describe different types of process organizations and the types of products for which each is suitable. In some cases more than one process organization is used to produce a set of goods and services. At Zytec, for example, transformers are manufactured in large batches and

---

[1] *CAD/CAM* refers to the integration of computer-aided design (CAD) and computer-aided manufacturing (CAM).

then transferred to a repetitive-flow line where they are assembled with other man-ufactured and purchased components.

The Continuum of Process Organizations

Traditional process organizations range from job shops to batch shops to repetitive-flow shops through to continuous-flow shops. This continuum was originally presented in Exhibit 1.6. The characteristics of these process organizations are described below.

Job-Shop Processes   When small volumes of a wide variety of customized products must be produced, firms such as Fujima often choose a **job-shop process** for its inherent flexibility. The support staff is small compared with the workforce, and communication between the workforce and management is informal. General-purpose equipment is operated by highly skilled workers and is arranged in a **process layout.**[2]

> **DEFINITION: A process layout is one in which similar items of equipment (such as lathes and sewing machines) or activities (such as accounting and field service) are placed together in work centers.**

A process layout is flexible because the routing of a job is not dictated by the layout of the plant. Jobs move from one work center to the next depending on their processing needs. Queues (waiting lines) tend to form in front of machines and create large work-in-process (WIP) inventories.

Bottlenecks are a common problem in process layouts.

> **DEFINITION: A piece of equipment or a group of workers is a bottleneck when its capacity is lower than that of any other element in the process.**

Bottlenecks are difficult to eliminate for several reasons. They are often caused by pieces of equipment that are expensive or come in increments that far exceed a firm's requirements. There may be difficulty in obtaining equipment or people because of an industrywide shortage. Finally, since the mix of equipment and workers varies from one job to the next, as does the job's processing time, bottlenecks may move. This problem is illustrated in Exhibit 9.5.

Developing a schedule detailing when each job is to be completed and which equipment will be used is a complex task in a job-shop environment. Not only must a large number of jobs be scheduled, but the type and length of processing required by each job vary and there are many possible job-equipment combinations to consider.

Intermittent-Flow Processes   **Intermittent-flow processes** are characterized by large batches of products produced with a combination of general-purpose and special-purpose equipment. As in a job-shop process, the labor content of each product is high and the workforce must be highly skilled and flexible. A narrower product line and larger batch sizes, though, make scheduling easier.

The equipment in an intermittent-flow process is often arranged in a process layout as in a job shop or, alternatively, in **group technology (cellular) layouts.** As is explained in the supplement to this chapter, *group technology* (GT) is based on

---

[2] The facility layout tools, such as CRAFT, that were reviewed in Chapter 8 are often used to design process layouts.

EXHIBIT 9.5   TOOLBOX: BOTTLENECK OPERATIONS

Shuttleworth Moulded Products is a custom builder of truck mufflers. The company manufactures the components needed to make mufflers and then assembles mufflers to order. As shown by the chart below, the time required to assemble mufflers varies by model.

TIME REQUIRED TO ASSEMBLE EACH MODEL

Model	Stuffer	Assembly	Welding	Painting	Boxing	Total Assembly Time
		Muffler Assembly Time, minutes				
2220	1.10	1.80	1.36	0.76	0.74	5.76
2240	1.80	1.36	1.30	0.76	0.74	5.96
2270	1.26	1.70	2.20	0.90	0.78	6.84
2350	1.80	1.80	1.68	1.08	0.80	7.16
3430	1.50	1.66	1.82	1.06	0.80	6.84
4000	2.06	1.30	1.36	0.76	0.74	6.20
Setup time	10	10	4	5	5	

What is the bottleneck assembly operation? If Shuttleworth assembles just one model, the bottleneck is the work center with the highest combined setup and cycle times. Consider model 2270, for example. If Shuttleworth makes a batch of 100 mufflers, the welding work center is the bottleneck.

ASSEMBLING 100 MODEL 2270 MUFFLERS
Assembly Times, minutes

	Stuffer	Assembly	Welding	Painting	Boxing
Assembly time	126	170	220	90	78
Setup time	10	10	4	5	5
Total	*136*	*180*	*224*	*95*	*83*

Suppose Shuttleworth has an order for 100 units of models 2220, 2240, and 2350; 50 units of models 2270 and 3430; and 200 units of model 4000 (product mix 1). The number of hours required at each work center is shown below. Note that the bottleneck now occurs at the stuffer work center, not the welding work center.

WORK CENTER REQUIREMENTS: PRODUCT MIX 1

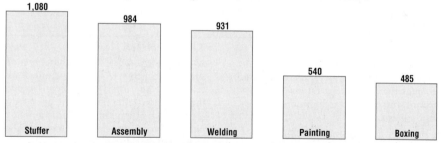

If Shuttleworth assembles 200 units of model 2220, 100 units of model 2240, 150 units of model 2350, and 50 units of models 2270, 3430, and 4000, the assembly work center becomes the bottleneck. *Thus, the bottleneck operation shifts as the product mix is modified.*

WORK CENTER REQUIREMENTS: PRODUCT MIX 2

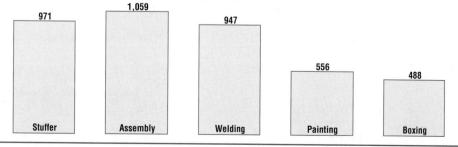

the notion of similarity, and the concept of *cellular manufacturing* has traditionally been associated with GT.

> **DEFINITION:** A cellular layout is one in which the equipment required to produce a specific set of parts is grouped together.

Parts grouped by design have corresponding shapes and sizes. Parts grouped by manufacturing characteristics require the same processing steps, materials, tooling, setup procedures, and/or labor skills.

Because parts move from one machine to another without waiting in queues, cells increase the speed with which products flow through the process. This results in much lower WIP inventories and simplifies production scheduling. Since similar parts are grouped together, equipment setup times are reduced and equipment utilization is increased. Two different types of cellular layouts (rabbit chase and U-line cells) are described in Exhibit 9.6.

Since there are many possible ways to group machines and tasks into cells, determining which cellular layout is the best is a time-consuming and challenging job. Cellular design is an excellent task for computer simulation. Simulation can assist firms in planning new manufacturing systems and deciding whether a new product-process design conforms to the existing manufacturing cell before a new system is adopted. An example of simulation applied to layout design appears in Exhibit 9.7.

Repetitive-Flow Processes When only a few standardized products are made, **repetitive-flow processes** are often used. An assembly line is the classic example of a repetitive-flow process. Special-purpose equipment is developed for the product and arranged into a set of sequentially dependent work centers. This arrangement is referred to as a **product layout.**

EXHIBIT 9.6 GROUP TECHNOLOGY CELLS

A. A Rabbit Chase Cell

The machines are arranged in a circle. If one operator is assigned to the cell, he or she loads and unloads every machine. If there are two operators, they move around the circle, one behind the other, sharing the equipment.

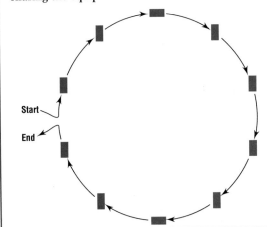

B. A U-Line Cell

As the name implies, the machines are arranged in the shape of the letter U. If one operator is assigned to the cell, he or she loads and unloads every machine. If there are two operators, each operator deals with a specified set of equipment. For example, one operator may tend to all the ▨ machines while another tends to the ▧ machines.

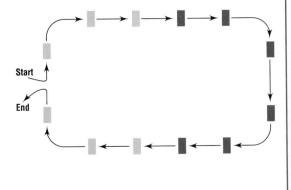

EXHIBIT 9.7   USING SIMULATION TO DEVELOP A CELLULAR LAYOUT

Industrial engineers at Gates Rubber Co. developed a simulation model to help convert a complex manufacturing process into a cellular layout. The model was built using the Micro Saint simulation tool.

Each task in the manufacturing process was represented by a node in the model's task network. Other information, such as the product mix, mean task time, and task order, was also fed into the model. Using Micro Saint's "what if" features, different processing configurations were generated and analyzed. The engineers were able to watch the rubber products proceed through the manufacturing process and identify potential bottlenecks. Different combinations of processing times, curing capabilities, and types of operations were employed.

The results of the simulations were used to present a complete proposal for a cellular design—including equipment specifications and labor power requirements based on different production levels—to management in just under three worker-weeks.

Source: Adapted from Hershell and Dahl (1988), pp. 40–45.

DEFINITION: A product layout is one in which the equipment required to produce a specific product is grouped together and arranged sequentially on the basis of that product's routing.

The workforce tends to be large in a repetitive-flow process, and each worker usually is assigned to a very narrow range of specialized tasks. Communication between the workforce and management tends to be formal and flows predominantly from the top down. The support staff is large compared with the workforce.

The production rate (capacity) of an assembly line can be varied by changing the way in which tasks are grouped together into work centers. The goal of **line balancing** is to group tasks into work centers so that the desired production rate is attained with maximum efficiency. In practice, line balancing involves compromises between labor, facilities, and equipment.

The Six-Step Line Balancing Procedure   The line balancing procedure can be thought of as a six-step process. Let us work through these steps using the company described in Exhibit 9.8.

Step 1. Define the tasks to be performed and obtain accurate time estimates for each task. Identify the precedence relationships among the tasks.

The Scott Snack Company has assembled a design team that includes an engineer and workers from the shop floor. The team has identified nine distinct tasks that must be performed. After analyzing the tasks, the team has developed comprehensive guidelines for performing each task and has estimated the time required for each one.[3] The task times are listed in Exhibit 9.8A.

Precedence diagrams are often used to visualize the sequence of tasks performed in the process. In the precedence diagram in Exhibit 9.8B, each circle (node) represents a particular task, the number inside the node represents the time required to complete that task, and each arrow represents a precedence relationship between two tasks. Task G, for example, cannot begin until tasks D and E have been completed.

Step 2. Specify the required daily output level. Calculate the cycle time that corresponds to the required daily output level.

[3] Over time these guidelines and time estimates will be updated to reflect improvements made to the process.

EXHIBIT 9-8 TOOLBOX: ASSEMBLY LINE PROBLEM

The Scott Snack Company is designing a process for its newest product. The process will consist of nine tasks.

A. Time Estimates

Task	Required Time, minutes	Immediate Predecessor
A	0.9	—
B	0.6	—
C	0.3	—
D	0.5	A
E	0.3	B, C
F	0.1	D
G	1.5	D, E
H	0.8	F, G
I	0.7	H
Total:	5.7	

B. Precedence Relationships

The precedence diagram below illustrates the order in which the tasks must be performed.

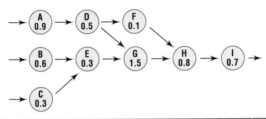

The ultimate goal is to group Scott's nine tasks into a set of work centers. To ensure that work flows smoothly through the process, each work center will be given the same amount of time to complete its tasks on a particular unit. This is referred to as the **cycle time.**

Suppose the nine tasks are grouped into two work centers and the cycle time is set at three minutes. Each product will spend three minutes in each work center, and a finished product will roll off the line every three minutes. Assuming that there are eight hours (480 minutes) in a day, the two processes could produce (480 minutes per day) ÷ (3 minutes per unit) = 160 units a day.

Given a desired output rate, equation (9.1) can be used to calculate the corresponding cycle time. Whenever the desired output rate changes, the corresponding cycle time has to change as well.

Required Cycle Time for a Given Daily Output Rate

$$C = \frac{AT}{OR} \tag{9.1}$$

where C = cycle time
AT = available operating time per day
OR = daily output rate

Suppose the desired output rate for Scott's new process is 240 units a day. Then the corresponding cycle time is (480 minutes a day) ÷ (240 units a day) = 2 minutes.

Note that the range of possible output rates is limited by the range of possible cycle times. The minimum cycle time is equal to the longest time required for a task in the process. The maximum cycle time is equal to the total time required to complete all operations.

In this example task G has the longest duration—1.5 minutes—and the total time required to complete all tasks is 5.7 minutes. Therefore, the process has an output range of 84 to 320 units per day.[4]

Step 3. Calculate the minimum number of work centers needed for the desired output rate.

Scott could group its nine tasks into one to nine work centers. Suppose all nine tasks are grouped into one work center. Since the total time needed to complete these tasks is 5.7 minutes, the cycle time must be at least 5.7 minutes. But to obtain the desired output rate of 240 units a day, the cycle time must be two minutes. Therefore, a one-work-center arrangement will not be feasible.

Now suppose that each of the nine tasks is assigned to its own work center. Each work center could complete its task within two minutes. However, as one can see in Exhibit 9.9A, since most of the work centers are idle most of the time, the process is very inefficient.

Reducing the number of work centers by grouping tasks together can reduce the idle time. For example, in Exhibit 9.9B, the number of work centers was reduced to six and the idle time was cut to 3.9 minutes.

The lower the number of work centers, the more efficient the line. For a desired output rate (and hence cycle time), one can use equation (9.2) to calculate the theoretical minimum number of work centers needed.

Theoretical Minimum Number of Work Centers

$$N = \frac{T}{C} \tag{9.2}$$

where N = number of work centers
T = sum of all task times
C = cycle time for desired output rate

The most efficient layout for Scott therefore includes only three work centers. (The number was rounded up because partial work centers are infeasible.)

$$N = \frac{5.7}{2} = 2.85$$

Step 4. Develop an initial layout by assigning tasks to work centers.

The actual number of work centers is usually higher than the theoretical minimum as a result of constraints on the ways in which tasks can be combined to form work centers. For example, precedence relationships must be preserved. Some tasks, such as sanding and painting in a repair shop, are not compatible and cannot be assigned to the same work center. If tasks require different types of labor skills, assigning them to the same work center may not be possible. The amount of floor space available and the facility's layout also restrict the way in which tasks are

[4] Since OR = 480 ÷ C, the minimum cycle time of 1.5 minutes corresponds to a daily output rate of 320 units. The maximum cycle time of 5.7 minutes corresponds to a daily output rate of 84 units.

EXHIBIT 9.9 TOOLBOX: ALTERNATIVE LAYOUTS

A. Nine-Work-Center Layout

If the cycle time for this layout is 2 minutes, every work center will have some idle time. In total, the process is idle 12.3 minutes of the 18 minutes (2 minutes per work center × 9 work centers) each product will spend in the process.

Work Center	Idle Time, minutes
1 (A)	1.1
2 (B)	1.4
3 (C)	1.7
4 (D)	1.5
5 (E)	1.7
6 (F)	1.9
7 (G)	0.5
8 (H)	1.2
9 (I)	1.3
Total:	12.3

Even if the cycle time is reduced to only 1.5 minutes (the length of the longest task), the process will be idle 7.8 minutes for every product.

B. Six-Work-Center Layout

The total idle time is now only 3.9 minutes when the cycle time is 2 minutes and only 3.3 minutes when the cycle time is reduced to 1.5 minutes.

combined. Determining the ideal number of workstations and task combinations is a complex problem that does not lend itself to optimization techniques.[5] Instead, heuristic-based computer programs are used.

Heuristic techniques often involve prioritizing tasks and then allocating tasks to work centers in priority order while obeying the precedence relationships. For example, tasks with the longest operation times can be assigned the highest priority and allocated first. Alternatively, as Kilbridge and Wester (1961) determine, the task with the lowest number of preceding tasks can be allocated first, the task with the second lowest number can be allocated next, and so on. Helgeson and Birnie (1961) also suggest that tasks whose followers have the largest total time can be allocated first.

Two different heuristics have been used to assign tasks to work centers for the Scott Snack Company (see Exhibit 9.10). Each heuristic yielded a slightly different layout, but both used four work centers. Because of the precedence relationships among the tasks, the theoretical minimum of three work centers was infeasible.

Step 5. Evaluate the current layout.

---

[5] Optimization techniques have been developed to balance even fairly large assembly lines [see, for example, Johnson (1988)], but simplifying assumptions must be made before these algorithms can be used.

Idle time at one or more work centers creates inefficiencies within the system. As was mentioned earlier, idle time results when the total task time at each work center is not the same. Morale problems may develop if idle times vary considerably from one work center to the next.

The efficiency of the selected layout is measured by the **balance delay** (D), which is the percentage of time that the process is idle and is calculated using equation (9.3). If the layout can be perfectly balanced, with each work center having exactly the same amount of work, then $NC = T$ and the balance delay will be zero.

Balance Delay

$$D = \frac{100(NC - T)}{NC} \tag{9.3}$$

where D = balance delay
N = number of work centers
C = cycle time for desired output rate
T = sum of all task times

The balance delay for all three work center layouts at Scott is 28.75 percent.

$$D = \frac{100(NC - T)}{NC} = \frac{100[(4)(2) - 5.7]}{(4)(2)} = 28.75$$

From a labor efficiency point of view, the fewer the work centers, the better. Recall, however, that the daily output decreases as tasks are arranged into fewer and

EXHIBIT 9.10 TOOLBOX: HEURISTIC TECHNIQUES

HEURISTIC 1: TASKS WITH THE LONGEST OPERATIONS TIMES HAVE THE HIGHEST PRIORITY
Step 1. Start with work center 1. The total available time at this and all work centers is equal to the cycle time for the desired output rate.
Step 2. Create a list of eligible tasks, that is, those tasks whose predecessors have all been assigned.
Step 3. Reduce the list to the tasks that can be completed in the time remaining at the current work center. If no tasks remain on the list, the work center is full. Return to step 2 and begin assigning tasks to the next work center.
Step 4. Select the task with the longest processing time. Assign it to the current work center. If all tasks have been assigned to work centers, stop. If not, go back to step 2.

The chart below demonstrates how tasks are assigned to work centers using heuristic 1.

Current Work Center	List of Eligible Tasks	Revised List	Selected Task	Time Remaining at Work Center
1	A, B, C	A, B, C	A (0.9)	2.0 − 0.9 = 1.1
1	B, C, D	B, C, D	B (0.6)	1.1 − 0.6 = 0.5
1	C, D	C, D	D (0.5)	0.5 − 0.5 = 0
2	C, F	C, F	C (0.3)	2.0 − 0.3 = 1.7
2	E, F	E, F	E (0.3)	1.7 − 0.3 = 1.4
2	F, G	F	F (0.1)	1.4 − 0.1 = 1.3
2	G	—		
3	G	G	G (1.5)	2.0 − 1.5 = 0.5
3	H	—		
4	H	H	H (0.8)	2.0 − 0.8 = 1.2
4	I	I	I (0.7)	1.2 − 0.7 = 0.5

(Exhibit 9.10 continues on next page)   **259**

EXHIBIT 9.10 *(continued)*

Layout Developed with Heuristic 1

HEURISTIC 2: THE TASK WITH THE LOWEST NUMBER OF PREDECESSORS IS ALLOCATED FIRST, THE TASK WITH THE SECOND LOWEST NUMBER NEXT, AND SO ON
[Kilbridge and Wester (1961)]

Step 1. Start with work center 1. The total available time at this and all work centers is equal to the cycle time.

Step 2. Calculate the number of predecessors for each task.

Step 3. Create a list of eligible tasks, that is, those tasks whose predecessors have all been assigned.

Step 4. Reduce the list to the tasks that can be completed in the time remaining at the current work center. If no tasks remain on the list, the current work center is full. Return to step 3 and begin assigning tasks to the next work center.

Step 5. Select the task with the lowest number of predecessors. If there is a tie, select the task with the longest processing time. Assign it to the current work center. If there is at least one unassigned task, return to step 3.

The predecessors for each of the tasks to be performed are listed in the table below.

Task	Predecessors	Number of Predecessors
A	—	0
B	—	0
C	—	0
D	A	1
E	B, C	2
F	A, D	2
G	A, B, C, D, E	5
H	A, B, C, D, E, F	6
I	A, B, C, D, E, F, G	7

The chart below demonstrates how tasks are assigned to work centers using the Kilbridge and Wester heuristic.

Current Work Center	List of Eligible Tasks	Revised List	Selected Task	Time Remaining at Work Center
1	A, B, C	A, B, C	A (0.9)	2.0 − 0.9 = 1.1
1	B, C, D	B, C, D	B (0.6)	1.1 − 0.6 = 0.5
1	C, D	C, D	C (0.3)	0.5 − 0.3 = 0.2
2	D, E	D, E	D (0.5)	2.0 − 0.5 = 1.5
2	E, F	E, F	E (0.3)	1.7 − 0.3 = 1.4
2	F, G	F	F (0.1)	1.4 − 0.1 = 1.3
2	G	—		
3	G	G	G (1.5)	2.0 − 1.5 = 0.5
3	H	—		
4	H	H	H (0.8)	2.0 − 0.8 = 1.2
4	I	I	I (0.7)	1.2 − 0.7 = 0.5

Layout Developed with Kilbridge and Wester Heuristic

fewer work centers. One alternative is to duplicate the line to increase output; the increased capital investment required for this alternative has to be weighed against the increased labor efficiency.

Another alternative for the Scott Snack Company is to choose the second layout illustrated in Exhibit 9.10 and decrease the cycle time to 1.8 minutes. This means that the line will have to run only (1.8 minutes per unit) $\times$ (240 units per day) = 432 minutes, or just over seven hours a day. Workers could spend the remaining time on preventive maintenance or other tasks.

From the point of view of morale, the second layout is preferable to the first because the work is more evenly distributed between the first two work centers. As was mentioned earlier, line balancing is really an attempt to attain the best compromise between labor, facilities, and equipment to achieve a given production rate.

Step 6. If possible, improve the layout by modifying it or using another heuristic to generate a new layout.

Scott's second layout, for example, can be improved by moving task C to work center 2 to more evenly divide the work between the first two centers. The cycle time can be reduced to 1.5 minutes, which means that the balance delay is only 5 percent and the line need run only six hours a day.

Most assembly lines use specially designed equipment. The cost and inflexibility of this equipment make process modifications and capacity increments time-consuming to implement and difficult to justify. Because products follow a predetermined route through a series of sequentially dependent work centers at a predetermined rate, scheduling is relatively simple.

Continuous-Flow Processes **Continuous-flow processes** are suitable for companies that produce commoditylike products. As in repetitive-flow processes, a process-oriented workforce is supplemented by a large support staff. The direct labor content of each product is low, and the dedicated equipment used is even more expensive and inflexible than that commonly found in repetitive-flow shops.

Job shops. Intermittent-flow shops. Repetitive-flow shops. Continuous-flow shops. These four process organizations represent useful reference points on a continuum of possible organizations, not discrete classifications. Furthermore, not all processes can be neatly slotted into a particular spot along the continuum by using the operating characteristics outlined in Exhibit 1.6. Many processes, for example, do not have a product, process, or group technology layout but a **fixed-position layout.** Pool cleaners, ship or house builders, and auditors have to move their equipment to the product's location.

Coordinating and controlling materials movement and storage and positioning equipment around the product are the prime concerns when a fixed-position layout is used. Space is usually limited, and the types of materials and workers needed change as work on the product progresses. Managers must make sure materials arrive just before use so that congestion and confusion are minimized. Materials are then positioned so that handling costs are minimized.

A mixed-model automobile assembly line is another example of a process that cannot be easily fitted into the continuum. Products still flow through sequentially dependent work centers in a predetermined manner, but batch sizes are relatively small and the process is relatively flexible. As the next section will show, advanced technology is further disrupting the continuum of process organizations.

The Link between Product and Process Life Cycles

Take another look at Exhibit 1.6. Note how the product variety that can be handled by the process narrows as one moves along the continuum from a job shop to a continuous-flow shop. General-purpose equipment is replaced by special-purpose equipment, production volumes increase, and support staffs become more important.

Chapter 1 presented the **product-process life cycle matrix** (reproduced in Exhibit 9.11) developed by Hayes and Wheelwright (1984). They suggested that as the product progresses through its life cycle, the process that best fits the needs of the firm also matures. Thus the firm's process has a life cycle as well, and a process' life cycle is closely related to its product's life cycle.

Abernathy and Utterback (1978) also characterized the relationship between life cycles in terms of a firm's shifting emphasis from product to process innovation. They presented this staged relationship between product and process innovation in their **dynamic model of product-process innovation** (see Exhibit 9.12).

EXHIBIT 9.11   THE PRODUCT-PROCESS LIFE CYCLE MATRIX REVISITED

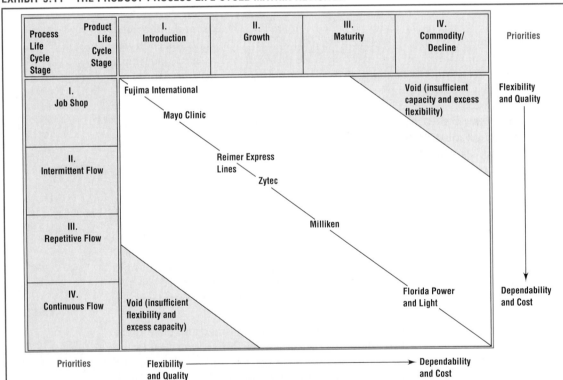

The job-shop organization is appropriate during a product's introductory stage. Production volumes are low, and the product is often customized. As the product progresses through the growth and maturity stages, it becomes more standardized and production volumes increase. Specialized equipment replaces general-purpose equipment, and the job shop is replaced by an intermittent (batch)-flow organization and then a repetitive-flow organization. Continuous-flow operations take over when the product becomes a commodity and the competitive focus shifts to price. Thus, the diagonal of the product-process life cycle matrix (called the production possibility frontier) represents the best set of product-process combinations.

Source: Adapted from Hayes and Wheelwright (1984), p. 216.

EXHIBIT 9.12   THE DYNAMIC MODEL OF PRODUCT-PROCESS INNOVATION

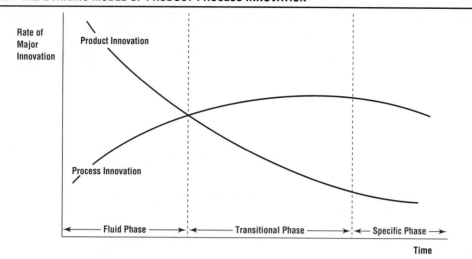

Innovation efforts are focused on the product until a dominant design emerges. The industry then moves into the transitional phase, and its innovation focus shifts to the process. Processes become efficient but too rigid and expensive to accommodate change easily. Radical process innovations are replaced by incremental innovations, and the industry enters the specific phase.

Source: Adapted from Abernathy and Utterback (1978).

The **fluid phase** occurs during the product's early life cycle stages and is characterized by high levels of product innovation. Once a dominant design emerges, the rate of product innovation drops off and the industry enters the **transitional phase,** during which innovation efforts are focused on the process. Equipment is developed specifically for the product and enables the firm to produce large volumes efficiently.

Toward the end of the product's life cycle, both product and process innovation are incremental and the industry enters the **specific phase.** The competitive emphasis is on cost reduction. Paradoxically, the efficient capital-intensive equipment developed is so rigid that the cost of change is extremely high. Firms find it difficult to adapt to environmental changes and are vulnerable to new products that render their existing products and processes obsolete.[6]

There are several important implications of the product-process life cycle matrix and the dynamic model of product-process innovation:

- Product and process life cycles are closely related.
- The type of process suitable for a product depends on that product's current life cycle stage.
- An **economies of scope** strategy should be followed when the competitive emphasis is on product variety and innovation. Firms that follow this strategy tend to produce a wide range of products with general-purpose equipment and multiskilled workers. Unit costs are lowered because the facility's fixed costs are spread over many products.

[6] Large integrated steel producers provide an example of how companies "locked" into inflexible processes can become vulnerable. By the 1980s, these companies were driven completely out of almost 40 percent of the steel market by minimills that had developed new ways of producing low-cost steel. Now Nucor Corp. and other minimills are threatening the remainder of their market by adopting even newer steel-making technologies.

- As the product matures, a strategy based on **economies of scale** should be pursued. Typically, the firm lowers its unit costs by mass-producing large volumes of standardized products with specialized equipment. The competitive emphasis shifts to process innovations that lower product costs.
- Firms can realize economies of scale *or* economies of scope, *but not both*. Process decisions involve strategic trade-offs between benefits of scope and scale economies, or between (1) flexibility and quality and (2) dependability and cost.

  DEFINITION: Economies of scope exist when the total cost of producing a given quantity of two or more products in one facility is less than or equal to the total cost of producing the same quantity of those products in a set of facilities each of which is dedicated to a single product.[7]

If there is a need to make strategic trade-offs between flexibility and quality and between dependability and cost, how can FROs compete simultaneously along the six dimensions of competition? This apparent contradiction can be addressed by examining the impact of advanced technology on process life cycles.

The Impact of Advanced Technology on Process Life Cycles

Advances in technology[8] have led to the development of general-purpose machines equipped with specialized software. These **flexible (software-driven) technologies** can produce a variety of customized products (characteristic of scope economies) and a large aggregate volume of low-cost products (characteristic of scale economies). Advanced technology has effectively eliminated the inherent incompatibility of scope and scale economies in the following ways:

- By allowing the specialization that has been built physically into a piece of equipment to be built into its computer software instead.
- By eliminating operating learning curve effects.[9] The computer software can perform its operations perfectly every time.
- By drastically reducing the time needed to switch over from one batch of products to another. This theoretically reduces the economic batch size to just one unit.[10]

Advanced technology is allowing many firms to move beyond the restrictions of the product-process life cycle matrix (Exhibit 9.11) and the dynamic model of product-process innovation (Exhibit 9.12). These firms are beginning to realize economies of integration.

Economies of Integration and Mass Customization

DEFINITION: *Economies of integration* refer to the simultaneous presence of economies of scale and economies of scope.

Consider a firm, such as the Cummins Engine Company in Exhibit 9.13, that has a proliferating product line. Economies of integration at Cummins allow the

---

[7] Just as *diseconomies of scale* set in once the production volume exceeds a certain level, *diseconomies of scope* appear when the product line is widened beyond a certain point.

[8] The supplement to this chapter provides an overview of different forms of advanced technologies.

[9] The learning curve ("practice makes perfect") effect is discussed in Chapter 10. As more units are produced by a process, the time required to make each unit decreases.

[10] The smaller the batch size, the less time items spend waiting on the shop floor between operations. This also means that the motivation to uncover and solve quality problems is high because there is little stock between operations.

EXHIBIT 9.13   ECONOMIES OF INTEGRATION AT CUMMINS ENGINE COMPANY

In the mid-1970s the Cummins Engine Company held more than half the diesel engine market with a relatively small stable product line. Ten years later, Cummins' catalog offered over 100,000 parts and markets were continuing to fragment. Customers were demanding a fast response to their individual needs, and the company was forced to reduce prices on new products 20 to 40 percent just to retain its market share.

In response to market and product line changes, most of Cummins' factories converted their production processes from high-volume transfer lines to conventional manufacturing cells. Large savings were realized in floor space, scrap, inventory levels, and indirect labor costs. But as the firm's product line proliferated and more parts were assigned to each manufacturing cell, the cells choked on low-volume parts with lengthy setup times. Cummins found it increasingly difficult to meet the new manufacturing challenges.

As Cummins studied its processes and the functional characteristics of its wide range of products, it realized that simply refocusing by product and by volume would not solve its problems. Now parts are assigned to particular types of processes [flexible machine cells, conventional cells, and computer numerical control (CNC) machines] on the basis of a number of criteria, including product volume, predictability of demand, and design stability. If a part's production requirements change, it moves from one type of process to another. The aim is to have total product quality, process uniformity, and the ability to respond quickly to customers' needs.

In some cases Cummins' new classification system violates conventional wisdom. For example, many parts with fairly high volumes are produced on flexible machines. The time required to produce each part is therefore relatively long, but new parts can be introduced quickly and design improvements can be incorporated easily. The customer gets a better product at a lower price sooner; Cummins gets flexible, efficient factories that have revived its competitiveness.

Source: Adapted from Unruh (1993), p. 29, and Venkatesan (1990), pp. 120–127.

company to cost-effectively produce a larger aggregate volume of a given product range. The corollary is also true: at any given level of aggregate production volume, Cummins can economically manufacture a larger variety of products.

Note that flexible technologies are not the only prerequisite for achieving economies of integration. The firm must also be flexible to strategically align activities within the firm and along the value chain.

Economies of integration give firms the speed, efficiency, and flexibility to pursue a strategy of **mass customization.**[11] The mass customization of consumer goods is a fairly new concept that is being recognized as the ultimate way to derive benefit from the flexibility inherent in advanced technologies [Noori (1990a)].

DEFINITION: Mass customization is the mass production of customized goods and services.

At GFT (Exhibit 9.1), for example, each production facility can produce very high quality designer clothing while remaining flexible enough to respond to changes in fashion trends and regional preferences. GFT can customize its clothing without sacrificing the cost efficiencies associated with mass production.

Firms pursuing a strategy of mass customization lower the cost of specialized products to a point where *cost*-conscious purchasers of the commodity product become *value*-conscious purchasers of the differentiated product. The global market for semiconductor chips is a good example. The Japanese dominate the world market with their high-volume production of commodity chips sold by the millions. Intel, Motorola, Cypress Semiconductor, and other American companies, however, are beginning to steal market share from the Japanese with designer chips produced in small batches by flexible manufacturing processes that suit specialized market needs.

[11] The term *mass customization* was used first by Davis (1987) and later by Pine (1993).

Since the price of these designer chips is not substantially higher than that of commodity chips, a **value gap** has been created.

This does not mean that high-volume dedicated processes are no longer viable. When these processes run at capacity, they can produce products at a lower total unit cost than can a similar process capable of producing highly differentiated batches of products. However, the more turbulent[12] the market is, the more likely it is that firms in the industry will move towards a mass-customization strategy. This requires a firm to increase its agility and flexibility.

How does the ability to achieve economies of integration and pursue a strategy of mass customization affect the product-process life cycle matrix? In Exhibit 9.14, economies of scope have been added to the upper left-hand corner of the matrix and economies of scale to the lower right-hand corner. The diagonal represents the traditional path of evolution from a job shop with its economies of scope to a continuous-flow shop with its economies of scale. The potential for economies of integration, however, has disrupted this path of evolution. The diagonal path has been pushed out to the bottom left, creating a decidedly concave production possibility frontier. This implies that three distinct operation strategies can be considered: a strategy based on economies of scope (variety), a strategy based on economies of scale (volume), and a strategy based on both economies of scope and scale (variety and volume) simultaneously.

In a market for product differentiation, the economies of integration may well be exploited, whereas price competition will force the company to run large batches of standard design and hence implement the economies-of-scale strategy.

---

[12] Highly turbulent markets exhibit some or all of the following characteristics: unstable and unpredictable demand levels; uncertain and quickly changing consumer needs and wants; high levels of price, quality, or fashion consciousness among consumers; powerful consumers; intense competition; and high rates of technological change.

EXHIBIT 9.14   THE REVISED PRODUCT-PROCESS LIFE CYCLE MATRIX

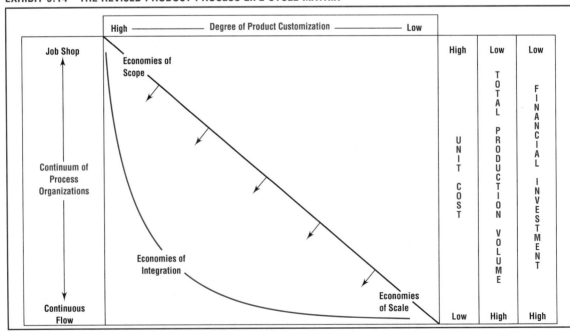

Note that the "product life cycle stage" and "process life cycle stage" labels have been removed from the matrix. This was done to emphasize the fact that *economies of integration have effectively decoupled the product and process life cycles.*

Fast-Response Process Capability   Decoupling the product and process life cycles means that the life cycle stage in which a product falls does not dictate the type of process that should be used to produce it. As illustrated in Exhibit 9.15, the life of a process can extend over several generations of similar products. Contrast this with the dynamic model of product-process innovation in Exhibit 9.12.

A flexible (software-driven) technology is reprogrammed, not ripped out and replaced, when one product or product family "dies" and is replaced by another. The changeover is quick and inexpensive. This ability is referred to as **fast-response process capability (FRPC).**

> **DEFINITION:** Fast-response process capability refers to the ability of a process to produce a number of products, both at once and over time and allow product testing, R&D, preventive maintenance, and other activities to be conducted without disrupting regular production.

The strategic implications of FRPC are clearly demonstrated by Chrysler's Bramalea assembly plant (see Exhibit 9.16). FRPC allows Chrysler to efficiently and effectively meet changing customer expectations with a flexible yet stable process.

Investments in Advanced Technology

Many strategic benefits are associated with economies of integration and fast-response process capability, but are these benefits outweighed by the enormous capital costs associated with advanced technology? In many cases the benefits out-

EXHIBIT 9.15   FAST-RESPONSE PROCESS CAPABILITY

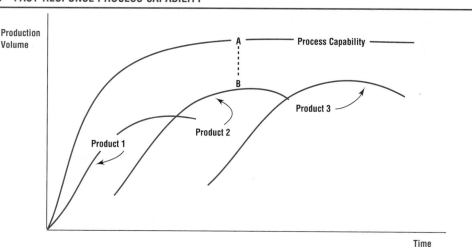

These product life cycle (PLC) curves are similar to the traditional PLC curves but are more compact and frequent, reflecting rapid changes in product design. Several generations of a product or product family can be accommodated by the same process; this is referred to as *fast-response process capability.*

The line AB represents underutilized process capability. This excess capacity can be used for a variety of strategic purposes, such as experimenting with design changes on existing products and further overlapping of product life cycles.

EXHIBIT 9.16 FAST-RESPONSE PROCESS CAPABILITY AT CHRYSLER

The flexible assembly line at Chrysler's automobile plant in Bramalea, Ontario, can handle four different models in the company's LH series. Since the time and costs associated with changing over from one model to the next are negligible, almost every vehicle produced is a different model from the one preceding it. Also, the total quantity produced of each model varies from day to day to meet consumer demand.

The Bramalea plant currently maintains excess capacity. This capacity is used for preventive maintenance, R&D, and on-line product testing and allows the firm to respond to increases in total demand.

The assembly line was originally set up to accommodate only three models. The inherent flexibility of the line, however, allowed Chrysler to add another model—the 1994 New Yorker—without disrupting regular production. Since the New Yorker was tested on the actual line during off hours, the length of its product development cycle was drastically reduced.

weigh the costs, but as is stressed in the supplement to this chapter, the financial measures commonly used to evaluate and compare capital expenditures cannot capture the true value of these benefits.

Are small firms capable of selecting, financing, and implementing advanced technology? Smaller firms often lack the resources to invest in advanced technology and survive unsuccessful ventures. They also lack the in-house expertise and the funds to hire consultants to carry out feasibility studies. It is not surprising that comparatively larger firms spend more on adopting advanced technology [Noori, (1992)].

Problems do exist for larger firms. Perhaps one of the more important barriers preventing large operating firms from acquiring advanced technologies is the inability of top management to realize the competitive potential of the technology. Several studies have explained why it is difficult to persuade senior managers to adopt advanced technology:

- Managers may be cautious about getting involved with equipment that may have unforeseen consequences and may cause labor unrest.
- Many executives perceive manufacturing as playing a supporting role and thus feel that technology does not influence the strategic plan. Discussions on advanced technology therefore focus on technical features rather than potential strategic benefits.
- Often executives lack a firm grasp of their competitors' manufacturing capabilities. This can lead to a sense of urgency below the level needed to get an advanced technology project "off the ground."
- Techniques for evaluating capital investment alternatives tend to emphasize short-term rather than long-term benefits.

The implementation or integration of technology with current operations requires decision making at the strategic level. For example, advanced technology allows a firm to produce a greater variety of products (marketing), challenges traditional capital justification methods to include intangible benefits (finance and accounting), and involves retraining the workforce and restructuring the reward system (human resources).

On the practical side, larger firms may experience sluggish implementation of technology because of bureaucratic deliberation and interdepartmental conflict. Lack of top management support, coupled with a negative attitude among workers and union resistance, makes implementation difficult.

Another factor making implementation of new technology difficult is an inability or reluctance on the part of managers to identify qualified suppliers. Most adopters of new technology know little about the technology and rely on vendor knowledge and support. The greater the user's uncertainty, the greater the reliance on suppliers. The greater the supplier's uncertainty, though, the less able the supplier is to support the user. Firms making breakthroughs on several dimensions—new technology, new environment, new use, new raw material—therefore require the greatest support but are the least likely to find it. This does not mean that they should not try the new process, although most commentators recommend incremental change and technology followership rather than leadership. It means that the new, radical adopter should be prepared for initial setbacks by having the resources to work through the difficulties and motivating managers and workers to work through the problems.

9.4 DESIGNING SERVICE PROCESSES

Process designers face special challenges in designing a process that produces services rather than goods. In many cases the customer exerts a great deal of influence on the process. Think about a bank, grocery store, or airline counter. The length of time needed to serve each customer is usually quite variable, as is the nature of the service demanded. The inability to create an inventory of services during low-demand periods to offset high-demand periods increases the difficulty of smoothing the production flow.

Usually it is possible to split a service operation into two identifiable parts: one that makes contact with the customer (**front office operation**) and one that is free from customer contact (**back office operation**). The split is important, for the more that can be placed in the back office and isolated from the customer, the more that can be managed and designed in the same way that a manufacturing operation works.

Think of a local McDonald's. The kitchen is designed and operated using industrial engineering and work study, while the order desk is designed using queuing theory. The inventory decoupling the back office from the front office is visible to all.

Designing Customer Contact Operations

Designing an operation with the psychological needs of the customer in mind is very important when the customer is involved in the process. The facility layout must take this into account, and the service providers have to be trained in interpersonal skills as well as in the technical details of their tasks.

Reducing variability is another key consideration in designing operations with a high degree of customer involvement. Let us quickly review some of the more commonly used tactics for doing this:

- Use a reservation system to smooth demand. Doctors, dentists, lawyers, and other professional services tend to use reservation systems.
- If a reservation system is not feasible, serving customers by numbers or having a centralized queue rather than a queue in front of every server can speed the flow of customers through the system.
- Cross-train employees and assign them to tasks on the basis of current customer demand.
- Design the process for peak load and have employees perform secondary functions during slow periods. Many banks have their tellers perform data entry and bookkeeping tasks when no customers are waiting.
- Segregate customers by the type of service they want. At airports, for example, many airlines have one area for ticket sales, another area for checking in for

people with large bags, and a third area for people checking in with carry-on luggage.

- Transfer routine tasks to the customer. Most banks, for example, have automated teller machines. When run-of-the-mill interventions are removed from the normal system, loads are reduced and the work is made more challenging for the service providers.

Shostack (1984) has developed a systematic approach to designing service processes that utilizes a special type of operating flow chart. Shostack's **service blueprint** is described in the next section.

Blueprint for Services

Shostack's approach to designing service processes is based on the need to develop a more objective and quantifiable approach to designing systems that have been acknowledged to require judgment and subjectivity in design. To explore all the issues inherent in creating or managing a service, Shostack suggests that the following four steps be taken.[13] Let us work through these steps by using a simple example.

> **Step 1. Identify processes. Develop a service blueprint (process flowcharts) for the total process, being careful to differentiate between activities performed in front of the customer and those performed out of the customer's sight. The line that separates the processes is called the "line of visibility."**

The blueprint in Exhibit 9.17A maps a face-painting business set up by a college student. Since the operation is so simple, the blueprint is straightfoward. Most services, however, are much more complex and result in complicated blueprints. The process must be analyzed carefully before being divided into a set of steps and required process inputs.

> **Step 2. Isolate fail points. Determine the points where the visible production system may fail. Build in corrective measures that make the system fail-safe.**

In the face-painting example the student may choose the wrong color, paint on the wrong design, or do a poor job of drawing the design. To avoid these types of errors, the student may choose to limit the variations of each color used, confirm which design has been chosen after the customer's face has been wiped, or keep referring to an example of the design being painted.

> **Step 3. Establishing a standard execution time for the process. Estimate the amount of time each step in the process should take under normal conditions and the maximum amount of time the customer is prepared to spend in the system. These times become service standards.**

The standard time to paint a face is 2 minutes 45 seconds. Market research can be used to find the length of time a customer is willing to wait before lowering his or her assessment of quality.

> **Step 4. Analyze profitability. Continuously monitor the profitability and the time taken to service each customer. Analyze in particular variances in time caused by failure and the point at which time delays result in unprofitable business.**

[13] See Shostack (1984), pp. 133–139.

EXHIBIT 9.17   TOOLBOX: SERVICE BLUEPRINT

A. A Service Blueprint for a Face-Painting Business

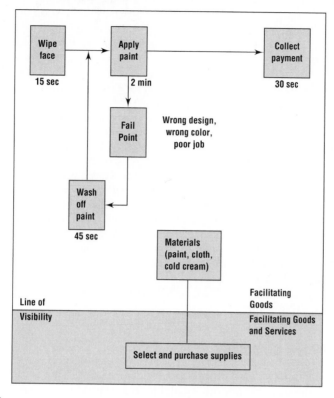

B. Profitability Analysis

Suppose the contribution margin (price minus variable costs) is $3 per painting, fixed costs are $20 per session, and demand is always greater than the face painter can meet.

	Execution Time		
	2.75 min	4 min	5 min
Number of faces painted per hour (approx.)	22	15	12
	× $3	× $3	× $3
Contribution margin	$66	$45	$36
Fixed costs	$20	$20	$20
Pretax profits	$46	$25	$16

Profits are almost halved when the execution time increases to an average of four minutes. After 5 minutes, the pretax profit becomes very small.

Source: Adapted from Shostack (1984), pp. 134–135.

Whatever its source, a delay can cause profits to decrease dramatically in a business that depends on time. As shown in Exhibit 9.17, mistakes cause significant time delays for the face painter. Since most faces are painted in the hour before a football game, wasted time results in lower profits (see Exhibit 9.17B).

Service blueprints can be used after the process has been designed to help managers analyze any problems that may arise and generate alternative solutions.

For every productive unit there is a specific product mix to be made within a specific corporate strategic context. This means that there is an appropriate manufacturing process by which the product mix should be made. The same is true of service processes. Process design should therefore be easy. Why, then, do so many managers make strange process design decisions?

The answer is that these decisions are not simple. The relationships among people, machines, and raw materials can be complex, and any change may lead to differences in these relationships of which a firm is not aware.

Remember, too, that the firm is concerned first with effectiveness and then with efficiency. Any process must produce the desired output. Then the firm can think about making the process better. In a quickly changing environment the firm will probably never reach the stage at which its processes will be perfect; the processes should therefore be designed in part for relatively short lives and for adaptation so that they can be changed rapidly. As the firm's knowledge expands and the need to be involved with smaller market segments grows, designing for flexibility will be the aspect of effectiveness that predominates.

Manufacturers no longer make a physical product and dump it into the marketplace; now there is a great deal of service content in a successful product. Of course, service organizations have always been concerned with service design, but now every organization has to be concerned with designing appropriate products and services. In high-contact service industries in particular, the effectiveness of the product is in the hands of the service provider. As part of the service process design, therefore, firms should ask themselves how they can more effectively support the front line staff.

CHAPTER SUMMARY

This chapter focused on process design. Process design is important because it influences the strategic options available to a firm. Major issues and points to remember from this chapter include:

- A process transforms selected resources into defined end products. It can be viewed as a series of discrete tasks or actions.
- Traditional process organizations range from job shops to batch shops to repetitive-flow shops through to continuous-flow shops.
- Job shops tend to produce a wide variety of customized products. General-purpose equipment is operated by highly skilled workers and arranged in a process layout.
- Intermittent-flow processes are characterized by large batches of products produced with a combination of general-purpose and special-purpose equipment. The equipment is often arranged in a process or group technology (cellular) layout.
- Repetitive-flow processes are used to produce a few standardized products. Special-purpose equipment is developed for the product and arranged into a set of sequentially dependent work centers (product layout). An assembly line is the classic example of a repetitive-flow process.
- Continuous-flow processes produce very large volumes of commoditylike products. In this case, a product layout is used.
- In the past the process life cycle was closely coupled with the product life cycle. Both the product-process life cycle matrix and the dynamic model of product-process innovation are based on this relationship. These models suggest that firms can achieve economies of scope *or* economies of scale but not both.

- Advances in technology have effectively eliminated the inherent incompatibility of scope and scale economies and have paved the way for economies of integration.

- Economies of integration refer to the simultaneous presence of both economies of scope and economies of scale. This means that a company can economically produce a larger aggregate volume of a given product range. The corollary is also true: at any level of aggregate production volume, the company can economically manufacture a larger variety of products.

- A firm that has achieved economies of integration is capable of following a mass-customization strategy.

- Flexible technologies do not automatically allow a firm to achieve economies of integration. All the firm's activities must be strategically aligned and integrated. Computer-integrated manufacturing can facilitate a firm's efforts to achieve economies of integration.

- The product and process life cycles have been decoupled. One process can now accommodate several generations of a product or product family. This ability is referred to as fast-response process capability.

- Smaller firms lack the resources to invest in advanced technology and survive unsuccessful ventures. Managers in small firms, however, often realize the competitive potential of technology. Managers in larger firms are not usually as quick to do this.

- People and equipment can be arranged in a product, process, group technology, or fixed layout.

- Process support systems include materials handling, inventory storage, inspection, forecasting-scheduling-controlling, training, and engineering and maintenance. The type of support system needed depends on the process organization and technology selected.

- The presence of the customer on the "shop floor" brings special challenges to the design of service-producing processes. Service processes can be split into front office and back office operations. Back office operations can be designed in the same way as a manufacturing process.

- A service blueprint can help designers identify fail points and introduce corrective measures to make the process fail-safe.

KEY TERMS

Process	Line balancing	Fluid, transitional, and	Mass customization
Job-shop process	Cycle time	specific phases	Value gap
Process layout	Balance delay	Economies of scope	Fast-response process
Bottlenecks	Continuous-flow process	Economies of scale	capability (FRPC)
Intermittent-flow process	Fixed-position layout	Flexible (software-driven)	Front office operation
Group technology	Product-process life cycle	technologies	Back office operation
(cellular) layouts	matrix	Economies of integration	Service blueprint
Repetitive-flow process	Dynamic model of		
Product layout	product-process		
	innovation		

DISCUSSION QUESTIONS

1. Compare and contrast job-shop, intermittent-flow, and continuous-flow processes.

2. Think of a local branch of a bank. What types of processes does it implement? Why?

3. What are the differences between economies of scale and economies of scope?

4. Explain the term *flexibility*. What is flexible automation?

5. Under what conditions do you recommend that a firm implement a strategy based on economies of scale? On economies of scope?

6. What type of process technologies are needed to support economies of scale? Economies of scope?

7. What are economies of integration? How do they affect Hayes and Wheelwright's product-process life cycle matrix?

8. Adopting flexible automation does not automatically allow the firm to achieve economies of integration. Why?

9. Who can benefit most from economies of integration? What changes are needed to transform the current environment to a situation suited for adopting economies of integration?

10. What is fast-response process capability? What is the significance of this concept? Should an FRO have this capability? Always?

11. Explain how fast-response process capability can be used to determine the degree of flexibility required in the technology used by a firm.

12. Explain the role of operations in determining a firm's technology strategy. Who should decide what flexible technology is needed and how much flexibility is needed?

13. Identify some of the intangible benefits of advanced operations technologies. How should these benefits be treated during the justification process?

14. Consider a service operation and propose a design for its process. Does the notion of customer service affect your design?

15. What is Shostack's approach to designing service processes? Is it an acceptable approach for creating a service department in a manufacturing company?

16. Can the notion of economies of scale, scope, and integration be used in services? How?

PROBLEMS

1. The following data apply to a work cell in which one operator tends four machines. Complete the operator-machine charts for an operator working at 133 and 167 percent, respectively, of the agreed-on labor standard for the work cell tasks. Use the chart for an operator at 100 percent as a guide. If 167 pieces are turned out each day, what can you say about the process?

Machine	Total Cycle Time	Machine Time	Total Operator Time	External Time	Internal Time
1	2.850	2.100	0.950	0.750	0.200
2	3.450	2.400	1.274	1.050	0.224
3	3.200	2.200	1.150	1.000	0.150
4	3.500	1.750	0.850	0.750	0.100

All times are given in minutes, and operations at the rate result in standard production of 100 pieces per day. In an eight-hour day the operator has been given allowances for personal time and the like totaling 12 percent. Internal time is for tasks performed while the machine is running; external time is for tasks that must be performed while the machine is not working, such as loading and unloading.

2. When you enrolled in this class, you had to go through a registration process. Think of this process from the viewpoint of the university. Identify elements of the process for which process design or redesign is needed.

3. Compare the process of making breakfast at home for yourself with the process of making breakfast for customers in a fast-food restaurant and in the local greasy spoon. What inputs are required in all three cases, and how do the inputs and processes differ?

4. Print Quick is evaluating four alternative investments in printing technology. Preliminary cash flow figures for each of four investment packages have been developed:

Investment	Cash Flow ($thousands) in Years 1 to 10									
	1	2	3	4	5	6	7	8	9	10
A	−10	2	2	2	2	2	2	2	—	—
B	−80	50	20	10	5	2	1	0.5	0.2	0.1
C	−80	10	20	40	80	80	—	—	—	—
D	−60	30	20	50	−40	−20	80	100	−80	100

What is the payback period for each investment? What is the net present value of each investment if the discount rate is 10 percent per year? What is the internal rate of return for each investment? Which of these investments would you recommend? Why? Would your recommendation change if you knew that investment B was the most likely to provide a good stepping-stone to the next new technology, one that would be important to invest in for longer-term survival in the industry? (See Chapter 7 for a review of capital budgeting techniques.)

5. Assume a desired output rate of 480 units per day and eight hours for each working day.
   a. Calculate the cycle time.
   b. Determine the theoretical minimum number of work centers.
   c. Develop two different layouts for the tasks in the precedence diagram below, using two different heuristics, and calculate the balance delay.

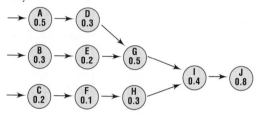

6. Adams Electronics has developed a new automatic sensing device that has been designed for assembly. The 11 assembly tasks, with their durations and precedence requirements, are:

Task	Performance Time seconds	Preceded by,
A	40	—
B	12	A
C	9	B
D	46	—
E	16	D
F	12	C
G	13	C
H	12	E
I	10	E
J	9	F, G, H, I
K	9	J

Adams requires a single-shift, 480-minute daily output of 600 units. What is the best line layout?

7. Adams Electronics has reviewed its work procedures and has reduced the time of task B to 11 seconds, that of task I to 9 seconds, and that of tasks J and K to 7 seconds each. Given the daily output in problem 6, what is the best line layout?

8. Adams Electronics wants to increase output to 625 units per day. How can this be achieved?

9. A redesign of the sensing device in problem 6 has allowed task D to be eliminated entirely while tasks C and G have been combined with a new total task time of 20 seconds; the new task times for B, I, J, and K are as in problem 7. The material cost increase for the new design is $0.435 per unit, and the all-inclusive assembly labor cost is $16.50 per hour. Is the new design economical?

10. What is your assessment of the redesign of Adams' sensing device if output has to be increased to 700 units per day? The overtime premium is $5.50 per hour.

11. A bracket casting is to be machined in a dedicated work cell. The company requires the production of 2,400 brackets per week, and the capacities of the various machines for this bracket are:

Lathe	40 per hour
Milling machine	30 per hour
Grinder	80 per hour
Drill press	60 per hour
Inspection (manual)	180 per hour

These capacities take into account run time and external time for the task. How many machines will be required for the cell?

12. The cell described in problem 11 has been built. Each casting has to be machined in the sequence shown above. The external time for each machine is 10 seconds for the lathe, milling machine, and drill press; for the grinder it is 15 seconds. Drilling and inspection are fully manual operations, and the others are automatic. The internal times for the automatic processes are eight seconds for each cycle. How many operators are required, and how should they be organized? How much inventory should be in the cell? Where? Why?

13. The firm can use robots to load the machines in the work cell in problem 11. Each robot has the reach to serve two machines; work pieces will be picked up from a small table and placed on a conveyor that automatically transfers pieces to the supply table serving the next process. The cycle time of the robots from picking up the finished piece to completing the positioning of the next piece to be machined is 35 seconds. How many robots and how many operators will be required?

14. If output has to increase to 3,600 pieces per week, what will be the new organization of the work cell in problems 11 through 13?

GROUP EXERCISES

Many of the tools and concepts discussed in this chapter are meant to be used in a team setting. The following problem is best solved by small groups of students. Ideally, each group should be composed of people with different backgrounds, interests, or areas of expertise.

The Cummins Engine Company was presented as an example of a company utilizing the notion of economies of integration (see Exhibit 9.13). Identify another company (service or manufacturing) that has realized economies of integration.

- What market (customers) does the firm serve?
- What kinds of technologies does the firm use?
- What type of organizational structure does it have?
- How quickly does it make the products?
- On what dimensions of competition does it concentrate?
- What cost analysis supports your contention that the firm *does* enjoy economies of integration?

REFERENCES AND SELECTED BIBLIOGRAPHY

Abernathy, W. J., and J. M. Utterback [1978], "Patterns of Industrial Innovation," *Technology Review* 80, no. 7, June–July, pp. 40–47.

Brockhouse, Gordon [1992], "Can This Marriage Succeed?" *Canadian Business,* October, pp. 128–136.

Davis, Stanley M. [1987], Future Perfect, Addison-Wesley, Reading, Mass.

Faltermayer, Edmund [1993], "Invest or Die," *Fortune,* Feb. 22, pp. 42–52.

Fine, C. H., and L. Li [1988], "Technology Choice, Product Life Cycles, and Flexible Automation," *Journal of Manufacturing and Operation Management,* vol. 1, no. 4, pp. 372–399.

Goldhar, J. E., and M. Jelinek [1983], "Plans for Economies of Scope," *Harvard Business Review,* March–April, pp. 75–81.

Hayes, R., and S. Wheelwright [1984], *Restoring Our Competitive Edge: Competing through Manufacturing,* Wiley, New York.

Helgeson, W. B., and D. P. Birnie [1961], "Assembly Line Balancing Using the Ranked Positional Weight Technique," *Journal of Industrial Engineering,* vol. 12, no. 6, pp. 394–398.

Hersell, J., and S. Dahl [1988], "Simulation Model Developed to Convert Production to Cellular Manufacturing Layout," *Industrial Engineering,* December, vol. 20, no. 12, pp. 40–45.

Howard, Robert [1991], "The Designer Organization: Italy's GFT Goes Global," *Harvard Busines Review,* September–October, pp. 28–44.

Johnson, Roger V. [1988], "Optimally Balancing Large Assembly Lines with 'Fable,' " *Management Science,* vol. 34, no. 2, pp. 240–253.

Kilbridge, M. D., and L. Wester [1961], "A Heuristic Model of Assembly Line Balancing," *Journal of Industrial Engineering,* vol. 12, no. 4, pp. 292–298.

Knight, David O., and Michael L. Wall [1989], "Using Group Technology for Improving Communication and Coordination among Teams of Workers in Manufacturing Cells," *Industrial Engineering,* January, pp. 28–34.

Lei, David, and Joel D. Goldhar [1990], "Multiple Niche Competition: The Strategic Use of CIM Technology," *Manufacturing Review,* vol. 3, no. 3, pp. 195–206.

Milas, G. H. [1990], "Assembly Line Balancing . . . Let's Remove the Mystery," *Industrial Engineering,* May, pp. 31–36.

Noori, H. [1990a], "Economies of Integration: A New Manufacturing Focus," *International Journal of Technology Management,* vol. 5, no. 4, pp. 577–587.

——— [1990b], *Managing the Dynamics of New Technology: Issues in Manufacturing Management,* Prentice-Hall, Englewood Cliffs, N.J.

——— [1991], "The Decouping of Product-Process Life Cycles," *International Journal of Production Research,* vol. 29, no. 9, pp. 1853–1865.

——— [1992], "Factors That Promote the Adoption of Advanced Manufacturing Technologies," in *Management of Technology III: The Key to Global Competitiveness,* Proceedings of the Third International Conference on Management of Technology, pp. 797–806.

———, and Kenneth J. Klassen [1993], "Fast Response Process Capability," Working Paper Series, Research Centre for the Management of Advanced Technology/Operations (REMAT), Wilfrid Laurier University, Waterloo, Ontario.

Pattison, D., and C. Teplitz [1989], "Are Learning Curves Still Relevant?" *Management Accounting,* February, pp. 37–40.

Pine, B. Joseph II [1993], *Mass Customization: The New Frontier in Business Competition,* Harvard Business School Press, Boston.

Schlender, B. R. [1991], "Chipper Days for U.S. Chipmakers," *Fortune,* Feb. 24, pp. 76–84.

Schlie, T. S., and J. D. Goldhar [1989], "Product Variety and Time Based Manufacturing and Business Management: Achieving Competitive Advantage through CIM," *Manufacturing Review,* vol. 2, no. 1, pp. 32–42.

Shostack, G. Lynn [1984], "Designing Services That Deliver," *Harvard Business Review,* January–February, pp. 133–139.

Skinner, Wickham [1974], "The Focused Factory," *Harvard Business Review,* May–June, pp. 113–121.

Thomson, Vince, and Udo Graefe [1989], "CIM: A manufacturing paradigm," *International Journal of Computer Integrated Manufacturing,* vol. 2, no. 5, pp. 290–297.

Unruh, B. [1993], "Cummins Engine Combines New Management and Technology to Develop Strategy for Future," *Industrial Engineering,* vol. 25, no. 8, pp. 29–31.

Venkatesan, Ravi [1990], "Cummins Engine Flexes Its Factory," *Harvard Business Review,* March–April, pp. 120–127.

Wall, T. [1986], "Advanced Manufacturing Technologies: The Case for the Operator and Wife," in H. Noori (ed.), *The* *Proceedings of Technology Canada Conference,* REMAT, WLU, Waterloo, May 21–22, pp. 311–323.

Welke, H., and J. Overbeeke [1988], "Cellular Manufacturing: A Good Technique for Implementing Just in Time and Total Quality Control," *Industrial Engineering,* vol. 20, no. 11, November, pp. 36–41.

SUPPLEMENT TO

CHAPTER 9

ADVANCED OPERATIONS TECHNOLOGIES

In describing the building blocks of a fast-response organization (FRO), Chapter 2 made it clear that the adoption of advanced technology is a structural prerequisite for an FRO. A transformation process designed to take advantage of advanced technology can drastically improve the quality of a firm's products and the speed with which they are designed and produced. Process flexibility and dependability are also increased.

What exactly *is* advanced technology? The term conjures up images of robots and other sophisticated computer-controlled pieces of equipment. Think back to this text's definition of technology and you will realize that physical equipment is only one element of technology: the hardware element.

> Reminder. *Technology* is the total body of knowledge brought to the transformation process; it can be divided into three interrelated elements: *hardware, software,* and *brainware.*[1]

This supplement describes several different forms of advanced operations technology used by both manufacturing and service firms. Since investments in advanced technology can be substantial, this supplement also looks at financial justification techniques and sources of financing.

S9.2 ADVANCED OPERATIONS TECHNOLOGIES

Although there are hundreds of different applications of advanced technology in the business world, this discussion is restricted to the **advanced operations technologies** shown in Exhibit 9S.1.

Computer-Aided Manufacturing (CAM)

Automation was first applied to very high volume and very low volume operations. In their drive to improve process efficiency, firms with high-volume operations implemented **fixed automation** extensively.

> DEFINITION: Fixed automation refers to a process that consists of equipment that can accomplish the only single task for which it was designed.

Machine utilization was increased and direct labor was minimized, but only a few different products or parts could be produced. Time-consuming manual adjustments were needed to change the process from one product to another.

The aerospace industry, which produced small volumes of a wide variety of products, began to apply **programmable automation** in the 1950's, using **numerical control (NC) technology.** NC technology uses prerecorded symbolic instructions to control and operate a machine that produces high-quality products.

> DEFINITION: Production equipment controlled by a program that can be modified is referred to as programmable automation. By reprogramming the machine instructions and changing the physical setup of the machines, the process can change over from one product to another.

Initially NC machines were hardwired, and instructions detailing how a specific part should be made were captured on punched cards, punched tape, or magnetic tape. Cards and tapes were easily damaged, however, and so **direct numerical contact** technology was developed in the late 1960s. Each NC machine was connected to a host computer which sent program instructions to individual machines in real time as needed. When the host computer failed (which occurred fairly often in the early days of computing), however, none of its NC machines were operable.

Rapid advances in computer technology led to the development of **computer numerical control (CNC)**. With CNC, each NC machine is equipped with its own microcomputer and thus is no longer dependent on a host computer. Today CNC technology goes far beyond controlling a single machining sequence for a particular part; it is essentially **flexible automation.**

> DEFINITION: Flexible automation is an extension of the programmable automation. A variety of products can be produced, and virtually no time is needed to change over from one product to the next.

CNC machines have one major drawback. Because each machine stores its own copy of a particular program, ensuring that all machines have the same version of the program can be difficult as products are modified over time. In response to this data management problem, **distributed numerical control (DNC)** was developed.

With DNC technology, CNC machines are connected to a host computer that stores all the programs.

---

[1] Technology *hardware* consists of the physical structure and logical layout of the equipment used to carry out a set of tasks. Technology *software* refers to the rules, guidelines, and algorithms that control and direct the hardware. Technology *brainware* is used to decide when, where, how, and why to use the technology.

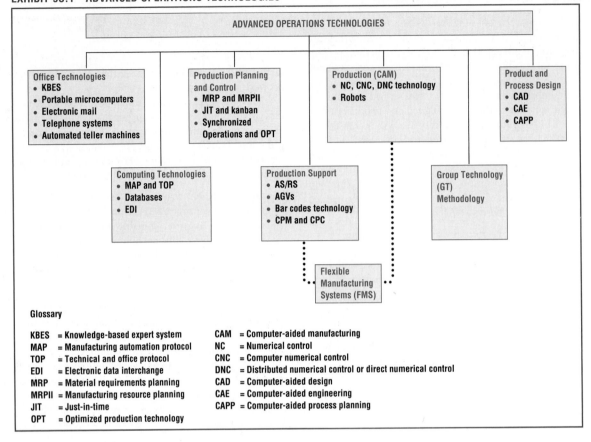

ADVANCED OPERATIONS TECHNOLOGIES

Office Technologies
- KBES
- Portable microcomputers
- Electronic mail
- Telephone systems
- Automated teller machines

Production Planning and Control
- MRP and MRPII
- JIT and kanban
- Synchronized Operations and OPT

Production (CAM)
- NC, CNC, DNC technology
- Robots

Product and Process Design
- CAD
- CAE
- CAPP

Computing Technologies
- MAP and TOP
- Databases
- EDI

Production Support
- AS/RS
- AGVs
- Bar codes technology
- CPM and CPC

Group Technology (GT) Methodology

Flexible Manufacturing Systems (FMS)

Glossary

KBES	= Knowledge-based expert system		CAM	= Computer-aided manufacturing
MAP	= Manufacturing automation protocol		NC	= Numerical control
TOP	= Technical and office protocol		CNC	= Computer numerical control
EDI	= Electronic data interchange		DNC	= Distributed numerical control or direct numerical control
MRP	= Material requirements planning		CAD	= Computer-aided design
MRPII	= Manufacturing resource planning		CAE	= Computer-aided engineering
JIT	= Just-in-time		CAPP	= Computer-aided process planning
OPT	= Optimized production technology			

The programs are downloaded to the CNC machines when required, and even if the host computer fails, the CNC machine is operable. Data can be passed up and down from the CNC machine, the DNC computer, and the firm's plant management computer.

Robots are multifunctional programmable machines that can perform a variety of direct production and production support tasks. These tasks include parts and materials handling, machine loading and unloading, heat treating, welding, spray painting, testing and inspection, die casting, assembling, and finishing. Robots are beginning to be seen in service roles as well; current applications of service robots include performing security functions, performing nursing activities in hospitals, and assisting handicapped individuals. Robots are also replacing people in dangerous, unpleasant, or boring jobs.

Enabling robots and other machines to sense and manipulate their environments intelligently is an important aspect of *artificial intelligence (AI)*. **Machine intelligence** is growing in importance; much research is being conducted in vision systems, range and proximity sensors, and contact sensors.

Advanced Technology for Production Support Functions

Advanced technology has been applied to many support functions essential to production. The first support function that comes to mind in this regard is materials handling and storage.

In an **automated storage and retrieval system (AS/RS)** parts are taken from input-output staging areas by storage-retrieval machines and loaded automatically into storage racks or bins. When they are needed, the parts are automatically unloaded and taken back to an input-output staging area, where they are transferred to conveyors, lift trucks, automatic guided vehicles, or other transport devices.

Bar code technology is used by storage-retrieval machines to identify the correct load to be picked. A bar code consists of a set of thin and thick black bars and spaces that can be read by an optical scanner. Product name, lot number, manufacturing location, shelf location, and price can be stored in a bar code. These codes can be printed directly on cartons, on the product, or on a label which is affixed to the product. Retailing and wholesaling operations use bar code technology as well.

The heart of AS/RS is the computer, which is used to record the location of every item in the warehouse and control the operation of the storage-retrieval equipment. If **automatic guided vehicles (AGVs)** are used, the AS/RS computer is often integrated with the computer used to control the operation of AGVs; sometimes the same computer controls both functions.

AGVs are driverless trucks or lifters controlled by central computers which dispatch carriers, track them, and govern their movements on guidepath loops. They can deliver inventory from holding to production areas or between workstations, replacing conventional forklifts and rigid transfer lines. They can also replace conventional industrial conveyor systems by acting as production platforms that support products while work is performed. Their principal advantage is their inherent flexibility.

Other production support activities that have been automated include **computer process monitoring (CPM)** and **computer process control (CPC)**. CPM systems gather information about the manufacturing process. The flow of information is one-way only—from the process being monitored to the computer. If process adjustments are made, they are accomplished by human operators.

Computer process control augments CPM and is used for monitoring and direct control of the manufacturing process. For example, when the computer realizes that a machine tool has worn beyond specified dimensions, it automatically shuts down the machine or even changes the tool. The information flow is two-way, and there is no need for process adjustments by human operators. The main benefit of CPM and CPC is improved product quality and production scheduling.

Production Planning and Control Systems

Advances in production planning and control include systems such as materials requirements planning, kanban, and optimized production technology. These systems are described briefly here. A detailed discussion appears in Chapters 15 and 16.

Materials Requirements Planning and Manufacturing Resource Planning
Material requirements planning (MRP) is an inventory ordering and scheduling technique. Using detailed information, including bills of material, inventory levels, and production lead times, MRP

expands the master production schedule[2] into a set of time-phased production orders. Thus, MRP acts as a link between computerized inventory systems and the scheduling function.

Although it can be implemented on its own, MRP is only one module in a much larger system called **manufacturing resource planning (MRPII)**. MRPII transforms MRP from a materials planning and control system to a companywide system that plans and controls all the firm's resources. For example, it may be used to schedule capacity, shipments, and maintenance. Projections of cash flows can be provided for financial planning. Estimates of future labor requirements can be used for human resources planning.

Just-in-Time and the Kanban System The **just-in-time (JIT)** management philosophy is one of the cornerstones of the famous Toyota production system. A more accurate translation of the Japanese term is "only-on-time," and this name more truly reflects the philosophy. All materials and resources should be available at the right time and in the right amount; any deviation results in waste. Toyota's goal was to develop a process that could economically produce a wide variety of automobiles in small volumes in response to customer demand.

Kanban is a manual information system that enables Toyota to "pull" specific types of cars through the production process in accordance with the final assembly schedule. Many North American companies have adapted kanban and JIT principles to their operations.

Synchronous Operations and Optimized Production Technology The **synchronous operations** philosophy emphasizes the importance of bottleneck resources and the need to focus a firm's efforts on maximizing their utilization. This emphasis on bottlenecks is reflected in a form of production planning and control software called **optimized production technology (OPT)**.

OPT increases shop floor throughput by scheduling variable batch sizes. Customer orders do not flow through the process in a large batch but are broken down into smaller batches. Therefore, very small batches are transferred from one operation to the next.

---

[2] The *master production schedule* specifies the quantity to be produced of each end item in each planning period.

This reduces production lead times, reduces work-in-process inventories, and smooths production. Individual batches are often combined at bottleneck operations, however, to increase bottleneck efficiency. Unlike schedules generated with MRP systems, OPT schedules are feasible because OPT directly considers capacity limitations. Since OPT schedules are so detailed, they can be used directly on the shop floor.

Computer-Aided Design

When the link between product and process design was examined in Chapter 5, it was emphasized that the quality (and production cost) of a product is largely determined by its design. Advanced technology has enabled engineers to generate and then alter high-quality designs for new and revised products quickly and inexpensively.

Computer-aided design (CAD) tools are used to create, store, and modify the designs of products, production processes, facility layouts, and equipment tooling. **Computer-aided engineering (CAE)** tools test designs to ensure that they do not violate any electrical, mechanical, heat, stress, or other engineering requirements. Many CAD software packages now include CAE capabilities.

Computer-Aided Process Planning and Group Technology

A process plan detailing the equipment to be used, the sequence of operations to be performed, the tooling needed, and the labor skills required must be developed for every new product. Whenever a product is modified or a firm's production capabilities change (e.g., after a new piece of equipment is purchased), the process plan must be updated.

Computer-aided process planning (CAPP) tools are **knowledge-based expert systems (KBES)** that generate standard process plans. (Like machine intelligence, knowledge-based expert systems are an application of artificial intelligence. Exhibit 9S.2 provides a brief description of how these systems work.)

Not only does CAPP increase the speed with which process plans can be completed, it helps make process plans consistent and increases process efficiency. Most CAPP systems simply modify an existing process plan to suit the new product; the existing plan is chosen in accordance with group technology principles.

Group technology (GT) is a methodology used to identify and organize parts with physical similarities. It facilitates the rapid retrieval of existing designs and the development of cellular layouts. Then, rather than design every part of a new product from scratch, designers can quickly retrieve the design of similar parts and start from there. The speed with which products can be designed is increased. Parts standardization also becomes easier to implement.

GT can be used to develop groups of parts or products that have similar production requirements. The firm can then arrange its production equipment and workers into **manufacturing cells** dedicated to the production of a part family.

> **DEFINITION:** A manufacturing cell is a group of equipment that produces a family of parts or products that have similar designs or processing requirements.

Manufacturing cells are both flexible and efficient. They are well suited for firms that produce small to medium batches of a variety of goods. They also play an important role in the successful implementation of just-in-time. Generally, when cells incorporate advanced technology and become part of an integrated system, the potential benefits are even greater.

In some instances benefits are not achieved because managers overlook an important issue: the specific tooling required by new machines and/or new products. Often tooling will dictate which machines are used and in what sequence. Some tools take a long time to make and may require specialist knowledge a firm does not possess.

Integrated Systems

One of the most important manufacturing advances has been the development of **flexible manufacturing systems (FMS)**.

> **DEFINITION:** A flexible manufacturing system is a group of workstations (such as CNC machines) integrated by automated materials handling equipment and controlled by a central computer.

Flexible manufacturing systems are designed to produce a family of parts and can produce different parts simultaneously and in random order. Improved product quality and consistency, increased productivity, reduced work-in-process and finished goods inventories, reduced labor costs, and reduced floor space requirements are the major benefits of these systems.

On their own, however, flexible manufacturing systems and other applications of advanced technology are simply "islands of automation." Integrating these islands can magnify the strategic benefits advanced technology offers. Firms such as Allen-Bradley (see Exhibit

Many problems are too poorly structured or too complicated or have too many possible solutions to be solved using conventional programming methods. The goal of artificial intelligence is to solve these types of problems with computer systems that can learn and reason in a manner similar to that of humans.

Knowledge-based expert systems use knowledge compiled by experts to solve problems in a particular domain. The solution provided by the system is not necessarily the optimal solution, but it should be a feasible one. Most systems are composed of the following interacting modules:

- Information (e.g., rules of thumb, relationships between objects, attributes of objects) about the problem domain is stored in a knowledge base. This information may be incomplete, uncertain, or rapidly changing.
- An inference engine monitors the facts in the database and manipulates the knowledge base to make inferences about the problem. The inference engine may ask the user for more information.
- A control mechanism guides the reasoning process.
- The user may query the explanation module to find out why a question was asked by the system or how the system arrived at its conclusion.

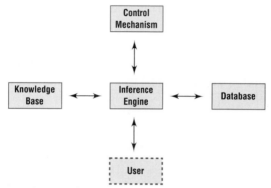

An expert system can increase productivity by (1) transferring the skill and knowledge of an expert to a novice without the usual training time lag, (2) quickly and accurately performing complex reasoning or reasoning that requires a scope of knowledge that exceeds that of any individual, and (3) coping with routine functions, allowing the expert to concentrate on exceptions.

Expert systems have a wide range of applications, including medical diagnosis; repair suggestions; program debugging, monitoring, interpreting, and controlling systems; and design work.

9S.3) are linking their manufacturing systems to each other, with other production activities, and even with other departments. Such an integrated system is also known as **computer-integrated manufacturing (CIM)**.

CIM is a flexible system in which a single database provides on-time information to all parts of the organization. Exhibit 9S.4 shows the progression from independent automated systems to flexible manufacturing systems and then to CIM.

> DEFINITION: Computer-integrated manufacturing refers to the use of computerized information systems and management philosophies to totally integrate all production-related activities from the customers' perceived need for a product on through product design, process design, production, and after-sales support.

Since all production-related activities are information-driven, it makes sense to use computers to integrate and control these activities. Computer-aided process planning and group technology help bridge the gap between computer-aided manufacturing and computer-aided design. Companywide systems such as MRPII integrate and connect computer applications throughout the firm. Telecommunication standards and computer databases (which are discussed in the next section) enable different computer software and hardware systems to "talk" to each other and share data.

Keep in mind, however, that CIM is not technology hardware per se. CIM is best suited to a well-integrated environment. As was discussed in Chapter 2, total integration requires changes in a firm's organizational structure, reward systems, and corporate culture.

Advanced Computing Technologies

To create a true CIM environment, different machines must be able to "shake hands," or communicate with each other. In practice, because their hardware

EXHIBIT 9S.3 INTEGRATING OPERATIONS AT ALLEN-BRADLEY

Integration of its production and information systems is giving Allen-Bradley the edge it needs to compete. Allen-Bradley is a worldwide manufacturer of industrial automation controls and systems that sells a wide range of products in relatively small quantities to a large number of customers. Flexibility, speed, and quality are essential.

At the company's EMS1 facility circuit boards are designed using computer-aided design (CAD) tools. Once a board has been designed, each of its components is automatically assigned to a process within the facility. The assignment is conveyed to the people who create the numerical control programs and related documentation for assembly. The manufacturing resource planning system is also informed of the assignment and schedules it for production.

The boards are produced on a computer-controlled continuous-flow assembly line that is linked with a conveyor system. A bar code identification system keeps track of the more than 1,500 components required to assemble the circuit boards. At each assembly line station, bar code readers are used to identify the component and download instructions from the center's database to the machine controls.

The system is very flexible, and as many as six different boards can be produced at one time. Throughput time is only one day, and the average work-in-process inventory is at most one day's work.

Source: Adapted from Blass (1992), pp. 26–29.

EXHIBIT 9S.4 COMPUTER-INTEGRATED MANUFACTURING (CIM)

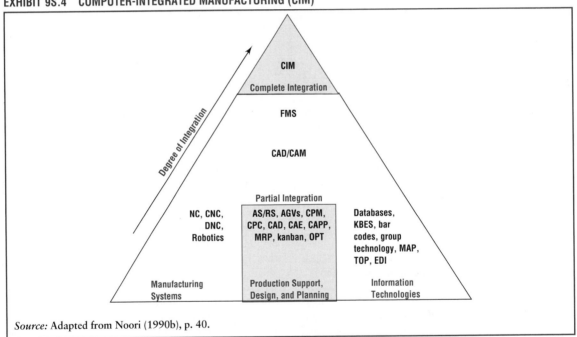

Source: Adapted from Noori (1990b), p. 40.

and/or software is incompatible, many computerized tools cannot communicate with each other or share data. To overcome this problem, network standards such as the **manufacturing automation protocol (MAP)** and the **technical and office protocol (TOP)** are being developed. These network standards conform to the seven-layer **open systems interconnection (OSI)** reference model proposed by the International Standard Or-

ganization. The goal is to provide protocols[3] that allow different manufacturers' products to be connected together and exchange information.

MAP was developed by General Motors and provides a common communications protocol for factory

---

[3] *Computer protocols* are rules that govern the format and sequence of electronic signals going from one computer to another.

computers, robots, and programmable controllers. It enables a firm to connect dissimilar machines in a single network. TOP was developed by Boeing as a developmental standard for office automation and to enable computers not involved in the transformation processes to communicate. Engineering, purchasing, materials management, accounting and sales computers, and workstations can be interconnected. It is therefore possible for an engineer to draft a product modification and have the change checked and authorized. Any new parts are recorded and then ordered electronically and in a fraction of the time manual action would take.

Centralized databases allow different computer applications linked together in a network to share data by storing the data in a central repository. In this case, a data file is no longer needed for each application, and all applications use the most up-to-date information.

A problem with centralized databases is that they require powerful computer hardware to store data and communicate with thousands of multiple users simultaneously. To combat this problem, **distributed databases** that can allocate data in the database among many computers are being developed. Since information is shared among these systems only when requested or required, computer hardware requirements are reduced and requests for data can be processed quickly.

Electronic data interchange (EDI) enables a firm's computers to exchange business information directly with the firm's suppliers' and customers' computers even if the computers have incompatible hardware or software. EDI translation software is used to translate data from the source computer into a standardized format developed by the Accredited Standards Committee, a group chartered by the American National Standards Institute. Once translated, the data are transferred to the destination computer, which uses translation software to convert the data into a suitable format for its own systems.

Purchase orders, advance shipping notices, and invoices are examples of EDI transactions. Since data are not entered twice (by the sender and then by the receiver) and do not have to travel by mail or courier, time and money are saved. The quality of information transfer is improved because fewer clerical errors can be made.

Office Technologies

Computers have been used for decades to automate information processing tasks. Advances in information technology have increased the speed of these applications and broadened the range of tasks that can be automated. Consider the following examples of **office technologies:**

- More powerful computers and the development of KBES are enabling firms to automate information processing tasks (e.g., debugging computer programs, diagnosing illnesses, and translating documents from one language into another).
- Word processing systems, electronic spreadsheets, computer graphics software, laser printers, and copying machines have increased the speed with which reports can be prepared and the quality of their presentation.
- Electronic mail systems allow people to send each other documents and messages immediately.
- Portable microcomputers are accessible at any location through the use of a telephone which can access other computers.
- Telephone systems are becoming increasingly sophisticated. Conference calling (allowing several people to talk at once), recording and playing of messages, and call forwarding are just a few of the features now found in many phone systems. Video conferencing, closed circuit television, and audio-video communication through electronic mail enable people to see each other while talking and may be used with electronic blackboards. *Electronic blackboards* are instruments that can be written on. The message is then transmitted and shown on a television screen in a different location. Facsimile machines allow hard-copy transmission of information over telephone lines.

These technologies have revolutionized the way in which many industries, especially the health care industry (see Exhibit 9S.5), manage and process information.

Advanced technology is also being used by service sector firms to transfer service tasks to the customer. Automatic teller machines, self-service gasoline pumps that take credit cards, and interactive tourist information computer terminals are examples.

S9.3 JUSTIFYING INVESTMENTS IN ADVANCED TECHNOLOGY

Advanced technology can provide a wide range of strategic benefits, some of which are outlined in Exhibit 9S.6. In practice, however, most managers face many obstacles when they attempt to invest in advanced technology, the largest of which is the firm's financial justification system.

Many firms evaluate and compare alternative technology investments by using financial measures such as

EXHIBIT 9S.5   INFORMATION TECHNOLOGY IN THE HEALTH CARE INDUSTRY

Perhaps no service industry has been affected by technological advances as much as has the health industry. Maintaining single patient records is a simple process with computers. These records can be linked electronically to the patient's family physician, attending surgeons, and other specialists. They can also be linked directly to health insurance organizations for direct payment of bills as the expenses are incurred. Patients are uniquely identified with a bar code, and bar code readers can be found throughout the hospital. The use of satellites and video conferencing enables medical professionals to exchange information quickly.

The availability of high-quality and high-capacity video, voice, and data communications has enabled the three major hospitals in London, Ontario, to operate as a highly coordinated unit. Each hospital provides specialized services to the others and the general community, reducing overall costs without compromising care. In addition, a reduced clerical workload allows the nursing staff to spend more time with patients, improving the psychological and the physical well-being of patients.

EXHIBIT 9S.6   THE BENEFITS OF ADVANCED TECHNOLOGY

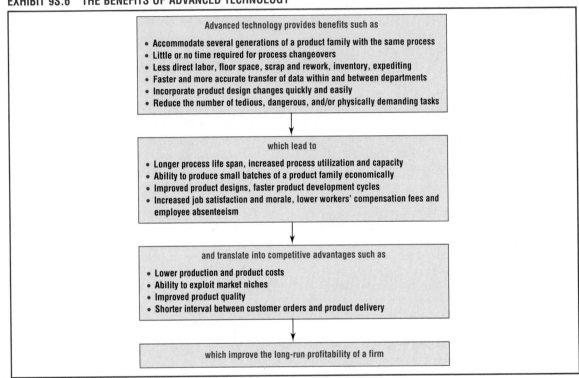

the ones discussed in Chapter 7. These measures, however, may not take into consideration all the technologies' tangible and intangible benefits.

S9.4   COMMON PITFALLS WHEN USING FINANCIAL MEASURES

All the financial measures discussed in Chapter 7 consider the net cash flows generated each year by the proposed investment. Annual cash outflows usually include maintenance and repair costs, insurance premiums, and other expenses generated by the investment. Many of these costs are relatively easy to identify. Cash inflows include salvage values, tax savings, and other inflows (savings) that can be traced back to the investment. Reduced direct labor costs, inventory levels, and floor space requirements are examples.

Software tools that can simulate conditions on the shop floor enable firms to estimate a widening range of cash flows generated through investments in advanced

286

technology. However, most of the benefits associated with advanced technology are still difficult to quantify. Look at the list of potential benefits in Exhibit 9S.6 again. How can a firm translate the ability to incorporate product design modifications quickly into a stream of cash inflows? What about increased job satisfaction? Closer ties with suppliers and customers? Even if intangible benefits can be quantified, how much confidence can be placed in these estimates and the final value of the financial measure being calculated? It is for these reasons that many managers include only easily quantifiable benefits in the estimated annual cash inflows. However, excluding the value of any potential benefit from the analysis is tantamount to assigning it a value of zero.

Investments in advanced technology tend to be too large to justify if the value of intangible benefits is ignored. The actual size and value of intangible benefits are likely to exceed those of easily quantifiable benefits. What, then, should the firm do? If financial measures must be used,[4] the firm should ask qualified individuals to make informed estimates of the dollar value of intangible benefits.

Another common mistake made in using financial measures such as NPV and IRR is to include an inflation component in the discount rate used in the calculation but not in the estimation of future cash flows. This biases financial analysis against making long-term in-

vestments (such as those in advanced technology), especially during inflationary periods.

An even more serious error is to compare the proposed investment to the current situation, or status quo. This assumes that competitors are not modernizing by investing in advanced technology and that customer demand is static. The actual situation is more like the one depicted in Exhibit 9S.7.

Rather being compared solely on the basis of financial measures, investments can be compared on the basis of their contribution to a firm's efforts to achieve its strategic goals and objectives. Chapter 19 presents a model that can be used to do this. First, the investment's expected benefits are listed. The cause-and-effect relationships between each benefit and each of the firm's goals are then evaluated.

S9.5 FINANCING ADVANCED TECHNOLOGY

Once an investment proposal has been justified, the firm focuses on raising the required funds. It was mentioned earlier that recent studies of manufacturing companies indicate that financing is the second most powerful factor slowing the rate of adoption of advanced technology. Hence, the issue of raising funds for technology development and acquisition is a major concern for management.

---

[4] An alternative to financial measures is described later in this section, but banks and other financing sources may still require a firm to use financial measures.

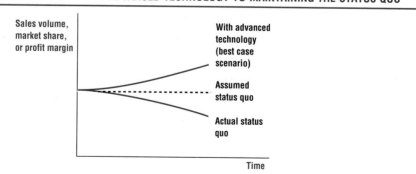

EXHIBIT 9S.7   A COMPARISON OF INVESTMENT IN ADVANCED TECHNOLOGY TO MAINTAINING THE STATUS QUO

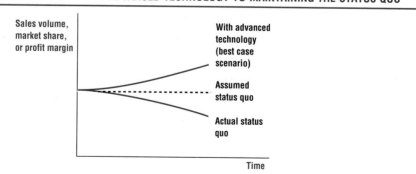

Message. Do not automatically assume that a firm's competitive position will remain as if investments in advanced technology are *not* made. Also, do not assume that if investments in advanced technology are made, the line will slope upward; these investments may be necessary just to maintain the status quo. The upward-sloping line may be the best case scenario. The true slope will depend on the success (or failure) of the implementation vis-à-vis the competition. The slope of the actual status quo will also be influenced by the actions of the firm's competitors.

Source: Adapted from Noori (1990b), p. 211.

acquisition of modern technology. Megagrowth technology companies that have current and projected sales growth rates of 40 to 50 percent per year also have difficulty acquiring financing. Because of the high growth rate, there is a low capital and retained earning level in such companies. External sources of financing include banks, term lenders, and venture capitalists.

Alternatives in funding methods differ depending on the size of the firm. Usually, it is smaller firms that lack the ability to internally raise the funds for a major

KEY TERMS

Technology hardware, software, and brainware
Advanced operations technologies
Fixed automation
Programmable automation
Numerical control (NC) technology
Direct numerical contact
Computer numerical control (CNC)
Flexible automation
Distributed numerical control (DNC)
Robots
Machine intelligence

Automated storage and retrieval system (AS/RS)
Bar code technology
Automatic guided vehicle (AGV)
Computer process monitoring (CPM)
Computer process control (CPC)
Material requirements planning (MRP)
Manufacturing resource planning (MRPII)
Just-in-time (JIT)
Kanban
Synchronous operations

Optimized production technology (OPT)
Computer-aided design (CAD)
Computer-aided engineering (CAE)
Computer-aided process planning (CAPP)
Knowledge-based expert systems (KBES)
Group technology (GT)
Manufacturing cell
Flexible manufacturing systems (FMS)
Computer-integrated manufacturing (CIM)

Manufacturing automation protocol (MAP)
Technical and office protocol (TOP)
Open systems interconnection (OSI) reference model
Centralized database
Distributed database
Electronic data interchange (EDI)
Office technologies
Payback period
Net present value (NPV)
Equivalent annual annuity value (EAAV)
Internal rate of return (IRR)

REFERENCES AND SELECTED BIBLIOGRAPHY

Ayres, R. V. [1986], "Computer Integrated Manufacturing and the Next Industrial Revolution," in J. Demer (ed.), *Competitiveness through Technology*, Lexington Press, Lexington, Mass., pp. 11–24.

Berliner, C., and J. A. Brimson [1988], *Cost Management for Today's Advanced Manufacturing*, Harvard Busines School Press, Boston.

Blass, Kim [1992], "World-Class Strategies Help Create a World-Class CIM Facility," *Industrial Engineering*, November, pp. 26–29.

Davis, E. W., and J. L. Goodhart [1988], "Integrated Planning Frontiers," in M. D. Oliff (ed.), *Intelligent Manufacturing, Proceedings from the First International Conference on Expert Systems and Leading Edge Production Planning and Control*, Benjamin/Cumming, Menlo Park, Cal., pp. 249–276.

Gray, Ann E., Abraham Seidmann, and Kathryn E. Stecke [1993], "A Synthesis of Decision Models for Tool Management in Automated Manufacturing," *Management Science*, vol. 39, no. 5, May, pp. 549–564.

Luconi, F., T. Malone, and M. Morton [1986], "Expert Systems: The Next Challenge for Managers," *Sloan Management Review*, Summer, pp. 3–13.

Noori, H. [1990a], "A Prototype Expert System for Technology Assessment," *IEEE Report*, April, pp. 8–14.

—— [1990b], *Managing the Dynamics of New Technologies: Issues in Manufacturing Managements*, Prentice-Hall, Englewood Cliffs, N.J.

—— and R. W. Radford [1990], *Readings and Cases in Management of New Technology: An Operation Perspective*, Prentice-Hall, Englewood Cliffs, N.J.

Veilleux, Raymond F., and Louis W. Petro (eds.) [1988], *Tool and Manufacturing Engineers Handbook*, 4th ed., vol. V, Manufacturing Management, Society of Manufacturing Engineers, Dearborn, Mich.

Warner, T. [1988], "Computers as a Competitive Burden," *Technology Review*, February–March, pp. 22–24.

Welch, Frank K., Jr. [1986], "MAP/TOP: Linking Factory and Office," *Production Engineering*, June, pp. 36–38.

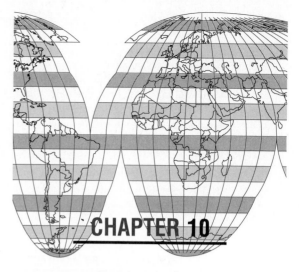

CHAPTER 10

JOB DESIGN

Enduring advantages result when a firm makes better use of its people. Designing jobs for people is a critical managerial task because it determines how people interact with technology, materials, and each other. Many planning and control parameters are based on job standards. As a consequence, managers have to ask themselves:

- What jobs should be analyzed and redesigned?
- How should jobs be analyzed?
- How should standards be set?

By the end of this chapter you will have been exposed to the benefits of effectively designed jobs and the means by which job design is carried out. You also will have read about why standards are necessary and how to establish the most frequently discussed standard: the time standard. Finally, you will have encountered one way of taking into account the impact of an FRO's managerial drive toward continuous improvement on time standards. That concept is referred to as the learning curve.

EXHIBIT 10.1 FRO MANUFACTURING PROFILE

Step inside Shell Canada's new lubricants plant, and the first thing that comes to mind is: Where are all the people?

The nine-month-old facility is the prototype of the new breed of a small, flexible factory fine-tuned for high productivity and short-run production. This ultramodern plant hums because highly skilled people are plugged into advanced computer technology and workplace ideas.

The plant's 75 employees are grouped into three teams called "job families." Each team manages a basic process: bulk handling and blending of the lubricants, packaging, or warehousing.

Every worker ("team operator") must master all the jobs within his or her team, plus at least one skill in each of the other two groups. Jobs change roughly every 18 months. Every operator is expected to understand all aspects of the business, including where materials come from and where final products go. He or she can tap into all information relevant to plant operations by using the plant's powerful network of five integrated computer systems. This allows employees to manage themselves as individuals and as team members.

If a problem arises, operators solve it on their own, even if that means calling a supplier. The teams are responsible for discipline and cost control (including absenteeism); they also arrange their own vacation and training schedules.

It is still early, but the system seems to work. Having started last April, the plant will not reach capacity for another few months. But the plant has already found customers in 44 countries, whereas three years ago an export order was a rarity. And staff absenteeism is running about one-third the normal rate in manufacturing.

Source: Adapted from Little (1993), p. B24.

EXHIBIT 10.2 FRO SERVICE PROFILE

Not only does the Zoological Society of San Diego face stiff competition from nearby Disneyland and Sea World, it must maintain high technical standards and a Caesar's-wife purity on environmental and other issues. But even with the recession, the San Diego Zoo has enjoyed a 20 percent increase in attendance.

The zoo is steadily remodeling to show its animals by bioclimatic zone (an African rain forest called Gorilla Tropics and Tiger River, an Asian environment) rather than by taxonomy (pachyderms, primates, etc.).

The way in which the zoo is managed has changed as well. Functional departments are invisible in the redesigned areas. Tiger River, for instance, is run by a team of mammal and bird specialists, horticulturists, and maintenance and construction workers. The four-year-old team, led by keeper John Turner, tracks its own budget on a PC that is not hooked up to the zoo's mainframe. Members are jointly responsible for the animal display, and it is hard to tell who comes from which department. For example, when the path in front of the aviary needed fixing last autumn, the horticulturist and the construction worker did it.

Seven people run Tiger River. When it started, there were 11, but as the team members learned one another's skills, they decided they did not need to replace workers who left. (They are all Teamsters.) Freed from managerial chores, executives can go out to drum up more interest in the zoo.

Source: Adapted from Stewart (1992), p. 98.

10.1 MANAGERIAL ORIENTATION

Chapter 9 presented an overview of process design and examined different types of process organizations and technology. There is more to designing a process, however, than installing equipment. Even ultramodern plants such as Shell Canada's lubricants plant (Exhibit 10.1) cannot be run without people.

The experience of fast-response organizations (FROs) indicates that people play fundamental roles in establishing and sustaining a firm's success. The "human element" must be considered in making almost every type of operations management decision. This chapter, however, will focus on job design, work measurement, and reward systems.

Well-designed jobs increase productivity and product quality and decrease unit costs. Naturally, that means eliminating tasks that do not add value to the firm's products. It also means that people are given productive jobs that they can perform effectively, efficiently, and willingly.

Job design philosophies have changed drastically since the industrial revolution. Shell Canada and the San Diego Zoological Society (see Exhibit 10.2) are among the many organizations around the world tapping into the potential contribution of their workforces. As competition continues to intensify, the role of the workforce will become even more important to a firm's efforts to satisfy its customers.

10.2 JOB DESIGN PHILOSOPHIES

DEFINITION: Job design refers to the synthesis of individual tasks or activities into a job which is assigned to an individual worker or a group of workers.

Early work on **job design** focused on the individual worker. Frederick Taylor concentrated on technological requirements in applying his principles of scientific management to job design at the turn of the century.[1] His theories are still reflected in the narrowly defined jobs found in traditional product-focused (i.e., high-volume, low-variety) operations. Workers are viewed as interchangeable extensions of machines. Each worker performs a narrow range of tasks over and over, while supervisors provide external direction, control, and policing.

Narrowly defined jobs appeal to many firms because they require workers who

---

[1] Taylor's work and major accomplishments are outlined in the Chapter 1 Supplement.

have few or no skills and are therefore less expensive than more skilled workers. Workers can be trained quickly for the tasks that constitute each job, and the potential work pace is relatively high. A high output can be produced in little time.

Narrowing the range of tasks performed by each worker does have disadvantages, however:

- It is often difficult to divide the work evenly among workers because each worker is so specialized. This means that at certain times some workers are idle.
- Since more people are working on each product, coordination and materials handling costs are high. Queues of partially finished products accumulate in front of people; in many cases this drastically increases the elapsed time required to produce each item.
- The highly repetitive work and the inability of workers to identify with the finished products lead to high employee absenteeism and turnover rates as well as poor quality. The adversarial relationship between workers and management compounds labor relations problems.

It became clear in the 1920s and 1930s that concentrating solely on the technical requirements of the process in job design is misleading and ineffective. Social as well as technical factors influence the productivity and quality of an operating process. If jobs are designed without consideration of the workers' social and psychological needs, the full potential of the organization cannot be met. Similarly, if jobs are designed with little consideration for the technical subsystem, the process will be ineffective and inefficient as well. This observation led to the development of the **sociotechnical approach** to job design by the Tavistock Institute.

DEFINITION: The sociotechnical approach to job design considers both the technical needs of the process and the social needs of the workers.

Exhibit 10.3 illustrates how organizational design mechanisms such as job design, work organization, and supervision connect the social and technical subsystems.

Since the social and technical subsystems are interdependent and complementary, the optimal job design is one that jointly optimizes both subsystems. A well-rounded

EXHIBIT 10.3 ORGANIZATIONAL DESIGN

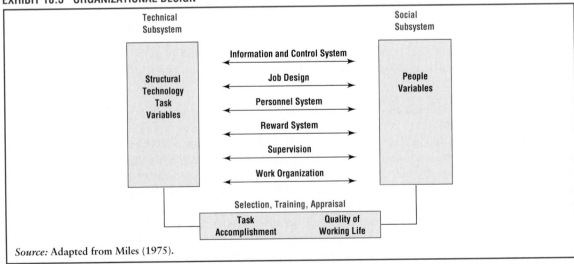

Source: Adapted from Miles (1975).

job pays equal attention to the characteristics of the human system and the critical requirements of the process technology.

The sociotechnical approach advocates the use of semiautonomous groups. Each group is given the responsibility for managing and performing a set of related tasks. Workers have an opportunity for sustained learning on the job and participate in decisions that affect their jobs.[2] The traditional view of workers (see Exhibit 10.4) must be replaced by a new, broader view. Workers must feel that their work is socially meaningful and that they have a future with the firm.

The sociotechnical approach is compatible with the needs of an FRO. Flexible processes require flexible workers who can perform a wide range of tasks. These tasks require increasingly higher levels of technical skill to deal with advanced technological processes. As middle management becomes leaner in an FRO, the firm depends more and more on its workforce for problem solving and continuous product and process improvements. The workforce becomes an asset rather than another cost of doing business.

In this new environment the workforce must be self-motivated and possess considerable analytic and interpersonal skills. Well-designed jobs are reasonably demanding, include a variety of tasks, and provide continuous opportunities to learn. They also provide "owned" areas of decision making. The elements of this new paradigm are:

- Workers with wide repertoires of skills and no specific job descriptions
- Lean and flexible management
- Labor-management relationships that tend toward mutuality
- Workers grouped into self-regulated teams with decision-making authority
- Ambitious and dynamic performance expectations that replace minimum work standards
- Compensation systems that emphasize learning and collaboration

The assumptions about the role of workers that underlie this new paradigm are reflected in the relationship between workers and process technology. In an FRO such as Shell Canada (see Exhibit 10.1) process technology supports the workers, not vice versa. Machine operators are trained in various aspects of operations sup-

---

[2] Expanding a job to include planning, organizational, and/or managerial tasks is referred to as **vertical job enrichment.** Simply increasing the number of different tasks assigned to a particular employee is called **horizontal job enrichment,** or **job enlargement.**

EXHIBIT 10.4 CHANGING ATTITUDES TOWARD WORKERS

Traditional View	FRO View
Workers are:	Workers are:
Passive and dependent	Active and independent
In need of structure and authority	Able to define their own structure and capable of internal control
Able to work only with answers and solutions provided by management	Able to solve problems
Able to make limited choices	Entitled to greater freedom of choice
Content with static skills	Interested in growth
Motivated primarily by money	Seeking self-actualization
Expendable parts	Resources to be developed
Extensions of machines	Complementary to machines

port, not merely in the operation of a machine. They are expected to manage the process and are encouraged to find ways to reduce waste and improve the process. The information provided by the machine is used by its operators, not restricted to specialists or supervisors. Operators are seen as **process midwives** rather than **process monitors.** Field research conducted by Wall (1986) suggests that the midwife approach, with its higher direct labor costs but lower indirect and labor support costs, leads to improved operator motivation and quicker, more appropriate decisions concerning process issues and problems.

10.3 METHOD STUDY

Job design involves the arrangement of a connected series of tasks in a logical, effective, and efficient manner, taking into account any preceding, concurrent, or subsequent activities.

A typical job is a collection of several different but related tasks. These tasks can be broken down into elements such as tightening a nut, flipping a hamburger, writing a journal entry, and making an incision. Elements can be broken down into a series of body motions (e.g., gripping an object).

The level of detail to which one should go in breaking down a job depends on the circumstances. Most people would not bother to think about breaking down the activity "throw a baseball," yet baseball coaches analyze the most minute details of a player's throwing mechanics, using super-slow-motion videos.

Dividing and analyzing jobs is referred to as **method study.** Frank and Lillian Gilbreth pioneered method study in their work on motion study.[3]

> **DEFINITION: Method study involves the systematic recording and critical examination of existing and proposed ways of doing work. The goal is to improve productivity by developing and applying easier and more effective work methods.**

The purpose of method study is to (1) improve operating processes and procedures, (2) make better use of materials, equipment, and labor, (3) improve the design of the plant and operating equipment as well as the plant layout, and (4) develop a better physical working environment for the employees.

The success of the job design techniques employed during method study is often attributed to this method's systematic approach to reducing wasted time, materials, and effort. This approach can be analyzed into the following seven-step procedure [International Labour Office, (1979)].

Step 1. Select the tasks to be studied.

Prime candidates for method study include tasks that are repeated frequently, bottlenecks that affect other operations, and tasks that require a great deal of labor time.

Step 2. Observe and document the correct method of performing the selected tasks.

Visual aids, such as the **operating,** or **outline, process chart** in Exhibit 10.5, are often used to document, analyze, and compare current and proposed methods.

---

[3] *Motion study* is the analysis of the body movements used to perform a task or set of tasks. Refer to the Chapter 1 Supplement for more details on the Gilbreths' work.

EXHIBIT 10.5 OPERATING PROCESS CHART: BUILDING A TABLE

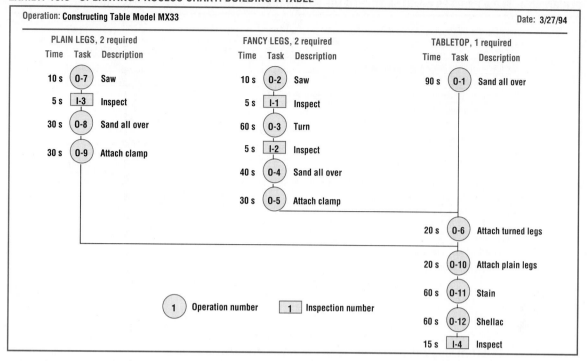

Operation: **Constructing Table Model MX33**   Date: **3/27/94**

Flow process charts are another common visual aid. These charts use symbols to represent a sequence of events graphically. The flow process chart in Exhibit 10.6, for example, depicts a visit to the pharmacy.

Since they are more detailed than operating process charts, flow process charts are usually developed for a single component of a product. These charts uncover hidden costs such as those generated by unnecessary material movements and operational delays.

Operator process charts record the actions of a single worker. The chart in Exhibit 10.7, whose codes are based on the Gilbreths' fundamental elements, breaks down these actions into those which are performed by each hand. These charts can be used to develop work center layouts, sequence activities, and provide motion guidelines.

Multiple-activity (worker-machine or gang) **charts** are multicolumn charts that show the activities of individual workers and/or machines. Each column shows the activities of a particular worker or machine. As illustrated in Exhibit 10.8, a common time scale is used to indicate the relative duration of each activity and show the interrelationships among activities.

Multiple-activity charts can be used to identify idle operator or machine time and to determine the best number (or group) of machines to assign to a single operator. They also can be employed to divide tasks among team members.

Travel charts present quantitative data about the movement of workers, materials, and equipment between two or more areas over a specific period. The charts used during facility layout analysis in Chapter 6 are travel charts.

Other visual aids include films, models, and string diagrams.

EXHIBIT 10.6 FLOW PROCESS CHART: A TRIP TO THE PHARMACY

EVENT	EVENT SYMBOL	TIME, min	DISTANCE, ft
Operation: Fill prescription			Date: 1/6/94
Open door, walk to pharmacy area of store	○ ➤ ▽ D □	0.8	50
Wait (for service)	○ ➤ ▽ D □	1	
Take prescription out of wallet or purse and give it to the pharmacist	○ ➤ ▽ D □	0.4	
Wait for pharmacist to fill prescription and calculate charge	○ ➤ ▽ D □	10	
Take credit card out of wallet or purse and give to pharmacist	○ ➤ ▽ D □	0.4	
Wait for pharmacist to complete credit card slip	○ ➤ ▽ D □	1	
Check credit slip	○ ➤ ▽ D □	0.2	
Sign credit slip	○ ➤ ▽ D □	0.1	
Wait for credit card slip to be returned and medicine to be placed in bag	○ ➤ ▽ D □	0.3	
Put card and slip back in wallet or purse	○ ➤ ▽ D □	0.2	
Pick up medicine and walk back to door	○ ➤ ▽ D □	0.8	50

Event Legend

○ = operation; ➤ = transportation;

▽ = storage; D = delay; □ = inspection

Process Summary	Event				
	○	➤	▽	D	□
Total number	1	2	3	4	1
Total distance (ft)	–	100	–	–	–
Total time (min)	0.1	1.6	1.0	12.3	0.2

EXHIBIT 10.7 OPERATOR PROCESS CHART: ASSEMBLY OF CABLE CLAMPS

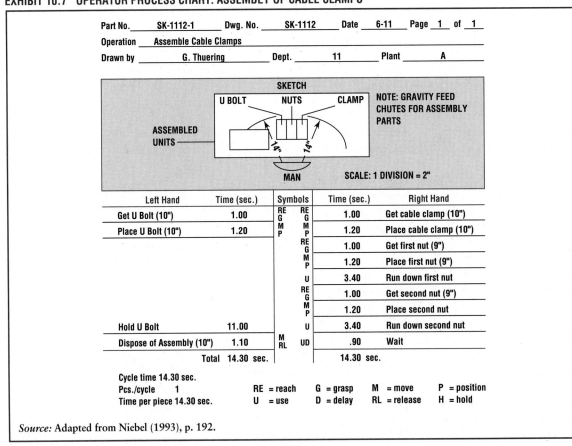

Part No. __SK-1112-1__ Dwg. No. __SK-1112__ Date __6-11__ Page __1__ of __1__

Operation __Assemble Cable Clamps__

Drawn by __G. Thuering__ Dept. __11__ Plant __A__

SKETCH

U BOLT   NUTS   CLAMP

ASSEMBLED UNITS

¼"   ¼"

MAN

NOTE: GRAVITY FEED CHUTES FOR ASSEMBLY PARTS

SCALE: 1 DIVISION = 2"

Left Hand	Time (sec.)	Symbols	Time (sec.)	Right Hand
Get U Bolt (10")	1.00	RE G M P	1.00	Get cable clamp (10")
Place U Bolt (10")	1.20	RE G M P	1.20	Place cable clamp (10")
		RE G M P	1.00	Get first nut (9")
			1.20	Place first nut (9")
		U	3.40	Run down first nut
		RE G M P	1.00	Get second nut (9")
			1.20	Place second nut
Hold U Bolt	11.00	U	3.40	Run down second nut
Dispose of Assembly (10")	1.10	M RL UD	.90	Wait
Total	14.30 sec.		14.30 sec.	

Cycle time 14.30 sec.
Pcs./cycle   1
Time per piece 14.30 sec.

RE = reach   G = grasp   M = move   P = position
U = use   D = delay   RL = release H = hold

Source: Adapted from Niebel (1993), p. 192.

Step 3. Examine the current method. Look for ways in which tasks can be eliminated, combined, rearranged, and simplified.

- What is the purpose of this operation?
- Why are tasks performed in this order?
- Who is currently performing each task, and why is it being done by that person?
- Where is the operation being performed, and why is it being done there?
- Why has this material been specified?

These are some of the questions typically asked in analyzing the current method.

The purpose of asking these questions is to identify opportunities for improving the current method. The procedure for building the table (see Exhibit 10.5), for example, can be improved by stacking and sawing the two legs in operations 2 and 7 simultaneously. The pharmacy visit (see Exhibit 10.6) can be shortened if the customer retrieves the prescription and credit card while waiting for the pharmacist to serve him or her. Dropping the prescription off and picking up the medicine later is an alternative for reducing the length of the visit; asking for the medicine to be delivered is another. Other improvements are possible for both the table and the pharmacy visit operations. (Do you have any suggestions?)

Step 4. Develop the best method under the prevailing conditions. Obtain approval for the new method.

Using the research compiled during steps 2 and 3, the analyst can now compare alternative methods and choose the best one—the most effective, efficient, and practical method. "Prevailing conditions" refers to factors or circumstances that cannot be changed at present. Examples include the firm's planning and scheduling system, the facility layout, the materials handling equipment, and the equipment used.

An important factor in analyzing current and proposed operating methods is work safety. The next section takes a closer look at this issue.

EXHIBIT 10.8 MULTIPLE-ACTIVITY CHART

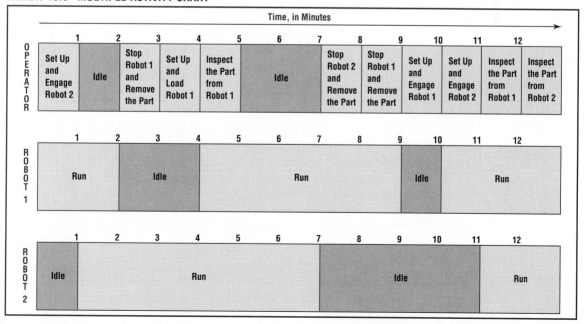

Step 5. Define the new method.

The purpose of carefully defining and documenting the new method is to ensure that it can be identified and followed. The definition includes standards for the tools and material to be used, the time and operator skill required, the working conditions, and so on.

Step 6. Implement the new method.

If the analyst is not the person who will use the new method, presenting the new method to the people who will be using it and gaining their acceptance is the next step. Workers must be retrained, and any changes in the equipment, the materials and tooling, the facility layout, and the like, must be made.

Step 7. Routinely verify that the new method is being followed correctly.

New methods and procedures are not always followed. The training might have been inadequate, the standards may be unclear, or the necessary support (e.g., new tooling, facility layout) might not have been implemented properly. The new method also may be inherently flawed, or changing circumstances may reduce its suitability.

Over time, the people using the new method will probably find ways to improve it. The cumulative effect of these small improvements is often significant. This chapter will examine the implications of these continuous improvements as part of the discussion of learning curves.

10.4 WORK SAFETY

Soaring workers' compensation rates and insurance premiums and increasing employee absenteeism are turning **work safety** into a very important issue. Work-related injuries and illnesses are costing North American firms billions of dollars a year and negatively affecting the quality of their goods and services. The range of compensatable injuries and work safety hazards is increasing. Franz Schneider of Humantech Inc. estimates that in the auto industry worker injuries account for $785 of the cost of a typical car.

Almost 60 percent of all occupational illnesses are *cumulative trauma disorders (CTDs)*, disorders of the musculo-tendinous-nervous system caused, precipitated, or aggravated by repeated exertions or movements of the body. Tendonitis, lower back pain, and carpal tunnel syndrome are examples of CTDs.[4]

What causes most CTDs and other work-related injuries? Usually poorly designed production equipment and processes are to blame. For example, research has shown that if a work surface is two inches too high, workers have to raise their shoulders and/or abduct their arms. This leads to muscular fatigue and results in at least a 20 percent drop in production efficiency [Alexander and Pulat (1985)]. To avoid work safety problems and improve efficiency, designers apply the principles of human factors engineering, or ergonomics.

Human factors engineering (ergonomics) applies knowledge of human capabilities and limitations to the design of products and processes.[5] Simple human factors

---

[4] Interestingly, CTDs have been around for decades. Insurance claims went unheeded, though, until professional and technical employees began to suffer from them as a result of using computers.

[5] Human factors engineering was discussed from a product design perspective in Chapter 5.

engineering principles include placing displays at eye level, making workstations height-adjustable, keeping frequently used parts within arm's length, and keeping heavy parts between shoulder and knuckle height.

What is eye level for most people? How far can most people reach? How much weight can most people comfortably lift? Designers rely on anthropometric and biomechanical data to answer these questions. Research has shown, for example, that the height (to eye level) of at least 25 percent of the population is less than 64 inches, while 5 percent of the population are over 69 inches tall. As demonstrated by Chrysler's Bramalea assembly plant (see Exhibit 10.9), everyone wins when processes are designed with this type of information in mind.

Environmental factors also influence worker safety and productivity. Lighting, temperature, humidity, and noise must be considered in designing the workplace.

What if the source of a safety problem cannot be eliminated? In practice, several approaches can be taken, including (1) separating the worker from the danger by automating the task, (2) rotating people through jobs so that exposure to a particular danger is limited, and (3) eliminating the need for the job completely through wholesale process redesign.

10.5 WORK MEASUREMENT

Method study alone is not sufficient for developing new or improved ways of doing a task or job; a firm must know how long it will take to do the job. This is important for a number of reasons, among the most common of which are deciding what resources will be required to meet specific capacity levels, deciding how much to pay people, assessing how much to charge customers, and choosing among alternative ways of doing a job. **Work measurement** is the term applied to the process of determining an appropriate task time.

EXHIBIT 10.9   HUMAN FACTORS ENGINEERING AT CHRYSLER

In the words of Terry Desjardins, human resources manager at Chrysler's Bramalea assembly plant, the factory has achieved an "excellent workers' compensation performance." So far its absenteeism rate of 1.9 percent is the lowest of any Chrysler assembly plant, well below the average 4.5 to 5 percent. And management is confident that the defects in the finished product will be fewer because the plant has been redesigned with the help of its full-time human factors engineer.

In a typical plant workers install underbody components such as engines and transmissions by fitting them upward through the underside of the car body. Working in awkward overhead positions with their arms constantly in the air, these workers suffer a disproportionate number of accidents and pain and strain injuries. At the Bramalea plant they now work with their arms at a comfortable level thanks to a new technique called pallet insertion assembly. The underbody components are assembled on a rectangular pallet. The entire pallet is then raised, and the underbody is clamped onto a waiting body.

Another example of human factors engineering at work is Bramalea's door-off assembly, in which a car's doors are removed before the interior components are installed. Not only does this ease access for workers, improving productivity, it also reduces the damage to the door that is done in traditional door-on assembly as workers constantly enter and exit the car, taking components and tools with them.

These and other changes have translated into a happier, healthier workforce and a better bottom line for the plant.

Source: Adapted from *Canadian Business* (1992), pp. 128–136, and *Globe and Mail* (1992), pp. B1, B6.

In small firms method study and work measurement are carried out by the same person or group of people. That means that the process described above has two extra steps: step 5A: Develop time standards; and step 8: Correct time standards. Even in large firms the separation of method study and work measurement into separate departments is somewhat artificial, as both groups of specialists have to know about and use each other's tools.

> **DEFINITION: Work measurement techniques are used to establish a time standard for a qualified worker to perform a specific job at a defined level of performance with the necessary tools in a normal job environment.**

Most jobs have standards associated with them, norms for what constitutes a reasonable effort in the short term and the long term. A disciplined approach to setting standards provides benchmarks better than those set casually or haphazardly. However, controversy often surrounds the employment of work measurement because time standards can be misused when one is determining worker compensation.[6] There are many valuable uses of time standards, though, including the following:

- Determining the cost of a product
- Providing information on which operations planning and scheduling can be based
- Balancing the work of team members so that they have tasks of equal duration
- Comparing the efficiency of alternative methods

The time needed to perform each work element can be determined in a number of ways. Potential sources of information include historical data, industry averages, published charts containing predetermined (or synthetic) time standards, and work sampling. The method most people think of is direct observation, the **time study.**

Time Study

> **DEFINITION: During time study, a stopwatch or other timing device is used to determine the exact time required to complete a specific set of tasks. The resultant time is adjusted for fatigue and other allowances and then becomes a time standard.**

The time study process can be analyzed into the following five-step procedure. Let us walk through this procedure using the simple assembly line job described in Exhibit 10.10.

> **Step 1. Observe someone performing the selected group of tasks several times. Break the tasks into a set of elements. For each element, obtain or prepare a complete description of what must be done and how it should be done.**

The assembly line job has been broken down into four elements. Note that each element has definite starting and ending points, and that each takes at least three seconds to perform. As a rule of thumb, avoid elements that take less than three seconds because they are difficult to time. Work elements should correspond to the standard work method that has been running smoothly for a while in a standard work environment.

---

[6] For example, workers may be unfairly penalized by conditions outside their control, such as machine breakdowns, poor scheduling, and holdups caused by a lack of raw materials.

EXHIBIT 10.10   TOOLBOX: TIME STUDY

John Williston is one of several people working on an assembly line for hand-held computer games. His job is to insert one of 15 different program modules into partially assembled units. John's job can be analyzed into the following set of elements:

1. Remove the game from the conveyor belt, identify the type of game, and place the game on the workbench.
2. Identify the corresponding program module. Retrieve it.
3. Insert the program module into the game.
4. Pick up the game and place it back on the conveyor belt. Step on the button to advance the conveyor belt.

PRELIMINARY OBSERVATIONS

Work Element

Observation Number	1. Remove Game from Belt		2. Retrieve Program Module		3. Insert Program Module		4. Return Game to Belt	
	$x_{1,j}$	$R_{1,j}$	$x_{2,j}$	$R_{2,j}$	$x_{3,j}$	$R_{3,j}$	$x_{4,j}$	$R_{4,j}$
1	4.1	100	4.7	100	10.1	110	3.2	100
2	5.0	100	5.2	90	8.5	105	4.5	100
3	3.7	100	4.2	100	11.2	105	3.6	100
4	4.8	100	5.9	100	9.2	110	2.8	100
5	4.2	100	5.5	90	7.9	100	3.4	100
6	3.9	100	4.8	100	8.3	100	2.9	100
7	4.2	100	16.2*	100	10.6	105	3.4	100
8	4.5	100	5.7	95	7.8	105	3.2	100
9	3.2	100	5.1	90	9.4	110	3.6	100
10	4.0	100	3.8	95	11.7	105	2.8	100
Total	41.6		61.1		94.7		27.1	

* Interrupted by another worker.

CALCULATION OF SAMPLE SIZE FOR ELEMENT 3

$$i = 3 \qquad m = 10$$

Substituting into equation (10.1) yields

$$s_3 = \sqrt{\frac{\sum\limits_{j=1}^{10} (x_{3,j})^2 - \dfrac{\left(\sum\limits_{j=1}^{10} x_{3,j}\right)^2}{10}}{10 - 1}}$$

$$\sum_{j=1}^{10} x_{3,j} = 94.7$$

$$\sum_{j=1}^{10} (x_{3,j})^2 = 10.1^2 + 8.5^2 + \cdots + 11.7^2 = 914.09$$

$$s_3 = \sqrt{\frac{914.09 - \dfrac{94.7^2}{10}}{10 - 1}} = 1.386$$

Therefore, the standard deviation of the sample of 10 observations is 1.386. The required number of observations can now be calculated using equation (10.1). John's manager has specified that she wants to be confident that 95 percent of the time the results of this time study are within ±5 percent of the true values. The z score associated with a 95 percent confidence interval can be found by using the standardized normal distribution table in Appendix B.

$$n = \left(\frac{(1.96)(1.386)}{(0.05)(9.47)}\right)^2 = 32.92$$

Since 10 observations have already been taken, only 23 more are needed.

(Exhibit 10.10 continues on next page)

EXHIBIT 10.10 *(continued)*

CALCULATION OF THE NORMAL TIME FOR ELEMENT 3

The normal time for work element 3 can be calculated using all 33 observations (not shown here) and equation (10.3).

$$NT_3 = \frac{(10.1)(110\%) + (8.5)(105\%) + \cdots + (9.3)(100\%)}{33} = 8.9$$

Summary of Allowances Made

Personal allowances	5%
Basic fatigue allowance	4%
Standing allowance	2%
Monotony allowance	1%
Unavoidable delays	6%
Total	18%

CALCULATION OF THE STANDARD TIME FOR ELEMENT 3

If the sum of the allowances for element 3 is equal to 18 percent, the standard time for element 3 is 10.85 seconds.

$$ST_3 = \frac{8.9}{1 - 0.18} = 10.85$$

Standard Times for Each Work Element

Element	Normal Time	Allowances	Standard Time
1	4.1	18%	5.0
2	5.3	18%	6.5
3	8.9	18%	10.9
4	3.5	18%	4.3
Total			26.7

Step 2. Select a worker to be timed. Collect an initial set of observations. Note the worker's pace for each observation.

Observing the worker who will be timed several times helps ensure that the standard work method is being followed. Record any information that may affect the work to be performed and the time it will take (e.g., working conditions, condition of tools used, operator's skill level). Incidental operations not normally involved in the task should be identified and separated from repetitive work.

The worker's pace should be rated for every observation. In the assembly line example 100 percent corresponds to a **normal pace.** This is a brisk pace that a trained, motivated worker can sustain, on average, without overexertion throughout the working day or shift. A performance rating above 100 percent means that the worker is working at a faster than normal pace. A value lower than 100 percent indicates that the worker is operating at a slower than normal pace.

Step 3. Calculate the number of work cycles that must be timed for each work element.

A **work cycle** is the sequence of elements which constitute the job or set of tasks under observation. The number of work cycles that must be timed depends on the degree of accuracy desired and the variability of the times observed during the preliminary study. It can be calculated using equations (10.1) and (10.2).

Estimate of the Standard Deviation of the Sample

$$s_i = \sqrt{\frac{\sum\limits_{j=1}^{m}(x_{i,j})^2 - \dfrac{\left(\sum\limits_{j=1}^{m}x_{i,j}\right)^2}{m}}{m-1}} \tag{10.1}$$

Required Number of Observations

$$n_i = \left(\frac{zs_i}{E\bar{x}_i}\right)^2 \tag{10.2}$$

where s_i = standard deviation of set of observations for work element i
m = number of preliminary observations made
$x_{i,j}$ = time recorded for work element i, observation j
n_i = number of observations required
z = z score corresponding to desired confidence level
E = allowable error
$\bar{x}_i$ = average observed value for work element i

In this example, John's manager wants to be confident that the results of this time study are within ±5 percent of the true values 95 percent of the time. Work element 3, for example, will therefore require 33 observations (see Exhibit 10.10).

Step 4. Make the required number of observations. Note the worker's pace for each observation. Calculate the normal time for each work element.

The **normal time** for each work element is found using equation (10.3).

Normal Time

$$\mathrm{NT}_i = \frac{\sum\limits_{j=1}^{n_i} x_{i,j}R_{i,j}}{n_i} \tag{10.3}$$

where NT_i = normal time for work element i
n_i = number of observations required
$x_{i,j}$ = time recorded for work element i, observation j
$R_{i,j}$ = rating for work element i, observation j

The mean actual time observed for work element 3 in the assembly line example is 8.1 seconds, but the normal time is 8.9 seconds.

Step 5. Calculate the standard time for each work element and for the complete set of tasks.

The **standard time** for each work element is longer than the normal time because allowances are made for worker fatigue, personal needs, poor working conditions, monotony, and the like. The International Labour Office has tabulated the effect of working conditions to arrive at the allowance factors (in percent) for personal delays and fatigue shown in Exhibit 10.11.

Unavoidable delays include factors such as talking with supervisors and other workers, material irregularities, and interference delays when a worker operates two

EXHIBIT 10.11   TABLE OF ALLOWANCES FOR PERSONAL DELAYS AND FATIGUE

A. Constant allowances			5. Atmospheric conditions (heat and	
1. Personal allowance	5		humidity)—variable	0–10
2. Basic fatigue allowance	4		6. Close attention	
B. Variable allowances			*a.* Fairly fine work	0
1. Standing allowance	2		*b.* Fine or exacting	2
2. Abnormal position allowance			*c.* Very fine or very exacting	5
a. Slightly awkward	0		7. Noise level	
b. Awkward (bending)	2		*a.* Continuous	0
c. Very awkward (lying, stretching)	7		*b.* Intermittent—loud	2
3. Use of force or muscular energy (lifting,			*c.* Intermittent—very loud	5
pulling, or pushing)			*d.* High-pitched—loud	5
Weight lifted, pounds:			8. Mental strain	
5	0		*a.* Fairly complex process	1
10	1		*b.* Complex or wide span of attention	4
15	2		*c.* Very complex	8
20	3		9. Monotony	
25	4		*a.* Low	0
30	5		*b.* Medium	1
35	7		*c.* High	4
40	9		10. Tediousness	
45	11		*a.* Rather tedious	0
50	13		*b.* Tedious	2
60	17		*c.* Very tedious	5
70	22			
4. Bad light				
a. Slightly below recommended	0			
b. Well below	2			
c. Quite inadequate	5			

Source: Adapted from Niebel (1993), p. 446.

sets of machines at the same time. In a typical shop unavoidable delays merit an allowance of around 6 percent.

    The **allowances** made vary from job to job. Five different allowances, totaling 18 percent, have been made for John Williston's job. The normal time assigned to each of the four work elements has been inflated using equation (10.4) to reflect these allowances.

Standard Time

$$ST = \sum_{i=1}^{m} ST_i = \frac{\sum_{i=1}^{m} (NT_i)}{1 - A_i} \tag{10.4}$$

where ST = standard time for set of *m* tasks
   ST_i = standard time for work element *i*
  NT_i = normal time for work element *i*
    A_i = allowances for work element *i* (expressed as a percentage)

    The time study method is time-consuming; it also tends to have a negative impact on the workers being timed. The next section will outline a popular alternative to direct observation: predetermined time standards.

DEFINITION: A predetermined time standard is the time assigned to a basic human motion or group of motions; it is based on studies of a large number of diversified operations.

Predetermined time standards (PTS), or synthetic time data, are usually presented in chart format and classified by the nature of the motion and the conditions under which it is made. Rather than conduct their own time study, analysts can use a PTS to develop a time standard for a group of tasks as follows:

1. Break down the tasks to a set of basic human motions such as reach and grasp.
2. Look up the time assigned to each basic human motion in the PTS tables.
3. Sum the times required for the basic motions.
4. Revise the total time required to reflect any allowances that must be considered.

Using PTS, trained analysts can develop reliable time standards quickly and easily. Because direct observation is not required, PTS can be used to develop a time standard before a production process is put in place.

The first PTS system was developed by Segur in the 1920s; today there are over 200 of these systems. This section will describe two widely used PTS systems; methods-time measurement and modular arrangement of predetermined time standards.

Methods-time measurement (MTM) is a family of PTS systems, each catering to a particular type of operation and intended use. MTM-1, for example, has been developed for manual work areas, while MTM-V is suitable for metal-cutting operations and MTM-C for clerical-related tasks. The table in Exhibit 10.12 is an MTM-1 chart that gives the *normal time* required to reach a certain distance for each of five different types of reaches.

There are also MTM-1 charts for move, turn and apply pressure, grasp, position, release, disengage, eye travel time and focus, and body, leg, and foot motions. The values in these charts are based on a work rate that can be sustained for eight hours a day, five days a week for the working life of a healthy person.

Because of its complexity, only qualified MTM technicians should use this system to establish time standards.

The **modular arrangement of predetermined time standards (MODAPTS)** system is simpler than MTM and has proved very effective at Ford and many other companies around the world. The MODAPTS system covers fewer than 50 different body movements. The time assigned to each movement is expressed in terms of multiples of a single unit of work called a *MOD*. One MOD is the time required to complete a single finger movement, that is, 0.00215 minute, or about one eighth of a second.

A major difference between MODAPTS and other PTS systems is that in MODAPTS the time assigned to a body movement is not a direct function of the distance moved. Instead, the body part moved is used to determine how much time is required. For example, a finger movement is assigned one MOD, while an arm movement is assigned four MODs.

Because distances are not measured and the system is fairly simple, standards for repetitive work can be established quickly and easily. Studies comparing MODAPTS standards with those derived from MTM-1 have found that the MODAPTS standards are usually 2 to 3 percent looser. The MODAPTS system is described further in the supplement to this chapter.

EXHIBIT 10.12   TOOLBOX: METHODS-TIME MEASUREMENT (MTM)

MTM-1 is a general system that is transferable throughout the world and applicable in all manual work areas. The chart below is one of many used in the MTM-1 system.

THE MTM-1 SYSTEM: REACH

Distance Moved, inches	Time TMU				Hand in Motion		Case and Description
	A	B	C or D	E	A	B	
3/4 or less	2.0	2.0	2.0	2.0	1.6	1.6	A. Reach to object in fixed loca-
1	2.5	2.5	3.6	2.4	2.3	2.3	tion or to object in other
2	4.0	4.0	5.9	3.8	3.5	2.7	hand or on which other hand
3	5.3	5.3	7.3	5.3	4.5	3.6	rests.
4	6.1	6.4	8.4	6.8	4.9	4.3	
5	6.5	7.8	9.4	7.4	5.3	5.0	B. Reach to single object in
6	7.0	8.6	10.1	8.0	5.7	5.7	location which may vary
7	7.4	9.3	10.8	8.7	6.1	6.5	slightly from cycle to cycle.
8	7.9	10.1	11.5	9.3	6.5	7.2	
9	8.3	10.8	12.2	9.9	6.9	7.9	C. Reach to object jumbled with
10	8.7	11.5	12.9	10.5	7.3	8.6	other objects in a group so
12	9.6	12.9	14.2	11.8	8.1	10.1	that search and select occur.
14	10.5	14.4	15.6	13.0	8.9	11.5	
16	11.4	15.8	17.0	14.2	9.7	12.9	D. Reach to a very small object
18	12.3	17.2	18.4	15.5	10.5	14.4	or where accurate grasp is
20	13.1	18.6	19.8	16.7	11.3	15.8	required.
22	14.0	20.1	21.2	18.0	12.1	17.3	
24	14.9	21.5	22.5	19.2	12.9	18.8	E. Reach to indefinite location
26	15.8	22.9	23.9	20.4	13.7	20.2	to get hand in position for
28	16.7	24.4	25.3	21.7	14.5	21.7	body balance or next motion
30	17.5	25.8	26.7	22.9	15.3	23.2	or out of way.

Suppose the worker must simultaneously reach 10 inches to pick up a bolt with the left hand and reach 16 inches with the right hand to pick up a nut. Both movements can be classified as case C. The left hand will need 12.9 TMUs, and the right hand will need 15.6 TMUs. (Each TMU is equal to 0.00001 hour.) Since the right hand is the limiting factor, the TMU value for the left hand is not used in calculating the time standard.

Source: Niebel (1993), p. 531.

Work Sampling

How often is a machine idle? What percentage of her time does a secretary spend photocopying? How often is a salesperson busy with a customer? These are the types of questions which can be answered using **work sampling.**[7]

DEFINITION: Work sampling involves the use of random samples to determine the proportion of total time spent on specified activities.

The manager in Exhibit 10.13, for example, is interested in the percentage of time one of her programmers, Sue Denton, spends performing user liaison duties. A preliminary study has shown that Sue spends about 40 percent of her day on these duties.

The next step is to make a series of random observations of Sue and record whether she is performing liaison duties. The number of observations that should be

---

[7] Work sampling is also known as activity sampling, ratio-delay sampling, the random observation method, and observation-ratio study.

made depends on the degree of accuracy wanted. The higher the degree of accuracy required, the higher the number of observations. Sue's manager, for example, wants to be confident that 95 percent of the time the results of the time study will be within ±5 percent of the true value. Therefore, using equation (10.5), 369 observations should be made.

Number of Observations Required

$$n = \frac{z^2 \hat{p}(1 - \hat{p})}{E^2}$$

(10.5)

where n = number of observations required

z = z score corresponding to desired confidence level

$\hat{p}$ = percentage of idle time (estimated)

E = allowable error

How should observations be made? Who should make them? How often should they be made each day? Observations can be made by the person being observed or by someone else. In Exhibit 10.13 a summer co-op student has created a list of random times based on a table of random numbers. At the appropriate time the worker walks over to Sue's desk and asks her what she is doing. The student then fills out the chart in the Exhibit 10.13.

An alternative is to have someone phone the person under observation at random intervals and ask what that person is doing. At the Texas Department of Human

EXHIBIT 10.13 TOOLBOX: WORK SAMPLING

The Hooper Company Ltd. develops and maintains its own set of computer programs for internal use. Sue Denton, one of the programmers, has been designated the "user liaison" and fields all computer-related questions. Her manager is interested in the percentage of her time Sue spends performing liaison activities.

During a preliminary study one of the firm's summer students randomly observed Sue 50 times. In 20 of the 50 observations Sue was performing liaison activities. Suppose Sue's manager wants to be confident that 95 percent of the time the results of the work sampling study are within ±5 percent.

The z score associated with a 95 percent confidence interval is 1.96. This value was found using the standardized normal distribution table in Appendix B.

Using equation (10.5), the number of required observations can be found:

$$n = \frac{(1.96)^2(0.40)(1 - 0.40)}{(0.05)^2} = 368.79$$

Using the daily observation sheet below, the summer student has made 369 random observations of Sue at work over a one-week period.

DAILY OBSERVATION SHEET
USER LIAISON STUDY (J123)

Date: 5 May 1993 Number of Observations: 74

Overall Time Period: 3 May 1993 to 7 May 1993 Total Observations: 369

Type of Activity Observed	Frequency	Total	Percentage
User liaison	卌 卌 卌 卌 卌 卌 l	31	41.89
Other	卌 卌 卌 卌 卌 卌 卌 卌 lll	43	58.11

EXHIBIT 10.14 WORK SAMPLING AT THE TEXAS DEPARTMENT OF HUMAN RESOURCES

Over 20,000 employees at the Texas Department of Human Services (TDHS) administer the yearly distribution of more than $8 billion in aid. Much of this aid is mandated by federal entitlement programs (Medicaid, AFDC, food stamps, etc.) that specify how program costs are to be divided between the federal and state governments.

Rather than keeping track of the time each employee spends on each program, TDHS uses the work sampling technique (called *random moment studies* in the public service sector) to determine how salaries and other overhead expenses should be allocated to individual programs.

Determining how observations should be made was a major problem for TDHS. Telephone surveys were not feasible because many employees are legitimately away from their desks a good deal of the time. And how honestly will a worker relaxing in the break room respond when his or her assistant announces that someone from the home office wants to know what case he or she is working on at that exact moment? If one analyzed data from telephone sampling, one might conclude that no one ever goes to the bathroom.

With employees scattered across the state (some in offices served by itinerant workers on a part-time basis), direct observation by another person was not a feasible option.

Giving selected employees a beeper and asking them to record current time and the cases on which they are working has proved to be cost-effective. The beeper sounds (or vibrates) at a specified average rate but at totally random times. Since the beeper is the size of a pager, it can be carried by the employee throughout the workday. And because the completed survey sheets are sent directly to the home office without a supervisor's assistance or interference, the survey results tend to be accurate.

Source: Adapted from Ramsay (1993), pp. 44–45.

Services (see Exhibit 10.14), the employee selected for observation carries a beeper that sounds at random intervals. When the beeper sounds, the employee records what he or she is doing at that exact moment.

Work sampling is fairly accurate if the sample size is relatively large and the study is done over a period that represents typical working conditions. Compared with continuous observation, work sampling is cost-effective.

10.6 IMPROVEMENT AND LEARNING

An FRO cannot be satisfied with the status quo and must search for continuous improvement of all its operations. With R&D and advanced technology, continuous improvement can be expected to lead to better cost and throughput conditions. R&D and investments in advanced technology create fundamental changes in the relationships among the resources used in the transformation process. Any changes in work practices and times will be the subject of specific job design activities, and managers will develop new plans that are based on changes in the supply conditions. How can a firm account for and measure continuous improvement?

Many firms are using the concept of the learning curve to predict reductions in operating times resulting from repetition of the task. This is important, for if a firm knows that the time it takes to do something will decrease at a certain rate, that firm should be able to predict the impact on cost. An effective *increase* in capacity should be experienced as time goes by. This observation was first documented by T. P. Wright of the Curtiss-Wright Corporation in 1936.

Wright noticed that the direct labor hours required to assemble each airplane decreased at a predictable rate as cumulative production increased. Every time the cumulative output doubled, direct labor hours declined by 20 percent. Therefore, if the first airplane took 1,000 hours to produce, the second would require (1,000) $(1 - 0.20) = 800$ hours, the fourth would require $(800)(1 - 0.20) = 640$ hours, and so on.[8] This phenomenon is referred to as the **learning curve effect**.

> **DEFINITION:** The learning curve effect shows that at each doubling of the cumulative production volume, the time required to produce the last unit diminishes at a constant rate.

The time required to produce a specific unit is often estimated by using equation (10.6) or the table of unit values in Appendix A. Appendix A also contains a table of cumulative values.[9]

Learning Curve Equation

$$Y_x = ax^b = ax^{\frac{\log \rho}{\log 2}} \tag{10.6}$$

where Y_x = number of hours required to produce xth unit
$\quad a$ = number of hours required to produce first unit
$\quad b$ = coefficient related to slope of curve
$\quad \rho$ = learning percentage

Consider the example outlined in Exhibit 10.15. Earl Rickman, a carpenter, has decided to specialize in a new type of desk. The first desk took Earl 50 hours to build. Using equation (10.6), Earl can estimate the time required to build each subsequent desk and then use this information to prepare a production schedule, make delivery promises, set prices, and develop budgets.

The learning curve effect is not limited to continuing reductions in direct labor hours (and hence costs) but has also been observed in studies of total costs for entire processes, plants, and industries. At the firm level, the term **progress curve** is used to describe these continuing cost reductions; at the industry level, the term **experience curve** is used.[10]

After reviewing more than 200 empirical and theoretical studies of progress curves, Dutton and Thomas (1984) made the following conclusions:

- Recorded progress rates vary across industries, processes, and products as well as among similar processes and products.
- The rate of progress is neither fixed nor automatic. In many instances it is an outcome of managerial policy decisions and is difficult to estimate with precision.

---

[8] Theoretically, the direct labor hours can decline to almost zero, but in practice, this is not realistic for several reasons. First, the output of a process is limited by market demand. (Remember that each doubling of cumulative output requires a corresponding doubling of cumulative demand.) Second, over time, significant changes will be made to the product and/or process; these changes will end the current labor-reduction sequence.

[9] The following equation can be used to *estimate* cumulative production times when x is greater than 100:

$$Y_t = \frac{ax^{1 - \left[\frac{\ln \rho}{\ln 2}\right]}}{1 - \frac{\ln \rho}{\ln 2}}$$

[10] In practice, the learning curve is frequently used to describe continuing cost reductions at the firm and industry level as well. To clarify the discussion, this text will use different terms to refer to each level.

EXHIBIT 10.15   TOOLBOX: THE LEARNING CURVE EFFECT

Earl Rickman designs and manufactures wooden desks. Lately Earl has been receiving a flood of orders for a hand-carved rolltop desk featured in a local trade show. The first desk took Earl approximately 50 hours to build, but each subsequent desk has taken substantially less time. Using his own experience and the data shown below, Earl estimates that his learning curve is about 90 percent.

Unit	Production Time, hours
1	50
2	45
3	42.3
4	40.5

How long will it take Earl to make the fifth desk? The tenth desk?

$$a = 50, x = 5, \rho = 0.9$$

Using equation (10.6),

$$Y_5 = (50)(5)^{\frac{\log 0.9}{\log 2}} = (50)(5)^{\frac{-0.4576}{0.30103}} = 39.14881$$

Therefore, it will take about 39 hours to make the fifth desk.

Rather than using equation (10.6), one can refer to the learning curve table of unit values in Appendix A. This table gives the value of x^b for various values of ρ. For example, if $\rho = 90$ percent and $n = 10$, then $x^b = 0.7047$. Therefore,

$$Y_{10} = 50x^b = (50)(0.7047) = 35.235$$

Similarly, the time required to produce any unit can be estimated. The first desk took Earl well over a week, but he can expect to finish the fifth desk in about a week and the twentieth desk in about 32 hours. His capacity is steadily rising.

The table of cumulative values in Appendix A can be used to calculate the total time required to complete n units if the first item takes 1 unit of time.

For example, if Earl wants to estimate the total time required to complete the first 20 desks, he simply multiplies the value found in the table by 20.

$$20(14.6078) = 292.156$$

Therefore, it will take about 292 hours to complete the first 20 desks.

The graph below compares Earl's 90 percent learning curve with an 80 percent learning curve.

EARL'S 90 PERCENT LEARNING CURVE

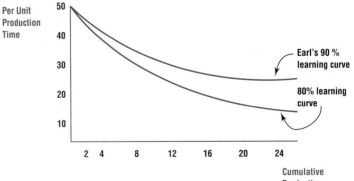

What happens if Earl discovers that his actual learning percentage is not 80 percent but 90 percent? Each desk will take longer than predicted, and Earl's schedule and delivery promises will be difficult to maintain.

- The factors that cause continuing cost reductions fall into four categories that vary in origin (internal or external to the firm) and type (autonomous or induced) (see Exhibit 10.16).
- Most causal factors in progress functions cut across functional boundaries.

In practice, this means that in contrast to the definition of the learning curve based on T. P. Wright's observation, learning is not constant or predictable. Therefore, managers should actively identify potential sources of improvement and then aggressively take advantage of them. This implies that the firm must invest in all four of the structural prerequisites presented in Chapter 2: (1) continuous improvement efforts, (2) research and development, (3) adoption of advanced technology, and (4) internal and external integration of people and systems.

Remember. Learning does not happen automatically; it must be actively sought and managed.

EXHIBIT 10.16 THE PROGRESS CURVE: SOURCES OF IMPROVEMENT

A progress curve aggregates the effects of many different sources of improvement. These sources can be classified by origin (internal or external to the firm) and type (autonomous or induced).

Internal sources of improvement result from employees learning and improving the designs of products, processes, and product support activities. *External* sources of improvement include suppliers, customers, competitors, and governments.

Autonomous sources of improvement appear as production is sustained over long periods. Additional investments in the current operating process are needed for *induced* souces of improvement.

To understand the different sources of improvement, or learning, look first at an individual activity: playing golf. What improves a person's golf game (as measured by the number of shots required to complete 18 holes on a particular course)? Factors such as practice, coaching, and equipment come to mind. Eight potential factors have been sorted using the classification system suggested above.

	Internal	External
Autonomous	• Practice • Improve physical fitness	• Periodically replace lost or damaged balls with higher-quality balls • Read golf magazines
Induced	• Change stance • Buy any clubs needed to complete the set	• Get coaching from a professional • Replace entire set of clubs with higher-quality clubs

The next step is to move to the work environment and think about organizational learning in the same way. A couple of examples for each cell in the matrix are listed below.

	Internal	External
Autonomous	• Direct labor learning resulting from the "practice makes perfect" principle • Improvements in production scheduling or inventory control	• Published information describing recent technological advances made by others • Periodic replacement of old equipment
Induced	• Changes to the product design that make the product easier and cheaper to manufacture • Improvements to the production process	• Copying and adapting a competitor's technological innovation • Incorporating product design changes demanded by consumers

The matrix illustrates a very important point: the way in which managers can help a firm take advantage of a potential source of improvement depends on the cell in which the improvement source lies.

10.7 REWARD SYSTEMS

Reward systems are used by managers to compensate their subordinates for acting in a manner consistent with the firm's goals and objectives. These systems are also used to attract and keep high-quality employees.

Rewards can be extrinsic or intrinsic. **Extrinsic rewards** include financial and nonfinancial rewards given to employees by the firm. Physical working conditions, job titles, and public recognition are nonfinancial rewards. **Intrinsic rewards** come from the work itself. A sense of challenge, accomplishment, and responsibility is an intrinsic reward. Although managers cannot hand out intrinsic rewards, they can ensure that jobs are designed so that employees have an opportunity to achieve these self-actualizing rewards.

Designing an effective reward system is complicated by the inherent differences between people. Everyone has his or her own set of needs, motivations, and responses to different types of rewards. Researchers, such as Herzberg, Vroom, Adams, Porter, and Lawler have developed a number of theories to explain motivation. Although their theories differ and conclusive results have not been obtained, several guidelines can be derived from their work:

- People must be aware of rewards and find them attractive.
- The relationship between a reward and the specific behavior that will lead to that reward must be strong and clearly articulated.
- People must believe that they are capable of the behavior required.
- The performance appraisal system must be perceived as one that can accurately and objectively measure the required behavior.

10.8 FINANCIAL REWARD SYSTEMS

Piece-rate systems, in which employees are compensated on the basis of individual output, are often used in manufacturing settings. The service sector version of this system—**commissions**—is common as well. Straight hourly pay and salaries are also popular compensation schemes.

The use of piece rates is based on reducing labor costs per item and thus reducing item costs. Where labor is only a small part of a product's costs, this may produce insignificant savings. The piece-rate system assumes that each worker is an *independent contractor,* however, and that makes coordinating production difficult. Inevitably, work-in-process inventories are significant and inventory costs may exceed labor cost savings.

The piece-rate system has been rightly criticized for setting worker against worker and worker against manager, for it is based on time standards that usually are set subjectively. There are, though, conditions under which piece rates are reasonable, including the following:

- Acceptance of the system by management, workers, and unions
- Accurate time standards with realistic allowances
- Well-trained workers
- Worker control of the pace of the operation
- Good equipment
- No outside interference with the ability to work

If any of these conditions is violated, a piece-rate system should not be used.

The first condition is the most critical, for belief in the fairness of the system is essential. At Lincoln Electric, the Cleveland, Ohio, firm that is acknowledged to produce the world's best and least expensive arc welding equipment, piece rates are used extensively. Every person in the organization accepts them, for every worker is selected in part because of a personal drive to make money. High work rates lead to less costly parts and products, a key element in Lincoln's strategy.

In most places in which a piece-rate system is used, however, the conditions *are* violated. Usually the violations are benign and understandable. Most clothing manufacturers use piece-rate systems, and the average number of piece rates in a factory is in excess of 5,000. Each new garment may have 20 different standards and rates, and even though standards are checked up to four times before being fully implemented, minor inaccuracies are almost inevitable. When they are reasonable, no problems are likely to occur. Sometimes, though, the violations are not subtle, resulting in problems for management. New technologies usually invalidate standards by reducing task times; sometimes management does not adjust the standards and ends up rewarding workers for equipment improvements. Management may try to *tighten* standards as workers improve their performance, penalizing workers for learning to do their jobs better or making improvements to processes. And management may interfere with output through poor planning, resulting in a lack of materials. Under each of these conditions some other form of reward system should be installed.

Another criticism of piece-rate systems is that they reward current output, not personal ability or potential. Accordingly, firms are investigating and implementing other forms of rewards. In some instances workers are paid straight salaries; doctors at the Mayo Clinic and operators at Fujima International, for example, are paid salaries instead of the traditional piece rates paid to their peers. In both instances this leads to cooperation and teamwork. Some firms also pay for knowledge and skill development rather than output, often adding increments for the acceptance of

EXHIBIT 10.17 PAY-FOR-KNOWLEDGE SYSTEMS

PAY FOR KNOWLEDGE AT GENERAL FOODS
At the General Foods plant in Topeka there is only one worker classification but four different pay rates. The starting rate is paid to new workers and those who have mastered one job. Once a worker has learned how to do all his or her teammates' jobs, his or her pay is increased to the team rate. Anyone who has learned all the jobs in the plant earns the plant rate. A person with special skills (e.g., electrical maintenance) qualifies for a special "add-on" rate. There are no limits on the number of people paid at any rate.
PAY FOR KNOWLEDGE AT GENERAL MOTORS
In many General Motors (GM) assembly plants workers are organized into teams of 10 or so. To receive a salary above the minimum, a worker must be able to do two of the jobs in the work group. The next salary increment comes when all these jobs are mastered. Promotion to group leader requires an individual to be able to do all the jobs in the "home" group and in another group in a different part of the plant. This requires a transfer and a program of learning and development for the individual.
The traditional path at GM was to stay at one job and receive annual increments. Promotion to leading hand was based on time and passing a course. Getting into the course was a matter of luck and favoritism. Now the incentive is still self-interest, but to gain promotion a worker has to have been trained in and have worked at every job in at least two work groups, thus becoming aware of the needs of other areas of the plant. This awareness sensitizes the members of the workforce to their individual and group impact on other parts of the plant and improves quality and productivity.
Source: Adapted from Nowlin (1990), p. 9.

added responsibility or for the achievement of specific market-related results. Two examples of pay-for-knowledge systems are described in Exhibit 10.17.

This book has consistently advocated teamwork, and rewarding individuals for team or group performance is widely practiced. These rewards, which include bonuses and profit sharing, are usually paid in addition to a salary or straight hourly wage. The group may be as small as a process work gang or as large as the entire firm, but research shows that extra reward schemes work best with small groups. They also work best when the reward is given as soon after the work performance as possible. Naturally, everyone involved must agree with the equity of the reward, and the reward for one group should be consistent with the rewards for other groups in the firm and with the firm's strategy.

MANAGERIAL IMPLICATIONS

Managers get things done through people. Job design is therefore an important part of operating process design and management. Proper job design allows an FRO to keep all types of costs under control and allows for improved operating system responsiveness, quality, and service. Further, keeping workers on the job means continuously improving performance.

Job design determines how individuals relate to the other elements in the transformation process: equipment, materials, time, and other people. Managers decide whether operators are slaves to the equipment or the equipment supports the operators. In an FRO the latter philosophy must prevail for it is only by supporting operators that managers assure that learning can occur.

Managers can assess and take into account the effect of continuous improvement by using the learning curve. Because the learning rate can be managed, any early assessment must be checked at the first opportunity and adjustments must be made. As most managers use the learning curve to predict when a job will end, a learning rate that is slower than assumed means that extra hours have to be made available to complete the job in the promised time.

Establishing standards, especially time standards, requires the active cooperation of and participation by the workforce. This is especially true as FROs organize around semiautonomous work groups. If the workforce does not trust or understand the efforts being made to analyze jobs and set standards, it is unlikely that the work study effort will be worthwhile.

CHAPTER SUMMARY

The focus in this chapter was on an important aspect of process design: job design. Major issues and points to remember include the following:

- Job design is the synthesis of individual tasks or activities into a job which is assigned to an individual worker or a group of workers. The sociotechnical approach to job design considers both the technical needs of the process and the social needs of the worker.
- Well-designed jobs are reasonably demanding, include a variety of tasks, provide continuous opportunities to learn and "own" areas of decision making, and are socially meaningful. Equipment operators should be equipment midwives rather than equipment monitors.
- The process of dividing and analyzing jobs is referred to as method study. Method study focuses on reducing unnecessary work content.
- Work measurement techniques are used to establish a time standard for a qualified worker to perform a specific job at a defined level of performance with the

necessary tools in a normal job environment. Time study, predetermined time standards, and work sampling are three work measurement techniques.

- During time study, a stopwatch or another timing device is used to determine the exact time required to complete a specific set of tasks. The resultant time is adjusted for fatigue and other allowances and then becomes a time standard.
- The predetermined time standard (PTS) technique develops time standards by analyzing a set of tasks into a set of basic human motions and then summing the times established for each motion. MTM and MODAPTS are PTS systems.
- Work sampling involves the use of random samples to determine the proportion of total time spent on specified activities.
- The learning curve principle states that at each doubling of the cumulative production volume, the time required to produce the last unit diminishes at a constant rate.
- At the firm level, the progress curve describes the continuing cost reductions that can be attributed to learning. The learning rate, however, is neither constant nor predictable.
- Reward systems are used to compensate employees for acting in a manner consistent with the firm's goals and objectives. Rewards can be intrinsic or extrinsic. There seems to be a trend toward rewards that focus on group rather than individual behavior.

KEY TERMS

Job design	Flow process chart	Work cycle	Work sampling
Sociotechnical approach	Operator process chart	Normal time	Learning curve effect
Vertical job enrichment	Multiple-activity chart	Standard time	Progress curve
Horizontal job enrichment (job enlargement)	Travel chart	Allowances	Experience curve
	Work safety	Predetermined time standards (PTS)	Reward systems
Process midwife	Human factors engineering (ergonomics)	Methods-time measurement (MTM)	Extrinsic rewards
Process monitor			Intrinsic rewards
Method study	Work measurement	Modular arrangement of predetermined time standards (MODAPTS)	Piece-rate system
Operating (outline) process chart	Time study		Commissions
	Normal pace		

DISCUSSION QUESTIONS

1. What *is* job design? Does it differ between manufacturing and service organizations? Why or why not?

2. Many companies are discovering that self-managed or cross-functional teams increase productivity. What do you think?

3. Explain what is meant by the operator midwife approach. Why do some firms consider it a superior alternative to monitoring?

4. Explain how job enlargement, job enrichment, and empowering people affect FROs.

5. Can unions play a role in designing jobs in today's environment? Explain.

6. Is the notion of time and motion study applicable in today's highly automated environment? If not, what alternative do you propose?

7. Concurrent engineering (see Chapter 7) is based on a team approach. How does this affect job design?

8. FROs strive for a flat organization and a team approach. What impact does this have on the traditional view of job design?

9. Is a working environment with highly automated machines more or less hazardous than a less automated environment? Explain.

10. A team approach and creating a flexible organization require, among other things, restructuring of

the workforce and building a sound and reliable communications channel. Do you agree? Why?

11. Chapter 2 differentiated philosophies of "static optimization" and "dynamic evolution." The latter relies on delegation of authority and the problem-solving approach; it strives to create knowledge managers. What changes would be necessary in a typical operation to promote this philosophy?

12. Consider a department store such as Wal-Mart. How often would you redesign jobs (or sets of tasks)? How would you fit job design into the firm's continuous improvement program? Who should be involved in the job design process?

13. Can and should a firm implement standardized work methods and times while pursuing a continuous improvements program on the shop floor?

14. Big, complex companies usually can't react fast enough. Small nimble ones may not have the muscle. What's the answer? A new form of organization called a 'virtual corporation' uses technology to link people, assets, and ideas in a temporary organization. After the business is done, it disbands. Can you think of an example? What effects might a virtual company have on job design? What are the disadvantages of this approach?

15. What types of jobs and circumstances are suitable for time study? Predetermined time standards? Work sampling? Explain.

16. What is the learning curve? What is the learning rate? Is the learning rate constant? What factors influence learning? Of what value is the learning curve to managers?

17. What is the progress curve? How does it differ from the learning curve? Of what value is it to managers?

18. What are extrinsic rewards? What are intrinsic rewards? Give examples of each?

19. Are piece-rate reward systems suitable for FROs? Why or why not?

20. What are the advantages and disadvantages of individual versus group reward systems?

21. Should reward systems favor long-term or short-term management action? Why?

PROBLEMS

1. You are part of a team conducting a mail questionnaire survey and want to know how many questionnaires can be prepared for mailing per day. You have made six observations of three people who work with you. The data are shown below.

Job Element/ Observation	Cycle Time, minutes						Performance Rating, %
	1	2	3	4	5	6	
Prepare questionnaire	0.5	1.0	0.5	0.75	3.0	1.0	110
Type envelope address	2.0	2.0	3.0	1.0	2.0	3.0	100
Stuff, stamp, and seal envelope	2.0	1.0	2.0	1.0	4.0	2.0	90

The arbitrary allowances factor is 15 percent. What is the standard time for the job?

2. An analyst at Acme Engineering wants to measure the percentage of downtime in one part of the blacksmith shop. The superintendent estimates the downtime to be about 25 percent. The desired results are to be accurate within ±5 percent of p, with a confidence level of 95 percent. How many observations will need to be made for this work sampling study? How will the study be conducted?

3. Using Exhibit 10.11, develop an allowance factor for an assembly element where the operator stands in an awkward position, regularly lifts a weight of 10 pounds, and has good light and atmosphere conditions. The attention required is fairly fine, the noise level is continuous at 60 decibels, and the mental strain and monotony are low, while the job is tedious.

4. A worker has been put in charge of four milling machines that together mill a casting. The standard times in minutes to complete each operation are shown in the chart below. Note that the machine must be stopped while the operator performs "external" tasks but can run while the operator performs "internal" tasks.

Operation	External Operator Time	Internal Operator Time	Machine Time
1	0.994	0.145	2.600
2	0.744	0.248	2.220
3	0.881	0.363	2.420
4	0.607	0.428	1.118

The operator has allowances that total 39 minutes in an eight-hour day.

a. How many units will be produced at standard in a day?

b. How many units will be produced when the operator works at 133 percent of standard? At 167 percent of standard?

5. The medication nurse in the intensive care unit of the local hospital has stated that advances in treatment have led to an increase in the time spent administering drugs. The nurse's assessment of the time spent in major activities each day is:

Drug administration	27 percent
Drug receipt	4 percent
Inventory control	7 percent
Record keeping	10 percent
Drug orders	5 percent
Discussions with patients	8 percent
Discussions with doctors	5 percent
Discussions with others	17 percent
Meals	15 percent

Given that 3 percent accuracy and a confidence interval of 95 percent are desired, how many observations will have to be made in a work sampling study to determine the validity of the nurse's assessment? What happens if after 15 observations it is found that the real percentage of time spent administering drugs is 40 percent?

6. A police officer walking a beat walks at a standard pace of 60 paces per minute and covers 0.75 meters per stride. On average, the officer checks the security of the shops he or she passes, trying to open the doors and shining a lamp through the windows to check for unlawful activity. This check occurs every 30 paces on average and takes about 10 seconds. How long is the beat if the police officer is expected to get around in one hour? How many shops are there?

7. An analyst working for the local hospital wants to set a standard in the pharmacy for counting and putting 100 pills in a bottle, capping the bottle, and putting on a label. Ten cycles were timed in a preliminary study, and the times recorded were (in seconds) 10, 7, 9, 11, 10, 24, 8, 11, 12, and 10. Calculate how many cycles will have to be timed in the full study if the allowable error is 5 percent and the confidence level is 95 percent.

8. A firm assembling vacuum cleaners assigns five people to the assembly line, where each person is expected to take 1.2 minutes to complete his or her tasks. The first vacuum cleaner took each person 2 minutes, and the tenth took 1.7 minutes. How long will it take each person to complete work on the two thousandth cleaner? How much time will each worker have spent in total assembling a run of 5,000 cleaners? How long should the run have taken at standard? If each worker receives $13 per hour, what is the total wage bill for the run and the average labor cost per cleaner? If there is a 40-hour week without overtime, when will the production run be completed? (The run starts at 7:30 a.m. on Monday, February 1.) What action should management take?

9. Suppose the system in question 8 is changed so that now each of the five workers assembles a complete cleaner. The planned assembly time is six minutes. Each person took 10 minutes on the first cleaner and 8.5 minutes on the tenth cleaner. How much time will each worker have spent in total assembling the run of 5,000 cleaners? If each worker receives $13 per hour, what is the total wage bill for the run and the average labor cost per cleaner? If there is a 40-hour week without overtime, when will the production run be completed? What action should management take?

10. A cost accountant was transferred from the central accounting office in the city to the firm's manufacturing plant in the country. On arrival, the accountant was sent to work in the foundry office in the center of the plant. The office was noisy, with almost constant high-pitched loud noises from the grinding wheels that cut off the risers from the bronze castings. Further, the room was moderately hot and humid and the light conditions were not quite what the accountant was used to in the air-conditioned office downtown. Given that the accountant will do exactly the same job as before, what do you think will happen to personal productivity? Why?

11. Given the allowance factor calculated in question 3 and the normal time calculated in question 5, what will be the time an operator takes for the job while working at 115 percent?

12. The worker in question 4 produces 800 pieces in a five-day week without working overtime. As the worker's supervisor, what would you do, and why?

13. Capping burning wells in Kuwait was very tricky work. Calculate from Exhibit 10.11 the personal and fatigue allowances for this type of work. Do you think they are enough? How confident are you that your allowances are reasonable? Why?

14. Because of time constraints, the analyst who developed a new flushing sequence for an oil pipeline can observe only 100 trials of the new procedure. If the procedure takes an average of 5 minutes with a standard deviation of 3.2 minutes over the first 20 observations, how confident can the analyst be that the error is only ± 3 percent?

15. Assembly of the first Volkswagen at a new Mexican plant took 100 hours. If the workers are experienc-

ing a 90 percent learning curve, how long will it take to produce the tenth unit?

16. In 1937 the eighth U-boat took German workers 28,718 hours to complete. The learning curve in the shipyard was 80 percent. How long did it take to produce the tenth U-boat?

17. Suppose Jones Engineering, a machine shop, has accepted an order for 10,000 units of a particular product. The order is due in six months. Jones used the learning curve for planning and costing and used a learning rate of 85 percent. One month into the project, the learning rate is found to be 90 percent. What is the effect of this discovery, and what can Jones do?

18. A machinist operates three machines in a work cell, progressively transferring a piece from one machine to the next; three pieces are being worked on at one time. The standards for the cell are:

| Machine | Cycle Time, minutes | |
	External Time (operator working on machine)	Internal Time (machine operating independently)
1	1.15	3.03
2	1.85	2.49
3	1.80	2.20

All operator time is included in the external time.

a. How many units will be produced in an eight-hour day at 100 percent standard?

b. If the operator can work at 115 percent of standard, how many units will be produced in a day?

c. If 130 units are produced in a day, how much of a bonus should the operator be paid if at 110 percent the operator would be paid a 10 percent bonus?

GROUP EXERCISES

Many of the tools and techniques discussed in this chapter are meant to be used in a team setting. The following problems are best solved by small groups of students. Ideally, each group should be composed of people with different backgrounds, interests, or areas of expertise.

1. Select a business (e.g., a hamburger stand) or activity with which you are familiar. What are some potential sources of improvement?

Develop a matrix similar to the one shown in Exhibit 10.16. Place each source of improvement in the appropriate matrix.

As a manager, how would you take advantage of each potential improvement source? Should your management approach vary depending on the cell in which the improvement source is found?

2. A U-bolt is inserted into a small flat plate, and a washer and then a nut are put on each leg. Each nut is tightened five times (each turndown after the first is M1G1 M1P0). The operator then stands up from the chair, walks five paces to a table, places the assembly on the table, returns to the workstation, and sits down. This ends the cycle.

All the parts are on the workstation bench. The U-bolt is about 12 inches away to the left; the plate is the same distance away to the right. The washers are one inch apart and six inches to the operator's front; the nuts are also one inch apart and slightly to the right of the washers.

Calculate the normal time for this activity. If a 15 percent allowance is used, how many assemblies can be done in an hour?

REFERENCES AND SELECTED BIBLIOGRAPHY

Alexander, David C., and Babur Mustafa Pulat [1985], *Industrial Ergonomics: A Practitioner's Guide,* Industrial Engineering & Management Press, Norcross, Ga.

Canadian Business [1992], vol. 65, no. 10, October, pp. 128–136.

Davis, Joyce [1993], "Are You As Good as the Best in the World?" *Fortune,* December, pp. 95–96.

Drucker, P. [1989], *The New Realities,* Harper & Row, New York.

Dutton, John M., and Annie Thomas [1984], "Treating Progress Functions as a Managerial Opportunity," *Academy of Management Review,* vol. 9, no. 2, pp. 235–247.

Globe and Mail [1992], June 30, pp. B1, B6.

Hellriegel, D., J. W. Slocum, and R. W. Woodman [1989], *Organization Behavior,* 5th ed., West, St. Paul, Minn.

Industrial Engineering [1993], Ergonomics Issue, vol. 25, no. 7, July.

International Labour Office [1979], *Introduction to Work Study,* 3d ed., Geneva, Switzerland.

Klatt, L., R. G. Murdick, and F. E. Schuster [1985], *Human Resource Management,* Charles E. Merrill, Columbus, Ohio.

Little, Bruce [1993], "How to Make a Small, Smart Factory," *Toronto Globe and Mail,* Feb. 2, p. B24.

Miles, Raymond E. [1975], *Theories of Management: Implications for Organizational Behavior and Development,* McGraw-Hill, New York.

Mishne, P. [1988], "A Passion for Perfection," *Manufacturing Engineering,* November, pp. 55–56.

Naderi, Babak, and Madina Baggerman [1992], "The Result of Ergonomics at the Forefront in Manufacturing: Quality," *Industrial Engineering,* April, pp. 42–46.

Niebel, Benjamin W. [1993], *Motion and Time Study,* 9th ed., Richard D. Irwin, Homewood, Ill.

Nowlin, William A. [1990], "Restructuring in Manufacturing: Management, Work, and Labor Relations," *Industrial Management,* November–December, pp. 5–9, 30.

Ramsay, George F., Jr. [1993], "Using Self-Administered Work Sampling in a State Agency," *Industrial Engineering,* February, pp. 44–45.

Shinnick, Michael D., and Walter W. Erwin [1989], "Work Measurement System Creates Shared Responsibilities among Workers at Ford," *Industrial Engineering,* August, pp. 28–30.

Stewart, Thomas A. [1992], "The Search for the Organization of Tomorrow," *Fortune,* May 18, pp. 93–98.

Trist, E. L. [1963], "The Sociotechnical Perspective," in A. H. Van de Ven and W. F. Joyce (eds.), *Perspective on Operations Design,* New York, Wiley.

van Beinum, H. [1988], "New Technology and Organizational Choice," *QWL Focus,* vol. 6, no. 1, pp. 3–10.

Wall, T. [1986], "Advanced Manufacturing Technologies—the Case for the Operator and Wife," in H. Noori (ed.), *The Proceedings of Technology Canada Conference,* RE-MAT, Wilfrid Laurier University, Waterloo, May 21–22, pp. 311–323.

SUPPLEMENT TO

CHAPTER 10

SETTING TIME STANDARDS

WITH

THE MODAPTS SYSTEM

The material in this supplement draws heavily on the
MODAPTS manual issued by the International MODAPTS
Association, Inc. (1991).

To design jobs and plan and control operations, managers need to know how long it should take an employee to complete a set of tasks. One way to establish time standards is to analyze a set of tasks into a set of body motions and then sum the times required to perform each motion. Rather than use a stopwatch to time each motion, a firm can use charts with **predetermined time standards (PTS)**. This supplement will present an overview of one of the more popular PTS systems: the **modular arrangement of predetermined time standards (MODAPTS)** system.

The popularity of the MODAPTS system stems from its simplicity, low cost, and diversity of applications, along with the speed with which time standards can be developed. Studies reveal that MODAPTS standards are comparable to those obtained using the more complex MTM-1 system and are usually 2 to 3 percent looser.

S10.2 AN OVERVIEW OF THE MODAPTS SYSTEM

MODAPTS was originally developed in Australia by G. C. Heyde in the 1960s for *manually controlled tasks*.[1] The times assigned to basic human motions in MODAPTS are expressed in a unit of time called a **MOD**. One MOD represents the time required to complete a single finger movement, that is, 0.00215 minute, or about an eighth of a second.

The time values assigned by MODAPTS and other PTS systems reflect a normal employee's performance. That is, they are the **normal times** required for a thoroughly experienced employee[2] working at a comfortable, sustainable pace in the customary work environment. The weight of the objects handled, the difficulty of the activity, the size of the parts, and the average distance moved have all been considered and embedded in the time values.

To develop a time standard for a set of tasks, analysts simply assign MODs to the basic motions or activities that constitute that set of tasks. Allowances for personal and unavoidable delays are added to the normal time estimates to arrive at the **standard time** that should be allocated for the set of tasks.

Fewer than 50 activities are used in the MODAPTS

system to describe basic body motions. These activities are grouped into the following three categories:

- **Movement activities.** Finger, hand, arm, shoulder, and trunk movements used to reach an object or move it to a destination.
- **Terminal activities.** Get and put activities performed at the end of a movement. Get activities involve gaining control of objects; put activities involve placing objects at their destinations.
- **Auxiliary activities.** Other activities, such as walking, bending, and inspecting.

Each activity has a corresponding icon (see Exhibit 10S.1) and is identified by a two-part code. The code consists of the first letter of the activity name and the number of MODs assigned to that activity. For example, the code M3 refers to a movement that takes three MODs, or 0.00645 minute, to complete.

The following sections will take a closer look at the activities that constitute the three MODAPTS categories of motion.

S10.3 MOVEMENT ACTIVITIES

Unlike MTM and other PTS systems, in MODAPTS movements are classified not by the distance of the move but by the body part used to complete the move.[3] Because each movement does not have to be measured, time standards can be developed relatively quickly.

When one is handling small objects, there are six possible types of movement. These movements are described in Exhibit 10S.2.

For example, a movement from the knuckle is called a finger movement, and the distance typically moved is one inch. A finger movement has been assigned one MOD of time, and its code is M1. The forward and backward movements needed to wind a watch while it is on a person's wrist, for example, are classified as M1 movements. If the watch is wound five times, ten M1's are awarded to the task (five for the forward movements and another five for the backward movements).

What if a person takes off the watch and then winds it? The forward and backward movements are then considered hand rather than finger movements. However,

---

[1] MODAPTS is not suitable for machine-paced tasks or those which involve highly repetitive short-duration activities such as the finger movements in piano playing and the leg movements of a cross-country runner.

[2] A thoroughly experienced person is someone who has taken an appropriate training program and reached a satisfactory level of competence.

[3] Because there is a relationship between the body part required to complete a move and the distance moved, MODAPTS does in effect take distances into consideration.

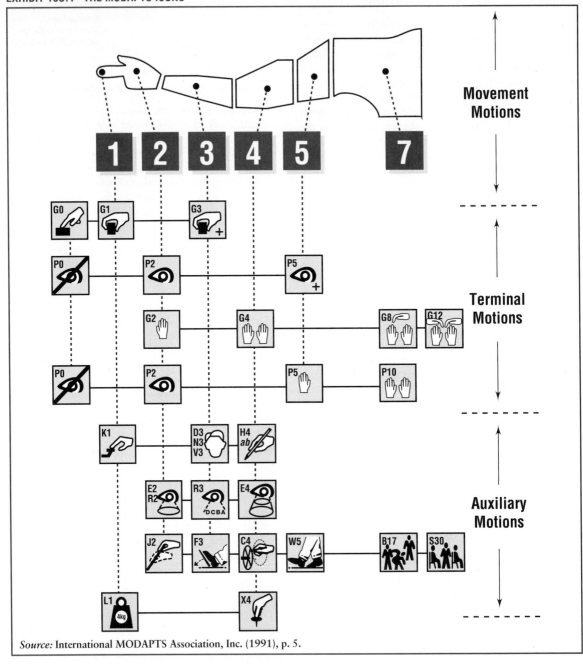

Source: International MODAPTS Association, Inc. (1991), p. 5.

since this task can be performed with finger movements, the correct classification is M1. *In general, the lowest movement type that can be used to complete the movement should be selected.*

If the object to be moved is large or heavy, the chart in Exhibit 10S.3 must be used. The times in this chart were developed for warehouse operations and should not be applied to other types of operations.

Since the purpose of a movement is almost always to grasp an object or place it somewhere, movements in MODAPTS are always combined with a get or a put terminal activity.

Terminal activities are activities which occur at the end of a movement activity; they are never performed on their own.

Get Activities

The purpose of a **get activity** is to gain control of an object after having reached toward it. The following **finger-controlled gets** are used to gain control of small/light objects.

 G0 Contact Get. The fingers touch the object but do not close around it. Example: depressing a key on a calculator.

 G1 Simple Grasp Get. The fingers close around the object. Example: grasping a pen from an uncluttered desk.

 G3 Get with Feedback. Sensual and/or visual feedback is required for the fingers to close around the object. Example: grasping a straight pin from a table.

When an object is large or heavy, one of the following **hand-controlled gets** is required to gain control over the object.

 G2 Get, One-Hand Engagement. Only one hand is used, but bracing is required. Example: grasping a knapsack from the floor.

EXHIBIT 10S.2   MOVEMENTS INVOLVING SMALL, LIGHT OBJECTS

Movement Type	Description	Typical Distance Moved, inches	Examples	Number of MODs	Movement Code
Finger	Movements from the knuckle	1	Winding a wristwatch, turning down a nut, squeezing a trigger, pressing a calculator key, writing a word	1	M1
Hand	Movements from the wrist. Hand or palm must move	2	Turning down a large nut, turning a part over, returning the pen to the beginning of a word just written	2	M2
Forearm	Movements from the elbow. Wrist must move	6	Turning over a page, drawing a six-inch-long line, moving hands from a keyboard to the desktop alongside the keyboard	3	M3
Whole arm	Movements from the shoulder directly forward. With or without body assistance. Elbow must move	12	Reaching forward to switch off a computer	4	M4
Extended arm	Movements from the shoulder fully to the left, right, or across the body. With or without body assistance. Shoulder must move	18	Reaching up to an object on a high shelf, moving an object across the body, reaching for control buttons located to the side of the workstation	5	M5
Trunk	Movements from the shoulder involving the body trunk. Upper body must move	30	Picking items from a pallet on the floor, picking up a dropped newspaper	7	M7

Source: Adapted from International MODAPTS Association, Inc. (1991), pp. 19–33.

The following chart should be used for the movement of large, heavy objects in warehouse operations. If an object is at least 16 inches in all three dimensions, it is considered large. Objects over 18 pounds are classified as heavy.

Movement		Maximum Weight Moved, pounds	Maximum Distance Moved, inches
Code	Description		
M2	Hand move, using only one hand	2	2
M3	Arm move, using only one arm	9	6
M4	Whole arm move		
	Using only one arm	18	12
	Using two arms	35	24
M5	Extended arm move		
	Using only one arm	18	18
	Using two arms	35	35
M7	Trunk move		
	Using two hands	136	39
	Using two hands combined with a put	57	59
	Trunk and foot move, using two hands, combined with a put	57	79

Source: Adapted from International MODAPTS Association, Inc. (1991), pp. 35 and 47.

 G4 Get, Two-Hand Engagement. Two hands are needed to get control of an unobstructed freestanding object. Example: grasping a heavy box from the floor.

 G8 Get, Three-Hand Engagement. Used when the object is slightly impeded by other objects. The object is typically pulled out with one hand and then grasped with two hands. Example: gaining control over a box that is sitting on a shelf with other boxes.

 G12 Get, Four-Hand Engagement. Used when the object is very much impeded by other objects. The object is typically pulled out with two hands and then grasped with two hands. Example: gaining control over a box that is between two others on a shelf.

G16 Get, Five-Hand Engagement. Used when the object is severely obstructed by other objects. The object is typically pulled out with two hands and then grasped with two hands. Bracing is required. Example: gaining control over a box that is wedged between two others on a shelf.

Put Activities

An action that places an object at a specific destination after moving it to a general area is called a **put activity**. The following three **finger-controlled puts** are used to control small/light objects.

 P0 Simple Put. The object is put to a general location without regard to its particular destination; eye control is not used. Example: tossing a pencil in a drawer.

 P2 Put with Feedback. The object is put to a defined location using feedback from one of the senses, usually the eyes. These puts involve *one* correction, a slight hesitation or repositioning to align, adjust, or orient the object. Maximum insertion is one inch.[4] Example: locating a Phillips screwdriver in a slot.

 P5 Put with Feedbacks. Like a P2 Put, but *more than one* correction, hesitation, or slight repositioning is required. Example: placing a nut on a bolt.

When an object is large or heavy, one of the following **hand-controlled puts** is used to place the object at its destination. Data for these puts are intended for use primarily in a warehouse and for objects that are not fragile.

 P0 Put, General Location. An object is put to a general location; orderliness is not required. Example: placing a box on an empty table.

---

[4] If the insertion is more than one inch, an additional move and put combination is required.

P2 Put with Orderliness. The object is put to a defined location but is not touched by the hands again once it has been placed down. Example: placing a box at the corner of a table.

 P5 Put, One New Contact. Like a P2, but one hand is used to place the object in an exact location once it has been set down. Example: placing a box on a table exactly in line with other boxes.

 P10, Two New Contacts. Like a P5, but two hands are used to position the object after it has been set down. Example: using two hands to position a heavy box on a table exactly in line with other boxes.

Move, get, and put activities are often performed simultaneously. The less conscious control is needed to perform an activity, the more likely it is that it will be performed at the same time as other activities.

S10.5 LOW-CONSCIOUS AND HIGH-CONSCIOUS CONTROL ACTIVITIES

A **low-conscious control activity** requires little muscular control, no visual control, and no mental control. Picking up a stapler from the top of an uncluttered desk is a low-conscious control activity. All movement activities and G0, G1, and P0 terminal activities are considered low-conscious control activities.

In contrast, a high degree of muscular control (often with visual or sensual assistance) is needed to complete a **high-conscious control activity** such as picking up a pin. P2, P5, and G3 are high-conscious control activities.

These two control categories are used to assign times to activities performed simultaneously by two different body parts.

S10.6 SIMULTANEOUS ACTIVITIES

While one hand performs a low-conscious control activity, it is possible for the other hand to perform a low- or even a high-conscious activity at the same time. For example, a pencil can be picked up by the right hand as a stapler is placed back on the desk by the left hand. MODs are awarded only for the move and the terminal activity that require the longest time.

Two high-conscious control activities cannot be performed simultaneously; time must be allowed for both activities. Suppose each hand is to perform an M4G3 activity. The two hands move out together, and then the two G3 gets are performed sequentially. As a general rule, an additional M2 move is added for the second get. That is, the task is coded as M4G3 M2G3.

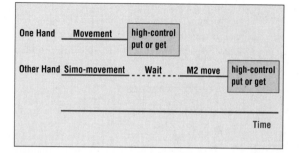

S10.7 AUXILIARY ACTIVITIES

Activities such as walking, bending, and inspecting are classified as auxiliary activities in MODAPTS and are briefly described below.

 R2 Read. Silently read one word in a group of familiar words to understand the overall message.

 R3 Read. Silently read one word in a group of words; each word has to register. Example: careful reading of instructions. One R3 is awarded for reading up to three digits. Reading the digits 1234 therefore requires two R3s.

 J2 Juggle. Change the position of an object currently grasped to gain better control of it. Example: repositioning a pen in the hand after picking it up to write with it. If the juggle is performed at the same time as another activity (such as a move), a juggle is not awarded to the action.

 X4 Extra Force. There is noticeable hesitation while pressure is applied to restrain an object, achieve control over it, or overcome resistance. Little or no motion is involved. Example: the final tightening of a screw with a screwdriver. Like the juggle, this activity is awarded only when all other activity stops.

Stepping forward, backward, or sideways and making a partial or complete turnaround of the body by means of the legs are classified as walking in MODAPTS. A side step made to balance the body is not considered a walk. The number of paces taken, not the distance traveled, is customarily used to calculate walk times.

 W5 Walk, Restricted Area. One W5 is awarded each time one foot passes the other (i.e., for each pace). Example: walking around boxes.

If a heavy/large object is being carried over a long distance (≥ 33 feet), the MOD value per pace is calculated as $W5 \times 295/(295 - M)$, where M is the weight of the object in pounds.

W4.5 Unrestricted walk. One W4.5 is awarded for each pace.

W5.5 Walk while pushing or pulling a small cart.

 F3 Foot Action. The foot moves, but the heel remains on the floor. One F3 is awarded for a movement in one direction. Example: depressing a foot pedal.

 B17 Bend and Arise, for production work. A down movement and an up movement are made, resulting in a vertical change in the upper part of the body. The hand must go below the knee. Following a Bend and Arise, all gets and puts are preceded by an M2 move.

B18 Bend and Arise, for office work.

 S30 Sit and Stand, for production work. This includes both the down and the up movements; it is recorded as one movement although other activities take place in between.

S48 Sit and Stand, for office work. Included are picking up a simple object from the desk and the overall interruption of having to get up.

C3 Crank, Wrist. The hand is moved in a circular path for more than one revolution. The maximum diameter of the crank handle is 3.5 inches. One C3 is awarded for each complete revolution.

 C4 Crank, Hand. The forearm is moved in a circular path for more than one revolution. One C4 is awarded for each complete revolution. Example: opening a window.

The use tool activity refers to a back-and-forth movement motion that does not terminate with a put activity or a get activity. Sawing, filing, rubbing, and polishing are all use tool activities.

U0.5 Use tool, finger motions. One U0.5 is awarded for a forward motion, and one for a backward motion.

U1 Use tool, hand motions.

U2 Use tool, forearm motions.

U3 Use tool, whole arm motions.

These are some other auxiliary activities included in the MODAPTS system:

E2 Eye fixation
E2 Eye travel

E4 Eye focus

H4 Write one character.
H5 Write one character in print style. Write one digit or symbol.

H6 Write one character in cursive style, uppercase.

H7 Write one character in print style, uppercase.

H21 Write one word in cursive style.

H26 Write one word in print style.

H35 Write one word in all uppercase.

L1 Load factor (added to put activities when the object being handled is heavy).

V3 Vocalize or speak one word or digit (or listening to someone else speak)

D3 Decide between two options.

N3 Count one item where items are arranged.

N6 Count one item where items are disarranged.

K1 Routine keys, little depression, no resistance on a compact keyboard.

K1.5 Routine keys, significant depression on a compact keyboard.

K2 Routine keys, significant depression, and some resistance on a compact keyboard.

K2.5 Nonroutine keys, little depression, and no resistance on a compact keyboard.

K3 Nonroutine keys, significant depression on a compact keyboard.

K4 Nonroutine keys, significant depression, and some resistance on a compact keyboard.

S10.8 DEVELOPING A TIME STANDARD USING MODAPTS: AN EXAMPLE

Let us take a simple task, such as sharpening a pencil with a desk-mounted manual sharpener, and develop a time standard for it.

EXHIBIT 10S.4 TOOLBOX: PENCIL-SHARPENING EXAMPLE

Actions	MODAPTS Code	MODs
1. Move left hand 5 inches to the pencil and pick up the pencil.	M3G1	4
2. Move the pencil to the sharpener and insert. (At the same time, the right hand moves to the crank of the sharpener and grasps it. No time awarded.)	M5P2	7
3. Rotate sharpener handle five times with the right hand.	Five C4s	20
4. Move the pencil to the paper (12 inches away) and place point on paper. (The pencil is transferred from the left hand to the right hand during this move. No time awarded.)	M4P2	6
5. Move the pencil back and forth on the paper once.	Two U1s	2
6. Move the left hand to the drawer and open it. (Move the right hand, which is holding the pencil, to the drawer area at the same time. No time awarded.)	M4G1 M3P0	8
Toss the pencil in the drawer.	M4P0	4
Close the drawer.	M3P0	3
7. Return hands to the desktop.	M4P0	4
	Total MOD Units	58

Barney is sitting at a desk. His pencil is 5 inches away to his left, and the sharpener is 12 inches away to his right. As one watches Barney, the following sequence of actions is noted:

1. Barney picks up the pencil in his left hand.
2. He moves the pencil to the sharpener and inserts it.
3. He turns the sharpener handle five times with his right hand.
4. He moves the pencil to a piece of paper directly in front of him.
5. He tests the lead by scribbling a line back and forth once on the paper.
6. He puts the pencil away in the top left drawer of his desk. He closes the drawer.
7. He returns his hands to the desktop in front of him.

One can assign times to each action by using the MODAPTS codes in Exhibit 10S.4.

Note that times were not assigned to every motion made by Barney because some of the motions were performed simultaneously with another motion. The move of the right hand to the crank of the sharpener occurred simultaneously with the move of the pencil in the left hand to the sharpener. The juggle of the pencil in the left hand is not recorded, nor is the transfer of the pencil from the left hand to the right hand during the movement back to the paper. The toss of the pencil into the drawer is done with the pencil in the right hand, which has to move across the body before the pencil is released; this involves the shoulder.

In total, 58 MODs have been assigned to the task. This translates into a normal time of 58×0.00215 minute, or 0.1247 minute. To convert the normal time to a standard time, it would be necessary to add allowances.

Determining the normal time for this task was relatively simple. However, training and practice are required before the MODAPTS system can be applied with confidence (and accepted) in a real-world setting.

KEY TERMS

Predetermined time standards (PTS)

Modular arrangement of predetermined time standards (MODAPTS)

MOD

Normal time

Standard time

Movement activities

Terminal activities

Auxiliary activities

Get activity

Finger-controlled get

Hand-controlled get

Put activity

Finger-controlled put

Hand-controlled put

Low-conscious control activity

High-conscious control activity

Simultaneous activity

REFERENCES AND SELECTED BIBLIOGRAPHY

Niebel, Benjamin W. [1993], *Motion and Time Study*, 9th ed., Richard D. Irwin, Inc., Homewood, Ill.

International MODAPTS Association, Inc. [1991], *MODAPTS: Modular Arrangement of Predetermined Time Standards*, Western Michigan University, Kalamazoo, Mich.

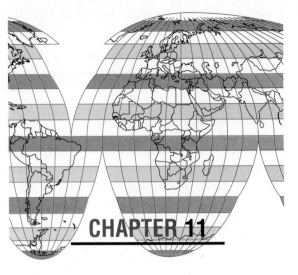

CHAPTER 11

PROCESS QUALITY AND IMPROVEMENT TOOLS

Chapter 9 explained that a firm can produce perfect products only if the product design is perfect and perfect resources are transformed in a perfect process. Managers should focus on elements they can influence rather than worrying about elements they cannot affect.

Managers in charge of operations need to ask the following questions:

- How does the firm define process quality?
- How might the firm's process affect product quality?
- How might the firm improve process quality?

In organizing for process improvement, managers must delegate the authority for initiating this improvement to the point at which it is best managed: the shop floor. Giving shop floor operators the tools, training, and authority to act is a fundamentally different way of managing a shop or office, but it must be done by a fast-response organization (FRO).

By the end of this chapter you will have been exposed to a wide range of tools and techniques for identifying, correcting, and preventing quality problems on the shop floor.

EXHIBIT 11.1 FRO PROFILE: MANUFACTURING

NCR Corporation's Engineering and Manufacturing Facility in West Columbia, South Carolina, manufactures (among other products) printed circuit boards (PCBs) for the firm's business information processing systems. This is a highly competitive area, and it is imperative that NCR strive for continuously reduced costs through product and process improvement. This drive led the Engineering and Manufacturing Facility to introduce statistical process control (SPC) in 1985. The first process on which SPC was tried was autoinsertion, where electronic components are automatically inserted into a PCB.

It is important for later assembly that each PCB be free of defects, and most defects detected by automatic testers must be reworked manually. For a PCB to be perfect, each component must be correctly positioned on the board and component leads must be inserted properly through the holes and cinched properly by the machines. In 1985 a substantial number of boards required rework, with the chances for rework increasing as the number of autoinserted components went from eight to several hundred per board.

A study of defects found that 40 percent were due to misinserted parts, 30 percent to broken parts, 10 percent to the wrong parts, and another 10 percent to missing parts. Solving the problems required SPC, taking regular (hourly) samples and analyzing the causes of defects when the process was shown to be out of control. Using this approach, the quality engineering staff and the line operators were able to identify a number of sources of the problems. As a consequence of this knowledge and of cooperative work on the causes, the number of defects has been reduced significantly.

Another important contribution of this first study to the acceptance of SPC across the corporation was the development of a database on the hourly process audits, which were extended to cover all the operations of the entire facility. This extensive database has been used to show the interconnectedness of all the processes in the value chain.

EXHIBIT 11.2 FRO PROFILE: SERVICE

After meeting with its customers and participating in a quality seminar, P∗I∗E Nationwide's executive officers became aware of the true cost of poor quality.

In response, P∗I∗E Nationwide (the fourth largest trucking company in the United States) has created a Blueprint for Quality. The blueprint maps out P∗I∗E's strategy for total quality and draws heavily on quality principles developed by the manufacturing sector. For example, P∗I∗E Nationwide is striving to build quality into its process by eliminating the source of potential failures with the help of statistical process control (SPC) tools.

(Exhibit 11.2 continues on next page)

EXHIBIT 11.2 *(continued)*

> Rating freight bills was the first process to which the company applied SPC. What type of errors are being made? How often are they being made? Why are they being made? How can these errors be prevented? What are the greatest opportunities for improvement? These are the questions teams of workers at P∗I∗E Nationwide answered, using control charts, cause-and-effect diagrams, and Pareto charts.
>
> As a result, the company was able to eliminate all auditors and inspectors and at the same time reduce the error rate from 10 percent to 0.8 percent in less than one year. Costs are also falling while customer service improves.
>
> *Source:* Adapted from Dondaro (1991), pp. 43–44.

11.1 MANAGERIAL ORIENTATION

This book has stressed the importance of product design by devoting several chapters exclusively to this topic. However, the quality of even a very well designed product depends on the quality of the transformation process.

> **DEFINITION:** *Process quality* is a measure of how well the goods or services provided by the transformation process conform to their design specifications.

Chapter 9 explored process design. This chapter will examine process control and improvement tools, drawing on the work of quality experts such as Deming, Juran, and Crosby.[1]

Let us begin with a review of a quality-control technique—acceptance sampling—that has been, and still is, popular in North America. Like many techniques, however, acceptance sampling was developed for a competitive environment markedly different from the one firms face today. This chapter will look at an alternative approach to acceptance sampling in which the firm attempts to monitor the process itself to identify and correct quality-related problems.

This chapter will describe tools and tactics for (1) identifying problems with the transformation process as early as possible, (2) solving these problems, and (3) improving the transformation process. As Toyota Canada (Exhibit 11.1) and P∗I∗E Nationwide (Exhibit 11.2) demonstrate, these tools can be very effective in the hands of well-trained and empowered workers.

Continuous efforts to improve the transformation process lead to improved product quality, a safer working environment, and lower production costs. In many cases a firm can increase its effective capacity without purchasing additional equipment, hiring new people, or enlarging its facilities.[2] The link between the quality of a firm's transformation process and that firm's ability to compete as a fast-response organization is strong and direct.

---

[1] Deming is credited with leading the Japanese quality revolution and is known for his 14-point total quality management program and his emphasis on statistical process control. Juran has also had a significant impact on Japanese quality. Juran defines quality as "fitness for use" and has developed a comprehensive approach to quality that covers a product's entire life span. Crosby is famous for his "quality is free" claim. Like Juran and Deming, he believes that quality improvement should be achieved through prevention rather than after-the-fact inspection.

[2] Process improvements at Florida Power and Light, one of the companies toured in the Startup Chapter, increased its capacity by 700 MW. This capacity gain resulted in a cumulative net revenue requirement reduction to customers of more than $300 million.

11.2 THE TRADITIONAL APPROACH TO QUALITY CONTROL: ACCEPTANCE SAMPLING

How can a firm ensure that the products flowing into, through, and out of its transformation process meet specified quality standards? One way is to inspect every product after every operation. This is expensive for companies that have relegated responsibility for quality to the quality-control department. For these companies, an attractive alternative to 100 percent inspection is to accept or reject an entire group of products on the basis of the quality of a sample drawn from the group. This alternative, called **acceptance sampling,** is presented briefly below; a detailed discussion of its mechanics appears in the supplement to this chapter.

An Overview of Acceptance Sampling

DEFINITION: Acceptance sampling is the evaluation of one or more random samples of items drawn from a group of items; the entire group is accepted or rejected on the basis of the quality of the items sampled.

The best way to understand the concepts underlying acceptance sampling is to work through a simple example. Suppose Mother Goose Toys (MGT) Ltd. purchases wheels for its toy trucks in lots of 5,000. Rather than inspect each wheel, MGT inspects a random sample of 50 from each lot. If more than one wheel is defective, the entire lot is rejected and sent back to the supplier; otherwise the lot is accepted. This is referred to as a single sampling plan.

Single sampling plans consist of a sample size (n) and an acceptance number (c). In this example, $n = 50$ and $c = 1$. The values used for n and c are not chosen arbitrarily but are based on the level of risk the people sending and receiving the goods are willing to assume.

Two types of risk are associated with acceptance sampling: the risk of rejecting a good lot and the risk of accepting a bad lot. In acceptance testing a lot is considered good if its quality exceeds a specified level called the **acceptable quality level (AQL).** A bad lot is one whose quality is worse than a predetermined value referred to as the **lot tolerance percent defective (LTPD).**

In this example the AQL has been set at 2 percent; that is, a lot is considered good if no more than 2 percent of its units are defective. The LTPD has been set at 4 percent. With the current sampling plan, the probability of rejecting a good lot is 0.264; the probability of accepting a bad lot is considerably higher at 0.406. Increasing the sample size (n) and/or decreasing the acceptance number (c) will decrease the probability of accepting a bad lot. However, the probability of rejecting a good lot will increase. Therefore, when one is designing a sampling plan, the two types of risk must be traded off against each other.

Acceptance Sampling in Today's Competitive Environment

Acceptance sampling is often used when (1) the cost of passing a limited number of defective products is low, (2) the number of products to be inspected is large, and (3) the process that produces the products is stable. If the only way in which a product can be inspected results in its destruction, 100 percent inspection is not feasible and acceptance sampling may be the only option.

Reread the first two conditions above. FROs are facing situations in which these conditions do not apply. Today the trend is toward very high quality levels and increasingly smaller lot sizes. AQL and LTPD values are being expressed in parts per million rather than parts per hundred. As these values approach zero, the sample size required becomes very close to, or equal to, the lot size; that is, 100 percent of the lot must be inspected.

Furthermore, acceptance sampling reflects a reactive attitude toward product quality. The underlying causes of quality problems are difficult to identify with postproduction inspection performed by quality-assurance specialists. A more proactive alternative is the prevention of product defects through monitoring, controlling, and improving the transformation process. Reducing process variation plays a key role in this approach.

11.3 IMPROVING PRODUCT QUALITY BY REDUCING PROCESS VARIATION

Process quality is perfect when every good or service produced by the transformation process meets every target value specified in the product design.[3] As was discussed in Chapter 6, the further a product deviates from its target values, the poorer its quality. The goal in process control therefore is to minimize these deviations. Unfortunately, eliminating all deviations from target values is an impossible task because the output from any process is subject to variation. This point will become clearer in the discussion of the two different types of variation in the next section.

Assignable and Natural Variation

Consider a process that consists of one machine and one operator and whose purpose is to drill a hole into a product. The exact size of the hole varies from one product to the next. Some of this variation can be traced to specific causes such as faulty setups, defective raw materials, tool wear, and poor training. These causes constitute **assignable variation.**

> **DEFINITION:** Assignable variation is the variation in a process that can be traced to specific causes.

After the variation resulting from assignable causes has been eliminated, variation will still be present. The source of this remaining variation is really a set of random factors. Individually, such random causes result in minute amounts of variation, but their joint interaction may lead to more substantial levels of variation. Examples of this **natural variation** include environmental changes (e.g., electrical fluctuations and changes in temperature and humidity) and the variation caused by the fitness of the technology and equipment being used.

> **DEFINITION:** Natural variation is the variation in a process that cannot be traced to specific causes.

Tracing and eliminating variation resulting from assignable causes can usually be done without major modifications to the equipment. This cannot be said for natural variation; in fact, totally eliminating such variation may be impossible.

Who is responsible for eliminating these two types of variation? The short answer is everyone. Deming suggests, though, that natural variation should be dealt with by management, and assignable variation by the workforce.

---

[3] For example, the product specifications for plastic tubing used for intravenous injections may state that the diameter must be 0.25 inch. A restaurant may specify that all customers must be served within five minutes of arrival.

The reasons for this are straightforward. Natural variation is a function of the process, and the only way to reduce it is to physically change the process. Strategic decisions requiring major technology investments are not normally delegated to operators, especially when major budgeting decisions are involved. Changes to the process may also require consequential changes in product design, materials, workforce skills, and job design. The implications of these changes make process replacement strategically sensitive.

Assignable variation occurs as a result of nonrandom change in a process. Those closest to the process are in the best position to recognize that variation is occurring. They also have the most intimate process knowledge and therefore can identify the cause of and then eliminate or reduce the assignable variation. For this to be successful, however, the workforce has to have training, authority, and confidence to act; otherwise little improvement or change will occur.

Reminder. When a number of processes can be improved, how does a firm decide *which* one to improve first? The answer is to improve the process that creates the biggest net positive gain for the customer. This may not be easy to identify at first, but with an improved understanding of the processes and customers, the task will get easier. The firm should, though, place some conditions on this statement: The benefit should be realized relatively quickly, result in *obvious* benefits to the customer, and fit in with the firm's long-term strategy. As pointed out in Chapter 3, making changes without reference to long-term objectives may erode a firm's core competency. This applies to the elimination of both assignable and natural causes of variation.

Process Improvement, People, and Total Quality Management

The definition of total quality management (TQM) in the Startup Chapter indicated that continuous process improvement is vital. Process improvement has been recognized as an important factor for many years. The way in which the improvement effort is organized and supported is important, and the next section will look at current practice. First let us briefly examine the philosophical underpinnings of process improvement organization and practice.

TQM may *seem* to be a relatively new concept, but its origins can be traced back more than 40 years to A. V. Feigenbaum and other noted American quality-control experts.[4] Feigenbaum (1983, p. 6) defined total quality control as "an effective system for integrating the quality-development, quality-maintenance, and quality-improvement efforts . . . so as to enable marketing, engineering, production, and service at the most economical levels which allow for full customer satisfaction."

Although Feigenbaum advocated the involvement of all departments in quality control, he assigned the central role to quality-control specialists. This view of quality control and management is still prevalent in many North American firms.

A much broader view of quality management, called *companywide quality control (CWQC)* by the Japanese, has emerged. The Japanese Industrial Standard Z8101-1981 defines quality control as "a system of means to economically produce goods or services which satisfy customers' requirements . . . [that] necessitates the cooperation of all people in the company, involving top management, managers, supervisors, and workers in all areas of corporate activity." Thus, everyone in the firm is

---

[4] W. Edwards Deming, Joseph Juran, and Philip Crosby, along with Feigenbaum, are the "big four" American masters of quality management.

involved in quality and every aspect of the value-added process is subject to quality improvement.

Ironically, the roots of CWQC can be traced back to an American, W. Edwards Deming. The U.S. government sent Deming to Japan in 1946 to assist in reindustrialization programs. Deming inspired the Japanese and sparked a quality revolution that is still thriving today. According to Deming's teachings, "quality is the predictable absence of error—a customer-oriented result achieved only when management decides to shake out the system-bound flaws in production, rather than blame employees for poor workmanship . . . this is a never ending process, continuous improvement, that will, in the long run, lower unit costs, improve productivity and, finally, profitability" [Loring (1990), p. 39]. Deming has condensed his philosophy into the 14 points outlined in Exhibit 11.3.

The implications of these new management philosophies regarding process improvement are important. Improvements are best made by people who have full knowledge of the effects and implications of the change. These people must have the authority to make the change; the support of superiors, subordinates, and peers; and a desire to improve continuously. The motivation for improvement must be supported by evaluation and reward systems that support success and accept, not penalize, improvement-motivated setbacks. With these necessary conditions in mind, let us look at how firms organize for continuous process improvement.

EXHIBIT 11.3   DEMING'S 14 QUALITY POINTS

Deming (1982) thinks that the following 14 points are essential to quality transformation in any organization in the service or manufacturing sector, regardless of its size.

1. Create constancy of purpose toward improvement of product and service, aiming to stay in business and provide jobs.

2. Adopt the new philosophy. This is a new economic age created by Japan. Transformation of the western style of management is necessary to halt the continued decline of industry.

3. Cease dependence on inspection to achieve quality. Eliminate the need for inspection on a mass basis by building quality into the product in the first place.

4. End the practice of awarding business on the basis of the price tag. Purchasing must be combined with design of the product, manufacturing, and sales, with the aim of minimizing total cost, not merely initial cost.

5. Improve constantly and forever every company activity that improves quality and productivity to constantly decrease costs.

6. Institute training and education on the job, including management.

7. Institute supervision. The aim of supervision should be to help people and machines and gadgets do a better job.

8. Drive out fear so that everyone may work effectively for the company.

9. Break down barriers between departments. People in research, design, sales, and production must work as a team to foresee problems in the production and use of the product or service.

10. Eliminate slogans, exhortations, and targets for the workforce that call for zero defects and new levels of productivity. Such exhortations only create adversarial relationships as the bulk of the causes of low quality and low productivity belong to the system and thus lie beyond the power of the workforce.

11. Eliminate work standards that prescribe numerical quotas for the day. Substitute aids and helpful supervision.

12a. Remove barriers that rob the hourly worker of his or her right of pride of workmanship. The responsibility of supervisors must be changed from sheer numbers to quality.

   b. Remove the barriers that rob people in management and engineering of their right of pride of workmanship. This means, among other things, abolishment of the annual or merit rating of management by objective and management by numbers.

13. Institute a vigorous program of education and retraining. New skills are required for changes in techniques, materials, and service.

14. Put everyone in the company to work in teams to accomplish the transformation.

The first step in eliminating variations is to get information about problems: what they are and where they are. It has been mentioned that because of their familiarity with the transformation process, shop floor employees can almost always identify causes for assignable variation and determine how to eliminate those problems. The important question, though, is what employees do with the information they collect. If this information is utilized properly, it can contribute significantly to the firm's continuous improvement efforts.

Consider Toyota Canada's plant in Cambridge, Ontario. Rather than hiring outside consultants to improve its production process, Toyota relies heavily on its employees to devise ways of doing their jobs more efficiently. In 1990 employee groups reduced total production time by 30 seconds per car while sustaining a high level of quality.

There are many different ways in which employees can be organized into groups and involved in process improvement efforts. The following sections will discuss two different types of employee groups: quality-control circles and superteams.

Quality-Control Circles

Quality-control (QC) circles originated in Japan as study groups in the early 1960s. The intent of these circles was to help shop floor workers learn and apply quality-control techniques. Facilitators trained the workers participating in the QC circles, ensured that things ran smoothly, and helped the workers present their proposals to management.

> **DEFINITION:** Quality-control circles are small groups of employees from the same work area who volunteer to meet regularly to discuss ways in which quality can be improved in their area.

QC circles in firms such as Toyota often generate thousands of suggestions, the majority of which are implemented. Cost savings have been measured in the millions of dollars.

In the United States the first formal use of QC circles was reported in 1974 at the Lockheed Missile and Space Co.'s plant in California. By the early 1980s QC circles could be found in over 90 percent of Fortune 500 companies. Initially, QC circles at many manufacturing and service sector firms were very successful. Unfortunately, this success was not sustained, and the vast majority of QC circles simply burned out.

This occurred because setting up QC circles does not magically improve a firm's operations. Ongoing management support and direction are essential to the success of QC circles, as is comprehensive training in problem-solving tools and techniques [Hart (1990)].

Without training and direction, workers find it difficult to select and solve problems. The training QC participants require, however, may be extensive. Hewlett-Packard, for example, found that most of its workers needed remedial education in mathematics before they could handle statistical calculations. Also, training in problem-solving tools must be supplemented with training in problem-solving methodologies.

The environment in which people work also must be considered. Companies just beginning to involve their workers in quality improvement programs may find that it takes years to overcome an adversarial relationship between labor and management. Some supervisors and managers may find it hard to solicit and accept ideas from their subordinates, especially when those ideas change the way in which they do their own work. If the ideas generated by a QC circle are not approved and implemented, the group's motivation tends to evaporate.

The composition of a QC circle is important as well. Initially, most groups in North American companies were composed of people from the same work area. Since people from downstream work areas were not included in the team, it was difficult for the team to identify ways in which they could improve quality. Unfortunately, it was easy for a team to slip into an "us versus them" mentality and consider its own well-being first. Teams therefore become gangs, with all the negative implications of that word.

Superteams

Today many North American firms are successfully implementing their own versions of QC circles: **superteams.**

> **DEFINITION: Superteams are small groups of self-managed employees that develop new ideas and concepts or deal with existing problems.**

As demonstrated in Exhibit 11.4, superteams can improve productivity dramatically. Like a QC circle, a superteam works on process and product improvements, but what distinguishes a superteam from a QC circle in North America is its ability to manage itself. A superteam arranges its own schedules, sets profit targets, orders material and equipment, has a say in hiring and firing team members, and in some cases devises strategy.[5]

Superteams are especially valuable when jobs are complex and highly interdependent. Product design is a good example; Chapter 5 discussed the advantages

---

[5] Refer back to Chapter 10 and you will notice that the superteam concept fits in well with the definition of a well-designed job.

EXHIBIT 11.4 SUPERTEAMS: EMPOWERING WORKERS

Superteams have been assembled in many North American firms, and half the 476 Fortune 1000 companies recently surveyed indicate that they will rely significantly more on superteams in the years ahead. As Corning CEO Jamie Houghton asserts, "If you really believe in quality, when you cut through everything, it's empowering your people, and it's empowering your people that leads to teams." Consider the following success stories:

- At a General Mills cereal plant in California superteams do almost everything middle management does elsewhere. The teams schedule, operate, and maintain machinery so effectively that the factory runs without managers during the night shift. Since teams have been introduced into the plant, productivity has risen 40 percent.
- Aetna Life & Casualty reduced its ratio of middle managers to workers from 1:7 to 1:30 *and* improved customer service after it organized its home office operations into superteams.
- Federal Express organized 1,000 clerical workers in Memphis into self-managing teams of 5 to 10 workers. These teams have helped Federal Express reduce service problems such as lost packages and incorrect bills by 13 percent. One team spotted and solved a billing problem that was costing the company over $2 million a year.
- A team of mill workers from Chaparral Steel traveled around the world evaluating new mill stands. The team chose a supplier and a particular model, negotiated the contracts, and then oversaw the installation. The mill stands, known as notoriously finicky pieces of machinery, worked as soon as they were turned on. The whole process, which can take as long as several years at other companies, took only one year.

Source: Adapted from Dumaine (1990), pp. 52–60.

associated with concurrent engineering and cross-functional design teams. When people from different jobs or functional areas work together on a project, the project tends to be completed much sooner and the quality of the work is often much higher.

On the shop floor superteams can be assembled temporarily to solve a specific problem or assembled on a permanent basis. As a permanent part of the workforce, they allow a firm to reduce the ratio of managers to workers. Fewer managers means less bureaucracy, and this improves the firm's ability to respond quickly; it also saves money. In most cases people on the shop floor find the additional responsibilities rewarding; this activates the "employee satisfaction ➤ employee retention ➤ customer retention" cycle. As employees become more satisfied with their jobs, they are less likely to quit or transfer to another area. Motivated, experienced, well-trained employees improve customer satisfaction and thus customer retention.[6] This is particularly important in service firms, where employees deal directly with customers.

11.5 PROCESS IMPROVEMENT TOOLS

A wide range of tools can be used by problem-solving teams to improve the transformation process. This section will present six of the "basic seven" quality improvement tools: flowcharts, check sheets, cause-and-effect diagrams, Pareto analysis, scatter diagrams, and histograms. These tools are simple and effective and are used extensively in practice. The seventh tool—the control chart—is more technical than the others and is described in detail in Section 11.6.

Process Flowcharts

Process flowcharts graphically represent the work performed on a product and the sequence in which it is performed. As was discussed in Chapter 10, process flowcharts help people understand and improve the process by highlighting operations that can be combined, simplified, reordered, or eliminated. Non-value-added activities become very visible. For example, a team at GE's Evendale, Ohio, plant developed several process maps to show how the manufacturing of a jet engine shaft can be improved. The original path reflected the plant's former emphasis on worker and machine efficiency. The team discovered that some of the existing practices actually hurt the efficiency of the plant's combined resources and accordingly suggested a revised path. The improved flow resulted in a 50 percent time savings, a $4 million drop in inventory, and a dramatic improvement in inventory turnover.

Check Sheets

Check sheets are used to record the occurrence of specific problems and the circumstances under which they occur. They can uncover problems, verify that a problem exists, determine the frequency of a problem, and provide insight into the possible causes of an observed problem.

The format of a check sheet differs depending on the type of data being collected. It may be a simple chart like the one illustrated in Exhibit 11.5 or a picture of the product that shows where defects occur and how frequently they occur.

Once a problem has been identified, its root cause or causes must be determined. Critical questioning and cause-and-effect diagrams are two helpful brainstorming techniques.

---

[6] Recall from Chapter 2 that it is more than six times more expensive to attract a new customer than to retain an existing one.

EXHIBIT 11.5 CHECK SHEETS

DAILY CHECK SHEET

Description: **Complaints for Product Line XXX**

Date: **12 January**   Telephone Representative: **W. Wheeland**

Type of Complaint	Tally	Subtotal
What's this charge?	＋＋＋＋ ＋＋＋＋ ＋＋＋＋ ＋＋＋＋ ⫼	23
Billing error	＋＋＋＋ ＋＋＋＋ ＋＋＋＋ ⫼	17
Where's my order?	＋＋＋＋ ＋＋＋＋	10
Shipping error	＋＋＋＋ ＋＋＋＋ ＋＋＋＋	15

Grand Total 118

Critical Questioning

When the root cause of a problem is not known, the **critical questioning** technique can be useful. It is a simple technique in which the problem-solving team asks why at least five times. For example, suppose a machine's motor habitually stops but no one knows what is causing the problem.

Question 1. Why did the motor stop?
Answer. There was an overload, and the fuse blew.
Question 2. Why was there an overload?
Answer. There wasn't enough lubrication on the shaft.
Question 3. Why wasn't there enough oil on the shaft?
Answer. The lubrication pump was not pumping at full volume.
Question 4. Why was the pump's output low?
Answer. The pump shaft was worn and rattling.
Question 5. Why was the shaft worn down?
Answer. There is no strainer in the oil fill tank, and metal shavings got mixed in with the oil.
Question 6. Why is there no strainer in the oil fill tank?
Answer. It was not designed to have a strainer.

After the team has asked why several times, the real cause of the problem becomes apparent: a flaw in the machine's design.

Cause-and-Effect Diagrams

Cause-and-effect diagrams are schematic representations of all the causes that contribute to a problem. As in critical questioning, these diagrams can help a problem-solving team determine the root cause of a problem. They are also good for organizing ideas, reducing costs, and shortening schedules.

Cause-and-effect diagrams are sometimes called fishbone diagrams, and the generic diagram in Exhibit 11.6A does resemble a fish skeleton. They are also referred to as Ishikawa diagrams, after their inventor.

The central spine of the diagram represents the principal problem. For example, in Exhibit 11.6B the principal problem is excess scrap. The main contributors to the problem are represented by the primary bones that radiate from the spine. As causes are more specifically defined, secondary and tertiary bones are added to the diagram.

Once the possible causes have been identified, Pareto analysis can help the team determine which causes to investigate further.

Pareto Analysis

Pareto analysis is a technique based on the Pareto principle of "the vital few and the trivial many." The Pareto principle is also called the 80-20 rule: approximately

EXHIBIT 11.6 CAUSE AND EFFECT DIAGRAMS

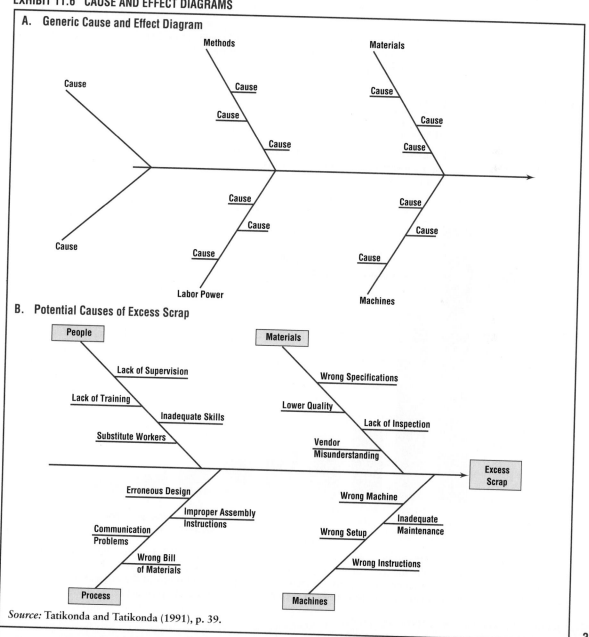

A. Generic Cause and Effect Diagram

B. Potential Causes of Excess Scrap

Source: Tatikonda and Tatikonda (1991), p. 39.

20 percent of a group of items, people, inventory, causes, and the like, accounts for approximately 80 percent of the worth, effort, problems, and so on.[7]

A **Pareto diagram** is a bar chart that illustrates the frequency of occurrence or the cost of a set of items. The items are shown in descending order of importance from left to right. By highlighting the most frequent or most costly items, Pareto diagrams can help a team focus its efforts. Exhibit 11.7 describes how one company used Pareto analysis (in conjunction with check sheets) to improve customer service.

Note that the most important or most visible problem is not always automatically targeted as the firm's first priority. A firm may choose to deal first with an issue of lower importance if it thinks it can resolve the issue quickly or with minimal resource utilization.

[7] This principle is based on Italian economist Vilfredo Pareto's (1848–1923) study of the distribution of wealth among various classes. This study revealed that roughly 20 percent of the people controlled 80 percent of the wealth.

EXHIBIT 11.7   PARETO ANALYSIS

Semantodontics sells dental products by catalog directly to dentists nationwide. When its major product line began to generate a larger than normal number of customer complaints, Semantodontics became concerned.

After reviewing the data compiled on daily check sheets by telephone representatives, the company organized the complaints into nine major categories. The number of calls corresponding to each category was then plotted on the Pareto diagram shown below.

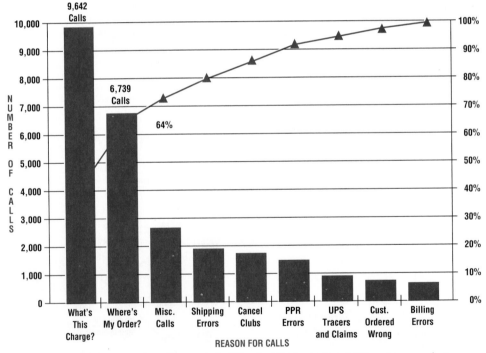

The company discovered that people calling to ask, What's this charge? and Where's my order? accounted for almost two-thirds of the calls logged. An investigation revealed that long production lead times meant that orders frequently appeared on a customer's invoice before the customer had received the order. Semantodontics solved this problem by applying just-in-time principles to drastically reduce the production lead time.

Source: Adapted from Conant (1988), pp. 34–37.

EXHIBIT 11.8   SCATTER DIAGRAM

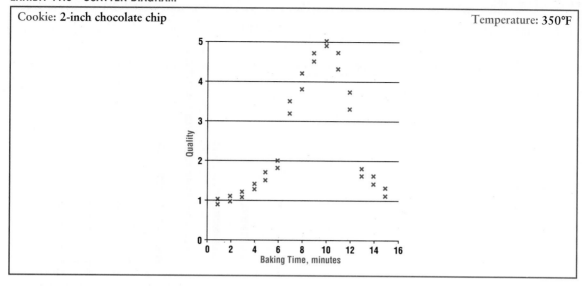

Cookie: 2-inch chocolate chip   Temperature: 350°F

Scatter Diagrams and Histograms

When investigating problems or potential process improvements, a team may suspect that there is a cause-and-effect relationship between two variables. This may call for some experimentation, and the group may decide to change one variable and note the changes in the other one. The results of this analysis can be plotted; one simple way to do this is with a **scatter diagram**. The scatter diagram in Exhibit 11.8 shows the relationship between baking time and cookie quality. This relationship can be examined further with statistical correlation analysis.

Histograms are bar graphs used to summarize and illustrate the variation in a set of data. Suppose a firm is interested in the width of a groove cut into wooden blocks and has taken 100 samples from the grooving operation. The observations range from 2 inches to $^{78}/_{100}$ of an inch. The observation range has been divided into eight intervals of equal size, and the number of observations recorded for each interval is shown in Exhibit 11.9A. This information is displayed graphically in the histogram in Exhibit 11.9B. Each vertical bar corresponds to a class interval, and the height of each bar indicates the frequency of observations in that interval.

Because histograms capture information visually, patterns and other clues about the parent population from which the sample was taken are relatively easy to identify.

11.6 STATISTICAL PROCESS CONTROL

The application of statistical techniques to the control of processes is referred to as **statistical process control (SPC)**. The **control chart** is a powerful SPC tool developed by Walter Shewhart of Bell Laboratories in the 1920s.[8] Its goal is to help differentiate between natural and assignable sources of variation in a process.

---

[8] The need to quicken and improve the inspection of urgently needed mass-produced products during World War II led to the spread of control charts and other statistically based control tools in the United States. After the war, however, American companies were swamped with pent-up demand and abandoned SPC tools in their quest to meet that demand. Ironically, it was the Japanese who adopted and implemented SPC in a systematic manner.

EXHIBIT 11.9   HISTOGRAMS

A. Data Collected from 100 Samples

Class Interval, hundredths of an inch	Class Midpoint	Number of Observations
0– 9.99	5	5
10–19.99	15	10
20–29.99	25	19
30–39.99	35	34
40–49.99	45	20
50–59.99	55	8
60–69.99	65	3
70–79.99	75	1

B. Frequency Histogram

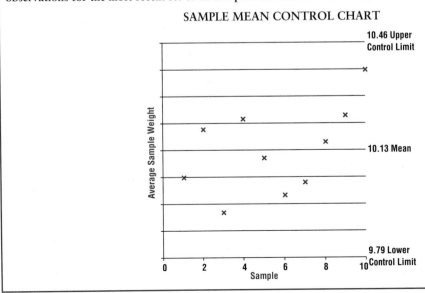

DEFINITION: Control charts are graphs that illustrate how a process performs over time with respect to a specific product characteristic and provide a statistical signal when assignable causes of variation are present.

The control chart in Exhibit 11.10, for example, is used to monitor a hopper that fills bags with potato chips. At predetermined time intervals five full bags are weighed. The average weight, the "sample mean," is plotted on the control chart.

EXHIBIT 11.10   SAMPLE MEAN CONTROL CHART

Potato chips are weighed and then placed in bags at the Grimm Potato Chip Company. Grimm monitors the weight of the chips its hopper places in bags by taking samples of five bags at predetermined time intervals. The observations for the most recent set of 10 samples are shown on the control chart below.

SAMPLE MEAN CONTROL CHART

If the sample means fall within the upper and lower control limits and if no discernible pattern is present, the process is **"statistically in control."** Otherwise, there is a high probability that assignable variation is present, and the cause of this variation should be investigated. Exhibit 11.11 shows several types of patterns.

The way in which control limits are set depends on the type of product characteristic under study. Control charts are used most often for **variable product characteristics,** that is, characteristics that are present in varying degrees. Examples include size, weight, and volume. The next section will examine control charts for variables. Afterward, control charts will be constructed for product characteristics that are **attributes.** These product characteristics are either present or absent or satisfactory or unsatisfactory. For example, a bottle may or may not have a cap, a plate of glass may or may not contain scratches, and a customer may or may not have been asked if he or she would like coffee and dessert after dinner.

The sampling scheme chosen influences the observed results and the chances of finding assignable causes. For example, suppose a process is fed by three preceding processes. The operator suspects that variation in this process can be traced back to differences between the parts produced by all of the preceding processes. In this case

EXHIBIT 11.11   DETECTING PATTERNS IN A CONTROL CHART

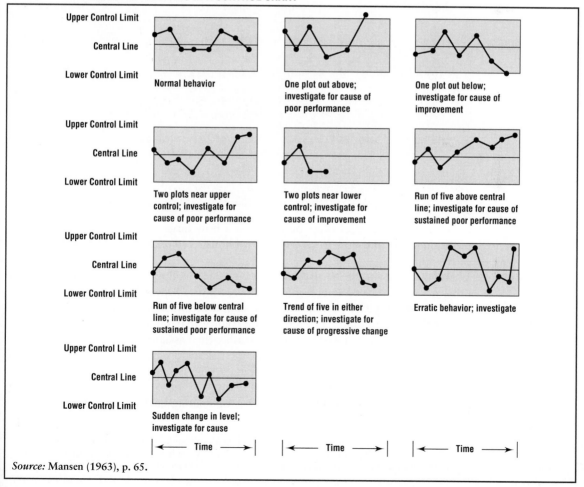

Source: Mansen (1963), p. 65.

each sample should contain parts produced by only one of the preceding processes. This segregation helps isolate differences in the quality of incoming parts.

Although the goal is to increase the chances of finding differences between samples, the chances of differences between individual products drawn for each sample should be minimized. If the products drawn for a sample have been produced under different conditions, the sample results will not be informative.

If an assignable cause is found, the process must be modified. Fresh samples are taken, and the charts are redrawn. The process may still be statistically out of control, however, and again potential sources of assignable variation must be investigated.

Control Charts for Variables

The control chart in Exhibit 11.10 is a **sample mean chart** that indicates changes in a central tendency. The last four average sample weights on the control chart in this exhibit are exhibiting an upward trend. In general, control chart trends may result from tool wear, gradual increases in temperature, or a new procedure.

The **center line** in a sample mean chart is usually the average of the sample means. If the standard deviation of the population is known, the standard deviation of the sampling distribution can be calculated by using equation (11.1). The **upper and lower control limits** can then be found by using equations (11.2) and (11.3).

Standard Deviation of the Sampling Distribution

$$\sigma_{\bar{x}} = \frac{\sigma_x}{\sqrt{n}} \tag{11.1}$$

Control Limits for the Sample Mean Chart (when $\sigma_{\bar{x}}$ is known)

$$\text{Upper control limit} = \bar{\bar{x}} + z\sigma_{\bar{x}} \tag{11.2}$$

$$\text{Lower control limit} = \bar{\bar{x}} - z\sigma_{\bar{x}} \tag{11.3}$$

where $\sigma_{\bar{x}}$ = standard deviation of sampling distribution
σ_x = standard deviation of population distribution
n = sample size
$\bar{\bar{x}}$ = mean of sample means
z = z score (number of normal standard deviations)

How many samples must be taken, and how large must each sample be? The traditional rule of thumb in setting control limits is to take 20 to 30 samples of four or five units.[9]

What value should be used for the z score? As illustrated in Exhibit 11.12, if only random variation is present, 95.5 percent of all the sample means should fall within $\pm 2\sigma_{\bar{x}}$ and 99.7 percent of all the sample means should fall within $\pm 3\sigma_{\bar{x}}$. The tighter the control limits, the higher the chance that sample observations that fall outside the limits are caused by random (rather than assignable) variation. Therefore, the tighter the control limits, the higher the risk of looking for assignable variation that does not exist (i.e., the risk of making a **type I error**). However, widening the control limits increases the risk of overlooking assignable variation (i.e., the risk of making a **type II error**). Hence, the cost of making each type of error must be

---

[9] Collecting this many preliminary observations is often a problem for firms that produce a wide variety of items in very small batches. Several techniques, such as combining observations of parts that require similar processing, can minimize this problem. See Evans and Hubele (1993) and Pyzdek (1993) for more information.

EXHIBIT 11.12   TOOLBOX: CONTROL CHARTS FOR VARIABLES

The most recent sample observations made by the Grimm Potato Chip Company are listed in the chart below. Past data indicate that the process variability is approximately normal and has a standard deviation of 0.25 ounce.

A. Sample Observations

Sample	Weight of Individual Observations, ounces					Average Sample Weight, $\bar{x}$	Sample Range, R
	1	2	3	4	5		
1	9.72	9.95	9.78	10.00	10.75	10.04	1.03
2	10.11	9.97	10.25	10.43	10.19	10.19	0.46
3	10.15	10.09	9.91	9.66	9.84	9.93	0.49
4	9.90	10.26	10.54	10.36	10.04	10.22	0.64
5	9.91	10.10	10.09	10.15	10.25	10.10	0.34
6	10.26	9.63	10.15	10.20	9.68	9.984	0.63
7	9.78	9.91	10.20	10.44	9.79	10.024	0.66
8	10.15	10.02	10.37	10.03	10.18	10.15	0.35
9	10.47	10.20	9.97	10.15	10.37	10.232	0.50
10	10.33	10.38	10.44	10.51	10.24	10.38	0.27
Average of the sample averages ($\bar{\bar{x}}$)						10.125	
Average of the sample ranges ($\bar{R}$)							0.537

CONTROL LIMITS FOR THE SAMPLE MEAN CHART

Given a sample size of five bags and the historical standard deviation of 0.25 ounce, the control limits for a sample mean chart were calculated as follows:

Using equation (11.2),

$$\sigma_{\bar{x}} = \frac{\sigma_x}{\sqrt{n}} = \frac{0.25}{\sqrt{5}} = 0.1118$$

The control limits were set at $\pm 3\sigma_{\bar{x}}$. As illustrated below, 99.7 percent of all $\bar{x}$ should fall within these limits.

STANDARDIZED NORMAL DISTRIBUTION

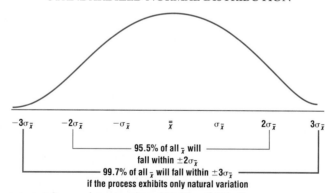

If the control limits are set at $\pm 3\sigma_{\bar{x}}$, using equations (11.3) and (11.4),

Upper control limit (UCL): $\bar{\bar{x}} + z\sigma_{\bar{x}} = 10.125 + 3(0.1118) = 10.4604$

Lower control limit (LCL): $\bar{\bar{x}} - z\sigma_{\bar{x}} = 10.125 - 3(0.1118) = 9.7896$

If the standard deviation of the process was not known, Grimm could have set its control limits using equations (11.5) and (11.6). The value of A_2 is a function of the size of each sample and can be found by using the chart below.

Upper control limit (UCL): $\bar{\bar{x}} + A_2\bar{R} = 10.125 + (0.577)(0.537) = 10.4348$

Lower control limit (LCL): $\bar{\bar{x}} + A_2\bar{R} = 10.125 - (0.577)(0.537) = 9.8152$

(Exhibit 11.12 continues on next page)

EXHIBIT 11.12   *(continued)*

B. Factors for Computing Control Chart Limits

Sample Size, n	A_2	D_3	D_4
2	1.880	0	3.268
3	1.023	0	2.574
4	0.729	0	2.282
5	0.577	0	2.114
6	0.483	0	2.004
7	0.419	0.076	1.924
8	0.373	0.136	1.864
9	0.337	0.184	1.816
10	0.308	0.223	1.777

CONTROL LIMITS FOR THE SAMPLE RANGE CHART

Using equations (11.6) and (11.7),

Upper control limit (UCL): $\qquad\qquad\qquad D_4\overline{R} = (2.114)(0.537) = 1.1352$

Lower control limit (LCL): $\qquad\qquad\qquad D_3\overline{R} = (0)(0.537) = 0$

The values of D_3 and D_4 are also a function of the size of each sample and can be found using the chart above.

C. Sample Range Chart

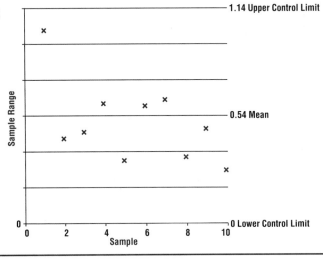

compared. If the cost of making a type I error is relatively low, it is more appropriate to set the control limits at ± 2 standard deviations than at ± 3 standard deviations.

If the standard deviation of the process is not known or is difficult to calculate, equations (11.4) and (11.5) can be used to set the upper and lower control limits. Note that these equations set the control limits at ± 3 standard deviations.

Control Limits for the Sample Mean Chart (when $\sigma_{\overline{x}}$ is unknown)

$$\text{Upper control limit: } \overline{\overline{x}} + A_2\overline{R} \qquad (11.4)$$
$$\text{Lower control limit: } \overline{\overline{x}} - A_2\overline{R} \qquad (11.5)$$

where $\overline{\overline{x}}$ = mean of sample means
$\quad\ \ \overline{R}$ = average range of samples

A_2 refers to the value obtained from the table in Exhibit 11.12B.

Significant changes in process uniformity can be identified with a **sample range control chart.** Possible causes of a loss of uniformity include a loose tool post, variability in the material used, and lack of concentration by the operator.

The sample range is the diffrence between the highest and lowest weights recorded for the sample and is plotted on the range control chart. The control limits can be set at ± 3 standard deviations using equations (11.6) and (11.7).

Control Limits for the Sample Range Chart

$$\text{Upper control limit: } D_4\overline{R} \tag{11.6}$$
$$\text{Lower control limit: } D_3\overline{R} \tag{11.7}$$

where $\overline{R}$ = average range of the samples

D_3 and D_4 are values obtained from the tables in Exhibit 11.12B.

Control Charts for Attributes: The p Chart

Control charts can also be drawn for product characteristics that are attributes. A **p chart** is used to monitor the percentage of defective units generated by a process. To use the p chart, it must be possible to count the number of defective and non-defective units. The Rochmer Insurance Company, for example, uses a p chart to monitor the quality of the policies issued by its automobile underwriting department (see Exhibit 11.13). P∗I∗E Nationwide (see Exhibit 11.2) used a p chart to track the proportion of freight bills that were defective.

The binomial distribution is the basis of the p chart because units are either defective or not defective. The upper and lower control limits are then set by using equations (11.8) and (11.9).

Control Limits for the p Chart

$$\text{Upper control limit: } p + z\sigma_{\overline{p}} \tag{11.8}$$
$$\text{Lower control limit: } p - z\sigma_{\overline{p}} \tag{11.9}$$

If p is not known, $\overline{p}$ can be used in its place:

$$\overline{p} = \frac{\sum_{i=1}^{m} d_i}{nm} \tag{11.10}$$

$\sigma_{\overline{p}}$ can be estimated using equation (11.11):

$$\sigma_{\overline{p}} = \sqrt{\frac{\overline{p}(1 - \overline{p})}{n}} \tag{11.11}$$

where p = average percentage defective for the process
z = z score (number of normal standard deviations)
$\sigma_{\overline{p}}$ = standard deviation of sampling distribution
$\overline{p}$ = average percentage defective in sample
d_i = number of defective units found in sample i
n = sample size
m = number of samples taken

347

EXHIBIT 11.13 TOOLBOX: CONTROL CHARTS FOR ATTRIBUTES (P CHARTS)

The Rochmer Insurance Company is monitoring the percentage of automobile policies issued with an incorrect rating classification. The results of 30 samples are shown below. Each sample consisted of 100 policies.

NUMBER OF DEFECTIVE POLICIES FOUND IN EACH SAMPLE

Sample	Number of Defectives	Sample	Number of Defectives	Sample	Number of Defectives
1	1	11	5	21	9
2	4	12	6	22	7
3	8	13	5	23	10
4	2	14	6	24	7
5	5	15	6	25	5
6	5	16	8	26	6
7	3	17	7	27	7
8	7	18	6	28	5
9	6	19	7	29	6
10	4	20	8	30	4

Total number of defective policies: 175

Average percentage defective in sample:

$$\bar{p} = \frac{\sum_{i=1}^{n} d_i}{nm} = \frac{175}{(100)(30)} = 0.0583$$

Standard deviation of the sampling distribution:

$$\sigma_{\bar{p}} = \sqrt{\frac{\bar{p}(1 - \bar{p})}{n}} = \sqrt{\frac{(0.0583)(1 - 0.0583)}{100}} = 0.0234$$

If the control limits are set at $\pm 3\sigma_{\bar{x}}$,

Upper control limit: $\qquad\qquad \bar{p} + 3\sigma_p = 0.0583 + 3(0.0234) = 0.1285$

Lower control limit: $\qquad\qquad \bar{p} - 3\sigma_p = 0.0583 - 3(0.0234) = -0.0119$

Since the lowest possible percentage defective is 0, the lower control limit is 0.

CONTROL CHART

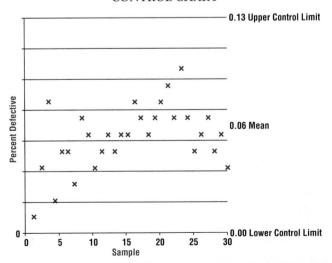

The sample size for attributes is usually much larger than the sample size for variables; it must be large enough to find at least one error in the sample. For example, if the process is in control and the estimated number of defective units is about 1 in every 200, the sample size must be at least 200 units.[10]

Control Charts for Attributes: The c Chart

A **c chart** is appropriate when a firm is interested in the number of defects per unit. The underlying distribution for the c chart is derived from the Poisson distribution, and the control limits are calculated using equations (11.12) and (11.13). As with a p chart, the sample size chosen must be large enough to catch at least one defect per unit or per area examined.

Control Limits for c Charts

$$\text{Upper control limit} = c + z\sqrt{c} \qquad (11.12)$$

$$\text{Lower control limit} = c - z\sqrt{c} \qquad (11.13)$$

If c is not known, $\bar{c}$ can be used in its place:

$$\bar{c} = \frac{\sum_{i=1}^{m} d_i}{m} \qquad (11.14)$$

where c = average number of defects for process
$\quad z$ = z score (number of normal standard deviations)
$\quad \bar{c}$ = average number of defects in sample
$\quad d_i$ = number of defects found in sample i
$\quad m$ = number of samples taken

Exhibit 11.14 describes how the Daiklen Glass Company uses a control chart to monitor the quality of glass tabletops.

Process Capability

The upper and lower control limits used in process control charts are frequently confused with the tolerance intervals set out in product specifications. For example, a product designer may specify that a plastic tube be 6 inches in diameter ± 0.15 inch. The target value is 6 inches, the lower tolerance limit is 5.85 inches, and the upper tolerance limit is 6.15 inches. *These tolerance limits are not the same as the upper and lower limits drawn on control charts.*

Remember that upper and lower control limits refer to the sample averages for a process or piece of equipment. If the process is statistically in control, only natural variation is present. However, the process still may not be able to meet the product's target specifications.

DEFINITION: The *process capability* of a process that is statistically in control is equal to its range of random variation, i.e., six standard deviations of its average value.

[10] As the percentage defective for an in-control process approaches zero, the sample size increases until it is close to or equal to the lot size.

EXHIBIT 11.14   TOOLBOX: CONTROL CHARTS FOR ATTRIBUTES (C CHARTS)

The Daiklen Glass Company is monitoring the number of scratches on its glass tabletops. The results of 20 samples are shown below.

NUMBER OF SCRATCHES FOUND ON EACH SAMPLE

Sample	Number of Scratches	Sample	Number of Scratches
1	1	11	2
2	0	12	1
3	3	13	5
4	4	14	1
5	2	15	3
6	2	16	4
7	2	17	3
8	4	18	5
9	2	19	3
10	6	20	1

Total number of scratches: 54

Average number of scratches in sample:

$$\bar{c} = \frac{\sum_{i=1}^{m} d_i}{m} = \frac{54}{20} = 2.7$$

If the control limits are set at $\pm 3\sigma_{\bar{x}}$,

Upper control limit (UCL): $\qquad c + 3\sqrt{c} = 2.7 + 3\sqrt{2.7} = 7.6295$

Lower control limit (LCL): $\qquad c - 3\sqrt{c} = 2.7 - 3\sqrt{2.7} = 2.2295$

Since the lowest possible number of defects is 0, the lower control limit is 0.

CONTROL CHART

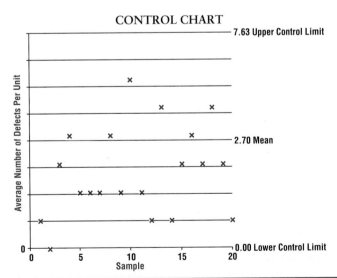

In general, if the limits of the process capability fit within the product's specification limits, the process is said to be capable. The capability of a process *with respect to a particular tolerance interval* can be measured by using the **capability index** given by equation (11.15). Alternatively, equation (11.16), which considers the process mean as well as the process range, can be used. In practice, this is the preferred index in the automobile industry.

Capability Index

$$C_p = \frac{UTL - LTL}{6\sigma_x} \qquad (11.15)$$

$$C_{pk} = \min\left(\frac{UTL - \mu}{3\sigma_x}, \frac{\mu - LTL}{3\sigma_x}\right) \qquad (11.16)$$

where C_p, C_{pk} = capability index
  UTL = upper tolerance limit
  LTL = lower tolerance limit
  σ_x = standard deviation of process
  μ = process mean

If C_p (or C_{pk}) ≥ 1, the process is capable.[11]
If C_p (or C_{pk}) < 1, the process is not capable.

Since a process's capability can be changed only through major modifications, the capability of an existing process must be known before it is chosen to produce a new or revised product. The examples in Exhibit 11.15 demonstrate how the capability index can be used to select a suitable process.

> **Reminder.** Ensuring that the process is capable and statistically in control does not ensure that product quality is perfect. A firm should strive to reduce variation around target values.

Continued efforts to improve the process lead to tighter and tighter control limits, effectively increasing the process's capability index. Eventually the firm reaches a point at which the capability index is very high and control charts are no longer necessary. Even in this case the firm has not reached the limits of process quality. Process quality can still be improved by preventing problems from occurring.

Motorola has formalized this objective in its "Six Sigma" campaign, aiming at defect rates of less than 3.4 parts per million. When suppliers can reach Motorola's standards, there are cost savings to both parties, as quality assurance and statistical process control cost both supplier and customer. And Motorola is not alone in setting extremely high standards—and reaping the benefits. Hewlett Packard and Baxter are two other companies whose primary facilities in Singapore have such high process capability that SPC is meaningless for table processes. This does not mean that SPC is never used; on the contrary, each time a process is changed or adjusted, SPC is strictly practiced until the required process capability is achieved.

---

[11] Some firms consider the process to be *barely capable* if $1 < C_p$ (or C_{pk}) ≤ 1.33 and *capable* if C_p (or C_{pk}) > 1.33. If fewer than 50 observations are used to determine the capability, the capability indexes can be modified by using $4\sigma_x$ instead of $3\sigma_x$ and a minimum acceptable C_p (or C_{pk}) of 1.5.

EXHIBIT 11.15   TOOLBOX: PROCESS CAPABILITY

The plastic tube used in one of Waldroff Inc.'s newest products must be 6 ± 0.15 inches in diameter. Which of the following processes can meet this specification?

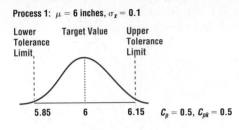

Process 1: $\mu = 6$ inches, $\sigma_x = 0.1$

Lower Tolerance Limit   Target Value   Upper Tolerance Limit

5.85   6   6.15 $C_p = 0.5$, $C_{pk} = 0.5$

This process is not capable. Its range of natural variation is wider than the tolerance interval. It would be almost impossible for the process to meet the product specifications.

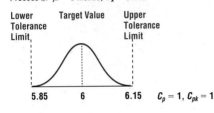

Process 2: $\mu = 6$ inches, $\sigma_x = 0.005$

Lower Tolerance Limit   Target Value   Upper Tolerance Limit

5.85   6   6.15 $C_p = 1$, $C_{pk} = 1$

The range of natural variation exhibited by process 2 is exactly the same as the product's tolerance interval. A very small percentage of values will fall outside the tolerance interval. The process is barely capable.

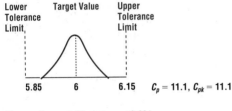

Process 3: $\mu = 6$ inches, $\sigma_x = 0.0045$

Lower Tolerance Limit   Target Value   Upper Tolerance Limit

5.85   6   6.15 $C_p = 11.1$, $C_{pk} = 11.1$

The range of natural variation is narrower than the product's tolerance interval. The process is capable.

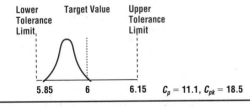

Process 4: $\mu = 5.9$ inches, $\sigma_x = 0.004$

Lower Tolerance Limit   Target Value   Upper Tolerance Limit

5.85   6   6.15 $C_p = 11.1$, $C_{pk} = 18.5$

The process is capable. But because the process mean is not equal to the target value, it is not as suitable as process 3. Of course, if the mean could be moved to 6 inches, this process would be superior.

11.7 PROBLEM PREVENTION

Eventually, through process change and/or continued process improvement, a company reaches the point at which process variation is so limited that even control charts are no longer required. Problem prevention then becomes the focus of the company's continuous efforts to improve its transformation process. For FROs, the way to improve the quality level is to eliminate the defects through prevention rather than continuing to rework the data [Boteler (1993)].

One way to prevent product defects is to use foolproof mechanisms that make it impossible to perform an operation incorrectly. If an operation does not lend itself to fail-safing, the firm can modify the process so that quality problems are detected at the source at a very low cost.

Foolproof Mechanisms (Poka-Yoke)

Applications of **foolproof mechanisms (poka-yoke)**[12] can be as simple as modifying a machine so that it will operate only if parts are inserted correctly. Adding a device to a drilling machine that counts the number of holes drilled into a part and buzzes if the part is removed before the correct number has been drilled is another example of poka-yoke. A combination of optical scanners and bar codes at the supermarket can nearly eliminate cash register keying errors. Including self-addressed, stamped envelopes with customer invoices reduces the chance of customers incorrectly addressing envelopes or forgetting to put a stamp on the envelope.

Autonomation

Autonomation[13] is a strategy for detecting and correcting production problems. It involves two mechanisms: one that detects abnormalities or defects and one that automatically stops the machine or process when a defect or abnormality is detected.

Machines can be designed to recognize abnormalities or defects and stop automatically when one is found. As a result, machines can run unattended and workers can perform other duties. Consider, for example, photocopiers that will automatically stop and tell the user what the problem is and how to correct it.

Human judgment also can be used to identify a problem and stop production. At Toyota Canada's Cambridge plant in Ontario, for example, each line worker has the authority to stop the line if a product defect is found. When the line stops, a bell sounds throughout the plant and a board suspended from the ceiling indicates the source of the problem. The line does not start again until the worker and his or her teammates have corrected the problem. Idled workers also can use the time to do maintenance or housekeeping work in their areas.

Lights, boards, or bells that indicate that the production process has been stopped by a worker are referred to as **andon.** They are examples of the visual controls often used when a firm is implementing autonomation.

Production control boards are also common visual control tools. They show the production schedule for the day and the actual production that has taken place. The board is updated throughout the day and makes any discrepancies immediately visible to everyone. The more immediate the feedback is, the smaller most problems will be and the more immediate and effective any corrective action will be.

Housekeeping

Good **housekeeping** practices can lead to early problem identification or prevention. Clean floors and equipment surfaces, for example, expose problems such as oil leaks and cracks quickly. Clean, well-tended machines also last longer and break down less frequently. Removing tools and materials that are no longer required makes the shop floor less cluttered and saves space. Moving parts and materials becomes much easier, and the danger of personal injury is reduced. Organizing tools so that those used most frequently are closest saves time. If tools are clearly organized, it is easy to see when one is missing. An organized work area also minimizes unnecessary reaching, bending, and fatigue.

---

[12] Poka-yoke techniques were developed and refined by the late Shingeo Shingo, who also developed the Toyota production system.

[13] The term *autonomation* was coined by Toyota.

These housekeeping principles can be summarized as (1) a place for everything, (2) everything in its place, (3) everything visible, and (4) everyone involved in cleaning, checking for damage, and anticipating problems.

The key to housekeeping is that it should be the responsibility of the shop floor workers and their immediate supervisors and should be heavily influenced by them.

Total Productive Maintenance

Good housekeeping practices are part of a proactive approach to equipment maintenance called **total productive maintenance (TPM)**. TPM represents a radical departure from a "fix it when it breaks" approach.

> **DEFINITION:** Total productive maintenance is a low-cost people-intensive system for maximizing equipment effectiveness by involving the entire company in a preventive maintenance program.[14]

TPM transfers the primary responsibility for maintaining equipment to the workers who operate the equipment. When fully trained, operators are expected to:

- Understand how their machines operate and be aware of telltale signs of imminent failure.
- Perform all routine preventive maintenance (e.g., lubrication, bolt tightening, cleaning).
- Inspect their machines daily. This allows operators to quickly identify and make necessary adjustments. This type of condition-based maintenance is sometimes referred to as *predictive maintenance*.
- Regularly clean their machines.
- Handle all basic repairs.

How often should routine preventive maintenance be done on a piece of equipment? It depends on the cost of maintenance, the expected cost of unexpected equipment failure, and the reliability of the machine. Exhibit 11.16 illustrates one way in which a minimum-cost maintenance policy can be found.

A TPM system cannot eliminate the need for maintenance workers. These workers will still be needed to train operators and help solve major equipment problems. They will also be expected to work with operators to identify and implement modifications that will improve equipment performance. *The goal of TPM is not only to keep processes operational but also to improve them continuously.*

A key measure of equipment performance is given by equation (11.17). Values in the range of 25 to 35 percent are common for average American plants, but firms using TPM report effectiveness values over 85 percent.[15] In addition to improved equipment effectiveness, TPM prolongs machine life and can lead to substantial savings in capital investments.

Equipment Effectiveness

$$\text{Equipment effectiveness} = \text{Machine availability} \times \text{Performance efficiency} \times \text{Rate of quality} \quad (11.17)$$

$$= \frac{PT - DT}{PT} \times \frac{TCT}{ACT} \times \frac{QP - D}{QP}$$

---

[14] This definition is based on Rodriguez (1990), p. 152.

[15] See Rodriguez (1990), p. 156.

EXHIBIT 11.16   TOOLBOX: SELECTING A MINIMUM-COST MAINTENANCE POLICY

Drayton Manufacturing Company (DMC) operates two eight-hour shifts per day, 360 days per year. In the past DMC adjusted and repaired its machines only when they failed. This policy is being revised; in the future all machines will be inspected and adjusted at regular intervals.

DEVELOPING A MAINTENANCE POLICY FOR A SPECIFIC MACHINE

Past data for one of DMC's machines indicate that it breaks down at least once every six shifts.

Hours between Failures	Probability
0–24	0.0
25–32	0.3
33–40	0.45
41–48	0.25

On average, each time the machine breaks down, emergency repairs costing about $42 are needed. The cost of inspecting and adjusting the machine is estimated to be about $10.

How often should a machine be inspected and adjusted? The table below shows the total cost associated with various maintenance intervals. For example, suppose the machine is inspected at the beginning of every fourth shift (every 32 hours). Only 180 inspections will be performed annually, at a cost of $1,800. The probability of failure will be 0.3, which translates into 54 expected failures per year. At a cost of $42 per failure, the annual failure cost is $2,268. The total cost associated with this maintenance interval is $1,800 + $2,268 = $4,068.

	Inspections		Failures			
(1) Maintenance Interval Once Every	(2) Number per Year	(3) Cost per Year, $	(4) Probability of Failure during Each Maintenance Interval	(5) Expected Number per Year	(6) Cost per Year, $	(7) Combined Cost, $
Shift (8 hours)	720	7,200	0.0	0	0	7,200
Second shift (16 hours)	360	3,600	0.0	0	0	3,600
Third shift (24 hours)	240	2,400	0.0	0	0	2,400
Fourth shift (32 hours)	180	1,800	0.3	54	2,268	4,068
Fifth shift (40 hours)	144	1,440	0.3 + 0.45 = 0.75	108	4,536	5,976
Sixth shift (48 hours)	120	1,200	0.3 + 0.45 + 0.25 = 1	120	5,040	6,240

Note: Column 3 = column 2 × $10.   Column 6 = column 5 × $42.
　　　Column 5 = column 2 × column 4.   Column 7 = column 3 + column 6.

The lowest-cost maintenance policy is to inspect this machine once every third shift.

where PT = planned time
　　 DT = downtime
　 TCT = theoretical cycle time (process time + extremely short setup times)
　 ACT = actual cycle time
　　 QP = quantity processed
　　　D = number of defects

Many Japanese and American companies are improving the effectiveness of their equipment by designing and manufacturing it themselves. This allows a firm to design equipment to meet its own needs and continually incorporate feedback from equipment operators and maintenance personnel.

TPM does create many time-consuming activities. Maintenance policies for each machine must be developed, preventive maintenance must be scheduled, spare parts inventories must be controlled, and machine operators must be trained. There are many potentially useful software tools available, however, to support these activities.

Ideally, a firm should inspect product samples to learn something about the operating *process*, not to make inferences about a batch of the product. The assumption ought to be that product that does not meet design specifications has been produced by an incorrect process. If the process is not operating as designed, it must be corrected. This means that inspection should be carried out as soon as possible after the process so that the amount of rework or scrapping of incorrect product is as small as possible. Inevitably this means sampling during many stages in the production process. The more confident a firm is about the stability of the process, the less it needs to sample. Managers should work with smaller sample sizes rather than reduce the frequency of sampling when they consider reducing the amount of inspection done.

If the process is operating as designed, thought should be given to improving the process further by eliminating variation among the individual items produced. This requires a very good undertanding of the product, the process, and the relationship between the two. Often, the best information is held by the process operators, and work should be or-ganized so that managers can make use of the knowledge and creativity of the whole workforce.

The seven basic problem-solving, or process improvement, tools can be used to solve over 85 percent of the variability problems or challenges faced by a firm and can be applied with great effectiveness by shop floor workers. Problem-solving teams consisting of line operators and representatives of all affected groups will be able to solve most of the variability for which a cause can be determined and provide valuable insights into problems which require more specialized training. Ideally, problems should be eliminated by foolproofing the process. Where this is not possible, inspection must be maintained. Again, the ideal people to conduct the inspections and investigations are the people closest to the process: the operators.

All that is required is to recognize the worth of the line operator as a thinking being and then provide appropriate training and encouragement. This is the key to an FRO: the utilization of all knowledge assets to their fullest in pursuit of ever-increasing effectiveness and efficiency.

CHAPTER SUMMARY

Process control and improvement tools were the focus of this chapter. Key points to remember from this chapter include the following:

- Acceptance sampling is the evaluation of one or more random samples drawn from a group of items; the entire group is accepted or rejected on the basis of the sample. Acceptance sampling is the traditional approach to quality control.
- There are risks associated with acceptance sampling. A good lot may be rejected, or a bad lot may be accepted. Before a sampling plan can be chosen, the producer and consumer must agree on acceptable levels of each type of risk.
- There are two categories of sampling plans: those for variable product characteristics and those for product characteristics that are attributes. Single or multiple sampling plans can be developed for each category.
- The operating characteristic curve illustrates the ability of a sampling plan to discriminate between good and bad lots. Sampling plans can also be evaluated on the basis of their average outgoing quality.
- Acceptance sampling is becoming less appropriate as a result of (1) the high cost associated with poor quality in today's competitive marketplace, (2) the trend toward very small lot sizes, and (3) the expression of acceptable quality limits in parts per million.
- Minimizing variation around target values leads to improved quality. Natural variation is random and extremely difficult to eliminate. Assignable variation, however, can be traced to specific causes. Control charts can provide a statistical signal when assignable causes of variation are present.

- Quality-control circles are small groups of workers from the same work area who meet regularly to discuss ways to improve quality in their work area.
- Superteams are small groups of employees who work together and manage themselves. They can be assembled temporarily to develop a new product or solve a particular problem or can be a permanent part of the workforce.
- Process flowcharts, check sheets, critical questioning, cause-and-effect diagrams, Pareto analysis, scatter diagrams, histograms, and control charts are problem-solving tools and techniques.
- After obvious quality-control problems have been solved, control charts can be used to identify less obvious problems.
- Control charts are graphs that illustrate how a process performs over time with respect to a specific product characteristic. Samples are taken periodically. If the sample weights fall within the upper and lower control limits and if no discernible pattern is present, the process is "statistically in control." Otherwise, there is a very high probability that assignable variation is present, and the cause of this variation should be investigated.
- Control limits are set using past data and a set of equations. The equations used depend on the type of control chart being drawn. Sample mean and range charts are used for variable product characteristics. The p chart is used to monitor the percentage of defective units generated by a process. The c chart is appropriate when a firm is interested in the number of defects per unit.
- The capability of a process that is statistically in control is equal to its range of random variation, that is, six standard deviations from its average value. The capability index measures the capability of a process with respect to a particular tolerance interval.
- Foolproof mechanisms (poka-yoke) are used to prevent errors from occurring. Autonomation is a strategy for detecting and correcting production problems. Andon lights and production control boards are examples of visual control tools used for implementing autonomation.
- Good housekeeping can reduce operating costs, expose problems, and improve worker safety.
- Total productive maintenance (TPM) transfers the primary responsibility for maintaining equipment to the workers who operate the equipment. The goal is to continually improve the production process. Benefits include prolonged machine life, lower production costs, higher product quality, and more stable shop floor operations.

KEY TERMS

Process quality	Critical questioning	Attribute	Process capability
Acceptance sampling	Cause-and-effect diagram	Sample mean chart	Capability index
Acceptable quality level (AQL)	Pareto analysis	Center line	Foolproof mechanisms (poka-yoke)
	Pareto diagram	Upper control limit	
Lot tolerance percent defective (LTPD)	Scatter diagram	Lower control limit	Autonomation
	Histogram	Type I error	Andon
Assignable variation	Statistical process control (SPC)	Type II error	Production control boards
Natural variation		Sample range control chart	
Quality-control (QC) circles	Control chart		Housekeeping
	Statistically in control	p chart	Total productive maintenance (TPM)
Superteams	Variable product characteristic	c chart	
Process flowchart			
Check sheets			

DISCUSSION QUESTIONS

1. What *is* quality control?

2. How has people's thinking about quality control changed over the last 30 years? What does this imply for operating managers?

3. Under what conditions would a multiple sampling plan be desirable? (Refer to the supplement to this chapter to answer this question.)

4. What is the most desirable sample size? Under what conditions? (Refer to the supplement to this chapter to answer this question.)

5. What *is* a sampling plan? How is one determined? (Refer to the supplement to this chapter to answer this question.)

6. How do variables and attributes differ from each other?

7. What is SPC? What is its focus?

8. How is the capability of a process determined? What is process capability?

9. How are the control limits for control charts established?

10. For the following processes, what critical characteristics *could* you measure? How *would* you measure them?
    a. Serving meals on an aircraft
    b. Operating a taxi

   c. Teaching a class
   d. Doing open-heart surgery
   e. Processing insurance claims

11. How does a firm know when a process is out of control? What should it do?

12. What would happen if the control limits in Exhibit 11.13 were set at ± 2 standard deviations from the mean of the sample means instead of ± 3 standard deviations? What if they were set at ± 1 standard deviation? Where would *you* set the control limits and why?

13. Why is housekeeping important?

14. How would you go about improving the performance of a bank teller?

15. What would you do to foolproof the following?
    a. Processing insurance claims
    b. Operating a supermarket checkout
    c. Telephone operator service
    d. Medical diagnosis
    e. Weather forecasting

16. Who should be responsible for controlling and managing the improvement process?

17. What are quality-control circles? How should they be organized?

PROBLEMS

1. ■ Brawer Ltd. manufactures bicycles. Currently all bicycles are inspected once they have been fully assembled. Ed Lawdoon, the production manager, is wondering if the frames should be inspected after they are welded together but before they are painted. A defective frame cannot be repaired; the cost of replacing it at this stage is $10. The cost of replacing a defective frame once the bicycle has been fully assembled is $15. Should the factory continue the current inspection if the actual percentage of defective frame is 1 percent? What if it is 3 percent? (Refer to the supplement to this chapter to solve this problem.)

2. ■ Kape City Inc. inspects random samples of its circuits before they are shipped to its customers. Each lot contains 6,000 circuits.
   a. Construct OC curves for the following sampling plans: (1) sample size = 150, acceptance num-

ber = 1; (2) sample size = 150, acceptance number = 3; (3) sample size = 100, acceptance number = 1.
   b. Suppose the entire lot is inspected if the number of defective circuits found is greater than the acceptance number. All defective circuits are replaced. What is the average outgoing quality if the sample size is 150 and the acceptance number is one? If the sample size is 100 and the acceptance number is one?
   c. Draw the average outgoing quality curve for the sampling plans described in part *b*. (Refer to the supplement to this chapter to solve this problem.)

3. Jerry Kamp Inc. purchases wine contained in two-gallon bottles from the local winery. Past records indicate that the volume of wine in each bottle is normally distributed with a standard deviation of

0.007 gallon. Both Jerry Kamp Inc. and the winery have agreed that the probability of accepting a good-quality lot (i.e., a lot whose average weight is at least two gallons) should be no less than 95 percent and that the probability of accepting lots with bad quality (i.e., a lot whose average weight is 1.9 gallons) should be no more than 10 percent. Develop a sampling plan for Jerry Kamp Inc. (Refer to the supplement to this chapter to solve this problem.)

4. 💾 The Happy Wanderer Travel Agency is monitoring the percentage of packaged holiday trips that contain errors. The results of 14 samples are shown below. Each sample contains 70 items.

Sample	Number of Defective Units	Sample	Number of Defective Units
1	6	8	7
2	5	9	3
3	7	10	5
4	5	11	7
5	6	12	2
6	4	13	3
7	5	14	6

What is the average percent defective? The standard deviation of the sampling distribution? The upper and lower control limits?

5. 💾 Clownburgers has a special machine that forms ground beef into hamburger patties. Patty weights are approximately normally distributed with a mean of 6 ounces and a standard deviation of 0.07 ounce. Twelve samples of 10 patties were taken during a shift, and the sample means are as follows: 6.01, 6.03, 5.97, 5.91, 6.04, 5.98, 6.05, 6.08, 6.04, 5.95, 6.02, 5.98. Draw a sample mean chart and a sample range chart. What are the upper and lower control limits on each chart? Is the process in control?

6. 💾 A drilling machine operator at Grey Roofing Products Ltd. is monitoring the diameter of the hole drilled by her machine. She has taken eight samples of eight parts. The sample means and ranges are shown below.

Sample	Mean	Range
1	5.020	0.0021
2	5.015	0.0022
3	5.012	0.0015
4	5.018	0.0021
5	5.015	0.0012
6	5.021	0.0018
7	5.019	0.0019
8	5.020	0.0012

Construct a sample mean chart and a sample range chart. Is the process in control?

7. 💾 A casting machine is used to make auto parts. Every two hours the operator inspects 15 parts. The results for 15 samples are given below.

Sample	Number of Defective Units	Sample	Number of Defective Units
1	1	9	3
2	3	10	2
3	2	11	3
4	0	12	1
5	2	13	1
6	2	14	0
7	3	15	1
8	0		

Construct a control chart. What are the upper and lower limits? Is the process in control?

8. 💾 Highest Fidelity Inc. manufactures complete stereo systems. Twenty-five systems were selected at random and inspected carefully. The numbers of defects found are listed below.

Sample	Number of Defects Found	Sample	Number of Defects Found
1	2	14	1
2	3	15	3
3	1	16	2
4	0	17	3
5	0	18	2
6	3	19	2
7	4	20	1
8	2	21	0
9	2	22	1
10	1	23	1
11	1	24	2
12	0	25	2
13	0		

Construct a control chart. Is the process in control?

9. 💾 A pharmaceutical company produces liquid cough medicine in eight-ounce bottles. Fifteen samples were randomly selected and weighed; each sample contains 80 bottles. The results are shown below.

Sample	Mean	Range	Sample	Mean	Range
1	302	5	9	300	3
2	297	3	10	298	5
3	303	6	11	299	4
4	305	7	12	302	6
5	299	4	13	301	3
6	297	6	14	298	5
7	304	5	15	303	4
8	302	4			

Develop a sample range chart and a sample mean chart. Is the bottling process under control?

10. Acme Pump Company makes a range of sealed pumps and currently has the largest market share of all major manufacturers. A new manufacturer has entered the market, however, and has a superior product that is threatening Acme's market share. A major problem is leaking seals and gaskets, which are caused by a number of factors. One is the trueness of the shafts, which are turned on a lathe. Another is the viscosity of the lubricant, which is a mixture of oils especially prepared for Acme by any of three oil companies. Another is the pump casting, which is made by one supplier but machined by another or by Acme's machine shop. The seals are stamped on Acme's presses and then force fitted to the shafts. The pump castings are in two pieces, which are bolted together; a purchased gasket of cork and copper is fitted between the two pieces. Each bolt has to be tightened within a range of pressures to ensure a good seal without overstressing the gasket or the castings. Prepare a cause-and-effect diagram for the leak problem.

11. Inspection over a three-month period has shown that 75 percent of the leaks at the driveshaft seal occur when the lubricant is off specification, 20 percent when the operating temperature of the liquid being pumped is too hot, and 5 percent when the pump is operating too fast. Draw a Pareto chart. What does it tell you?

12. A friend of yours who waits on tables in a top-class restaurant is interested in increasing the tip take per

week. Prepare a cause-and-effect diagram to help your friend think through this problem.

13. Your friend from problem 12 has brought in a scatter diagram that shows the tip size in relation to the distance from the kitchen. Can you offer any explanation why the diagram looks the way it does? How would you suggest your friend try to stratify the data to gain more insight?

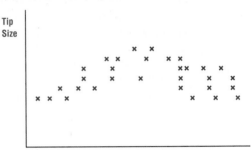

14. You and your friends are sitting around thinking about how to improve the quality of education, especially in operations management. You suggest making a cause-and-effect diagram. Construct the diagram.

15. One of the issues, of course, is how you measure the quality of education. What are the five most critical measures of quality? What criteria did you use to decide on these five? Devise a sampling plan to actually get the measurements you want.

GROUP EXERCISES

Many of the tools and techniques discussed in this chapter are meant to be used in a team setting. The following problem is best solved by small groups of students. Ideally, each group should be composed of people with different backgrounds, interests, or areas of expertise.

Select a local business (e.g., a hamburger stand or dry cleaner) that seems to be losing business or has just been forced out of business. Use a cause-and-effect diagram to determine the root cause of that business's problems. What other tools could you use to identify and solve these problems?

REFERENCES AND SELECTED BIBLIOGRAPHY

Boteler, James L. [1993], "Using Prevention Techniques," *Quality Progress*, vol. 26, no. 7, pp. 105–107.

Conant, Ronald G. [1988], "JIT in a Mail Order Operation Reduces Processing Time from Four Days to Four Hours," *Industrial Engineering*, September, vol. 20, no. 9, pp. 34–37.

Crosby, P. B. [1979], *Quality Is Free*, McGraw-Hill, New York.

Deming, W. Edwards [1982], *Quality, Productivity, and Competitive Position*, Massachusetts Institute of Technology Press, Cambridge, Mass.

Dobbines, J. G., and W. J. Padgett [1993], "SPC in Printed Circuit Board Assembly," *Quality Progress*, July, pp. 65–67.

Dondaro, Cort [1991], "SPC Hits the Road," *Quality Progress*, January, pp. 44–45.

Dumaine, Brian [1990], "Who Needs a Boss?" *Fortune,* May 7, pp. 52–60.

Evans, Mark E., and N. Faris Hubele [1993], *A Case Study of Family Formation for Statistical Process Control in Small-Batch Manufacturing: Presentation and Discussion with Questions and Answers,* Society of Manufacturing Engineers, Dearborn, Mich.

Feigenbaum, A. V. [1983], *Total Quality Control,* 3d ed., McGraw-Hill, New York.

Hart, M. K. [1990], "Education in Quality Control: The Evolution of Quality Control Circles and the Implications for the U.S. Colleges of Business," *Midwest Business Administration Association: Production and Operations Management Proceedings,* March, pp. 32–39.

—— [1991], "Quality Control Training for Manufacturing," *Production and Inventory Management Journal,* vol. 32, no. 3, pp. 35–40.

Heidenreich, P. [1989], "Supplier SPC Training: A Model Case," *Quality Progress,* July, pp. 41–43.

Huge, Ernest C. [1990], "Quality of Conformance to Design," in E. Huge (ed.), *Total Quality: An Executive's Guide for the 1990s,* Business One–Irwin, Homewood, Ill., pp. 132–151.

Ishikawa, K. [1985], *What Is Total Quality Control? The Japanese Way,* translated by David J. Lu, Prentice-Hall, Englewood Cliffs, N.J.

Juran, Joseph M., and Frank M. Gyrna, Jr. [1980], *Quality Planning and Analysis,* McGraw-Hill, New York.

Lawler, Edward E. III, and Susan A. Mohrman [1985], "Quality Circles after the Fad," *Harvard Business Review,* January–February, pp. 65–71.

Loring, John [1990], "Dr. Deming's Traveling Quality Show," *Canadian Business,* September, pp. 38–42.

Mansen, B. L. [1963], *Quality Control: Theory and Application,* Prentice-Hall, Englewood Cliffs, N.J.

Marshall, Robert, and Tawnya Seamans [1992], "TEAM Maintenance Management System," *APICS,* December, pp. 47–50.

McDougall, Bruce [1991], "The Thinking Man's Assembly Line," *Canadian Business,* November, pp. 40–44.

Mizuno, Shigero [1988], *Company-Wide Total Quality Control,* Asian Productivity Organization, Tokyo.

Pyzdek [1993], "Process Control for Short and Small Runs," *Quality Progress,* April, pp. 51–60.

Quality Progress [1989], "One-Person Assembly Line Benefits All," October, p. 19.

Rodriguez [1990], "Total Productive Maintenance," in E. Huge (ed.), *Total Quality: An Executive's Guide for the 1990s,* Business One–Irwin, Homewood, Ill., pp. 152–161.

Stewart, Thomas A. [1991], "GE Keeps Those Ideas Coming," *Fortune,* Aug. 12, pp. 41–49.

Tatikonda, Lakshmi, and Rao J. Tatikonda [1991], "Overhead Cost Control—through Allocation or Elimination?" *Production and Inventory Management Journal,* First Quarter, pp. 37–41.

SUPPLEMENT TO
CHAPTER 11

ACCEPTANCE SAMPLING

S11.1 MANAGERIAL ORIENTATION

Acceptance sampling refers to the evaluation of one or more random samples of items drawn from a group of items; the entire group is accepted or rejected on the basis of sample results. During the brief overview of acceptance sampling in Chapter 11, it was mentioned that if certain conditions are met, acceptance sampling can be used as an alternative to 100 percent inspection. These conditions are as follows: (1) The cost of passing a limited number of defective products is low, (2) the number of products to be inspected is large, and (3) the process that produces the products is stable. If the only way in which a product can be inspected results in its

destruction, 100 percent inspection is obviously not feasible and acceptance sampling may be the only option.

S11.2 PRODUCER AND CONSUMER RISKS (TYPE I AND TYPE II ERRORS)

As was mentioned earlier, there are risks associated with acceptance sampling. Since the entire lot is rejected

EXHIBIT 11S.1 TOOLBOX: A DOUBLE SAMPLING PLAN

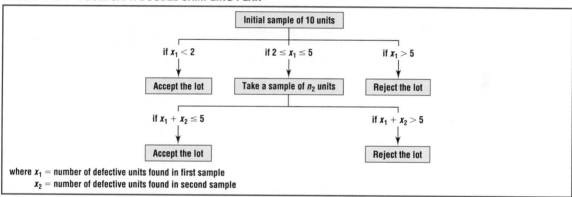

where x_1 = number of defective units found in first sample
x_2 = number of defective units found in second sample

EXHIBIT 11S.2 TOOLBOX: A SEQUENTIAL SAMPLING PLAN

In sequential sampling a series of one-unit samples are taken from the lot. The steps outlined below are followed until the entire lot is accepted or rejected.

1. Randomly select a unit from the lot.

2. Calculate the total number of defective units found so far.

3. Find the point on the graph to the right that corresponds with the number of units inspected and the number of defective units found.

If the point falls in an area marked "reject" or "accept," stop. If not, return to step 1 and continue sampling.

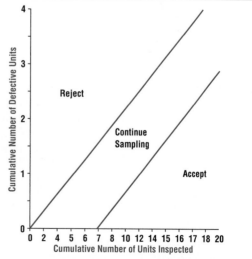

For example, suppose that you have taken eight samples from the lot and the only defective unit found was in the sixth sample. If the ninth sample is defective, the lot is rejected. If the ninth sample is good, however, at least one more sample must be taken.

If the quality of the lot is borderline, the entire lot may be sampled.

Mother Goose Toys (MGT) Ltd. manufactures a wide range of toys and has just expanded its product line to include miniature trucks. The wheels for the trucks will be purchased from Wheels Inc. in lots of 5,000 units.

Suppose MGT inspects a random sample of 50 wheels from each lot of 5,000. If more than one wheel is defective, the entire lot is rejected. Otherwise, the lot is accepted.

Since wheels are either good or bad and since the sample size is small relative to the lot size (i.e., less than 5 percent), the binomial distribution can be used to find the probability of finding exactly i defective units in a sample of n units and the probability of finding up to c defective units in a sample of n units.

$$P(i) = p^n (1 - p)^{n-i} \frac{n!}{i!(n - i)!}$$

where $P(i)$ = probability of finding exactly i defective wheels in sample
   p = probability that any wheel will be defective
   n = number of wheels in sample

When the sample size is large ($n > 20$) and the actual fraction defective is small ($p < 0.05$), the Poisson distribution can be used as an approximation of the binomial formula.

The cumulative Poisson table in Appendix D shows the probability of $i \leq c$ for specified values of n, c, and p. Each row in the table corresponds to a particular mean ($\mu = np$), and each column to a particular value of c. The probability of $i \leq c$ for a particular mean is given in the intersection of row μ and column c.

For example, $p(i \leq c) = 0.910$ when $c = 1$, $n = 50$, and $p = 0.01$. The relevant portion of the cumulative Poisson table is shown below.

					c			
$\mu = np$	0	1	2	3	4	5	6	$\cdots$
.								
.								
.								
0.5	0.607	0.910	0.986	0.998	1.000	1.000	1.000	
.								
.								
.								

or accepted on the basis of a randomly drawn sample, a good lot may be rejected or a bad lot may be accepted.

A lot is considered *good* if its quality meets or exceeds a specified level called the **acceptable quality level (AQL)**. For the purposes of acceptance sampling, the AQL is considered a satisfactory value of the process average. If the AQL is 1 defective unit per 100 units (AQL = 0.01), a lot of 500 is good if it contains 5 defective units or fewer. Rejecting a lot whose actual quality is better than, or equal to the AQL is a risk the producer wishes to minimize.

DEFINITION: Rejecting a lot whose quality is equal to or better than the acceptable quality limit is called a *type I error* in acceptance sampling.

DEFINITION: The *producer's risk* (α) is the probability of making a type I error.

While minimizing type I errors is important, the firm or department receiving the lot is more concerned about accepting a bad lot. In acceptance sampling, a *bad lot* is a lot whose quality is worse than a predetermined value referred to as the **lot tolerance percent defective (LTPD)**.

DEFINITION: Accepting a lot whose quality is equal to or worse than the lot tolerance percent defective is referred to as a *type II error* in acceptance sampling.

DEFINITION: The *consumer's risk* (β) is the probability of making a type II error.

Similarly, the cumulative Poisson table can be used to find the probability that the sampling plan will accept lots with other values of p.

Percent Defective, p	$\mu = 50p$	$P(i \leq 1)$
0.005	0.25	0.974
0.01	0.5	0.910
0.02	1.0	0.736
0.03	1.5	0.558
0.04	2.0	0.406
0.05	2.5	0.332
0.06	3.0	0.199
0.07	3.5	0.137

It is now possible to draw the operating characteristic curve for this plan.

OPERATING CHARACTERISTIC CURVE, $n = 50, c = 1$

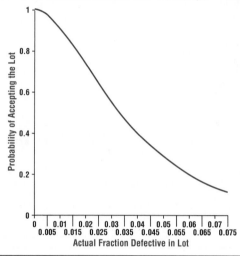

There are two categories of acceptance sampling techniques: those developed for product characteristics that are attributes and those developed for variable product characteristics.[1]

S11.3 SAMPLING PLANS FOR ATTRIBUTES

Types of Sampling Plans

Sampling plans for attributes range from single sampling plans to multiple sampling plans. In a single

[1] Product characteristics that are attributes are either present or absent or satisfactory or unsatisfactory. For example, a bottle may or may not have a cap, a plate of glass may or may not contain scratches, and a customer may or may not have been asked if he or she would like coffee and dessert after dinner. Variable product characteristics such as size, weight, and volume are present to varying degrees.

sampling plan one sample of n units is taken at random from the lot. Each product in the sample is examined. Any product that contains one or more **defects** is labeled defective, and the number of **defective products** is tallied.

DEFINITION: A defect is a flaw in a product.

DEFINITION: A defective product is a product that contains one or more defects.

If there are more than a specified number of defective units (say, c) in the sample, the entire lot is either rejected or fully screened. By contrast, if up to c defective units are found, the lot is accepted.

In a **double sampling plan** the entire lot is accepted or rejected on the basis of one or two relatively small random samples. For example, in the sampling plan in

Mother Goose Toys Ltd. is considering the following three sampling plans:

Plan 1: $n = 50, c = 1$
Plan 2: $n = 100, c = 1$
Plan 3: $n = 50, c = 3$

Using the cumulative Poisson table, the probability of accepting lots of various quality levels with each sampling plan has been calculated. An OC curve for each plan follows.

OPERATING CHARACTERISTIC CURVES

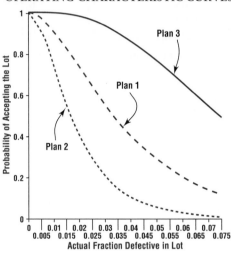

Suppose the AQL = 2 percent and the LTPD = 4 percent. The producer's risk and consumer's risk associated with each sampling plan are shown in the chart at the right.

Sampling Plan	Producer's Risk (α)	Consumer's Risk (β)
$n = 50, c = 1$	$1 - 0.736 = 0.264$	0.406
$n = 100, c = 1$	$1 - 0.406 = 0.594$	0.092
$n = 50, c = 3$	$1 - 0.981 = 0.019$	0.857

Exhibit 11S.1 a random sample of 10 units is taken. If fewer than two defective units are found, the lot is accepted; if more than five defective units are found, the lot is rejected. If 3 or 4 defective units are found, another sample of 10 units is selected at random. The lot is accepted if the total number of defectives found in the two samples does not exceed five; otherwise the entire lot is rejected or fully screened.

In a **triple sampling plan,** up to three random samples are taken but the size of each sample is smaller than it is in a double sampling plan. The concept of multiple sampling can be extended to a point where the sample size is equal to 1. This is referred to as **sequential sampling** (see Exhibit 11S.2).

The Operating Characteristic Curve

Suppose a firm has decided to use a single sampling plan. The best sampling plan is one that minimizes the average number of items inspected yet discriminates

well between good and bad lots. How can sampling plans be evaluated, and how can the optimal values of n and c be found?

The ability of a sampling plan to discriminate between good and bad lots can be illustrated by its **operating characteristic (OC) curve.**

> DEFINITION: An operating characteristic curve shows the probability that lots of various quality levels will be accepted.

An OC curve has been constructed for the sampling plan ($n = 50, c = 1$) in Exhibit 11S.3. With this sampling plan, the probability of accepting a lot whose actual percent defective is 2 percent is 0.736. If the AQL is 2 percent, the producer's risk (i.e., the risk of rejecting a good lot) is $\alpha = 1 - 0.736 = 0.264$. Suppose the LTPD is set at 4 percent. The consumer's risk (i.e., the risk of accepting a bad lot) is $\beta = 0.406$.

Note that increasing the sample size, *n*, increases the producer's risk (α) but decreases the consumer's risk (β) and that increasing the acceptance number, *c*, decreases the producer's risk (α) and increases the consumer's risk (β).

If the sample size is increased to the lot size, both the producer's risk and the consumer's risk will be eliminated (assuming no inspection errors are made). The operating characteristic curve for this perfect sampling plan is shown below.

OPERATING CHARACTERISTIC CURVE
FOR A PERFECT SAMPLING PLAN

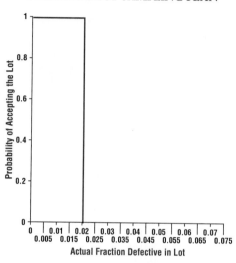

However, acceptance testing is used to avoid 100 percent inspection. This means that it is necessary to accept some level of producer's risk and consumer's risk.

What happens if the sample size is increased from 50 to 100 units? As illustrated in Exhibit 11S.4, the producer's risk soars to $\alpha = 0.594$ but the consumer's risk falls to $\beta = 0.092$. What if the sample size is reset to 50 units but the acceptance number increases from one to three? The consumer's risk now increases to $\beta = 0.857$, while the producer's risk decreases to $\alpha = 0.019$.

Which of the three plans ($n = 50, c = 1; n = 100, c = 1; n = 50, c = 3$) is the best plan when the AQL is set at 2 percent and the LTPD is set at 4 percent?[2] The producer obviously prefers the third ($n = 50, c = 3$) because it has the lowest α value. The second plan ($n = 100, c = 1$), however, has the lowest β value and

thus is preferred by the consumer. Therefore, before a sampling plan can be chosen, the producer and consumer must agree on the specific values of α and β.

Once values for AQL, LTPD, α, and β have been chosen, a sampling plan whose OC curve contains the points (AQL, $1 - \alpha$) and (LTPD, β) must be found. Originally, a trial-and-error approach had to be used to find such a sampling plan. This approach was used to find a sampling plan for Mother Goose Toys Ltd. in Exhibit 11S.5. In this exhibit, note how the sample size rapidly increases as the values of AQL and LTPD approach zero.

The trial-and-error approach has been simplified by the development of special tables such as the 1963 Military Standard Sampling Procedures and Tables for Inspection by Attributes (MIL-STD-105D) published by the U.S. Government Printing Office. Computer software packages are widely available as well (see, for example, ©OM-Expert).

---

[2] These values were chosen because they highlight the differences between the three plans. Of course, such high fraction defective levels are no longer acceptable in most competitive environments.

Wheels Inc. supplies Mother Goose Toys Ltd. (MGT) with wheels. It estimates that on average, only 1 percent of its wheels are defective. After meeting together, MGT and Wheels Inc. agree that the probability of accepting a lot whose actual fraction defective is high (i.e., exceeds 4 percent) should be only 0.10. The probability of accepting a lot with 1 percent or fewer defective wheels, however, should be 0.95.

Therefore, the sampling plan chosen must meet the following two conditions.

$$P(i \leq c) = 0.10 \text{ when } p = 0.04 \text{ (LTPD) (Condition 1)}$$
$$P(i \leq c) = 0.95 \text{ when } p = 0.01 \text{ (AQL) (Condition 2)}$$

where p = actual fraction defective in lot
i = number of defective wheels in sample
c = acceptance number

Using the cumulative Poisson table, different combinations of n and c are tried until a combination that satisfies both conditions is found. The last sampling plan ($n = 200$, $c = 4$) in the table at the right is such a combination.

SAMPLING PLAN COMBINATIONS

Sampling Plan (n, c)	$p = 0.01$ $\mu = np$	$p = 0.01$ $P(i \leq c)$	$p = 0.04$ $\mu = np$	$p = 0.04$ $P(i \leq c)$
35, 1	0.35	0.951	1.4	0.592
95, 1	0.95	0.754	3.8	0.107
80, 2	0.80	0.953	3.2	0.380
135, 2	1.35	0.845	5.4	0.095
200, 4	2.00	0.947	8.0	0.100

Using the cumulative Poisson table, the probability of accepting lots of various quality levels for the sampling plan $n = 200$, $c = 4$ can be calculated.

Actual Fraction Defective in Lot, p	$\mu = np = 200p$	Probability of Accepting the Lot, $P(i \leq 4)$
0.005	1	0.996
0.01	2	0.947
0.015	3	0.815
0.02	4	0.629
0.025	5	0.441
0.03	6	0.285
0.035	7	0.173
0.04	8	0.100
0.045	9	0.055

Average Outgoing Quality

Sampling plans also can be evaluated on the basis of their **average outgoing quality** (AOQ). The smaller the AOQ value, the better the average outgoing quality.

DEFINITION: The average outgoing quality is the fraction defective in an average lot of goods inspected through acceptance sampling.

Suppose Mother Goose Toys Ltd. has decided to draw a random sample of 200 units from each lot of 5,000 wheels. If more than four wheels are defective, the entire lot is inspected and all defective units are repaired or replaced. If there are 100 lots to be inspected

and the actual percent defective in each lot is 2 percent, the AOQ is calculated as follows:

- Since the actual percentage of defective units is 2 percent, the probability of finding four or fewer defective units in the sample is 0.629 (see the table in Exhibit 11S.6). This means that about 63 of the 100 lots will be accepted.
- The remaining 27 lots will be fully screened and will contain no defective wheels; neither will the sampled portions of the 63 accepted lots.
- Two percent of the unsampled portions (5,000 − 200 = 4,800 wheels per lot), however, will remain

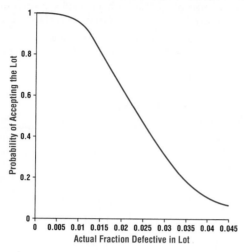

OPERATING CHARACTERISTIC CURVE
FOR THE SAMPLING PLAN ($n = 200$, $c = 4$)

What happens if MGT and Wheels Inc. agree to lower the values of the AQL and LTPD? As can be seen in the chart below, the sample size rapidly increases as these values approach zero.

AQL, LTPD	Sample Size, n	Acceptance Level, c
0.01, 0.032	330	6
0.0075, 0.0222	530	7
0.005, 0.013	1,100	9

defective. This means that a total of $(0.02 \times 4,800 \times 63) = 6,048$ defective wheels will pass the inspection.

- The AOQ in this case will be $6,048 \div (5,000 \times 100) = 0.012096$.

Alternatively, the AOQ value can be set at $p = 2$ percent by using equation (11S.1).[3]

---

[3] Note that if the lot size is very large relative to the sample size, the term $(N - n)/N$ will be very close to 1. In this situation this term is often omitted from equation 11S.1.

Average Outgoing Quality (AOQ)

$$AOQ = (p)(P_{ac})\left(\frac{N - n}{N}\right) \qquad (11S.1)$$

where p = fraction defective in incoming lot

P_{ac} = probability of accepting a lot whose fraction defective is p

N = lot size

n = sample size

Suppose Mother Goose Toys Ltd. (MGT) and Wheels Inc. agree to the following sampling plan.

Randomly select 200 wheels from every lot. If four or fewer defective wheels are found, repair or replace those wheels and accept the remainder of the lot without further inspection. If more than four defective wheels are found in the sample, inspect the entire lot. Repair or replace any defective wheels found.

Before equation (11S.1) can be used to find the AOQ for various values of p, the probability of accepting the lot for each value of p must be calculated. The chart below is used to construct the OC curve for this sampling plan.

Actual Fraction Defective in Lot, p	Probability of Accepting the Lot, $P(i \le 4)$	AOQ
0.005	0.996	0.0034
0.01	0.947	0.0076
0.015	0.815	0.0098
0.02	0.629	0.0101
0.025	0.441	0.0088
0.03	0.285	0.0068
0.035	0.173	0.0048
0.04	0.100	0.0032
0.045	0.055	0.0020

The worst AOQ (i.e., the highest fraction defective) occurs when p is about 0.02. Therefore, the AOQL is about 0.0101.

AVERAGE OUTGOING QUALITY CURVE

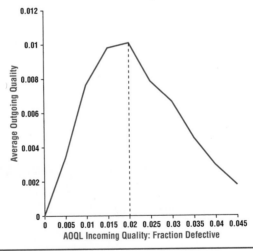

AOQL Incoming Quality: Fraction Defective

A. Current Sampling Plan

Lopez Ltd., a manufacturer of jams and jellies, purchases all its sugar from a single supplier. It currently uses the following sampling plan.

Randomly select 135 sacks and weigh each sack. If a sack weighs less than 97 pounds, it is defective. If the sample contains more than three defective sacks, reject the lot.

With the current sampling plan, the probability of accepting a high-quality shipment (i.e., one that meets or exceeds the AQL) is 0.95. Shipments with light sack weights are accepted no more than 10 percent of the time.

AQL = 0.01   (i.e., 1 percent of bags weigh less than 97 pounds)
LTPD = 0.049 (i.e., 4.9 percent of bags weigh less than 97 pounds)

$P(i \leq 3) = 0.95$ when $p = 0.01$
$P(i \leq 3) = 0.10$ when $p = 0.049$

B. Revised Sampling Plan

Assume that the sack weights follow the normal distribution, with a standard deviation of 2.05 pounds. A high-quality shipment is one whose mean weight is at least 100 pounds. These shipments should be accepted 95 percent of the time. Therefore, 95 percent of the distribution shown below must be to the left of the point marked 100 pounds. When values are normally distributed, this point corresponds with $\mu + 1.645\sigma_{\bar{x}}$:

$$\mu + 1.645\sigma_{\bar{x}} = 100 \tag{1}$$

A shipment with a mean weight of 97 pounds is the lowest acceptable level and shoud be accepted no more than 10 percent of the time. Therefore, 10 percent of the distribution shown above must be to the left of the point marked 97 pounds. When values are normally distributed, this point corresponds with $\mu - 1.28\sigma_{\bar{x}}$ on a normal distribution:

$$\mu - 1.28\sigma_{\bar{x}} = 97 \tag{2}$$

Since $\sigma_{\bar{x}} = \sigma_x \div \sqrt{n}$ and $\sigma_x = 2.05$, equations (1) and (2) become equations (1b) and (2b).

$$\mu + \frac{1.645(2.05)}{\sqrt{n}} = 100 \qquad \therefore \mu = 100 - \frac{3.37225}{\sqrt{n}} \tag{1b}$$

$$\mu - \frac{1.28(2.05)}{\sqrt{n}} = 97 \qquad \therefore \mu = 97 + \frac{2.624}{\sqrt{n}} \tag{2b}$$

To find a sampling plan that satisfies both conditions, solve equations (1b) and (2b) for the value of n:

$$100 - \frac{3.37225}{\sqrt{n}} = 97 + \frac{2.624}{\sqrt{n}}$$

$$100\sqrt{n} - 3.37225 = 97\sqrt{n} + 2.624$$

$$3\sqrt{n} = 5.99625$$

$$n = 3.995$$

Therefore $n = 4$. If one substitutes $n = 4$ in equation (1b) and solves for μ, $\mu = 98.31$.

This means that Lopez Ltd. should randomly select four sacks from every lot. If the average weight of those four sacks equals or exceeds 98.31 pounds, the lot should be accepted. Otherwise, the lot should be rejected.

Therefore, the AOQ when $p = 0.02$ is[4]

$$AOQ = (0.02)(0.63)\frac{5,000 - 200}{5,000} = 0.012096$$

The AOQ curve in Exhibit 11S.6 was constructed by calculating the AOQ for various values of p.

If the quality of the incoming lot is very high, the quality of the average outgoing lot will also be very high. Since all rejected lots are fully screened, the average outgoing lot will be of high quality if the income lot is of very poor quality. The highest (or worst) value for the AOQ is referred to as the **average outgoing quality limit (AOQL)**.

The AOQL differs for each plan and occurs at different values of p. From the consumer's perspective, the higher the AOQL, the worse the sampling plan. The AOQL for Mother Goose Toys Ltd.'s sampling plan is about 0.0101. If the company feels that this level is too high, it must go back to its supplier and renegotiate the sampling plan parameters (i.e., AQL, LTPD, α, and β) until an acceptable AOQL is found.

S11.4 SAMPLING PLANS FOR VARIABLES

So far this supplement has discussed single and multiple sampling plans developed for product characteristics that are attributes. However, these sampling plans also can be used for product characteristics that are variable. Consider Lopez Ltd., a manufacturer of jams and jellies that uses a variable sampling plan to evaluate incoming shipments of sugar. A random sample of 135 sugar sacks is taken from each shipment and weighed. If more than three sacks are underweight, the entire shipment is rejected. The details of the sampling plan are shown in Exhibit 11S.7A.

Lopez Ltd. is evaluating incoming sugar shipments on the basis of only one product characteristic: weight. Since weight is a variable, not an attribute, it is possible to construct a sampling plan that meets Lopez Ltd.'s requirements but calls for a sample of only four sugar sacks. This can be done because a measurement gives more information than does a simple good/bad evalu-

ation. Therefore, the same discriminating power associated with a good/bad sampling test can be obtained by using a much smaller value for n.

A variable sampling plan consists of a sample size (n) and an acceptance average (μ) for the sample. For example, Lopez Ltd. will randomly select n sacks of sugar from an incoming shipment. Each sack will be weighed, and the average weight will be calculated. If this average is above the predetermined acceptance average, the lot is accepted. Otherwise, the lot is rejected.

To develop a variable sampling plan, the type of distribution that the value of individual observations will follow must be known. Continuing with the sugar example, suppose Lopez Ltd. buys all its sugar from a single supplier. On the basis of past experience, Lopez Ltd. estimates that the sack weights follow the normal distribution and that the standard deviation of those weights is relatively constant and is equal to 2.05 pounds.

Since the sack weights are normally distributed, the sample sack weight is also normally distributed.[5] The standard deviation of the sample is equal to the standard deviation of the process divided by the square root of the sample size [equation (11S.1)].

The revised sampling plan requirements for Lopez Ltd. are derived in Exhibit 11S.7B. They state that Lopez Ltd. needs a value of μ that satisfies the following two conditions: (1) 95 percent of the distribution should lie to the left of the point $\mu + 1.645\sigma_{\overline{X}} = 100$ and 10 percent of the values should fall to the left of the point marked $\mu - 1.282\sigma_{\overline{X}} = 97$. Solving the two equations simultaneously yields a value of 4 for the sample size (n) and 98.31 pounds for the mean of the sample means (μ). Exhibit 11S.7B walks through these calculations.

Therefore, Lopez Ltd. should randomly select four sacks from every lot. If the average weight of the four sacks equals or exceeds 98.31 pounds, the lot should be accepted. Otherwise, the lot should be rejected. An operating characteristic curve for this sampling plan can be drawn.

Variable sampling plans can also be created for variables that must fall within specified upper and lower boundaries. These plans have an acceptance average for both the upper and lower boundaries. Other variable sampling plans include those created for measurements expressed in terms of percent defective and those for which the standard deviation is unknown and may be variable.

---

[5] Even if the population from which a set of samples is drawn is *not* normally distributed, the central limit theorem states that the distribution of the sample means roughly follows a normal curve.

[4] Note that once again P_{ac} has been rounded upward.

KEY TERMS

Acceptance sampling
Acceptable quality level (AQL)
Type I error
Producer's risk (α)

Lot tolerance percent defective (LTPD)
Type II error
Consumer's risk (β)
Single sampling plan

Defect
Defective product
Double sampling plan
Triple sampling plan
Sequential sampling plan

Operating characteristic (OC) curve
Average outgoing quality (AOQ)
Average outgoing quality limit (AOQL)

REFERENCES AND SELECTED BIBLIOGRAPHY

Evans, James R., and William M. Lindsay [1993], *The Management and Control of Quality*, 2d ed., West, St. Paul, Minn.

Feigenbaum, Armand V. [1983], *Total Quality Control*, 3d ed., McGraw-Hill, New York.

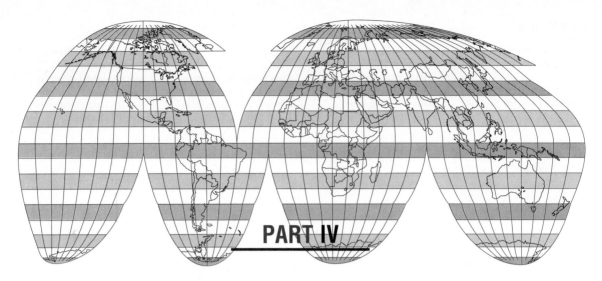

PART IV

PLANNING AND CONTROLLING IN
FAST-RESPONSE ORGANIZATIONS

Firms intent on succeeding in the modern competitive environment must understand the new character of competition. These firms also have to internalize the new drivers or levers of competition and advantage and learn how to use them in this environment. Until these things are done, building an enterprise that can sustain growth will be difficult.

Part IV continues this book's focus on competitive levers by looking at the allocation of people and materials to operating processes to meet customers' time and quantity requirements for products. These requirements are derived from customers' order or from surrogates for those orders such as marketing forecasts and distributor requirements.

Part IV consists of eight chapters. Chapter 12 deals with projects, an increasingly common form of operations organization. The remaining chapters deal with more permanent forms of operations organization, although the lessons taught there can be useful for managers in project settings.

Chapter 13 deals with determining how much to make and when to make individual lots of a product demanded by stakeholders outside the firm. The level and timing of this demand are directly influenced not by the firm's actions but by the independent actions or needs of a number of customers. In most cases this demand has to be forecast so that the products can be available at the time and in the quantity required.

Chapter 14 is concerned with providing the detailed capacity required to satisfy the lot sizing and timing decisions made in Chapter 13 and with providing the flexibility to manage the inevitable short-term changes that occur between planning and production.

Chapters 15 and 16 deal with the management of internal demand, or demand created as a result of the firm's making the lot sizing and timing decisions for the final products demanded by customers. This planning must take into account the demand created at each step in the production process and is therefore time-phased to follow the sequence of production. A firm cannot meet customer demand if it does not have the appropriate components at the right place at the right time. These chapters investigate models that allow a firm to achieve the necessary degree of coordination at the lowest reasonable level of working capital.

Chapter 17 takes planning a step further by describing allocation of production to specific machines or work cells. This process, which is called scheduling, is the last internal planning process; after scheduling comes the control of physical operations, which is beyond the scope of this book.

Chapter 18 does extend the scope, though, by looking at managing materials beyond the boundary of physical operations. It looks at the management of suppliers and of the distribution chain, arguing that the whole chain must be managed as a coordinated unit.

Chapter 19 continues this theme of inclusion by looking at total performance measurement. A firm cannot manage what it does not measure, and it cannot manage effectively unless it takes a holistic view of its operations. Without measurement there can be no control.

The focus of Part IV is on improving efficiency and getting "better." This means meeting customer needs and expectations at progressively lower costs and in shorter times. Each of these elements on its own can improve a firm's competitive position. Together, they provide a superior position that the firm's competitors will find difficult to overcome.

The planning discussed in Part IV is critical to the success and survival of a contemporary enterprise. Good planning *integrates* a firm with its market and suppliers and effectively uses the flexible resources a firm has at its disposal to meet market needs. The flexibility is enhanced by the presence and use of appropriate hard and soft technologies and through continuous improvement of new products and processes. Planning is only one part of the management portfolio, but like all others, it is an integral and often misused element.

CHAPTER 12

PROJECT MANAGEMENT

Chapter 5 mentioned projects but did not ask two important questions:

- How are projects managed?
- Is project management in fast-response organizations different from traditional project management?

These questions are addressed in this chapter, starting with a discussion of projects in general and then moving to project design, management, and control. This is followed by a technical discussion of project design and planning techniques. By the end of the chapter you will be able to plan, design, and manage a project.

The chapter ends with a discussion of the implications of the project management in today's environment, focusing on the challenges and benefits of managing *across* projects in fast-response organizations.

EXHIBIT 12.1   FRO MANUFACTURING PROFILE

Over the last seven or eight years the Lockheed Missiles and Space Co. has increased its square footage by 70 percent with an investment of over $1 billion. During this build-out program, the company's Facility Operations Division has developed a project management strategy that enables it to construct high-quality facilities quickly and on budget.

By almost completely overlapping work on facility design, permitting, and construction, Lockheed cuts project durations in half, but "fast-tracking" construction projects in this manner puts additional pressure on project planning and control. The Facility Operations Division has developed a project management strategy composed of the following seven elements:

- Staffing, or getting the right people on the project team
- Determining project priorities
- Defining project requirements
- Selecting a contracting method, contractor, and contract structure that best suit the project
- Utilizing project controls for scheduling and budgets
- Managing the design process
- Managing the construction process

Source: Adapted from Adams (1991), pp. 1–6.

EXHIBIT 12.2   FRO SERVICE PROFILE

When New York State decided to establish its Excelsior Award for quality, the launch was planned and executed as a project. The award was designed and delivered by the Executive Committee, a group of 18 volunteers who met monthly from project inception to completion. Each step required for the success of the project was identified by the Executive Committee, and once the priorities were established, each task was made the responsibility of an identified individual or group.

Each process was assigned milestone and completion dates, and the assigned team was responsible for managing the task to ensure that deadlines were met. The monthly meetings could thus be used for coordination and forward planning, separating the planning and management issues. Major tasks that formed parts of the project included the identification, selection, and training of judges and examiners; initial marketing and promotion of the award; identification of the award criteria; and the review process. The time spent in planning was repaid handsomely when the award was established in only 15 months.

Source: Adapted from Luther (1993), pp. 38–43.

12.1 MANAGERIAL ORIENTATION

Projects are probably the oldest form of organized work. All seven wonders of the ancient world were individually manufactured products, and even today a large percentage of business activity takes the form of individual projects.

> **DEFINITION:** A project is a set of finite activities that is usually performed only once and has well-defined objectives.

Projects are not confined to large construction efforts such as building dams, ships, and office towers. Writing an essay, planning a vacation, preparing an advertising campaign, organizing an audit, and purchasing a piece of equipment are also projects.

A recent survey [Wallace and Halverson (1992), p. 48] found that almost 60 percent of senior managers in the manufacturing, electronics, and financial services industries view their work in terms of projects; many indicated that **project management** is a critical success factor for their organizations.

> **DEFINITION:** Project management involves planning and controlling a project; its goal is to ensure that the project's objectives are achieved on time and on budget.

The direct relationship between good project management and customer satisfaction is clearly illustrated by Lockheed Missiles and Space Co.'s Facility Operations Division (see Exhibit 12.1).

In a fast-response organization (FRO) operations managers are members of cross-functional teams involved in large-scale strategic projects such as developing new products, processes, and facilities. They are also involved in smaller tactical-level projects in their own areas. Examples include launching a new program (see Exhibit 12.2), purchasing a piece of equipment, and redesigning a process layout.

This chapter begins with a review of issues facing managers as they organize and control individual projects. Several valuable tools and techniques to support these efforts are presented, including the well-known PERT and CPM techniques. The chapter then examines how firms can select and manage a large portfolio of projects.

12.2 THE PROJECT LIFE CYCLE

Projects are finite. They have a clear beginning and a clear end and often seem to take on a life of their own. It is thus appropriate to think of a project as having a natural life cycle consisting of four phases: *conception, formative, operational,* and *termination.*

> **DEFINITION:** During the *conception phase,* the idea for a project is studied. If it appears beneficial and feasible, the idea is turned into a project proposal. A "go" or "no go" decision is then made.

Project proposals include the expected benefits, estimates of the resources (people, money, equipment, etc.) required for the project, and the project's duration.

A proposed project is not evaluated on its individual merits alone. The degree to which it supports the firm's strategy and fits in with other projects currently under way is considered, and the proposal is compared with other proposals. Which projects get added to the firm's portfolio of projects and when they will commence are strategic decisions.

Once a proposal has been approved, the project moves into the formative phase.

DEFINITION: During the *formative phase* the objectives of the project are clearly defined, the type of project organization is selected, and a project manager is appointed. The proposal is transformed into a master project plan. Detailed schedules, resource requirements, and budgets are developed.

The intention of project planning is to ensure that the right resources are available at the right time and to anticipate problems. This means that all interested constituents must be involved during project planning.[1]

Project planning can be time-consuming, difficult, and expensive, especially if details about the tasks to be performed are not clear. Planning the development of a new product that requires process technology that has not yet been invented, for example, is challenging. In these situations only general project plans can be made initially. As the project progresses, however, more specific plans must be made.

As illustrated in Exhibit 12.3, many of the tools that will be presented here can be used during both the formative and operational phases of a project.

DEFINITION: By the *operational phase,* the project team has been assembled. Work on the project now begins.

Monitoring progress, updating project plans, and keeping the team on track are key managerial responsibilities during this stage. Dealing with requests for changes

---

[1] Think back to the discussion of concurrent engineering in Chapter 5. Involving representatives from various functional areas from day one saves time and results in higher-quality but less expensive products.

EXHIBIT 12.3 THE PROJECT LIFE CYCLE

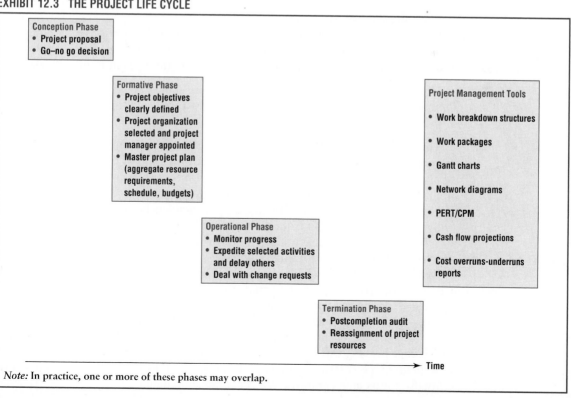

Note: In practice, one or more of these phases may overlap.

in the work to be done or in the project objectives is perhaps the most challenging task of all.

> **DEFINITION:** By the *termination phase,* work on the project has been completed (or prematurely halted). During this phase, the successes and failures of the project (including its organizational structures) are analyzed, a detailed report for future project teams is prepared, and team members are assigned to other tasks.

Although projects tend to be unique in one aspect or another, a good postcompletion audit can help managers. Good analysis and understanding create knowledge that is useful now. And avoiding past mistakes as well as taking advantage of improved organizational forms, planning and control techniques, and management styles helps a firm design and manage projects more effectively in the future.

12.3 ORGANIZING PROJECT ACTIVITIES

The first step in project organization is to identify the activities that must be completed and the relationships among those activities. This step is very important, for mistakes made here may result in poor resource allocations, budgets, and schedules. **Work breakdown structures (WBS)** are an excellent tool for identifying activities, which can then be grouped into logical sets, or **work packages,** and assigned to specific people.

Even in a relatively small project the relationships among the project activities can be complex. Illustrating the project with a set of **network diagrams** can help clarify these relationships and help schedule activities and prepare budgets.

Work Breakdown Structures

Suppose the Mayo Clinic is completely revamping major portions of its computer systems—a massive undertaking that will take several years. The major components of this information systems project are illustrated in the WBS in Exhibit 12.4A.

> **DEFINITION:** A work breakdown structure shows the project as a set of major components progressively broken down into smaller and smaller elements.

The **product-focused WBS** in Exhibit 12.4A is the most useful form of breakdown structure. In this form, the project is represented at the top of the pyramid. Below it are clearly defined major components of the project. This subdivision is repeated until the finest concrete or measurable element of the project *worthy of the attention of the managers for whom the WBS is being drawn* has been defined.

By analyzing the project from the top down rather than simply generating a list of activities, the project team is less likely to omit project components. It is also easier to establish the relationships among those components.

Exhibit 12.4B shows a **process-focused WBS** for the information systems project in Exhibit 12.4A. The project is analyzed into a series of major processes (e.g., researching, designing, and programming). A process-focused WBS groups tasks by type, not by project segment. Given the scope of the project, it is unlikely that work on all segments can occur simultaneously. It is also difficult to see if any activities are missing. Leaving out an activity can result in an underestimation of resource needs (and hence cost) or, worse, a distortion of the sequence of activities and eventually a misstatement of the project completion date.

EXHIBIT 12.4   TOOLBOX: WORK BREAKDOWN STRUCTURE

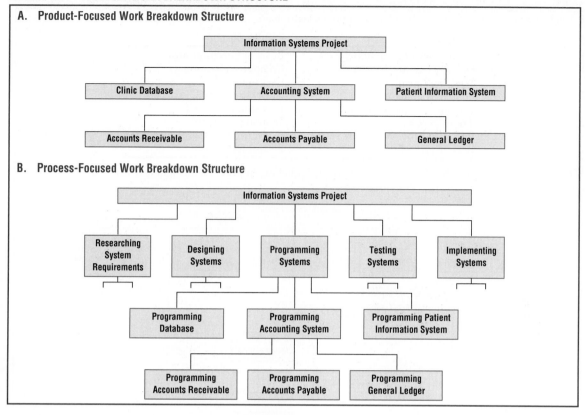

A. **Product-Focused Work Breakdown Structure**

B. **Process-Focused Work Breakdown Structure**

Note. A process-focused WBS provides little or no help in planning and managing the activities to be performed. It is discussed here solely as an example of the *wrong* way to break down the project.

As has been indicated, the WBS and the activity list derived from it are developed for a particular level of management, not necessarily for a complete project. The WBS in Exhibit 12.4A, for example, is suitable for the Mayo Clinic's upper management, while the more detailed WBS in Exhibit 12.5 is preferred by the General Ledger project manager.

Subordinate managers must be able to link their products and activities to higher-level products; this is essential for coordination and integration. Thus, each succeeding level of management will have WBSs and networks integrated with those above and below it in the management hierarchy.

Work Packages

The products that constitute the General Ledger project in Exhibit 12.5 will probably be grouped into work packages.

DEFINITION: A work package describes the set of activities assigned to a specific group of people.

Not only do work packages describe the work to be done, they also include estimated task durations and the resources (e.g., people, equipment, and finances) for doing the work in the estimated time. Time estimates are often made by the

The General Ledger project can be analyzed into the eight major activities listed below.

Activity	End Product
Determine system requirements	Business specifications
Develop computer programs	Computer programs
Write user manual	User manual
Prepare training material	Training material
Conduct acceptance testing	User group sign-off
Train users	Training seminar
Install and convert to new system	Conversion and implementation
Review project	Postproject report

The corresponding work breakdown structure is shown below. In practice, all eight activities would be broken down into tasks.

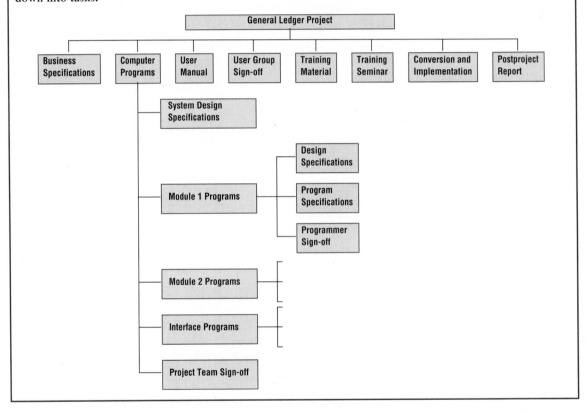

person assigned to the activity or the person in charge of the activity. The importance of proper time estimates cannot be overstated; poor time estimation is the most common cause of schedule slippage.

Milestones or activity deliverables, the person in charge of the work, and other information may also be included in the work package. A work package for the module 1 programs of the General Ledger project appears in Exhibit 12.6.

Network Diagrams

Once the project has been divided into a set of activities and work packages have been created, the project planners develop a preliminary schedule. Before they can do this, they need to establish the precedence relationships among the project activ-

EXHIBIT 12.6 TOOLBOX: WORK PACKAGE FOR A PORTION OF THE GENERAL LEDGER PROJECT

The computer program portion of the General Ledger project can be subdivided into several work packages. For example, the module 1 programs, module 2 programs, interface programs, system design specifications, and team sign-off can each constitute a work package. A work package for module 1 programs is shown below.

Product: Module 1 Programs
Team Leader: Susan Smith (team designer)

General Resource Requirements
* One designer, one programmer
* Two mainframe computer terminals, access to word processing package, electronic mail and testing environment
* Occasional access to a meeting room that holds up to five people

Total Estimated Duration: 17 days

Activity	Required Personnel	Estimated Duration
1. Design module 1		
• Prepare initial design specifications	• Team designer	• 2 days
• Walk through design	• Team programmer and designer, user representative, one designer from module 2 and interface teams	• ¼ day (includes preparation time)
• Modify design specifications if necessary	• Team designer	• ¾ day
2. Program module 1		
• Prepare initial program specifications	• Team programmer	• 5½ days
• Walk through program	• Team programmer and designer, user representative, one programmer from module 2 and interface teams	• ¼ day (includes preparation time)
• Modify program specifications if necessary	• Team programmer	• 1¼ days
• Write program	• Team programmer	• 2 days
3. Test and debug module 1	• Team programmer	• 5 days

ities. These relationships indicate which activities must be completed before other activities can begin and which can be performed concurrently.

In the General Ledger project, the system requirements must be completed before work on the computer programs can begin. Once the computer programs have been developed, the user manual can be written and the training material can be prepared. If enough resources are available, the user manual and training material can be developed concurrently.

Even in small projects precedence relationships can become complex. A network diagram of the project can help project managers sort out and understand these relationships. Network diagrams consist of a series of circles, or nodes, connected with arrows. An **activity-on-node (AON) network diagram** depicting the major activities of the General Ledger project appears in Exhibit 12.7A.[2]

---

[2] A separate network diagram can also be drawn for every major activity in the General Ledger project. For example, a network diagram illustrating the 12 tasks that constitute activity B of the project will be presented later in this chapter. As with WBSs, the level of detail presented depends on the needs of the people for whom the diagram is being drawn.

EXHIBIT 12.7   TOOLBOX: NETWORK CONSTRUCTION

The precedence relationships among the eight major activities in the General Ledger project are listed below.

Activity	Activities that must be completed before work on this activity can begin	Immediate Predecessor(s)
A. Determine system requirements	—	—
B. Develop programs	A	A
C. Write user manual	A, B	B
D. Prepare training material	A, B	B
E. Conduct acceptance testing	A, B, C	C
F. Train users	A, B, C, D, E	D, E
G. Install and convert to new system	A, B, C, E	E
H. Review project	A, B, C, D, E, F, G	F, G

A. Activity-on-Node Network Diagram

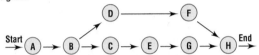

B. Activity-on-Arrow Network Diagram

Illustrating activities A, B, and C on an AOA network is relatively easy.

The difficulties start with activities D and E. If the network is drawn as shown below, the diagram implies that activities D and E both precede activities F and G. But activity G can begin before activity D has been completed.

Incorrect

To avoid this problem (which is not uncommon in drawing AOA diagrams), a dummy activity must be added to the network. Dummy activities are typically represented by arrows with broken lines.

Correct

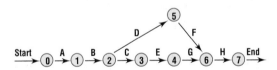

DEFINITION: In an activity-on-node network diagram each activity is represented by a circle, or node. Arrows running between the nodes indicate the order in which the activities must be performed.

Alternatively, an **activity-on-arrow (AOA) network diagram** for the General Ledger project can be drawn (see Exhibit 12.7B).

DEFINITION: In an activity-on-arrow network diagram each activity is represented by an arrow connecting two nodes. In these networks there is only one beginning and one ending for the project.

Note that in the AOA network the firm needs a special type of activity to show that the training material must be completed before the users are trained but need not be completed before the new system can be installed. This type of activity is called a **dummy activity.**[3]

> **DEFINITION:** Dummy activities are inserted in AOA networks to preserve the precedence logic and/or ensure that each activity has a unique pair of starting and ending nodes.

In practice, each activity in an AOA network is usually assigned a unique pair of start and end nodes; if a computer is used to draw the network, this is essential. As illustrated in Exhibit 12.8, dummy activities may be needed to ensure that each activity has its own unique start and end nodes.

The nodes in an AOA network are numbered from left to right. Numbering the nodes in a simple AOA network diagram is straightforward. As the network becomes larger and more complex, a node-numbering algorithm such as the one in Exhibit 12.9 becomes a valuable tool.

Section 12.4 will show that network diagrams can be used in conjunction with scheduling tools such as Gantt charts and PERT/CPM.

12.4 SCHEDULING PROJECT ACTIVITIES

Gantt charts and **PERT/CPM network diagrams** are popular tools for scheduling projects; they can also be used to help monitor and control a project once it begins.

[3] Later, when activity durations are added to the network, all dummy activities will be assigned a duration of zero.

EXHIBIT 12.8   TOOLBOX: DUMMY ACTIVITIES

Suppose a project consists of four activities. The first three activities (A, B, and C) all immediately precede activity D.

Activity	Immediate Predecessor
A	—
B	—
C	—
D	A, B, C

All three activities could be drawn as activity (0, 1) in a three-node network, as shown below.

Incorrect

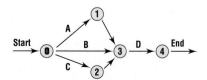

This is confusing, however, and it is impossible for a computer to follow the order. To overcome this problem, two nodes and two dummy activities are added. Now each of the four activities has a unique pair of start and end nodes.

Correct

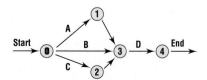

EXHIBIT 12.9 TOOLBOX: ACTIVITY-ON-ARROW NODE-NUMBERING ALGORITHM

NETWORK DRAWING CONVENTIONS

- The head of the arrow should be to the right of the tail.
- The node at the tail of an arrow should have a lower number than the node at the head.

NODE-NUMBERING ALGORITHM

1. Locate the starting node and number it 0.
2. Move along the uppermost path. Number the nodes in sequence. At any diverging node take the topmost path.
3. At any converging node, stop. *Do not* number the converging node. Trace back from the converting node along any path with nonnumbered nodes until a numbered node is located. Trace forward along the "unmarked" path, numbering nodes in sequence from the last number used.
4. If a converging node is encountered, repeat step 3 as many times as necessary until all paths entering the converging node have been numbered. Number the converging node and carry on through the network.
5. When the ending node has been numbered, stop.

EXAMPLE

Consider the network below. The starting node is labeled 0. Then, proceeding along the path A→C→G, number the nodes 1 and 2. Since G ends at a converging node, stop.

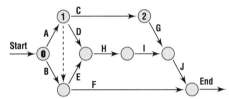

Trace back along the only unnumbered path entering G, that is, back through activity I then activity H. At the start of H, there is another converging node.

Going back through activity D, one finds a numbered node. If one goes back through activity E, however, one encounters an unnumbered node. This is the terminal point for activity B and a dummy activity. Since the heads of both activities have already been numbered, one can safely number their tails. The last number used was 2 (at the head of activity C), so this node is numbered 3.

It is now possible to trace forward through the unnumbered path E→H→I and number the nodes 4, 5, and 6.

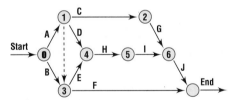

Moving forward from node 6 through activity J, one encounters another converging node. All the preceding nodes have been numbered already, however, and one can safely number the node at the tail of activity J 7. Since all the nodes are now numbered, stop.

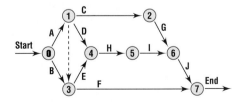

Gantt Charts

Gantt charts are visual aids named for their creator, Henry Gantt, who developed the concept in the United States early in the twentieth century.

> **DEFINITION:** A Gantt chart is a horizontal bar chart with activities listed down the vertical axis and dates displayed along the horizontal axis.

Each bar on a Gantt (scheduling) chart represents the duration of an activity, with the start and finish of the bar standing for the estimated start and finish dates of the activity. A Gantt chart for the General Ledger project is shown in Exhibit 12.10.

The earlier starting activities are at the top of the chart, with the later-starting activities displayed progressively lower down the vertical axis. This makes the chart

EXHIBIT 12.10   TOOLBOX: GANTT CHART

The team assigned to the General Ledger project has estimated the duration of each of the eight major activities.

A. Activity List for the General Ledger Project

Activity	Immediate Predecessor(s)	Activity Duration, days
A. Determine system requirements	—	10
B. Develop programs	A	31
C. Write user manual	B	10
D. Prepare training material	B	5
E. Conduct acceptance testing	C	5
F. Train users	D, E	3
G. Install and convert to new system	E	4
H. Review project	F, G	2

The team has prepared the Gantt chart shown below. Activity A is scheduled to begin on day 0; all other activities begin as soon as they can.

B. Simple Gantt Chart for the General Ledger Project

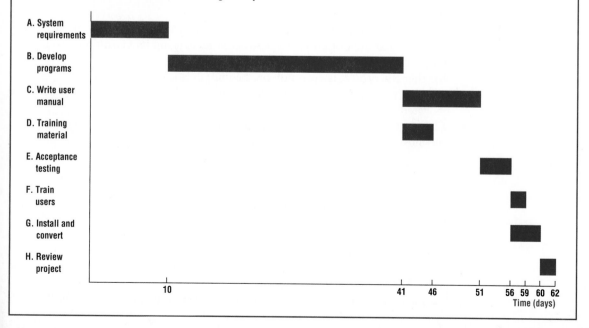

look like the side view of a mountain stream and explains why Gantt charts are sometimes called "cascade" charts. In addition to the flow from top left to bottom right, an idea of sequence can be gained by placing the number or letter of the immediately preceding activity at the left-hand end of the activity bar.

Gantt charts are very popular and practical project management tools. Not only are they easy and inexpensive to develop, they can convey a large amount of information. For example, progress can be recorded as the project proceeds by shading in the area under the bar depicting a particular activity. By dropping a line down from the current day's date on the chart, a manager can immediately see which activities are ahead of schedule and which are behind.

Generally, the larger the project is, the more difficult it is to develop and maintain up-to-date Gantt charts. On large projects, though, they can still be useful at the subtask level or at the highest level to provide a broad overview of the project. A more serious drawback is that Gantt charts do not indicate which activities can be deferred or extended without affecting the duration of the project.

PERT/CPM Networks

Network-based scheduling tools such as PERT and CPM can be used in conjunction with or instead of Gantt charts. PERT (program evaluation and review technique) was developed by the Special Projects Office of the U.S. Navy in conjunction with Booz, Allen, and Hamilton in 1958 to plan and control the Polaris missile program. CPM (critical path method) was developed in the 1950s by duPont and Remington Rand to assist in the building and maintenance of chemical plants. Today the two acronyms are used as if the two techniques were the same, and they now closely resemble each other.

PERT/CPM network diagrams are better than Gantt charts for illustrating the sequence of activities to be performed; they also indicate which activities can and cannot be performed concurrently. Other information that can be derived from these networked-based scheduling tools includes:

- The project's estimated completion date.
- Activities that are critical (that will delay the entire project if they are delayed).
- Activities that are not critical. These activities can run late (within reason) without delaying the project's completion.
- Whether the project is currently on, behind, or ahead of schedule.
- Whether the money spent to date is equal to, less than, or greater than the budgeted amount.
- Whether there are enough resources available to finish the project on time.
- The most inexpensive way of shortening the estimated duration of the project.

Six steps are common to both PERT and CPM:

1. Define the project and all its significant activities or tasks.
2. Determine the relationships among the activities. Decide which activities must precede and which must follow others.
3. Draw a network connecting all activities.
4. Assign time and/or cost estimates to each activity.
5. Compute the time required to complete the activities on each path through the network.
6. Use the network to help plan, schedule, monitor, and control the project.

Today the only major difference between PERT and CPM relates to the estimated *duration*[4] of each activity: CPM uses a single-point time estimate of activity duration, while PERT uses three (earliest likely, probable, latest likely).

The next several sections will work through the six-step procedure outlined above. In practice, computer software packages such as ©OM-Expert are used to draw the networks and make the tedious calculations.

Single-Point Time Estimates   The first three steps in the General Ledger project have been completed. Usually neither an AOA or an AON diagram is used to draw the project network. *Both* types will be used here to familiarize you with them. The network diagrams for the General Ledger project appear in Exhibit 12.11A.

A single-point estimate of the duration of each General Ledger activity is shown in Exhibit 12.10A. The sum of these activity durations is 70 days, but because some activities can be performed concurrently, the entire project can be completed in less time. The estimated duration of the entire project can be found by calculating the **earliest start and finish times** for each activity in the project.

If it is assumed that each activity is begun as soon as possible and is completed in exactly the estimated time, equation (12.1) can be used to find the earliest finish time for each activity. The earliest finish time for the project is the earliest finish time for the last activity.

Earliest Finish Time for an Activity

$$EF_i = ES_i + t_i \tag{12.1}$$

where EF_i = earliest finish time for activity i
ES_i = earliest time activity i can be started, given that all its predecessor activities have started as early as possible and have been completed on time
t_i = duration of activity i

The earliest start and finish times for each of the eight General Ledger activities have been calculated in Exhibit 12.11B. On the basis of these times, the General Ledger project can be completed in 62 days.

Take another look at the earliest start and finish times on the network diagrams in Exhibit 12.11B. Note that activity D is finished on day 46 but that the next activity, activity F, does not begin until day 56.[5] Therefore, the project manager can choose to delay activity D by up to nine days without delaying the entire project. Activity D is said to have **activity slack time.**

DEFINITION: The slack time for an activity is the maximum time an activity can be delayed without delaying the entire project.

To find the slack time for each activity in the network, one must first calculate the **latest start and finish times** for each activity. This is done by working backward through the network (see Exhibit 12.11C). The latest start time for an activity is equal to its latest finish time minus its duration [equation (12.2)]. The slack time for that activity is then calculated by using equation (12.3) or equation (12.4).

---

[4] Note that in project management any reference to "time" implies "duration."

[5] This disparity is caused by activity E, which also directly precedes activity F. Activity E is not finished until day 56.

EXHIBIT 12.11   TOOLBOX: ADDING TIME ESTIMATES TO NETWORK DIAGRAMS

A. Network Diagrams

Activity-on-Arrow Network

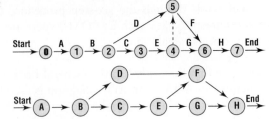

Activity-on-Node Network

B. Finding the Earliest Start and Finish Times

Activity	Activity Duration, days
A	10
B	31
C	10
D	5
E	5
F	3
G	4
H	2

The earliest start times for each activity can be found by moving from the starting activity A through to the ending activity H. Since A is a starting activity, it can begin at time zero.* Its duration is 10 days; thus, EF_A is 10.

Activity B can begin as soon as activity A is finished, and so ES_B is 10. EF_B is 41 ($ES_B + t_B = 10 + 31 = 41$). Activity B immediately precedes activities C and D, and so ES_C and ES_D are both 41. The earliest C can finish is day 51, while D can finished by day 46.

* Calendar dates can be used as well.

Activity E follows C, which means that $ES_E = 51$ and $EF_E = 56$. Activity F cannot begin until both D and E are finished. EF_D is 46 but EF_E is 56, and so ES_F is 56. F takes three days, making EF_F equal to 59.

Activity G must wait for activity E to finish as well, and so ES_G is also 56. Activity G cannot finish until day 60 ($ES_G + t_G = 56 + 4 = 60$).

Activity H can begin when F and G are finished, which is not until day 60. Activity H takes two days, and the earliest it can finish is day 62 ($EF_H + t_H = 60 + 2 = 62$). Therefore, the earliest day the General Ledger project can be completed is day 62.

		Earliest	
Activity, *i*	Duration, t_i	Start Time, ES_i	Finish Time, EF_i
A	10	0	10
B	31	10	41
C	10	41	51
D	5	41	46
E	5	51	56
F	3	56	59
G	4	56	60
H	2	60	62

C. Finding the Latest Start and Finish Times

To find the latest time each activity can start and finish, trace backward through the network:

Activity H: The latest H can finish is set equal to the earliest day it can finish: day 62. Thus, $LF_H = 62$.

$LS_H = LF_H - t_H$ therefore $LS_H = 62 - 2 = 60$.

Activities F and G: Both activities immediately precede H, and so $LF_F = LF_G = LS_H = 60$. $LS_F = 60 - 3 = 57$. $LS_G = 60 - 4 = 56$.

Activity E: E precedes both F and G. The latest F can start is day 57, but G must start by day 56. Therefore, $LF_E = 56$ and $LS_E = 56 - 5 = 51$.

Activity D: D immediately precedes F, and $LF_D = LS_F = 57$. $LS_D = 57 - 5 = 52$.

Activity C: C immediately precedes E, so $LF_C = LS_E = 51$. $LS_C = 51 - 10 = 41$.

Activity B: B precedes activities C and D. $LS_C = 41$, and $LS_D = 52$; therefore, $LF_B = 41$ and $LS_B = 41 - 31 = 10$.

Activity A: A immediately precedes B, and so $LF_A = LS_B = 10$ and $LS_A = 10 - 10 = 0$.

		Earliest		Latest		
(1) Activity, i	(2) Duration, t_i	(3) Start Time, ES_i	(4) Finish Time, EF_i	(5) Start Time, LS_i	(6) Finish Time, LF_i	(7) Slack, S_i
A	10	0	10	0	10	0
B	31	10	41	10	41	0
C	10	41	51	41	51	0
D	5	41	46	52	57	11
E	5	51	56	51	56	0
F	3	56	59	57	60	1
G	4	56	60	56	60	0
H	2	60	62	60	62	0

D. Network Diagrams with Start and Finish Times

The earliest start and finish times are shown above the activity letter. The latest start and finish times are shown below the activity letter.

Activity-on-Arrow Network

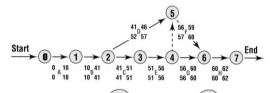

Activity-on-Node Network

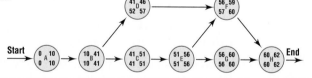

Latest Start Time for an Activity

$$LS_i = LF_i - t_i \qquad (12.2)$$

Slack Time for an Activity

$$S_i = LS_i - ES_i \qquad (12.3)$$
$$S_i = LF_i - EF_i \qquad (12.4)$$

where LS_i = latest time activity i can be started without delaying entire project

391

LF_i = latest finish time for activity i
S_i = activity i slack time
t_i = duration of activity i
EF_i = earliest finish time for activity i
ES_i = earliest time activity i can be started given that all its predecessor activities have started as early as possible and have all been completed

(A→B→D→F→H), (A→B→C→E→F→H), and (A→B→C→E→G→H) are the three distinct paths through the network diagram for the General Ledger project. Every activity along the third path has a slack time of zero; this path is called a **critical path.**

> **DEFINITION:** The critical path is the longest time path through a network. Every activity that lies on a critical path has a slack time of zero.

The first and second paths are not critical paths because each one contains some **path slack time** (11 days and 1 day, respectively).

> **DEFINITION:** The path slack time is the amount of time the activities along the path can be delayed without delaying the entire project.

Note that the path slack is not necessarily equal to the sum of the activity slacks along its path. For example, the sum of the activity slacks along the first path is 12 days ($S_A + S_B + S_D + S_F + S_H = 0 + 0 + 11 + 1 + 0 = 12$). But if activity D is deferred 11 days and activity F 1 day, the entire project will be 1 day late because the activity slack calculation assumes that all other activities along its path are started as soon as possible. The actual slack for the set of activities along the first path is 11, not 12, days.

Probabilistic Time Estimates Realistically, activity times cannot be predicted with 100 percent accuracy. It was mentioned earlier that PERT addresses this problem by using three estimates of activity duration: *earliest likely, most likely,* and *latest likely.*

> **DEFINITION:** *The earliest likely (optimistic) time* is the time required to complete the activity under the most favorable conditions.

> **DEFINITION:** *The most likely (probable) time* is the time required to complete the activity under normal conditions.

> **DEFINITION:** *The latest likely (pessimistic) time* is the time required to complete the activity under the most unfavorable conditions.

The expected duration of an activity is the weighted average of the three time estimates [equation (12.5)]. This equation is based on the beta statistical frequency distribution and implies that the most likely time (m) is four times more likely to occur than are the earliest likely and latest likely times.[6] The variability of an activity's expected duration is given by equations (12.6) and (12.7).

---

[6] The beta distribution was chosen by the originators of PERT because it appeared to be the most appropriate for their purposes. PERT was developed for project management in the aerospace industry; because most activities in aerospace projects occur just once, insufficient data were available to choose a distribution based on empirical evidence. The beta distribution is a unimodel distribution (i.e., it has a single peak value) with finite endpoints. It can be skewed to the right, skewed to the left, or evenly distributed.

Expected Average Time

$$ET_i = \frac{a_i + 4m_i + b_i}{6} \tag{12.5}$$

Variance of the Expected Average Time

$$\sigma_i^2 = \left(\frac{b_i - a_i}{6}\right)^2 \tag{12.6}$$

Standard Deviation of the Expected Average Time

$$\sigma_i = \frac{b_i - a_i}{6} \tag{12.7}$$

where ET_i = expected average time to complete activity i
a_i = earliest likely time to complete activity i
m_i = most likely time to complete activity i
b_i = latest likely time to complete activity i
σ_i^2 = variance of expected average time to complete activity i

Because variance is a measure of dispersion, the greater its value, the less reliance can be put on the probability that the actual activity time will be ET_i.[7]

In addition to the variance of individual activities, project managers are interested in the total variance of the time estimates for activities along a path. This variance can be calculated by using equation (12.8).

Variance of the Expected Average Time to Complete the Activities along a Chosen Path

$$\sigma_{cp}^2 = \sum_{i=1}^{n} \sigma_i^2 \tag{12.8}$$

where σ_{cp}^2 = variance of chosen path
σ_i^2 = variance of expected average time to complete activity i on chosen path
n = number of activities on chosen path

In the General Ledger project, the earliest likely, most likely, and latest likely times for each activity are shown in Exhibit 12.12A. Using this data, one can calculate the expected time and the variance of the expected time for each activity.

The next step is to recalculate the earliest start, earliest finish, latest start, and latest finish times for each activity, using the expected times calculated in Exhibit 12.12A. These revised times can be found on the AOA network diagram in Exhibit 12.12B. Note that the expected duration of the project has grown from 62 to 68.5 days. The standard deviation of the critical path is 7.79 days.

What is the probability of finishing the General Ledger project in, say, 70 days? To answer this question, use the standardized normal distribution table in Appendix

---

[7] Paths that are not critical but have a high variance may become critical as the project progresses. By running a simulation, it is possible to work out how many times in 100, say, a noncritical path is likely to become critical. If the ratio is high, it signals managers to pay as much attention to items on that near-critical path as they do to those which lie on "true" critical paths.

EXHIBIT 12.12   TOOLBOX: PROBABILISTIC TIME ESTIMATES

A. Probabilistic Time Estimates for the General Ledger Project

(1) Activity, i	(2) Earliest Likely Time, a_i	(3) Most Likely Time, m_i	(4) Latest Likely Time, b_i	(5) Expected Time, ET_i	(6) Variance of Expected Time, σ_i
A	6	10	14	10	1.78
B	24	31	68	36	53.78
C	7	10	13	10	1.00
D	3	5	7	5	0.44
E	3	5	13	6	2.78
F	2	3	4	3	0.11
G	2	4	9	4.5	1.36
H	1.5	2	2.5	2	0.03

Column 5 = [column 2 + 4 (column 3) + column 4] ÷ 6.
Column 6 = [(column 4 − column 2) ÷ 6]².

B. Activity-on-Arrow Network Diagram for the General Ledger Project Based on Probabilistic Time Estimates

The critical path is A→B→C→E→G→H, and its expected duration is 68.5 days. The standard deviation of the critical path is

$$\sigma_{cp} = \sqrt{\sigma_A^2 + \sigma_B^2 + \sigma_C^2 + \sigma_E^2 + \sigma_G^2 + \sigma_H^2}$$

$$= \sqrt{1.78 + 53.78 + 1.0 + 2.78 + 1.36 + 0.3} = 7.79$$

B.[8] The z score will be equal to the desired date minus the expected date divided by the standard deviation of the project's critical path:

$$z = \frac{\text{Desired date} - \text{Expected date}}{\text{Standard deviation of critical path}}$$

$$= \frac{70 - 68.5}{7.79} = 0.19$$

It is important to know the area under the normal curve associated with the z score that has been calculated. The area under the normal curve for $z = 0.19$ is 0.5753. The probability of completing the project by day 70 is therefore 57.53 percent. Similarly, it can be shown that the probability of finishing the project by day 80 is approximately 93 percent.

PERT/CPM: Limitations and Extensions   Although PERT/CPM can be a very valuable tool for planning and controlling projects, it is not suitable for every type of

---

[8] The expected project length was calculated by summing the expected durations of each activity. The duration of each activity is an independent random variable. The central limit theorem states that the sum of a large number of independent random variables is approximately normally distributed regardless of the distribution of the individual random variables.

project. The project must consist of a set of well-defined activities each of which can be started and stopped independently of the others. The precedence relationships among these activities must be known, and realistic time estimates must be available for each activity.

A common criticism of PERT/CPM involves its emphasis on critical paths. In practice, activities that are *not* on a critical path often cause the entire project to be extended. As was mentioned earlier, managers must monitor near-critical paths as well as critical paths.

The use of three time estimates and the beta distribution has also been criticized. People often find it difficult to make one accurate time estimate for each project activity, let alone three. Even if all three estimates are reasonably accurate, the expected time is only an approximation and is subject to errors on the order of 5 to 10 percent.[9] If errors of this magnitude are significant for a project, other formulas which reduce the statistical error can be used [see Moder and Rodgers (1968) and Perry and Greig (1975)].

In response to these limitations, PERT/CPM has been modified and extended. Three examples are listed below:

- **Precedence networking** allows for three additional types of precedence relationships: (1) start to start; activity B cannot start until n days after activity A has been started, (2) finish to finish; activity B cannot be finished until n days after activity A has been completed, and (3) start to finish; activity B cannot finish until n days after activity A has been started.
- **Decision CPM** permits sets of alternative activities to be included in the network diagram and analysis. This allows planners to examine the scheduling implications of alternative activities before a final choice is made.
- **GERT** (Graphical Evaluation and Review Technique) does not assume that all activities will take place but that each activity has a probability of occurrence. This implies that not all activities in the network may be completed. Also, looping back to redo the previous activities is permitted.

Resource-Constrained Schedules

When people are asked to provide time estimates for project activities, they must make assumptions about the availability of the resources (e.g., people, equipment, money) that will be required. For example, consider activity B—develop the computer programs—of the General Ledger project. Its total duration of 31 days is based on several assumptions. It is assumed that three programmers will be available and that the person who programs a particular module will also test and debug that module. It also assumes that other team members will be able to prepare for and attend program walkthroughs. When considered in isolation, these assumptions make sense. But what if the team is assigned only two programmers and three programming activities are scheduled for the same time?

Not only do resources tend to be limited, their availability often changes over time. Project managers must schedule (and reschedule) around these limitations. The net effect of resource constraints may be to delay some activities and possibly the project.

Let us return to activity B of the General Ledger project. The estimated duration of each of the 12 tasks that constitute activity B is given in Exhibit 12.13A. As shown

---

[9] In extreme cases the PERT formulas can lead to absolute errors in the estimated activity time on the order of 30 percent. See MacCrimmon and Ryavec (1964).

in the corresponding network diagram in Exhibit 12.13B, if three programmers are available, the entire activity can be completed in 31 days.

Suppose two, not three, programmers are available to work on the General Ledger project. As illustrated by the resource requirement charts in Exhibit 12.13C, if all the activity B tasks are started as early as possible, the number of programmers required exceeds the number available on six days.

It is possible to reschedule activities—by delaying tasks B7 and B10, for example—to meet the resource constraints and not delay the project beyond the planned completion time.

> **DEFINITION:** *Resource leveling* is the process of rescheduling activities to smooth resource requirements while extending the length of the project as little as possible.

The activity B tasks of the General Ledger project have been rescheduled using the **minimum slack time decision rule** described below:

- Allocate resources period by period.
- Whenever resource requirements exceed the resources available, list the activities competing for a resource in order of their slack time, lowest first.

EXHIBIT 12.13   TOOLBOX: RESOURCE CONSTRAINTS

Activity B of the General Ledger project—develop the programs—consists of the 12 tasks described below.

A. Resource Requirements for Activity B

		Staff Required		Duration,	Start Date	
Task	Description	Designers	Programmers	days	Early	Late
B1	Design the General Ledger system	1	—	4	10	10
B2	Design module 1	1	—	3	14	14
B3	Design module 2	1	—	2	14	19
B4	Design system interface	1	—	2	14	30
B5	Program module 1	—	1	9	17	17
B6	Program module 2	—	1	6	16	21
B7	Program system interface	—	1	4	16	32
B8	Test and debug module 1	—	1	5	26	26
B9	Test and debug module 2	—	1	4	22	27
B10	Test and debug system interface	—	1	3	20	23
B11	Conduct system testing	1	2	8	31	31
B12	Conduct intersystem testing	1	1	2	39	39

B. Network Diagram for Activity B

Note that one or more programmers are needed for each of the shaded nodes.

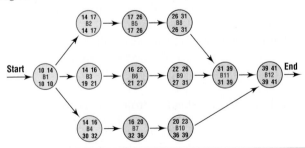

Suppose only two programmers are available. As shown below, more programmers are needed than are available. Under the earliest start scenario, the team is short one programmer on days 17 to 22. Under the latest start scenario, the team is short one programmer on days 33 to 38.

C. Resource Requirement Charts

ACTIVITIES START AS EARLY AS POSSIBLE

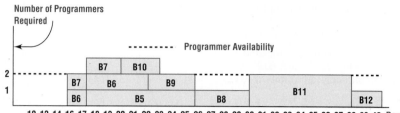

ACTIVITIES START AS LATE AS POSSIBLE

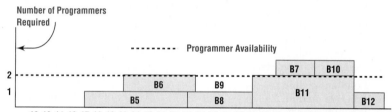

By deferring some of the activity B tasks, however, the team can complete activity B only one day late with two programmers.

D. Revising the Schedule Using the Minimum Slack Time Decision Rule

Using the decision rule for the minimum slack time, the available programmers are allocated to tasks as follows:

Day 16:
  • Activities eligible to start: B6, B7
  • Allocation: one programmer to B6, one to B7

Day 17:
  • Activities eligible to start/continue: B5, B6, B7
  • Slack values: B5 = 0, B6 = 5, B7 = 16
  • Allocation: one programmer to B5, one to B6
  • Defer remaining three days of B7

Day 18, 19, 20, 21: same as day 17

Day 22:
  • Activity B6 has been completed
  • Activities eligible to start/continue: B5, B7, B9
  • Slack values: B5 = 0, B7 = 11, B9 = 5
  • Allocation: one programmer to B5, one to B9
  • Defer B7

Day 23, 24, 25: same as day 22

Day 26:
  • Activities B5 and B9 have been completed
  • Activities eligible to start/continue: B7, B8
  • Allocation: one programmer to B7, one to B8

Day 27, 28: same as day 26

Day 29:
  • Activity B7 has been completed
  • Activities eligible to start/continue: B9, B10
  • Allocation: one programmer to B9, one to B10

Day 30: same as day 29

(Exhibit 12.13 continues on next page)

EXHIBIT 12.13   *(continued)*

Day 31:	• Activity B8 has been completed • Activities eligible to start/continue: B10, B11 (which requires two programmers) • Slack values: B10 = 5, B11 = 0 • Allocation: two programmers to B11

Day 32, 33, 34, 35, 36, 37, 38: same as day 31

Day 39:	• Activity B11 has been completed • Activities eligible to start: B10 • Allocation: one programmer to B10
Day 40:	• Activity B10 has been completed • Activities eligible to start: B12 • Allocation: one programmer to B12

Day 41: same as day 40

Day 42:	• All activities have been completed

REVISED SCHEDULE

Task	Description	Duration, days	Scheduled Dates
B1	Design the General Ledger system	4	10–13
B2	Design module 1	3	14–16
B3	Design module 2	2	14, 15
B4	Design system interface	2	14, 15
B5	Program module 1	9	17–25
B6	Program module 2	6	16–21
B7	Program system interface	4	16, 26–28
B8	Test and debug module 1	5	26–30
B9	Test and debug module 2	4	22–25
B10	Test and debug system interface	3	29, 30, 40
B11	Conduct system testing	8	31–38
B12	Conduct intersystem testing	2	40, 41

PROGRAMMER REQUIREMENTS FOR THE REVISED SCHEDULE

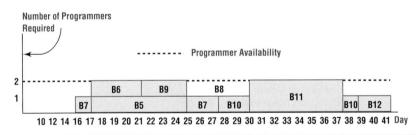

- The resource is allocated to the activity with the least slack time, then to the one with the second least slack time, and so on. The activities with the most slack may have to be rescheduled.
- The firm should try to reschedule activities that are not on a critical path to free resources for activities that do lie on a critical path.

Exhibit 12.13D walks through the procedure day by day. To simplify the discussion, it is assumed that programmers are the only limited resource for the project.

In the last section aggregate resource requirements were used to test the feasibility of the project schedule and revise the schedule to meet resource limitations. Aggregate resource requirements are also needed by project managers when they prepare budgets and cash flow estimates.

Projecting Cash Flows

Let us return to the General Ledger project and focus again on Activity B: develop the computer programs. The cost of each of the 12 tasks that constitute activity B has been estimated and is shown in Exhibit 12.14A. The daily cost associated with each task has been calculated by dividing the total task cost by its estimated duration.[10]

With the daily cost data, it is possible to develop a cash flow chart that shows the cumulative cash flow if each task is started as early as possible. It is also possible to develop a cash flow chart that shows the cumulative cash flows if each task that is not on the critical path (tasks B3, B4, B6, B7, B9, and B10) is delayed as long as possible. These cumulative cash flow scenarios (see Exhibit 12.14D) provide the envelope within which costs are expected to move.

If activity times are not known with certainty, beginning at the earliest start time provides a safety margin. This margin is not free, however. Heavier cash outflows early on mean borrowing earlier, and this increases the cost of financing the project. The cost of financing may in fact cause the project manager to delay activities as much as possible. A cap on monthly expenditure may be demanded by the lender (or by senior management), and this may lead to an early start for some activities and the movement of others to spread the outlays more uniformly across the duration of the project.

---

[10] In practice, this assumption of linearity does not always hold. If the actual daily or weekly costs are known, they should be used.

EXHIBIT 12.14   TOOLBOX: CASH FLOW ANALYSIS

The estimated costs of all 12 activity B tasks are shown below. The estimated daily cost is the total estimated cost divided by the activity duration.

A. Estimated Costs for Activity B Tasks

Task	Description	Total Estimated Cost, $	Duration, days	Estimated Daily Cost, $
B1	Design the General Ledger system	1,170	4	292.5
B2	Design module 1	875	3	291.67
B3	Design module 2	580	2	290
B4	Design system interface	580	2	290
B5	Program module 1	2,440	9	271.11
B6	Program module 2	1,625	6	270.83
B7	Program system interface	1,085	4	271.25
B8	Test and debug module 1	1,355	5	271
B9	Test and debug module 2	1,085	4	271.25
B10	Test and debug system interface	815	3	271.67
B11	Conduct system testing	5,690	8	711.25
B12	Conduct intersystem testing	860	2	430

(Exhibit 12.14 continues on next page)

EXHIBIT 12.14 *(continued)*

B. Network Diagram for Activity B

Note that once again it is assumed that three programmers are available.

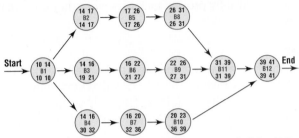

B1→B2→B5→B8→B11→B12, B1→B3→B6→B9→B11→B12, and B1→B4→B7→B10→B12 are the three paths through the network. By deferring activities along the second and third paths until their latest start date, the team can also defer cash flows.

C. Early and Late Cash Flows

	Earliest Start			Latest Start		
Days	Ongoing Activities	Daily Cost	Cumulative Cost to Date	Ongoing Activities	Daily Cost	Cumulative Cost to Date
10–13	B1	292.5	292.5, 585, 877.5, 1170	B1	292.5	292.5, 585, 877.5, 1170
14 and 15	B2, B3, B4	871.67	2041.67, 2913.34	B2	291.67	1461.67, 1753.34
16	B2, B6, B7	833.75	3747.09	B2	291.67	2045.01
17 and 18	B5, B6, B7	813.19	4560.28, 5373.47	B5	271.11	2316.12, 2587.23
19	B5, B6, B7	813.19	6186.66	B5, B3	561.11	3148.34
20	B5, B6, B10	813.61	7000.27	B5, B3	561.11	3709.45
21	B5, B6, B10	813.61	7813.88	B5, B6	541.94	4251.39
22	B5, B6, B10	813.61	8627.49	B5, B6	541.94	4793.33
23–25	B5, B9	542.36	9169.85, 9712.21, 10254.57	B5, B6	541.94	5335.27, 5877.21, 6419.15
26	B8	271	10525.57	B8, B6	541.83	6960.98
27–29	B8	271	10796.57, 11067.57, 11338.57	B8, B9	542.25	7503.23, 8045.48, 8587.73
30	B8	271	11609.57	B8, B9, B4	832.25	9419.98
31	B11	711.25	12320.82	B11, B4	1001.25	10421.23
32–35	B11	711.25	13032.07, 13743.32, 14454.57, 15165.82	B11, B7	982.50	11403.73, 12386.23, 13368.73, 14351.23
36–38	B11	711.25	15877.07, 16588.32, 17299.57	B11, B10	982.92	15334.15, 16317.07, 17299.99
39 and 40	B12	430	17729.99, 18159.57	B12	430	17729.99, 18159.99

D. Cumulative Cash Flows

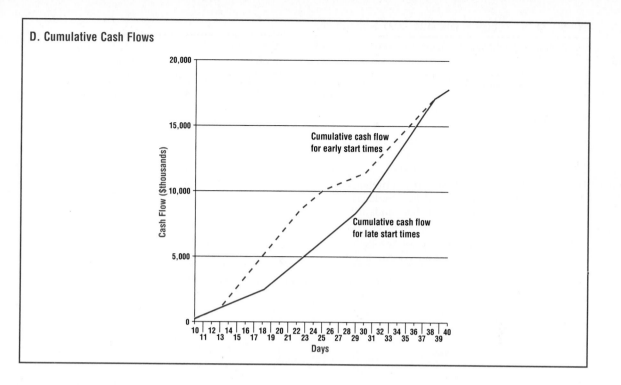

Minimum-Cost Scheduling

Project activities can often be expedited if more resources are assigned to them. An important managerial concern is whether the benefits of completing the project more quickly outweigh the associated costs. Of course, allocating additional resources increases the direct costs of the project. However, if the project duration is reduced, the indirect project costs (e.g., management support and other overhead allocations) decrease. There may be penalties if the project is completed after a due date, and bonuses may be paid if the project is completed earlier. If the savings in indirect project costs (and avoided penalty costs) combined with any early completion bonuses more than offset the increase in direct costs, expediting the project makes economic sense.

Not all activities can or should be expedited ("crashed"). As a rule of thumb, it is a waste of money and resources to crash activities that have plenty of slack time. Only critical activities need to be crashed.

DEFINITION: *Minimum-cost scheduling* involves expediting selected activities to reduce total project costs.

Let us walk through the following seven-step procedure to find the minimum-cost schedule for the General Ledger's activity B tasks.

Step 1. Develop a network diagram and preliminary schedule. Activities should be assigned their normal resources and should start as early as possible.

An AON network diagram and a preliminary schedule for the activity B tasks appear in Exhibit 12.15A. Each task is scheduled to begin as early as possible.[11]

---

[11] The same preliminary schedule would have been developed if an AOA diagram had been drawn instead.

EXHIBIT 12.15   TOOLBOX: MINIMUM COST SCHEDULING

A. Preliminary Schedule for Activity B Tasks (Based on Earliest Start Times)

Task	Description	Earliest Start Time	Duration	Earliest Finish Time
B1	Design the General Ledger system	10	4	14
B2	Design module 1	14	3	17
B3	Design module 2	14	2	16
B4	Design system interface	14	2	16
B5	Program module 1	17	9	26
B6	Program module 2	16	6	22
B7	Program system interface	16	4	20
B8	Test and debug module 1	26	5	31
B9	Test and debug module 2	22	4	26
B10	Test and debug system interface	20	3	23
B11	Conduct system testing	31	8	39
B12	Conduct intersystem testing	39	2	41

NETWORK DIAGRAM FOR ACTIVITY B TASKS

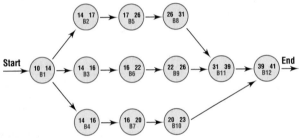

B. Cost and Duration of Activity B Tasks

The next table shows the normal cost and duration of the activity B (develop programs) tasks. Some tasks can be performed more quickly (i.e., crashed) if people are authorized to work overtime, but at an increased daily cost. Note that tasks B3, B4, and B12 cannot be crashed.

The overhead cost associated with activity B is $220 per day. Since the entire activity is expected to take 31 days, the total expected overhead cost is $6,820.

	Normal		Crash			
(1) Task	(2) Total Cost, $	(3) Duration, days	(4) Total Cost, $	(5) Total Premium, $	(6) Duration, days	(7) Daily Crash Premium
B1	640	4	840	200	3	200
B2	480	3	560	80	2	80
B3	320	2	—	—	—	—
B4	320	2	—	—	—	—
B5	1,260	9	1,470	210	6	70
B6	840	6	980	140	4	70
B7	560	4	630	70	3	70
B8	700	5	840	140	3	70
B9	560	4	630	70	3	70
B10	420	3	490	70	2	70
B11	3,360	8	3,940	580	6	290
B12	280	2	—	—	—	—
Total	9,740					

Column 5 = column 4 − column 2.   Column 7 = column 5 ÷ (column 3 − column 6).

The total direct costs ($9,740) plus the total overhead costs ($6,820) equal $16,560.

C. Finding the Minimum-Cost Schedule

Iteration 1
Path 1 (B1→B2→B5→B8→B11→B12) duration: 31 (critical path)
Path 2 (B1→B3→B6→B9→B11→B12) duration: 26
Path 3 (B1→B4→B10→B12) duration: 15
Crash alternatives along path 1: B1 ($200), B2 ($80), B5 ($70), B8 ($70), B11 ($290)
Least-cost alternatives: B5 and B8

Let us arbitrarily choose B8 and crash it by one day.

Iteration 2
Path 1 duration: 30 (critical path)
Path 2 duration: 26
Path 3 duration: 15
Crash alternatives along path 1: B1 ($200), B2 ($80), B5 ($70), B8 ($70), B11 ($290)
Least-cost alternatives: B5 and B8

Let us arbitrarily choose B8 and crash it by one day. Note that task B8 has now been reduced from five days to three days and cannot be expedited further.

NETWORK DIAGRAM FOR ACTIVITY B TASKS AFTER ITERATIONS 1 AND 2

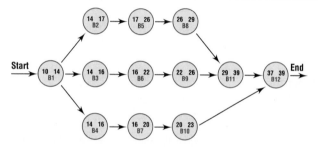

Iteration 3
Path 1 duration: 29 (critical path)
Path 2 duration: 26
Path 3 duration: 15
Crash alternatives along path 1: B1 ($200), B2 ($80), B5 ($70), B11 ($290)
Least-cost alternative: B5

Iterations 4 and 5
The same alternatives as in iteration 3 are available, and the same selection—B5—is made. B5 can be expedited only three days.

NETWORK DIAGRAM FOR ACTIVITY B TASKS AFTER ITERATIONS 1 TO 5

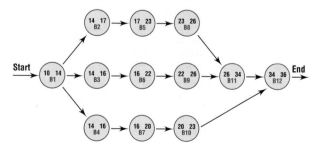

Iteration 6
Path 1 duration: 26 (critical path)
Path 2 duration: 26 (critical path)
Path 3 duration: 15

(Exhibit 12.15 continues on next page)

EXHIBIT 12.15 *(continued)*

There are now two critical paths. Therefore, to reduce the duration of activity B by one day, the team must reduce the durations of both path 1 and path 2 by one day.

Crash alternatives: B1 ($200) or B11 ($290) or [B2 ($80) + B6 ($70)] or [B2 ($80) + B9 ($70)]

Least-cost alternatives: [B2 + B6] and [B2 + B9]

Let us arbitrarily choose B2 and B6.

NETWORK DIAGRAM FOR ACTIVITY B TASKS AFTER ITERATIONS 1 TO 6

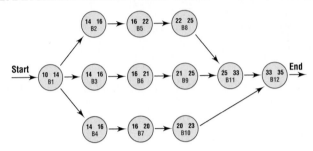

Iteration 7
Path 1 duration: 25 (critical path)
Path 2 duration: 25 (critical path)
Path 3 duration: 15
Crash alternatives: B1 ($200) and B11 ($290)
Least-cost alternative: B1

Iteration 8
Path 1 duration: 24 (critical path)
Path 2 duration: 24 (critical path)
Path 3 duration: 15
Crash alternative: B11 ($290)

Since the cost of crashing task B11 one day exceeds the daily savings of $220, task B11 should not be crashed. The minimum-cost schedule has been found and is illustrated by the network diagram below.

MINIMUM-COST SCHEDULE FOR ACTIVITY B

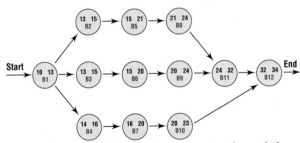

The crash premiums associated with each of the seven iterations are shown below. Reducing the duration of activity B from 31 to 24 days results in an overhead allocation savings of $1,540 ($220 per day times seven days) and a crash premium of $700. The net saving is $840.

Iteration	Task(s) Crashed	Crash Premium, $	Cumulative Crash Premium, $	Activity B Duration
1	B8	70	70	30
2	B8	70	140	29
3	B5	70	210	28
4	B5	70	280	27
5	B5	70	350	26
6	B2 and B6	70 + 80 = 150	500	25
7	B1	200	700	24

The direct, indirect, and total costs associated with every possible project duration are shown below.

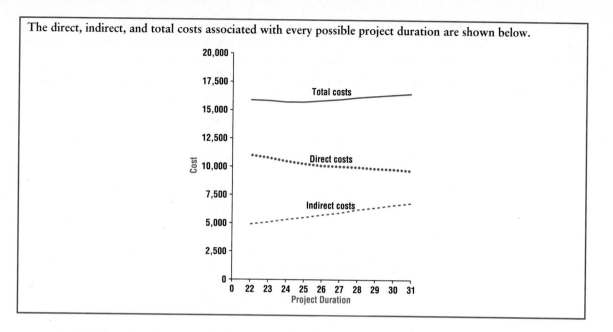

Step 2. Calculate the cost of the project. This will serve as an upper limit.

The normal direct cost of each activity B task is the labor cost of the person or persons assigned to that task multiplied by the duration of the task. The daily overhead cost is $220 per day; this brings the total costs associated with activity B up to $16,560.

Step 3. Identify activities that can be crashed and determine the shortest time each activity requires (crash time) and the daily cost of expediting the activity (crash premium).

The table in Exhibit 12.15B shows the daily cost of expediting each task. Note that tasks B3, B4, and B12 cannot be crashed.

Step 4. Calculate the length of each path through the network and identify the critical path(s). The length of the critical path(s) is the expected project duration.

There are three paths through the activity B network:

Path 1 (B1→B2→B5→B8→B11→B12) is 31 days long and is the critical path.
Path 2 (B1→B3→B6→B9→B11→B12) is 26 days long.
Path 3 (B1→B4→B10→B12) is only 15 days long.

Step 5. Generate a list of activities that lie on a critical path and can be crashed. If there are no such activities, the minimum-cost schedule has been found. Stop.

Use the list to develop sets of one or more activities on parallel critical paths that when simultaneously reduced by one day[12] will reduce the duration of all critical paths by one day. If there are no such sets, the minimum-cost schedule has been found. Stop.

[12] Any unit of time can be used (e.g., week, month).

Since path 1 (B1→B2→B5→B8→B11→B12) is the critical path, the duration of this path is shortened to shorten the duration of activity B. Note that with the exception of task B12, all activities along the path can be crashed.

Step 6. Select the activity (or set of activities with the lowest (combined) crash premium. Compare the premium with the daily penalty. If it exceeds the daily penalty, the minimum cost schedule has been found.

Tasks B5 and B8 both have the lowest daily crash premium: $70. Since this premium is less than the $220 daily overhead cost, the minimum cost schedule has not been found. Let us arbitrarily choose B8.

Step 7. Crash the selected activity (or set of activities) by one day. Return to step 4.

Activity B8 has been crashed by one day, and the activity B network diagram has been updated in Exhibit 12.15C. After seven more iterations through steps 4 to 7 (see Exhibit 12.15D), the minimum-cost schedule is found.

When the General Ledger project was crashed (see Exhibit 12.15) to minimize the cost of the project, the number of critical paths was increased from one to two. In general, as project activities are crashed, the number of critical paths increases.

Each critical path requires close attention by the management, for any delay in an activity along a critical path will delay the project. Therefore, the more critical paths there are, the more managers' time will be required.[13] Therefore, for a small management team there should be a minimum number of critical paths, perhaps one or two. Larger management teams may be able to handle more critical paths.

Because of the unpredictability of many projects, a project manager should have a small surplus of management time available for emergencies such as noncritical activities that suddenly become critical and activities that were not in the original work plan. Thus, managers should strive to limit the number of critical paths even when well-designed information and control systems are in place.

Monitoring Cash Flows

As the project progresses, costs have to be monitored and compared to the budget. Any cost overruns or underruns must be identified so that appropriate actions can be taken.

Suppose the General Ledger project has been under way for 30 days. The system specifications were completed in only nine days, one day less than expected. Activity B—programming the system—has been started but appears to be taking much longer than expected. The lead designer has supplied the data in Exhibit 12.16A.

Since tasks B1, B2, B3, and B4 have already been completed, it is easy to identify any cost overruns or underruns by comparing the actual amount spent on a task with the amount budgeted for that task. Task B1, for example, has an overrun of $285.

What about tasks that have not been completed? Task B5, for example, is 50 percent complete. If it is assumed that costs are incurred at the same rate at which work is completed, equations (12.9) and (12.10) can be used to estimate whether task B5 is running over (or under) budget.

---

[13] In practice, management costs do not rise in proportion to the number of critical paths. If the number of critical paths is doubled, for example, the increased need for communication and coordination across activities tends to increase management costs by closer to three times the original costs.

EXHIBIT 12.16   TOOLBOX: BUDGETARY CONTROL

A. Status Report for Activity B Tasks as of Day 26

Task	Scheduled Start	Scheduled Finish	Actual Start	Actual Finish	Percentage Completed	Expenditures, $ Budget	Expenditures, $ Actual
B1	10	14	9	14	100	1,170	1,455
B2	14	17	14	19	100	875	1,455
B3	14	16	14	17	100	580	870
B4	14	16	14	18	100	580	1,165
B5	17	26	19	—	50	2,440	1,900
B6	16	22	17	23	100	1,625	1,625
B7	16	20	18	21	100	1,085	815
B8	26	31	—	—	0	1,355	—
B9	22	26	23	—	40	1,085	815
B10	20	23	21	24	100	815	815
B11	31	39	—	—	0	5,690	—
B12	39	41	—	—	0	860	—

B. Cost Report for Activity B Tasks

Task	Percentage Completed	Expenditures, $ Budget	Expenditures, $ Actual	Value of Work Completed	Cost Overrun (Underrun)
B1	100	1,170	1,455	1,170	285
B2	100	875	1,455	875	580
B3	100	580	870	580	290
B4	100	580	1,165	580	585
B5	50	2,440	1,900	1,220	680
B6	100	1,625	1,625	1,625	0
B7	100	1,085	815	1,085	(270)
B8	0	1,355	—	—	—
B9	40	1,085	815	434	381
B10	100	815	815	815	0
B11	0	5,690	—	—	—
B12	0	860	—	—	—

Value of Work Completed

$$V_i = \left(\frac{P_i}{100}\right)B_i \qquad (12.9)$$

Cost Overrun/Underrun

$$D_i = C_i - V_i \qquad (12.10)$$

where V_i = value of work completed for activity i
P_i = percentage of work completed for activity i
B_i = budget for activity i
D_i = cost overrun (underrun if its value is negative)
C_i = actual expenditure on activity i

Calculations of the cost overrun/underrun for each task completed or currently under way on the General Ledger project are shown in Exhibit 12.16B. Note that four of the seven completed tasks incurred cost overruns and that both of the tasks currently in progress are incurring overruns; there is cause for alarm. Task B9, a task on the critical path, should now be finished but is only 40 percent complete. Every additional day spent on this task lengthens the project duration by one day. Action to bring the project back on line may call for even heavier expenditures on tasks B5, B8, B11, and B12 to expedite (or crash) activity B.

12.6 MANAGING A PORTFOLIO OF PROJECTS

The tools and techniques described in this chapter are relatively old, and only marginal improvements have been made to them. Their widespread use has been facilitated by inexpensive software that runs on personal computers.

What has changed is the need for fast-response organizations (FROs) to effectively manage a *portfolio of projects*. Remember that in an FRO there is always a wide range of ongoing projects. Some of these projects reflect the FRO's commitment to delighting its customers with a steady stream of new and improved products. As was discussed in Chapter 7, the fastest way to develop high-quality, low-cost products that meet market needs is to create product development teams composed of cross-functional and external (customer and supplier) representatives. In addition to product development teams, people throughout the firm are actively involved in projects to continually improve the FRO's operations and eliminate waste.

With so many projects, an FRO must establish a **continuous project support system.** A project selection process must be established, and a relatively large pool

---

MANAGERIAL IMPLICATIONS

When one sees a building being erected or a computer system being installed, one is looking only at the tip of the iceberg from a project management point of view. For many projects the execution phase is not the longest phase or the most critical as far as costs and customer satisfaction are concerned. There is a parallel between the stages of a project life cycle and the stages of a product life cycle, and the lessons to be learned are similar.

If sufficient time and effort are not devoted up front to properly designing the project and obtaining the necessary approvals, the project is likely to be compromised. As with a product, it is much more costly to redesign a project once it has started than to design it properly in the first place. That does not mean the whole project need be tightly designed before it starts. Firms are beginning to recognize the value of leaving design commitment until the last minute. Firms have to become good at designing flexible interfaces between project elements so that they can keep element/stage design unfrozen for the longest possible time.

This presents real problems for project planning, for the firm has to commit resources (including cash) before it can begin a specific phase. Detailed planning therefore takes place much closer to the time of execution than was previously the case.

Of course, delaying planning as long as possible should make project management much simpler, for there should be less uncertainty about the physical execution. The further ahead the planning takes place, the greater the likelihood of change and disruption. As disruption causes cost increases, better and later planning should minimize cost overruns.

This would be challenging enough if a firm had to be concerned only with one project. Managing multiple projects will be the order of the day for many firms in the future, however, and juggling resources to suit changing customer requirements while trying to retain efficiency will be a major challenge. Perhaps the surest way of managing under these conditions is to co-opt customers and suppliers to form a larger but looser project organization.

Managing complete project value chains—or at least the elements that are both critical and uncertain—should result in more effective project management and therefore more effective projects. If *everybody* is committed to a common vision and mutually set objectives, it is easier to design, plan, and execute the whole project. And if the project is executed properly, it should be much easier to learn the appropriate lessons from it. These lessons can be carried forward to subsequent projects.

of potential project team members and leaders must be created. Maintaining this resource pool requires ongoing training and development of critical communication, problem-solving, and leadership skills.

Part of this continuous project support system is an information system which allows the FRO to manage *across* projects. Since time is important and resources are limited, managers must know how best to allocate resources. An information system that allows managers to make online queries and play "what if" games is very valuable. For example, suppose project A begins to fall behind schedule. Managers may ask the system to project the impact of doing nothing, expediting key activities, or transferring resources from another project. If transferring resources is an option, managers need to know the effect of this on both projects. They also need to know which activity paths can be crashed, which are critical, and which are near-critical.

Frequent information exchanges also take place between people on different teams. An information system that makes this exchange fast, simple, and painless is essential.

An information system that establishes a corporate project memory for an FRO saves time by avoiding the pitfall of continually reinventing the wheel. New teams can draw on this memory when they break down the project into activities, determine the relationships between those activities, and decide what resources will be needed and how long they will be needed. Actual activity durations reported by previous projects can be used in subsequent projects as a basis for time estimates. Requiring design teams to report on their organizational and operational effectiveness also improves the effectiveness of future teams.

CHAPTER SUMMARY

As more work is done in a team setting, the need for project management skills becomes more important. This chapter discussed the four phases of projects—conception, formative, operational, and termination—and the key managerial concerns associated with each one. It also reviewed the following tools and techniques that help managers organize and control projects:

- Work breakdown structures can be used to analyze a project into a set of activities. Activities can then be grouped into logical sets, or work packages, and assigned to specific people.
- The relationships between activities in even a relatively small project can become complex. Network diagrams help clarify and illustrate these relationships.
- Activity-on-arrow and activity-on-node diagrams are two formats for drawing network diagrams.
- A Gantt chart is a horizontal bar chart that shows the expected start and finish dates of each project activity. By adding the actual start and finish dates, managers can easily see which activities are ahead of schedule and which are behind.
- PERT/CPM network diagrams illustrate the relationships among project activities. They also show the earliest (and latest) start and finish times for each activity. PERT and CPM techniques are very similar. The major difference is that PERT uses three probabilistic time estimates for each activity, while CPM uses only one.
- If an activity can be delayed without delaying the entire project, it has slack time. If a path in a project network can be delayed without delaying the entire project, it has slack time. A path without slack time is a critical path.

- Project managers are often interested in the cash flow associated with a project plan. Limited finances may force project managers to delay activities as much as possible.
- Even if an activity is not complete, project managers can predict whether it will incur a cost overrun or underrun by using the formula for the value of work completed.
- Project resources (e.g., people and equipment) are usually limited. The minimum slack rule can help managers reschedule activities to smooth resource requirements while extending the length of the project as little as possible.
- Minimum-cost scheduling involves expediting selected activities to reduce total project costs.

Because there will always be a wide range of ongoing projects in a fast-response organization, such a firm has to establish a continuous project support system. An information system that allows the firm to manage across projects and establish a corporate project memory is an important part of this continuous support system.

KEY TERMS

Project
Project management
The conception phase
The formative phase
The operational phase
The termination phase
Work breakdown structure (WBS)
Work package
Network diagram
Product-focused work breakdown structure

Process-focused work breakdown structure
Activity-on-node (AON) network diagram
Activity-on-arrow (AOA) network diagram
Dummy activity
Gantt chart
PERT/CPM network diagrams
Earliest start and finish times

Activity slack time
Latest start and finish times
Critical path
Path slack time
Earliest likely (optimistic) time
Most likely (probable) time
Latest likely (pessimistic) time

Precedence networking
Decision CPM
GERT
Resource leveling
Minimum slack time decision rule
Minimum-cost scheduling
Continuous project support system

DISCUSSION QUESTIONS

1. Why will projects become more important in the future? What is likely to be the trend in average project duration?

2. Two friends of yours who are starting a catering business ask how network planning could possibly be of importance to them. What do you tell them?

3. In response to your well-reasoned response to their previous question, the same two friends say that all they need to do is buy a computer network planning package and everything will be easy. How do you respond to that statement?

4. Projects have one start point and one finish point. Under what circumstances could these rules be violated. What would be the management implications of doing this?

5. Of the two network techniques, which is better: CPM or PERT? How do you judge this?

6. Is it possible to manage a project using CPM and PERT network diagrams? What, if any, are the limitations of network diagrams from a management point of view?

7. For any project, what factors limit the number of levels in the work breakdown structure (WBS)? Is the depth of the WBS important?

8. What *is* the critical path in a network? How is it identified? How are "near-critical" paths identified?

9. Having identified near-critical paths, what should you do about them and why?

10. Why does the direct cost of projects tend to be lower when there are fewer critical paths?

11. In an R&D project in which two different approaches are tried in parallel, how would you allocate scarce resources such as technicians?

12. What resource do you think is most frequently the constraining resource on a project? How can this constraint be overcome?

13. What exactly is a work breakdown structure? How is it organized? What method of organizing a WBS is least appropriate, and why?

14. If uncertainty exists in any project, how might a firm best minimize the degree of uncertainty?

15. What is the relationship between a process flowchart and a network diagram? What can you learn from one that you can apply to the other? Why is this issue becoming important?

16. What are the four basic ways of forming project teams? What differentiates one from another? (See the supplement to this chapter to answer this question.)

17. What type of project team would you form for the following activities?
    a. Organizing the company picnic
    b. Selecting a new paper machine for a paper mill
    c. Designing a dam to be built in another country
    d. Building the dam
    e. Working on a business process reengineering project
    f. Assembling an automobile
    (See the supplement to this chapter to answer this question.)

18. What are the essential differences between "lightweight" and "heavyweight" project teams? Which one is better? (See the supplement to this chapter to answer this question.)

19. With what issues are project managers most concerned? Why? Does the type of project team influence the issues and their importance? (See the supplement to this chapter to answer this question.)

20. What are the characteristics of a good project manager? Which do you think is the most important? (See the supplement to this chapter to answer this question.)

21. Project managers are born, not made. Comment on this statement. (See the supplement to this chapter to answer this question.)

22. This chapter described how project teams are formed. How do you think teams of project team managers are formed? Would there ever be teams of project team managers? (See the supplement to this chapter to answer this question.)

23. If a feasible scenario has most future business organized along project lines, what implications should that have for the education of students and faculties of management and business schools? (See the supplement to this chapter to answer this question.)

PROBLEMS

1. A work breakdown structure (WBS) can be prepared for "house projects" as well as corporate projects. Design a WBS with no more than five levels for the following projects.
   a. Organizing a backyard barbeque
   b. Planning a one-month trip to Europe and Asia

2. Hanover Manufacturing Company is planning to install a closed circuit television (CCT) in its Alabama plant. The CCT will connect the following five departments: design, manufacturing, marketing, finance, and central purchasing. The company's director of design has been assigned the responsibility for completing the project in six months.
   a. Draw a WBS for the project. Consider activities such as procurement, location selection, wiring, installation, testing, and commissioning.

   b. Develop a corresponding network diagram for the project.

3. 🔲 A project includes 10 activities. Using the information in the table below, draw a PERT network diagram to represent the project. What is the estimated duration of the project?

Activity	Time, days Pessimistic	Probable	Optimistic	Preceding Activities
A	10	6	5	—
B	2	1	1	—
C	3	2	1	A
D	20	18	17	A
E	31	26	21	B
F	15	12	10	C, D, E
G	20	15	13	D, E
H	6	5	4	B
I	4	2	2	G
J	5	3	2	F, H, I

4. 💾 Identify the critical path in each of the following PERT networks.

a.

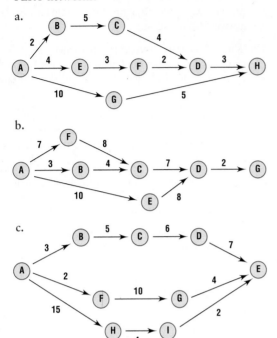

b.

c.

5. 💾 Mitusho Information Systems has received an order for a transportation information control system. The project manager has analyzed the project into a set of six activities and has prepared the time and cash flow estimates shown below.

Activity	Preceding Activity	Time Estimates, months			Cost Estimates, $ thousands per month		Maximum Months Activity Can Be Crashed
		a_i	b_i	m_i	Normal	Crash	
A. Design, code, and test software	—	12	16	14	20	30	1
B. Design, develop, and test hardware	—	1	5	3	15	20	1
C. Integrate hardware and software	A, B	2	5	5	50	70	2
D. Design and fabricate chassis	B	5	15	7	10	14	2
E. Integrate and test system	C, D	2	6	4	10	15	1
F. Deliver and perform customer test	E	6	14	10	20	40	2

What is the normal duration and cost of the project? Can the project be completed earlier at a lower cost? If so, what is the minimum cost?

6. Nova Bank is considering an innovative deposit scheme to attract middle-class salaried employees. Management has been asked by the board to conduct market research and establish the profit portential. The president of the bank has hired you to coordinate the work and ensure that a report is ready within the next six months. Using the flowchart below, determine how many people will be needed to complete the report on time. Develop a detailed schedule for each person.

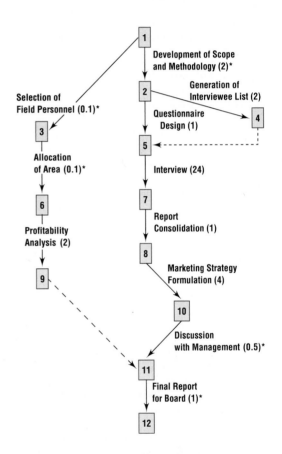

The numbers in parentheses are the time durations required for each activity in person-months (e.g., an activity requiring 24 person-months can be completed in six months by four persons). Starred activities cannot be crashed by adding people.

7. Krystal Enterprises Ltd. is conducting a feasibility study for a new product concept. The marketing

department has generated the following information regarding the various activities involved in the study, including cost and time estimates.

	Time Estimates, months		Cost Estimates, $ thousands per month		Preceding
Activity	Normal	Crash	Normal	Crash	Activity
A. Review technology and literature	2	1	20	45	—
B. Market analysis	3.5	2	80	150	—
C. Select an optimum technology	2	0.5	20	30	100%A, 50%B
D. Business analysis (ROA and net present value)	1.5	1	30	50	B, C
E. Develop project specifications	0.5	0.5	5	5	C
F. Determine marketing technology and production strategy	2	1	40	60	C, D
G. Develop project schedule	2	1	20	50	E, F
H. Initiative work	—	—	—	—	—

a. Prepare a project schedule. Present the schedule as a Gantt chart.

b. The time estimates assume that only one person is assigned to each activity. What is the minimum number of people required to achieve the above schedule?

c. Assess the impact of allocating only one manager and one assistant to the whole project. The assistant can help the manager with activities A, B, and G. What is the new project schedule?

d. Assume that labor costs are the same throughout the project. What is the optimal number of people who should be assigned to the project?

8. The Oguchi Trading Company is a wholesaler of home appliances and hardware products. The company is expanding its receiving area to facilitate the handling of large boxes. The civil contractor has prepared time and cost estimates for the expansion project as shown in the next table.
   a. What is the minimum time in which the project can be completed?
   b. What is the minimum cost schedule?

	Time, Days		Cost, $ thousands		Preceding
Activity	Normal	Crash	Normal	Crash	Activities
A. Mark out site	1	0.5	10	30	—
B. Dig foundation B	4	2	40	60	A
C. Concrete foundation B	3	2	30	60	B
D. Mold plinth	3	2	10	12	—
E. Mold tower A	3	2	10	12	—
F. Mold tower B	3	2	10	12	—
G. Mold span	3	2	10	12	—
H. Erect plinth	2	1	10	15	C, D
I. Erect tower B	1	0.5	5	10	F, H
J. Dig foundation A	2	1	20	30	A
K. Concrete foundation A	1	0.5	10	20	J
L. Complete base A	1	0.5	10	20	K
M. Erect tower A	1	0.5	5	10	E, L
N. Erect span	1	0.5	5	10	G, M

9. This flowchart shows production of a high-pressure boiler vessel. Parenthetical numbers indicate the number of days required for an activity.

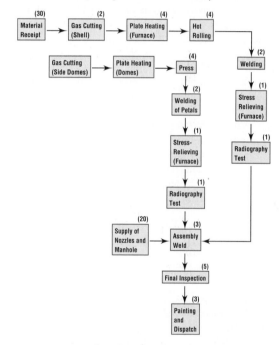

a. Determine the critical path, assuming that unlimited resources are available.
b. Will this change if there is only one furnace for heating the plates and stress relieving the structures and only one job can be loaded at one time?
c. Suppose the company has orders for 10 boiler drums. Develop a delivery schedule.

10. An oil company is considering a new offshore production project. Using the information in the table below, determine how long the project should take. Which activities are critical? Why are they critical?

Activity	Preceding Activity	T_p	T_o	T_m
		Estimated Time		
A. Predrilling survey	—	8	3	5
B. Exploratory drilling	A	12	6	8
C. Preliminary environmental assessment	—	6	4	4
D. Oil discovery	B	7	3	5
E. Preliminary construction survey	C, D	4	2	3
F. Platform design	C, D	10	7	8
G. Platform fabrication	F	14	10	11
H. Platform fabrication	F	14	10	11
I. Pipeline layout	D	12	8	10
J. Offshore facilities	H	6	3	5
K. Instrumentation	J, N	7	4	5
L. Production commencement	K, Q	—	—	—
M. Pilot plant	C, D	8	5	6
N. Crude testing	M	2	1	1
O. Contract negotiation with government	C, D	20	4	11
P. Comprehensive environmental assessment	C, D	16	12	14
Q. Government approval	P, Q	10	5	8

a. Using the information above, draw a network diagram for the project. What is the critical path?

b. If the project cost of $20 million is to be paid 20 percent with order, 65 percent on delivery, and the balance on completion of tests and commissioning, generate a monthly cash flow requirement for the project period.

c. If the board is willing to give approval on the basis of the initial discussion (E and I) and the vendor is willing to reduce the lead time by half, what will be the impact on the cost of the project?

d. Consider the impact on project cost if the bank delays financing arrangements by four months.

12. ⊞ Hitech Controls Inc. has launched a project to develop an intelligent neural controller for marine robots. The prototype development phase has been analyzed into the 13 activities shown below. Prepare a project schedule.

Activity	Preceding Jobs	Optimistic	Pessimistic	Probable
		Time Estimates, days		
A. Preliminary technology search	—	2	4	3
B. Labor manpower and funding approval	—	0.5	1	0.5
C. Project group selection	A	0.5	0.5	0.5
D. Hydrodynamic studies	C	4	8	7
E. Control theory development	D	3	6	5
F. Artificial intelligence	C	6	8	7
G. Neutral network development	C	8	15	12
H. Hardware testing	G	4	8	7
I. Software coding	F	7	8	7
J. Field test	E	3	4	3
K. Prototype design	H, F	6	8	7
L. Simulation	I, J	3	4	3
M. Final testing	K, L	5	9	7

11. The Kay Export Company is modernizing its facilities with computer-integrated office systems. The projected budget for the project is $20 million. A consultant has been hired to coordinate the project. She is charging the company $500,000 plus a monthly monitoring fee of $10,000. Twenty percent of the lump sum fee is payable on signing the contract, and the rest is to be paid in four installments at the completion of each of the four phases. The details of the activities are given below.

	Time, months	Preceding Work
Phase I		
Technology assessment	4	—
Preliminary discussion with vendors	3	A
In-house discussion	2	A
Preparation and submission of report	1	B, C
Phase II		
Board approval for project	1	D
Negotiations with vendors	3	D
In-house layout design	2	E
Purchase recommendations report	1	F, G
Phase III		
Purchase approvals	1	H
Financing arrangements with bank	1	I
Order placement	1	I, J
Delivery of equipment	9	K
In-house layout modifications	5	I, J
Phase IV		
Installation of equipment	2	L, M
Test and commissioning	2	N
Preparation of control manuals	12	K

13. A project has been proposed, and some initial estimates have been made. The information made available so far is shown below.

Task	Immediate Predecessor	a_i	m_i	b_i
		Time Estimate, days		
A	—	3	4	7
B	—	4	9	12
C	A	5	11	15
D	A	3	5	8
E	B	5	7	12
F	D, C	3	4	7
G	D, C	2	3	4
H	E	7	11	18
I	E	7	10	14
J	F	4	6	9
K	G	5	7	9
L	H, I	2	3	5
M	J, K	7	8	9
N	L	1	3	4
O	M, N	14	17	23

a. Find the critical path. What is its expected length?
b. If you want to be at least 95 percent confident of completing the project on time, what completion date would you quote?
(Note. Assume a five-day working week.)

14. Given the project in problem 13, what happens if tasks B, C, and D have to be carried out by the same indivisible group of people? What is the probability of completing the project by the 95 percent probability date calculated in problem 13?

15. ⌨ A firm adopts the program for the project in problem 14. After six weeks of working on the project you look at the cost position. Prepare a report that reflects the overruns and underruns for the total cost and for each activity. Assume that it will cost $1,000 per day for each day the project is delayed beyond the expected completion date and that it costs $800 per day to crash an activity. The firm can crash all activities except activity 0, but only by the difference between m_i and a_i for that activity. The current cost position is as follows.

Activity	Cost Incurred to Date, $	Budget, $	Percent Complete
A	22,000	25,000	100
B	48,000	45,000	100
C	75,000	100,000	100
D	20,000	20,000	100
E	14,000	20,000	100
F	94,000	85,000	100
G	47,000	40,000	100
H	125,000	120,000	100
I	109,000	100,000	95
J	97,000	100,000	100
K	87,000	100,000	70
L	0	25,000	0
M	0	75,000	0
N	0	73,000	0
O	0	197,000	0

Note. For simplicity, use the m_i time estimates from problem 13 for planning and reporting.

GROUP EXERCISES

Many of the tools and concepts discussed in this chapter are meant to be used in a team setting. The following problems are best solved by small groups of students. Ideally each group should be composed of people with different backgrounds, interests, or areas of expertise.

1. Visit a local company that has just finished or is in the process of undertaking a major project. Discuss with the project manager the planning, conduct, and control of the project, particularly the management of changes that occurred during the project.

   Take one discrete aspect of the project and try to develop a precedence activity list and time estimates for each activity. Knowing the resources available, schedule the resources without taking any other projects into consideration.

   If the information is available, take the scarcest resource and allocate it across all the projects with which the firm is involved. What impact does cross-allocation have on project completion? What options for crashing or project alteration are available? How does the company make these decisions?

2. Visit a large hotel or convention center. Before you go, list all the major activities you can identify that would be necessary in preparing to host a major conference. On site, discuss with the management the process of planning a major conference. See how many of these items you have included on your list. How accurate was the time estimate you made?

REFERENCES AND SELECTED BIBLIOGRAPHY

Adams, J. G. [1991], "Project Management at Lockheed Missile and Space Co.," *Site Selection and Industrial Development,* September–October, vol. 160, no. 5, pp. 1–6.

Clayton, E. R., and L. J. Moore [1972], "PERT vs. GERT," *Journal of Systems Management,* vol. 23, February, pp. 11–19.

Kerner, Harold [1989], *Project Management: A Systems Approach to Planning, Scheduling and Controlling,* 3d ed., Van Nostrand Reinhold, New York.

Luther, David B. [1993], "How New York Launched a State Quality Award in 15 Months," *Quality Progress,* May, pp. 38–43.

MacCrimmon, K. R., and C. A. Ryavec [1964], "An Analytical Study of the PERT Assumption," *Opus Research,* January–February, pp. 16–37.

McFarlane, D. [1993], "Enterprise-Wide Project Management," *Industrial Engineering,* vol. 25, no. 6, p. 44.

Moder, J. J., and E. G. Rodgers [1968], "Judgement Estimates of the Moments of PERT Type Distributions," *Management Science,* October, vol. 15, no. 2, pp. B76–B83.

Perry, C., and I. D. Greig [1975], "Estimating the Mean and Variance of Subjective Distributions in PERT and Decision Analysis," *Management Science,* August, vol. 21, no. 12, pp. 1477–1485.

Project Manager's Guide [1977], June, Technical Document 108, Naval Ocean Systems Center, San Diego, p. XXI–I.

Radford, R. [1986], *The Impact of Management on the Introduction of Process Technology in a Process-Oriented Firm,* unpublished doctoral dissertation, Harvard Business School, chap. 6, pp. 207–261.

Rogers, T. [1993], "Project Management: Emerging as a Requisite for Success," *Industrial Engineering,* vol. 25, no. 6, pp. 42–43.

Roman, D. [1986], *Managing Projects: A Systems Approach,* Elsevier, New York, chap. 5.

Spirer, H. F. [1982], "The Basic Principles of Project Management," *Operations Management Review,* vol. 1, no. 1, pp. 8–10 ff.

Wallace, Ron, and Wayne Halverson [1992], "Project Management: A Critical Success Factor or a Management Fad," *Industrial Engineering,* April, pp. 48–50.

Wiest, J. D., and F. K. Levy [1977], *A Management Guide to PERT/CPM,* Prentice-Hall, Englewood Cliffs, N.J.

SUPPLEMENT TO
CHAPTER 12

FORMING AND MANAGING
PROJECT TEAMS

S12.1 MANAGERIAL ORIENTATION

Chapter 5 stated that product development is best carried out by a multidisciplinary project team, and Chapter 12 explained that FROs are moving toward a form of organization based partly on technologies and partly on the short-lived coalitions called project teams. These teams will be involved with planning *and* with the implementation of projects. An important management issue is how these teams are to be formed. This supplement looks at that issue and then at the implications for operations managers of managing through projects.

Remember that there is a big difference between a team and a work gang or group. Work groups are assigned to processes and are organized around those processes; teams are essentially multifunctional and are not concerned directly with accomplishing specific value-added tasks or activities. A machine crew in a paper mill is a work group tasked with making paper to predetermined specifications. Each member of that crew may also be a member of a team attempting to improve operational effectiveness, but other people (for example, engineers and marketing product specialists) are also members of the team.

S12.2 THE COMPOSITION OF PROJECT TEAMS

Remember that a project team is multifunctional and that each function or group with a current or future stake in the project is represented on the team. In a product development project, therefore, one can expect to see a change in the composition of the project team as the project progresses. At the beginning the team consists of marketing, engineering, design, manufacturing, purchasing, and external stakeholders, with the marketing and design groups perhaps the most heavily represented. As the project moves closer to production,

EXHIBIT 12S.1 PROJECT TEAM

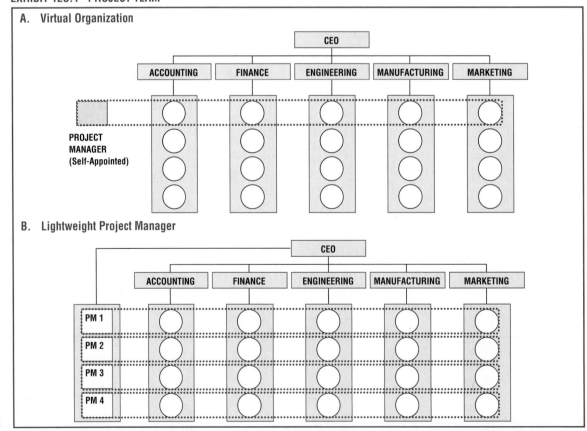

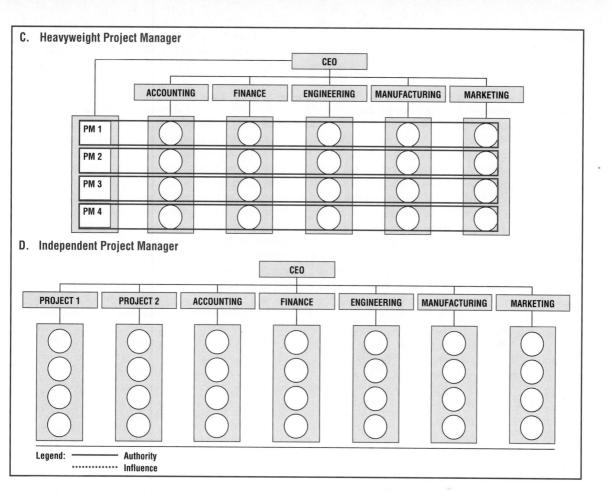

C. Heavyweight Project Manager

CEO

ACCOUNTING | FINANCE | ENGINEERING | MANUFACTURING | MARKETING

PM 1
PM 2
PM 3
PM 4

D. Independent Project Manager

CEO

PROJECT 1 | PROJECT 2 | ACCOUNTING | FINANCE | ENGINEERING | MANUFACTURING | MARKETING

Legend: ——— Authority
·············· Influence

the marketing numbers will decrease and the engineering and manufacturing representation will increase.

In some instances there may be a tendency to disband the team when production starts or once the product reaches maturity. Given the short product life cycles that are likely in the future and the need to keep products abreast or ahead of market expectations, the move to disband a project team before the end of the product's life cycle will be premature. Project teams will have to be kept as small as possible, though, especially if the firm expects to have an increasing number of projects and to devote an increasing amount of personnel time to projects.

S12.3 ESTABLISHING PROJECT TEAMS

There are basically four ways to establish project teams, and the model chosen depends largely on the relative strength of the managers to whom the project members report (see Exhibit 12S.1). The exhibit shows a project team being formed from within a traditional functionally organized firm. Exhibit 12S.1A shows what might be called the **virtual team,** or the "coffee club," in which a project leader is appointed who has no authority over any of the team members. This form of team is the norm when a superior asks a subordinate to carry out a task and the subordinate co-opts others to help. The team leader does not have delegated authority, only influence. Typically, the number of people involved and the duration of the project are minimal.

This project form is also employed in research laboratories in which every researcher has a set amount of time that can be devoted to **informal projects,** or work on new ideas that have not been discussed with or approved by more senior managers. The advocate must bring others to the project purely on the strength of the idea and his or her personality and must keep important team members interested. Because management is not **419** aware of the project, the team can be destroyed if enough official tasks are given to the members to make them unavailable. The greater the project scope, the greater the number of people involved, and the longer the time required for the project, the greater the probability of unwitting management interference.

The next form (see Exhibit 12S.1B) is what Clark and Fujimoto (1990) call the **lightweight project manager.** Although the appointment is official, the project manager has no authority over the people appointed to the project by functional managers. These functional representatives become little more than liaison officers, and their meetings tend to be little more than information-gathering, conflict-resolving, and coordinating sessions. Many committees suffer this fate, with their mandate for action being undermined by members who cannot make a commitment without asking their departments. This can be contrasted with the heavyweight project team shown in Exhibit 12S.1C. This looks the same as the lightweight project team but is much more dynamic. A **heavyweight project manager** has authority over the project and thus has more power than do the individual team members' functional superiors. This form of project team was used by Northern Telecom when Harmony telephones were designed and built and was used by Honda in the development of the Accord.

As Clark and Fujimoto (1990) point out, it is easy to see the difference between a lightweight and a heavyweight project manager in action. Lightweight project managers essentially *push paper* and attend meetings; heavyweight managers physically walk around visiting their team members and other stakeholders, ensuring that decisions are made and timelines and budgets are met. If a heavyweight project manager has a clear project vision and communicates clearly with team members, the project is more likely to be properly completed on time and within budget.

All three models discussed so far involve project managers who cannot totally control the time and energy of the appointed team members. The project manager must therefore negotiate the time allocated to the project with each functional manager and must negotiate overall **project parameters**—cost, time, success criteria—with senior management. Even though a heavyweight project manager is a senior manager, poor use of team members' time and knowledge will quickly lead to dissatisfaction among the members and consequent attempts to relegate the project manager to the lightweight role. This will undermine the integrity of the project and perhaps the integrity of the firm.

The final model is the independent team shown in Exhibit 12S.1D. In these teams the project manager has complete line authority over the team members. Many physical construction projects are of this type, especially if carried out a long way from the construction firm's home base. For the construction of the SkyDome in Toronto, the construction contractor, Ellis-Don, established a fully **independent project management team.**

In this model, the authority of the project leader is unequivocal but the cost of establishing dedicated support elements (personnel, purchasing, design) may be very high and may rob the firm of flexibility. The extreme case would have every person in the firm dedicated to individual projects, leaving the firm totally inflexible. Nonetheless, this is an important project management form if a project is critical or is so large that full-time management is essential.

Although the first three models in Exhibit 12S.1 show a matrix, this matrix has been created within a traditional functional organization. There are instances, though, of what are essentially matrix organizations getting involved in projects, particularly in professional service organizations. Management consultancies, R&D laboratories, and public accounting firms are the most obvious examples, but consulting engineering offices and even faculties of management are effectively designed in this way. This form appears to be best suited for conditions in which all the firm's business is episodic and therefore project-oriented and each project requires a broad range of skills.

In any matrix, though, one manager (usually the functional manager) is responsible for allocating people to projects, ensuring in the process that specialists are not overloaded. This manager is also responsible for developing and evaluating the specialists in the particular function and developing long-range human resource plans. The appointed project team leader is responsible for negotiating with the specialist managers to get the individuals desired for the team and for operationalizing and managing the project. The individual team members probably will work on several projects at any time, and each has a responsibility to ensure that he or she contributes effectively to all the projects.

S12.4 PROJECT MANAGER CHARACTERISTICS

When a project has a finite life, once the project is complete, team members revert to the full control of their functional managers. Team members and functional managers know this and, as suggested above, lose no time in undermining the project if they feel their long-term interests are being threatened. Project managers must therefore be selected with care. First, a project manager must be a generalist rather than a technical specialist and must have had a broad range of experience. This experience can be gained through projects or through job rotations throughout the firm. Second, the project manager must be a good facilitator and be able to manage the relationships among senior management, the team members, their functional superiors, and customers. Third, the project manager must have sufficient technical expertise to understand the specialists and the overall implications of changes made during the project. Fourth, as outlined above, the project manager must focus on task completion. The project manager must be a leader rather than a supervisor.

Because many projects, especially product development projects, take a long time and require a changing team structure, the question arises, Who should manage the project? Should the project manager have a marketing, design, or production background? Should the manager have had previous experience in all aspects of the project? Should the manager be changed as the project moves through its phases? Individual firms have their own answers to these questions.

A single manager should be appointed for the duration of the project, since changing managers in mid-course can create problems. Not the least of these problems is the tendency for a team that changes to fragment, a process that may be exacerbated by the change in personality and style of the project manager. The manager should have experience in the various aspects and functions involved in the project, and this implies something about the development of project managers.

Firms should expect that every manager will become a project manager and should therefore arrange their experiences around projects. Working on projects will give managers the experience they will need when they are made project managers. This exposure will also allow senior managers to evaluate these managers for suitability to manage projects, thus reducing the risk of poor project management in the future. Perhaps the greatest resource shortage in the future will be one of good project managers; their grooming and selection are critical to the maintenance and increase of a firm's capacity and capability.

KEY TERMS

Virtual team	Lightweight project manager	Project parameters	Independent project
Informal projects	Heavyweight project manager		management team

REFERENCES AND SELECTED BIBLIOGRAPHY

Clark, Kim B., and Takahiro Fujimoto [1990], "The Power of Product Integrity," *Harvard Business Review,* vol. 68, no. 6, November–December, pp. 107–118.

Davis, Stanley M., and Paul R. Lawrence [1977], *Matrix,* Addison-Wesley, Reading, Mass.

Galbraith, Jay [1973], *Designing Complex Organizations,* Addison-Wesley, Reading, Mass.

Kerzner, Harold [1989], *Project Management: A Systems Approach to Planning, Scheduling and Controlling,* 3d ed., Van Nostrand Reinhold, New York.

Roman. D. [1986], *Managing Projects: A Systems Approach,* Elsevier, New York.

CHAPTER 13

MANAGING INVENTORIES: INDEPENDENT DEMAND SYSTEMS

In every operating firm raw materials and parts flow forward to, within, and from the firm. Control of this flow is important because it directly affects the costs, the revenues and, ultimately, the success of the firm.

This chapter deals with the accumulation and control of inventory levels. Inventory is the stock of materials and subcomponents held by a firm to respond to market demand. Whether the firm produces goods for the final customers directly or serves as a supplier to another production unit, it must address the following questions:

- How many units (or raw materials) should be ordered?
- When should the order be placed?
- How often should the order be placed?
- How much and where should inventory be held?

The answers to these questions constitute the firm's inventory policy. Various types of inventory policies under deterministic (known) and probabilistic (uncertain) demand will be discussed, along with an examination of the relationship between a firm's inventory levels and its ability to compete.

EXHIBIT 13.1   FRO MANUFACTURING PROFILE

Historically, the appliance industry has endorsed the theory that a loaded dealer is a loyal dealer. If a dealer's warehouse is full of a manufacturer's product, the argument goes, the dealer will be committed to that manufacturer's product line because there is no room for goods from anyone else. Therefore, dealers get the best price when they buy a full truckload of appliances.

In the late 1980s General Electric (GE) abandoned the loaded-dealer concept and reinvented the way in which it makes, sells, and distributes appliances. Under GE's new Direct Connect system, retailers no longer maintain inventories of major appliances. They rely instead on GE's "virtual inventory," a computer-based logistics system that allows stores to operate as if they had thousands of ranges and refrigerators in the back room when in fact they have none.

Dealers now have instantaneous computer access to GE's on-line order-processing system 24 hours a day. They get GE's best price, regardless of order size and content, as well as next-day delivery. Since the hassles and cost of maintaining inventory have been eliminated, dealers' profit margins have soared.

Virtual inventory works better than real inventory for both dealers and customers. "Instead of telling a customer I have two units on order," says one dealer, "I can now say that we have 2,500 in our warehouse. I can also tell a customer when a model is scheduled for production and when it will be shipped. If the schedule doesn't suit the customer, the GE terminal will identify other available models and compare their features with competitive units."

GE gets about half the dealer's business and a 12 percent reduction in distribution and marketing costs. GE has captured a valuable commodity from its dealers as well: data on the movement of its products. The company now in effect manufactures in response to customer demand instead of for inventory.

Source: Adapted from Treacy and Wiersema (1993), pp. 86–87.

EXHIBIT 13.2   FRO SERVICE PROFILE

The customer is in a rush. Quebec's legendary potholes have claimed a wheel on his 1989 Honda Civic, and he is desperate for a replacement. The request is not a big deal for the saleswoman behind the counter in the neon-lit showroom of Pintendre Auto Inc. She calmly punches the make, model year, and coded part number into a computer terminal. Within

(Exhibit 13.2 continues on next page)

EXHIBIT 13.2 *(continued)*

seconds she confirms that Pintendre has a dozen such wheels in its vast stock of used parts. The screen flashes the range of prices and conditions as well as the location of each wheel on Pintendre's rambling premises. It is another small coup for Quebec's largest used auto parts dealer, whose stock in trade is as much information and inventory control as crankshafts and oil pans.

Pintendre's flexible information system tracks and manages an inventory of more than 200,000 parts. "Without the computers," confesses Mr. Carrier, one of the firm's founders, "it would be hell." He adds, "People often ask me what I would buy first if I were just starting out. It would be a computer—not a building, not a tow truck."

Bolstered by this technology, Pintendre can offer fast and reliable service—24-hour delivery anywhere in the province—and guarantee everything it sells. Customers such as Pierre Mayrand, purchasing manager at a major Quebec City auto body shop, says that the quality of Pintendre's parts and service keeps them coming back: "We order a side panel or a door in the morning, and we get it in the afternoon."

Source: Adapted from McKenna (1993), p. B24.

13.1 MANAGERIAL ORIENTATION

When one is shopping, it is annoying to find that a desired item is out of stock. Within a firm, too, running out of needed parts and materials is frustrating, but how can a firm avoid stockouts? Holding relatively large amounts of inventory has been the traditional strategy to cushion a firm against uncertainty. In practice, however, large inventories increase costs while diminishing a firm's responsiveness to its markets.

Fast-response organizations (FROs) are improving their ability to compete simultaneously along the six competitive dimensions by reducing their need to hold inventory. General Electric's "virtual inventory" system (see Exhibit 13.1) demonstrates the impact on competitiveness of lowering inventory levels. The need for effective inventory control is not limited to firms in the manufacturing sector. The relationship between inventory control and competitiveness at Pintendre Auto Inc. (see Exhibit 13.2), for example, is quite clear.

This chapter will examine models used to control inventory levels and costs and touches on the potential of advanced technology to help reduce inventory-related costs. It also discusses how a firm can reduce its inventory levels by reducing the *need* for inventory. Let us begin by reviewing the functions served by inventories.

13.2 INVENTORY FORMS AND FUNCTIONS

Inventory can be classified by its form, its function, or the nature of its demand.

Classifying Inventory by Its Form

In a typical operation inventory is held in three different forms: as **raw materials, work-in-process (WIP),** and **finished goods inventories.** Raw material inventories may also be kept by the supplier for the firm; finished goods inventories are frequently held throughout the firm's distribution channels. Semicompleted goods (work-in-process inventories) accumulate at various points in the production process.

Classifying Inventory by Its Function

One of the most common functions served by raw materials, work-in-process, and finished goods inventories is to guard against future uncertainty.

DEFINITION: *Safety,* or *buffer, inventory* is inventory held to offset the risk of unplanned production stoppages and/or unexpected increases in consumer demand.

The key word here is *unplanned* or *unexpected.* If everything were certain, managers would be able to eliminate safety inventory (safety stock). When firms produce to sales forecasts, however, and must be able to supply from stock, safety stock has to be carried to cover the variability of demand. The more volatile the demand is, the greater the amount of safety stock that has to be carried if targets for the service level are to be met. Buffer inventories can also be carried in raw materials to offset problems with supplier performance and in work in process to allow the plant to continue operations while a machine is repaired or a replacement operator is found to substitute for an absent worker. All safety stock increases costs and working capital requirements.

DEFINITION: *Decoupling inventory* is inventory required between adjacent processes or operations whose production rates cannot be synchronized; it allows each process to operate as planned.

The key word here is *planned,* for the required amount of decoupling inventory can be calculated accurately. An example of decoupling inventory is the inventory of steel ingots between an electric arc furnace making a batch of 180 ingots once every three hours and a machine converting one ingot a minute into reinforcing rods. Buildups of decoupling inventory also occur in advance of planned machine down-time for major periodic maintenance.

DEFINITION: *In-transit (pipeline) inventory* is created by materials moving forward through the value chain; these are items that have been ordered but not yet received.

The key word here is *moving.* Inventory is transferred from suppliers to plants, to and from subcontractors, from one operation to the next within the plant, and from the plant to the firm's distribution channels. Gas in a pipeline is in-transit inventory, as is the pizza crust on a truck traveling between a distribution center and a McDonald's restaurant. The longer the flow time through the value chain, the larger the in-transit inventory.

DEFINITION: *Cycle inventory* results when, in order to reduce unit purchase costs (or increase production efficiency), the number of units purchased (or produced) is greater than the firm's immediate needs.

The key word concept is *economy.* This is the only inventory form to which lot sizing is applied. It may be more economical for purchasing to order a large quantity of units and store some for future use than to make a series of smaller orders. With some items the firm may be forced to purchase a minimum quantity. Production lot sizes that exceed immediate requirements are frequently chosen to offset the cost of lengthy process setups.

DEFINITION: *Anticipatory,* or *seasonal, inventory* accumulates when a firm produces more than its immediate requirements in low-demand periods to meet the needs of high-demand periods.

The key word here is *seasonal.* By building up its anticipatory inventory, the firm smooths its production requirements. Anticipatory inventory is frequently accumulated when demand is very seasonal.

Caution. An item of inventory can be performing more than one function at any time. This makes determining the amount of inventory to be carried a more complicated task than it might otherwise appear.

Classifying Inventory by the Nature of Its Demand

Inventory can also be classified by the nature of its demand into **independent inventory** and **dependent inventory.**

> **DEFINITION:** The demand for an item is *independent* when it is unrelated to the demand for other items produced by the firm.

> **DEFINITION:** The demand for an item is *dependent* when it can be derived from the demand for other items produced by the firm.

Demand for finished goods (e.g., cars, televisions, hamburgers) and replacement parts (e.g., mufflers, shoelaces, batteries) is independent demand. During production planning the demand for these items must be forecast.

The demand for dependent demand items, however, does not have to be forecast; it can be calculated from the demand for end items and from production decisions. For example, an automobile manufacturer develops a production schedule for automobiles (an independent demand item) on the basis of the forecast demand. The production schedule can then be used to calculate *how many* tires, mufflers,[1] and tailpipes will be needed and *when* they will be needed.

Retailers, wholesalers, and manufacturers all have to deal with inventories of independent demand items. The systems presented later in this chapter are intended for this type of inventory.

Manufacturers also have to be concerned with inventories of dependent demand items. Because the demand for these items can be calculated rather than forecast, special inventory systems have been developed to manage them. Chapter 15 will take a close look at managing inventories of dependent demand items in its examination of material requirements planning.

13.3 INVENTORY COSTS

In many operating systems inventory costs represent a significant proportion of total production costs. The higher the average inventory level, the higher the total production cost. Typically, inventory-related costs include item costs, ordering (process setup) costs, holding costs, and stockout (shortage) costs.

- **Item costs** refer to the purchase price of something a firm buys or the cost of something it manufactures. For purchased goods, the total price is the list price plus shipping and handling costs plus taxes, tariffs, and duties. The book cost of items manufactured in-house traditionally includes the cost of raw materials, the cost of labor, and an overhead allocation.
- **Ordering costs** are the costs of placing an order for an item purchased from a supplier. **Process setup costs** are the costs of changing the production process from one product to another. These costs are expected to be reasonably constant each time they are incurred for a particular product regardless of the quantity purchased or manufactured.

---

[1] Mufflers have been used here as an example of both an independent and a dependent demand item. It is not uncommon for a firm to sell parts that it also uses to produce other products.

Ordering costs include purchasing activities such as preparing specifications and tender documents, writing purchasing orders, monitoring suppliers, inspecting orders once they arrive, and maintaining documentation.

Process setups may take minutes, hours, or even days to complete. The production order must be prepared, scheduled, and monitored. Jigs, fixtures, and cutting tools may have to be changed as the production process switches from one order to the next. Equipment may have to be cleaned or sterilized.

Ordering and setup costs should include the relevant costs incurred by all functional departments, not just purchasing and operations, when a purchase or production order is made.

- **Holding costs** are the expenses incurred when items are kept in inventory. Examples include rent, electricity, taxes, shrinkage, obsolescence, insurance premiums, and labor costs for people to monitor and move inventories. Capital costs which reflect a loss in earning power, or an "opportunity" cost, must also be included in the cost of holding inventory; if the money tied up in inventories had been invested elsewhere, a return on investment would have been expected.
- **Stockout (shortage) costs** are incurred whenever a firm cannot fulfill a customer's order. The firm loses the contribution margin for that sale and may lose the contribution margin for future sales. In some cases penalties have to be paid.

Stockout costs are difficult to establish because customers may or may not switch permanently to a competitor or a substitute product.

Running out of the raw materials or components used to produce end items also incurs costs. The supplier may charge a premium to make an emergency delivery, inferior items may have to be used, the production process may be idle while waiting for the missing item, and so on.

Many firms use computerized inventory systems to monitor inventory levels and costs. The cost of these systems can be significant and must be considered in calculating total inventory costs and developing an **inventory policy.**

DEFINITION: An inventory policy is a procedure put in place to help managers answer questions such as, How much should the firm order? When should it order? and How often should it order?

When the demand for an item is known and is relatively constant, the economic order quantity model or one of its variations can be used to develop an inventory policy for that item. When demand is independent but is not known with certainty, reorder point systems such as the (s,S) system and the P system are more appropriate. These and other systems are discussed in the next several sections.

13.4 INVENTORY REPLENISHMENT SYSTEMS WHEN DEMAND IS KNOWN

In certain situations a firm can assume that demand is known and constant. For example, demand for several products can be aggregated over several sales districts and several time periods. As was discussed in Chapter 4, when demand is aggregated, individual variations offset one another. The aggregate demand may be relatively predictable and constant. The demand for toothpaste, for example, may be quite stable, while the demand for particular tube sizes and flavors from one manufacturer may be very volatile.

The most widely used inventory model for items whose demand is known and constant is the economic order quantity model.

Economic Order Quantity Model

First developed in 1915 by Ford Harris,[2] the **economic order quantity (EOQ) model** calculates the best quantity to order (or produce) by minimizing inventory ordering costs and inventory carrying costs. The EOQ model is based on the following simplifying assumptions:

- The demand rate for the item is constant now and in the future. The demand for one product does not influence the demand for another.
- The item is produced or purchased in lots. There are no constraints on the size of each lot, and an ordered lot is received all at once.
- There is no uncertainty in demand, supply, or lead times. Stockouts do not occur.
- There are only two relevant costs: the inventory holding cost and the ordering (or process setup) cost. The cost to hold one unit in inventory for one period does not vary with the amount held; the cost of ordering (or setting up the process) does not vary with the order size.

With these assumptions, the inventory level will change at a constant rate (see Exhibit 13.3). Suppose 1,000 units are ordered each period. The inventory level is therefore 1,000 units at the beginning of the period and is depleted at a constant rate throughout the period. The average inventory level is one-half the quantity ordered (or produced) each period, or 500 units. The annual cost of holding inventory is given by equation (13.1).

Annual Holding Costs

$$\text{Annual holding costs} = H\frac{Q}{2} = iC\frac{Q}{2} \qquad (13.1)$$

where H = inventory holding costs ($) for one year for one unit
  Q = quantity ordered each period, in units
  i = carrying cost rate expressed as a percentage of inventory dollar value per year
  C = per unit cost of item ($)

[2] Wilson (1934) is also recognized for his contribution to this subject. In fact, EOQ is sometimes referred to as the *Wilson lot size technique.*

EXHIBIT 13.3   INVENTORY LEVELS UNDER THE EOQ ASSUMPTIONS

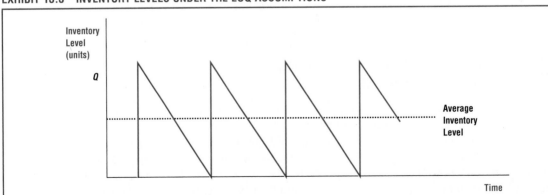

The solid line represents the inventory level. In every period Q units are ordered and arrive all at once. Since the demand rate is constant, the inventory is depleted at a constant rate. The average inventory on hand (shown by the dotted line) is half the quantity ordered in each period (Q).

The annual ordering (or setup) cost is equal to the cost of making each order (or setup) multiplied by the number of orders (or setups) made during the year. It is given by equation (13.2).

Annual Ordering (or Setup) Cost

$$\text{Annual ordering cost} = S\frac{D}{Q} \qquad (13.2)$$

where S = cost of making each order (or setup) ($)
$\quad D$ = annual demand, in units
$\quad Q$ = quantity ordered each period, in units

The total relevant cost of inventory [equation (13.3)] is the sum of holding and ordering (or setup) costs.

Total Relevant Cost of Inventory

$$\text{TRC} = H\frac{Q}{2} + S\frac{D}{Q} \qquad (13.3)$$

where TRC = total relevant cost of inventory ($)
$\quad H$ = inventory holding costs ($) for one year for one unit
$\quad Q$ = quantity ordered each period, in units
$\quad S$ = cost ($) of making each order (or setup)
$\quad D$ = annual demand, in units

Note that as the quantity ordered increases, holding costs *increase* but ordering costs *decrease*. As illustrated in Exhibit 13.4, the minimum total relevant cost occurs at the point where the annual holding cost and the ordering cost are equal. The order quantity at this point is the EOQ [equation (13.4)].

Economic Order Quantity

$$\text{EOQ} = \sqrt{\frac{2DS}{H}} = \sqrt{\frac{2DS}{iC}} \qquad (13.4)$$

where EOQ = economic order quantity, in units
$\quad D$ = annual demand, in units
$\quad S$ = cost ($) of making each order (or setup)
$\quad H$ = inventory holding costs ($) for one year for one unit
$\quad i$ = carrying cost rate, expressed as a percentage of inventory dollar value per year
$\quad C$ = per unit cost of item ($)

The economic order quantity is calculated for a television retailer in Exhibit 13.5.[3] Note that ordering and holding costs for the year are equal when the EOQ system is used but are quite different under the store's current monthly ordering system.

Once the EOQ has been calculated, equations (13.5) and (13.6) can be used to find the **average number of purchase (production) orders per year** and the average time between orders. If 1,500 units must be ordered annually and the average lot

[3] The equations presented in this section have been used to calculate the EOQ and other relevant data. Alternatively, the EOQ module of ©OM-Expert would have been employed.

EXHIBIT 13.4 TOTAL RELEVANT COST OF INVENTORY

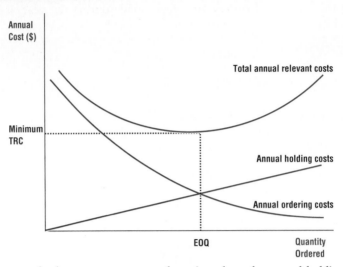

Note that the minimum total relevant cost occurs at the point where the annual holding cost and the annual ordering cost are equal. To find this point, set the annual holding cost equal to the annual ordering cost and then solve for Q:

$$\text{Annual holding cost} = \text{Annual ordering cost}$$

$$H\frac{Q}{2} = S\frac{D}{Q}$$

$$Q^2 = \frac{2DS}{H}$$

$$Q = \sqrt{\frac{2DS}{H}}$$

EXHIBIT 13.5 TOOLBOX: ECONOMIC ORDER QUANTITY

As part of its drive to reduce waste, Thompson's TV is trying to reduce its large inventories. Ted Thompson currently orders his stock once per month but suspects that he can save money by converting to an EOQ system. Using the X2400 model as an example, let us compare the inventory costs under Ted's current system with the costs associated with an EOQ system.

BACKGROUND INFORMATION

The monthly demand for model X2400 is about 50 units and varies little from month to month. The retail price is $1,499 but Ted buys them for $890 each. The ordering cost is $10 plus a $5 per unit freight charge. It takes two days for the order to be filled, and both Thompson's TV and its supplier are open seven days a week.

Last year, the average inventory level for this model was 25 units and the average per unit cost was $835. About $1,875 of last year's storage fees (rent, insurance, labor, and shrinkage) can be allocated to the X24000 model. The store's cost of capital was 12 percent.

$$\text{Annual demand } (D) = 50 \text{ units} \times 12 = 600 \text{ units}$$
$$\text{Ordering cost } (S) = \$10$$
$$\text{Unit cost } (C) = \$890 + \$5 = \$895$$
$$\text{Carrying cost } (H) = iC = 895i$$

The inventory carrying cost rate (i) can be found as follows:

$$\text{Annual capital cost last year} = \text{Average inventory value} \times \text{Cost of capital}$$
$$= 25 \text{ units} \times \$835 \text{ per unit} \times 12\%$$
$$= \$2,505$$

Annual carrying cost = Annual capital cost + Annual storage cost
= \$2,505 + \$1,875 = \$4,380

$$\text{Carrying cost rate} = \frac{\text{Annual carrying cost}}{\text{Average inventory value}}$$

$$= \frac{\$4,380}{\$20,875} = 0.21$$

CALCULATE THE EOQ

All the data needed to calculate the EOQ have been collected.

$$\text{EOQ} = \sqrt{\frac{2DS}{iC}} = \sqrt{\frac{(2)(600)(10)}{(895)(0.21)}} = 7.99$$

Therefore, the best order quantity is eight units.

CALCULATE THE REORDER POINT, AVERAGE NUMBER OF ORDERS PER YEAR, AND AVERAGE ORDER INTERVAL

$\bar{d}$ = 600 units per year ÷ 365 days per year = 1.64 units per day

L = 2 days

$R = \bar{d} \times L = 1.64 \times 2 = 3.28$ units

$$m = \frac{D}{\text{EOQ}} = \frac{600}{8} = 75 \text{ orders}$$

$$t = \frac{1}{m} = \frac{1}{75} = 0.0133 \text{ year, or } 4.87 \text{ days}$$

Therefore, when only three units are left, eight more should be ordered. About one order will be placed every five days, and 75 orders will be placed each year.

COMPARE THE CURRENT SYSTEM WITH THE EOQ SYSTEM

Under the current system Ted orders 50 units of model X2400 once a month, or 12 times a year. The average inventory level is 25 units. Under the EOQ system, Ted would place 75 orders a year and the average inventory level would drop to four units.

	Current System	EOQ System
Holding costs per unit	\$187.95	\$187.95
Average inventory level	×25	×4
Annual holding costs	\$4,698.75	\$751.80
Cost per order	\$10.00	\$10.00
Orders per year	×12	×75
Annual ordering costs	\$120.00	\$750.00
Total relevant costs	\$4,818.75	\$1,501.80

The savings in total relevant costs generated by the EOQ system is \$3,316.95 for model X2400 alone.

size is 100 units, 15 orders will be placed during the year. The **average order interval** (cycle time) is one-fifteenth of a year, or about 24 days.

Average Number of Orders per Year

$$m = \frac{D}{\text{EOQ}} = \sqrt{\frac{HD}{2S}} \qquad (13.5)$$

Average Order Interval

$$t = \frac{1}{m} = \frac{EOQ}{D} = \sqrt{\frac{2S}{HD}} \qquad (13.6)$$

where m = average number of orders per year
D = annual demand, in units
EOQ = economic order quantity, in units
H = inventory holding costs for one unit for one year
S = cost ($) of making each order or setup
t = average order interval (in fraction of a year)

If the EOQ is ordered, the **total relevant cost** can be calculated by using equation (13.7).[4]

Total Relevant Cost of Inventory When the EOQ Is Ordered

$$TRC = \sqrt{2DSH} \qquad (13.7)$$

where TRC = total relevant cost ($)
D = annual demand, in units
S = cost ($) of making each order (or setup)
H = inventory holding costs ($) for one year for one unit

Normally, there is a time lag between placing the order and receiving the purchase order or between scheduling production and receiving the items. This lag is referred to as the **lead time.** Since the EOQ model assumes that the lead time is constant, equation (13.8) can be used to calculate the point at which the order must be placed (the **reorder point**).

Reorder Point (Constant Demand Rate, Constant Lead Time)

$$R = \bar{d}L \qquad (13.8)$$

where R = reorder point, in units
$\bar{d}$ = average daily demand, in units
L = lead time, in days

When the lead time is less than the average order interval, at most a single order will be outstanding. If the lead time is *greater* than the time it takes to draw down one lot, however, there will be at least one order outstanding. Suppose for example the lead time for Thompson's TV (see Exhibit 13.5) increased from two days to six days. Since the average order interval is about five days, Thompson's TV will make its next order before the last one has been delivered.

One of the difficulties in using formulas such as the EOQ is accurately estimating parameter values (in the EOQ these are H, i, C, S, and D). The less accurate the parameter estimates, the less reliable the solution.

In the case of the EOQ, however, extreme accuracy may not be vital. Look at the shape of the total cost function in Exhibit 13.4. Note that it is quite flat around the point of lowest cost. This means that small variations or errors in cost estimates will not significantly affect the EOQ value. The EOQ calculated for Thompson's TV, for example, is valid for ordering costs between $8.83 and $11.29 (see Exhibit

[4] Equation (13.7) was derived by substituting the EOQ for Q into equation (11.3).

13.6). Even if Thompson's TV orders slightly more or less than the EOQ, the total relevant cost of inventory will not vary significantly.

How much can parameter estimates vary from their true value before the EOQ is affected, and how much can the actual order quantity vary from the EOQ before the total relevant costs of inventory increase significantly? **Sensitivity analysis** can provide answers to these questions.

DEFINITION: Sensitivity analysis deals with the impact of varying one or more cost parameters on the EOQ and TRC.

EXHIBIT 13.6   TOOLBOX: SENSITIVITY OF THE EOQ TO PARAMETER VALUES

A. EOQ for Various Ordering Costs

The EOQ for Thompson's TV model X2400 has been recalculated using different values for the ordering cost. The EOQ of 10 units is valid for ordering costs between $8.83 and $11.29.

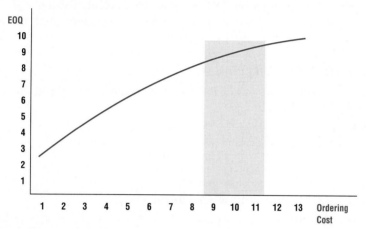

B. Total Relevant Costs for Various Order Quantities

The following graph shows the total relevant cost (TRC) that corresponds to various order quantities. Note that the TRC for model X2400 is relatively insensitive to small changes in the order quantity. Therefore, if the ordering cost estimate is off by even 50 percent, the difference in TRC will be small.

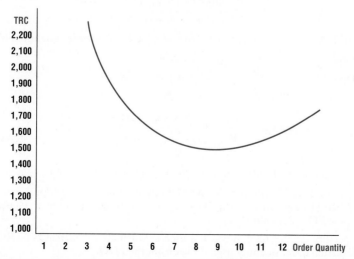

Exhibit 13.6 examined the impact of changes in parameter values by recalculating the EOQ and TRC. The change in TRC for any given change in order size, however, can be easily calculated using equation (13.9) [see Silver and Peterson (1985)].

Percentage Cost Penalty

$$PCP = \frac{50p^2}{1 + p} \tag{13.9}$$

where PCP = percentage cost penalty in total relevant costs
p = percentage deviation of order size used (Q) from the EOQ, i.e.,

$$p = \frac{Q - EOQ}{EOQ}$$

For example, suppose Thompson's TV ordered 10 units rather than the EOQ quantity of 8 units, an increase of 25 percent in order quantity. The corresponding percentage increase in TRC is only 2.5 percent. Exhibit 13.7 walks through the calculations for this and other examples of sensitivity analysis.

EXHIBIT 13.7   TOOLBOX: PERCENTAGE COST PENALTY

Ted Thompson of Thompson's TV is studying the impact of certain environmental changes on the EOQ and TRC values for model X2400.

Recall these amounts:

Annual demand (D)	600 units
Holding cost per unit per year (H)	$187.95
Cost of making each order (S)	$10
Economic order quantity	8 units

Scenario 1. A minimum order quantity of 10 units is introduced.

This new rule will not affect the EOQ but will increase the TRC.

The percentage deviation from the EOQ is

$$p = \frac{10 - 8}{8} = 0.25$$

$$PCP = \frac{50p^2}{1 + p} = \frac{(50)(0.25)^2}{1 + 0.25} = 2.5$$

Therefore, the TRC will increase 2.5 percent as a result of the minimum order quantity policy.

Scenario 2. The demand forecast is increased by 25 percent.

A change in the demand forecast will affect the EOQ as well as the TRC.

The revised EOQ is

$$EOQ = \sqrt{\frac{2DS}{iC}} = \sqrt{\frac{(2)(600)(1.25)(10)}{187.95}} = 8.93$$

The revised TRC is

$$TRC = \sqrt{2DSH} = \sqrt{(2)(600)(1.25)(10)(187.95)} = 1,679.06$$

The 25 percent increase in demand will increase the EOQ by only one unit (12.5 percent) while the TRC will increase by only $177.26 (12 percent). In fact, if the demand forecast is within ± 11 percent of the original forecast of 600 units, the EOQ does not change.

The percentage cost penalty (PCP) equation was not used to calculate the increase in TRC. The PCP equation is used only when the actual order quantity used differs from the EOQ.

Variations on the EOQ Model

In reality, the simplifying assumptions in the EOQ model rarely hold. This section will examine the effect that relaxing these assumptions has on the EOQ formulation and on TRC.

EOQ with Quantity Discounts Companies often save time and money by producing items in large quantities. With fewer changeovers to equipment, the production of large quantities that require long production run times increases worker efficiency and lowers per unit costs (fewer setup costs and higher productivity). To pass on some of the costs savings, suppliers may offer discounts on goods that are ordered in large quantities. Typically, these discounts are price incentives to induce customers to purchase large quantities of inventory.

Discount policies include one or more breakpoints which correspond to changes in the unit price. In the **all-units discount** illustrated in Exhibit 13.8A, the discount is applied to all the units in the order. If 50 units are ordered, the total purchase price is 50 × $5 = $250. If 150 units are ordered, the total purchase price is 150 × $4 = $600.

Under an **incremental discount** scheme, the discount applies only to the units which exceed the discount quantity. An incremental discount is depicted in Exhibit 13.8B. The total purchase price is still $250 for 50 units (50 × $5). If 150 units are ordered, however, the total purchase price is equal to (100 × $5) + (50 × $4) = $700.

A **carload discount** is illustrated in Exhibit 13.8C. A fixed cost is charged per unit until the cost of a full carload is covered, and the firm is not charged for any additional units carried in the carload. The same process is repeated if a second carload is needed [see Nahmias (1993)]. If 150 units are ordered under this discount scheme, $1\frac{1}{2}$ carloads are needed. Therefore, the firm will pay $5 × 80 = $400 for the first carload and $5 × 50 = $250 for the second carload.

Of the three discount policies outlined above, the all-units discount is the most widely used. Under an all-units discount, a four-step procedure is used to find the best order quantity (see Exhibit 13.9).[5]

Step 1. Calculate EOQs for each price range. Reject an EOQ which is not in a feasible quantity range for the price used.

There are three price ranges in this example. The EOQ for the second range is the only feasible EOQ.

Step 2. For allowable EOQs, calculate the total annual inventory cost.

Since the unit cost varies with the size of the purchase order, the total inventory cost must include the purchase cost of the order. The total annual inventory cost associated with the EOQ quantity of 538 units is $7,703.11.

Step 3. Calculate the total annual inventory cost associated with all higher-quantity ranges that have infeasible EOQs. For each quantity range, use the lowest allowable order quantity for that range.

There is only one higher quantity range in this example: the 1,000 or more range. The total inventory cost associated with ordering lots of 1,000 units is $7,230 per year.

---

[5] The EOQ with Discount module of ©OM-Expert follows this procedure as well.

EXHIBIT 13.8   ALTERNATIVE DISCOUNT POLICIES

A. All-Units Discount Policy

Order Quantity	Per Unit Cost, $
0 to 99	5
100 to 199	4
200 or more	3

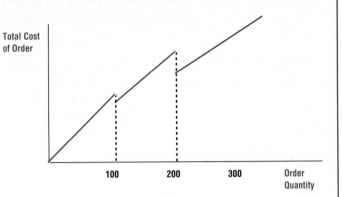

B. Incremental Discount Policy

Order Quantity	Per Unit Cost, $
0 to 99	5
100 to 199	5 for first 99
	4 for next 100
200 or more	5 for first 99
	4 for next 100
	3 for the remainder

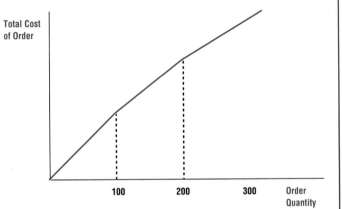

C. Carload Discount Policy

Order Quantity	Per Unit Cost, $
0 to 99	5 for first 80
	Units 81 to 99 are free
100 to 199	5 for first 80
	Units 81 to 99 are free
	5 for units 100 to 180
	Units 181 to 199 are free
200 to 300	5 for first 80
	Units 81 to 99 are free
	5 for units 100 to 180
	Units 181 to 199 are free
	5 for units 200 to 280
	Units 281 to 299 are free

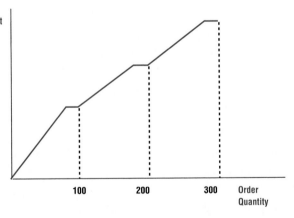

Step 4. Compare the total annual inventory costs calculated in steps 2 and 3. The quantity with the lowest total annual cost is the true EOQ.

In this example the true EOQ is 1,000 units.

EOQ with a Maximum Time Supply or Capacity Restriction In certain situations a firm may not be able to order the entire EOQ value. For example, if the shelf life of the product is shorter than the interval between orders, then, as demonstrated in Exhibit 13.10, the best order quantity is less than the EOQ quantity. The firm should order the maximum quantity that can be held before the product perishes or becomes obsolete.

EXHIBIT 13.9   TOOLBOX: ECONOMIC ORDER QUANTITY WITH PRICE DISCOUNTS

Suppose that Zytec employs the EOQ model to calculate the best order quantity for some of the parts used to build its power supplies. One of its suppliers has offered Zytec the following price break.

Quantity Range	Price per Item, $
1–499	1.60
500–999	1.50
1,000 or more	1.40

Other relevant information is as follows:

Ordering cost (S)	$11
Annual demand (D)	5,000 units a year
Carrying cost rate (i)	25 percent

To calculate the best order quantity, first calculate the EOQ associated with each quantity range.

(1) Quantity Range	(2) $2 \times D \times S$	(3) iC	(4) EOQ
1–499	(2)(5,000)(11) = 110,000	(0.25)(1.60) = 0.4	524
500–999	(2)(5,000)(11) = 110,000	(0.25)(1.50) = 0.38	538
1,000 or more	(2)(5,000)(11) = 110,000	(0.25)(1.40) = 0.35	561

Column 4 = $\sqrt{(\text{column } 2 \div \text{column } 3)}$ rounded.

The EOQ for the quantity range 1–499 is not valid because it does not fall within the range. The EOQ for the 500–999 range is feasible, but the EOQ for the 1,000 or more range is not feasible.

TOTAL COST ASSOCIATED WITH EOQ IN THE 500–999 RANGE

Total cost = Ordering cost + Inventory holding cost + Purchasing cost

$$= iC\frac{Q}{2} + S\frac{D}{Q} + DC$$

$$= (0.25)(1.50)\frac{(538)}{2} + 11\frac{(5,000)}{538} + 5,000(1.50)$$

$$= 7,703.11$$

TOTAL COST ASSOCIATED WITH 1,000 RANGE PRICE BREAK

Total cost = Ordering cost + Inventory holding cost + Purchasing cost

$$= (0.25)(1.40)\frac{(1,000)}{2} + 11\frac{(5,000)}{1,000} + 5,000(1.40)$$

$$= 7,230.00$$

The true EOQ is 1,000 since its total annual cost is lower than the total annual cost associated with an order quantity of 538 units.

(Exhibit 13.9 continues on next page)   **437**

EXHIBIT 13.9 *(continued)*

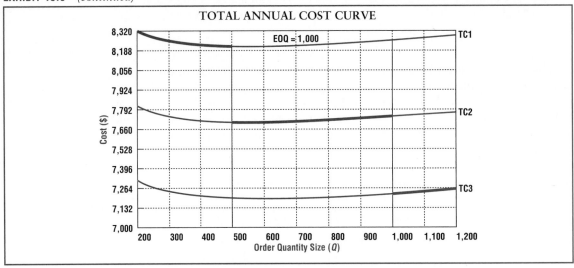

TOTAL ANNUAL COST CURVE

EXHIBIT 13.10 TOOLBOX: BEST ORDER QUANTITY UNDER TIME OR CAPACITY RESTRICTION

Suppose the pharmacy at the Mayo Clinic uses the EOQ model to calculate the best order quantity for some of the drugs it keeps on hand. Daily demand for one of these drugs is about five bottles, and the EOQ is 350 units. The EOQ quantity will last 70 days. If the drug's shelf life is only 60 days, how much should be ordered?

The EOQ in this case is not the best order quantity since $5 \times 10 = 50$ bottles will spoil during each order cycle. The best order quantity is the quantity that will last the same amount of time as the drug's shelf life: 60 days. Therefore, only $5 \times 60 = 300$ bottles should be ordered.

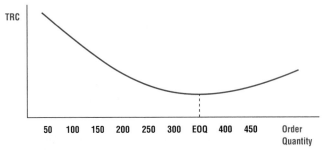

Alternatively, suppose the pharmacy has room only for 250 bottles. As shown by the graph above, the best order quantity is then 250 bottles.

The EOQ quantity may also exceed the storage capacity available for the product or the available space on the shop floor. The best EOQ value in these cases is the maximum amount that will not exceed the firm's space limitations.

EOQ with Gradual Order Delivery One assumption of the EOQ model is that once a replenishment order has been placed, the inventory quantity arrives all at once. Suppose, for example, that the EOQ is 400 units and the demand rate is 20 units per week. The supplier will deliver 400 units every 20 weeks, and the inventory level will gradually decrease from 400 to zero, at which point the supplier will deliver another 400 units.

Now suppose that the supplier delivers the EOQ quantity in smaller batches, say, 50 a week for eight weeks. As illustrated in Exhibit 13.11, since the firm is using 20 units a week, the inventory will grow at a rate of 30 units per week. After the eight-week delivery period, the inventory will decline, as before, at a rate of 20 units a week.

The best order quantity when the amount ordered arrives (or is produced) gradually is called the **economic lot size** (the finite replenishment economic order quantity) and is calculated by using equation (13.10). The maximum inventory level is no longer equal to the best order quantity but tends to be considerably lower.

Economic Lot Size

$$ELS = \sqrt{\frac{2DS}{H\left(1 - \dfrac{D}{P}\right)}} = \frac{EOQ}{\sqrt{1 - \dfrac{D}{P}}} \qquad (13.10)$$

Maximum Inventory Level

$$Q_{max} = ELS\left(1 - \frac{D}{P}\right) \qquad (13.11)$$

where ELS = economic lot size, in units
  D = demand, in units per year
  S = cost ($) of making each order (or setup)
  P = production rate of machine used to produce item (or delivery rate), in units per year
  H = inventory holding costs ($) for one year for one unit
  Q_{max} = maximum inventory level, in units

As demonstrated in Exhibit 13.11, as the value of P decreases, the best order quantity increases but the maximum inventory level falls. When P is just slightly higher than D, the best order quantity is significantly higher than the EOQ; the machine has to produce parts almost continuously (or the supplier must continuously deliver parts) to meet the demand. Finally, note that P must be greater than or equal to D. If P is less than D, the capacity of the machine (or the arrival rate of the components) will always be insufficient to meet the demand.

EXHIBIT 13.11 TOOLBOX: ECONOMIC LOT SIZE

Suppose Milliken purchases 1,040 units of a product each year. The EOQ, assuming that the order quantity arrives all at once, is 400 units. If the supplier delivers 50 units a week, however, the best order quantity is no longer 400 units.

A weekly delivery rate of 50 units converts to an annual rate of 2,600 units. If $P = 2,600$,

$$ELS = EOQ \times \frac{1}{\sqrt{1 - \dfrac{D}{P}}} = 400 \times \frac{1}{\sqrt{1 - \dfrac{1,040}{2,600}}} = 516$$

The maximum inventory level at this delivery rate is

$$Q_{max} = ELS\left(1 - \frac{D}{P}\right) = 516\left(1 - \frac{1,040}{2,600}\right) = 310$$

Therefore, the supplier delivers 50 units a week until the best order quantity (516 units) has been delivered. At this point the inventory is at its maximum level of 310 units. Once this inventory has been depleted, the supplier will resume weekly deliveries of 50 units.

(Exhibit 13.11 continues on next page)

EXHIBIT 13.11   *(continued)*

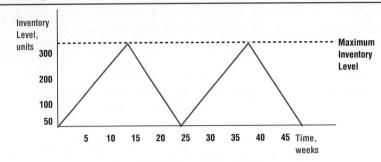

WEEKLY DELIVERY RATE OF 25 UNITS

A weekly delivery rate of 25 units converts to an annual rate of 1,300 units. If $P = 1,300$,

$$\text{ELS} = 400 \times \cfrac{1}{\sqrt{1 - \cfrac{1,040}{1,300}}} = 894$$

The maximum inventory level at this delivery rate is

$$Q_{\text{max}} = 894\left(1 - \frac{1,040}{1,300}\right) = 179$$

The following graph illustrates how the inventory level changes over time.

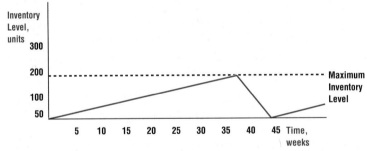

Note that the value of the best order quantity moves inversely to the delivery rate: the inventory grows more slowly as the delivery rate decreases. This reduces the holding costs. Since the minimum TRC occurs when the holding costs are equal to the ordering costs, the quantity ordered increases to lower the annual ordering cost to the value of the annual holding cost.

WEEKLY DELIVERY RATE OF 15 UNITS

Milliken purchases 1,040 units annually and uses them at a constant rate of 20 units a week. A weekly delivery rate of 15 units is therefore insufficient for Milliken's needs. If the formula is used, the term $1 - D/P$ will have a negative value and the answer will be undefined.

13.5 INVENTORY REPLENISHMENT SYSTEMS WHEN DEMAND IS UNCERTAIN

Note that the amount ordered under the EOQ system remains the same from one period to the next, as does the length of the interval between orders. This is due to the EOQ's assumption of a known, constant demand rate. This assumption, however, is not valid in most real-life situations. In these situations a firm is left with the two general options depicted in Exhibit 13.12.

EXHIBIT 13.12 AN OVERVIEW OF CONTINUOUS REVIEW AND PERIOD REVIEW SYSTEMS

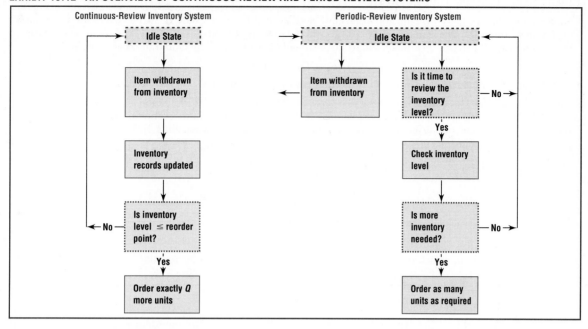

First, the firm can continuously review the inventory level and place an order whenever it falls to a predetermined level (the *reorder point*). Alternatively, it can review the inventory periodically and place an order at that time if one is needed.

In both cases firms often carry safety stocks to protect themselves from unexpected increases in demand while they are waiting for purchase (or production) orders to arrive. The amount of safety stock held is a function of the **service level** the firm wishes to maintain.

A high service level implies that a high percentage of customers can be served by the available inventory. For example, if a firm chooses a 95 percent service level, enough inventory of a product must be available to fill 95 percent of the demand during every inventory cycle.[6] But as service levels increase, so does the firm's investment in inventory.

Continuous-Review Strategy and the Fixed-Quantity Reorder Point System

In a **continuous-review strategy** the amount of inventory on hand is monitored constantly and is recalculated whenever items are added to or removed from stock. The amount of inventory on hand includes any amount on order but not yet received, minus any unfulfilled customer order or commitment. The fixed-quantity reorder point system is a widely used inventory policy based on continuous review strategy.

In the **fixed-quantity reorder point system,** when the inventory position falls to a predetermined reorder point, R, an order for Q units is placed. Note that as a result of the random nature of the demand, the time between orders will vary. For

---

[6] Note that service level (SL) can be defined in different ways. For example, SL can equal the percentage of time customers are satisfied. Alternatively, it can represent the percentage of total demand that should be satisfied. Each definition has its own impact on the size of the buffer stock. For more information, see Haehling von Lanzenauer and Noori (1986).

EXHIBIT 13.13 TOOLBOX: THE (Q,R) SYSTEM

Suppose the average daily demand for disposable needles at the Mayo Clinic is 50 per day with a standard deviation of 5 needles. The lead time is two days, and the EOQ is 300 needles. If the desired service level during the lead time is 90 percent, how much safety stock should be held and what should the reorder point be?

$$R = D_L + z_k \sigma_L$$

The demand during the lead time, D_L, is 50 needles per day times two days, or 100 needles.

To find the z score associated with a service level of 90 percent, turn to the standardized normal table in Appendix B and look for 0.90. The closest value is 0.8997, which is in the intersection of the 0.08 column and the 1.2 row. The value of z is the sum of the column heading and the row heading: 1.28.

It is also necessary to know the standard deviation of demand during the two-day lead time. Using equation (13.13),

$$\sigma_{2 \text{ days}} = \sigma_{1 \text{ day}} \times \sqrt{\frac{2}{1}} = 5\sqrt{2} = 7.07$$

It is now possible to calculate the buffer stock quantity and the reorder point:

$$R = 100 + (1.28)(7.07) = 109.05$$

Therefore, whenever the stock of needles falls to 109, a replenishment order for 300 more needles should be placed.

this policy, the values of R and Q are treated as independent decision variables and determined in advance. This (continuous-review) policy is also referred to as the **(Q,R) system,** or the Q system.

For example, in Exhibit 13.13 the Mayo Clinic orders the EOQ of 300 units whenever the inventory level falls to 109 units. This reorder point includes nine units of safety stock to protect the clinic from unexpected increases in demand during the purchase lead time.

The reorder point was calculated using equation (13.12), which assumes that demand follows the normal distribution.[7]

Reorder Point When Demand Is Normally Distributed

$$R = D_L + z_k \sigma_L \qquad (13.12)$$

where R = reorder point, in units
D_L = average demand, in units, during lead time
z_k = z score associated with desired service level k during the lead time
σ_L = standard deviation of demand during lead time

Note that the standard deviation of demand must be calculated for the lead time interval. If the standard deviation of demand is known but is at a time interval different from the lead time, use equation (13.13) to express the data in the same time measure.

Converting the Standard Deviation of Demand over Another Time Period

$$\sigma_T = \sigma_t \sqrt{\frac{T}{t}} \qquad (13.13)$$

[7] Other distributions can be used, but the normal distribution is the most popular.

where σ_T = standard deviation of demand over time period T
$\quad\sigma_t$ = known standard deviation of demand over time interval t
$\quad T$ = time period, expressed in the same time interval as σ_t

Suppose, for example, the standard deviation of daily demand is 10 units but the lead time is nine days. Therefore, the standard deviation of demand during the lead time is 30 units:

$$\sigma_L = 10\sqrt{\frac{9}{1}} = 30$$

Periodic-Review Strategy and Variable Order Quantity Reorder Point Systems

In a **periodic-review system** the inventory level is checked at fixed intervals (say, once a week) rather than continuously. Depending on the inventory level, a replenishment order may or may not be issued. The optional replacement system is a widely used periodic-review inventory policy.

The Optional Replacement (s,S) System   If an **optional replacement system** (also called an **(s,S) system**) is used, up to S units are ordered if the inventory level is below s. Otherwise, an order is not made. The Mayo Clinic, for example, may review its inventory of needles once a week and order up to 410 if the inventory level does not exceed 110.

How can a firm determine the best values for s and S? In practice, this is difficult. As a result, a number of approximation methods have been suggested [see Porteous (1985)]. One method uses the (Q,R) values that were determined in the previous section. In this case, $s = R$ and $S = R + Q$. This approximation is widely used and gives reasonable results in many cases.

The importance of choosing appropriate values for s and S is illustrated in Exhibit 13.14. Look at the inventory level at the end of week 5. It is just over the s value of 110 units, and so an order is not placed. As a result, a stockout occurs in week 6.

The P System   The **P system** is a variation of the optional replacement (s,S) system. The inventory is reviewed periodically as in the (s,S) system, but an order is always placed at the time of review to increase the stock to a predetermined target level T.

To approximate the length of the review interval P, divide the EOQ by the annual demand.[8] Calculating the target inventory, T, however, is more involved. The **target inventory level** must be large enough to cover the average demand over the review interval period and the lead time for the subsequent order as well as any unexpected variations in demand.[9]

---

[8] This is the same formula used to calculate the average order interval when demand is known and constant [equation (13.6)].

[9] If the standard deviation of demand over the combined period $(P + L)$ is not known, use this variation of equation (13.13) to approximate its value:

$$\sigma_{P+L} = \sigma_t\sqrt{\frac{P + L}{t}}$$

EXHIBIT 13.14 TOOLBOX: THE OPTIONAL REPLACEMENT SYSTEM

Suppose the Mayo Clinic uses the optional replacement system to manage its inventory of disposable needles. Every week the inventory is counted. If there are 110 or fewer needles, then (410 − inventory level) are ordered. If the inventory level is greater than 110, an order is not made.

The graph below depicts what can happen over a 10-week period.

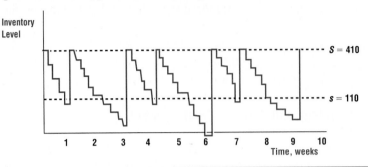

Target Inventory Level

$$T = D_{P+L} + z_k \sigma_{P+L} \qquad (13.14)$$

where T = target inventory level, in units
D_{P+L} = demand, in units, during review period and lead time
z_k = z score associated with desired service level k during lead time
σ_{P+L} = standard deviation of demand during review period and lead time

Under the P system, the Mayo Clinic, for example, may review its stock of disposable needles every six days and then order enough to increase the inventory level to 418 units (see Exhibit 13.15).

A Comparison of Continuous-Review and Periodic-Review Strategies

Which approach is better: continuous review of inventory levels or review at predetermined time intervals? Circumstances dictate the answer.

Continuous-review systems are appropriate when running out of a particular item has grave consequences and when the item is sensitive or expensive. Relatively low levels of safety stock are required, but this is offset by the cost of maintaining the perpetual inventory records. The fixed lot sizes can be set to obtain quantity discounts; they also can be set to reduce inventory and thus reduce warehousing requirements.

Periodic-review systems are appropriate for inexpensive or relatively unimportant items or when there are no physical or financial constraints on storage. Record-keeping costs are low. Since orders are placed at specific intervals, multiple orders for the same supplier can be combined.

Hybrid Systems

In practice, hybrid systems that incorporate features of both periodic-review and continuous-review systems are also used. One of these systems is called the **base stock system**. Here the idea is to place a replenishment order each time there is a

EXHIBIT 13.15   TOOLBOX: THE P-SYSTEM

Suppose the average daily demand for disposable needles at the Mayo Clinic is 50, the lead time is two days, and the EOQ is 300 needles. The desired service level during the lead time is 90 percent. If the clinic wishes to implement a periodic review system in which an order is always placed at review time, how often should it review its stock and what should the target inventory be?

LENGTH OF THE REVIEW PERIOD

$$P = EOQ \div D = 300 \div 50 = 6 \text{ days}$$

TARGET INVENTORY LEVEL

$$T = D_{P+L} + z_{90\%}\, \sigma_{P+L}$$

The demand over the review period and lead time is 50×8 days $= 400$ units. The firm knows that the z score associated with 90 percent is 1.28, but it is necessary to calculate the standard deviation of demand over the eight-day period. The standard deviation of *daily* demand is five needles.

$$\sigma_{8 \text{ days}} = \sigma_{1 \text{ day}} \times \sqrt{\frac{8}{1}} = 5\sqrt{8} = 14.14$$

The clinic now has all the data it needs to calculate the target inventory.

$$T = 400 + 1.28(14.14) = 418.099$$

Therefore, the clinic should review its stock every six days and order enough new stock to increase the inventory level to 418 units.

The following graph illustrates what can happen to the inventory level under this system over a six-week period.

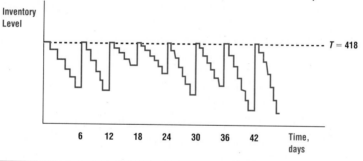

withdrawal. The order quantity (Q) is the same as the withdrawal quantity. Thus if there is a withdrawal of 15 units, a replenishment order is placed for 15 more. Inventory is kept at a base stock level that is equal to the expected demand during the lead time plus the safety stock.

The base stock level is equivalent to the reorder point in a (Q,R) system [equation (13.12)]. However, to keep the inventory equal to R at all times, order quantities vary. Since this is the least inventory a firm can hold while maintaining a specified service level, the base stock system can be seen as a way to minimize cycle inventory. Only enough inventory is held to satisfy the maximum demand, and so orders for small quantities are placed frequently. This is ideal for firms that buy expensive parts.

A second hybrid system is the **visual hybrid system,** in which there are no records of current inventory levels. Here the usage rate is reconstructed from past purchase orders. Low-value items such as nuts and bolts are the types of items for which this system is appropriate. Overstocking of low-value items is acceptable since the extra holding cost is nominal.

One version of the visual hybrid is called the **single-bin system.** A maximum level is marked on a shelf or bin which is filled periodically. Gas tanks and shelves in supermarkets are examples. Usage of inventory is determined by examining purchase orders since records of receipts are not usually kept.

In a **two-bin system** an item's inventory is stored at two different locations. The first bin is the place to go if withdrawals of inventory are necessary. If this bin is empty, the second bin can cover demand until new inventory arrives. As the first bin becomes empty, a new order (equivalent to the size of the bin) is placed, and the arriving shipment restores the second bin to its normal level. Any leftovers are then deposited into the first bin. With this version of the Q system the normal level in the second bin is the reorder point. It is recommended that the order quantity last much longer than the replenishment lead time. This system is effective only if there is no more than one order outstanding at a time.

The Newsboy Problem: A Special Case of Uncertain Demand

What happens when demand for a single product is to be met *only* over one season (e.g., Christmas) or over a given time period (e.g., one week)? What happens if the product will be obsolete when the season is over? These types of situations are often referred to as **newsboy problems** or "Christmas-tree" problems. Picture a corner newsstand. If the stand does not buy enough papers, sales are lost. However, if there are too many papers, excess costs are incurred because no one will buy a day-old paper. The objective is to find the order quantity which maximizes the expected profit.

Determining the best order quantity is difficult. In practice, a payoff matrix (see Exhibit 13.16) is often used. Each column in the matrix represents a different demand level, and each row represents a different order quantity. Each cell contains the payoff (net profit) that results from that quantity demanded–quantity ordered combination. This payoff is calculated by using equation (13.15). Note that the opportunity cost of ordering less than the quantity demanded is not usually considered.

Newsboy Problem Payoff Matrix

$$\begin{aligned} R_{i,j} &= PQ_i && \text{if } Q_i \leq D_j \\ &= PD_i - L(Q_i - D_j) && \text{if } Q_i > D_j \end{aligned} \tag{13.15}$$

where $R_{i,j}$ = payoff associated with order quantity i and demand level j
P = profit (\$) per unit sold during season
L = loss (\$) per unit not sold during season
Q_i = order quantity, in units: $i = 1$ to n
D_j = quantity demanded, in units: $j = 1$ to m

The expected payoff associated with each order quantity is calculated by using equation (13.16). The best order quantity is the quantity with the highest expected payoff.

Expected Payoff Associated with Each Order Quantity

$$EP(Q_i) = \sum_{j=1}^{m} p_{D_j} R_{i,j} \tag{13.16}$$

where $EP(Q_i)$ = expected payoff associated with order quantity i
p_{D_j} = probability of demand level j occurring
$R_{i,j}$ = payoff associated with order quantity i and demand level j

EXHIBIT 13.16   TOOLBOX: PAYOFF MATRIX FOR THE NEWSBOY PROBLEM

The Atwood department store sells Halloween costumes every year. Each costume costs the store $5 but sells for $15. The costumes can be sold for $3 once Halloween is over. Given the various demand levels and associated probabilities below, how many costumes should be ordered?

Demand	Probability of Demand Materializing
50	0.1
60	0.1
70	0.2
80	0.3
90	0.2
100	0.1

PAYOFF MATRIX

The payoff matrix is constructed using equation (13.15). For example, if $Q = 60$ and $D = 90$, the payoff is $(10)(60)$, or $600. Now suppose the order quantity exceeds the demand level, say, $Q = 60$ and $D = 50$. The payoff is $(10)(50) + (5 - 3)(60 - 50)$, or $480.

Purchase	Demand Level					
Quantity	50	60	70	80	90	100
50	500	500	500	500	500	500
60	480	600	600	600	600	600
70	460	580	700	700	700	700
80	440	560	680	800	800	800
90	420	540	660	780	900	900
100	400	520	640	760	880	1,000

EXPECTED PAYOFF FOR EACH ORDER QUANTITY

The expected payoff for each order quantity is found by using equation (13.16). For example, the expected payoff if 60 costumes are ordered is

$$480\,(0.1) + 600\,(0.1) + 600\,(0.2) + 600\,(0.3) + 600\,(0.2) + 600\,(0.1) = 588$$

Order Quantity	Expected Payoff, $
50	500
60	588
70	664
80	716
90	732
100	724

The highest expected payoff occurs when 90 costumes are ordered.

13.6 CONTROLLING INVENTORY AT AN AGGREGATE LEVEL

The inventory models that have been discussed all deal with the timing and quantity of individual purchases (or production runs). In practice, however, managers are often more concerned with their aggregate inventory positions than with individual ordering policies.

Trade-off, or exchange, curves allow managers to control inventory at an aggregate level [Tersine (1988)]. If the firm assumes that ordering costs and carrying cost percentages are the same for all items in inventory, aggregate inventory levels can be determined without summing the inventory levels for each individual item.

The average investment for a single inventory item is equal to its unit cost (C) times its average inventory level (EOQ/2), which is equivalent to

$$\sqrt{\frac{S}{i}} \times \sqrt{\frac{CD}{2}}$$

Since it is assumed that the ordering costs (S) and the carrying cost percentage (i) are the same for all inventory items, the total average inventory investment (U) is given by equation (13.17).

Total Average Inventory Investment

$$U = \sqrt{\frac{S}{i}} \sum_{j=1}^{n} \sqrt{\frac{C_j D_j}{2}} \tag{13.17}$$

Total Number of Annual Replenishments

$$V = \sqrt{\frac{i}{S}} \sum_{j=1}^{n} \sqrt{\frac{C_j D_j}{2}} \tag{13.18}$$

Trade-off Curve

$$UV = \left(\sum_{j=1}^{n} \sqrt{\frac{C_j D_j}{2}} \right)^2 \tag{13.19}$$

Trade-off Curve Ratio

$$\frac{U}{V} = \frac{S}{i} \tag{13.20}$$

where U = total average inventory investment
V = total number of annual replenishments
S = cost of making each order or setup ($)
i = carrying cost rate, expressed as a percentage
j = 1, 2, 3, . . . , n, represents the set of inventory items
C_j = per unit cost of item j ($)
D_j = annual demand for item j, in units

The number of replenishment orders for a single inventory item is equal to its annual demand (D) divided by its EOQ value, which is equal to

$$\sqrt{\frac{i}{S}} \times \sqrt{\frac{CD}{2}}$$

If it is assumed again that S and i are the same for all inventory items, the total number of annual replenishments (V) is given by equation (13.18).

The trade-off curve is found by multiplying U by V [equation (13.19)]. Note that the values of U and V are dependent on the ratio S/i. The division of both sides of equation (13.17) by V gives equation (13.20), which is known as the **trade-off curve ratio.**

Of what value are the trade-off curve and trade-off curve ratio? As demonstrated in Exhibit 13.17, managers can select a desirable inventory level (U) and implicitly define a value for S/i. The S/i ratio can then be used to determine the order quantities for individual inventory items. These order quantities result in an inventory that displays the characteristics (i.e., U and V values) selected.

EXHIBIT 13.17   TOOLBOX: TRADE-OFF (EXCHANGE) CURVE

McCaffery Ltd. has six different items in inventory. The number of units demanded of each item and its unit cost are shown in the table below.

Item	Annual Demand, D	Unit Cost, C	$\sqrt{CD/2}$
1	20,000	$5.29	230
2	50,000	1.60	200
3	30,000	1.50	150
4	80,000	2.56	320
5	90,000	2.42	330
6	60,000	2.43	270
Total			1,500

The trade-off curve, UV, that corresponds to this inventory system is

$$UV = \left(\sum_{j=1}^{6} \sqrt{\frac{C_j D_j}{2}} \right)^2 = 1,500^2 = 2,250,000$$

McCaffery Ltd. has not estimated its ordering or holding costs. However, it has set its average inventory level at $15,000. Using the trade-off curve equation, it can solve for V.

$$15,000V = 2,250,000$$
$$V = 150$$

Now that U and V are known, the value of S/i can be calculated using the exchange curve ratio.

$$\frac{U}{V} = \frac{15,000}{150} = 100 \qquad \frac{U}{V} = \frac{S}{i} \qquad \therefore \frac{S}{i} = 100$$

What happens if the average inventory investment is decreased to $10,000? As shown on the following graph, replenishment orders are made more often (225 times a year) and the value of S/i falls to 44.44.

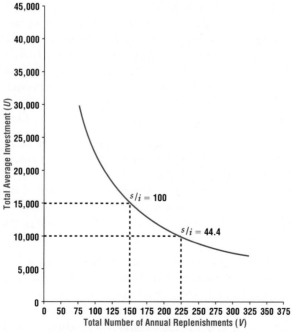

EXCHANGE CURVE FOR UV = 2,250,000

How will McCaffery Ltd. use the S/i value? Suppose the S/i value is 100. Recall that the EOQ is calculated:

$$EOQ = \sqrt{\frac{2DS}{iC}} = \sqrt{\frac{S}{i}} \times \sqrt{\frac{2D}{C}}$$

(Exhibit 13.17 continues on next page)

EXHIBIT 13.17 *(continued)*

The EOQ quantity for each inventory item is shown in the table below.

(1) Item	(2) Annual Demand, D	(3) Unit Cost, C	(4) $\sqrt{2D/C}$	(5) EOQ
1	20,000	$5.29	86.96	870
2	50,000	1.60	250	2,500
3	30,000	1.50	250	2,500
4	80,000	2.56	200	2,000
5	90,000	2.42	272.73	2,727
6	60,000	2.43	222.22	2,222

Column 5 = column 4 × 100, rounded.

13.7 ISSUES IN MANAGING INVENTORY SYSTEMS

The inventory models discussed so far trade off several costs to determine the best inventory policy for a particular item. There are, however, many other issues in inventory management.

In a typical operation numerous parts and materials are required to produce goods and services. Running out of some of these items may be disastrous, while running out of others may be merely inconvenient. Some may be very expensive, others relatively cheap. Obviously, the importance of closely monitoring and controlling inventory items varies from one item to the next. One widely used method of differentiating inventory items is the ABC inventory classification system.

ABC Inventory Classification

If a typical manufacturer ranks every item in its inventory on the basis of its annual dollar volume (unit cost × yearly demand), it will probably find that a small number of items account for a large dollar volume and that a large number of items account for a small dollar volume. This observation is depicted in Exhibit 13.18A and is the basis of the **ABC inventory classification system.**

The single-criterion ABC classification system assigns each inventory item to one of three categories on the basis of its annual dollar volume:

- Category A items are items whose cumulative value is about 75 to 80 percent of the total value of annual inventory purchases. Typically, 15 to 20 percent of the items fall into this category.
- Category B is composed of the 30 to 40 percent of inventory items that account for about 15 percent of the inventory's total value.
- The remaining inventory items are found in category C. These items represent only 5 to 10 percent of the total value of inventory.

This classification system helps managers control inventory and inventory-related costs by putting their time and effort where they will have the biggest payoff. Items in category A should be reviewed more frequently than items in categories B and C, for example, and more detailed inventory records should be kept for them.

Because cost is not the only important criterion in inventory management, the ABC classification system is often extended to include criteria such as the consequences of running out of an item, how quickly an item can be purchased, and the availability of substitute items. The table in Exhibit 13.18B shows how inventory items can be classified by dollar usage and criticality. Each of the nine combinations

EXHIBIT 13.18   THE ABC CLASSIFICATION SYSTEM

A. Single-Criterion ABC

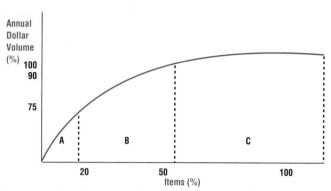

B. Multiple-Criteria ABC

Rather than simply classifying inventory items on the basis of dollar volume, the firm can classify them on both dollar volume and criticality. Separate inventory policies can then be assigned to each of the nine categories.

Dollar	Criticality		
Usage	I	II	III
A	1	2	3
B	4	5	6
C	7	8	9

can be assigned a specific inventory management policy or grouped into three or four major classifications.

Inventory Turnover

Inventory turnover is a widely used performance measure that reflects the liquidity of a firm's inventory and the speed with which inventory is converted into sales. It indicates the number of times the inventory is sold—or turned over—during a stated period. For example, if the firm's annual cost of goods sold is $500,000 and its average inventory value is $50,000, the inventory turns over 10 times. If the cost of goods sold rises to $1 million and the inventory value remains as is, the turnover ratio jumps to 20.

Inventory Turnover

$$\text{Inventory turnover} = \frac{\text{Cost of goods sold}}{\text{Average inventory value}} \qquad (13.21)$$

Inventory turnover is related to actual sales. Therefore, high inventory levels are not penalized when sales levels are high and low inventory levels are not rewarded when sales levels are low.

The higher the number of turnovers, the less time each item, on average, remains in the firm's inventory and the more liquid the inventory is. The cash flow needed to finance the inventory also decreases as the number of inventory turnovers increases.[10]

---

[10] Consider an analogy. Suppose you spend $2,000 a year on groceries. The more often you buy groceries, the smaller the value of the food you have in the house at any time and the smaller the cash flow needed to finance your grocery purchases.

Inventory turnovers vary from firm to firm and from industry to industry. Typical high-tech firms have 5 or 6 turnovers a year, while some Japanese automobile firms experience 40 a year. As will be discussed in the next section, firms today are striving to reduce their investment in inventories and increase their inventory turnover.

The Drive to Reduce Inventory Levels

This chapter began with a discussion of the different functions served by inventories within a firm: guarding against uncertainty, offsetting the high cost of product changeovers, protecting current throughput by decoupling operations, and smoothing production levels. On the surface, the functions performed by inventories seem

EXHIBIT 13.19   THE DRIVE TO REDUCE INVENTORY LEVELS

Canberra Industrial Products Ltd. manufactures products A, B, and C in a three-work-center production process. The annual demand for each product is about 3,000 units, holding costs are $4.80 per unit per year, and process setup costs are $20 an hour. Currently, each setup requires 10 hours.

The EOQ for each product is therefore 500 units:

$$EOQ = \sqrt{\frac{2DS}{H}} = \sqrt{\frac{(2)(3,000)(200)}{4.80}} = 500$$

$$TRC = H\frac{Q}{2} + S\frac{D}{Q} = 4.80\left(\frac{500}{2}\right) + 200\left(\frac{3,000}{500}\right) = 2,400$$

Each product is manufactured in a three-work-center production process. The per unit processing times for each product at each work center are shown in the table below.

	Hours Required per Unit		
Product	Work Center 1	Work Center 2	Work Center 3
A	0.4	0.3	0.15
B	0.3	0.3	0.10
C	0.4	0.3	0.15

Although it takes 10 hours to set up each work center, the second and third centers can set up their equipment before the arrival of each batch. The Gantt chart below illustrates the movement of products A, B, and C through the three work centers. Note that it takes 805 hours for the set of three batches to flow through the process.

GANTT CHART AND CORRESPONDING WIP INVENTORY FOR EOQ OF 500 UNITS

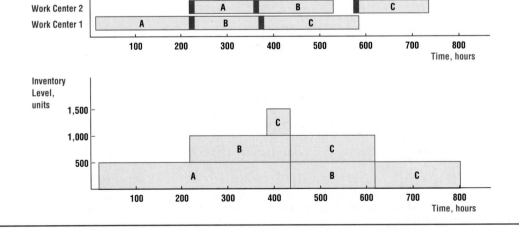

Suppose Canberra can reduce its setup time to 2½ hours. The setup cost drops to $50, and the EOQ falls to 250 units.

$$EOQ = \sqrt{\frac{(2)(3,000)(50)}{4.80}} = 250$$

$$TRC = 4.80\left(\frac{250}{2}\right) + 50\left(\frac{3,000}{250}\right) = 1,200$$

As shown below, it now takes 395 hours to produce a batch of product A, B, and C and only 677.5 hours to produce 500 units of each product. Note that the new setup time for each work center is short and not drawn on the Gantt chart. The setup times, however, were incorporated in the calculation of total production hours. The corresponding WIP inventory has been reduced drastically.

GANTT CHART AND CORRESPONDING WIP INVENTORY LEVEL FOR EOQ OF 250 UNITS

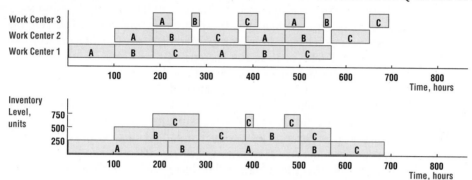

As Canberra reduces its setup times, the EOQ falls. Smaller batch sizes translate into lower WIP inventory, lower inventory costs, and faster throughput times. When the batch size is 10 units, it takes just over 555 hours to produce 500 units of each product, compared with the original throughput time of 805 hours. Canberra has effectively increased its capacity.

Setup Time, hours	Batch Size (EOQ), units	Throughput time, hours	
		For 500 Units of Each Product	For One Set of Products A, B, and C
10	500	805	805
2.5	250	677.5	395
0.1	50	575.5	77.8
0.004	10	555.1	15.51
0.001	5	552.6	5.51

to be essential. In fact, how could a firm survive *without* substantial inventory levels?

Managers in many firms, however, have recognized that holding large inventories impedes their ability to compete simultaneously on cost, time, quality, service, flexibility, and dependability. To understand why this is so, take another look at the EOQ formula.

Recall that the EOQ is the quantity at which ordering (or process setup) and holding costs are equal. What would happen if one of these costs—say, the ordering (or process setup) cost—was drastically reduced? In Exhibit 13.19 the process setup time for Canberra Industrial Products Ltd. is reduced from 10 hours to 2.5 hours. As a result, the EOQ and total relevant costs are cut in half.

Lower inventory-related costs are not the only benefits that accrue to Canberra

Ltd. as it reduces its batch sizes and inventory levels. Other advantages of lower inventory levels include the following:

- **Shorter production lead times.** If it is assumed that Canberra operates two 8-hour shifts a day, seven days a week, the original production lead time for product A is about five weeks. Once the batch size is cut in half, product A's lead time falls to 215 hours, or just under two weeks. Cutting the batch size down to 50 units reduces product A's lead time to approximately $2\frac{1}{2}$ days.

- **More stable production schedules, smaller buffer inventories, lower holding costs, and more reliable delivery promises.** A reduction in the production lead time enables the firm to use shorter-range, and hence more accurate, forecasts. The firm may even be able to produce to order rather than to stock. The more reliable the forecast, the more stable the production schedule and the smaller the need for safety stock in the finished goods inventory. The risk of inventory obsolescence falls, as do inventory holding costs. Customers receive their orders sooner, and delivery promises become more realistic.

- **More reliable delivery of purchased goods.** A more stable production schedule also allows the firm to pass on better information to its suppliers. This should improve the ability of the suppliers to supply the right items at the right times and reduce the firm's level of safety stock for purchased goods.

- **Quicker incorporation of product modifications.** Suppose the firm wishes to improve product A. An engineering change is drafted and sent to the shop floor. It is unlikely that the change will be incorporated until the next batch of product A is produced. In the first scenario this may take about seven weeks. With batch sizes of 50 units, product A is produced daily and the engineering change can be implemented almost immediately.

- **Improved product quality.** Look again at the first Gantt chart in Exhibit 13.19. Suppose a problem at work center 1 results in two defective units of product A which are discovered at work center 3. What is the probability that the cause of the problem can and will be found? The units were processed at work center 1 one or two weeks ago, and the operator has 498 other units. The manager may feel that a 4 percent defect rate is acceptable and may simply increase the safety buffer and thus the batch size. If the batch size is only 50 units, it will take just one day for the defective units to arrive at work center 3. Hence, there is a better chance that the source of the problem will be discovered. The manager will feel more motivated to solve the problem because the lower WIP inventory magnifies its impact.

- **Simpler inventory management and production control systems and reduced production costs.** Lower inventories, more stable production schedules, and higher-quality products also reduce the need for complex inventory management and production control systems. Fewer people are needed to track and expedite orders. There is less of a need for expensive equipment to move inventory from one work center to the next. Work centers can be moved closer together, saving floor space and improving shop floor communication. These savings become more significant as the number of products and processes increases.

Thus, as a firm reduces its inventory levels, its ability to compete is improved. Fast-response organizations (FROs) are reducing inventory levels by drastically reducing or even eliminating the *need* for inventory. They do this by improving product and process quality, reducing process setup and ordering costs, improving information systems, and working more closely with their suppliers and customers.

Caution. The ultimate goal is to improve the firm's ability to compete and satisfy its customers, not to drive inventory levels to zero.

The goal is to make inventory management subservient to customer service and to drive inventory down to a "perfect" level.

Improving Inventory Control

Historically, the average inventory accuracy of facilities in the United States has been low, at around 60 to 70 percent [Martinka (1993)]. The drive to reduce inventories increases the need for accurate, timely inventory records. How can a firm ensure that its records are accurate and minimize the cost of keeping them accurate? Certainly, safeguards such as limiting access to storerooms are essential in many situations, but the vast majority of inaccuracies in inventory records are caused by mistakes made in recording transactions. A firm can reduce these inaccuracies with a bar coding system and identify their causes much sooner with cycle counting. Both systems reduce the cost of monitoring and controlling the inventory.

Bar Coding   As was mentioned in the Chapter 8 Supplement, a **bar code** is a set of thick and thin black bars and spaces which contain information such as the product's name, lot number, location, and price. The code is printed directly on the product or on its packaging. When an optical scanner is used, this information can be read quickly into a PC or mainframe computer.

Advances in bar code technology continue to be made as bar coding becomes more popular and is used by a wider range of industries and environments. Some of the latest advances include the following.

- **Code 49.** This bar code symbol was developed for the electronics and health care industries, where most inventory items are too small to carry conventional bar codes. Instead of just one row, two to eight adjacent rows are used. Thus more information can be encoded in a smaller area.
- **Portable data collection terminals.** These terminals enable people in remote locations to collect information. Then, through either a modem or a radio link, employees can download relevant data to the mainframe or host computer.
- **Electronic article surveillance (EAS).** EAS equipment can read bar codes at the checkout counter while simultaneously deactivating an antishoplifting signal which is built into the bar label. Alligator chips attached directly to clothes in retail stores are an example of EAS.

Bar coding offers firms more than a handy way to manage finished goods. If everything—parts, components, finished goods—is coded, information accuracy will be improved *everywhere*. Reduced inventory uncertainty means smaller safety stocks and lower costs. Therefore, firms that use bar codes to manage finished goods inventory *are* also using them elsewhere.

Cycle Counting   Bar coding is just one way to improve the accuracy of inventory data. Canceling the traditional annual comparison of recorded versus actual inventory levels and implementing a **cycle counting** system can also achieve this. Rather than physically counting inventory items once per year, the firm checks a portion of the inventory on a regular basis (e.g., daily or weekly).

The annual inventory count is very expensive, and the information derived from it is not very timely. When inventory items are counted more often, the records become more accurate. This means that every system that uses the inventory is also more accurate. Since discrepancies between actual and recorded inventory levels are found more quickly, the chances of finding the causes of these inaccuracies are much higher.

Cycle counting tends to be less expensive than annual inventory counts because it can be performed on regular time by existing employees. It also reduces the costs of unexpected inventory excesses and shortages.

How are items selected for counting? Every item should be counted at least once every fiscal year, but some should be counted much more frequently than others. For example, items that have a relatively large number of inventory transactions or are relatively important (e.g., category A items), should be counted more often. Reconciling the inventory record with the actual amount on hand also makes sense when the inventory record has a zero balance or the material dispensing area reports that an insufficient quality of an item is on hand to fill an order.

MANAGERIAL IMPLICATIONS

Most firms *have* to carry inventory to be fully effective. It is management's obligation to make sure the firm carries the smallest dollar value of inventory while remaining effective. Unfortunately, most firms carry too much inventory. One major reason for this is the way in which managers are evaluated and rewarded. When managers are evaluated according to their ability to keep operators and equipment busy, there is an incentive to maintain excessive inventory. This is compounded by the fact that many managers do not know how to determine why they are holding inventory or how much they should hold.

All the models used to decide how much and when inventory should be ordered or produced trade off the costs of ordering or making against the costs of holding the inventory. The more complicated models take into account other costs as well, particularly the costs of maintaining and controlling inventory. These more elaborate models also recognize resource or capacity constraints and restraints. Without a doubt, the greatest and most overlooked cost and constraint in the inventory management process is the lack of managerial resources.

Models cannot manage inventory; only managers can. If the managers are worked beyond their limits, the inventory will not be managed effectively. That is why many firms use inventory models and rules that seem at first to be inefficient. They are, but using them instead of elegant but unmanageable models makes them effective. In all things, firms need first to be effective; only then can they worry about being efficient. As a firm's ability to manage information becomes better, though, its management of its inventories should continually improve.

CHAPTER SUMMARY

The focus in this chapter was on inventory: why it is kept, how it can be managed, and its impact on a firm's ability to compete.

- Inventory can be classified by its form (raw materials, work-in-process, finished goods), by its function (safety, in-transit, cycle, decoupling, anticipation), or by the nature of its demand (dependent, independent).

- Inventory-related costs include item, ordering (or process setup), holding, stock-out, and monitoring costs.
- An inventory policy is a procedure put in place to help managers answer questions such as: How much should the firm order? When should it order? How often should it order?
- When the demand for an item is known and is relatively constant, the economic order quantity (EOQ) model or one of its variations can often be used to develop an inventory policy for that item.
- The economic order quantity (EOQ) model calculates the best quantity to order (or produce) by minimizing the sum of inventory ordering and carrying costs.
- Sensitivity analysis deals with the impact of varying one or more cost parameters on the EOQ and total relevant costs.
- Variations of the EOQ model include EOQ with quantity discounts, inclusion of a maximum time supply or capacity restriction, and gradual delivery.
- When demand is independent but is not known with certainty, reorder point systems such as the (s,S) and P systems are more appropriate. Safety, or buffer, stock is needed to protect the firm from unexpected increases in demand during the purchase (or production) lead time.
- Under the (Q,R) system the inventory level is monitored continuously. Whenever the inventory level falls to R, an order for Q more units is placed.
- Under the (s,S) system the inventory level is reviewed periodically. Up to S more units are ordered if the inventory level is less than s; otherwise an order is not made.
- The P system is a variation of the optional replacement (s,S) system. The inventory is reviewed periodically as in the (s,S) system, but an order is always placed at the time of review to increase the stock position to a predetermined target level T.
- The base stock system and the visual hybrid system are examples of hybrid systems.
- If the demand for a single product is to be met *only* over one season or over a given period and if the product will be obsolete when the season is over, the newsboy problem payoff matrix can be used to calculate the best order quantity.
- Trade-off (exchange) curves allow managers to control inventory at an aggregate level. The total average inventory investment is set first, and then order quantities for individual items are calculated on the basis of the selected investment level.
- The ABC inventory classification system can help managers decide which inventory policy to apply to each type of inventory item.
- Inventory turnover is a widely used performance measure that reflects the liquidity of a firm's inventory and the speed with which inventory is converted into sales.
- Reducing the need for high cycle, buffer, and decoupling inventories by improving its production process enables a firm to improve its ability to compete on cost, quality, time, dependability, and flexibility.
- The accuracy of inventory records, and hence the quality of inventory control, can be improved through the use of bar codes and cycle counting.

Inventory management is a tactical issue that must be subservient to a firm's strategy for improving customer satisfaction. Chapter 14 will discuss aggregate planning, another important determinant of a firm's ability to satisfy its customers.

KEY TERMS

Raw materials inventories
Work-in-process (WIP) inventories
Finished goods inventories
Safety (buffer) inventories
Decoupling inventory
In-transit (pipeline) inventory
Cycle inventory
Anticipatory (seasonal) inventory
Independent demand inventory
Dependent demand inventory

Item costs
Ordering costs
Process setup costs
Holding costs
Stockout (shortage) costs
Inventory policy
Economic order quantity (EOQ) model
Average number of purchase (production) orders per year
Average order interval
Total relevant cost
Lead time
Reorder point

Sensitivity analysis
All-units discount
Incremental discount
Carload discount
Economic lot size
Service level
Continuous-review strategy
Fixed-quantity reorder point system
(Q,R) system
Periodic-review system
Optional replacement (s,S) system
P system

Target inventory level
Base stock system
Visual hybrid system
Single-bin system
Two-bin system
Newsboy problems
Trade-off (exchange) curves
Trade-off curve ratio
ABC inventory classification system
Inventory turnover
Bar code
Cycle counting

DISCUSSION QUESTIONS

1. Why would a firm want to hold inventory?

2. Independent demand inventory is important for manufacturers. How important is it for service organizations? Is it necessary to think differently about inventory for service firms? If so, how?

3. Give me a decent forecast and I'll give you a decent inventory policy. What do you think of this statement? Is anything else required to develop a reasonable inventory policy? Why or why not?

4. What are the five functions inventory performs? Can you think of examples of all five for each of the companies visited in the Startup Chapter?

5. How can a firm decide how much decoupling, anticipatory, and pipeline inventory to hold? Who should be involved in making these decisions?

6. In addition to the five functions, there are three forms of inventory [raw materials, work-in-progress (WIP), and finished goods]. Can you draw a three-by-five matrix of forms and functions and find examples for each cell?

7. Under what conditions will an item of inventory be simultaneously raw material, WIP, and finished goods inventory? What are the implications of this for management?

8. What assumptions underlie the EOQ model? How can these assumptions be relaxed? What happens if all of them are relaxed?

9. The EOQ model has been described as insensitive. When is it insensitive? When is it very sensitive? What are the management implications of this?

10. What advantages do fast-response organizations have over their competitors in managing independent demand inventory?

11. Why is the newsboy problem different from the general inventory problem? Can you think of circumstances in which the newsboy problem exists?

12. What is an exchange curve? Under what circumstances would you use one?

13. How does advanced technology help with inventory management? In what settings can advanced technology be beneficial?

14. How low can a firm drive its finished goods inventory and still be an FRO? What are the implications of this?

15. What is the ABC classification system? Under what circumstances is it beneficial to a firm?

PROBLEMS

1. 💾 The demand for sofas at the Brocktown Furniture Store is 800 units per year. It costs $100 to hold one sofa in the store's inventory for one year and $15 for each replenishment order. The replenishment lead time is five days. The average cost of each sofa is $500. Find the following:

a. Economic order quantity
b. Reorder point
c. Annual purchasing cost
d. Annual ordering cost
e. Annual holding cost
f. Total annual cost

2. In problem 1, assume that the supplier has instituted a minimum order quantity of 20 units. By what percentage will the total relevant costs increase?

3. ⌨ Five pounds of material is required for each unit of product A. The demand for product A is about 50,000 units a year and varies little from month to month. The material costs $8 to purchase and arrives in seven days. The ordering cost is $42 per order, and the holding cost is 30 percent of the purchase cost per unit per year.
   a. How many pounds of material should the company purchase each time?
   b. At what inventory level does the company need to reorder the material?
   c. What is the total annual cost of inventory?

4. ⌨ In problem 3, assume that the demand for product A increases by 20 percent and the lead time drops to five days.
   a. By what percentage will the EOQ change?
   b. By what percentage will the total relevant costs change?

5. ⌨ In problem 2, assume that the supplier offers a per unit discount of 20 cents for orders over 6,499 units and a discount of 40 cents per unit for orders exceeding 7,999 units. What is the best order quantity in this situation?

6. ⌨ The Five Corners Garage changes car tires for its customers free of charge if they buy the tires from the garage. The forecast demand for tires is 6,000 units next year. The garage buys tires for $25 each and pays a transportation fee of $3 per tire. The ordering cost is $100 per order, and the lead time is six days. The holding cost is 35 percent of the acquisition cost.
   a. How many tires does the garage have to order to achieve the lowest inventory cost?
   b. How long is the ordering interval?
   c. What is the economic order quantity?
   d. What is the total annual holding cost?

7. A sportswear store sold 8,500 baseball caps last year. Based on past records, $2,100 of last year's inventory holding costs can be allocated to the caps. The store places an order once a month at a cost of $10 and is charged $7 plus a delivery charge of 10 cents per hat. The lead time is three days. Both the supplier and the sportswear store are open seven days a week. The demand forecast for this year is 5 percent higher than last year's demand, but the unit costs have not changed.
   a. How can the store manager reduce inventory-related costs for baseball caps?
   b. How much money can be saved?

8. ⌨ Computers for the Home, a computer retailer, buys directly from manufacturers. The demand for its most popular model, the Orange, is forecast to be about 5,000 units next year. The retailer has a markup of $200 per computer. Each order costs about $50, and the annual holding cost per computer is 25 percent of its cost. To encourage its customers to order larger quantities, the manufacturer has developed the following discount policy.

Order Quantity Range	Price per unit, $
1–29	850
30–49	835
50 and over	820

How many computers should the store order at one time? How many times per year should it order?

9. ⌨ Gimbley's Supermarket sells about 200,000 gallons of milk annually. The milk is purchased for $4 per gallon. Holding costs are $1.40 per gallon per year. Each order costs $35. If the shelf life of the milk is only five days, how many gallons should be ordered at a time?

10. ⌨ The clerk at Metals Inc. has estimated that the annual demand for a particular raw material is 600 tons and that the EOQ is 80 tons. If the supplier delivers 30 tons each week, what is the best order quantity? What will the maximum inventory level be if this quantity is ordered?

11. ⌨ The Future Shop, a department store, sells television sets which it purchases for $300 per unit. The average daily demand is 10 units with a standard deviation of 2 units. The holding cost is 30 percent of the acquisition cost. The ordering cost is $40, and orders arrive in three days.
    a. What is the EOQ?
    b. What is the reorder point (assume a 90 percent service level)?
    c. What is the total annual cost?

12. ⌨ Household Hardware carries an extensive line of plumbing supplies. The average demand for sinks is 20 units per day with a standard deviation of 4 units. Other related information is listed below.

Purchasing cost	$40 per unit
Holding cost	$9 per unit per year
Ordering cost	$60
Lead time	three days

Determine the EOQ and the reorder point if the service level is 85 percent, 90 percent, or 95 percent.

13. The Care Cookie Company uses about 2,000 eggs per day with a standard deviation of 150 eggs. The inventory is checked weekly, and an order is made if the inventory falls below 500 eggs. The order lead time is two days, and the desired service level is 95 percent. Is this the best purchasing policy? Can you suggest a better policy?

14. ⌷ Given the following information, can you devise a periodic-review inventory policy? The desired service level is 95 percent.

Part	Average Daily Demand	Standard Deviation	Current Inventory Level	Lead Time
L2005	25	4	80	5
L2006	18	3	50	5
S3008	23	5	40	5

15. The manager of a drugstore is wondering how many Christmas Cards to order before Christmas. Each card costs $1.30 but retails for $2.20 if sold before Christmas. After Christmas the store reduces the price by 60 percent. On the basis of past records, the manager has developed the following table.

Demand	Probability
3,000	0.05
3,500	0.15
4,000	0.25
4,500	0.25
5,000	0.15
5,500	0.15

How many cards should be ordered?

GROUP EXERCISES

Many of the tools and concepts discussed in this chapter are meant to be used in a team setting. The following problem is best solved by small groups of students. Ideally, each group should be composed of people with different backgrounds, interests, or areas of expertise.

For this exercise colored blocks and a die are required. The group should decide on the general demand profile for the products that will be manufactured by the group. Demand will range from uniform to highly irregular, with or without seasonality and/or trend. A "customer" will throw the die each period, probably once a minute, and the result of the throw will indicate how far the actual demand will vary from the "forecast" profile. The group should determine what the "error" should be; for example, 1 and 6 could be 10 percent above and below the forecast, respectively; 2 and 5 could be 5 percent; and 3 and 4 could be on forecast.

Each color can be used to represent the same product, but different lot sizing techniques are employed. The lots can be manufactured, with the time to make a batch being one second for each item. The exercise should be run for about 20 minutes at a minimum. The inventory position and the ability to supply the market should be monitored at all times and plotted at the end of the exercise.

The setup and holding costs per period can each be agreed on at the beginning of the exercise. As a variant, the same lot sizing technique can be used for each color, with the setup cost being varied for each color. Again, the inventory and market satisfaction should be continually monitored through the exercise, and the group can discuss the implications of the outcomes. Finally, the same exercise can be run several times to see how the outcomes vary with each simulation.

REFERENCES AND SELECTED BIBLIOGRAPHY

Backes, Robert W. [1980], "Cycle Counting: A Better Method for Achieving Accurate Inventory Records," *Management Accounting,* January, pp. 226–234.

Beddingfield, Thomas W. [1992], "Reducing Inventory Enhances Competitiveness," *APICS,* September, pp. 28–31.

Bell, P. C., and H. Noori [1985], "Managing Inventories

through Difficult Economic Times: A Simple Model," *Interfaces,* vol. 15, no. 5, pp. 39–45.

Czaplicki, D. [1988], "New Developments in Bar Coding Lead to Greater Efficiencies in the Work Place," *Industrial Engineering,* October, pp. 12–15.

Flores, B. E., and D. C. Whybark [1987], "Implementing Multiple Criteria ABC Analysis," *Journal of Operations Management,* vol. 7, no. 1, pp. 79–85.

Haehling von Lanzeauer, C., and H. Noori [1986], "Fiscal-Period-Based Level Constraints and Safety Stock Requirements," *International Journal of Production Research,* vol. 24, no. 3, pp. 483–492.

Harris, F. W. [1915], *Operations and Cost,* Factory Management Series, Shaw, Chicago.

Martinka, John P. [1993], "Management Facilities Regarding Inventory Accuracy," *APICS,* June, p. 53.

McKenna, Barrie [1993], "More Than the Sum of Its Parts," *Toronto Globe and Mail,* Feb. 23, p. B24.

Morgan, J. I. [1963], "Questions for Solving the Inventory Problem," *Harvard Business Review,* July–August, pp. 95–110.

Nahmias, S. [1993], *Production and Operations Analysis,* 2d ed., Richard D. Irwin, Homewood, Ill.

Neeley, Parley S. [1989], "Let's Take the Cycle Out of Cycle Counting," *P & IM Review,* November, pp. 40–42.

Noori, H., and F. Anatol [1989], *Decision Inventory Package: Reference Manual,* Institute of Industrial Engineers, Industrial Engineering Management Press, Atlanta, Georgia.

Paris, W. F. III [1988], "Automated Warehouse System Expedites Medical Resupply to Hospital Departments," *Industrial Engineering,* October, pp. 36–39.

Porteous, E. L. [1985], "Numerical Comparisons of Inventory Policies for Periodic Review Systems," *Operations Research,* vol. 33, pp. 134–152.

Schaeffer, Randall [1993], "A New View of Inventory Management," *APICS,* January, pp. 21–24.

Silver, E., and R. Peterson [1985], *Decision Systems for Inventory Management and Productivity Planning,* Wiley, New York.

Tersine, R. J. [1988], *Principles of Inventory and Materials Management,* North-Holland, New York.

Treacy, Michael, and Fred Wiersema [1993], "Customer Intimacy and Other Value Disciplines," *Harvard Business Review,* January–February, pp. 84–93.

Waigh, Martin O. [1992], "Inventory Management: The Need for New Rules," *APICS,* April, pp. 48–51.

Wilson, R. H. [1934], "A Scientific Routine for Stock Control," *Harvard Business Review,* vol. 13, pp. 116–128.

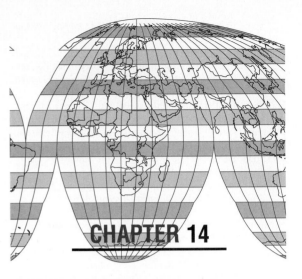

CHAPTER 14

AGGREGATE PLANNING

THE LEARNING PROCESS

The link between the operating system (value-added elements in a service or manufacturing organization) and its environment (suppliers and customers) is the planning and control information system. Top-level planning is essential for smooth operations.

This chapter looks at operational (intermediate-term) planning, relating the known and expected demand for a firm's products to its ability to deliver. Invariably, the firm has to balance capacity with need and address questions such as:

- How much capacity is needed?
- How will the required capacity be provided?
- How will demand needs be balanced across several periods?

By the end of this chapter you will have been introduced to a general plan of action for production and staffing. You will also be familiar with several techniques that simplify operational planning.

EXHIBIT 14.1   FRO MANUFACTURING PROFILE

With four factories supplying over 100 sales distribution points (SDPs) with hundreds of different sizes, colors, and types of tile, the American Olean Tile Company (AO) found that its manual production planning system was inadequate.

A new computer-based system is being implemented at AO. Already coordination and communication between production, marketing, and the SDPs have improved. Production and distribution costs have been reduced through improved short-term scheduling and by more closely matching demand patterns within each SDP area.

The new planning system integrates intermediate-term and short-term planning:

- The forecast sales for the year are allocated to AO's 10 product families and then apportioned to the 120 SDPs.
- A monthly production plan is developed for each plant on the basis of sales allocations and seasonal inventory targets and demand patterns.
- Each individual plant production plan is then converted into a master production schedule for the whole plant, using firm customer orders and short-term forecasts for each product stockkeeping unit (SKU) submitted by the SDPs.
- The master production plan then drives the short-term schedules. Basing the production plan on the demands of individual sales territories allows plants to be more responsive to local needs while substantially lowering costs.

Source: Adapted from Liberatore and Miller (1985), pp. 1–11.

EXHIBIT 14.2   FRO SERVICE PROFILE

The way in which managers view aggregate planning in a hospital setting is changing. Hospitals are being forced to think of themselves as producers of a range of product families, not as resource or service centers. No longer can forecast patient days be used as a basis for resource planning, because the American government has introduced a new reimbursement scheme for Medicare patients.

A hospital now receives payments that are based on the diagnostic-related group (DRG) in which a patient is classified. A DRG is composed of a group of specific diagnoses whose treatments involve similar resource consumption patterns and thus similar hospital costs. Since the reimbursement payment is not based on the amount of services consumed by the patient or the length of the hospital stay, planning and control are essential.

By viewing a hospital as a producer of a range of product families, managers can apply planning and control techniques commonly used in manufacturing environments. Managers now realize that they must increase their throughput (i.e., reduce the average length of a patient's hospital stay) and lower costs while maintaining a high-quality product.

(Exhibit 14.2 continues on next page)

EXHIBIT 14.2   *(continued)*

> Since resource demands vary widely from one type of illness to another, intermediate planning based on aggregate patient days is inadequate. DRGs are now being combined into major diagnostic categories (MDC) for purposes of aggregate planning. The demand for each MDC is then forecast, and time-phased resource requirements are derived from the forecasts. Resources can be put in place only when and where they are needed.
>
> *Source:* Adapted from Roth and Van Dierdonck (1991).

14.1 MANAGERIAL ORIENTATION

- How much does the firm need to produce next year?
- What is the capacity of its resources?
- How will the firm vary the monthly production level to meet demand?
- How many people should it hire?
- What types of goods and service must the firm purchase and in what quantities?

These are the types of questions addressed by managers as they prepare operational plans.

A formal, complex operational planning system is needed by companies such as American Olean Tile Company (Exhibit 14.1), Milliken, and the Mayo Clinic.[1] These firms have large product lines and multiple production facilities. At the opposite extreme, small companies with a very limited product line (such as a dental office, a shoe repair shop, and a family farm) may find that an informal, simple system is adequate. Almost all firms, however, find that their operational plans affect their ability to compete (see Exhibit 14.2).

As illustrated in Exhibit 14.3, operational plans bridge the gap between long-range and short-range production plans. This chapter will focus on the topics in the shaded boxes: aggregate and resource planning, rough-cut capacity planning, and master production scheduling.

Note that production managers are not the only managers interested in operational plans. These plans affect the work of marketing, purchasing, finance, and human resources managers as well. The input of all these managers is needed to ensure that the plans are feasible and make the best use of the firm's resources. The need to involve managers from a variety of functional areas becomes clearer when one reviews the typical inputs and outputs shown in Exhibit 14.4.

14.2 THE SIX-STEP AGGREGATE PLANNING PROCESS

> **DEFINITION:** The *aggregate production plan* specifies how a firm will provide the capacity to meet demand in the intermediate term.

The aggregate production plan developed by the American Olean Tile Company for each of its plants gives managers a "big picture" look at the demand for the firm's product families over the next year and the resources available to satisfy that demand. The year is divided into monthly time periods, and the production plan is usually updated every several months.

Developing product groups and dividing the intermediate planning horizon into a set of shorter time periods is the first step in the aggregate planning process.

[1] Milliken and the Mayo Clinic were toured in the Startup Chapter.

EXHIBIT 14.3   THE OPERATIONS PLANNING HIERARCHY

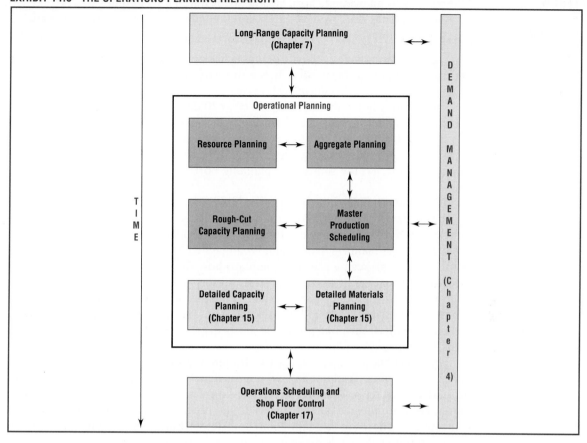

EXHIBIT 14.4   OPERATIONAL PLANNING: INPUTS REQUIRED AND OUTPUTS EXPECTED

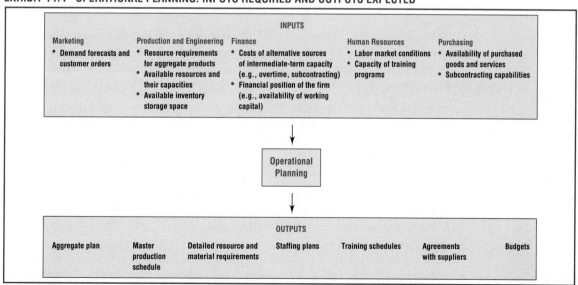

Step 1. Select a planning horizon and divide it into a set of time periods (time buckets). If the firm produces a variety of goods or services, create aggregate product groups.

Typically, firms have aggregate **planning horizons** that coincide with their budget cycles, usually 12 to 18 months. It is customary to update the plan several times (e.g., every three months) during this cycle.

The planning horizon is divided into 10 to 20 **time buckets,** or planning intervals. More than that and the detail and sensitivity become overbearing; less than that and it is difficult to plan by allocating resources. Typically, the length of a time bucket is one month or one week. The more flexibility a firm has in adjusting intermediate sources of capacity, the shorter the planning horizon and the time buckets tend to be.

Aggregate products rather than individual products are used at this level because, in general, demand forecasts for groups of products over the intermediate term are more accurate than are forecasts for individual products. Also, by using aggregate product groups, planners avoid being swamped with unnecessary details. Since the purpose of the aggregate plan is to map out how the firm will manipulate its intermediate-term sources of capacity, product groups are sufficient.

An aggregate product group usually consists of goods or services that have common processing, labor, and/or material requirements. A paper product company, for example, may have one group for all its disposable diapers and another for its facial tissues.

The experience of many American hospitals testifies to the need to aggregate goods and services. Traditionally, all intermediate-term planning has been based on forecast patient days. Resource demands, however, vary widely with the patient's illness. For example, the billable materials and procedures for a coronary bypass are contrasted to those for a major joint/limb reattachment in Exhibit 14.5. Widely varying resource demands make it difficult to translate forecast patient days into a set of resource requirements.

When treatments with similar resource consumption patterns are grouped and aggregate plans are based on those groups, estimates of resource requirements become more accurate. Intermediate-term planning then becomes easier and more meaningful.

What happens if a set of products require the same scarce resource but differ greatly in the amount of other resources consumed per unit? How should they be grouped? In this situation managers should aggregate by using the resource that causes the least overall distortion as a base.

Step 2. Develop a forecast of the estimated demand for each aggregate product group in every period of the planning horizon. Translate the demand forecasts into resource requirements.

Consider the DaCorté Bicycle plant (see Exhibit 14.6). The company has divided its product line into three aggregate groups and has forecast the monthly demand for each aggregate group over the next year. The production manager has translated demand into monthly labor requirements by multiplying the monthly demand for each product group by its average labor requirements.. The total labor requirements for each group are then summed.

The aggregate plan for DaCorté Bicycle Ltd. is stated in terms of labor hours. Some firms use the dollar value of monthly output or the number of units produced.

EXHIBIT 14.5 RESOURCE CONSUMPTION IN A HOSPITAL

Billable Materials and Procedures	Standard Service Units*	
	Coronary Bypass	Major Joint/Limb Reattachment
Room-board/PVT	17	14
ICU/surgical	8	—
Pharmacy	692	236
Drugs/generic	3	—
Drugs/nongeneric	53	2
Drugs/other	14	6
IV solutions	14	—
Med-surg supplies	294	87
Laboratory	395	59
DX x-Ray	26	7
DX x-Ray other	2	—
Nuclear med/DX	1	1
OR services	2	1
Anaesthesia	2	1
Blood/storage procedure	5	4
Blood/administration	2	3
Respiratory services	270	64
Physical therapy	11	30
Emergency room	1	—
Cardiac cath lab	401	—
Recovery room	2	1
EKG/ECG	17	3
Telemetry	1	—
Perivascular lab	6	1

* Service units vary by material and procedure. For example, the service unit for the pharmacy may be dispensations and that for the lab may be the number of tests.

Source: Adapted from Roth and Van Dierdonck (1991), p. 30.

The key is to choose a homogeneous unit of measurement that is commonly understood by the managers who will be using the plan.

Step 3. If the production requirements vary widely from one period to the next, consider using pricing, promotion, and other techniques for altering the timing and level of demand.

As a general rule, the smaller the variation in production requirements from one period to the next is, the easier it is to match capacity to demand in the intermediate term. When production requirements vary widely throughout the planning horizon, firms often try to adjust the demand for their goods and services.

Offering price discounts, producing complementary products, and increasing promotional efforts are common techniques for altering demand. Hotels, for example, may offer discount packages in the winter, and a snowmobile manufacturer may also produce engines for personal watercraft. Advertising, direct mail, and in-store promotions are often used to increase demand during slack periods.

Capacity requirements can be reduced by transferring work to the customer (e.g., automated teller machines and self-service gas stations). Providing routine informa-

DaCorté Bicycle Ltd. produces 25 different bicycle models, using a labor-intensive process. After analyzing the processing requirements of each model, DaCorté has created three aggregate product groups: tricycles, standard adult, and customized adult. Capacity is measured in terms of available labor hours, and the required labor hours for each aggregate product group are shown below.

REQUIRED LABOR HOURS FOR EACH AGGREGATE PRODUCT GROUP

Aggregate Product Group	Required Labor Hours per Unit
Tricycles	0.75
Standard adult	1.00
Customized adult	1.50

The marketing department has supplied the following monthly forecast of next year's demand. The production manager has used the required labor hours per unit listed above to convert the demand forecasts into labor requirements.

DEMAND FORECAST AND LABOR REQUIREMENTS

	Demand, units			Labor Hours Required			(8)
(1) Month	(2) Trikes	(3) Std.	(4) Custom	(5) Trikes	(6) Std.	(7) Custom	Total Labor Requirements
Jan.	4,800	2,795	1,070	3,600	2,795	1,605	8,000
Feb.	3,600	2,100	800	2,700	2,100	1,200	6,000
Mar.	5,000	2,750	1,000	3,750	2,750	1,500	8,000
Apr.	7,800	4,600	1,700	5,850	4,600	2,550	13,000
May	11,400	6,655	2,530	8,550	6,655	3,795	19,000
June	12,000	6,500	3,000	9,000	6,500	4,500	20,000
July	12,600	7,200	2,900	9,450	7,200	4,350	21,000
Aug.	11,000	7,700	2,700	8,250	7,700	4,050	20,000
Sept.	9,000	5,550	1,800	6,750	5,550	2,700	15,000
Oct.	5,600	4,300	1,000	4,200	4,300	1,500	10,000
Nov.	6,000	3,550	1,300	4,500	3,550	1,950	10,000
Dec.	8,400	3,000	1,800	6,300	3,000	2,700	12,000
Totals	97,200	56,700	21,600	72,900	56,700	32,400	162,000

Column 5 = column 2 × 0.75 hour per unit.
Column 6 = column 3 × 1 hour per unit.
Column 7 = column 4 × 1.5 hours per unit.
Column 8 = column 5 + column 6 + column 7.

tion through signs, pamphlets, and information kiosks also reduces capacity requirements.

Step 4. For each planning period, compare the current capacity with production requirements. If there are mismatches between the capacity required and the capacity available, generate alternatives for adjusting capacity. Estimate the cost of each alternative.

Even after demand has been manipulated, there are usually mismatches between the required capacity and the available capacity in one or more planning periods. Some of the many ways in which firms can adjust capacity in the intermediate term are listed below. Note that each alternative has advantages and disadvantages.

- **Adjust the workforce level.** Occasionally hiring or firing full-time employees can be very effective. When done excessively, it may increase the difficulty of attracting quality employees at competitive wages. The impact on the community and the morale of the workforce must be considered as well. Hiring part-time or temporary employees is another option. Nonprofit organizations such as the Heart & Stroke Foundation use volunteers during campaign drives to increase capacity.

- **Arrange for overtime, undertime, or temporary layoffs.** Many workers welcome limited amounts of overtime. Using overtime may allow a firm to avoid hiring workers who will be fired in the slow season. Excessive overtime, however, may result in fatigue, reduced morale, and decreased product quality. The use of undertime (workers are paid but are idle or temporarily assigned to other duties) may be less expensive than laying off workers for short periods. It also reduces the chances of losing skilled workers and does not create the same morale problems and loss of community goodwill as the layoff and hire/fire options. Employees can be asked to take their vacations during periods of low demand.
- **Adjust the length of the workday.** Some firms ask employees to work longer hours during the busy season in exchange for shorter hours during slow periods.
- **Share capacity.** If one firm cannot provide a specific service or is at full capacity, it can subcontract work to local competitors. Accounting firms, for example, occasionally "lend" employees from a branch office in one country to a branch office in another to take advantage of differing tax seasons. Cross-training its employees also enables a firm to transfer excess capacity from one area to another. Using a multiskilled floating staff is another option.
- **Accumulate anticipatory inventories.** Inventory can be accumulated in the off-season to meet peak demand requirements in subsequent periods. These inventories can include finished goods or components that can be assembled quickly.
- **Allow customer orders to backlog or use waiting lists.** Customers may agree to wait a short time before their orders are filled or to be placed on a waiting list. This practice is common in service industries (e.g., elective surgery in a hospital, routine checkup at the dentist). If the industry has excess capacity and competition is fierce, however, this option may lead to lost sales now and in the future.
- **Subcontract work to other firms.** Paying another firm to make the product may be more profitable than losing current (and possibly future) sales. The firm usually has less control over quality levels and delivery schedules, however.
- **Stockouts.** The firm may choose not to satisfy all demand. Prestigious private schools, restaurants, and resorts use this option extensively. Once again, depending on the competitive environment, the firm may lose current and future sales.

The current capacity at DaCorté Bicycle Ltd. is compared with its required capacity in Exhibit 14.7. The histogram illustrates the significant capacity gap during the summer months. The firm has five feasible alternatives for altering its capacity in the intermediate term, but the extent to which each alternative can be used is restricted.

In general, the range of capacity-generating alternatives available to a firm is limited by the following constraints:

- The type of workforce required, the available labor pool, and union contracts
- The type of product sold and the process by which it is made
- The firm's competitive strategy and competitive environment
- The firm's position in the community

For example, a firm cannot easily adjust the production rate through frequent changes in workforce size if the workforce is highly skilled and the labor pool is

EXHIBIT 14.7   TOOLBOX: INTERMEDIATE-TERM SOURCES OF CAPACITY

A. Available versus Required Capacity

The DaCorté Bicycle Ltd. plant can accommodate up to 85 employees. Currently there are only 70 full-time employees working eight hours a day, five days a week. As shown in the table below, the number of working days per month varies.

CURRENT CAPACITY WITH ONE SHIFT OF FULL-TIME WORKERS

(1) Month	(2) Working Days*	*Regular Hours Available*		
		(3) Per Worker	(4) With 70 Workers	(5) With 85 Workers
Jan.	16	128	8,960	10,880
Feb.	14	112	7,840	9,520
Mar.	21	168	11,760	14,280
Apr.	22	176	12,320	14,960
May	22	176	12,320	14,960
June	20	160	11,200	13,600
July	22	176	12,320	14,960
Aug.	22	176	12,320	14,960
Sept.	20	160	11,200	13,600
Oct.	22	176	12,320	14,960
Nov.	19	152	10,640	12,920
Dec.	21	168	11,760	14,280
Totals	*241*	*1,928*	*134,960*	*163,880*

* Includes all American national holidays and vacation time (taken in January and February).

The total annual capacity with 70 workers (134,960 hours) is insufficient to meet next year's production demands. If the plant moves to a full complement of 85 workers, however, capacity just exceeds demand.

The forecast labor requirements are compared with the available capacity in the following histogram. The labor requirements reflect the highly seasonal demand, which peaks in the summer months. There is a large capacity gap in the summer, but even with all vacation time scheduled in January and February, there is still excess capacity in the first quarter of the year.

MONTHLY LABOR REQUIREMENTS AND AVAILABLE CAPACITY

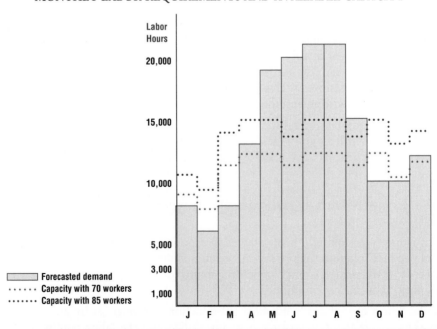

B. Options for Adjusting Capacity in the Intermediate Term

The production manager at DaCorté Bicycle Ltd. has generated the following list of feasible options for adjusting the plant's capacity.

Option	Costs	Limitations
Hire/fire full-time employees Hire students during summer months	Hiring and training per employee: $1,200 Firing per employee: $900 Hourly labor cost per employee: $10	Company policy is to maintain a core workforce year-round. Hiring someone who will be fired within a year is not encouraged. The plant can accommodate up to 85 workers. The union contract allows for summer students only. Students are available from May to August.
Overtime and undertime	Overime labor cost per hour per worker: $15 Undertime labor cost per hour per worker: $10	Overtime is limited to 30 percent of regular time (12 hours per week) in the union contract.
Accumulate inventory during slow demand periods	Inventory cost per bicycle per month: $3 (or roughly $3 per labor hour with current product mix)*	The plant (and distribution channels) can accommodate up to about 14,000 finished bikes. This equates to about 15,200 labor hours with current product mix.*
Subcontract standard models	Marginal cost per bicycle: $19 (or $19 per labor hour)	The subcontractor accepts orders only in lots of 100 standard adult bicycles. This equates to 100 labor hours. The maximum quantity that can be subcontracted is 5,000 labor hours per month.

* Current product mix: 55 percent tricycles, 33 percent standard adult, and 12 percent custom adult. Therefore, the labor requirement for an "average" bicycle is $(55\% \times 0.75) + (33\% \times 1) + (12\% \times 1.5) = 0.9225$ hour.

small, the process is a continuous-flow operation, or the workforce has a powerful union. If the product is a service or a perishable good, inventory cannot be used to smooth production levels. Only a limited amount of inventory can be accumulated if the product is customized or subject to rapid obsolescence. Backlogs and waiting lists cannot be used extensively if there is excess capacity in the industry and competition is fierce. Finally, a firm that is the major employer in an area has less flexibility in releasing employees than does a firm that is one of many employers in a large city. This is especially true when the economy is in a downturn, for laid-off employees will find it very difficult to get other jobs.

Step 5. Select an aggregate planning strategy.

Should the firm try to match capacity to demand in every aggregate planning period (**chase strategy**), try to maintain a stable production rate (**level strategy**), or use a combination of both strategies (**mixed strategy**)?

DEFINITION: When following a chase strategy, a firm adjusts the output rate in each aggregate planning period to match the demand rate in that period.

DEFINITION: When following a level strategy, a firm maintains the same output rate in every aggregate planning period.

The aggregate plan for DaCorté Bicycle Ltd. in Exhibit 14.8 is a chase strategy, with the production level for each period equal to the demand for that period. The production level is varied by making adjustments in the workforce level, using overtime and undertime, subcontracting, and the like. Anticipatory inventory does not accumulate from one period to the next.

Contrast the aggregate plan in Exhibit 14.8 with the plan in Exhibit 14.9. The latter reflects a level strategy; the daily production rate is 672 labor hours per day every day of the year. Inventory is accumulated during slow periods and drawn down in high-demand periods. Another option is to let customer orders backlog during high-demand periods.

Rather than adopting a pure chase or level strategy, many firms combine elements from both. For example, a firm may decide to (1) build up anticipatory inventory in slack periods, (2) allow only a few workforce changes each year, (3) utilize overtime to increase capacity during busy periods, and (4) allow customers' orders to backlog. An aggregate plan that reflects a mixed strategy for DaCorté Ltd. is shown in Exhibit

EXHIBIT 14.8 TOOLBOX: THE CHASE STRATEGY

The aggregate plan below reflects a chase strategy used by DaCorté Bicycle Ltd. With a combination of workforce changes, overtime, undertime, and subcontracting, the production rate is varied from month to month to match demand.

	\multicolumn{12}{c}{*Month*}											
	Jan.	Feb.	Mar.	Apr.	May	June	July	Aug.	Sept.	Oct.	Nov.	Dec.
Required production to meet demand	8,000	6,000	8,000	13,000	19,000	20,000	21,000	20,000	15,000	10,000	10,000	12,000
Sources of production												
Regular time	8,000	6,000	8,000	12,320	14,960	13,600	14,960	14,960	13,600	10,000	10,000	11,760
Overtime	—	—	—	180	3,040	3,400	3,040	3,040	1,400	—	—	—
Subcontracting	—	—	—	500	1,000	3,000	3,000	2,000	—	—	—	240
Average daily rate (hours)	500	429	381	568	818	850	818	818	750	455	526	560

Note that:

1. All figures are given in labor hours.
2. Seventy workers are employed year-round. In the summer months (May to August), however, 15 additional workers are hired.
3. The number of working days varies from month to month.
4. In some months the regular production time scheduled is less than the regular time available.

Month	Scheduled Undertime	Month	Scheduled Undertime
Jan.	960	Apr.–Sept.	—
Feb.	1,860	Oct.	2,320
Mar.	3,760	Nov.	640
		Dec.	—

5. The daily production rate ranges from a low of 381 hours in March to a high of 850 hours in June.

$$\text{Daily production rate} = \frac{\text{Regular time} + \text{Overtime}}{\text{Number of working days}}$$

EXHIBIT 14.9   TOOLBOX: THE LEVEL STRATEGY

Rather than chase the monthly demand, DaCorté Bicycle Ltd. can try to level the daily production rate. Anticipatory inventory is accumulated at the beginning of the year and used during the summer months. Work is also subcontracted during the summer.

The total capacity requirement for the year at DaCorté Bicycle Ltd. is 162,000 labor hours, and there are 241 working days in every year. The daily production rate is therefore 162,000 ÷ 241 days = 672.2 units. If each employee works eight hours a day, 84 employees are required.

						Month						
	Jan.	Feb.	Mar.	Apr.	May	June	July	Aug.	Sept.	Oct.	Nov.	Dec.
Required production to meet demand	8,000	6,000	8,000	13,000	19,000	20,000	21,000	20,000	15,000	10,000	10,000	12,000
Sources of production												
Regular time	10,752	9,408	14,112	14,784	14,784	13,440	14,784	14,784	13,440	14,784	12,768	14,112
Subcontracting	—	—	—	—	—	—	—	2,936	6,560	—	—	—
Inventory level												
Beginning	—	2,752	6,160	12,272	14,056	9,840	3,280	—	—	—	4,784	7,552
Change	2,752	3,408	6,112	1,784	(4,216)	(6,560)	(3,280)	—	—	4,784	2,768	2,112
Ending	2,752	6,160	12,272	14,056	9,840	3,280	—	—	—	4,784	7,552	9,664

Note that:

1. All figures are given in labor hours.
2. The number of working days varies from month to month.

14.10. The daily production rate associated with this plan is compared with that of the chase and level plans in Exhibit 14.11.[2]

As illustrated by the matrix below, a chase strategy is an option for most firms. Mixed and level strategies, however, are restricted to firms that can hold an inventory of their product and/or can defer demand by allowing customer orders to backlog (or use waiting lists).

Can an inventory of finished goods be accumulated?

		Yes	No
Are the customers prepared to go on a waiting list?	Yes	Chase Mixed Level (make-to-order and/or make-to-stock) Examples: book publisher, mass footwear manufacturer	Chase Mixed Level (make-to-order only) Examples: custom tailor, custom furniture manufacturer
	No	Chase Mixed Level (make-to-stock only) Examples: grocery store, gas station	Chase Examples: electricity generation, newspaper publisher

Any firm in the yes/yes quadrant of the matrix can choose any strategy. Many service sector firms and manufacturers of customized goods fall in the no/no quadrant; they *must* chase or lose business. If an inventory of finished goods can be accumulated,

---

[2] The term *pure strategy* can also refer to an aggregate plan that adjusts only one variable (e.g., the workforce level) to meet fluctuations in demand. If a combination of variables is used, the strategy is sometimes referred to as a *mixed strategy*.

EXHIBIT 14.10 TOOLBOX: MIXED STRATEGY

This aggregate plan for DaCorté Bicycle Ltd. combines elements of both a chase strategy and a level strategy. The daily production rate is level thoughout the winter (560 hours) but varies during the summer, when demand is high.

						Month						
	Jan.	Feb.	Mar.	Apr.	May	June	July	Aug.	Sept.	Oct.	Nov.	Dec.
Required production to meet demand	8,000	6,000	8,000	13,000	19,000	20,000	21,000	20,000	15,000	10,000	10,000	12,000
Sources of production												
Regular time	8,960	7,840	11,760	12,320	14,960	13,600	14,960	14,960	11,200	12,320	10,640	11,760
Overtime	—	—	—	—	2,488	2,080	2,488	2,488	1,896	—	—	—
Subcontracting	—	—	—	—	2,000	2,000	2,000	2,000	—	—	—	—
Inventory level												
Beginning	—	960	2,800	6,560	5,880	6,328	4,008	2,456	1,904	—	2,320	2,960
Change	960	1,840	3,760	(680)	448	(2,320)	(1,552)	(552)	1,904	2,320	640	(240)
Ending	960	2,800	6,560	5,880	6,328	4,008	2,456	1,904	—	2,320	2,960	2,720
Average daily rate	560	560	560	560	793	784	793	793	655	560	560	560

Note that:

1. All figures are given in labor hours.
2. Seventy workers are employed year-round. In the summer months (May to August), however, 15 additional workers are hired.
3. The number of working days varies from month to month.

EXHIBIT 14.11 A COMPARISON OF THE CHASE, LEVEL, AND MIXED PRODUCTION PLANS

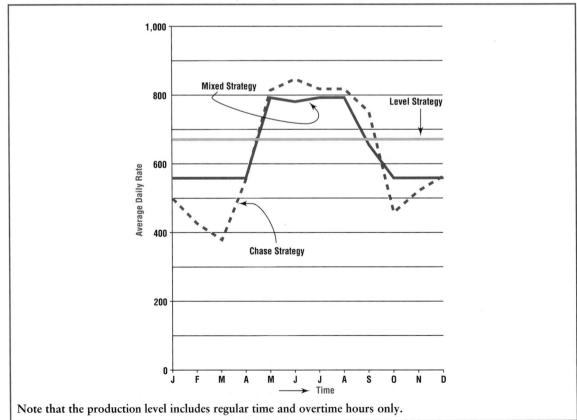

Note that the production level includes regular time and overtime hours only.

the firm can use excess capacity in one period to satisfy the demand forecast in a future period (i.e., **make-to-stock**). If customers are prepared to go on a waiting list, the firm can use excess capacity in one period to satisfy the demand from a previous period (i.e., **make-to-order**).

Which strategy should a firm adopt? Generally, the most suitable strategy depends on the capacity adjustment options available to the firm, the relative costs of those options, and the firm's competitive situation. Union agreements and inflexible production equipment, for example, may preclude the firm from following a pure chase strategy. A level strategy may not be feasible for firms like DaCorté Ltd., which must contend with seasonal demand and high inventory costs.

Step 6. Develop the aggregate plan by using optimization or heuristic techniques.

Once a general aggregate planning strategy has been selected, the aggregate plan can be developed. The goal is to find the lowest-cost plan that supports the firm's competitive emphasis on flexibility, timeliness, quality, service, and dependability. It is not unusual for a firm to modify the original plan several times before it is accepted.

If the firm has decided to follow a pure level strategy, developing the aggregate plan is relatively simple. The production rate is established, and then the way in which that rate will be achieved (e.g., the number of workers and shifts) is determined.

Developing an aggregate plan is much more difficult, however, when a chase or mixed strategy has been selected and there are many options for adjusting capacity in the intermediate term. The next section describes a variety of techniques, ranging from sophisticated mathematical models to a simple trial-and-error approach, that can be used by aggregate planners.

14.3 AGGREGATE PLANNING TECHNIQUES

All the aggregate planning techniques that will be discussed fall into two broad categories: those which use optimization models to find the "best" production plan and those which use heuristics (rules of thumb) to arrive at a feasible plan.

Optimization Techniques

HMMS (Linear Decision Rules)   One of the first attempts to develop an aggregate production planning model that could simultaneously consider several parameters was made by Holt, Modigliani, Muth, and Simon in the 1950s. Their **HMMS model** (linear decision rules) was developed for a paint company and reflected the close relationship between production and employment levels over a series of time periods.

The HMMS model uses a single quadratic cost function that includes payroll, inventory, hiring, layoff, overtime, back order, and setup costs. A pair of linear equations are derived from this total cost function and are used to determine the best aggregate production level and workforce size for the upcoming month in accordance with the forecast demand for the planning horizon. The HMMS model does not directly consider constraints such as limited overtime capacity and maximum inventory levels.

In practice, once the quadratic cost function is obtained, it can be used repeatedly as long as the underlying cost structure does not change. When the cost structure changes, however, the cost estimates and quadratic cost function also must be revised.

An inability to consider constraints frequently encountered by firms and the difficulty of making modifications severely limit the value of this model to fast-response organizations (FROs). The HMMS model is used occasionally, however, as a benchmark against which heuristic models are compared.

Linear Programming and the Transportation Method   Linear programming (LP) is another optimization tool.[3] LP can be used to determine the impact of a variety of costs and restrictions on production alternatives and to find the "optimal" production plan.

The DaCorté plant is analyzed as a linear programming problem in Exhibit 14.12. The goal is to minimize production costs for the year, subject to constraints such as limitations in regular time capacity, overtime capacity, inventory storage space, and capacity available through subcontracting. Note that the problem has 96 variables and 180 constraints.

The **transportation method** greatly simplifies the problem. The DaCorté problem is reformulated as a transportation problem in Exhibit 14.13.

The major drawback with LP and other optimization models is that they oversimplify the problem. For example, LP models assume that the relationships among the variables are all linear and deal only with a single objective (e.g., minimizing costs or maximizing profits).[4] Some constraints and objectives are often left out of the model. Therefore, the "optimal" solution provided by these models may not even be feasible.

Optimization models do have practical value in aggregate planning, however. As one can see in the DaCorté example, the solution derived using linear programming provides an excellent initial plan that can be modified until it becomes a good, realistic plan. Sensitivity analysis can be used to examine how much values can be varied without changing the optimal solution.

Heuristic Techniques

Unlike optimization models, the intent of heuristic techniques[5] is to generate a good, feasible aggregate plan quickly and cost-effectively. This may or may not be the optimal plan.

Management Coefficients Model   The **management coefficients model** [Bowman (1956)] uses past decisions regarding workforce and production levels to suggest the levels at which these variables should be set in the future. The reasoning and rules of thumb behind past decisions, however, are not identified directly. Instead, multiple regression analysis using past data is employed to develop a general decision rule.[6]

---

[3] See the accompanying *OM-Companion* for a broad overview of linear programming and the transportation method.

[4] Even goal programming models, which can consider multiple objectives, cannot incorporate every criterion an aggregate planner must consider.

[5] See *OM-Companion* for a review of heuristics and heuristic techniques.

[6] The general decision rule is

$$P_t = aW_{t-1} - bI_{t-1} + cF_{t+1} + K$$

where P_t = production rate set for period t
W_{t-1} = workforce in previous period
I_{t-1} = ending inventory for previous period
F_{t+1} = forecast of demand for the next period

a, b, c, and K are constants derived through multiple regresson analysis using historical values for P, W, I, and F.

EXHIBIT 14.12   TOOLBOX: LINEAR PROGRAMMING

Using the options listed in Exhibit 14.7, the DaCorté Bicycle Ltd. aggregate planning problem can be expressed as follows.

PROBLEM FORMULATION

Let

W_t = number of workers employed at beginning of month t
H_t = number of workers hired immediately before month t
F_t = number of workers fired immediately before month t
R_t = number of regular time hours scheduled in month t
V_t = number of overtime hours scheduled in month t
U_t = number of idle time hours scheduled in month t
I_t = number of labor hours in finished goods inventory at the end of month t
S_t = number of labor hours subcontracted in month t

Objective: Minimize the annual production costs equal to

$$\sum_{t=1}^{12} (10R_t + 15V_t + 10U_t + 19S_t + 1.5I_t + 1.5I_{t-1} + 1{,}200H_t + 900F_t)$$

Subject to the following constraints for $t = 1, 2, 3, \ldots, 12$

- Workforce level

$$W_0 = 70$$
$$W_t = W_{t-1} + H_t - F_t$$
$$W_t \leq 85$$
$$H_2 = H_3 = H_4 = H_8 = H_9 = H_{10} = H_{11} = H_{12} = 0$$

- Regular time and idle time

$$R_t + V_t = W_t \times \text{ number of regular production hours available per employee in month } t$$

e.g., $R_2 + V_2 = W_2 \times 112$

- Overtime

$$V_t \leq W_t \times 0.30 \times \text{ number of regular production hours available per employee in month } t$$

e.g., $V_2 \leq W_2 \times 0.30 \times 112$

- Number of labor hours supplied in total*

$$R_t + V_t + I_{t-1} - I_t + S_t = \text{ demand in month } t$$

e.g., $R_2 + V_2 + I_1 - I_2 + S_2 = 6{,}000$

(Note that the company is being forced to meet 100 percent of its demand.)

- Inventory level

$$I_0 = 0$$
$$I_t \leq 15{,}200$$

- Unit subcontracted

$$S_t \leq 5{,}000$$

- All variables must have nonnegative values

$$R_t, V_t, U_t, S_t, I_t, L_t, H_t, F_t, W_t \geq 0$$

---

* The company is being forced to meet 100 percent of its demand requirements. If lost sales are allowed, the following adjustments must be made.
1. Add a variable (L_t) that represents the demand, in labor hours, not met.
2. Calculate a cost for each lost labor hour of sales and add this cost to the objective function.
3. Change the labor hours constraint to $R_t + V_t + I_{t-1} - I_t + S_t = (\text{demand in month } t) - L_t$.

EXHIBIT 14.13 TOOLBOX: TRANSPORTATION METHOD

The initial workforce of 70 workers has been increased to 85 in May and reduced back to 70 in September in the problem formulation. The cost in each cell is the cost per labor hour.

Production Period		Sales Period					Unused	
Month	Source	Jan.	Feb.	Mar.	. . .	Dec.	Capacity	Capacity
Jan.	Regular time	10	13	16		43	10	8,960
	Overtime	15	18	21		48	0	2,685
	Subcontract	19	21	25		52	0	5,000
Feb.	Regular time	M	10	13		40	10	7,840
	Overtime	M	15	18		45	0	2,352
	Subcontract	M	19	21		49	0	5,000
Mar.	Regular time	M	M	10		37	10	11,760
	Overtime	M	M	15		42	0	3,528
⋮	Subcontract	M	M	19		46	0	5,000
Dec.	Regular time	M	M	M		10	10	11,760
	Overtime	M	M	M		15	0	3,528
	Subcontract	M	M	M		19	0	5,000
Demand		8,000	6,000	8,000		12,000	86,864	248,864

We used the ©OM-Expert transportation module to solve this problem. The optimal solution is shown below.

	Month											
	Jan.	Feb.	Mar.	Apr.	May	June	July	Aug.	Sept.	Oct.	Nov.	Dec.
Required production	8,000	6,000	8,000	13,000	19,000	20,000	21,000	20,000	15,000	10,000	10,000	12,000
Sources of production												
Regular time	8,960	7,840	11,760	12,320	14,960	13,600	14,960	14,960	11,200	10,000	10,240	11,760
Overtime	—	—	—	—	480	4,080	4,488	4,488	3,360	—	—	—
Subcontracting	—	—	—	—	—	—	1,552	552	437	—	—	—
Inventory level												
Beginning	—	960	2,800	6,560	5,880	2,320	—	—	—	—	—	240
Change	960	1,840	3,760	(680)	(3,560)	(2,320)	—	—	—	—	240	(240)
Ending	960	2,800	6,560	5,880	2,320	—	—	—	—	—	240	—

Note that:

1. All figures are given in labor hours.
2. Seventy workers are employed year-round. In the summer months (May to August), however, 15 additional workers are hired.
3. In October and November the regular production time scheduled is less than the regular time available (2,320 and 400 hours, respectively).
4. The number of working days varies from month to month.

Total production costs

Hiring costs (15 workers at the beginning of May): $1,200 × 15	$	18,000
Firing costs (15 workers at the end of August): $900 × 15	$	13,500
Regular-time wages = total regular time worked during the year × $10 = 142,560 × $10	$1,425,600	
Overtime wages = total overtime worked during the year × $15 = 16,896 × $15	$	253,440
Undertime wages = total undertime worked during the year × $10 = 2,720 × $10	$	27,200
Inventory costs = average inventory in each month × $3 = 16,114 × $3	$	48,342
Subcontracting costs = total number of units subcontracted × $19 = 2,541 × $19	$	48,279
Total	$1,842,299	

Unfortunately, this production plan is not feasible because all subcontracting must be done in lots of 100 hours. It is, however, a good starting point.

Bowman compared the performance of his model with that of the HMMS model in the paint company for which the HMMS model was developed; the results showed that the management coefficients model was superior.

Search Decision Rules The **search decision rules (SDR) model** [Taubert (1968)] uses cost equations of any form to conduct a systematic search for the minimum-cost combination of workforce (W) and production (P) levels over the planning horizon. A trial set of values for workforce size and production rate in each period of the planning horizon is selected. The computer evaluates this plan and makes small changes to it in the most promising direction. If the changes result in a lower-cost plan, they are adopted. If the new plan is more costly, the changes are not made. This cycle is repeated until no more improvements can be made. As with all heuristic techniques, there is no guarantee that the optimal solution has been found.

Knowledge-Based Expert Systems A relatively new advancement in computing—**knowledge-based expert systems (KBESs)**—provides another tool for aggregate planners. A KBES uses knowledge compiled from experts to solve problems in a particular domain.[7]

In an aggregate planning context, experienced planners develop a set of rules that will be stored in the system's knowledge base. Then, during an interactive session, the KBES develops the aggregate plan. The user can override decisions made by the system and ask the system to explain the reasoning behind its decisions.

Unlike the formal models described here, expert systems can incorporate the wide range of constraints typically found in operating environments. The ease with which these systems can be updated to reflect changes in a firm's environment, though, is perhaps their most attractive benefit. In the dynamic competitive environment in which firms are finding themselves this flexibility is very important.

Many expert systems can now access data from the firm's corporate database and "talk" to other computerized tools used by the firm. This allows a firm to examine the cascading effects on lower levels of decisions made on one level and facilitates internal integration. In short, KBESs are emerging as a very promising aggregate planning tool.

The other sophisticated models and techniques discussed here are used by relatively few firms because they require a firm to spend a significant amount of time and effort to develop the model and obtain or approximate the cost data used in the model. The firm's forecasting procedures often need to be upgraded as well. Even then, the optimal solution generated by the model may not be practical or realistic. Planners do more than look for a solution that is close to optimal under favorable conditions; they also want a solution that is robust under a wide range of conditions. Experienced planners find that with the help of powerful computer spreadsheets, they can develop reasonable (and feasible) aggregate plans quickly by using the trial-and-error approach.

The Trial-and-Error Approach

The **trial-and-error approach** is a conceptually simple and popular aggregate planning technique. Using heuristics based on past experience, simple cost data, and intuition, planners generate and evaluate several aggregate plans. Graphs are often

[7] Refer back to the Chapter 9 Supplement for a general description of the interacting modules that constitute KBESs.

used to illustrate alternative plans and compare the capacity each plan generates with the forecast demand.

Some simple heuristics for DaCorté Bicycle Ltd. appear in Exhibit 14.14. With these heuristics, an aggregate plan that could be used as a starting point to generate a better, lower-cost plan was developed. The calculations are straightforward, though they become repetitive and time-consuming as alternative plans are evaluated. This problem can be alleviated if a computer spreadsheet is used.

14.4 THE MASTER PRODUCTION SCHEDULE

Detailed short-term plans are needed on the "shop floor" to guide operations. All the aggregate plans developed for DaCorté Bicycle Ltd. are much too general to be used for short-range planning. In practice, the aggregate plan is usually disaggregated into a **master production schedule (MPS)**. The MPS is the driving force behind detailed capacity planning, materials planning, and eventually the daily production schedule used on the shop floor.

> **DEFINITION:** A master production schedule details, usually on a weekly or even daily basis, the quantity of specific products or product groups to be produced.

An MPS for DaCorté Bicycle Ltd. appears in Exhibit 14.15. It shows the quantity of each product group to be produced in each of the next six weeks. Each week the MPS is rolled forward by one week and updated to reflect any new information received.

The products listed in the MPS are usually end products, that is, products sold to the firm's customers. Components rather than end products are often specified in MPS in companies that assemble a few basic components into a wide variety of products in accordance with customer specifications. In this case a final assembly schedule for finished products is needed by these companies.

Look again at the MPS in Exhibit 14.15. Several batches of each end product will be made each month, and the batch size varies from month to month. If the firm produces to customer specifications (i.e., makes to order), the size of each batch size corresponds to the size of customer orders. Make-to-stock companies often use rules (or algorithms) to determine how large each batch should be; some of these rules were examined in Chapter 13.

The planning horizon of an MPS depends on the amount of time needed to obtain the required parts and materials, produce the product, and ship it to the customer. The planning horizon should be at least as long as the longest cumulative lead time for the items in the MPS. This means that the MPS may be less than a week for some firms and much longer for others.

14.5 ROUGH-CUT CAPACITY PLANNING

Is the MPS a realistic plan? Does the firm have enough of the right resources available at the right time? **Rough-cut capacity planning (RCCP)** examines the feasibility of the MPS by looking ahead to see if the people on the shop floor will have problems implementing the plan.

> **DEFINITION:** Rough-cut capacity planning is used to examine the effects of a proposed MPS on key work centers, departments, and machines.

EXHIBIT 14.14 TOOLBOX: TRIAL AND ERROR TECHNIQUE

The aggregate planners at DaCorté Ltd. have developed the following heuristics by analyzing cost data, company policy, and their own experience.

- The cheapest source of labor hours is regular-time production used in the current month at $10 per hour. There are two sources of regular-time production: permanent workers and summer students. Summer students cost $2,100 to hire and then fire. New permanent workers cost $900 to hire but will be idle almost five months of the year. Therefore, it is better to hire students.
- If a student works for four months during the summer, the $2,100 cost translates into a premium of $3.05 per labor hour. Hire as many students as possible.
- If the production requirements for a particular month cannot be met with regular-time production from both permanent workers and summer students, increase regular-time production in the previous month.
- If demand is still greater than capacity in a particular month, use overtime during that month. Although the union contract allows for up to 30 percent overtime, no more than 20 percent should be used each month. This keeps product quality high (by limiting worker fatigue) and gives production managers flexibility in the short run.
- If demand is still greater than capacity in a particular month, increase regular-time production in the second or third month before that month.
  It is better to let a worker be idle than to let him or her work on a bicycle that will be in the inventory for more than $3\frac{1}{3}$ months
- If demand is greater than capacity, subcontract the standard adult model. This must be done in lots of 100 hours. (If necessary, readjust the previous allocation.) Using these rules, the planners have developed the following aggregate plan.

						Month						
	Jan.	Feb.	Mar.	Apr.	May	June	July	Aug.	Sept.	Oct.	Nov.	Dec.
Required production	8,000	6,000	8,000	13,000	19,000	20,000	21,000	20,000	15,000	10,000	10,000	12,000
Sources of production												
Regular time	8,000	7,650	11,760	12,320	14,960	13,600	14,960	14,960	11,200	10,000	10,240	11,760
Overtime	—	—	—	—	2,990	2,720	2,940	2,940	2,200	—	—	—
Subcontracting	—	—	—	—	—	—	3,100	2,100	1,600	—	—	—
Inventory level												
Beginning	—	—	1,650	5,410	4,730	3,680	—	—	—	—	—	240
Change	—	1,650	3,760	(680)	(1,050)	(3,680)	—	—	—	—	240	(240)
Ending	—	1,650	5,410	4,730	3,680	—	—	—	—	—	240	—

Note that:

1. All figures are given in labor hours.
2. Seventy workers are employed year-round. In the summer months (May to August), however, 15 additional workers are hired.
3. In January, February, October, and November the regular production time scheduled is less than the regular time available (960, 190, 2,320, and 400 hours, respectively).
4. The number of working days varies from month to month.

Total production costs

Hiring costs (15 workers at the beginning of May): $1,200 × 15	$ 18,000
Firing costs (15 workers at the end of August): $900 × 15	$ 13,500
Regular-time wages = total regular time worked during the year × $10 = 141,410 × $10	$1,414,100
Overtime wages = total overtime worked during the year × $15 = 13,790 × $15	$ 206,850
Undertime wages = total undertime worked during the year × $10 = 3,870 × $10	$ 38,700
Inventory costs = average inventory in each month × $3 = 15,710 × $3	$ 47,130
Subcontracting costs = total number of units subcontracted × $19 = 6,800 × $19	$ 129,200
Total	$1,867,480

This is a fairly good, feasible plan, but it calls for quite a bit of overtime throughout the summer. The aggregate planners may want to modify the plan to include more subcontracting.

EXHIBIT 14.15   TOOLBOX: MASTER PRODUCTION SCHEDULE

End Product	Weekly Production Level, units					
	1	2	3	4	5	6
Tricycles	1,200	1,200	1,200	1,200	1,170	1,170
Standard adult	700	700	700	700	680	680
Customized adult	265	265	265	265	430	430
Total	*2,165*	*2,165*	*2,165*	*2,165*	*2,280*	*2,280*

During rough-cut capacity planning work centers (departments or machines) whose capacity is insufficient are identified. The capacity required at each selected work center is then calculated using the proposed MPS. If the required capacity exceeds the available capacity at one or more work centers, the MPS must be modified and/or the available capacity must be increased. Even if the available capacity is adequate, the MPS may be unacceptable because it makes poor use of the firm's resources.

Every time the MPS is amended, its effects on key resources must be reexamined. Thus, RCCP is an iterative process for which the computer is well suited. The process ends when the MPS appears to be feasible.

How is the expected workload for a work center estimated during RCCP? Several methods can be used, the simplest of which is the overall factors method.

The **overall factors method** uses past data to determine the percentage of total production hours that can be attributed to each work center [equation (14.1)]. These percentages are used to estimate the expected workload at each work center for each MPS time period [equation (14.2)].

Overall Factors Method

$$H_t = \sum_{p=1}^{n} q_{p,t} h_p \qquad (14.1)$$

$$l_{w,t} = H_t r_w \qquad (14.2)$$

where H_t = total number of production hours required for week t
$q_{p,t}$ = number of units of product p to be produced during week t
h_p = total production hours required by product p
n = number of products to be produced
$l_{w,t}$ = expected workload at work center w during week t
r_w = percentage of total production hours assigned to work center w during previous period

The overall factors method was used to examine the feasibility of DaCorté Ltd.'s MPS in Exhibit 14.16.

The overall factors method for estimating expected workloads is easy to use and requires a minimal amount of data. However, it assumes that the product mix is similar to last year's mix and remains constant from one MPS period to the next. If this is not the case, the more complicated but more accurate capacity bill method may be more appropriate.

The **capacity bill method** estimates the expected workload at each work center w for each MPS time period t, using equation (14.3).

EXHIBIT 14.16   TOOLBOX: OVERALL FACTORS METHOD

Suppose only three work centers—welding, painting, and assembly—are classified as key work centers at DaCorté Bicycle. Tricycles require 0.5 hour in total at these work centers, the standard adult model requires 0.7 hour, and the customized version requires 1.3 hours.

Using equation (14.1) and the previously developed master production schedule, it is possible to calculate the number of production hours required each week. In week 1, for example, 1,200 tricycles, 700 standard adult bikes, and 265 customized bikes are to be produced. The total number of production hours required in week 1 is therefore

$$(1,200)(0.5) + (700)(0.7) + (265)(1.3) = 1,435$$

The requirements for the remaining weeks are calculated in the same way and are shown in the table below.

NUMBER OF PRODUCTION HOURS REQUIRED EACH WEEK

End Product	Required Labor Hours Each Week					
	1	2	3	4	5	6
Tricycles	600	600	600	600	585	585
Standard adult	490	490	490	490	476	476
Customized adult	345	345	345	345	559	559
Total	1,435	1,435	1,435	1,435	1,620	1,620

The percentage of total production hours assigned to each work center last year is shown below.

Work Center	Number of Hours	Percentage of Total Hours
Painting	12,500	12.5
Welding	37,500	37.5
Assembly	50,000	50
Total	100,000	100

Using equation (14.2) and the percentages listed above, DaCorté can allocate production hours to specific work centers.

Since the painting work center accounted for 12.5 percent of the weekly production hours last year, it is allocated 12.5 percent of the production hours required each week. In week 1, for example, it is allocated 12.5 percent × 1,435 = 179 hours.

Work Center	Required Labor Hours Each Week					
	1	2	3	4	5	6
Painting (12.5%)	179	179	179	179	202	202
Welding (37.5%)	538	538	538	538	608	608
Assembly (50%)	718	718	718	718	810	810
Total	1,435	1,435	1,435	1,435	1,620	1,620

The capacity of each work center is shown below. Since the expected production requirements are less than the capacity of each work center, the MPS appears to be feasible.

	Weeks 1 to 4		Weeks 5 and 6	
Work Center	Capacity	Estimated Weekly Production Requirements	Capacity	Estimated Weekly Production Requirements
Painting	450	179	400	202
Welding	750	538	650	608
Assembly	1,025	718	900	810
Total		1,435		1,620

Capacity Bill Method

$$l_{w,t} = \sum_{p=1}^{n} q_{p,t} h_{p,w} \qquad (14.3)$$

where $l_{w,t}$ = expected workload at work center w for week t
$q_{p,t}$ = number of units of product p to be produced during week t
$h_{p,w}$ = number of production hours required by product p
        at work center w
n = number of products to be produced

The feasibility of DaCorté Ltd.'s MPS using the capacity bill method is examined in Exhibit 14.17. Note that the expected total weekly production hours are the same for both the overall factors method and the capacity bill method. The key difference between the two methods lies in the allocation of these hours to individual work centers.

The capacity bill method shows that the capacity of the welding work center is exceeded. Therefore, the trial MPS is not feasible. The MPS must be revised and/or the capacity of the welding work center must be increased.

It has been assumed that products can be started and completed during one MPS time period. However, if these periods are short compared with production lead times, the projections of capacity requirements should be time-phased to reflect the lead times.

14.6 FAST-RESPONSE AGGREGATION

Traditionally, the production planning process has begun with longer-term aggregate plans and has progressed through successive iterations to very short term and detailed plans for each product. This process of *top-down aggregation* made sense when planning was done by hand. The advent of powerful computer systems now allows firms to question the necessity of this time-consuming approach and has enabled them to plan accurately for the immediate future and then for the medium term. It makes sense to have a planning system that allows a firm to integrate sales and marketing activities with manufacturing activities.

Most sales forecasters first concentrate on the near term and then extrapolate to the longer term. The closer the forecast horizon is, the more accurate the forecast is likely to be, and so it makes sense for marketers to develop very detailed forecasts by individual product for the near term and more general forecasts for the longer term, aggregating to the product group or higher level. If manufacturing followed this logic, the manufacturing planning process would concentrate first on the detailed near-term forecast and then work in the medium-term and longer-term future in a more general and aggregate manner.

This approach to manufacturing planning can be called **bottom-up aggregation** to differentiate it from the traditional, top-down long- to short-term planning philosophy. By working with detailed forecasts coupled with detailed and accurate knowledge of resource requirements at each stage of the manufacturing process for each product (including transportation and storage requirements), planners can quickly develop feasible production plans that take into account the latest market and manufacturing status information. This approach to scheduling and planning benefits from the ability to run simulations that enable the planners to "see" operational and logistics problems rather than waiting to experience those problems.

EXHIBIT 14.17   TOOLBOX: CAPACITY BILL METHOD

Further investigation of production data at DaCorté Bicycle reveals the following standard time data.

End Product	Standard Labor Hours Required Per Unit		
	Painting	Welding	Assembly
Tricycles	0.1	0.2	0.2
Standard adult	0.1	0.2	0.4
Customized adult	0.1	0.7	0.5

During week 1, for example, the MPS calls for 1,200 tricycles, 700 standard adult models, and 265 customized models. Therefore, using equation (14.3), the expected workload at the assembly work center during week 1 is 653 hours:

$$l_{3,1} = \sum_{p=1}^{3} q_{p,1}\, h_{p,3}$$
$$= (1,200)(0.2) + (700)(0.4) + (265)(0.5)$$
$$= 240 + 280 + 132.5 = 652.5$$

End Product	Weekly Production Hours Required					
	1	2	3	4	5	6
Painting						
Tricycles	120	120	120	120	117	117
Standard adult	70	70	70	70	68	68
Customized adult	27	27	27	27	43	43
Total	217	217	217	217	228	228
Welding						
Tricycles	240	240	240	240	234	234
Standard adult	140	140	140	140	136	136
Customized adult	186	186	186	186	301	301
Total	566	566	566	566	671	671
Assembly						
Tricycles	240	240	240	240	234	234
Standard adult	280	280	280	280	272	272
Customized	133	133	133	133	215	215
Total	653	653	653	653	721	721
Grand total	1,436	1,436	1,436	1,436	1,620	1,620

The capacity bill method reveals that the capacity of the welding work center is exceeded by its scheduled workload in weeks 5 and 6. Therefore, this MPS is not feasible.

Work Center	Weeks 1 to 4		Weeks 5 and 6	
	Capacity	Estimated Weekly Production Requirements	Capacity	Estimated Weekly Production Requirements
Painting	450	217	400	228
Welding	750	566	650	671
Assembly	1,025	653	900	721
Total		1,436		1,620

DaCorté Bicycle has several options in this situation, including the following:

- Increase the capacity at the welding work center during February.
- Customized bicycles require 0.7 hour of welding versus 0.2 hour for standard adult bicycles and tricycles. If DaCorté produces 90 fewer customized bicycles per week, capacity will not be exceeded.
- There is excess capacity in weeks 1 to 4. The quantity of standard adult bicycles and tricycles could be increased in weeks 1 to 4 and decreased in weeks 5 and 6.

The cost of these (and other) options should be investigated.

Bottom-up aggregation relies on new software that can quickly manipulate large databases. These databases contain detailed orders and forecast demands for every product and very detailed resource and capacity requirements for every operation for every product, including inspection, transportation, and material handling. In addition, the database contains detailed information on the actual capacities of each process, machine, and department and the decision rules for deciding how temporary capacity adjustments should be made. The process of using this software to plan is called *finite capacity scheduling,* as actual capacities are used and detailed production schedules are produced. Scheduling and scheduling decision rules are discussed in Chapter 17.

Given the appropriate software, plans can be regenerated whenever the sales staff makes new forecasts. The desired approach is to have new forecasts made each scheduling period, which should be weekly or even daily. The more detail required, the greater the computer time required and the greater the cost of producing the schedule. Hence, it makes sense to limit the number of detailed planning periods and to switch to more aggregate planning as soon as possible. Beyond the detail "fence" it is possible to use rough-cut capacity planning, which requires far less computer resources than does the finite capacity scheduling that is necessary for detailed planning. It is up to marketing and operations to negotiate the frequency of forecasts and the number of periods over which detailed forecasts are made; the latter should never be fewer than the number required to build a product from scratch. Of course, it is possible to generate new plans whenever planning and order information changes. Regenerating the schedules as needs change is called *real-time scheduling*; in most instances temporary adjustments to capacity are not possible in the short term, but the need for costly adjustments should be markedly reduced.

Bottom-up aggregation is not a pipe dream but a reality. IBM uses finite capacity planning to schedule weekly and monthly production on a high-technology and highly customized circuit panel manufacturing line in its plant in Endicott, New York. The time required to generate production planning information has been reduced by 60 percent, and the labor needed to generate the monthly plan has been reduced by 80 percent. Customer service has also been improved through improved delivery performance and by identifying problems before production starts, thus allowing customers to be involved in rescheduling decisions. Vendor support has been similarly improved. The finite capacity planning software has been integrated into the plant's MRP system (see Chapter 15). Even though MRP is an integrative approach to planning, the detailed accurate planning afforded by the finite capacity scheduling module has improved the accuracy and responsiveness of the MRP system and of the IBM plant.

Bottom-up aggregation is therefore a reasonable approach for fast-response organizations, since the use of more accurate and timely data allows better short-range resource allocation decisions to be made than is possible with top-down aggregation. More accurate resource and capacity allocation means higher capacity utilization and less of a need for buffer inventory, reducing direct and allocated product costs. More detailed knowledge makes it possible to quickly determine the ability to respond to sudden changes in customer needs and assess the implications of making changes. Fast-response organizations can also improve their responsiveness by continually working to reduce their manufacturing lead times. This is important not just for responsiveness but also for the cost of producing the schedule.

When a firm becomes involved in aggregate planning, it is dealing with approximations of activities that will take place in the future. The further into the future a firm has to plan and the more aggregate the information, the less accurate the forecast is apt to be. The firm must accept this and determine:

- How much of the firm's resources, especially managerial, can be devoted to managing aggregate planning activities?
- How much inaccuracy can the firm tolerate in its intermediate-term planning?

Naturally, managers should work to improve the planning process continually so that lesser degrees of aggregation are usable. But managers have to recognize *current* limits to effective management and the limits of flexibility of their systems or they will not be able to adjust effectively when production actually begins.

With the ability to process and manage information through increasingly powerful and less expensive computers, most organizations can now plan at the product level rather than at higher levels of aggregation. As a firm disaggregates, however, managers have to realize that their planning is only as accurate as their information. Now they must have *very* accurate information about demand for individual products. That means the firm needs better information from the markets (through the marketing function) and a shortened planning horizon.

CHAPTER SUMMARY

The focus in this chapter was on intermediate-term plans, such as aggregate production plans and master production schedules, that bridge the gap between a firm's strategic plans and short-range production schedules.

- Intermediate-term production plans are of interest to managers throughout the firm because they influence production costs and flexibility, product quality, and the speed with which customer orders can be filled. They are also used outside the production area to create budgets, develop training programs, negotiate contracts with suppliers, make customer promises, and so on.
- The aggregate planning process can be divided into six steps.
- **Step 1.** Select a planning horizon and divide it into a set of time periods. If the firm produces a variety of goods or services, create aggregate product groups. Aggregate plans tend to be about 12 to 18 months in length and are divided into monthly time periods. In choosing aggregate product groups, ensure that the aggregate plan can be disaggregated for shorter-term planning.
- **Step 2.** Develop a forecast of the estimated demand for each aggregate product group in every period of the planning horizon. Translate the demand into resource requirements.
- **Step 3.** If the production requirements vary widely from one period to the next, consider using pricing, promotion, and other techniques for altering the timing and level of demand. As a general rule, the smaller the variation in production requirements is from one period to the next, the easier it is to match capacity to demand in the intermediate term.
- **Step 4.** Compare current capacity with production requirements. If there are mismatches between required capacity in a planning period and available capacity, generate alternatives for adjusting capacity. Estimate the cost of using each alternative. Options for adjusting capacity include changes in workforce level, overtime, undertime, temporary layoffs, sharing capacity, accumulating anticipatory inventories, subcontracting work, and allowing customer orders to backlog.

- **Step 5.** Choose a chase, level, or mixed aggregate planning strategy. When a firm follows a chase strategy, the production level for each period is set equal to the demand for that period. Anticipatory inventory does not accumulate from one period to the next. The production level remains the same from one day to the next with a level strategy. Inventory is accumulated during slow periods and used during high-demand periods. A mixed strategy combines elements from the chase and level strategies.

- **Step 6.** Develop the aggregate plan by using optimization or heuristic techniques. Linear programming, the transportation method, and the HMMS model are optimization techniques. The management coefficients model, search decision rules, and knowledge-based expert systems use heuristic techniques. Usually more than one aggregate plan is developed and evaluated. The plan that best meets the firm's strategic goals is the best plan.

- The aggregate production plan is usually disaggregated into a master production schedule which is used to calculate detailed materials requirements and daily production schedules.

- The feasibility of an MPS is examined during rough-cut capacity planning. Either the capacity bill method or the overall factors method can be used.

- Developing an aggregate plan and then disaggregating it into an MPS is referred to as top-down planning. Bottom-up aggregation begins at the individual product level and then groups the requirements for individual products to develop a more general plan. Many professional services use the bottom-up approach.

Chapter 15 will continue the discussion of the MPS. The focus, however, will be on detailed materials planning.

KEY TERMS

Aggregate production planning	Make-to-stock	Search decision rules (SDR) model	Rough-cut capacity planning (RCCP)
Planning horizon	Make-to-order	Knowledge-based expert	Overall factors method
Time buckets	HMMS model	system (KBES)	Capacity bill method
Aggregate products	Linear programming (LP)	Trial-and-error approach	Bottom-up aggregation
Chase strategy	Transportation method	Master production	
Level strategy	Management coefficients	schedule (MPS)	
Mixed strategy	model		

DISCUSSION QUESTIONS

1. What is operational planning? Where does it fit in the hierarchy of plans, and how are operational plans integrated into the corporate planning process?

2. What is aggregate planning? Why does a firm make an aggregate plan? How often?

3. What are the steps in the aggregate planning process? Does it matter if any steps are left out?

4. What does it mean to aggregate? Are there any rules a firm should use when deciding how to aggregate?

5. What would you use as the aggregation metric in the following sites?
   a. A general-purpose machine shop
   b. An automobile assembly plant
   c. A trucking company
   d. A general hospital
   e. A bank branch

6. Who in the firm should be involved in aggregate planning? Why?

7. What is the aggregate planning horizon? The planning time unit? Why do firms use these time intervals?

8. What is the relationship between a firm's aggregate plan and its ability to compete on the six competitive dimensions (cost, quality, dependability, flexibility, time, and service)?

9. How would a firm use the transportation method in aggregate planning? What are its limitations?

10. How useful is the trial-and-error method for aggregate planning? What are its limitations? How can a firm overcome them?

11. In what ways can a firm make temporary changes in capacity so that it can better accommodate actual or anticipated orders?

12. One way to adjust capacity is to manipulate the workforce. What means are available to adjust workforce capacity? Under what conditions is workforce adjustment difficult?

13. What is the master production schedule? How is the MPS developed, and to what uses is it put?

14. What is rough-cut capacity planning? Why do firms do rough-cut capacity planning?

15. What general rules can a firm develop from an analysis of the rough-cut capacity planning techniques discussed in this chapter?

16. What is the role of knowledge-based expert systems in aggregate planning? What must a firm have in place before it can use this type of system for its planning?

17. What are the pure strategies for production planning? Why are pure strategies almost never used in job-shop or batch operations?

18. What production strategies are available to a firm if it cannot hold inventories and customers will not back order? What strategies are available if the firm can hold inventories and customers will back order? Can you give two examples of firms in these situations?

PROBLEMS

1. 💾 Hightech Ltd. produces three different types of cameras. The hours required to produce each model are listed below.

	Model A	Model B	Model C
Hours required	1.6	1.8	2.3

As of January 1 there are 105 permanent workers and an average of 165 production hours available per worker per month. The hourly labor cost is $12, and the overtime rate is $18 per hour. It costs $1,300 to hire and train a worker and $800 to fire a worker. The forecast demand for each model in the first half of next year is shown below.

Model	Month					
	1	2	3	4	5	6
A	5,000	5,600	5,300	5,100	4,500	4,000
B	3,500	4,300	4,500	4,600	4,000	4,080
C	1,000	1,200	1,250	1,340	900	1,100

a. Prepare an aggregate plan that reflects a chase strategy. Compute the total production cost.
b. Prepare an aggregate plan that reflects a level strategy. Compute the total production cost.
c. Assume that company policy is to hire no more than 10 workers per month. Prepare an aggregate plan that does not violate this condition. Compute the total production cost.

2. In problem 1, assume that Hightech Ltd. can subcontract work at $16 per hour. Prepare another aggregate plan and compute the total production cost.

3. 💾 Solid Furniture Ltd. has 70 full-time employees. The regular-time pay is $11 per hour, and each employee works eight hours a day. Overtime pay is $1\frac{1}{2}$ times regular pay. It costs $900 to hire an employee and $800 to fire one. The inventory cost is $0.90 per hour per month. The forecast demand and available working days in each month are shown below.

Month	Demand, labor hours	Working Days in Month
1	11,700	20
2	12,350	19
3	12,110	22
4	11,700	21
5	12,890	22
6	11,694	22
7	13,820	21
8	12,795	23
9	13,946	21
10	14,853	21
11	15,560	20
12	11,070	20

Prepare an aggregate plan, bearing in mind the following restrictions:

- The company wants to keep its inventory level as low as possible. At the same time, however, it wishes to maintain a relatively stable workforce.
- It is difficult to arrange overtime work.
- The company wants to keep production costs low.

4. 🔲 Solid-Made, a plastics manufacturer, produces five different types of containers. At present it has 50 employees. The forecast demand and labor requirements for each container are shown below.

Month	Type A	Type B	Type C	Type D	Type E	Available Working Days
1	15,660	3,560	3,870	1,230	368	21
2	18,730	3,870	2,680	1,890	687	22
3	19,300	2,340	3,520	1,000	498	22
4	17,460	3,840	4,350	2,630	758	21
5	17,650	3,080	2,970	1,090	670	23
6	12,004	3,920	3,560	1,980	453	21
7	15,670	3,290	3,370	1,850	567	21
8	10,980	3,780	4,450	1,560	378	20
9	11,460	4,590	4,090	1,760	790	20
10	15,000	2,890	4,100	1,600	500	20
11	15,000	2,800	4,400	1,790	430	19
12	16,700	3,800	4,100	2,450	340	22
Labor standard	0.2	0.3	0.35	0.4	0.45	

Relevant cost data:

Regular pay rate	$9/hour
Overtime pay rate	$13.50/hour
Firing cost	$1,000 per worker
Hiring cost	$1,200 per worker
Inventory cost	$1.20 per hour per month

Assume that each working day is eight hours long. Prepare two different aggregate plans and compute the cost of each one. Can the plans be improved?

5. 🔲 Danielle Fashions, a leather jacket manufacturer, has prepared the following demand forecast.

	Month					
	1	2	3	4	5	6
Units	2,800	3,200	4,500	3,800	3,000	3,200

It takes 1.5 hours to make each jacket. The regular labor cost is $9 an hour, and overtime costs 1.5 times the regular rate. Firing and hiring costs are $700 and $900, respectively, per employee. The inventory cost is $3 per jacket per month. The current number of employees is 25, and the beginning inventory is 500 jackets. Assume that there are 170 available hours per employee per month.

a. Develop an aggregate plan using a chase strategy. Develop another using a mixed strategy.
b. Compute and compare the production costs.

6. Assume that as a result of a shortage of skilled laborers, Danielle Fashions (problem 5) cannot find additional employees. Also assume that overtime is limited to 20 percent of regular time and that the company can find a subcontractor who charges $21 per jacket. Develop a feasible plan and compute the production cost.

7. 🔲 Pearl Computers Ltd. serves a local market composed primarily of university students. The market demand, production costs, and other relevant information are given below.

Demand

Month	Units	Month	Units
1	350	7	505
2	370	8	530
3	380	9	650
4	385	10	655
5	400	11	680
6	495	12	480

	Assembly per Unit	Test per Unit	Packing per Unit
Hours needed	5	0.5	0.1
Labor cost	Regular time	$14/hour	
	Overtime	$21/hour	
	Hiring and training	$2,500	
	Firing cost	$900	
Inventory	Beginning inventory	50 units	
	Inventory cost	$9 per month per unit	
	Number of employees	15	
	Available regular hours per worker per month	160	

Would a chase, level, or mixed strategy result in the lowest production cost?

8. Assume that Pearl Computers Ltd.'s (problem 7) maximum inventory storage capacity is 500 units because of limited space and material handlers. Also assume that workers cannot be fired but can be laid off (they then collect 70 percent of their regular pay). Recalculate the total cost of your recommended production plan and compare the different results. Comment on the limited resources.

9. 🔲 The forecast demand for the last six months of the year is shown for Isocontrol, a manufacturer of control devices. The beginning inventory is 800 units.

Month	Expected Demand	Desired Safety Stock	Working Days
July	5,000	1,000	21
August	6,000	1,200	13
September	10,000	2,000	20
October	8,000	1,600	23
November	8,000	1,600	21
December	6,000	1,200	20

Hiring and training a worker costs $220, while laying off a worker costs $240. Each worker can produce four units per day. Subcontracting costs $20 per unit above the manufacturing cost. The wage rate is $8 per hour.

a. Prepare a chase strategy that varies only the workforce.

b. Prepare a chase strategy that varies only the quantity subcontracted each month.

10. 🔲 A city administrator is calculating the personnel requirements for firefighters in the upcoming year. Past years' demand and growth trends suggest the following needs.

Jan.	Feb.	Mar.	Apr.	May	June
27,000	22,000	23,000	24,000	25,000	29,000

July	Aug.	Sept.	Oct.	Nov.	Dec.
30,000	32,000	28,000	21,000	19,000	26,000

The figures are in labor hours. Current work levels can provide 25,000 labor hours per month of regular time at a rate of $6 per hour. Overtime costs are $9 per hour but can provide only up to 10 percent more hours per month. Part-time firefighters can be used. These people are not as well qualified and cost $7 per regular hour and $10.50 on overtime. Training costs are $500 per firefighter; layoff costs for full-time firefighters are $300 per person (there are no layoff costs for part-timers).

a. What should the monthly numbers of firefighters be? What is the annual cost?

b. What criteria were important in making your decision?

11. 🔲 Able Box Co. Inc. is developing an aggregate plan for the last six months of the year. The forecasted demand is as follows.

July	Aug.	Sept.	Oct.	Nov.	Dec.
1,000	1,000	1,200	1,100	1,200	1,300

There are 22 working days per month. The beginning inventory is 100 units; the inventory carrying cost is $8 per unit per month, and the stockout cost is $20 per unit per month. There are currently 10 workers paid $12 per hour on regular time and $18 per hour on overtime; the firm can work a maximum of 25 percent overtime per month. The hiring cost per worker is $200, and the layoff cost is $300. There are two labor hours per unit. Subcontracting costs $80 per unit above material costs.

a. What is the cost of a pure chase strategy in which the workforce is varied?

b. What is the cost of a strategy of maintaining a level workforce of 10 people and using overtime and subcontracting to vary the labor supply?

12. What is the best strategy for problem 11, and what is its cost?

13. 🔲 The Frosty Snowblower Manufacturing Co. has decided to build small rotary hoes to balance production on its lines. The best forecasts for the first year show dealer demand at the following levels.

Jan.	Feb.	Mar.	Apr.	May
500	600	700	800	500

Each month has 22 working days except February, which has 20. Frosty currently employs 30 workers who are paid a salary of $1,000 a month. Each unit's manufacture is expected to involve two labor hours. Hiring costs are $400 per person, with layoff costs of $500. The inventory carrying cost is only $5 per unit per month, but the stockout costs are approximately $100 per unit per month. Which of the following plans is better?

a. Varying the workforce to meet demand.

b. Maintaining a level workforce and using inventory and stockouts to absorb demand fluctuations.

14. What is the best strategy for Frosty? What criteria are important? Per unit labor costs are $50 on regular time and $75 on overtime. Overtime is limited to an average of two hours per day.

15. 🔲 What happens when Frosty suddenly discovers in early February that demand for the rotary hoes doubles each month in March through May, with demand in June and July of 800 and 600 units, respectively? In June and July Frosty had expected to make 300 and 400 snowblowers, each of which takes 1.5 hours of labor. Parts for the rotary hoes can be found from suppliers, and there is enough capacity in the shop to manufacture the units. A subcontractor has been found, though, who would charge $150 per unit in addition to material charges, if any. What is the best strategy, and how much will it cost?

GROUP EXERCISES

Many of the tools and concepts discussed in this chapter are meant to be used in a team setting. The following problem is best solved by small groups of students. Ideally, each group should be composed of people with different backgrounds, interests, or areas of expertise.

Your firm manufactures white goods: washing machines, clothes dryers, refrigerators, freezers, and dishwashers. Manufacturing input data are as follows.

Product	Sheet Metal, m^2	Labor, hours	Material Cost, $
Basic washer	6	2.00	100
Premium washer	6	3.50	115
Basic dryer	6	1.20	90
Premium dryer	6	1.50	100
Small refrigerator	5	3.00	105
Medium refrigerator	7	4.00	125
Large refrigerator	9	5.00	140
Chest freezer	9	2.50	95
Upright freezer	9	3.00	110
Dishwasher	6	3.00	130

The plant has four lines, each of which can assemble any of your products. Each line has a maximum capacity of 1,000 labor hours per week for a normal 40-hour week; 20 percent overtime can be worked per week at a 50 percent premium of $8 per hour. The premium is not charged on the hourly benefits of $5. The inventory carrying charge is 12 percent, and manufacturing overhead is allocated at 110 percent of direct labor. The labor hiring cost is $1,500 per person; this does not take into account the fact that new hires are on average only 75 percent effective for the first four weeks of employment. Layoff costs are $800 per person regardless of the length of time worked. All sheet metal passes through the electrostatic painting area,

where it takes seven seconds per square meter to apply the paint powder.

Divide the products up among the group and find out from local businesses what the seasonal demand profile looks like for each product over a typical year. Each member should then produce a monthly forecast for each of the products for the next 18 months. For the third month provide *daily* demand figures as well.

a. From these detailed forecasts prepare the aggregate plan for the plant for the next year, working in monthly time buckets. Assume that you start with inventory of 25 of each product, 3 people in the paint shop, and 15 people on each line. Explain your reasons for choosing the aggregation "representative" product or products.

b. Using the daily demand figures, do some more detailed capacity scheduling for the paint shop, which is the bottleneck. Assume that you produce all your products in three colors (white, black, and beige) and that the color demand proportions for each product are constant at 60 percent, 15 percent, and 25 percent, respectively. The changeover time between colors is one minute, and the application time for the paint powder is 6.7 seconds per square meter. Every 2,000 square meters there is a 10-minute changeover time from an empty to a full container of powder. One person operates the hand spray nozzle. How different is the plan, and what is the change in painting capacity utilization? What are the implications for the firm of the new information, and how might you manage them? You will not be able to adjust capacity except through overtime, which in this operation is limited to a maximum of two hours per day.

REFERENCES AND SELECTED BIBLIOGRAPHY

Bowman, E. H. [1956], "Production Planning by the Transportation Method of Linear Programming," *Journal of Operations Research Society,* February, pp. 100–103.

Brill, S. [1993], "Finite Scheduling Helps IBM Satisfy Its Panel Products Customers," *APICS,* October, pp. 66–69.

Gordon, J. R. M. [1966], *A Multi-Model Analysis of an Aggregate Scheduling Decision,* unpublished Ph.D. thesis, Sloan School of Management, MIT, Cambridge, Mass.

Gutis, P. [1988], "Grumman Says It Will Reduce Jobs by 2,300," *The New York Times,* March 10, p. B3.

Hakanson, W. P. [1993], "MES: Taking the Kinks out of Managing Manufacturing Operations," *APICS,* October, pp. 43–47.

Hesket, J. L., E. Sasser, Jr., and C. W. L. Hart [1991], *Service Breakthroughs,* The Free Press, New York.

Holt, C. C., F. Modigliani, J. F. Muth, and H. A. Simon [1960], *Planning Production, Inventories and Workforce,* Prentice-Hall, Englewood Cliffs, N.J.

Huettel, J. [1993], "Finite Capacity Scheduling: Just a Luxury, Right?" *APICS,* June, pp. 37–39.

Kotlowitz, A. [1987], "Firms Alter Production Strategies to Cope with Sweeping Job Pledges in Contracts," *The Wall Street Journal,* Sept. 21, p. 10.

Liberatore, M. J., and T. Miller [1985], "A Hierarchical Production Planning System," *Interfaces,* vol. 15, no. 4, pp. 1–11.

MacLain, J. O., and L. J. Thomas [1977], "Horizon Effects in Aggregate Production Planning with Seasonal Demand," *Management Science,* vol. 23, March, pp. 728–736.

Posner, M. E., and E. Szwarc [1983], "A Transportation Model with Backordering," *Management Science,* vol. 29, February, pp. 188–199.

Roder, P. I. [1993], "Finite Scheduling Systems," *APICS,* August, pp. 40–42.

Roth, A., and R. Van Dierdonck [1991], *DRGS and Hospital Service Requirements Planning,* paper presented at the Decision Science Institute's First International Meeting, Brussels, Belgium, June.

Silverman, Barry G. (ed.) [1987], *Expert Systems in Business,* Addison-Wesley, Reading, Mass.

Taubert, W. H. [1968], "A Search Decision Rule for Aggregate Scheduling Problems," *Management Science,* vol. 14, no. 6, February, pp. B343–B359.

Vollman, T. E., W. L. Barry, and D. C. Whybark [1992], *Manufacturing Planning and Control Systems,* 3d ed., Business One, Irwin, Homewood, Ill.

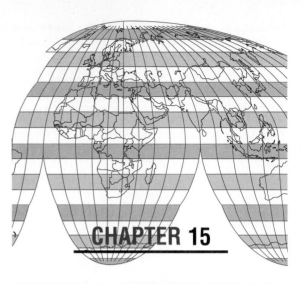

CHAPTER 15

MATERIAL REQUIREMENTS PLANNING

Materials and components directly related to the demand for final products are known as dependent demand inventory. Despite the known relationships between the demand for these products and the demand for final products, managing dependent demand inventory is a constant cause of concern. Managers continue to ask the following questions:

- How can work-in-process (WIP) inventory be reduced without compromising customer demand?

- What can be done to smooth out production and gain control of the operating system?

Material requirements planning (MRP) is a popular technique for planning and controlling dependent demand inventory items. By the end of this chapter you will be familiar with basic MRP techniques and concepts and their strengths and weaknesses.

EXHIBIT 15.1   FRO MANUFACTURING PROFILE

After Mixer Systems Inc. went on-line with an MRPII system in 1988, it tried to sell the 23 file cabinets containing its old filing system, but there were no takers. "It was like selling buggy whips," recalls the vice president of operations, John Cherba. "We ended up donating them."

Like its old filing system, the company was falling behind its fast-moving market. Customers had to wait up to six weeks for replacement parts for their mixing machines (some of which dated back to the 1970s), the sales staff could not get reliable information, and report preparation was a long and tedious manual chore. Inventory control was a guessing game; in some cases the company operated on a shortage list, and in others employees would overorder to avoid running out.

Now, using the information generated by the MRPII system, Mixer minimizes inventory at all levels, including raw materials, work in process, and finished goods. "We've been very successful at minimizing inventory levels. We were struggling to track only 18,000 parts in 1987, and today we're successfully maintaining over 70,000 on the computer," says Cherba. Computerization has allowed Mixer to nearly triple its business while minimizing the need for additional personnel.

What makes the system so valuable is the way it enables Mixer to respond rapidly to customers' orders. Ninety percent of service part orders are now filled within 10 days. Cherba wonders how he was able to do his job without the cost reports generated by the system within a day of the completion and shipping of a project. This rapid feedback helps Cherba find problems that might have gone unnoticed for weeks before computerization.

Source: Adapted from Capel and Kades (1992), pp. 40–41.

EXHIBIT 15.2   FRO SERVICE PROFILE

When Eastman Kodak's Imaging Group committed itself to becoming a class A MRPII user, it did not stop at the factory door. Instead, the group made the marketing division an integral part of the system and the implementation process, with marketing activities being included as levels in the MRP plan.

The marketing activities include the distribution network, the marketing companies throughout the world that support the group's sales efforts, and the group's marketing team. Working across the major functions, the planning process that drives the MRP system operates on a four-week cycle, once every four weeks, and plans to an 18-month time horizon. The four week sequence is as follows:

- Week 1. Demand data are gathered from the field and integrated with financial inputs.
- Week 2. Aggregate demand and inventory positions are checked and current plans are approved at sales review meetings.

(Exhibit 15.2 continues on next page)

EXHIBIT 15.2 *(continued)*

- Week 3. Positions identified in week 2 are discussed with each major manufacturing plant, and initial production plans are made.
- Week 4. The plans made in week 3 with individual plants are reviewed at regional and then worldwide levels to balance aggregate supply and demand.

The integration of the service elements into the MRP plan has led to improved customer service at the same time that inventories and lead times have been reduced. In addition, forecast accuracy has been improved along with communications throughout the marketing and manufacturing organizations. Although most firms look for savings inside the manufacturing organization when MRP is implemented, the Imaging Group has demonstrated that significant savings can be found within the marketing and service organizations as well.

Source: Adapted from Miller (1993), pp. 55–57.

15.1 MANAGERIAL ORIENTATION

Eliminate inventory. This has become a common battle cry in many North American firms. However, as was discussed in Chapter 13, the goal of a fast-response organization (FRO) is to improve its ability to compete and satisfy its customers, not to drive inventory levels of zero. Inventory serves legitimate functions, such as guarding against uncertainty, decoupling operations, and smoothing production requirements. Reducing the *need* for inventory and eliminating all unnecessary inventory are the strategies followed by FROs.

Even if they do not hold inventory, most firms have to plan and control the flow of inventory through the value chain. Consider firms such as Ford, Milliken,[1] and General Electric (Exhibit 13.1). Like Mixer Systems Inc. (Exhibit 15.1), not only must they manage inventories of end products, they also have to plan and control the hundreds (sometimes thousands) of parts and materials that make up these end products. As Eastman Kodak has discovered (Exhibit 15.2), influences on inventory levels of finished goods and parts extend beyond the factory walls.

The size of parts and materials inventories is not the only reason why managing inventories is challenging. Each part can be used in more than one end product and by more than one work center. If a product takes several days to produce, some parts may be needed the first day while others are not needed until the final assembly process.

If the **master production schedule (MPS)** calls for the same mix of end products each day, demand for parts and raw materials is relatively constant and the EOQ or one of the other independent demand inventory control models discussed in Chapter 11 may be adequate. However, when end products are produced periodically in batches, the demand for their component parts is lumpy.

> **DEFINITION:** *Lumpy demand* is demand that varies significantly from one period to the next, with many periods having no demand.

When demand is lumpy, independent demand inventory control models are not suitable for component parts. Consider the example in Exhibit 15.3. If Vermeer Ltd. uses the EOQ model to determine the timing and quantity of lock production, it will be faced with very high inventory levels and/or a high probability of stocking out.

[1] Milliken is one of the firms toured in the Startup Chapter.

EXHIBIT 15.3   INDEPENDENT VERSUS DEPENDENT DEMAND

Vermeer Ltd. designs and manufactures briefcases. The graph below illustrates the demand for one of its more popular models. Since demand varies so little from day to day, the firm simply manufactures the EOQ every three days.

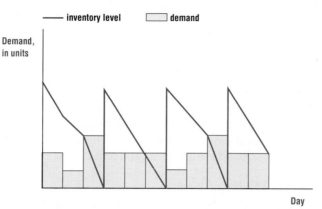

The demand for one of the locks used by Vermeer is illustrated below. Note the large variations in day-to-day demand. If the EOQ model is used to calculate the best order quantity and order interval for this lock, very large buffer inventories will be needed to prevent stockouts.

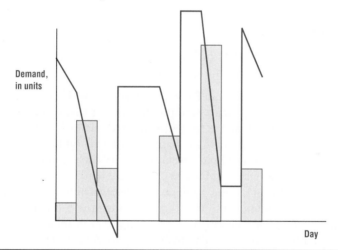

Using the EOQ model in this situation cripples Vermeer's efforts to compete simultaneously along the six dimensions of competition.

Instead of estimating the demand for component parts and materials, a firm can accurately calculate demand from the master production schedule by using a **material requirements planning (MRP)** system. MRP systems represent a major step forward in operations planning because they help lower inventory levels while ensuring that the right quantities of each item are on hand when required.

How do MRP systems fit into the operations planning hierarchy? Turn back to Exhibit 15.3. An MRP system is a detailed time-phased materials planning system. It converts the master production schedule into a detailed set of material requirements that can be used on the shop floor to schedule and control production.

15.2 THE BASICS OF MATERIAL REQUIREMENTS PLANNING

The master production schedule specifies the quantity required of each end item in each planning period; it is a set of time-phased requirements for end items. But the firm also needs a set of time-phased requirements for the parts and raw materials that make up those end items.

> **DEFINITION:** Material requirements planning is a production planning and control technique in which the master production schedule is used to create production and purchase orders for dependent demand items.

The production orders are used to schedule production on the shop floor, and the purchase orders are used by purchasing to ensure that the right quantities of components are delivered when needed. Thus, MRP acts as a link between a firm's intermediate-term and short-term production planning and scheduling functions.

Information Requirements

As illustrated in Exhibit 15.4, the master production schedule is just one of the major inputs in a typical MRP system. Information contained in bills of material and inventory files is required as well. These inputs will be described in the next two sections.

Bills of Material

> **DEFINITION:** The *bill of material (BOM)* lists the component parts that make up one unit of a particular product.

The small wooden table illustrated in Exhibit 15.5 consists of four legs clamped to a tabletop. All the parts are purchased, but two of the four legs are turned on a wood lathe. The legs are turned, inspected, clamped onto the table, and inspected again. The plain legs are then clamped onto the table.

Since the firm can hold inventories after each step in the building sequence, the eight part codes listed in Exhibit 15.6A are used.

The BOMs in Exhibit 15.6B are single-level bills of material. Each BOM contains a list of the components that directly constitute the part, along with the quantity required of each component. For example, each table (part A) is made up of one part B and two parts C. The BOM for part B states that each part B is made up of

EXHIBIT 15.4   MRP: MAJOR INPUTS AND OUTPUTS

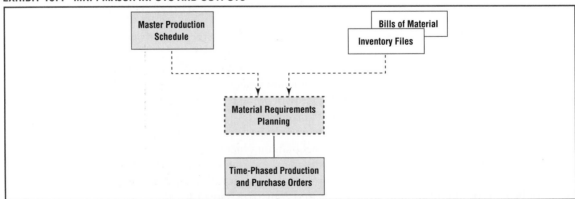

EXHIBIT 15.5   DRAWING AND PARTS LIST FOR TABLE X31

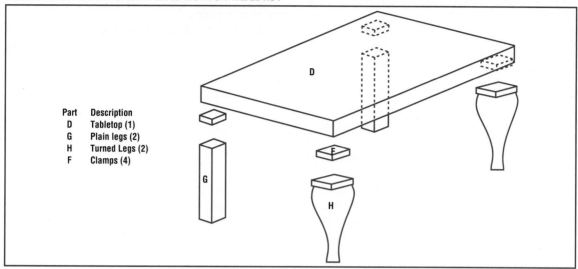

Part	Description
D	Tabletop (1)
G	Plain legs (2)
H	Turned Legs (2)
F	Clamps (4)

EXHIBIT 15.6   BOMS FOR TABLE X31

A. Part Codes for Table X31

Part Code	Description
A	Complete table
B	Tabletop with turned legs attached
C	Plain leg assembly
D	Tabletop
E	Turned leg assembly
F	Clamp
G	Plain leg
H	Turned leg

B. Five Single-Level BOMs

Note that each BOM lists only the parts or components that are directly used in a parent item.

```
A
  B(1)
  C(2)
B
  D(1)
  E(2)
C
  G(1)
  F(1)
E
  H(1)
  F(1)
H
  G(1)
```

C. Indented (Multilevel) BOM

This indented BOM is a list of parts and components from the end item all the way down to purchased parts and raw materials.

```
A
  B(1)
    D(1)
    E(2)
      H(1)
        G(1)
      F(1)
  C(2)
    G(1)
    F(1)
```

one part D and two parts E. Contrast this with the multilevel indented BOM in Exhibit 15.6C, which includes all eight part codes.

The BOM also can be drawn as a product structure tree or chart. In Exhibit 15.7 the product structure tree for the table indicates the sequence in which the parts are used and the level of the BOM at which each component is held. Note that the higher the level, the lower its level number and the more complete the item. In this example there are five levels. The completed table (part A) is at level zero, while plain legs (part G) are at level 4.

As with the other BOMs, the number of parts needed is shown in brackets. Thus, two plain leg assemblies (part C) are needed to make a table but only one plain leg (part G) is used to make a plain leg assembly.

Inventory Files Information on each part is also stored in a series of inventory files that usually reside in a database that is accessed and updated by several different computer applications. The MRP system requires two different types of data: (1) production (or purchasing) lead times and (2) the actual and projected end-of-period inventory balances for each period in the planning horizon.[2]

The component lead times listed in Exhibit 15.8A were used to convert the

---

[2] Data regarding the demand for each part in the past may be needed if certain lot sizing rules are used by the system. Lot sizing rules are discussed later in this chapter.

EXHIBIT 15.7   PRODUCT TREE FOR TABLE X31

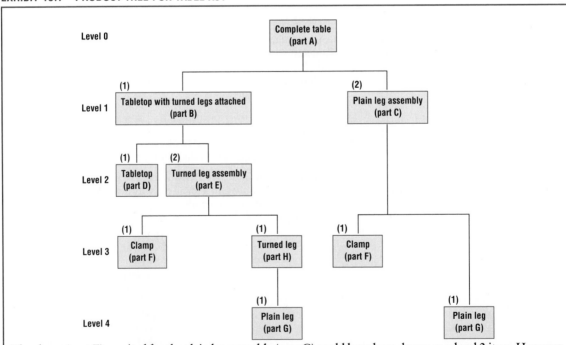

The clamp (part F) required for the plain leg assembly (part C) could have been drawn as a level 2 item. However, when all requirements for a particular part are held at the lowest level at which that part appears in the BOM, computer searches become more efficient. If the computer locates an item at one level, it does not have to look for that item again at the lower levels of the BOM that it is currently searching. Since the clamp required for the turned leg (part H) is on level 3, the clamp required for the plain leg assembly is placed on level 3 as well.

EXHIBIT 15.8   TIME-PHASED BUILD PROGRAM FOR TABLE X31

A. Component Lead Times

Part		Lead Time, weeks
A	(complete table)	1
B	(tabletop with turned legs attached)	2
C	(plain leg assembly)	1
D	(tabletop)	2
E	(turned leg assembly)	1
F	(clamp)	2
G	(plain leg)	1
H	(turned leg)	1

B. Time-Phased Build Program

product structure tree for table MX301 into the time-phased build program in Exhibit 15.8B.

Component lead times and inventory balances are used in an MRP as it "explodes" the BOM to calculate the demand for each component part in each planning period.

Exploding the Bill of Material

To ensure that the end product can be produced as required, each component part must be available at the right time and in the right quantities. The desired quantity of each component part is calculated by using the MPS in a process known as **bill of material explosion.**

Chapter 12 stated that the MPS indicates the required quantity of each end product in each period. The demand for the components of an end product is found by multiplying the MPS quantity by the component usage quantity specified in the BOM. This demand is reduced by any available inventory or scheduled receipts.

Finally, to ensure that a component is available when needed, its net requirements must be offset by its lead time.

Let us work through a simple example to clarify these concepts. Suppose a firm is planning a barbecue for its employees for Saturday and estimates that the guests will eat about 50 hamburgers. If each hamburger contains ¼ pound of beef, the *gross requirements* are 12½ pounds of ground beef and 50 hamburger buns. But if there is already three pounds of beef in the freezer (on-hand inventory) and someone has promised to bring the buns (scheduled receipt), the *net requirement* is 9½ pounds of ground beef. If it takes one day for the groceries to be delivered, the order for ground beef must be placed on Friday, not Saturday.

Before moving to a more complicated example, let us formally define several terms.

> **DEFINITION:** The *gross requirements* for a component consist of the quantity required of that component during each period to produce the end items specified in the master production schedule.

> **DEFINITION:** *Scheduled receipts* are existing replenishment orders for a component that have been released to the shop floor (or the supplier) and are due at the beginning of each period.

> **DEFINITION:** The *projected inventory balances* are the quantities expected to be on hand at the end of each period after the replenishment orders have been received and gross requirements have been satisfied.

> **DEFINITION:** *Planned order receipts* are replenishment orders for the component due at the beginning of each period that have not yet been released.

> **DEFINITION:** *Planned order releases* are replenishment orders for a component due to be released to the shop floor (or the supplier) at the beginning of each period.

A portion of the MPS for table X31 is shown in Exhibit 15.9A. Assume that it is now week 1 and that the first seven weeks of the MPS are "frozen" (i.e., not allowed to change). Note that the frozen portion of the MPS should extend from the current date out past the cumulative lead time of the end product. Every week the plan is updated, and the frozen portion of the schedule is automatically rolled out by one more week.

In week 7 the MPS calls for 20 completed units of model X31. Therefore, the *gross* requirement for part A, the completed table, is 20 units. Since there are no scheduled receipts in week 7 and since the projected inventory at the end of week 6 is zero, the *net* requirement is 20 units as well.

Assume that the size of each production (or purchase) order for a component is equal to the net requirements for the period. The planned order receipt for part A in week 7 is then 20 units. The lead time for part A is one week, and so the planned order should be released at the beginning of week 6. *The planned order release lags behind the planned order receipt by the component's production or purchase lead time.* Once the planned order is released to the shop floor, it becomes a scheduled receipt.

To start making the 20 units of part A in week 6, one part B and two part C's must be available. *Gross requirements at a lower level relate to planned order releases at the next higher level.* A two-week lead time for part B means that the planned release date for the part B production order will be week 4. The planned release date

EXHIBIT 15.9   TOOLBOX: EXPLODING THE BOM

A. A Portion of the Master Production Schedule

	Quantity Required in Week								
End Product	1	2	3	4	5	6	7	8	. . .
Tables									
X30	10	20	40	10	20	40	20	10	. . .
X31	20	—	—	—	—	—	20	40	. . .
⋮									
Recliners									
P12	20	20	16	30	60	20	16	30	. . .
P13	16	16	24	8	20	16	24	8	—
⋮									

B. Exploding the BOM for Table X31 in Week 7

Level 0
Part A, table

Lead time: 1 week	Quantity Required in Week						
	1	2	3	4	5	6	7
MPS for Table X31	20	—	—	—	—	—	20
Gross requirements	20	—	—	—	—	—	20
Scheduled receipts	12	—	—	—	—	—	—
Projected ending inventory |8	—	—	—	—	—	—	—
Net requirements	—	—	—	—	—	—	20
Planned order receipts	—	—	—	—	—	—	20
Planned order releases	—	—	—	—	—	⟨20⟩	—

The planned order release in week 6 for 20 units of part A results in gross requirements in week 6 for parts B
(20 × 1 each = 20) and C (20 × 2 each = 40).

Level 1
Part B, tabletop with turned legs

Lead time: 2 weeks	Quantity Required in Week						
	1	2	3	4	5	6	7
Gross requirements	—	—	—	—	—	⟨20⟩	—
Scheduled receipts	—	—	—	—	—	—	—
Projected ending inventory |0	—	—	—	—	—	—	—
Net requirements	—	—	—	—	—	20	—
Planned order receipts	—	—	—	—	—	20	—
Planned order releases	—	—	—	20	—	—	—

Level 1
Part C, plain leg assembly

Lead time: 1 week	Quantity Required in Week						
	1	2	3	4	5	6	7
Gross requirements	—	—	—	—	—	40	—
Scheduled receipts	—	—	—	—	—	—	—
Projected ending inventory |0	—	—	—	—	—	—	—
Net requirements	—	—	—	—	—	40	—
Planned order receipts	—	—	—	—	—	40	—
Planned order releases	—	—	—	—	40	—	—

The planned order release for 20 units of part B (tabletop with turned legs attached) in week 4 results in gross
requirements for part D (tabletop) and part E (turned leg with clamp attached). Twenty tabletops and 40 turned
legs must be available at the beginning of week 4.

(Exhibit 15.9 continues on next page)

EXHIBIT 15.9 *(continued)*

Level 2 Part D, tabletop Lead time: 2 weeks	Quantity Required in Week						
	1	2	3	4	5	6	7
Gross requirements	—	—	—	20	—	—	—
Scheduled receipts	—	—	—	—	—	—	—
Projected ending inventory |0	—	—	—	—	—	—	—
Net requirements	—	—	—	20	—	—	—
Planned order receipts	—	—	—	20	—	—	—
Planned order releases	—	20	—	—	—	—	—

Level 2 Part E, turned leg assembly Lead time: 1 week	Quantity Required in Week						
	1	2	3	4	5	6	7
Gross requirements	—	—	—	40	—	—	—
Scheduled receipts	—	—	—	—	—	—	—
Projected ending inventory |0	—	—	—	—	—	—	—
Net requirements	—	—	—	40	—	—	—
Planned order receipts	—	—	—	40	—	—	—
Planned order releases	—	—	40	—	—	—	—

The planned order release in week 3 for 40 units of part E results in gross requirements in week 3 for part H (40 × 1 turned leg each = 40).

Level 3 Part H, turned leg Lead time: 1 week	Quantity Required in Week						
	1	2	3	4	5	6	7
Gross requirements	—	—	40	—	—	—	—
Scheduled receipts	—	—	—	—	—	—	—
Projected ending inventory |0	—	—	—	—	—	—	—
Net requirements	—	—	40	—	—	—	—
Planned order receipts	—	—	40	—	—	—	—
Planned order releases	—	40	—	—	—	—	—

Part F is used by both part C and part E. The planned order release in week 5 for 40 units of part C results in a gross requirement of 40 units (40 × 1 clamp each) for part F in week 5. The planned order release in week 3 for 40 units of part E results in a gross requirement of 40 units (40 × 1 clamp each) in week 3.

Level 3 Part F, clamp (1 required) Lead time: 2 weeks	Quantity Required in Week						
	1	2	3	4	5	6	7
Gross requirements	—	—	40	—	40	—	—
Scheduled receipts	—	—	—	—	—	—	—
Projected ending inventory |0	—	—	—	—	—	—	—
Net requirements	—	—	40	—	40	—	—
Planned order receipts	—	—	40	—	40	—	—
Planned order releases	40	—	40	—	—	—	—

Part G is used by both part C and part H. The planned order release in week 5 for 40 units of part C results in a gross requirement of 40 units (40 × 1 plain leg each) for part G in week 5. The planned order release in week 2 for 40 units of part H results in a gross requirement of 40 units (40 × 1 plain leg each) in week 2.

Level 4 Part G, plain leg Lead time: 1 week	Quantity Required in Week						
	1	2	3	4	5	6	7
Gross requirements	—	40	—	—	40	—	—
Scheduled receipts	—	—	—	—	—	—	—
Projected ending inventory |0	—	—	—	—	—	—	—
Net requirements	—	40	—	—	40	—	—
Planned order receipts	—	40	—	—	40	—	—
Planned order releases	40	—	—	40	—	—	—

C. Exploding the BOM for Table X31 in Week 8

Level 0
Part A, table
Lead time: 1 week

	Quantity Required in Week						
	2	3	4	5	6	7	8
MPS for table X31	—	—	—	—	—	20	40
Gross requirements	—	—	—	—	—	20	40
Scheduled receipts	—	—	—	—	—	—	—
Projected ending inventory |0	—	—	—	—	—	—	—
Net requirements	—	—	—	—	—	20	40
Planned order receipts	—	—	—	—	—	20	40
Planned order releases	—	—	—	—	20	40	—

The planned order release in week 7 for 40 units of part A results in gross requirements in week 6 for parts B (40×1 each $= 40$) and C (40×2 each $= 80$).

Level 1
Part B, tabletop with turned legs
Lead time: 2 weeks

	Quantity Required in Week						
	2	3	4	5	6	7	8
Gross requirements	—	—	—	—	20	40	—
Scheduled receipts	—	—	—	—	—	—	—
Projected ending inventory |0	—	—	—	—	—	—	—
Net requirements	—	—	—	—	20	40	—
Planned order receipts	—	—	—	—	20	40	—
Planned order releases	—	—	20	40	—	—	—

Level 1
Part C, plain leg assembly
Lead time: 1 week

	Quantity Required in Week						
	2	3	4	5	6	7	8
Gross requirements	—	—	—	—	40	80	—
Scheduled receipts	—	—	—	—	—	—	—
Projected ending inventory |0	—	—	—	—	—	—	—
Net requirements	—	—	—	—	40	80	—
Planned order receipts	—	—	—	—	40	80	—
Planned order releases	—	—	—	40	80	—	—

If the firm continues to explode the BOM for week 8 of the MPS, it will eventually arrive at the following requirements for part G. Note that the replenishment order for 40 units in week 2 is now a scheduled rather than planned order receipt.

Level 4
Part G, plain leg
Lead time: 1 week

	Quantity Required in Week						
	2	3	4	5	6	7	8
Gross requirements	40	80	—	40	80	—	—
Scheduled receipts	40	—	—	—	—	—	—
Projected ending inventory |0	—	—	—	—	—	—	—
Net requirements	—	80	—	40	80	—	—
Planned order receipts	—	80	—	40	80	—	—
Planned order releases	80	—	40	80	—	—	—

for part C will be week 5, and 40 units (2×20 units) will be required. The calculations for parts D, E, F, G, and H appear in Exhibit 15.9B.

Note that MRP combines the requirements for different end products. If, for example, any of the other table models require the same plain leg or there are customer orders for replacement parts, the gross requirements for the plain leg will increase. And each week, the plan is updated by one week. Some of the calculations for week 8 appear in Exhibit 15.9C; you will complete the remaining calculations as an exercise at the end of this chapter.

15.3 BATCH SIZING TECHNIQUES

How much should the firm make or buy at one time? and When should the firm make or buy? are questions that apply to every level in the BOM. For every item, therefore, the firm has to determine what lot size it should use, keeping in mind two objectives: minimizing costs and maintaining a reasonable and realistic plan.

When the BOM was exploded for the table, it was assumed that the batch size for any part was equal to the amount required of that part for the period. This lot sizing technique is the first of several that will be discussed in this section.

Lot for Lot

Lot-for-lot batch sizing is the simplest lot sizing technique. The rule here is to supply in this period what is demanded in this period. In the MPS in Exhibit 15.10A, the BOM for table X31 has been exploded again. The planned order releases for part C, based on the lot-for-lot rule, are shown in Exhibit 15.10B.

Lot-for-lot batch sizing results in minimal inventory holding costs. Note that the projected inventory at the end of each week is zero in Exhibit 15.10B. However, lot for lot means setting up to manufacture (or purchase) once for each period in which the item is required, no matter how many are required. When setup (or purchase order) costs are low and inventory carrying costs are high, lot for lot frequently results in the lowest inventory costs.

Because lot for lot is simple, it can be calculated quickly. This is important if the firm has many lot sizing decisions to make each time it runs or regenerates its MRP schedules. Lot for lot results in the lowest demand on computer time, which may be a major cost element in a firm's material management system.

EXHIBIT 15.10   TOOLBOX: THE LOT-FOR-LOT RULE

A. MPS for Table X31 for Week 7 to Week 15

			Quantity Required in Week						
	7	8	9	10	11	12	13	14	15
X31	20	40	10	10	40	20	10	10	20

The bill of material was exploded to arrive at the following requirements for part C (plain leg assembly). Every week the planned order receipt is equal to the net requirements for that week.

B. Lot for Lot

					Quantity Required in Week					
	5	6	7	8	9	10	11	12	13	14
Gross requirements	—	40	80	20	20	80	40	20	20	40
Scheduled receipts	—	—	—	—	—	—	—	—	—	—
Projected ending inventory |0	—	—	—	—	—	—	—	—	—	—
Net requirements	—	40	80	20	20	80	40	20	20	40
Planned order receipts	—	40	80	20	20	80	40	20	20	40
Planned order releases	40	80	20	20	80	40	20	20	40	—

Economic Order Quantity

In some circumstances the **economic order quantity (EOQ)** may yield the least-cost component inventory lot size. Recall from Chapter 11 that the EOQ is the least-cost position if all the assumptions of constancy of cost and certainty of demand and delivery are satisfied. The firm may have items, such as packaging material, whose demand, when measured across all its products, is more or less constant.

Although the demand for part C varies from one period to the next, for illustrative purposes the EOQ was used to regenerate the set of planned order receipts and projected inventory levels in Exhibit 15.11. Only three batches of part C are ordered using the EOQ batch sizing technique, and inventory is much higher than it was when the firm used the lot-for-lot technique.

Period Order Quantity

The **period order quantity (POQ)** technique maintains the fixed order period of the EOQ while adjusting the amount manufactured or purchased each time. First, the EOQ and the expected number of orders placed each year are calculated. In this example the EOQ is 125 units. Since annual demand is 2,225 units, about 18 orders $(2,225 \div 125 = 17.8)$ are placed each year. This means that one order is placed approximately every three weeks. Therefore, the POQ for part C is equal to the sum of the requirements for the next three weeks. For example, in week 6 the POQ is $40 + 80 + 20 = 140$. In week 9 the POQ is 140 units as well, but it falls to 60 units in week 12. The resultant inventories (see Exhibit 15.12) are much lower than they were when the EOQ technique was used.

Part Period Algorithm

The **part period algorithm (PPA)** attempts to balance setup (or ordering) and holding costs dynamically rather than in the static manner of the EOQ. Unlike the EOQ technique, the PPA uses projected demand rather than past average demand.

EXHIBIT 15.11   TOOLBOX: ECONOMIC ORDER QUANTITY RULE

Recall from equation (11.4) that the economic order quantity is calculated as follows:

$$EOQ = \sqrt{\frac{2DS}{H}}$$

On the basis of past records, the annual demand (D) for part C is about 2,225 units. The holding cost (H) for part C is $5.70 per part per year, and the production setup cost (S) is $20 per setup. Therefore,

$$EOQ = \sqrt{\frac{(2)(2,225)(20)}{(5.7)}} = 124.96$$

In week 6, 40 units are required but there are no scheduled receipts and the projected inventory at the end of week 5 is zero. Therefore, 125 units are ordered. The projected inventory at the end of the week is $(125 - 40 = 85)$.

		Quantity Required in Week								
	5	6	7	8	9	10	11	12	13	14
Gross requirements	—	40	80	20	20	80	40	20	20	40
Scheduled receipts	—	—	—	—	—	—	—	—	—	—
Projected ending inventory │0	—	85	5	110	90	10	95	75	55	15
Net requirements	—	40	—	15	—	—	30	—	—	—
Planned order receipts	—	125	—	125	—	—	125	—	—	—
Planned order releases	125	—	125	—	—	125	—	—	—	—

EXHIBIT 15.12   TOOLBOX: PERIOD ORDER QUANTITY

Economic order quantity					125 units					
Annual demand					2,225 units					
Number of EOQ orders per year					2,225 ÷ 125 = 17.8, or one every 3 weeks					
Period order quantity					Enough to cover requirements for the next 3 weeks					

		Quantity Required in Week								
	5	6	7	8	9	10	11	12	13	14
Gross requirements	—	40	80	20	20	80	40	20	20	40
Scheduled receipts	—	—	—	—	—	—	—	—	—	—
Projected ending inventory |0	—	100	20	—	120	40	—	60	40	—
Net requirements	—	40	—	—	—	—	—	—	—	—
Planned order receipts	—	140	—	—	140	—	—	60	—	—
Planned order releases	140	—	—	140	—	—	80	—	—	—

A part period is the equivalent of holding one unit of inventory for one period or any similar combination. Thus, holding one unit for two periods and holding two units for one period are both equal to two part periods. The **economic part period** (**EPP**) is the number of part periods required to equate setup (or ordering) costs and holding costs.

Economic Part Period

$$EPP = \frac{S}{H} \qquad (15.1)$$

where EPP = economic part period
     S = setup or ordering cost
     H = holding cost per unit per period

Continuing with the example, the setup cost for part C is $20 and the weekly inventory holding cost is $0.11 per unit. If the firm holds inventory for only one EPP, the two costs are about equal when the inventory level is 182 units ($20 ÷ $0.11). By grouping the period requirements until the combined requirements are as close to the EPP value of 182 units as possible (but not over it), the firm can balance the holding and setup costs. As demonstrated in Exhibit 15.13, the requirements for weeks 6 to 9 should be grouped together, as should the requirements for periods 10 to 13.

Which of these four techniques is the best? The holding and ordering costs associated with each one are shown in Exhibit 15.14.

The PPA results in the lowest combined holding and ordering costs. The most costly solution was obtained using the lot-for-lot technique. But note that the PPA solution is the lowest-cost solution for only this very small part of the production planning problem. It may not necessarily be the best solution for the entire problem.

Grouping the requirements for several periods increases the lumpiness of demand, that is, increases the variation from one period to the next. This lumpiness creates surges in demand for items in lower levels of the BOM. These surges often exceed the available capacity. Modifications to the schedule may have to be made to ensure that the schedule is feasible. Imagine the difficulty of using the "lumpy" techniques for every end product and component part. The time and effort required to develop a feasible schedule would be prohibitive. Accordingly, even if the lot-for-lot batch

EXHIBIT 15.13 TOOLBOX: PART PERIOD ALGORITHM

Ordering cost per order	$20	
Holding cost per unit	$5	
Economic part period	$20 ÷ $0.11 = 181.82	

Periods Grouped	Batch Size	Number of EPPs
6	40	0
6 and 7	120	0 + 80(1) = 80
6, 7, and 8	140	80 + 20(2) = 120
6, 7, 8, and 9	160	120 + 20(3) = 180
6, 7, 8, 9, and 10	240	120 + 20(4) = 200

Therefore, group the requirements for weeks 6, 7, 8, and 9.

Periods Grouped	Batch Size	Number of EPPs
10	80	0
10 and 11	120	0 + 40(1) = 40
10, 11, and 12	140	40 + 20(2) = 80
10, 11, 12, and 13	160	80 + 20(3) = 140
10, 11, 12, 13, and 14	240	140 + 40(4) = 300

Therefore, group requirements for weeks 10, 11, 12, and 13. Although the 40 units required in week 14 will probably be grouped with the requirements for subsequent weeks, week 14 is considered to be the third grouping.

	Quantity Required in Week									
	5	6	7	8	9	10	11	12	13	14
Gross requirements	—	40	80	20	20	80	40	20	20	40
Scheduled receipts	—	—	—	—	—	—	—	—	—	—
Projected ending inventory |0	—	120	40	20	—	80	40	20	—	—
Net requirements	—	40	—	—	—	80	—	—	—	40
Planned order receipts	—	160	—	—	—	160	—	—	—	40
Planned order releases	160	—	—	—	160	—	—	—	40	—

EXHIBIT 15.14 TOOLBOX: COMPARING THE COST OF VARIOUS LOT SIZING TECHNIQUES

		Orders Placed	Inventory Accumulated		
(1) Technique	(2) Number	(3) Total Ordering Cost, $	(4) Number of Part Periods	(5) Total Inventory Cost, $	(6) Total Cost, $
Lot for lot	9	180	0	0	180
Economic order quantity	3	60	540	59.40	119.40
Period order quantity	3	60	380	41.80	101.80
Part period algorithm	3	60	320	35.20	95.20

Column 3 = $20 × column 2.
Column 5 = $0.11 × column 4.

size is not used at the highest level of the BOM, in most cases it is used at every other level.

Other Techniques

Other lot sizing techniques are used in MRP systems. The best known is the Wagner-Whitin algorithm, which generally yields a lower-cost solution than do those discussed so far. It is, however, computationally complex and requires an appreciable amount of computer time.

In practice, scheduling is performed in a dynamic rather than static environment. Several master production schedules may have to be developed before a feasible schedule is found, and even then the schedule is amended periodically to reflect changes in demand or shop floor conditions. Therefore, while many algorithms can potentially provide a lower-cost solution, the time and effort needed to keep updating the solution may outweigh the savings generated by the lower-cost solution.

15.4 CAPACITY REQUIREMENTS PLANNING: CLOSING THE MRP LOOP

One of the most important assumptions made in a typical MRP system is that capacity is unlimited. In practice, this is almost always a poor assumption. To improve its usefulness, therefore, MRP has been extended to include a **capacity requirements planning (CRP)** module.

> **DEFINITION:** The capacity requirements module uses the production orders generated by MRP to calculate the labor and machine resources required at each work center during each planning period. The required capacity is then compared with the available capacity.

The CRP module requires two product files: the routing file and the resource bill file. The product routing file contains the sequence of departments, work centers, and machines that the product follows as it is manufactured. The resource bill lists the standard resource requirements needed to manufacture each component.

CRP is similar to but goes well beyond the rough-cut capacity planning described in Chapter 14. For example, CRP considers the time-phased production orders for all components, not just for the end items specified in the MPS. It also compares required and available capacity at every work center, not just at key work centers. Some CRP modules even consider setup and maintenance schedules as well as planned labor downtime.

If the capacity of one or more resources is overloaded by the MPS, the MPS is not feasible and must be manually adjusted. CRP can identify the components that are causing the overload and trace (peg) those components back up to the end product to which they belong.

The inclusion of the CRP module creates a feedback mechanism which "closes the loop" in the MRP system and transforms MRP into the iterative process illustrated in Exhibit 15.15.

> **DEFINITION:** A *closed-loop MRP* system is an MRP system which has both production planning and execution functions and in which feedback on the plans generated flows back up the planning system.

Most closed-loop MRP systems consist of a collection of modules, each of which performs a major planning or control function. By packaging functions into modules, firms can choose only those which they need and can easily update the modules. A brief description of typical closed-loop MRP modules appears in Exhibit 15.16.

A wide range of reports can be produced by MRP systems, but the most common ones are notices of orders that can now be released, notices of order cancellations, suspensions or due date changes, inventory status reports, performance reports, exception reports, and planning reports.

EXHIBIT 15.15 CLOSING THE LOOP IN AN MRP SYSTEM

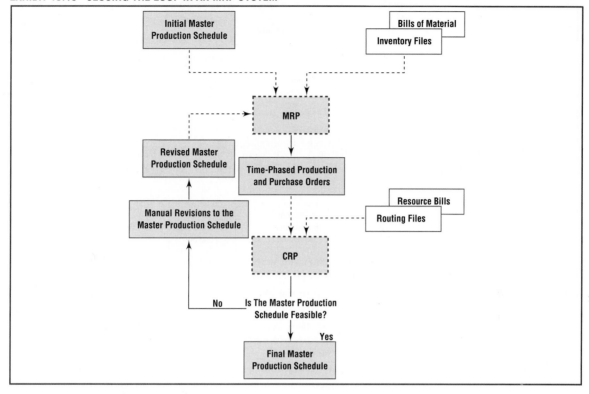

Caution. If it is assessing computer files with old or inaccurate data, even a closed-loop MRP system cannot ensure that the MPS is feasible or that reports are reliable.

15.5 REGENERATIVE AND NET CHANGE SYSTEM UPDATES

To be reliable, the information contained in MRP files must be kept up to date. The arrival of scheduled receipts must be recorded, as must changes in customer orders or due dates, stock level corrections, and scrap. Of course, all these changes affect the planned production and purchase orders generated by the MRP system. Updating these orders can be done by reexploding the entire MPS or a portion of the schedule.

DEFINITION: The master production schedule is totally reexploded in a *regenerative system update*.

DEFINITION: In a *net change system update* a partial explosion is made for the parts and materials affected by the changes.

The time required for a regenerative system update can be prohibitive. An update for a moderate-sized operation, for example, often requires over 12 hours of CPU time. New developments in computer software, however, are drastically reducing CPU times [Gunn (1992)]. In practice, although both net change and regenerative updates can be made relatively quickly, updates tend to be done on a periodic rather than a continual basis to avoid **system nervousness**.

511

EXHIBIT 15.16 MODULES TYPICALLY FOUND IN A CLOSED-LOOP MRP SYSTEM

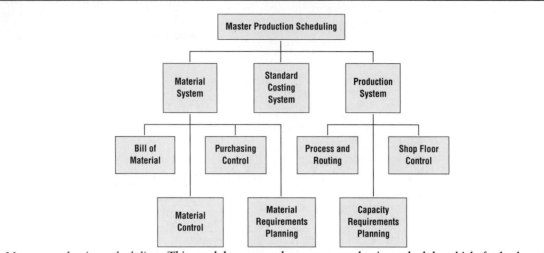

Master production scheduling. This module creates the master production schedule which feeds the other modules. Actual performance can be compared with planned performance.

Material system. The material system is composed of the bill of material system (BMS), the material control system (MCS), material requirements planning (MRP), and the purchasing control system (PCS).

The bill of material system is used by the MRP module to create a set of time-phased production orders that are based on the master production schedule. It is also used by engineering when product designs are created and revised and by accounting when products are costed.

The material control system maintains extensive database files on the status of inventories as well as material planning information. It provides answers to questions such as, Will there be a shortage of any materials or components? When will each customer order be completed? and Which orders are late and require rescheduling?

The purchasing control system (PCS) links supply requisitions generated by the MRP or MCS module to contracts or purchase orders. PCS helps identify orders which will be late; it can also be used to analyze vendor performance.

Standard costing system. Using the database files maintained by other modules, the standard costing system generates product costs. Costs can then be analyzed and budgets can be recalculated if necessary.

Production system. Process and routing systems describe the sequence of operations required to produce each part. Work center capabilities, labor and tooling requirements, and alternative routings are often included. This information is used for scheduling, product costing, performance measurement, lead time calculations, and work center loading.

The capacity requirements planning system is used to test the feasibility of the master production plan by estimating the expected workload at key work centers.

The shop floor control system is used to implement the master production schedule. This system monitors shop floor performance and creates shop floor documentation.

DEFINITION: System nervousness occurs in an MRP system when relatively small changes in the MPS (or in higher-level planned order releases) result in significant timing and/or quantity changes in lower-level planned order releases.

15.6 SAFETY STOCK AND SAFETY LEAD TIMES

In some cases the exact *quantity* of an item that is required is uncertain. This uncertainty may arise from frequent unplanned usages caused by scrap or spare part demand, for example. To guard against this uncertainty, the MRP system can build in a level of **safety stock**.

> **DEFINITION:** Safety stock in an MRP system is inventory held in addition to that needed to satisfy gross requirements.

As demonstrated in Exhibit 15.17A, if a safety stock of 10 units is desired for part G, the projected ending inventory should never fall below 10 units.

Safety lead times tend to be used when the *timing* of supply is uncertain (e.g., because of an unreliable vendor).

EXHIBIT 15.17 TOOLBOX: SAFETY STOCK AND SAFETY LEAD TIME

The quantity required of part G (plain leg) for table X31 in weeks 2 to 8 is shown below. The lot-for-lot rule has been applied.

Level 4
Part G, plain leg
Lead time: 1 week

	Quantity Required in Week						
	2	3	4	5	6	7	8
Gross requirements	40	80	—	40	80	—	—
Scheduled receipts	40	—	—	—	—	—	—
Projected ending inventory |0	—	—	—	—	—	—	—
Net requirements	—	80	—	40	80	—	—
Planned order receipts	—	80	—	40	80	—	—
Planned order releases	80	—	40	80	—	—	—

A. Safety Stock

Suppose a safety stock of 10 units has been specified for part G (plain leg) of table X31. This means that the projected ending inventory is not allowed to fall below 10 units. The revised planned order receipts and releases are shown below.

Level 4
Part G, plain leg
Lead time: 1 week
Safety stock: 10 units

	Quantity Required in Week						
	2	3	4	5	6	7	8
Gross requirements	40	80	—	40	80	—	—
Scheduled receipts	40	—	—	—	—	—	—
Projected ending inventory |10	10	10	10	10	10	10	10
Net requirements	—	80	—	40	80	—	—
Planned order receipts	—	80	—	40	80	—	—
Planned order releases	80	—	40	80	—	—	—

B. Safety Lead Time

Now suppose a safety lead time of one week has been specified for part G (plain leg) of table X31. This means that each order should be received one week earlier than necessary. The revised planned order receipts and releases are shown below. (Note that the safety stock requirement has been removed.)

Level 4
Part G, plain leg
Lead time: 1 week
Safety lead time: 1 week

	Quantity Required in Week							
	1	2	3	4	5	6	7	8
Gross requirements	—	40	80	—	40	80	—	—
Scheduled receipts	—	40	—	—	—	—	—	—
Projected ending inventory |0	—	—	—	—	—	—	—	—
Net requirements	—	—	80	—	40	80	—	—
Planned order receipts	—	80	—	40	80	—	—	—
Planned order releases	80	—	40	80	—	—	—	—

DEFINITION: When a safety lead time is used, purchase (or production) orders are scheduled to arrive one or more periods before they are needed to satisfy gross requirements.

Suppose a safety lead time of one week is specified for part G. All planned order receipts are scheduled to arrive one week before they are needed (see Exhibit 15.17B). As a result, the planned order release date is pushed forward one week. The net effect of this may be to extend the total lead time required to produce the product.[3]

Caution. Neither safety stocks nor safety lead times should be used permanently. They increase costs without improving a firm's competitiveness. Although there may be circumstances in which these devices may be used temporarily, the *need* for them must be eliminated as soon as possible.

15.7 IMPLEMENTING AN MRP SYSTEM

What type of operating processes can be best served by MRP systems?

In general, the benefits of MRP are greatest when a firm produces a large variety of products, the average number of product BOM levels is high, and batch sizes are large. A computerized system to monitor and control the large number of inventory items is often warranted under these conditions. Large batch sizes result in lumpy component demand; this means that the potential savings generated from replacing an independent demand system with MRP can be high. Therefore, MRP systems work best in intermittent-flow and repetitive-flow shops where large volumes of fairly standardized products are made to stock.

Most make-to-order companies do not use MRP because they do not maintain BOMs of their end products. This makes sense when products are always customized, for a new bill must be created each time an order is taken and that bill is thrown out once the product is complete. As part of the quotation process, however, and before a job can be started, bills of material, labor bills, routing sheets, and capacity availabilities must be checked before a price can be quoted and a delivery date guaranteed. When responsiveness to requests for quotations, reductions in planning time, and/or savings in design and engineering time are critical, computer-driven product configuration is required.

The key component of this approach is a *product configurator*. This is an expert system containing company-specific decision rules that identifies key descriptors in the customers' product definition and then uses its own logic to design the product and produce all the necessary documentation for manufacture. Digital Equipment's XCON expert system configures VAX computers and produces all the documentation, including detailed wiring diagrams. The costs of manufacture are developed accurately. Panasonic's individually customized bicycle that is built within three hours of the receipt of an order is configured electronically; the configurator automatically releases the bicycle into production and transmits detailed instructions to each workstation.

The development cost for a product configurator can be high, especially when a large number of interrelated conditional decision rules are required. The strategic

---

[3] If the lead time for part C of the table is extended by one week, for example, the total lead time is still six weeks. If the lead time for part G is extended by one week, however, the total lead time is also extended by one week.

EXHIBIT 15.18 APPLYING MRP LOGIC TO SERVICES

Chapter 14 described how some hospitals are using diagnostic related groups, or DRGs (groups of diagnoses whose treatments entail similar resource consumption patterns and hence hospital costs), for aggregate planning purposes. For shorter-term planning, Roth and Van Dierdonck (1991) suggest that hospitals consider using MRP logic. Each DRG can be treated as an end product, and a time-phased bill of resources can replace the standard bill of material used by manufacturers.

The treatment required for an aneurysm (DRG111), for example, can be divided into seven distinct stages. Preoperative testing is stage 1; its resource bill calls for (1) a primary MD and cardiologist for two hours, (2) treadmill, CT scan, EKG, and arteriogram (one unit of each), (3) lab tests (eight units), and (4) radiology (two units).

Rather than using a master production schedule, a hospital can develop an anticipated discharge schedule by using its projected admissions for each DRG. Then, working backward from the discharge schedule, the hospital can create a set of time-phased resource requirements. For example, it is known that an operating room and a surgeon are needed during stage 3 of the aneurysm treatment. Since stage 3 occurs nine days before the aneurysm patient's anticipated discharge date, the operating room and surgeon can be booked at the right time.

---

benefits of rapid, accurate quotations of price and delivery date, though, coupled with automatic integration with MRP and CAD/CAM systems, are attractive.

In some cases MRP techniques can be used to plan and control services. Exhibit 15.18 shows how hospitals can apply MRP techniques to their operations.

Although there have been success stories, the vast majority of companies implementing MRP systems report more problems than successes. It seems that MRP's inherent weaknesses, combined with poor implementation, are responsible for this. Let us take a close look at some of these weaknesses.

- **The use of predetermined standard lead times.** The largest component of production lead time is not processing time but waiting time. Although processing time may be predictable, waiting time is not. Waiting times are a function of conditions on the shop floor: the more congested the shop floor, the longer the waiting time. To protect the system against possible material or component shortages, MRP uses generous estimates of the lead time. This results in higher than necessary inventories and decreased system throughput.
- **An inability to directly consider resource capacity limitations and alternatives as the MPS is developed.** Although the CRP module gives schedulers some feedback, it provides little guidance regarding possible alternatives and the quality of each alternative. Since MRP/CRP is an iterative process, it is often too time-consuming to allow schedulers to investigate all the alternatives.[4]
- **An inability to deal with complex situations and circumstances on the shop floor.** Infeasibilities are often left to the shop floor to resolve where informal systems should be developed that bypass the MRP system. These informal systems undermine user confidence in the MRP system and reduce the chances of MRP output being used and MRP data being kept up to date. As inaccuracies creep into the system, it becomes less and less reliable. The integrity of the system is slowly eroded, and this lowers the users' confidence.

As was pointed out earlier, without accurate and up-to-date inventory and BOM files, MRP systems cannot function effectively. However, ensuring that these files are

---

[4] Some firms have addressed this problem by developing MRP software (called *capacity optimized planning and scheduling*) that directly considers capacity and material constraints in detail as the MPS is developed [see Sharma (1993)].

"clean" when the MRP system is first installed is time-consuming and frustrating. Because BOM files frequently do not reflect the engineering changes that have been made, they are usually out of date. Inventory levels include items that are obsolete or damaged and those which have been pilfered. Some items are listed under several different part numbers, and inventory transactions are often entered incorrectly. Much of the time required to implement an MRP system (typically about five years) is spent cleaning up the data and convincing users of the need to keep the data current and accurate.

Problems also arise when MRP is treated as just another computer software package and is implemented in isolation. MRP is much more than this; it is a management information system that must be integrated with other information systems and activities within the firm. The MRP implementation starts with top management commitment (see Exhibit 15.2).

15.8 MANUFACTURING RESOURCE PLANNING

MRP is continually evolving and expanding to include more business functions. As illustrated in Exhibit 15.19, it has been transformed from a material planning and control system to a companywide system capable of planning and controlling almost all the firm's resources. A new term—**manufacturing resource planning (MRPII)**—has been coined to describe this expanded system.

> **DEFINITION:** Manufacturing resource planning (MRPII) is composed of a wide range of integrated functions which together plan and control all the resources of a manufacturing firm.

MRPII can be used to schedule capacity, shipments, and maintenance, for example. Projections of cash flows can be provided for financial planning. Estimates of future labor requirements can be used for human resources planning. Since it is a companywide system, an MRPII often has a built-in simulation capability that allows the firm to ask "what if" questions.

EXHIBIT 15.19 THE EVOLUTION OF MRP INTO ELP

MRP (BEFORE: 20 YEARS AGO)	MRPII (NOW)	ELP (FUTURE: ONE TO FIVE YEARS)
• Material requirements planning • Capacity requirements planning	• Material requirements planning • Capacity requirements planning • Order entry • Forecasting • Distribution requirements planning • Resource requirements planning • Shop floor control • Purchasing • Cost accounting	• Material requirements planning • Capacity requirements planning • Order entry • Forecasting • Distribution requirements planning • Resource requirements planning • Shop floor control • Purchasing • Cost accounting • More sophisticated shop floor control, financial planning, and simulation capabilities • Ties to customers and suppliers

Source: Adapted from Gunn (1992), p. 20.

MRPII facilitates internal integration (one of the four structural prerequisites of an FRO) by coordinating the activities performed by the firm's various functional areas and providing a common database. This ensures that everyone is using the same up-to-date information and working from the same script.

A logical extension of MRPII—**enterprise logistics planning (ELP)** systems—is emerging as well. The goal is to tie the entire value chain, from the firm's suppliers to the firm's customers, into an integrated system. Digital Equipment Corporation, Xerox, and Sony are among the firms moving toward the ELP vision. Exhibit 15.19 indicates the broad range of integrative activities being carried out by ELP systems.

In the future the scope of ELP systems will widen. For example, as firms join together temporarily to form a **virtual plant/company** to produce a specific product, they will have to be able to share information quickly and easily. ELP systems will probably be extended to facilitate this intercompany communication.

MANAGERIAL IMPLICATIONS

Time-phased material management and production planning systems (of which MRP is the best known) make firms more effective and efficient by imposing a discipline on the entire process and integrating activities at each step in the production process. MRP systems can be regenerated whenever assumptions that were made during planning turn out to be incorrect.

However, a firm should ensure that the assumptions it uses for planning are correct. It can guarantee this only if three conditions are met: (1) the end item demand is accurate, (2) the supply conditions are accurate, and (3) the firm's knowledge of internal conditions is accurate.

The only way to do this is to ensure that the total production cycle time is as short as possible and that the suppliers and customers are integrated into the firm's systems. This is where ELP becomes essential.

Like everything else, effective internal planning or integrated value chain planning through ELP requires top management's commitment. This is not an easy task, for the changes required are great. The benefits of integrated planning can be assessed by looking at firms that have successfully implemented MRP.

CHAPTER SUMMARY

The focus in this chapter was on material requirements planning (MRP). The intent of MRP is to systematically plan and control dependent demand inventory items. The general procedure is outlined below.

- The gross requirements for each item in each planning period are calculated by exploding the bill of material for every parent product specified in the master production schedule.
- The gross requirements for each item are reduced by the projected on-hand inventory or any scheduled receipts to yield the net requirements for the period.
- The size and timing of each planned production or purchase order are determined by using a lot sizing rule, such as lot for lot, the economic order quantity, the period order quantity, and the part period algorithm.
- A planned order receipt is offset by the production or purchase lead time to create a planned order release.
- If the timing of supply is uncertain, safety lead times may be added temporarily. If the quantity of supply is uncertain, safety stocks may be added.

- The planned order receipts and releases are updated regularly to reflect changes in the master production schedule, inventory levels, and so forth. A regenerative or net change update can be done.

When it generates production and purchase orders, MRP assumes that there are no restrictions on the quantity that can be ordered, that is, that capacity is infinite. The capacity requirements planning module compares the capacity required to carry out the detailed production plan with the available capacity. This feedback loop transforms MRP into closed-loop MRP. Manufacturing resource planning transforms closed-loop MRP into a companywide system that can plan and control all the firm's resources. Enterprise logistics planning extends MRPII to include the entire value chain from suppliers to customers.

KEY TERMS

Master production schedule (MPS)	Projected inventory balance	Part period algorithm (PPA)	Net change system update
Lumpy demand	Planned order receipt	Economic part period (EPP)	System nervousness
Material requirements planning (MRP)	Planned order release	Capacity requirements planning (CRP)	Safety stock
Bill of material (BOM)	Lot-for-lot batch sizing	Closed-loop MRP	Safety lead time
Bill of material explosion	Economic order quantity (EOQ)	Regenerative system update	Manufacturing resource planning (MRPII)
Gross requirements	Period order quantity (POQ)		Enterprise logistics planning (ELP)
Scheduled receipts			Virtual plant/company

DISCUSSION QUESTIONS

1. What is dependent demand? What are the differences between dependent demand and independent demand?

2. What is MRP? Why should inventories be reduced once MRP is implemented? What forms and functions of inventory are influenced by MRP?

3. What is closed-loop MRP? What is MRPII? How are these systems different from basic MRP?

4. If, on doing a BOM explosion, a firm finds a negative on-hand balance for a component in week zero, what does that mean? What can the firm do about the problem?

5. Which is the best lot sizing technique to use with MRP? What is the basis for your decision?

6. How should MRP be implemented? What importance does the context have?

7. Which forms of operating organizations are best served by MRP? What alternatives for managing dependent demand are available? Under what circumstances is each suitable?

8. How does MRP relate to aggregate planning? How should the two processes be linked?

9. Can MRP be extended beyond the operating system? In what ways might it be extended?

10. MRP is ostensibly for manufacturing enterprises. Can it be used by service firms? Where in service firms might one find dependent demand inventory?

11. How much stock should be carried to cover uncertainty in an MRP system? How should this stock be managed?

12. How can the ability to deexpedite be as helpful as the ability to expedite? Why should a firm need to do either in an MRP system?

13. A friend suggests that MRP is simple and does not need to be computerized. What do you say?

14. MRP was designed for an environment in which every promise is broken and everything breaks down. Comment on the validity of this statement. What is the *ideal* environment for MRP, and why?

15. If MRP is such a powerful tool, why don't people use it at home?

PROBLEMS

1. In Exhibit 15.9 calculate the requirements for parts D, E, and F.

2. Product A is composed of one B assembly, one C assembly, and one D assembly. B assembly is made of two E subassemblies and one F subassembly. D assembly is made of one J subassembly. E subassembly is made of one K part and two L parts. F is made of two M parts. G is made of two N parts and one P part. H subassembly is made of one R part and two M parts. J is made of two T parts and one L part. Draw a product structure tree and calculate the quantity of each item that will be required for each product A.

3. Product EL731 has the following product structure tree. Determine what quantity of each item is required to make 500 units of EL731.

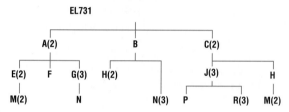

4. Using the following information about parents and components, construct a product structure tree and calculate the quantity of each item that will be required to make 200 units of end product M.

M	A	B	C	F	I
A(2)	D(2)	F(3)	I(1)	D(2)	E(2)
B(1)	E(1)	G(2)	J(3)	K(2)	L(3)
C(3)		H(2)			

5. 🖳 The forecast weekly demand for a product over the next six weeks is 700, 600, 550, 800, 660, and 690 units. Assuming that beginning inventory is 1,500 units and safety stock is 150 units, develop a net requirements schedule for the product.

6. Statistical order-level systems sometimes try to store enough safety stock so that there is no stockout for a specified percentage of the time. If enough safety stock is maintained so that each of items A, B, C, and D will not stock out over 90 percent of the time, what is the probability that the firm will be able to produce end item X?

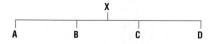

7. Using the following product structure tree, design the associated bill of materials, showing the hierarchy and components at the correct levels. Use low-level coding.

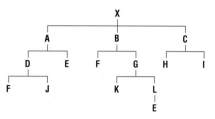

8. Time-phase the net requirements for component H in problem 7 by placing the appropriate net requirements in the correct time buckets.

		Week				
	1	2	3	4	5	6
Gross requirements	42	65	70	18	27	37
Scheduled receipts	23	34				
On hand	25					
Net requirements						

9. 🖳 Suppose a lead time of one week applies to the orders in problem 8. Time-phase the planned order releases to satisfy net requirements. Use the lot-for-lot technique.

10. 🖳 Suppose the order lot size of item H in problem 7 is 35 units. Specify the planned order release for problem 8, assuming a lot size of 35.

11. 🖳 An end item Y consists of two main subassemblies, A and B. To produce A components, C, D, and two units of E are required. To make B components, F and three units of G are required. Component F requires two units of component H.
   a. Construct the product structure tree for Y.
   b. Determine the quantities of each component required to produce 1,200 Y's.

12. 🖳 Student Audio Services has just designed a state-of-the-art CD system and has won a major contract with Combined University Bookstores. Demand of 52,000 is expected in the year, spread evenly over the year. The system consists of the plastic case, a carrier strap, and the cardboard box in which the unit is packed. Inside the plastic case are a power supply, two speakers, and the control unit. The control unit consists of the switch, the volume control, the playing laser head, and the printed circuit board assembly, which also acts as the mounting base for the components in the control unit.

a. Develop your own master production schedule for a planning horizon of 10 weeks.
b. Specify the product structure tree.
c. Given a lead time of two weeks on power supplies and three weeks on all other components, develop an MRP plan for production. With no on-hand inventories, when could the first units be shipped?
d. If it takes five minutes to assemble the control unit, three minutes to assemble the player in the plastic case, 30 seconds to box the items, 15 seconds to place the box in a packing case, and 25 seconds per item to receive, check, and place the purchased components on the shelves, how many people will be needed to meet the delivery schedule? Assume that no training is required.

13. 💾 Product X is made of three units of W and two units of Y. Annual demand for X is uniform at 48 units per week in a 50-week year. The setup cost for production is $40. Product X costs $24 per unit, and the inventory carrying cost is 30 percent of the product's direct cost.
a. Determine the EOQ lot size for X.
b. Assuming a lead time of one week for X, two weeks for W, and three weeks for Y, create a complete MRP schedule for all three items for an eight-week period. There is no on-hand inventory.

14. 💾 The master scheduler for Monopoly Company would like to determine the amount and date of planned order releases for all components, including end item 413 shown below. All lead times are in weeks. There are no on-hand inventories or scheduled receipts. Can item 413 be shipped at the end of eight weeks? What would happen if the lead

time of item 944 was extended from one week to two weeks?

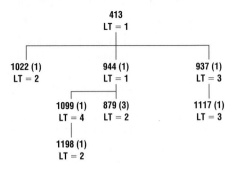

15. The master scheduler for Monopoly Company in problem 14 would also like to determine the capacity requirements in each of the four departments that are involved in the production of item 413. The table below shows the time requirements in weeks for each component in each of the four departments. Given the MRP schedule for problem 14, determine the total requirements in weeks in each department over the planning horizon used. Assume that departmental loads are calculated during the single week in which a planned order release for a given component is executed.

	Department			
Component	1	2	3	4
1022	0	0.005	0	0.001
944	0.001	0	0	0
937	0.001	0.0007	0.002	0.0001
1099	0.001	0.0005	0.0008	0.0002
879	0.0004	0.0006	0.0002	0.0005
1117	0.0008	0.002	0.001	0.0025
1198	0.001	0.001	0.002	0.001

GROUP EXERCISES

Many of the tools and concepts discussed in this chapter are meant to be used in a team setting. The following problems are best solved by small groups of students. Ideally, each group should be composed of people with different backgrounds, interests, or areas of expertise.

1. As a group, find a local firm that is a class A MRPII user. Visit the firm and discuss planning and MRP. You should discuss the following topics:

• How long it took from initial installation to the present or to class A status, whichever came first
• What the initial implementation process plan was and what changes were made during implementation

• From which vendor the MRP system was purchased and what modifications were made to the software to suit the firm
• What the MRP system is used for: scheduling, production control, materials management, and so on
• How well the MRP system is integrated into other information systems and how effectively MRP is integrated with vendor and customer systems
• What problems the firm currently has with planning and what developments are in store for the MRP system

2. Identify as many MRP system vendors as possible

and obtain from three of them documentation on their MRP software. Focus on the following:

- The modules and functions that form part of the MRP system
- The time suggested for installation and the suggested implementation process
- The types of support available from the vendor during installation and in operation

- The rate of modification of the system
- The ability to customize the system to users' needs
- The availability of finite capacity scheduling and real-time scheduling (see Chapter 14)

Identify the types of operations best suited to each of the systems you have investigated and suggest which system is the "best."

REFERENCES AND SELECTED BIBLIOGRAPHY

APICS Dictionary, 6th ed. [1987], American Production and Inventory Control Society, Falls Church, Va.

Anderson, J. C., and R. G. Schroeder [1984], "Getting Results from Your MRP System," *Business Horizons,* May–June, pp. 57–64.

Bourke, Richard W. [1993], "Configurators: Ruled-Based Product Definition," *APICS,* December, pp. 51–64.

Cambell, Kevin [1993], "Manufacturing Enterprise Management in the Aerospace and Defense Industry," *APICS,* February, pp. 50–52.

Capel, David, and Deborah Kades [1992], "A Small Manufacturer Makes a Concrete Investment in MRP," *APICS,* September, pp. 40–41.

Fox, Kenneth A. [1984], "MRP II Providing a Natural 'Hub' for Computer-Integrated Manufacturing System," *Industrial Engineering,* October, pp. 44–50.

Gunn, Thomas G. [1992], "Logistics Planning," *OR/MS Today,* October, pp. 16–28.

Kamenetzky, R. D. [1985], "Successful MRP II Implementation Can Be Completed by Smart Scheduling, Sequencing Systems," *Industrial Engineering,* October, pp. 44–52.

Karmarkar, Uday S., and Indur M. Shivdasani [1989], "Closed Loop Integration of MRP, Scheduling and Shop Floor Control," working paper, Graduate School of Business, University of Rochester, Rochester, N.Y.

Lieberman, Mark [1992], "Configuration Control: A New Way to Look at MRPII Manufacturing," *APICS,* March, pp. 35–38.

Miller, S. [1993], "MRP II at Eastman Kodak," *APICS,* August, pp. 55–57.

Orlicky, J. [1975], *Material Requirements Planning,* McGraw-Hill, New York.

Roth, A., and R. Van Dierdonck [1991], *DRGS and Hospital Service Requirements Planning,* paper presented at the Decision Science Institute's First International Meeting, Brussels, Belgium, June.

Sharma, Ken [1993], "Adding 'Intelligence' to MRP Systems," *APICS,* March, pp. 53–58.

Vollman, T., W. Berry, and D. Whybark [1992], *Manufacturing Planning and Control Systems,* 3d ed., Richard D. Irwin, Homewood, Ill.

Wight, O. W. [1981], *MRPII: Unlocking America's Productivity Potential,* Oliver Wight Ltd. Publications, Williston, Vt.

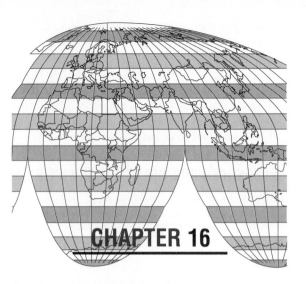

CHAPTER 16

JUST-IN-TIME AND SYNCHRONOUS OPERATIONS

No matter how successful a firm is, its managers must continually ask questions such as the following:

- How can the firm improve its operations?
- How can the firm utilize its resources more effectively to satisfy customers' needs?

This chapter will present two relatively new operations management philosophies—just-in-time and synchronous operations—that can help managers answer these questions. By the end of this chapter you will understand the fundamentals of these philosophies and know how their underlying concepts can be applied to every area of a firm.

EXHIBIT 16.1   FRO MANUFACTURING PROFILE

Because its antennas are used by the U.S. military in airborne radar and missile applications, product quality is very important at Texas Instruments' (TI) Antenna Department. At the same time, the downsizing of the military budget has forced TI to become a low-cost producer.

Initially, high product quality was maintained through a series of 100 percent inspections as the antennas flowed through the production process. When defects were found, the product would be reworked or scrapped. Because items were constantly going on hold for rework or being scrapped, material flow was not consistent. Work-in-process inventories were high, and the theoretical lead time of eight hours was inflated to 60 days.

In 1990 TI began to implement JIT concepts to improve product quality and decrease costs. The following changes were made:

- A series of modifications were made to the process to improve its reliability.
- Batch sizes were reduced.
- Operators were cross-trained.
- The shop was reconfigured into U-line layouts.
- A closer relationship was established with TI's suppliers.

After two years, the number of product defects has been reduced tenfold and both WIP and lead time have been reduced by about two-thirds. Operator morale is up, and product costs are down.

Source: Adapted from Ellis and Conlon (1992), pp. 16–19.

EXHIBIT 16.2   FRO SERVICE PROFILE

Hospitals must be able to supply materials as their surgical and medical staffs require it, yet many items are expensive, their use is occasional, and their shelf life is limited, making hospital material management an expensive proposition. Despite the sensitive nature of hospital supply, many hospitals are investing in just-in-time resupply. One successful partnership is that between Littleton/Porter Hospital and Emery Medical Supply in Denver, Colorado. Emery supplies the hospital (and three others) twice daily, basing its deliveries on the hospital's twice-daily orders. Electronic data interchange (EDI) allows the hospital to place the orders electronically and enables Emery to generate pick lists for the required stock. All the stock, placed in small totes or small bags, is delivered directly to the supply lockers around the hospital, not to a central store. This includes supplies for the emergency room and the same-day surgery center, both areas of high variability in supply usage. The hospital still has a central storage area, but it is for emergency supplies only, with a total content value of about $10,000. And the hospital was able to sell back to Emery stock that was beyond its requirements.

The move has resulted in area, inventory, and personnel savings for Littleton/Porter. Costs have increased for Emery, for the firm now operates from 4 a.m. to 9 p.m. daily, not the previous 8 a.m. to 5 p.m. Overall, the cost savings to the hospital are projected to be around 10 percent annually.

16.1 MANAGERIAL ORIENTATION

This book has discussed many North American companies (see Exhibits 16.1 and 16.2) that have been pressured to increase the quality of their products while lowering product costs and increasing the speed with which customer orders are filled. To meet these challenges, firms are examining new approaches to operations management. This chapter will present two relatively new yet widely used operations philosophies: **just-in-time** (JIT) and **synchronous operations**.

JIT focuses on the elimination of **waste** from all areas of the company. Synchronous operations concentrates on the effective management of **capacity-constrained resources**. Both can be viewed as alternatives to material requirements planning (MRP)[1] but are not incompatible with MRP. At the end of this chapter the three approaches will be compared and the way in which a fast-response organization (FRO) can draw on the strengths of all three approaches will be discussed.

16.2 THE JUST-IN-TIME (JIT) PHILOSOPHY

DEFINITION: Just-in-time is an operations philosophy based on continuous improvements in and elimination of waste from all areas of a company.

The goal of JIT is to produce only the necessary item in the necessary quantity at the necessary time. Achieving this goal can radically increase the responsiveness of a company to the demands of its customers and improve its ability to compete on cost, quality, dependability, flexibility, and time.

The concept of having parts and raw materials flow into the production process as they are needed is not new. Henry Ford constructed his assembly lines in the 1920s with this idea in mind; it is also the intent of MRP systems. However, the JIT philosophy involves more than the timing of materials flow.

The JIT philosophy was pioneered by Toyota Motor Company and forms one of the cornerstones of the **Toyota production system.** This system became the focus of attention in Japan in the early 1970s, when the company was able to generate huge profits while other Japanese firms, faced with the same skyrocketing fuel and raw material costs, sustained substantial losses. Companies around the world have since adapted Toyota's ideas.

The evolution of the Toyota production system is shown in Exhibit 16.3. The intent of this system was to develop a process that could economically produce a wide variety of automobiles in small volumes.[2]

Note how Toyota has attacked different types of waste: time and money spent to produce products not demanded by its customers, switching from one product to another, storing items, reworking (or even discarding) poor-quality products, equipment failures, and the like. Let us examine the principles used by Toyota to improve its productivity and the quality of its products.

Reduce the Economic Batch Size by Reducing Equipment Setup Times

Toyota started to implement its JIT system by drastically reducing the time needed to switch from one product (or part) to another. The discussion of the

---

[1] Chapter 15 has a detailed review of MRP.

[2] Toyota has achieved economies of integration (the simultaneous presence of both economies of scale and economies of scope) and is able to compete on service as well as cost, quality, dependability, flexibility, and time. Refer to Chapter 9 for a review of economies of scale, scope, and integration.

EXHIBIT 16.3 THE EVOLUTION OF THE TOYOTA PRODUCTION SYSTEM

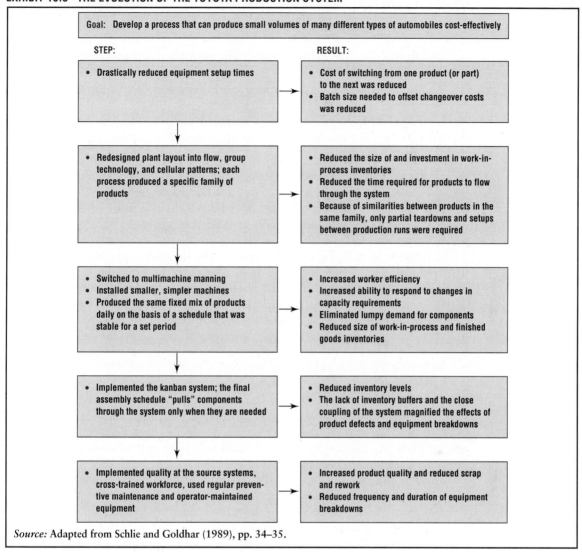

Goal: Develop a process that can produce small volumes of many different types of automobiles cost-effectively

STEP:

- Drastically reduced equipment setup times

RESULT:

- Cost of switching from one product (or part) to the next was reduced
- Batch size needed to offset changeover costs was reduced

STEP:

- Redesigned plant layout into flow, group technology, and cellular patterns; each process produced a specific family of products

RESULT:

- Reduced the size of and investment in work-in-process inventories
- Reduced the time required for products to flow through the system
- Because of similarities between products in the same family, only partial teardowns and setups between production runs were required

STEP:

- Switched to multimachine manning
- Installed smaller, simpler machines
- Produced the same fixed mix of products daily on the basis of a schedule that was stable for a set period

RESULT:

- Increased worker efficiency
- Increased ability to respond to changes in capacity requirements
- Eliminated lumpy demand for components
- Reduced size of work-in-process and finished goods inventories

STEP:

- Implemented the kanban system; the final assembly schedule "pulls" components through the system only when they are needed

RESULT:

- Reduced inventory levels
- The lack of inventory buffers and the close coupling of the system magnified the effects of product defects and equipment breakdowns

STEP:

- Implemented quality at the source systems, cross-trained workforce, used regular preventive maintenance and operator-maintained equipment

RESULT:

- Increased product quality and reduced scrap and rework
- Reduced frequency and duration of equipment breakdowns

Source: Adapted from Schlie and Goldhar (1989), pp. 34–35.

economic order quantity or batch size in Chapter 11 stated that the EOQ balances the cost of inventory with the cost of setting up the production process. *The lower the setup costs, the lower the EOQ.*[3]

Setup times at Toyota are often a small fraction of what they have been tradi-

[3] Suppose that the annual demand (D) is 10,000 units and the inventory holding cost for one unit for one year (H) is $100. The setup cost ($S$) is $40, because it takes one operator four hours to set up the process and the operator is paid $10 per hour.

$$EOQ = \sqrt{\frac{2DS}{H}} = \sqrt{\frac{(2)(10,000)(40)}{100}} = 89.44$$

If the setup time is reduced to one hour, the setup cost falls to $10 and the EOQ drops to 45 units:

$$EOQ = \sqrt{\frac{(2)(10,000)(10)}{100}} = 44.72$$

tionally in American and European automobile companies. The goal at Toyota is **single-digit setup times,** or setups less than 10 minutes long. Setup times can be reduced in a number of ways:

- Modifications can be made to reduce the need for time-consuming adjustments to a machine and its tooling.
- Modifications can be made to allow more setup actions to be performed while the machine is processing the previous batch.
- The fastest setup routine can be documented and posted on the wall.
- Workers can be given an opportunity to practice and improve setups.

Lowering setup times and costs enables a firm to economically reduce batch sizes; this results in substantially reduced cycle inventories and increased system throughput.[4] Short lead times allow a firm to use actual rather than forecast demand for its detailed production scheduling. This increased certainty results in lower finished goods inventories. Maintaining excess capacity also enables a firm to meet unexpected surges in demand without stockpiling substantial inventories.

In addition to reducing cycle inventories, the JIT philosophy advocates continually reducing buffer inventories *bit by bit*. This exposes problems which can then be attacked and eliminated. Product quality increases while inventory investment decreases. As the firm reduces its need for inventory, its ability to compete and satisfy customers improves. Reducing inventory levels to zero, however, is not the ultimate objective. In many cases small amounts of inventory are necessary and beneficial.

Redesign the Plant Layout and Increase Process Flexibility

Redesigning a plant into product or group technology (cellular) layouts[5] also leads to lower inventory levels and faster system throughput. Similarities between products in the same family mean that only partial teardowns and setups are needed between production runs. Once work on a product is begun, that product moves quickly from one machine to the next in the cell. Very little work-in-process (WIP) inventory accumulates between the machines.

Cross-training the workforce and establishing **U-form cells** increase the flexibility of the system; the production level can be changed easily in response to changes in demand by increasing or decreasing the number of workers assigned to each combination of cells. Exhibit 16.4 illustrates how three U-form cells can be combined into one unit and how the number of workers can be varied.

Small, simple machines allow a firm to increase or decrease its capacity in very small chunks.

Use a Pull System on the Shop Floor and Smooth Production Requirements

To ensure that only the products demanded by the customer are produced, a final assembly schedule that is based on customer orders "pulls" components through the production process.

Push versus Pull Systems   It is important to understand what is meant by the pull system and, by implication, the push system of shop floor control. Although the techniques of shop floor control are discussed in Chapter 17, it is appropriate to deal

---

[4] Exhibit 13.19 illustrates how smaller batch sizes led to smaller cycle inventories and increased system throughput.

[5] Chapter 9 provides a detailed description of various layout patterns.

EXHIBIT 16.4 TOOLBOX: INCREASING OUTPUT IN A PRODUCTION LINE

The production lines shown below for product families A, B, and C are group technology layouts and are referred to as U-form lines. The first and last operations in each line are located beside each other. These operations are usually performed by the same person.

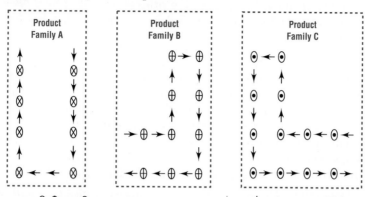

Legend: ⊗, ⊕, and ⊙ are machines   →, ←, ↑, and ↓ indicate the operating flow

This layout allows the firm to vary the number of people working on the line. In the first diagram below five workers are assigned to the three production lines. In the second diagram one more worker has been assigned to the lines. Increasing the number of workers increases the capacity of the process.

LAYOUT 1: FIVE WORKERS

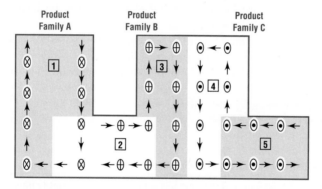

LAYOUT 2: SIX WORKERS

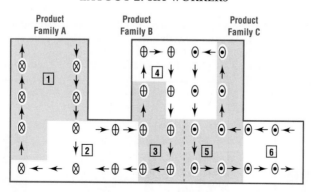

Source: Adapted from Monden (1983), pp. 106–107.

with the philosophies of the two systems here. It is also necessary to understand the circumstances in which each system is preferable. Let us begin with the traditional push system.

> **DEFINITION:** In a production process controlled by a *push* system, items are produced at times specified by a schedule that has been prepared in advance.[6]

Push systems are driven by the release of the necessary instructions to make the components of a product and to assemble the components until the product is completed. As a work center completes its task on a piece, that piece is "pushed" into the work center that will work on it next. Push systems are often viewed as synonymous with MRP systems; they are also used with the synchronous operations systems that will be described later in this chapter and in manually scheduled job shops and batch operations. Exhibit 16.5 illustrates a push system; the barbecue production schedule given to Sue is the driving force that pushes production.

> **DEFINITION:** In a production process controlled by a *pull* system, an item is produced only when a signal is received from its user.[7]

Pull systems, which are often viewed as synonymous with JIT operations, are fundamentally different from push systems. The assembly line in Exhibit 16.5 has been converted to a pull system in Exhibit 16.6. The driving force in the system is no longer the production schedule developed by the host; it is now the guests removing the food from the buffet table.

In practice, a final assembly schedule that is based on customer orders pulls parts and products through the production process. Only the last work center in the process is given a copy of the final assembly schedule. That center signals its require-

[6] See *APICS Dictionary* (1992), p. 40.
[7] See *APICS Dictionary* (1992), p. 40.

EXHIBIT 16.5   A SIMPLE EXAMPLE OF A PUSH SYSTEM

Suppose you are at a backyard barbecue and the host has set up a simple assembly line. Sue is grilling hamburgers and hot dogs, Brian is assembling the hamburgers and hot dogs, and Chris is spooning out salad. Sixty guests have been invited.

The host has asked Sue to begin barbecuing at six-thirty. Batches of six hamburgers and six hot dogs are to be alternated, starting with hamburgers. As soon as each batch is ready, Brian puts each hamburger or hot dog in a bun and onto a plate. Once Brian has finished, Chris adds salad to the plate. Half the plates get coleslaw, and the other half get potato salad. After all six plates have salad, Chris carries them to the buffet table.

EXHIBIT 16.6 A SIMPLE EXAMPLE OF A PULL SYSTEM

What changes if an assembly line is converted to a pull system in Exhibit 16.5? A small, predetermined amount of inventory is kept before each operation on the buffet table. Suppose someone takes a hamburger and potato salad plate from the table. The following chain of events occurs:

- Chris takes another hamburger and potato salad plate to the buffet table.
- Chris takes a hamburger plate from Brian's inventory area, adds potato salad, and puts the completed plate in his own inventory area.
- Chris asks Brian to make another hamburger plate.
- Brian takes a hamburger from Sue's inventory area, puts the burger in the bun, puts the bun on the plate, and puts the plate in his own inventory area.
- Brian asks Sue to make another hamburger.
- Sue moves a hamburger to the warming rack and puts another hamburger patty on the grill.

The people eating the food are the driving force in this system.

---

ments to the preceding work centers and so on back through the process, using cards (also called **kanbans**[8]), empty containers, or empty squares taped to the floor.

Unlike a push system, production schedules for each work center are not issued. Daily reports that compare actual performance with planned performance are also not required.

The need for fewer production schedules and production reports is only one of the benefits of a pull system. Firms that have switched from a push system to a pull system have reported significant reductions in inventory costs, production costs, and production lead times. At the same time, product quality and customer responsiveness have improved.

The potential benefits of a pull system are very attractive, but many firms do not use such a system. In North America many companies are moving toward a pull system, but creating the required environment often takes years. Also, in some cases it is almost impossible to provide all the prerequisites for a pull system. Consider the major system prerequisites listed below:

- The risk of equipment failures must be very low.
- The quality of the parts and components produced by the system must be very high.
- To produce very small batches economically, equipment setup times must be extremely short.
- The quality of raw materials and purchased parts must be very high. Suppliers must be able to deliver items in very small quantities just before they are needed. This calls for close relationships with suppliers.

Production Smoothing When a variety of products are made with the same process, each product usually has similar but not identical resource requirements. Some product models may require extra time at a particular work center or may require special materials. If large quantities are required infrequently, the demand for some resources and materials will be lumpy. Lumpy demand violates the prerequisites of smoothed production.

The consequences of lumpy component demand are severe because a pull system is a reactive system. If a subsequent work center withdraws parts in fluctuating

---

[8] *Kanban* is the Japanese word for "card."

quantities and rates, the work center must hold large quantities of WIP inventory for each part to meet demand peaks. The magnitude of these fluctuations increases as they filter back through the system.

If large WIP inventories are not held, whenever demand exceeds supply at a work center, production soon stops at the subsequent centers. Thus, to minimize WIP inventories and work center idle time, the final assembly schedule must be carefully prepared and smoothed.

How is **production smoothing** done? The answer varies from one situation to another and from one company to the next. Toyota, for example, does this in two ways. First, the quantity to be produced of each product model is the same from one day to the next during the frozen portion of the final assembly schedule. Second, the models are made in very small batches and the same sequence of models is produced repeatedly throughout the day. The sequence is developed by a heuristic computer program which attempts to level work center requirements as much as possible.

Suppose an operating process builds three products. Next week 1,200 units of A, 600 units of B, and 200 units of C must be produced. Thus, in a five-day week 240 units of A, 120 units of B, and 40 units of C must be built daily. Suppose engineering studies show that the best sequence is AA-B-AA-B-AA-B-C. If it takes 12 minutes to produce each sequence set, five sets will be made each hour. The daily production requirements will be met in eight hours.

The unchanging production pattern provides the certainty that suppliers need to time their deliveries properly, but the production sequence is valid only for the frozen portion of the final assembly schedule. In the next period the sequence may be different. Toyota started with a six-week frozen schedule. In at least two of its Japanese plants Toyota is now offering customers five-day guaranteed delivery of vehicles with their specified options. In fact, the production cycle time in these plants is less than two days and the plants routinely schedule every day for the following two days.

Increase Process Quality and Dependability

This chapter has mentioned several ways in which WIP inventories can and should be lowered. There is a danger, however, associated with holding very low WIP inventories. The system is so tightly coupled that a problem at one work center affects subsequent work centers very quickly. This danger is minimized when the firm detects and solves problems as soon as possible and prevents problems from occurring in the first place. This can be accomplished with the following tools and strategies.[9]

- **Foolproof mechanisms (poka-yoke)** that make it impossible to perform an operation incorrectly.
- Automated and manual mechanisms that prevent the continued production of defective work (**autonomation**). An autonomous machine has a stopping device attached to it which prevents a large number of defects from being produced and checks machine breakdowns. With more manual systems workers can push a button to signal for help or even stop the line.
- **Housekeeping practices** that lead to early problem identification and prevention. Clean floors and equipment surfaces, for example, expose problems such as oil leaks and cracks quickly. They also reduce the risk of personal injury.

[9] Chapter 11 provides a detailed review of these tools and strategies.

- Transferring the primary responsibility for equipment maintenance to the operators and implementing other elements of a **total productive maintenance** program.

Because defects are spotted almost immediately and can easily be traced back to their source, the consequences of poor-quality work are visible very quickly in a closely coupled operation. Thus, workers in a JIT environment are more aware of the importance of their work and are motivated to avoid errors and improve their performance. This increased sense of commitment and responsibility has led workers in many Japanese firms to create quality circles.

Improve Supplier Relationships

In addition to a dependable production process, JIT calls for dependable suppliers. Poor-quality materials and components will disrupt the production process, as will late deliveries.

The supplier must be able to make frequent deliveries of small quantities of items at the correct time. This means that the firm must share production planning information with the supplier.

Frequent deliveries and small lot sizes often necessitate changes in the way a supplier operates, and the supplier may need managerial support from the firm. The supplier may even change location to be closer to the firm.

In short, supply decisions, the choice of suppliers, and supplier partnering are important considerations for FROs. A successful JIT system entails a long-term relationship with suppliers.

Implementing a JIT System

Regardless of the manufacturing or service focus of an operation, the JIT production philosophy cannot be implemented overnight. It took Toyota more than 20 years to develop the JIT system, and most firms need years of continuous improvements before they can successfully implement a JIT system suitable to their own operations. Some of the changes a firm must make to its operations are outlined below:

- Management must be supportive of the JIT philosophy. This includes a willingness to delegate more responsibility and authority to shop floor workers.
- A spirit of cooperation between management and the workers must be achieved and maintained. The need for flexible workers may reduce the number of worker classifications. Reward systems may have to be restructured.
- The facility layout must accommodate JIT deliveries. The way in which people and their equipment are arranged must be modified to accommodate a pull system. Machines must be flexible enough to produce several different products, and workers must be able to perform a variety of tasks.
- The time required to change over from one job to the next must be reduced drastically to make small batch sizes feasible.
- Machine reliability must be very high. Preventive maintenance is very important.
- Changes in product design may be needed, such as increased use of standardized parts.
- Suitable suppliers must be found, and a close relationship must be developed.

Implementing a JIT system calls for continued improvements to the process and the way in which workers and management interact and deal with each other and the operating process.

EXHIBIT 16.7   THE INTERLOCKING ELEMENTS OF JIT

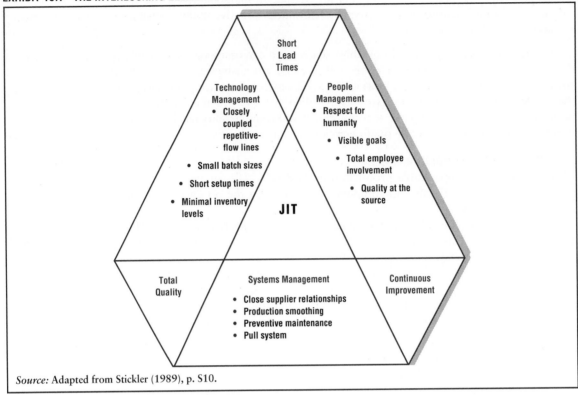

Source: Adapted from Stickler (1989), p. S10.

The interlocking elements of JIT are illustrated in Exhibit 16.7. Implementing some or all of these elements has enabled North American firms to realize substantial benefits, including higher-quality products, lower production costs, and improved market responsiveness. Harley-Davidson (Exhibit 16.8), for example, has adapted many JIT concepts to its own operations in its materials as needed (MAN) program.[10]

The Hytrol Conveyor Company, Inc., is another firm that has benefited from a partial implementation of JIT concepts. An important part of its marketing strategy is delivery within 24 hours of any of its 50 different conveyor belt models, which are available in over 2,200 sizes. Hence, unlike Toyota, Hytrol retains a relatively large finished goods inventory. However, since the early 1970s the firm has implemented JIT concepts such as drastically reducing setup times and cross-training workers. These improvements have contributed significantly to Hytrol's success.

Not all attempts to implement JIT, however, have been successful. The failure of JIT in some firms can be traced to the "romanticized" vision of the system in the popular American literature [Zipken (1991)]. Senior managers who are far removed from the shop floor fail to acknowledge the breadth of changes required to implement JIT and the time required to make those changes. Firms that take a more pragmatic approach and prepare thoroughly before slowly and carefully implementing JIT principles fare much better than do their romantic counterparts. It is important to

[10] IBM's version of JIT is called *continuous-flow manufacturing (CFM)*. Motorola has dubbed its version *inventory productivity process (IPP)*.

EXHIBIT 16.8 JIT AT HARLEY-DAVIDSON

Known for quality, durability, and value, Harley-Davidson once controlled the market for large-displacement motorcycles worldwide. Yet like many other North American companies, Harley-Davidson failed to react to economic and social changes. Even with its new, modernized plant in York, Pennsylvania, the firm continued to lose market share to Japanese competitors that could provide higher-quality motorcycles at competitive prices.

By 1982 staggering losses had put Harley-Davidson's survival in question. Poor parts control meant that production was based on part availability rather than the master schedule. Fewer than 70 percent of the motorcycles produced on the assembly line came off complete. Overtime was a way of life. These conditions prompted the firm to adopt a JIT approach.

After studying the JIT system at Toyota, Harley-Davidson implemented its own version, *materials as needed* (MAN). Quality was the primary goal. Accompanied by advanced manufacturing techniques such as statistical process control and a strong emphasis on employee involvement, Harley-Davidson's MAN program has turned the firm around. Inventory has been reduced by two-thirds, productivity has been increased by 50 percent, and the number of manufacturing errors and product defects has been lowered significantly.

Source: Adapted from Sepheri (1987), pp. 87–93.

recognize that the makeup of JIT systems may differ depending on the firm size and the type of process employed [see White (1993)].

An operating philosophy that draws on both JIT and MRP concepts is known as the synchronous operations philosophy.

16.3 THE SYNCHRONOUS OPERATIONS PHILOSOPHY

DEFINITION: Synchronous operations is a philosophy that emphasizes the importance of bottleneck resources and the need to focus the firm's efforts on maximizing their utilization [Goldratt and Cox (1992)].

The **synchronous operations philosophy** builds on Goldratt's theory of constraints and is reflected in his production planning and control software, optimized production technology (OPT).[11] This philosophy focuses on bottleneck and capacity-constrained resources.

DEFINITION: A bottleneck resource is a resource whose capacity is lower than the demand placed on it.

DEFINITION: A capacity-constrained resource is a resource whose capacity is just sufficient to meet the demand placed on it. If it is not scheduled carefully, a capacity-constrained resource can become a bottleneck.

Firms focus on bottlenecks and capacity-constrained resources because the capacity of the entire operating process is determined by the management of these resources. The objective of the synchronous operations philosophy is to increase the throughput of the operating process while reducing inventory levels and operating expenses.[12]

If bottleneck resources govern the system's throughput, why not just obtain additional resources? First, additional resources may be scarce or expensive or may

---

[11] OPT software is discussed in more detail in Chapter 17.

[12] *Throughput* is defined by Goldratt and Cox (1992) as the rate at which a firm generates money through sales. *Inventory* represents all the money the firm invests in purchasing things it intends to sell, while *operating expenses* are the funds spent to turn inventory into throughput.

take too long to incorporate into the operating process. Second, the bottleneck resource may shift as the product mix is modified because of differing resource requirements for each product.[13] Finally, as discussed below, additional capacity often can be squeezed out of a bottleneck resource quickly and inexpensively.

Basic Synchronous Operations Principles

This section will familiarize you with some of the basic principles of the synchronous operations philosophy. These principles are reflected in the nine rules of synchronous operations summarized in Exhibit 16.9.

Principle 1. Let the bottleneck resource or resources set the production pace.

When the capacity of each work center varies, work-in-process (WIP) inventories often accumulate in front of some work centers. Goldratt and Cox suggest that these inventories can be reduced by balancing the flow of work through the process, with the bottleneck resource setting the production pace. Balancing the flow of work rather than fully utilizing the capacity of each work center is the first rule of synchronous operations.

Bottleneck resources are scheduled by the OPT software using market demands and a simple job priority system.[14] This ensures that the maximum amount of work flows through bottleneck resources. Since the bottlenecks determine the real capacity of the process, they must be as productive as possible. *An hour lost at a bottleneck is an hour lost for the total process.*

The schedules for the bottleneck work centers are then used to derive schedules for the succeeding work centers. The schedules for preceding work centers are developed by working backward from the bottleneck schedules. Work centers that do not feed a bottleneck or are not fed by a bottleneck are scheduled backward from the final assembly schedule.

Thus, the rate at which the first operation is allowed to release work to the process is dictated by the rate at which the bottlenecks can work.[15] Since work is

---

[13] Exhibit 9.6 shows how a bottleneck can shift.

[14] Bottleneck resources can be viewed as the drum that strikes the beat which the rest of the production process must follow. The production schedule is like a rope that synchronizes production: it prevents resources with excess capacity from starting jobs too early. Strategically placed WIP is the buffer which protects the productivity of bottleneck resources.

[15] The bottleneck operation drives preceding operations just as the final assembly schedule drives a production line that uses the kanban system.

EXHIBIT 16.9   THE NINE RULES OF SYNCHRONOUS OPERATIONS

1. Balance flow, not capacity.
2. The level of utilization of a nonbottleneck is determined not by its potential but by another constraint in the system.
3. The utilization and the activation of a resource are not synonymous.
4. An hour lost at a bottleneck is an hour lost for the total system.
5. An hour saved at a nonbottleneck is a mirage.
6. Bottlenecks govern both throughput and inventories.
7. The transfer batch may not, and often should not, be equal to the process batch.
8. The process batch should be variable, not fixed.
9. Schedules should be established by looking at all the constraints simultaneously. Lead times result from a schedule and cannot be predetermined.

Source: Goldratt and Cox (1992), p. 179.

never released just to keep workers or equipment busy, work centers that are not bottlenecks have idle time.

Principle 2. Use variable batch sizes to limit WIP inventories and system throughput.

WIP inventories are reduced by limiting the size of process batches at nonbottleneck work centers. As was discussed earlier in this chapter, small batch sizes keep the flow of materials smooth and balanced. Since nonbottleneck work centers have excess capacity, the additional setup time resulting from a larger number of batches does not affect the flow of work through the process. Goldratt and Cox (1992) claim that efforts to reduce setup times here are wasted, for "an hour saved at a nonbottleneck is just a mirage."

Throughput can also be increased by increasing the size of process batches at bottleneck work centers. By combining batches or selected portions of batches that require similar processing a firm can increase work center efficiency. The grouping of batches can be varied from one operation to the next and over time. Customer due dates, however, must be considered when a firm combines batches.

Principle 3. Focus on increasing the capacity of the bottleneck resource or resources.

A simple way to increase the capacity of a bottleneck work center is to ensure that it is always staffed, even during breaks and shift changes. Cross-training workers reduces the chance of idle time caused by employee absenteeism. Reducing setup time, improving the bottleneck process, and increasing preventive maintenance can increase the bottleneck's available processing time. Careful inspection of parts immediately before the bottleneck can prevent wasting valuable time processing defective parts.

Principle 4. Protect the productivity of bottleneck resources with strategically placed inventories.

Because bottleneck resources govern the output of the process, protecting their productivity is important. Goldratt and Cox (1992) suggest that buffer inventories be strategically placed at various points in the process. First, every bottleneck operation must have a buffer in front of it. This protects the bottleneck from any disruptions to the systems that lead to bottleneck idle time. Second, as shown in Exhibit 16.10, an inventory buffer must also be placed in front of every assembly operation that requires a part from a nonbottleneck operation. This protects the final assembly schedule by ensuring that there is not a shortage of parts that do not flow through a bottleneck resource.

The contents of these inventory buffers change constantly. For example, consider the daily schedule for the bottleneck work center in Exhibit 16.11. Suppose the firm has chosen to maintain a two-day buffer inventory in front of this work center. The planned buffer contents on Monday morning, therefore, are composed of the work that this work center is scheduled to perform on Monday and Tuesday. By Tuesday morning the buffer should no longer include the work scheduled for Monday. Instead, it should include the work scheduled for Tuesday and Wednesday.

Principle 5. Use the actual contents of inventory buffers to direct continuous improvement efforts.

EXHIBIT 16.10   SYNCHRONOUS OPERATIONS: INVENTORY PLACEMENT

In the following production process the product is composed of three parts which are assembled at the last work center.

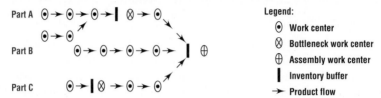

Legend:
- ⊙ Work center
- ⊗ Bottleneck work center
- ⊕ Assembly work center
- ▎ Inventory buffer
- → Product flow

Inventory buffers are strategically located in front of all bottleneck work centers. The final assembly work center is also protected with a buffer of parts that do not flow through any bottleneck work centers, that is, an inventory of part B.

Source: Adapted from Goldratt and Cox (1992), p. 103.

The actual contents of a buffer can help identify areas that will benefit the entire system the most if they are improved. For example, if the actual buffer is less than the planned buffer—for example, only half the 17 part B's have arrived—the firm knows that a disruption has occurred: there is a problem at an upstream work center. Severe disruptions may result in some jobs being expedited. The more severe the impact is, the more important it is to eliminate the source of the problem. Thus, the buffer contents act as an alarm that draws attention to urgent problems and directs the focus of the continuous improvement program. Compared with lengthy reports that list deviations from planned production, buffer contents can be analyzed quickly and easily.

If more items are found in the buffer than had been expected—for example, part E's are found in Monday's buffer—then work is being released to the initial work centers too early. If the actual buffer contents usually contain less than the planned contents and if the bottleneck becomes starved for work, the buffer should be increased. However, as improvements to the system are implemented, fewer disruptions occur and the firm can reduce the size of the buffer. The smaller the buffer, the shorter the production lead time.

Implementing a Synchronous Operations System

Implementing a synchronous operations system involves more than spending a few months installing the OPT software and placing strategic inventory buffers at various points in the process. Process improvements, changes in the product mix, and changes in the marketplace may cause bottlenecks to move; this means that the way in which the shop is run has to change. Successful implementaton requires a change in management style as well as in performance measures and reward systems. For example, workers and machines will have, and should have, idle periods throughout the day. Thus, measuring and rewarding schedule attainment rather than machine or labor utilization makes sense.

The way in which product mix decisions are made is also affected. As demonstrated in Exhibit 16.12, the most profitable product mix is the one which makes the most profitable use of bottleneck resources.

The weaknesses of synchronous operations include the high cost of the OPT software and the difficulty of making delivery promises. Since lead times are variable, the only way to determine whether a due date can be met is by simulating a schedule.

EXHIBIT 16.11   SYNCHRONOUS OPERATIONS: BUFFER CONTENTS

Westlake Ltd. has one bottleneck work center. Next week's schedule for that work center is shown below.

Day	Part to Be Processed at Bottleneck	Quantity	Hours Required at Bottleneck
Monday	A	10	5.25
	D	4	2.25
Tuesday	D	6	3.00
	B	17	4.50
Wednesday	B	3	0.75
	E	10	2.25
	C	17	4.50
Thursday	C	4	1.00
	A	5	2.75
	D	7	3.75
Friday	B	10	2.75
	E	15	4.00
	C	2	0.75

To ensure that the bottleneck work center has no unplanned idle time, an inventory buffer has been placed in front of it. The buffer should contain the work scheduled for the bottleneck on the current day and the work scheduled for the next day. The expected buffer contents for Monday, Tuesday, and Wednesday are:

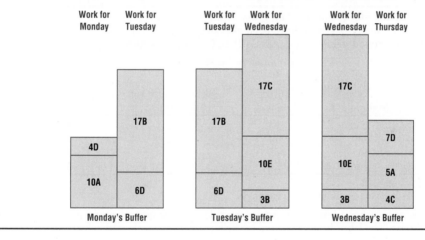

Variable lead times also complicate purchasing if certain raw materials or components have particularly long purchasing lead times.

16.4 MRP, JIT, OR SYNCHRONOUS OPERATIONS: WHICH IS BEST?

MRP, JIT, and synchronous operations. Which approach to inventory planning and control is best for a fast-response organization (FRO)? Unfortunately, there is no best approach. Although these systems differ significantly and have been compared extensively, their underlying philosophies are not mutually exclusive. Nor are they the only three possible approaches.

The key features of MRP, JIT, and synchronous operations are summarized in Exhibit 16.13. Note that all three systems are meant to reduce WIP inventory levels, lower costs, and reduce cumulative production lead times.

Also note that each system has been developed for a specific operating environment. MRP and synchronous operations have been designed to manage intermittent-flow shops, while JIT's kanban system works best in repetitive-flow shops. Stories of companies moving from an MRP system to a kanban system are common today, but this does not represent the only natural progression. Some companies that use the kanban system are moving in the opposite direction as they broaden their product lines and produce made-to-order products. Wherever its process lies on the continuum of operating environments, however, an FRO can derive significant benefits by adapting concepts from each of the three approaches to its production planning and inventory control system.

As the range of products offered by a firm increases and the life span of each product decreases, the firm's operating environment tends to become more complex. The more complex the operating environment is, the more complex the control systems must be.

MRP and MRPII are complex computer-based systems designed to handle the large number of products, components, and materials in intermittent- and repetitive-flow shops. Since an MRP system can plan for, not just react to, schedule changes, it can be valuable as a central planning tool. At the operational level it can monitor

---

EXHIBIT 16.12 TOOLBOX: SELECTING THE PRODUCT MIX

Suppose a firm can produce four products. The gross profit associated with each product is shown below. Although direct labor and factory overhead have been allocated on a per unit basis, these costs are essentially fixed for the next planning period. Direct labor costs will be $69,100, and factory overhead will be $207,300.

(1) Product	(2) Sales Price, $	*Manufacturing Costs*			(6) Gross Contribution, $	(7) Gross Profit, $
		(3) Raw Materials, $	(4) Direct Labor, $	(5) Factory Overhead Allocation, $		
A	300	60	54	162	240	24
B	375	211	34	102	164	28
C	325	115	45	135	210	30
D	350	215	25	75	135	35

Column 6 = column 2 − column 3.
Column 7 = column 2 − (column 3 + column 4 + column 5).

Suppose the operating process has a bottleneck work center. During the next planning period this work center has 2,800 available hours. The labor hours required by each product at this bottleneck are shown below.

(1) Product	(2) Forecasted Demand, units	*Labor Hours at Bottleneck*	
		(3) Per Unit	(4) Total
A	500	1.7	850
B	400	1.4	560
C	300	2.1	630
D	600	2.2	1,320
			3,360

Column 4 = column 2 × column 3.

PRODUCT MIX BASED ON THE TRADITIONAL COST ACCOUNTING METHOD

The traditional cost accounting method advocates the selection of product mixes on the basis of per unit *gross profit*, or contribution to general overhead expenses. In this case, since product D has the highest gross profit, as many units of D should be produced as possible, followed by the maximum number of product C, then B, and then finally A.

Product	Forecast Demand	Hours Available at Bottleneck	Quantity Selected	Bottleneck Hours Required
D	600	2,800	600	600 × 2.2 = 1,320
C	300	2,800 − 1,320 = 1,480	300	300 × 2.1 = 630
B	400	1,480 − 630 = 850	400	400 × 1.4 = 560
A	500	850 − 560 = 290	170	170 × 1.7 = 289

Therefore, 600 units of D, 300 units of C, 400 units of B, and 170 units of A should be produced.

PRODUCT MIX BASED ON SYNCHRONOUS OPERATIONS

An alternative method advocated by the synchronous operations philosophy selects the product mix on the basis of *gross contributions per bottleneck unit.* This system recognizes the fact that direct labor and factory overhead are essentially fixed for the next planning period.

(1) Product	(2) Gross Contribution per Unit, $	(3) Labor Hours at Bottleneck per Unit	(4) Gross Contribution per Bottleneck Hour, $
A	240	1.7	141.18
B	164	1.4	117.14
C	210	2.1	100.00
D	135	2.2	61.36

Column 4 = column 2 ÷ column 3.

Since product A has the highest contribution per bottleneck hour, as many units of A should be produced as possible. The firm should then produce the maximum number of product B, then C, and finally D.

Product	Forecast Demand	Hours Available at Bottleneck	Quantity Selected	Bottleneck Hours Required
A	500	2,800	500	500 × 1.7 = 850
B	400	2,800 − 850 = 1,950	400	400 × 1.4 = 560
C	300	1,950 − 560 = 1,390	300	300 × 2.1 = 630
D	600	1,390 − 630 = 760	345	345 × 2.2 = 759

Therefore, the firm should produce 500 units of product A, 400 units of product B, 300 units of product C, and only 345 units of product D.

The profit (before interest and taxes) associated with each product is shown on the statement below. Note that the cost accounting method resulted in a loss of $26,000 but the alternative method generated a profit of $18,775.

	Traditional Cost Accounting Method		Synchronous Operations Method	
Sales revenue				
Product A	$ 51,000		$150,000	
Product B	150,000		150,000	
Product C	97,500		97,500	
Product D	210,000		120,750	
Total		$508,500		$518,250
Manufacturing costs				
Raw materials				
Product A	$ 10,200		$ 30,000	
Product B	84,400		84,400	
Product C	34,500		34,500	
Product D	129,000		74,175	
Direct labor	69,100		69,100	
Factory overhead	207,300		207,300	
Total		$534,500		$499,475
Profit (Loss)		($26,000)		$ 18,775

EXHIBIT 16.13   A COMPARISON OF MRP, JIT, AND SYNCHRONOUS MANUFACTURING

Material Requirements Planning (MRP)	Just-in-Time (JIT)	Synchronous Operations
Focus		
• Improved production planning and control	• Elimination of all waste	• Increased throughput and reduced inventory and operating expenses
Intended Operating Environment		
• Intermittent- or repetitive-flow processes	• Repetitive-flow processes*	• Intermittent- and repetitive-flow processes
Key Features		
Reduces inventory by supplying only what is needed when it is needed		
• Generates planned order releases based on the master production schedule, BOMs, and standard lead times • Complex, computer-based system with rich databases	• Reduces inventory by decreasing batch sizes and equipment setup times • Emphasis on continuous improvements, total quality control, and active employee involvement	• Emphasizes 100 percent utilization of bottleneck resources • Reduces inventory by limiting output of all resources to bottleneck capacity and using variable batch sizes
Scheduling Capabilities		
• Yields a production plan that may not be feasible and is time-consuming to produce • Scheduling on the shop floor is required • Is a push system	• Shop floor activity is not scheduled directly but is activated by a pull system such as kanban • Manual system • Level daily production schedule	• OPT software generates a detailed, feasible schedule quickly • Uses both push and pull
Implementation		
• Requires vast amounts of accurate data • Requires expensive software and hardware • Average total installation time: 5 years	• Requires reorganization of the shop floor, setup time reductions, very reliable processes • Average total installation time: 5 to 10 years	• Modest data requirements • OPT software is expensive but can be installed in a relatively short time; organizational changes (e.g., changes in performance measures, reward systems, cost accounting systems) may take much longer

* JIT concepts have been applied successfully to processes that have been traditionally intermittent flow, effectively transforming them into repetitive-flow processes.

operating processes and inventory levels and ensure that the correct materials and components are available when required. When demand is not smooth and lead times are long, this capability is essential.

Advanced planning is also required for new production introductions, a new model mix, major product improvements, new processes, and new facilities. MRPII systems can support advanced planning for these events as well. Since MRPII systems link many of a firm's information systems and provide a common database, they can be instrumental in the firm's efforts to integrate its functional areas. When the MRPII system is used, each functional area can assess and share up-to-date accurate data. The integration of information is a key prerequisite for internal integration.

As was discussed in Chapter 15, the key weaknesses of MRP systems include inflexibility, lack of natural incentives to reduce lead times, and inability to consider capacity limitations directly. Many of these weaknesses can be minimized by introducing JIT concepts to reduce lead times and simplify operations. Consider the following examples:

- Introducing shop floor incentives to reduce setup times and costs will reduce batch sizes and ultimately production lead times.
- The use of modular design concepts will decrease the total number of parts required and increase the number of standardized components. Group technology layouts can then replace some or all process layouts. This reduces the number of possible product routings and simplifies scheduling.
- Increasing maintenance efforts will prolong machine life, increase machine dependability, and minimize disruptions on the shop floor.

Simplifying job-shop processes will reduce the complexity of managing the process and may make an MRP system feasible. Simplifying intermittent-flow processes can result in a process that more closely resembles a repetitive-flow process. In these cases a **hybrid MRPII/kanban system** can be implemented.

It is common for companies to implement either MRPII or kanban material control. However, neither approach alone adequately addresses the more complex needs of an FRO and the requirement for better service, greater product variety, and increased productivity. The operations solution to this problem is the mixed model (hybrid system) of operations flow control that combines the strength of MRPII and kanban [see Samitt and Barry (1993)].

In an MRPII/kanban hybrid system, many of the shop floor control functions are managed by the simple kanban pull system while MRPII handles higher-level planning and control tasks. If implemented properly, such a system can provide the best of both worlds.[16]

Planned order releases and dispatch lists are still used for the intermittent-flow portions of the process, and as before, inventory records are updated after each operation. To derive the greatest benefit from drastically reduced setup times, MRP time buckets are often changed from weekly to daily periods.[17]

The repetitive-flow operations in the hybrid environment are driven by the pull signals that originate from the final assembly schedule. Inventory transactions are posted only after the product passes through its final assembly stage. At this point the bill of material is exploded to determine the quantity of materials and components used. Inventory levels are then reduced accordingly. This process is referred to as *backflushing,* and it eliminates a major shop floor data collection task. Bar coding is sometimes used to track customer orders.

Closer relationships with vendors, another JIT concept, can lessen supply uncertainties in all operating environments, reducing lead times and inventory levels. Obviously, a program of continuous improvements and waste reduction can also benefit any type of operation, as can more cooperative relationships between the workforce and management.

---

[16] See Sharma (1993), Karmarker (1989), and Flapper and associates (1991) for additional information on hybrid systems and their implementation.

[17] As setup times and costs are reduced, producing only what is required during the period becomes the best alternative. Suppose 100 units of a part are needed on Monday, Wednesday, and Friday. If weekly time buckets are used, the lot size is 300 and inventory accumulates during the week. The firm can avoid this accumulation by producing batches of 100 units on Monday, Wednesday, and Friday. Since setup times and costs are negligible, smaller batch sizes and daily time buckets are more advantageous.

Hybrid systems can also take advantage of synchronous operations principles. One of their most valuable contributions can be directing continuous improvement efforts to areas in which the system can benefit the most. Synchronous operations emphasizes another management concept important to all firms: Although the role of a manager is to improve the area under his or her control, the goal should be to optimize the performance of the system as a whole. A machine operating at peak efficiency is not contributing to the firm's success if it is producing items in the wrong amounts or at the wrong times.

MANAGERIAL IMPLICATIONS

The aim of all operations managers is to integrate their operations with the rest of the organization and the rest of the value chain as efficiently as possible. There are two basic approaches to this challenge. One is to eliminate all uncertainty and variability, making the integration relatively straightforward. The second is to develop complicated information processing systems capable of handling the complex, information-intense "real world," where change in the internal and external environments is expected to happen constantly. In reality, neither pure form is capable of supporting operations of all types and at all times. Thus the JIT system introduced by Toyota in the 1970s has been modified to let more uncertainty from the external environment affect it, and OPT has been introduced to provide a less information-intensive yet flexible computer-based integration system. Signif-

icantly, each system has scenarios in which it operates better than does the other system.

This is the most important implication for managers. Each operation requires some means of planning and controlling worker attention, and the system chosen must be able to handle the complexities managers have decided to allow the operating system to encounter. The level of complexity depends on the corporate strategy. Of course, this level may change over the course of a year and will definitely change over the life of the products and the firm. Some form of combined or hybrid system may therefore be called for in many firms. Remember, though, that the system must first be effective, and this probably means holding inventory until the firm gets good enough to eliminate all but the essential minimum.

CHAPTER SUMMARY

Two relatively new operations philosophies were presented in this chapter: just-in-time (JIT) and synchronous operations.

The goal of JIT is to produce only the necessary items in the necessary quantities at the necessary time. Any deviations constitute waste; waste elimination lies at the heart of the JIT philosophy. Ways in which waste can be reduced include the following:

- Reduce WIP inventory levels and increase the speed with which products flow through the process by using very small batch sizes and arranging the process into group technology cells. Economic batch sizes can be lowered by reducing equipment setup times.
- Reduce the buffer inventories by a small amount to expose problems with the process. Correct the problem and then lower buffer inventories again. Continue this process. This increases process dependability and product quality.
- Cross-train workers and establish U-form cells to increase the flexibility of the system.

- Develop a final assembly schedule that is based on customer demand and let this schedule pull work through the production process. This helps ensure that the right products are produced at the right time.
- Lower WIP inventories by smoothing production requirements.
- Increase the dependability of the process by actively involving all workers in process improvement efforts, utilizing autonomation, and training workers to perform daily maintenance work on their machines.
- Increase product quality by encouraging quality at the source and working closely with suppliers.

The synchronous operations philosophy emphasizes the importance of bottleneck resources and the need to focus a firm's efforts on maximizing their utilization. WIP inventories and process throughput can be increased by doing the following:

- Letting bottleneck resources set the production pace
- Using variable batch sizes
- Increasing the capacity of bottleneck resources
- Protecting the productivity of bottleneck resources with strategically placed inventories
- Using the contents of buffer inventories to direct continuous improvement efforts

JIT and synchronous operations are sometimes viewed as alternatives to material requirements planning systems, but the three approaches are not incompatible. Hybrid systems are possible, and almost every operation can draw on concepts from each approach.

KEY TERMS

Just-in-time (JIT)	Toyota production	Production smoothing	Total productive
Synchronous operations	system	Foolproof mechanisms	maintenance
Waste	Single-digit setup times	(poka-yoke)	Synchronous operations
Capacity-constrained	U-form cells	Autonomation	philosophy
resources	Kanbans	Housekeeping practices	Hybrid MRPII/kanban
			system

DISCUSSION QUESTIONS

1. What is JIT? How does it differ from MRP? Can the two systems coexist?

2. Responsiveness is critical for an FRO. Can an FRO use MRP? Can it use JIT? What other characteristics should the dependent demand inventory management system display? Why?

3. What is the synchronous operations philosophy? On what does it focus? Does this make sense? Why or why not?

4. Identify areas in a typical manufacturing company where waste and wasteful practices may exist. Do the same for a service organization. Consider inventory, materials handling, quality, information management, and so on.

5. What characteristics should an operating system that uses JIT possess? Which of these characteristics are critical, and which are merely desirable?

6. MRP was designed with expectations of uncertainty, while JIT was designed with expectations of certainty. What does this statement mean, and is it essential that the JIT environment be more certain than that of MRP?

7. How could JIT be used in the following operating settings?
   a. General hospital
   b. Engineering consultancy
   c. Insurance company
   d. Petroleum refinery
   e. Automobile service center
   f. Underground mine

8. People tend to think of JIT as being used in linear processes. Can it be used in processes in which the product passes more than once through the same work center? What modifications to the control system might the firm have to make?

9. Can JIT be used when product has to be shipped between dispersed factories? When the two factories are on different continents? What changes might a firm have to make to accommodate this geographic dispersion?

10. Can the synchronous operations philosophy be used in a service setting? If so, what service settings are appropriate?

11. Under what circumstances would a firm want to have the bottleneck operation as the last operation in a process? As the first operation?

12. Is it possible to use the synchronous operations philosophy across a network of plants? What safeguards would a firm need to adopt?

13. What are the key considerations in implementing the synchronous operations philosophy? Who should be involved in its implementation?

14. How important is environmental certainty in synchronous operations? How can uncertainty be accommodated?

15. Can JIT and the synchronous operations philosophy be used together? Under what circumstances would this be possible?

PROBLEMS

1. Suppose a series of changes, including cross-training workers, has enabled the firm in Exhibit 16.12 to increase its capacity. It can now meet demand for all four of its products.
   a. What constraints, if any, does the firm now face?
   b. Three different raw materials are used to produce the firm's four products. The quantity used in each product is shown below.

Raw Materials	Cost, per unit, $	Quantity of Each Raw Material, in units, Used to Produce Each Product			
		A	B	C	D
1	10.00	2	8	5	8
2	1.10	—	110	50	100
3	5.00	8	2	2	4

   (1) Suppose the available supply of raw material 1 is limited to 7,500 units. How many units of each product should the firm produce?
   (2) The firm's purchasing department has uncovered another source of supply for raw material 1. How much should the firm be willing to pay for each additional unit?
   (3) What does this example illustrate regarding the strategic linkages between operations and purchasing?

2. In an automobile assembly plant three models of a vehicle are built on the same line. Demand for these vehicles over the next four-week planning horizon is as follows:

Model A	6,400
Model B	2,400
Model C	800

The plant works a single shift of eight hours five days a week. Develop the build module for this planning cycle. How long will each module take to build at each work center?

3. Each workstation in the plant in problem 2 is resupplied every two hours. What is the size of the lot for each of the models? What happens if the resupply schedule is reduced to every hour?

4. Adirondack Iron Works has developed an annual plan for its 10 standard products:

Product A	150,000 units
Product B	140,000 units
Product C	125,000 units
Product D	110,000 units
Product E	49,000 units
Product F	8,000 units
Product G	6,000 units
Product H	5,000 units
Product I	4,000 units
Product J	3,000 units

The plant works five days a week for 50 weeks a year. During each of the eight hours worked per day the single line process can produce 300 units. Using a batch size of 100 units, determine the production plan.

5. Ever-Shine, a brush company produces four different models of a hairbrush. The forecasts of demand for the next year, which fill capacity, are as follows:

Model 1	7,500
Model 2	12,500
Model 3	30,000
Model 4	70,000

a. Using a 250-day year and an eight-hour day, determine the level master schedule for a daily batch, an hourly batch, and mixed-model production with minimum batch sizes.

b. What would the schedule look like for an eight-hour day using mixed-model production? How long would each module take to produce?

6. Model 3 and model 4 brushes in problem 5 use the same handle but different bristles. Model 3 uses a nylon bristle, and model 4 a hair bristle. If bristle sets and handles are supplied every two hours to the line, what would the resupply pattern be if all three items were individually supplied in containers of 50 items?

7. Lulu's Luxuries has installed a machine to make two components installed in all products on the final assembly line. The output rate is 100 units per hour for either component. The setup time is one hour, and the lot size is 500 units. Forty units per hour for each component are required. The company has just learned of an inexpensive second-hand machine, selling price $3,500, that could produce either unit at 50 units per hour. No additional people would be required. If each component is worth $10 at this stage in the process, is it worthwhile to purchase the new machine? The first machine is 25 percent depreciated.

8. John's Junction Boxes has implemented a JIT program that uses kanbans to signal the movement and production of product. The average inventory levels have been reduced to the point where they are roughly proportional to the number of kanbans in use. For one of its products, usage averages 100 units per day, container size is 20 units, there is no safety stock, and lead time has been five working days (one week). The process engineers, having improved the process, propose that the lead time be reduced to three days. What would the percentage change in inventory be?

9. An automobile manufacturer building cars for the North American market decides that a thicker seal will be placed on each car to be sold in northern regions and very dusty regions. Forecasts indicate that 1 vehicle in 100 will be sold in the north and 1 in 80 will be sold in dusty regions. Each seal has to be identified because the glue that attaches the seal to the door is applied by the manufacturer. The glue for the northern cars is different from the glue used in other areas. The plant is supplied on a two-hour cycle by all outside suppliers, among which is the door seal manufacturer. What size container would you use for the seals if vehicles were assembled at a rate of 60 per hour? How would you ensure that the correct door seals were placed on each vehicle?

10. A hard rock mining company plans to open a new horizontal drive and calculates that the rate of progress will be 10 feet per eight-hour shift; three shifts will work each day, seven days a week, for the next three months. Maintenance crews will lay rail, bolt the roof, and hang air ducting as the drive is extended.

The mine is supplied solely by rail, as there is no road access. The supply elevator from the surface to the working levels of the mine operates during the night shift only and can handle all the supplies required. Unfortunately, the elevator can bring items for the new development down on only one day per week.

If rail comes in 50-foot lengths, air ducting in 30-foot lengths, and roof bolts in boxes of 50 (averaging 3 roof bolts per foot of drive), how will you organize inventories and resupply of these items?

11. A manufacturer of pharmaceuticals has a plant in New York City producing two popular cold remedies on the same line. Annual demand for the drugs in the metropolitan area is 100 million units each, with the demand peaking in the spring and autumn; demand in October–December and April–June is three times as high as in the other months. The plant has an annual (50-week) sustained capacity, working three shifts over seven days, of 430 million units. Each drug contains an ingredient that quickly loses its effectiveness, and thus minimum inventories should be held in the pipeline. Changeover between products takes one full shift, principally for cleaning the equipment and ensuring that it is thoroughly dry before the start of a production run.

Given that the forecasts are accurate and that demand during each of the four "seasons" is the same each day of the week, what production schedule should be followed to ensure JIT supply from the plant to the distributors? Daily supply to the distributors from the plant can be arranged; the distributors traditionally cover their customers every two days with these products.

12. The plant manager of the New York City manufacturing plant in problem 11 suddenly discovers that one critical piece of equipment, the blister packag-

ing equipment, has begun to break down. Unplanned downtime is averaging five minutes per hour. All equipment in the process has the same sustained capacity. What impact will this have on the policies developed in problem 11?

13. Wacky Watchworks produces 2,800 watches per eight-hour day on one line, with each watch taking the same amount of time at each station. There are four bands, five faces, five types of glass, and six different bodies available; any combination can be ordered. All the bands are manufactured on one line; the line operates at a rate of 6,000 units per day, and the changeover time between band types is two minutes. The same situation applies to the other components. The assembly schedule is made 30 minutes ahead for the next 30 minutes. What lot size should be used for making components, and how many containers of each component type should be in the system?

GROUP EXERCISES

Many of the tools and concepts discussed in this chapter are meant to be used in a team setting. The following problem is best solved by small groups of students. Ideally, each group should be composed of people with different backgrounds, interests, or areas of expertise.

Set up a simple linear operating system that manufactures two products. One suggestion is to move small lots of flat toothpicks representing one product and round toothpicks representing the other product. Another (more expensive) suggestion is to use children's building blocks in two different colors. Seed the system by pushing product through the process, ensuring that each workstation has three lots of each product in front of it at steady state. Demand for each product should be the same. Use a cycle time of 5 seconds per item in a lot; a lot of six items requires 30 seconds of "work" at each workstation. There should be one person per workstation, and one person should represent the market.

Two dice will be needed, one for the customer and one for any one of the workstations except the last. The customer should toss a die every 30 seconds and should be given six products. The product mix demanded depends on the die throw, with the rules having been devised by the group. As an example, the die throw could be the number of flat toothpicks demanded each 30 seconds, with round toothpicks making up the difference between the total demand of six products and the number of flat toothpicks demanded. The other die will be thrown during the manufacture of each lot at the "problem" workstation, and again the rules chosen will determine the outcome. For example, a double throw could be made of the die, and a lot might not be made if the throws resulted in a double one or a double six. The impact of these rules on the push system can be observed; the rules can be changed to determine the impact of higher or lower quality or more or less reliable equipment.

The impact can be monitored continually by keeping a running score sheet of customer demand, supply to the customer, and inventory status at each workstation. The group can also time how long it takes for any one product to go through the complete process. This series of status checks should continue throughout the exercise and should provide useful information with which to critically analyze the implications of every process and procedure change.

The system can then be changed to a pull system with a buffer of two lots between workstations. The impact of a breakdown on the pull system can then be observed.

Finally, one of the products can be replaced by a new product. Demand for the new product can be forecast to be 50 percent higher than that for the replaced product. The group should figure out how to introduce the new product while continuing to pull through the original product.

The group should switch to pull production once the system has been fully seeded with the new product. Once pull production has been started, the group should experiment with inventory reduction to assess the impact on the overall system.

This exercise can last as long as the group wants but will take at least 90 minutes.

REFERENCES AND SELECTED BIBLIOGRAPHY

Ahmadian, R. A., and W. D. Chandler [1990], *Readings in Production and Operations Management: A Productivity Perspective,* Allyn & Bacon, Boston.

APICS Dictionary, 6th ed. [1987], American Production and Inventory Control Society, Falls Church, Va.

Burgan, John W. [1993], "JIT and MRPII Could Make Beautiful Music Together," *APICS,* November, pp. 25–29.

Bose, Gerald, and Ashok Rao [1988], "Implementing JIT with MRP II Creates Hybrid Manufacturing Environment," *Industrial Engineering,* September, pp. 49–53.

Ellis, Scott, and Bill Conlon [1992], "JIT Points the Way to Gains in Quality, Cost and Lead Time," *APICS: The Performance Advantage,* August, pp. 16–19.

Flapper, S. D., G. J. Miltenburg, and J. Wijngaard [1991], "Embedding JIT into MRP," *Internal Journal of Production Research,* vol. 29, no. 2, pp. 329–341.

Fox, Kenneth A. [1984], "MRP II Providing a Natural Hub for Computer-Integrated Manufacturing System," *Industrial Engineering,* October, pp. 44–50.

Fox, Robert E. [1983], "OPT vs. MRP: Thoughtware vs. Software," American Production and Inventory Control Society, Inc., 26th Annual International Conference Proceedings, November, pp. 693–715.

Goldratt, Eliyahu M., and Jeff Cox [1992], *The Goal,* 2d ed., North River Press, Croton-on-Hudson, N.Y.

Harvard Business Review [1984], "Just-in-Time Production Controlled by Kanban," pp. 1–10.

Jacobs, R. [1984], "OPT Uncovered: Many Production Planning and Scheduling Concepts Can Be Applied with or without the Software," *Industrial Engineering,* October, pp. 32–41.

Karmarkar, Uday [1989], "Getting Control of Just-in-Time," *Harvard Business Review,* September–October, pp. 121–132.

Lee, Terry N., and G. Plenert [1993], "Optimizing Theory of Constraints When New Product Alternatives Exist," *Production and Inventory Management Journal,* vol. 34, no. 3, pp. 51–57.

Monden, Yasuhiro [1981], "Adaptable Kanban System Helps Toyota Maintain Just-in-Time Production," *Industrial Engineering,* May, pp. 29–46.

——— [1983], *Toyota Production System,* Industrial Engineering and Management Press, Atlanta, Ga.

Noori, H. [1990], "A Reference to Just-in-Time Literature," *Operations Management Review,* vol. 7, nos. 3 and 4, pp. 36–41.

Plenert, Gerhard, and Thomas D. Best [1986] "MRP, JIT, and OPT: What's Best?" *Production and Inventory Management,* second quarter, pp. 22–27.

Samitt, M., and A. Barry [1993], "Mixed Model Operations: Solving the Manufacturing Puzzle," *Industrial Engineering,* vol. 25, no. 8, pp. 46–50.

Schlie, T. S., and J. D. Goldhar [1989], "Product Variety and Time Based Manufacturing and Business Management: Achieving Competitive Advantage through CIM," *Manufacturing Review,* vol. 2, no. 1, pp. 32–42.

Schonberger, R. J. [1984], "Just-in-Time Production Systems: Replacing Complexity with Simplicity in Manufacturing Management," *Industrial Engineering,* October, pp. 52–63.

Sepehri, M. [1987], "Manufacturing Revitalization at Harley Davidson Motor Co.," *Industrial Engineering,* August, pp. 87–93.

Sharma, Ken [1993], "Adding 'Intelligence' to MRP Systems," *APICS,* March, pp. 53–58.

Stickler, Michael J. [1989], "Going for the Globe, Part I: Assessment," *P&IM with APICS News,* October, pp. S6–S10.

Vollman, Thomas E., William L. Berry, and D. Clay Whybark [1992], *Manufacturing Planning and Control Systems,* 3d ed., Richard D. Irwin, Mass.

Wantuck, K. A. [1981], "The ABC's of Japanese Productivity," *P&IM Review,* September, pp. 25–34.

White, Richard E. [1993], "An Empirical Assessment of JIT in U.S. Manufacturers," *Production and Inventory Management,* vol. 34, no. 2, pp. 38–42.

Zipken, Paul [1991], "Does Manufacturing Need a JIT Revolution?" *Harvard Business Review,* January–February, pp. 40–50.

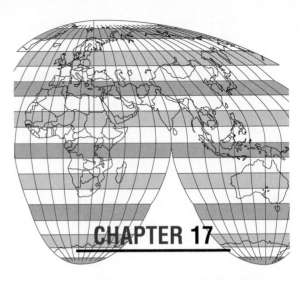

CHAPTER 17

SHOP FLOOR MANAGEMENT

Chapter 14 examined several ways in which a firm can manipulate capacity in the intermediate term to satisfy the demand for its goods and services. The result is an aggregate plan that can be used to develop a much more detailed production plan called the master production schedule. The focus of this chapter is on the execution and management of the master production schedule on the shop floor.

In the short term managers on the shop floor need to address the following questions:

• What delivery date should be promised for each product?

• When should each job be started?
• How can the firm ensure that each job is completed on time?

By the end of this chapter you will be familiar with shop floor management issues in various operating environments and will understand why shop floor control is critical to a firm's quest to achieve the six competitive capabilities. You will also be aware of several popular techniques that help managers organize and control activities on the shop floor.

EXHIBIT 17.1   FRO MANUFACTURING PROFILE

Precision Packaging Products manufactures molded plastic products to customer specifications. "You want it *when*?" might have been its slogan two years ago, when production schedules were "squeaky-wheel-driven." Production schedules were developed manually and updated daily, sometimes hourly, to accommodate new customers' orders. Large quantities of raw materials were ordered far in advance to satisfy expected demand.

Customer service suffered and costs were high under Precision's fly-by-the-seat-of-the-pants shop floor control system. A new scheduling system was a must.

A computer-based scheduling tool is at the heart of Precision's new scheduling system. The computer-generated schedule is based on customer due dates, and because it takes people, materials, and machines into consideration, the schedule is realistic. Now the sales force can give customers firm target due dates that are based on the company's current workload. Since raw materials are ordered in small quantities as they are needed, the average inventory level has been cut in half. Thus, cash flow has improved along with customer service.

Source: Adapted from Ciaramello (1992), pp. 47–49.

EXHIBIT 17.2   FRO SERVICE PROFILE

Customer service is the key concern of Urgences Santé, the public agency responsible for coordinating ambulances in the Montreal area of Quebec, Canada. The agency does not own its own ambulances but rents them from 15 different private companies and is responsible for designing the work schedules for the approximately 700 technicians employed by those companies.

The scheduling problem is complex; the following represents some of the constraints faced by Urgences Santé:

• The demand for ambulances is quite variable. Demand is higher at the end of the week and during the winter.
• Provisions of the union contract must be met. For example, the lunch period is 30 minutes long and must begin and end within an hour of the shift midpoint. Shifts must be either 8 or 10 hours long.
• There must be a fair distribution of service hours assigned among the 15 different companies.

(Exhibit 17.2 continues on next page)

EXHIBIT 17.2 *(continued)*

With ambulance rental fees of over $55 an hour, a daily excess of 10 hours represents more than $200,000 a year. Thus Urgences Santé must ensure that its schedules keep costs as low as possible while maintaining a high level of emergency care.

Urgences Santé's scheduling problem is too complex for mathematical or heuristic techniques alone; the firm has developed a system that combines both techniques. The new system has lowered costs by approximately $250,000 a year and increased the quality of a typical technician's schedule. It is also flexible enough to accommodate changes in union contracts, rental agreements, and operational methods over time.

17.1 MANAGERIAL ORIENTATION

Have you ever arrived on time for a doctor's appointment only to wait an hour to see the doctor? Or tried to pick up a watch from the repair shop on the promised date only to find out that it has not been touched? Or stood in a growing line at the supermarket and wondered why only half the checkouts were open?

Frustrating customers is not the only consequence of poor scheduling. Product costs soar and quality suffers when feasible schedules cannot be developed and executed. In a typical operation it is not uncommon for jobs to spend over 80 percent of their time on the shop floor simply moving or waiting in a queue for the next value-added operation. As Precision Packaging Products (see Exhibit 17.1) and Urgences Santé (see Exhibit 17.2) demonstrate, there is a direct link between a firm's ability to compete and its shop floor operations.

DEFINITION: *Shop floor control (SFC)* refers to the detailed short-term planning, execution, and monitoring of the activities required to fulfill the production plan.

Executing production plans developed during operational planning with detailed daily production schedules is a key responsibility of SFC systems (see Exhibit 17.3). However, SFC involves much more than deciding what to produce and when to produce it. SFC systems must also schedule resources such as labor, machines, tooling,[1] and material receipts as well as preventive maintenance. Problems such as machine breakdowns, employee absenteeism, defects, and inadequate materials must be solved swiftly and effectively. (These types of problems can easily result in confusion, inefficiency, and overall shop floor congestion.) Data on the status of jobs, resource usage, and the validity of the standards used must be collected. Production must be in constant communication with marketing, purchasing, distribution, and other areas of the firm.

This chapter focuses on the scheduling aspect of shop floor control. Chapter 11 presented a wide range of tools and techniques for identifying, correcting, and preventing product and process quality problems on the shop floor.

17.2 SCHEDULING IN VARIOUS OPERATING ENVIRONMENTS

The characteristics that differentiate a process organization affect the focus of that organization's shop floor management system. These characteristics also affect the tools and techniques used to schedule operations.

---

[1] *Tooling* refers to a wide variety of equipment accessories and attachments required to perform specific operations or sets of operations.

EXHIBIT 17.3 THE OPERATIONS PLANNING HIERARCHY

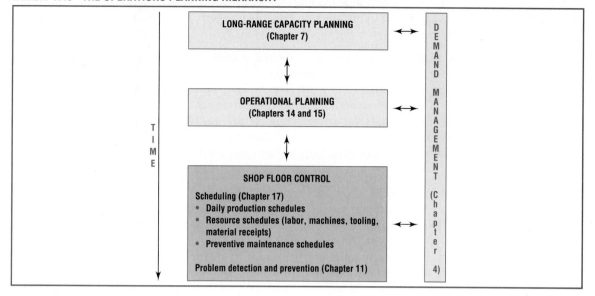

Scheduling in Job Shops

Picture a job shop such as Fujima International[2] or Precision Packaging Products (Exhibit 17.1) or an accounting firm such as Ernst & Young. Typically, the plant (or office) is arranged in a process layout: similar pieces of equipment (or types of accountants) are grouped together. Since each customer order is unique, orders can flow through the plant in many ways. The time, materials, equipment, and labor skills required by each customer order vary as well.

Scheduling in a job-shop environment is a complex problem. Consider the following types of decisions that must be made on a routine basis:

- Which operations must be performed for each customer order (or job)? How long should each take? What materials, tooling, and labor skills are needed, and when?
- To which work centers should the job be assigned? In what order should the job visit those centers?
- When should the job be released to the shop floor?
- In what order should jobs at a specific work center be processed?

In most job shops, there are millions of ways in which a set of jobs can be loaded and sequenced.[3]

DEFINITION: *Loading* refers to the assignment of jobs to specific work centers, people, or machines.

DEFINITION: *Sequencing* is the ordering of the jobs to be processed by a specific work center, person, or machine.

---

[2] Fujima International was toured in the Startup Chapter.

[3] Suppose a firm has three similar work centers in its welding area. If there are 15 jobs to be processed, there are 3^{15}, or over 14 million, ways in which the set of jobs can be loaded.

The sheer number of loading and sequencing combinations is not the only problem encountered by production schedulers. Other complicating factors include the following:

- Capacity restraints such as limited tooling and equipment and workers with specific skills cannot be violated.
- The workload at each work center must be reasonable.
- Similarities in equipment setups should be taken advantage of to increase productivity. At the same time unnecessarily large work-in-process (WIP) inventories should not be allowed to accumulate.
- Customer orders must be ready on time, not too early or too late.

The workforce has to be scheduled as well. People have to be assigned to shifts and then to specific shop floor tasks.

In practice, computerized scheduling systems that employ heuristic techniques (e.g., Johnson's rule) and/or optimization techniques (e.g., linear programming) are used. Scheduling at Urgences Santé (see Exhibit 17.2) is so complex that a combination of both techniques is employed. A wide range of scheduling tools and techniques are examined in Section 17.4.

Because there tend to be so many jobs on the shop floor at one time, job shops require complex information systems. An important component of many of these systems is the **shop packet** that accompanies jobs as they travel from work center to work center on the shop floor.

> **DEFINITION:** A shop packet is a package of documents used to monitor and control a job as it passes through the shop floor.

The shop packet includes a **production order** prepared manually or by a computerized system such as material requirements planning (MRP).

> **DEFINITION:** A production order is a document or group of documents that authorize the manufacture of a specified quantity of a particular item.

A **routing file** is often included in the shop packet as well.

> **DEFINITION:** A routing file describes the operations to be performed at specific work centers, the sequence in which operations should be performed, and setup and process times.

Paper or computerized routing files usually exist for routine parts but may have to be prepared for new parts or variants of standard parts. Other items frequently included in the shop packet are pick lists for the materials and components required and technical information such as customer specifications and blueprints.

The **daily dispatch list** (see Exhibit 17.4) is another component of a shop floor information system. A daily dispatch list is prepared for each work center.

> **DEFINITION:** A daily dispatch list shows the jobs that are currently at a specific work center or are expected to arrive there in the next few days. Information such as the customer due date and the priority ranking may be included for each job.

The daily dispatch list may specify the order in which jobs should be processed. Alternatively, the work center may use local priority rules (e.g., first come, first served) to decide which job on the list to process next. A variety of local priority rules are discussed later in this chapter.

EXHIBIT 17.4 DAILY DISPATCH LIST

DAILY DISPATCH LIST FOR DAY 150 AT WORK CENTER 1068

Start Date	Job Number	Processing Time	Due Dates Operation	Due Dates Customer
148	C8185	18.6	151	154
150	C8189	3.4	151	156
150	C8195	2.9	151	160
151	C8174	0.9	152	155
151	C8190	4.8	152	157
151	C8193	2.7	152	153
152	C8196	1.3	152	155
152	C8199	12.5	154	156

As the job passes through the work centers on the shop floor, data are collected about its progress and resource usage. These data are used to compare actual progress with scheduled progress, highlight out-of-control situations, and generate reports on shop performance. Out-of-control situations may be a result of equipment break-downs, employee absenteeism, bottleneck operations, restricted tooling capacity, or problems with purchased materials.

In addition to developing production schedules, shop floor control systems provide feedback to other departments and other information systems. This feedback includes information on shop floor conditions, the status of the master production plan's execution, and the validity of the time standards used.

Scheduling in Intermittent-Flow Shops

Scheduling in an intermittent-flow shop tends to be less complex than scheduling in a job shop. Not only is the range of products narrower, there are fewer routing options. The sequence in which jobs are scheduled is still a major concern, and many of the tools and techniques used to sequence production in a job shop are also used in an intermittent-flow shop. The information system employed to monitor and control shop floor operations tends to be similar as well.

Products are usually produced in small to medium batches in an intermittent-flow shop. There is often pressure to enlarge batch sizes as much as possible to increase process utilization and efficiency rates. But as was discussed in Chapter 13, smaller batches result in lower inventory-related costs and improved responsiveness. Determining the best batch size is therefore a major control issue in intermittent-flow shops. Lot sizing rules include the economic order quantity, lot for lot, and the period order quantity.[4]

Scheduling in Repetitive-Flow and Continuous-Flow Shops

Production scheduling in a repetitive-flow or continuous-flow environment tends to be less complex than scheduling in job shops and intermittent-flow shops. There are fewer end products, parts, and raw materials to schedule, monitor, and control, and individual jobs do not have to be assigned to work centers; all products follow a predetermined route along the shop floor.

If products flow continuously through the process from start to finish, the entire process can be scheduled as a single unit. Alternatively, the process can be broken

---

[4] Chapters 13 and 15 discuss these rules.

down into stages separated by WIP inventory. In this case a production schedule is needed for each stage. The production schedule usually is based on short-term demand forecasts and/or actual customer orders. Suitable scheduling techniques include capacity-constrained load sequencing scheduling and process flow scheduling. These techniques will be described below.

Rather than control production directly with a production schedule (i.e., with a **push system**), a firm can employ a **pull system** for repetitive-flow processes.

17.3 SCHEDULING TOOLS AND TECHNIQUES

This section will present a wide range of scheduling tools and techniques, all of which can be used by firms in both the service sector and the manufacturing sector. Of course, the usefulness of a tool or technique differs from firm to firm, depending on the operating process and the competitive environment.

Sequencing Heuristics

The heuristics presented in this section are used to specify the order in which a set of jobs at one or more work centers are to be processed.

Local Priority Rules: n Jobs, One Work Center In many job shops and intermittent-flow shops the order in which jobs are processed at a work center is not predetermined and controlled centrally. After finishing each job, the operator uses a **local priority rule** to determine which of the jobs in the queue in front of the work center should be processed next.

Many different priority rules can be used, including the following:

- **First come, first served (FCFS).** Sequence the jobs in the same order in which they arrived at this work center.
- **Shortest processing time (SPT).** Sequence the jobs in processing time order for this work center, shortest first.
- **Earliest due date (EDD).** Sequence the jobs in customer due date order, earliest first.
- **Least order slack (LS).** Sequence the jobs in slack order, lowest first. The **job slack** can be calculated by using equation (17.1).

> **Job Slack**
>
> $$S_k = AT_k - TRT_k \qquad (17.1)$$
>
> where S_k = slack time for job k
> AT_k = shop time available to complete job k (between current date and customer due date)
> TRT_k = shop time required to complete job k (includes all setup, processing, moving, and waiting time at all work centers that still have to process job k)

A negative slack value means that the job will not be finished on time under the current schedule. A slack value of zero means that it will be finished on time, and a positive slack value means that it will be finished before the customer due date.

- **Critical ratio (CR).** Sequence the jobs in critical ratio order, least first. The critical ratio for each job can be calculated by using equation (17.2).

Critical Ratio

$$CR_k = \frac{AT_k}{TRT_k} \qquad (17.2)$$

where CR_k = critical ratio for job k
AT_k = shop time available to complete job k
TRT_k = shop time required to complete job k

A critical ratio below 1 means that the job will not be finished on time under the current schedule. A ratio of 1 means that it will be finished on time, and a ratio over 1 means that it will be finished before the customer due date.

The scheduling module of ©OM-Expert can be used to apply these priority rules to the jobs waiting at a single work center (see Exhibit 17.5).

Advantages and disadvantages are associated with each priority rule. Some criteria used to compare them are listed below:

- **Average flow time.** The average amount of time jobs spend in the shop
- **Average number of jobs in the system.** The average number of jobs in the shop daily
- **Average job lateness.** The average amount of time by which each job's actual completion date exceeds its promised due date

The primary limitation of the first come, first served rule is that long jobs tend to delay other jobs and increase machine idle time for downstream work centers. The main advantage of FCFS is its simplicity. Customers often view this as the fairest rule.

Application of the SPT rule results in the lowest average completion time and work-in-process inventories. It can provide the lowest average lateness and offer better customer service. SPT decreases downstream idle time and reduces congestion in the work area because a lower average number of jobs are completed. However, SPT makes long jobs wait, perhaps too long.

The earliest due date rule directly addresses due dates and minimizes lateness. Since it does not take processing time into account, it can leave jobs waiting a long time, adding to in-process inventories and job congestion.

The least order slack and critical ratio rules often force the designated job sequence to change after a given operation. This makes it difficult to predict when a job will get through the system.

In practice, the priority of jobs at a work center is often modified by the status of jobs at upstream and/or downstream work centers. For example, the priority of a job that is moving to a congested work center may be reduced while the priority of a job moving to an idle center may be increased.

Johnson's Rule: n Jobs, Two Work Centers   Johnson's rule [see Johnson (1954)] is a simple heuristic used to sequence a set of jobs through two adjacent machines or work centers. Its goal is to minimize the total time needed to process the entire set of jobs. For this heuristic to be used, the following conditions must be met:

- The time needed to complete each job at each work center must be known, constant, and independent of the job sequence.
- All jobs must follow the same two-step work sequence.
- All jobs are of equal priority.

EXHIBIT 17.5 TOOLBOX: LOCAL PRIORITY RULES

It's Tuesday, March 10, and Kelly Anderson, a manager at the Riley and O'Brian accounting firm, has five jobs waiting to be reviewed. She has estimated the time she will need to review each job and the total time her staff needs to complete the job.

Job	Hours Required to Review the Job	Total Hours Needed to Complete the Job	Date Job Put in Input Basket	Customer Due Date
A	10	30	March 5	March 16
B	12	80	March 10	March 31
C	6	50	March 9	March 23
D	8	60	March 10	March 30
E	4	14	March 6	March 13

Using the shortest processing time (SPT) rule, Kelly should review the jobs in this order: E, C, D, A, B.

If Kelly uses the first come, first served (FCFS) rule, the jobs are reviewed in this order: A, E, C, D, B.

The earliest due date (EDD) rule results in yet another job sequence: E, A, C, D, B.

Sequencing the jobs using the least order slack (LS) rule is a bit more involved. Refer to the table below to calculate the number of business days remaining for each job (column 2 minus today's date minus weekends). Then convert this figure into hours (column 3 × 8). The slack for each job is equal to the time remaining for that job (column 4) minus the total time required by Kelly and her staff to complete the job (column 5).

(1) Job	(2) Customer Due Date	(3) Business Days Remaining	(4) Time Remaining, hours	(5) Time Required, hours	(6) Slack, hours
A	March 16	6 − 2 = 4	32	30	2
B	March 31	21 − 6 = 15	120	80	40
C	March 23	13 − 4 = 9	72	50	22
D	March 30	20 − 6 = 14	112	60	52
E	March 13	3 − 0 = 3	24	14	10

Therefore, using the LS rule, the jobs should be reviewed in this sequence: A, E, C, B, D.

The critical ratio of each job is simply the time remaining divided by the time Kelly and her staff need to complete the job. Therefore, the jobs should be reviewed as follows: A, C, B, E, D.

(1) Job	(2) Time Remaining, hours	(3) Time Required, hours	(4) Critical Ratio
A	32	30	1.07
B	120	80	1.50
C	72	50	1.44
D	112	60	1.87
E	24	14	1.71

Johnson's rule is a three-step procedure which is repeated until every job has been scheduled. Let us work through this procedure using the example in Exhibit 17.6.

Step 1. After listing the jobs and their time at each work center, select the shortest operation time. If a tie exists, arbitrarily choose a job.

There are seven jobs to be completed, and the shortest processing time is one hour for job J7.

Step 2. If the job with the shortest time is at the first work center, schedule it first. If the shortest time is at the second work center, schedule that job in the last available position.

EXHIBIT 17.6   TOOLBOX: JOHNSON'S RULE, *N* JOBS, TWO WORK CENTERS

The Solid Life Insurance Company Ltd. customizes its group life insurance policies. The following seven policies must be scheduled through a two-stage process so that the total completion time is minimized.

	Processing Time, hours	
Job	Stage 1	Stage 2
J1	8	6
J2	3	2
J3	3	4
J4	4	6
J5	5	7
J6	6	4
J7	2	1

The shortest processing time is one hour for job J7. Since it occurs at stage 2, the job is scheduled in the last available position.

Current job sequence: ___, ___, ___, ___, ___, ___, J7

The shortest processing time is now two hours for job J2. Since it occurs at stage 2, the job is scheduled in slot 6, the last available position.

Current job sequence: ___, ___, ___, ___, ___, J2, J7

Job J3 has the next shortest processing time—three hours at stage 1—and is scheduled in the first available position.

Current job sequence: J3, ___, ___, ___, ___, J2, J7

Jobs J4 and J6 both have four-hour processing times. The firm arbitrarily chooses J4 and schedules it in the first available position. Job J6 is then scheduled in the last available position.

Current job sequence: J3, J4, ___, ___, J6, J2, J7

Job J5 has the next shortest processing time and is scheduled in the first available position. This leaves J1 in the only remaining position.

Final job sequence: J3, J4, J5, J1, J6, J2, J7

The final job sequence is illustrated by the Gantt chart shown below and was generated by ©OM-Expert. All seven jobs will be completed in 33 days.

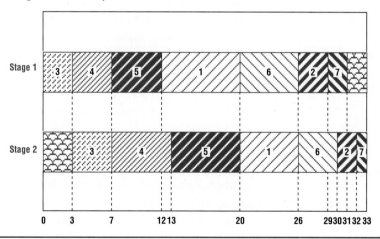

Job J7 requires one hour of processing time at the second processing stage; therefore, it is scheduled in the last available position.

Step 3. Remove the assigned job from further consideration. Return to step 1 if any jobs are left to be scheduled.

There are six jobs left to be scheduled, and so the firm must return to step 1. Exhibit 17.6 walks through steps 1, 2, and 3 for each of the remaining six jobs.

Johnson's Rule: n Jobs, Three Work Centers If one or both of the following conditions are met, Johnson's rule can be used to schedule a set of jobs at three work centers.

- The shortest job duration on machine 1 is at least as great as the longest job duration on machine 2.
- The shortest job duration on machine 3 is at least as great as the longest duration on machine 2.

Using the Rocky Crest Manufacturing Company in Exhibit 17.7, let us work through the following procedure.

EXHIBIT 17.7 TOOLBOX: JOHNSON'S RULE, *N* JOBS, THREE WORK CENTERS

A three-stage process is used to produce souvenir beach towels at the Rocky Crest Manufacturing Company. The following five jobs must be scheduled using Johnson's rule.

	Processing Time, minutes		
Job	Work Center 1 (t_1)	Work Center 2 (t_2)	Work Center 3 (t_3)
J1	4	1	6
J2	5	3	8
J3	5	1	8
J4	6	4	7
J5	7	1	6

The problem has been converted into a two-work-center problem by combining processing times.

	Processing Time, minutes	
Job	Pseudo Work Center 1 ($t_1 + t_2$)	Pseudo Work Center 2 ($t_2 + t_3$)
J1	5	7
J2	8	11
J3	6	9
J4	10	11
J5	8	7

Using Johnson's rule, the jobs are sequenced as follows:

- Job J1 has the shortest processing time. Since this processing time is for pseudo work center 1, this job is scheduled first. Job J3 has the next shortest processing time and is scheduled in the first available slot.

  Current job sequence: J1, J3, ——, ——, ——
- Job J5 has the next shortest processing time and is scheduled in the last available slot.

  Current job sequence: J1, J3, ——, ——, J5
- Job J2 is scheduled next, followed by job J4.

  Final job sequence: J1, J3, J2, J4, J5

Therefore, the five jobs will be processed by work center 1, work center 2, and work center 3 in the following order: J1, J3, J2, J4, and finally J5.

Step 1. Convert the problem into a two-work-center problem by combining the time required at work centers 1 and 2 for each job and combining the time required at work centers 2 and 3 for each job.

Two pseudo work centers have been created for Rocky Crest Manufacturing by combining processing times in Exhibit 17.7.

Step 2. One by one, sequence jobs using the three-step procedure for the two-work-center problem.

The five jobs are scheduled in Exhibit 17.7 one by one in operation time order at the *pseudo work centers,* shortest first.

The CDS Algorithm: n Jobs, m Work Centers In practice, scheduling problems typically involve a large number of jobs that must be processed by many work centers. In these cases Johnson's rule is obviously inadequate. Johnson's rule has been extended, however, by Campbell, Dudeck, and Smith (1970) to sequence a set of n jobs through a set of m work centers. Their heuristic, the **CDS algorithm,** systematically combines work centers into two work centers and then applies Johnson's rule.

- Consider only the first and last work centers. Solve the problem using Johnson's rule.
- Create two pseudo work centers by using the following two equations. Solve the problem using Johnson's rule.

$$t_{i,p1} = t_{i,1} + t_{i,2} \qquad t_{i,p2} = t_{i,m-1} + t_{i,m}$$

where $t_{i,j}$ = time required at center m (j = 1 to m refer to actual work centers, j = $p1$ refers to pseudo work center 1, j = $p2$ refers to pseudo work center 2)
- Create two pseudo work centers by using the following two equations. Solve the problem using Johnson's rule.

$$t_{i,p1} = \sum_{j=1}^{3} t_{i,j} \qquad t_{i,p2} = \sum_{j=m-2}^{m} t_{i,j}$$

- Continue to create pseudo work centers in the same manner until $m - 1$ problems have been solved. In the final problem, the following two equations are used to create the pseudo work centers.

$$t_{i,p1} = \sum_{j=1}^{m-1} t_{i,j} \qquad t_{i,p2} = \sum_{j=2}^{m} t_{i,j}$$

- For each of the problem solutions, calculate the total completion time. Select the solution with the lowest total completion time.

General-Purpose Tools Applied to the Scheduling Problem

Throughout this book general-purpose tools such as **linear programming** have been applied to a variety of operations management problems. This section[5] will describe how some of these tools can be used to solve the scheduling problem. Let us begin with linear programming.

---

[5] Refer to the accompanying *OM-Companion* for a detailed review of the techniques discussed in this section.

Linear Programming and the Assignment Method   If the following conditions are met, linear programming can be used to load and sequence jobs:

- Each job–work center combination has an associated cost (or profit). This cost (or profit) is known, constant, and independent of the job sequence.
- All jobs are of equal priority.
- The goal is to find the optimal set of job–work center combinations, that is, the set that minimizes the sum of the job–worker center combinations (or maximizes the sum of the profits).

If the number of jobs to be scheduled equals the number of work centers (machines or people) available, a special form of linear programming called the **assignment method** can be used. With the help of ©OM-Expert, the same problem has been solved with both techniques in Exhibit 17.8.

EXHIBIT 17.8   TOOLBOX: LINEAR PROGRAMMING APPLIED TO THE SCHEDULING PROBLEM

Dana Reisse must assign the following four jobs to the four lawyers on her staff. Her goal is to minimize the total completion time for all four jobs. Since each lawyer has his or her own area of expertise, the time required to complete each job depends on the person assigned to that job. Each person must be assigned to one job.

TIME REQUIRED TO COMPLETE EACH JOB IN HOURS

	Staff Members			
Job	Ann Bourque	Glen Wesley	Kathy Janney	Dave Christian
A	5	12	12	14
B	7	15	20	15
C	5	10	14	5
D	20	12	10	7

Mathematically, the problem can be stated as follows:

Let c_{ij} represent the time required by person i to do job j
$x_{ij} = 1$ if person i is assigned to job j
$x_{ij} = 0$ if person i is not assigned to job j

Objective function

$$\text{Minimize} \sum_{i=1}^{4} \sum_{j=1}^{4} x_{ij} c_{ij}$$

Constraints

$$\sum_{i=1}^{4} x_{ij} = 1 \qquad j = 1, 2, 3, 4$$

$$\sum_{j=1}^{4} x_{ij} = 1 \qquad i = 1, 2, 3, 4$$

Note that since each person is assigned only one job and each job is done completely by one person, there is no need for sequencing in this situation.

This problem can be solved using ©OM-Expert. The optimal solution is as follows:

$x_{12} = 1$	(Ann Bourque is assigned to job B)
$x_{21} = 1$	(Glen Wesley is assigned to job A)
$x_{34} = 1$	(Kathy Janney is assigned to job D)
$x_{43} = 1$	(Dave Christian is assigned to job C)

All other values of $x_{ij} = 0$, and the total completion time is 34 hours.

Since each person must be assigned to one job and the number of jobs is equal to the number of people, the assignment method can be used to solve this problem. It is much simpler and more efficient (see the accompanying *OM-Companion*). The answer, of course, is the same as the answer shown above.

Simulation   Computer **simulation models** are mathematical models of a system that can be used to experiment with that system. On the shop floor production schedulers can use simulation models to examine the impact of different schedules on due date performance, throughput rates, resource utilization, and so on.

Simulation models can be used to periodically develop and update production schedules. They can also be linked to the shop floor information system and can be run in parallel with real time. Whenever an event occurs (e.g., machine breakdown, material shortage, engineering change) that upsets the current production schedule, the model can be employed to evaluate options for modifying the schedule.

One of the major problems with on-line simulations is the time required to generate and evaluate alternative solutions. To combat this problem, software developers are combining simulation models with knowledge-based expert systems. The simulation model is used to predict the performance of an alternative, which is then evaluated by the expert system.

Knowledge-Based Expert Systems   **Knowledge-based expert systems (KBESs)** use knowledge compiled by human experts to solve problems in a particular domain. The solution provided by the system is not necessarily optimal, but it should be a good, feasible solution.[6]

The more complex the scheduling problem is (i.e., the more variables, constraints, and objectives that must be considered), the more difficult it is to solve the problem with a mathematical model. A KBES, however, can handle very complex scheduling problems, even ones that involve incomplete, uncertain, or rapidly changing information. Because they are able to explain the reasoning in KBESs, users' confidence in them tends to be high. Exhibit 17.9 describes how a company with a wide product range and an intermittent-flow process uses a KBES to schedule operations.

Finite Capacity Scheduling   The KBES referred to in Exhibit 17.9 falls into a new category of planning software and protocols called **finite capacity scheduling** (introduced in Chapter 14). Most finite capacity scheduling systems contain detailed resource and capacity requirements for every operation performed on every product produced by the firm, including inspection, transportation, and other material handling. Setup and labor constraints are also included. The system also contains detailed information on the actual current capacities of each process, department, and machine, as well as the decision rules for deciding how temporary capacity adjustments should be made. When, as at CarTech, the system operates constantly to determine the optimal sequence of jobs, the practice is called **real-time scheduling.** Most finite capacity scheduling systems are not "real time" or interactive; IBM's Endicott, New York, plant regenerates its finite capacity scheduling system weekly.

The advantages of finite capacity planning are due to the wealth of detail in the various databases and the power of the computer and the software. IBM has reduced the time required to produce detailed production plans and schedules by 60 percent and the labor required for production planning by 80 percent. Customer service and vendor support have improved markedly. Improved integration of vendors and customers into the planning process is possible because potential problems can be identified as schedules are being produced and can be discussed and resolved with customers and vendors. The plant's overall responsiveness has improved because the lead times for planning—and hence production—have been reduced by weeks.

[6] Refer to the Chapter 9 Supplement for a general discussion of KBESs.

EXHIBIT 17.9 TOOLBOX: KNOWLEDGE-BASED EXPERT SYSTEMS

The Carpenter Technology (CarTech) Corporation manufactures specialty metals. Production scheduling is complex at CarTech, especially for its hot rolling mill: the Specialty Metals Producer Number 5 Mill. The mill heats billets and ingots to the required temperature and then runs them through rolls to reduce the cross-sectional areas of the material to the customer-specified size. Production schedulers must cope with a wide product range, 50 different heating cycles covering 350 grades of steel, processing temperatures ranging from 1,500°F to 2,425°F, a variety of throughput rates, and 13 furnaces.

After investigating mathematical algorithms and simulation models, CarTech discovered that only a knowledge-based expert system (KBES) was powerful enough to model the mill, account for all the important variables and constraints, and deliver an achievable schedule.

A KBES consists of several separate but interacting modules. CarTech's *knowledge base* contains information about the shop floor (e.g., the capacity of each furnace), production goals, constraints, and procedures. Rules for splitting orders, the time each lot should spend in the furnace, the best temperature at which to process particular metals, and so on, are also included in the knowledge base. Because the knowledge base is written in "natural" language, operators on the shop floor can easily read and modify its contents.

The *database* module contains information about customer orders downloaded from CarTech's MRP system. The *inference engine* monitors the facts in this database and manipulates the knowledge base as it develops the production schedule. The *control mechanism* guides the reasoning process.

Source: Adapted from Martin (1992), pp. 37–39.

Push Scheduling Systems

In a push system production schedules are prepared centrally and then released to the shop floor. There are many different ways in which these schedules can be developed. Note that all these systems are **off-line scheduling** systems.

> DEFINITION: Off-line scheduling systems consider the conditions in the entire shop as they load and sequence jobs at all work centers on the shop floor.

An important characteristic of off-line scheduling is its ability to produce good, *feasible* schedules.

Capacity-Constrained Load Sequencing Scheduling

Capacity-constrained load sequencing scheduling (CCLSS) is a finite loading system which produces a set of start and finish times for each operation at each work center. Jobs are scheduled one by one in job priority order. All the operations for a specific job are scheduled at one time, with resource constraints and the other jobs to be scheduled taken into consideration.

Job priorities are established using factors such as customer due dates and earliest start dates. The operations required for a specific job can be scheduled using either a forward or a backward scheduling technique. In both cases all capacity constraints are directly considered; this means that all the schedules will be feasible. The individual job schedules are combined into a production schedule, which is then used to develop a detailed material requirement plan.

> DEFINITION: *Forward scheduling* is a scheduling technique where the scheduler begins with a preestablished start date for the first operation. The start and end dates for each operation are computed by working forward through the process.

> DEFINITION: *Backward scheduling* is a scheduling technique where the scheduler begins with a preestablished end date for the final operation. The

start and end dates for each operation are computed by working backward through the process.

Seven jobs going through a five-work-center process have been scheduled using the backward scheduling technique in Exhibit 17.10.

The CCLSS approach yields a detailed, feasible schedule that is computationally efficient and is understandable to and controllable by operations personnel. Firms that have implemented CCLSS [see White and Hastings (1986)] report that schedules can be developed quickly with relatively few resources. These schedules are generally stable and can be readily adapted to reflect the needs of management. Jobs due dates are generally met, and average flow times (i.e., the time each job spends in the shop) are good.

Optimized Production Technology Optimized production technology (OPT) is one of many commercially available off-line scheduling software packages. OPT focuses on the utilization of bottleneck resources (resources whose capacity is less than the demand placed on them).[7]

Together, four modules—BUILDNET, SERVE, SPLIT, and OPT—create a production schedule by using the following six-step procedure [see Fry, Cox, and Blackstone (1992)].

Step 1. Create an engineering network that represents a model of the shop floor environment.

The BUILDNET module creates the engineering network by using information such as bills of material, product routings, resource descriptions, customer orders and due dates, and current inventory levels.

Step 2. Identify bottleneck resources.

Using the information provided by the BUILDNET module, the SERVE module develops a production schedule by working backward from customer due dates. Lot-for-lot batch sizing is used, and all resources are assumed to have infinite capacity. Resources that are utilized at close to or over 100 percent are classified as bottlenecks.

Step 3. Split the shop floor operations into two networks: an O-net and an S-net.

The SPLIT module first identifies critical operations, that is, operations that require bottleneck resources or are performed after an operation that requires bottleneck resources. Critical operations are placed in the O-net, and noncritical operations are placed in the S-net (see Exhibit 17.11).

Step 4. Schedule all bottleneck operations in the O-net.

The OPT module produces a production schedule for each bottleneck operation as follows:

1. The software uses customer orders, bills of material, and current inventory balances to calculate the quantity required of each part produced by the system.
2. For each part required, the transfer batch size is calculated. A transfer batch size is the quantity of parts moved between resources.

---

[7] OPT was created by Eliyahu Goldratt, the developer of the synchronized operations philosophy (see Chapter 16), and is used to implement this philosophy on the shop floor.

EXHIBIT 17.10   TOOLBOX: CAPACITY-CONSTRAINED LOAD SEQUENCING SCHEDULING

Seven jobs must be scheduled through the shop's five work centers. The time, in hours, required at each work center by each job is shown below. The jobs have been listed in descending order of priority. Assume that there is only one eight-hour shift daily and that all jobs flow through the work centers in the same order (1 to 2 to 3 to 4 to 5).

JOB SEQUENCE AND WORK CENTER REQUIREMENTS

Job	Due Date	Work Center 1	2	3	4	5
C	298	4	4	6	6	2
A	297	2	2	4	4	4
B	299	6	4	2	6	—
F	299	2	2	4	4	6
G	300	2	4	4	2	6
D	301	2	6	—	2	2
E	301	6	4	2	6	4

Jobs are scheduled one by one in job priority order. For each job, operations are scheduled by working backward through the shop (i.e., work centers 5, 4, 3, 2, 1), using the customer due date as the expected finish time at work center 5.

The first job to be scheduled is job C. Since it must be completed by day 298, it is assigned to work center 5 for the last two hours of day 297. To be ready for work center 5, job C must begin to be processed at work center 4 the first thing in the morning on day 297. This means that work center 3 must complete its work on job C by the end of day 296 and work center 2 must be finished with job C by the end of hour 2 that morning. To be ready for work center 2 on time, job C must be released to work center 1 by the beginning of the third hour of day 295.

The remaining jobs are scheduled in the same way, and the resultant schedule is illustrated by the following Gantt chart.

GANTT CHART SCHEDULE

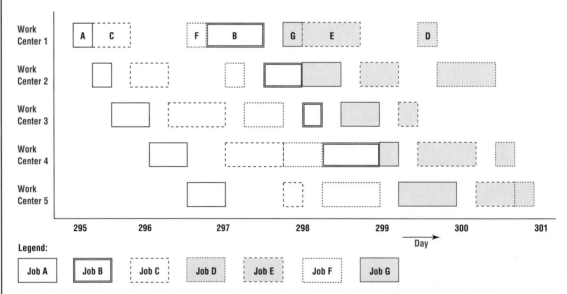

Note that because job B takes so long at work center 1, job F must leave work center 1 two hours before it will be processed at work center 2. Also note that the "holes" in the schedule are characteristic of horizontal loading.

EXHIBIT 17.11 TOOLBOX: OPT

In the following production process the product consists of three parts which are assembled together at the last work center.

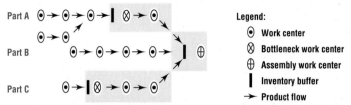

Inventory buffers are strategically located in front of all bottleneck work centers. The final assembly work center is also protected by a buffer of parts that do not flow through any bottleneck work centers, that is, an inventory of part B.

The SPLIT module has divided the process into two networks. The shaded network represents operations contained in the O-net, and the remaining operations form the S-net.

The size of the transfer batch is influenced by a set of management-supplied parameters, including the minimum time a bottleneck resource spends producing a batch of any part.

Breaking down customer orders into small transfer batches reduces production lead times and WIP inventories and smooths production.

3. For each part required, the process batch size is calculated. It is the number of parts a machine processes before being set up for a new part and is equal to one or more transfer batches. Combining transfer batches at bottleneck operations increases bottleneck efficiency.

To calculate process batch sizes, OPT performs a series of detailed simulations of the shop floor. These simulations consider machine availability, setup times, and inventory buffers.

Calculating the process batch sizes requires OPT to sequence the transfer batches and results in a detailed production schedule for the bottleneck resource.

Step 5. Calculate the earliest completion date for each customer order.

If none of the parts required by a customer order flow through the O-net, the earliest completion date is equal to the customer due date. OPT calculates the earliest completion date for the remaining customer orders by forward scheduling from bottleneck operations. Resource constraints, inventory buffers, setup times, and process times are all considered. In some instances the earliest completion date may not be the same as the customer due date. In such cases a new due date must be negotiated with the customer.

Step 6. Back schedule each customer order by using the completion dates and the bottleneck schedules.

The SERVE module schedules noncritical operations by working backward from the order completion dates through to the bottleneck operations. Upstream operations are scheduled backward by using the bottleneck schedules developed by the OPT module. Since noncritical operations have excess capacity, resource constraints are not considered directly.

The completed production schedule can be evaluated by using OPT's on-line interactive program and can be supplemented with a wide range of reports.

Since OPT directly considers capacity limitations, its schedules are feasible. Since the schedules are so detailed, they can be used directly on the shop floor. Companies that use OPT software report lower WIP inventories and shorter production lead times. However, they also feel the results are not intuitive, maintenance costs are high, and the system requires extremely accurate and timely feedback to be effective.

The Kumera Oy System   Rather than use one of the general approaches presented so far, many firms have developed their own production planning and control systems. One of these firms is Kumera Oy. This Finnish firm manufactures a broad range of custom-made gear-driven power transmissions by using an intermittent-flow process. The company attributes much of its success to the simple but effective **Kumera Oy system (periodic control system).**

The periodic control system developed at Kumera Oy begins with the firm's annual plan, which specifies the number of units to be produced of each product group during the year. Product groups are referred to as production sets. The year is divided into five-week periods, and each production set is scheduled once during any given five-week period. Customer orders are assigned to a specific production set, with actual orders replacing the period quantities used for planning. Exhibit 17.12 gives a more detailed account of how periodic control works.

Process Flow Scheduling   It was mentioned earlier that if products flow continuously through the process from start to finish, the entire process can be scheduled as a single unit. Alternatively, the process can be broken down into stages separated by WIP inventory. These processes can be scheduled by using the process flow scheduling approach. During **process flow scheduling,** scheduling calculations are guided by the process structure.

The Coors Brewing Company has divided its beer-making process into three stages (see Exhibit 17.13). A production schedule based on demand forecasts pushes production through stage 1, the brewing stage. A packaging schedule based on customer orders, however, pulls the required end products through the remaining two stages.

Because the production equipment used at all three stages is expensive, Coors schedules its equipment first to minimize idle time. Material, transportation, and labor requirements are then derived from the equipment schedules. This is referred to as *process-dominated scheduling (PDS).*

Taylor and Bolander (1991) suggest that PDS be used for a production stage when (1) capacity is relatively expensive at that stage, (2) the stage is a bottleneck, or (3) production setups are expensive. Alternatively, if (1) materials are relatively expensive, (2) there is excess capacity, or (3) setup costs are negligible, a materials-dominated schedule (MDS) is recommended.

Pull Scheduling Systems

In a production process controlled by a pull system an item is produced only when a signal is received from its user. This signal may take the form of a card, an empty square on the floor, or an empty container. Alternatively, a telephone or computer terminal may be used to communicate a user's needs to an upstream work area.

Two-Card Kanban Systems   Toyota, one of the pioneers of the pull system for repetitive-flow processes, utilizes a two-card **kanban system** on its shop floor. **With-**

EXHIBIT 17.12   PERIODIC CONTROL AT KUMERA OY

THE ANNUAL PRODUCTION PLAN

The following annual production plan specifies the quantity that must be produced of each product group. Fifty units of product group A, for example, will be produced once every five weeks.

Product Group	Annual Forecast	Periodic Quantities (based on five-week periods)
A	500	50
B	100	10
C	1,000	100
D	2,000	200
E	1,500	150

THE MASTER PRODUCTION SCHEDULE

The master production schedule (MPS) below indicates when each product group will be produced. The next batch of 100 units of product group C, for example, will be assembled during week 3.

The MPS is distributed throughout Kumera Oy, to its customers, and to its key suppliers. Note that the production sequence does not vary from one period to the next.

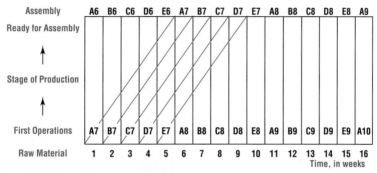

Customer orders are assigned to a specific production set, with actual orders replacing the period quantities used for planning. No more orders than the period quantity can be allowed into a production set. Once this quantity is reached, the next customer order is delayed until a later production set or exchanged for one already included in an earlier set.

If the period quantity is not met, marketing can pull up an order from a subsequent production set. The other option is to produce a smaller period quantity.

Bills of material are prepared for the orders in the production set, and actual inventories are checked against computer records before net requirements are calculated. Purchased items are scheduled to be received as needed or in the week before production. Purchase and shop orders are released at the same time.

The shop orders for a specific production set all have the same implicit due date of five weeks after their release. The orders are numbered consecutively, and the shop floor priority rule is simply to work on the lowest numbered item next. The assembly line supervisor can schedule the assembly sequence for the orders in the production set to take advantage of production efficiencies.

Parts that fall behind may not require special expediting since their order numbers will be relatively low and hence they have priority. Emergency orders (e.g., an order for a part needed immediately for a customer because his or her machine is down) are assigned very low numbers. Low-priority items are assigned high numbers.

Source: Adapted from Whybark (1984), pp. 74–76.

EXHIBIT 17.13 TOOLBOX: PROCESS FLOW SCHEDULING

The Coors Brewing Company brews seven different brands of beer by using the three-stage process depicted below.

THE PROCESS

During stage 1 raw materials are combined during the brewing and malting process to produce wort. The wort is fermented and then transferred to aging tanks.

During stage 2 the beer is blended to achieve the desired alcohol content, filtered, and then moved to a finishing facility.

During stage 3, the beer is packaged in bottles, cans, or kegs and then moved to distribution.

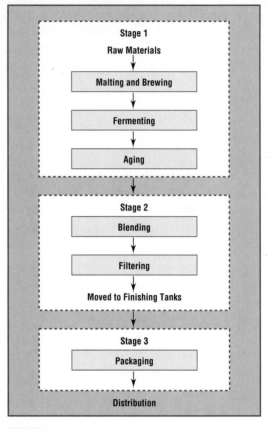

SCHEDULING: STAGE 1

The brewing schedule based on demand forecasts is developed first. The fermentation schedule is derived directly from the brewing schedule, and then the aging schedule is derived from the fermentation schedule. Once these schedules have been made, a materials schedule is developed. If the materials schedule is not feasible, the brewing schedule is revised.

SCHEDULING: STAGES 2 AND 3

The packaging schedule is developed first, using actual customer orders that have accumulated during the previous week. This schedule specifies the quantity of each package-brand combination required and the sequence in which the products should be made. The blending and filtering schedules are then developed.

Once the packaging, blending, and filtering schedules have been developed, transportation and material schedules are created. If the transportation and/or material schedules are not feasible, the packaging schedule is revised until all schedules are both feasible and acceptable.

Source: Adapted from Taylor and Bolander (1990), pp. 3–5.

drawal (move) kanbans specify the quantity of a product that can be withdrawn from a work center by a subsequent work center. **Production kanbans** specify the quantity of a product that should be produced by a work center. A withdrawal kanban and a production kanban are illustrated in Exhibit 17.14.

Let us walk through a simple example to explain the mechanics of a two-card kanban system. Consider the process illustrated in Exhibit 17.15A. Work center 8 receives production kanbans from work center 9. Production kanbans are attached to its receiving post but are transferred to its production ordering post and sequenced in first come, first served order. If there are no production kanbans on the post, no items can be produced.

Suppose the next production kanban authorizes the production of one container of item K by work center 8. Each container of K is made with one container of part A and one container of part B.

As illustrated in Exhibit 17.15B to D, the following chain of events will occur:

- A carrier for work center 8 removes a withdrawal kanban for part A from the work center 8 withdrawal post.

    He or she takes the withdrawal kanban and an empty container designed for part A back to work center 5.

    After leaving the empty container at a designated spot, he or she locates a full container of part A in the work center 5 store. The full container has a production kanban card attached to it. The carrier carefully compares his or her withdrawal kanban with this production kanban to ensure that he or she has located the correct container.

EXHIBIT 17.14   WITHDRAWAL AND PRODUCTION ORDERING KANBAN CARDS

WITHDRAWAL KANBAN	
Store Shelf No.: SE215 Item Back No.: A2-15	Preceding Process: Forging B-2 Subsequent Process: Machining M-6
Item No.: 35670507 Item Name: Drive Pinion Car Type: SX50BC	

Box Capacity	Box Type	Issue No.
20	B	4/8

The withdrawal kanban is used by the machining work center to obtain a box containing 20 drive pinions from location B-2 at the forging work center.

PRODUCTION ORDERING KANBAN	
Store Shelf No.: F26-18 Item Back No.: A5-34	Process: Machining SB-8
Item No.: 56790-321 Item Name: Crankshaft Car Type: SX50BC-150	

The production kanban shown above authorizes the production of one container of crankshafts for car type SX50BC-150.

Source: Adapted from Monden (1983), p. 15.

EXHIBIT 17.15 TOOLBOX: A TWO-CARD KANBAN SYSTEM

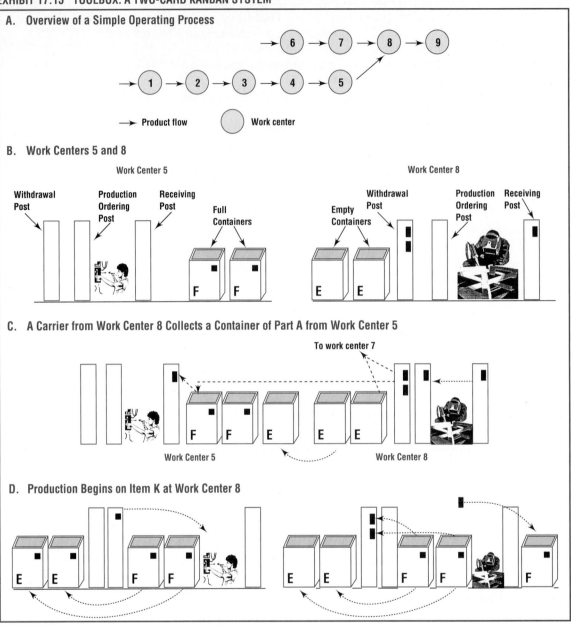

A. Overview of a Simple Operating Process

Product flow / Work center

B. Work Centers 5 and 8

Work Center 5

Withdrawal Post / Production Ordering Post / Receiving Post / Full Containers

Work Center 8

Empty Containers / Withdrawal Post / Production Ordering Post / Receiving Post

C. A Carrier from Work Center 8 Collects a Container of Part A from Work Center 5

To work center 7

Work Center 5 / Work Center 8

D. Production Begins on Item K at Work Center 8

Once the carrier has located the correct container, he or she removes the production kanban and places it on the work center 5 receiving post.

The withdrawal kanban is placed on the full container and is taken to work center 8.

- The same process is repeated at work center 7 for part B.
- Work center 8 now has the parts needed to build one container of item K.
- The production kanban for item K is removed from the production post and follows item K through the process. The quantity produced of item K must be

exactly the quantity specified on the production kanban. A kanban should always be attached to the physical product.

- The withdrawal kanbans for parts A and B are returned to the withdrawal post once their containers have been emptied.
- Once work on item K is completed, the production kanban is attached to the completed container of K and the container is placed in the work center 8 store.

If the production quantity is large and the production velocity is rapid, a special kind of production kanban—a **signal kanban**—is used. The containers for the item are stacked on pallets in the work center store. The signal kanban is attached to the edge of the pallets at the reorder point. The signal kanban is moved to the reorder point post once the inventory level is reduced to the reorder point and authorizes the production of the item.

An **express kanban** is used when there is a shortage of a part. The work center will produce this part immediately and deliver it to the subsequent work center. Express kanbans are issued temporarily and are needed only in extraordinary situations.

At Toyota, suppliers are also issued kanban cards along with a copy of the monthly production plan and the daily sequence schedule. This information is used by suppliers to plan their own production schedules as well as the required deliveries to Toyota.

The larger the number of kanban cards, the larger the inventory. When setup times are short and work centers are close together, the total number of production kanbans is given by equation (17.3).

Number of Production Kanbans Issued

$$K = \frac{\overline{d}\,L(1 + s)}{CC} \tag{17.3}$$

where K = total number of kanbans that corresponds to maximum inventory level

$\overline{d}$ = average daily demand

L = lead time, which consists of processing time, waiting time, conveyance time, and kanban collecting time

s = safety coefficient

CC = container capacity, usually restricted to less than 10 percent of daily demand

For example, if daily demand is 1,200 units, the lead time is 0.1 day, the safety coefficient is 4 percent of daily demand, and each container holds 25 units, five cards will be issued. If daily demand drops to 960 units, one card should be removed. Thus, small changes in demand can be accommodated by changes in the number of kanbans allowed on the shop floor.

The size of the safety coefficient reflects the variation in daily demand and lead time. As was discussed in Chapter 16, firms use a variety of tactics to minimize this variation (production smoothing, short setup times, close supplier relationships, very high product and process quality).

CONWIP In a traditional kanban system, each part has its own card (container, space on the floor, etc.) and a small amount of WIP inventory is held for each part. What if a very wide range of products are produced? Holding inventory of each and every part would be prohibitive. In this situation the **constant work-in-process (CONWIP) system** [see Spearman, Woodruff, and Hopp (1990)] is a viable alternative.

CONWIP is a generalized form of kanban in which production cards are assigned to the production process and are not part-specific. The CONWIP system works as follows:

- The master production schedule is used to develop a list of parts that must be produced. This is called the backlog list.
- The part on the top of the list is assigned to a production card. The card is attached to a standard container and released to the production process when work is needed for the first work center.
- After flowing through the process, the card is removed from the container and sent back to the start of the production process. It is then assigned to the next part on the backlog list.
- Under no conditions can work begin on a part or product that does not have a production card.
- The level of WIP inventory is controlled by the number of cards released to the process. The more cards released, the higher the WIP inventory.

The CONWIP system is also suitable for production environments in which it is difficult or impossible to eliminate lengthy process setups. Schedulers using this system can take advantage of similarities in production setups by manipulating the production sequence on the dispatch list.

17.4 SCHEDULING HUMAN RESOURCES

The aggregate staffing plan specifies the workforce levels required in each planning period. In the short term, however, operations must determine which workers will be assigned to each shift and which workers will perform each job.

Workforce scheduling is relatively simple in an office setting where workers are assigned to the same routine operations daily and there is only one shift. Many firms, though, have to schedule a wide range of tasks and personnel.

Scheduling also becomes more complicated when demand patterns vary from day to day (e.g., in a hospital) or when there are daily demand peaks. Options such as having workers on call and assigning workers to low-priority work until demand increases are often used. Department stores, fast-food restaurants, and retail banks employ these tactics.

Satisfying daily workforce requirements is complicated by a number of constraints. For example, hourly workers must be paid overtime if they work more than a set maximum number of hours per week. If workers are not given two consecutive days off, overtime payments may be excessive. Schedulers must also consider statutory holidays, vacations, and other provisions in the union contract. If more than one shift is regularly scheduled per day, most firms must ensure that employees rotate from one shift to the next during the period and are given adequate time between shift rotations to adapt.

Traditionally, assigning people to jobs was relatively straightforward, for people were as specialized as machines. In these days of the multiskilled worker, this is no longer the case. Bank clerks and police officers, for example, are expected to perform many tasks. Work groups are composed of people who are all able to do every task assigned to the group and more. Many front-line service or production workers form emergency response teams and problem-solving teams. How should people be assigned work in this scenario? Managers in many firms are establishing work priorities and letting small work groups allocate tasks among themselves.

There are computerized packages that employ mathematical and/or heuristic techniques to develop workforce schedules. A simple heuristic used to schedule people over a seven-day week so that each person receives two consecutive days off is shown in Exhibit 17.16.

17.5 SCHEDULING HIGH-CONTACT SERVICES

If the firm provides a high-contact service, scheduling is further complicated by variable customer arrivals and service times. Effective forecasting methods for demand are essential. Long waiting lines put pressure on service personnel and lead to customer dissatisfaction. **Queuing theory** is often used to determine the amount of capacity needed to keep waiting lines to a reasonable size without excessive system idle time.[8]

Reservation systems are often employed in the entertainment, food, travel, and accommodation industries. Reservations enable managers to obtain a good estimate of demand and minimize customer disappointment. Even with reservations, scheduling is complicated by customers who do not arrive. Hotels handle no-shows by deliberately overbooking. Overflows are diverted to nearby hotels at no cost to the customer. Theaters reduce the impact of no-shows by not refunding tickets if patrons do not arrive.

Appointment systems are an effective way to reduce probable client waiting time and increase capacity utilization. Complicating factors include late arrivals, no-shows, emergencies, and clients who arrive without an appointment. Some doctors and dentists reduce the number of no-shows by reminding patients of upcoming appointments.

Two sets of rules are required for an appointment system: rules that govern the timing and duration of the scheduled appointment and rules for processing clients once they arrive. Some firms assign a client to one of several categories on the basis of the service to be provided and allocate the mean service time for that category to the appointment. For example, a hairstylist allocates more time for a perm than for a simple shampoo and cut. The strategy used by many doctors is to schedule two patients at the start of each hour and one at every 15 minutes thereafter. Patients are then processed in accordance with a processing rule such as first come, first served or longest expected service time first.[9]

Appointment scheduling is more difficult when the schedules of several professionals must be coordinated. Scheduling an operation in a hospital is a good example. Surgeons, anaesthetists, and nurses must be scheduled, along with the operating room and postoperative care facilities. Room must be left in the schedule for emergency operations. Scheduling a court case is another example.

---

[8] Queuing systems are described in the accompanying *OM-Companion.* ©OM-Expert includes an extensive module on queuing systems.

[9] Noori (1984) used simulation to compare the results of different combinations of several scheduling and processing rules in a family doctor's office. His results indicate that patient waiting time can be reduced as much as 58 percent if patients are scheduled using mean service categories and then processed on a first come, first served basis.

EXHIBIT 17.16   TOOLBOX: WORKFORCE SCHEDULING

When the number of people needed each day varies and everyone must have two consecutive days off each week, the following procedure can be used. It consists of three steps repeated for each employee to be scheduled.

Step 1. Look at every pair of consecutive days. Choose the pair with the lowest total labor requirements. If a tie exists, choose the pair with the lowest requirements on an adjacent day. If a tie still exists, choose the first of the available tied pairs.

Step 2. The chosen pair becomes the employee's "weekend." Schedule the employee to work the remaining days.

Step 3. Update the labor requirements. If there are employees left to be scheduled, return to step 1.

Suppose there are ten employees to be scheduled and labor requirements for the following week are:

Monday	Tuesday	Wednesday	Thursday	Friday	Saturday	Sunday
7	5	6	7	8	8	9

Tuesday and Wednesday have the lowest combined total labor requirements: 11 days. Therefore, employee 1 will be scheduled to work every day but Tuesday and Wednesday. The labor requirements are updated by subtracting 1 from every day employee 1 is working.

Employee	Monday	Tuesday	Wednesday	Thursday	Friday	Saturday	Sunday
	7	5	6	7	8	8	9
1	x	—	—	x	x	x	x
	6	5	6	6	7	7	8

There are two pairs of days (Monday and Tuesday, Tuesday and Wednesday) that have the lowest combined total. Which pair has the lowest adjacent value?

The first pair is adjacent to Sunday (8) and Wednesday (6). The second pair is adjacent to Monday (6) and Thursday (6). Once again there is a tie. Therefore, choose the first available pair.

Employee	Monday	Tuesday	Wednesday	Thursday	Friday	Saturday	Sunday
	6	5	6	6	7	7	8
2	—	—	x	x	x	x	x
	6	5	5	5	6	6	7

Once again there are two pairs with lowest total labor requirements: Tuesday and Wednesday, Wednesday and Thursday. There is also a tie with the requirements for adjacent days. Choose the first available pair.

Employee	Monday	Tuesday	Wednesday	Thursday	Friday	Saturday	Sunday
	6	5	5	5	6	6	7
3	x	—	—	x	x	x	x
	5	5	5	4	5	5	6

The remaining employees are scheduled as shown below.

Employee	Monday	Tuesday	Wednesday	Thursday	Friday	Saturday	Sunday
	5	5	5	4	5	5	6
4	x	x	—	—	x	x	x
	4	4	5	4	4	4	5
5	x	x	x	—	—	x	x
	3	3	4	4	4	3	4
6	—	—	x	x	x	x	x
	3	3	3	3	3	2	3
7	x	x	x	x	—	—	x
	2	2	2	2	3	2	2
8	—	—	x	x	x	x	x
	2	2	1	1	2	1	1
9	x	x	—	—	x	x	x
	1	1	1	1	1	0	0
10	x	x	x	x	x	—	—
	0	0	0	0	0	0	0

Source: Adapted from Browne and Tibrewala (1975), pp. 22–23.

That is, of course, only the public aspect of the job. How should doctors, dentists, lawyers, and other high-contact professionals schedule themselves? The following rules can help:

- Schedule as the first priority joint professional activities: operations, court schedules, and the like.
- Schedule office hours around joint professional activities. If the joint professional schedule changes later (i.e., surgery lasts longer than anticipated), office hours are extended and the customers will be inconvenienced.
- Schedule professional development activities independently of the above.
- Schedule customers so that noncritical contact work can be performed on one while the service professional is performing critical contact work on another.
- Perform support activities—record keeping and the like—as time permits during the day.
- Never put off until tomorrow what has been scheduled for today, including ancillary paperwork. This may mean working through lunch or staying late, but the business of the day must be concluded. That includes preparation for the following day.

MANAGERIAL IMPLICATIONS

Short-range production or activity planning should be a simple extension of prior planning activities. That this is often not true is often a cause for concern. In fact, one frequently sees continual efforts to change the plan because of changes in the planning parameters. These changes are sometimes due to unrealistic promises to customers and sometimes due to the sudden breakdown of equipment or the absence of operators.

To best handle this a firm must use simple rules and have surplus capacity in the system. It can use the computer to recast the priority system at each work center and then calculate the new due dates for jobs. And the firm can often "find" extra time through overtime or even send urgent jobs out to other firms that have the capacity to finish the job

in the required time. Extra capacity costs, though and the ideal is to have a costless capacity buffer.

If the lead times are sufficiently long, the firm can build in the flexibility. Customers, however, want their products within a reasonable time, and the safety lead time may not be an option. One option in many job shops and batch operations, though, is to plan on using only about 70 percent of the shop's capacity for planning. Any urgent jobs or slow jobs can then use the extra capacity without disrupting other jobs. As it is the domino effect of expediting a job that is the most critical issue, the capacity cushion should be a valuable device. Of course, as the firm gets better at what it does and as its production cycles get shorter, the need for this capacity will be reduced.

CHAPTER SUMMARY

An excellent shop floor control system is a necessity for fast-response organizations in both the manufacturing and service sectors. The best type of shop floor control system for a firm, however, depends on the operating environment.

- In a job shop or intermittent-flow shop push systems are often used: items are produced at times specified by a schedule that has been prepared in advance. A production order accompanies each job through the shop from start to finish. A daily dispatch list is developed for each work center; it shows the operation start and end dates for each job currently at the work center or expected to arrive in the next few days.

- In a repetitive-flow or continuous-flow shop, the equipment is usually arranged in a product layout and work flows rapidly through the shop. Scheduling systems are simpler because individual operations do not have to be scheduled separately.
- The output rate of an assembly line is dictated by the way in which tasks are grouped into work centers and the time each product spends in each center. The goal is to attain the desired output rate with the maximum possible efficiency.
- Pull systems are often used in repetitive-flow shops: an item is produced only when a signal is received from its user. Kanban and CONWIP are two ways in which a pull system can be implemented.
- Smoothing production to limit work-in-process inventories and maintaining high levels of product and process quality are very important in a pull system.
- Local priority rules such as first come, first served can be used to sequence a set of jobs through one work center. Johnson's rule and the CDS algorithm can be used to sequence a set of jobs through two or more work centers.
- Examples of general-purpose tools applied to scheduling include linear programming, simulation, and knowledge-based expert systems.
- An off-line scheduling system considers the conditions of the entire shop floor as it loads and sequences jobs at all work centers on the shop floor.
- Capacity-constrained load sequencing, optimized production technology, Kumera Oy's periodic control system, and process flow scheduling are off-line scheduling systems.
- Workforce scheduling is simple in an office setting but is more complicated when demand patterns vary, there is more than one shift, and the firm operates seven days a week. Union contracts and workforce legislation also increase the difficulty of scheduling human resources.
- In high-contact service industries scheduling is further complicated by variable customer arrivals and service times. Queuing theory is often used to determine how much capacity is needed to keep waiting lines to a reasonable size without excessive system idle time. Appointment and reservation systems are common in high-contact services.

KEY TERMS

Shop floor control (SFC)	Shortest processing time (SPT)	Finite capacity scheduling	Process flow scheduling
Loading	Earliest due date (EDD)	Real-time scheduling	Kanban system
Sequencing	Least order slack (LS)	Off-line scheduling	Withdrawal (move) kanbans
Shop packet	Job slack	Capacity-constrained load sequencing scheduling (CCLSS)	Production kanbans
Production order	Critical ratio (CR)		Signal kanban
Routing file	Johnson's rule	Forward scheduling	Express kanban
Daily dispatch list	CDS algorithm	Backward scheduling	Constant work-in-process (CONWIP) system
Push system	Linear programming	Optimized production technology (OPT)	Queuing theory
Pull system	Assignment method	Kumera Oy system (periodic control system)	Reservation systems
Local priority rules	Simulation models		Appointment systems
First come, first served (FCFS)	Knowledge-based expert systems (KBESs)		

DISCUSSION QUESTIONS

1. What shop floor control process would you use in the following operations?
   a. A three-chair hairdressing salon
   b. A plant baking the same type of cookies 24 hours a day
   c. A plant making seats for an auto assembly plant

d. A woodworking plant making customized office furniture

2. Why is shop floor control an important managerial concern?

3. Is shop floor control more difficult in a job shop or a repetitive manufacturing facility? Why?

4. What is OPT? Could this technique be used in service operations? Which ones? How?

5. What is the kanban control system? How does it operate? Could kanban be used in service operations? Which ones?

6. Why does the periodic system developed by Kumera Oy work? Where else might this system work? Why?

7. What are the potential disadvantages of using the first come, first served dispatching rule? The shortest processing time rule? Which of the dispatching rules should be given precedence? Why?

8. Can the dispatch rules used in manufacturing be employed by service operations? What modifications, if any, are required?

9. What means are available to reduce uncertainty and confusion in the scheduling of service operations? Are there disadvantages to reducing uncertainty?

10. Could simulation be used to help with scheduling operations?

11. Can emergency response units be rescheduled? If so, under what conditions? What form would the rescheduling take?

12. How can uncertainty be reduced in manufacturing operations? What will the impact be on the scheduling of operations?

13. What happens if operators at each work center are empowered to schedule their own operations?

14. Under what conditions could different scheduling systems be combined? What would the managerial implications be?

15. Is it worth pursuing perfect dispatching scheduling or loading decision rules? Why or why not?

16. In certain situations jobs are expedited, that is, given a higher priority and rushed through the shop floor. What are the dangers of excessive expediting? How can an FRO minimize the need for expediting?

PROBLEMS

1. █ You are given the following information concerning five jobs that are waiting for processing through a machine.

Job Number	Processing Time, days	Due Date, days
1	6	17
2	7	20
3	5	25
4	8	28
5	12	39

Sequence the jobs using the shortest processing time and the earliest due date.

2. █ The production workshop has received five orders from customers. The information concerning the jobs is given below.

Job Number	Remaining Shop Time, days	Date Order Received	Customer Due Date, days
1	13	101	155
2	5	103	120
3	8	105	121
4	7	107	123
5	9	110	140

Today is day 111.

a. Sequence the jobs using the shortest process time and the earliest due date.

b. For each of the methods in part a, determine the average completion time, the number of jobs in the system daily, and the average job lateness.

3. █ Study the information concerning jobs below:

Job Number	Processing Time, days	Date Order Received	Customer Due Date, days
1	3	3	15
2	6	4	28
3	5	5	24
4	2	6	23
5	7	7	30

Today is day 8.

a. Sequence the jobs using (1) shortest processing time, (2) earliest due date, (3) least order slack, (4) critical ratio, and (5) first come, first served.

b. For each of the methods in part a, determine the average completion time, the number of jobs in the system daily, and the average job lateness. 577

4. ■ The following jobs need to be processed through two work centers. Develop a processing sequence that minimizes total completion time.

	Processing Time, hours	
Job Number	Work Center 1	Work Center 2
1	9	7
2	5	8
3	6	2
4	4	7
5	3	1
6	2	5

5. ■ The parts in the table below have to be machined by two different machines. First, they need to be planed, and then they must be ground. The processing times through the two machines are:

	Processing Time, hours	
Job Number	Planing Machine	Grinder
1	2	3
2	4	2
3	1	5
4	3	4
5	2	6
6	3	2

a. Determine a job sequence that minimizes total completion time.
b. Calculate the idle time for the grinder.

6. ■ A machining shop has the following parts. All parts go first through a milling machine and then through a boring machine. It is known that the milling machine can work only 4 hours and then has to be stopped for maintenance for 10 hours. Develop a job sequence that entails the shortest completion time.

	Processing time, hours	
Job Number	Milling Machine	Boring Machine
1	7	6
2	3	5
3	2	6
4	2	4
5	5	2
6	4	5
7	5	6

7. ■ A workshop has three jobs that must be scheduled to go through three work centers. The specific information about the three jobs is given below. Determine a job schedule using the earliest due date method and the least slack first method.

Job Number	Due Date, days	Work Center and Processing Time, days		
		1	2	3
1	15	2	4	5
2	16	4	5	4
3	17	5	3	1

8. ■ Given this information concerning four jobs that have to go through three work centers, develop a job schedule using the earliest due date method and the shortest processing time.

Job Number	Due Date, days	Work Center and Processing Time, days		
		1	2	3
1	15	2	4	3
2	16	4	4	4
3	17	2	5	2
4	24	2	5	2

9. ■ A company makes parts for an auto manufacturer. The company recently received five orders from the manufacturer for five different types of parts. All five types of parts must go through forging, machining, and heat treatment. Any one of the three work centers can process only one type of part each time. Develop a job schedule using the earliest due date method and the least slack first method, given this information about the five jobs:

Job Number	Due Date, days	Work Center and Processing Time, days		
		1	2	3
1	29	7	3	2
2	20	3	5	4
3	17	3	9	3
4	22	5	4	2
5	15	4	2	4

10. ■ A toy production line is composed of three workstations. Four types of toys are waiting for processing. Develop a job schedule using the earliest due date method and the least slack first method, given this information about the four jobs:

Job Number	Due Date, days	Work Center and Processing Time, days		
		1	2	3
1	35	8	6	3
2	42	9	2	7
3	56	3	4	7
4	24	5	8	4

11. 🔲 Four jobs are on the desk of the scheduler for Jones Construction Co. Each job is done in the sequence masonry-carpentry-wiring. The jobs and their estimated times in weeks for each trade are:

Job	Masonry	Carpentry	Wiring
20	2	3	1.5
21	1	1.5	1
22	3	2	3
23	5	0.5	1.5

If each trade must complete its whole job, what is the best sequence of jobs? What criteria did you use? Explain.

12. Suppose that in problem 11 each job can be broken into 0.5-week blocks, with subsequent trades being able to start after 0.5 week of the start of the prior trade. None of the subsequent trades can finish within 0.5 week of the finish of a prior trade. What difference does this make to your schedule?

13. What is the impact on your schedule when you find that, given the whole job limitation in problem 12, the wiring work can be done before the carpentry but the carpentry time is increased by 0.5 week if this happens?

14. 🔲 Prepare a dispatch list for the following vehicle repair tasks. Use at least two rules and state your decision criteria. It is day 0 at 7:30 a.m., and you work, alone, an eight-hour day.

Job	Due Date	Remaining Time, hours
1	1	7
2	0	8
3	2	28
4	−1	2
5	2	15

15. What happens to your decision in problem 14 if you can hire help at $100 per day and your costs of being late are $20 per hour?

16. 🔲 Three faculty members teach five courses as a team and have decided to split the grading of each of the five final exams. Professor A marks part I of each exam, professor B marks part II, and professor C marks part III. The time (in hours) required by each professor to mark his or her portion of each exam is shown below.

	Professor		
Exam	A	B	C
1	10	8	12
2	5	9	10
3	7	4	8
4	12	15	6
5	8	6	6

Assume that each exam must be marked in order (i.e., part I, part II, then part III) and that the professors work eight hours a day. If they wish to minimize the total time required to mark the five exams, in what order should the exams be marked? What is the total completion time?

17. 🔲 If the individual parts of each exam in problem 16 can be marked in any sequence, in what order should the exams be marked? What is the total completion time?

18. 🔲 A metal machining job shop has four lathes, each with a dedicated machinist. Each machinist has over the years developed a particular specialty. Today, Monday, April 1, the production supervisor has eight jobs that must be processed at each lathe in the following order: A, B. C, D. The time (in hours) required for each job at each lathe is listed below. These times include allowances for setting up the lathe and transporting the batch of pieces to and from the lathe to storage.

	Job							
	1	2	3	4	5	6	7	8
Lathe A	—	12	17	10	11	21	16	18
Lathe B	11	15	22	12	10	13	17	—
Lathe C	—	14	11	13	14	—	12	—
Lathe D	5	10	12	8	12	6	17	—

In what order should the jobs be processed? When will all eight jobs be completed? Assume that the shop works an eight-hour day, five days a week.

19. 🔲 Suppose three different areas (kitchen/bathroom, basement, and exterior) must be painted in seven new houses. Each area is painted by a different crew of workers, and because of access and safety considerations, no two crews can be in a house at the same time. The houses must be completed in the following order: 1, 2, 3, 4, 5, 6, 7. The painting contractor wants to have the houses finished as quickly as possible. The time required by each crew in each house is shown below.

	House						
	1	2	3	4	5	6	7
Kitchen	2	2	3	4	1	4	3
Basement	1	3	2	4	2	3	2
Exterior	3	3	3	3	3	4	1

a. How long will it take to completely paint all seven houses? In what order will each crew visit the seven houses?

b. What changes to the plan need to be made if the contractor decides that the kitchen crew must be finished as soon as possible?

20. Calculate the number of kanbans required for the following situation:

	Product A	Product B
Usage per day	120	800
Lead time (hours)	2	1
Container size (units)	4	10
Safety stock (percent)	5	0

21. Calculate the number of kanbans required for the following:

	A	B
Usage	100 per week	100 per day
Lead time	1 week	2 weeks
Container size	2 units	50 units
Safety stock	20 percent	0 percent

GROUP EXERCISES

Many of the tools and concepts discussed in this chapter are meant to be used in a team setting. The following problem is best solved by small groups of students. Ideally, each group should be composed of people with different backgrounds, interests, or areas of expertise.

The group operates a metal machining job shop consisting of three departments: milling, turning, and drilling. The shop makes to order only and quotes a lead time of processing time plus one week from the time the job is released to the shop floor, although customers regularly set due dates that bear no relationship to the published lead times. Each department contains two identical machines, and the shop works a single shift, five days a week. Overtime is allowed and is paid at $5 per hour for the first three hours per day and $7 per hour for the next five hours. A maximum of 15 hours of overtime per week is allowed. Extra shifts can be worked at a cost of $15 per week but must be worked for a minimum of four weeks. Every day or part of a day that a shipment is late, there is a $35 penalty.

The market is represented by one "customer," whose requirements for each order are communicated by card. Each card, which can be made up in advance or by the customer in "real time," contains the following information:

- Order number (beginning at 001)
- Date required (the exercise starts on January 1)
- Number of items required

- Sequence through departments
- Time required for operating on an item in each department

The customer should place orders at a rate roughly equal to 80 percent of the shop's capacity; this means that the total hours of operation given to the shop each week should average around 65 hours.

Setup time for each machine is two hours, with two hours needed to transport each batch from one department to another or to shipping for instantaneous delivery to the customer. The working day is four minutes long, although this can be adjusted to suit the abilities of the group members. A timekeeper should be appointed to keep accurate records of time, overtime hours and costs, second shift costs, and late delivery penalties.

The group members representing the management of the shop are free to use whatever scheduling rules they wish and to treat departments as independent or interdependent. There will be more learning if the simulation occurs at least twice using exactly the same order sequence, but with different scheduling rules in place each time. It will be advantageous to use the "weekends" to catch one's breath and review performance.

The exercise can be made as simple or complicated as the group desires, although simplicity makes for better understanding. One option is to have only two possible sequences of machines and to rearrange the shop into a group technology layout for the second simulation.

REFERENCES AND SELECTED BIBLIOGRAPHY

Brill, S. [1993], "Finite Scheduling Helps IBM Satisfy Its Panel Products Customers," *APICS*, October, pp. 66–69.

Browne, J. J., and R. K. Tibrewala [1975], "Manpower Scheduling," *Industrial Engineering*, August, pp. 22–23.

Campbell, Herbert G., Richard A. Dudek, and Milton L. Smith [1970], "A Heuristic Algorithm for the *n* Job *m* Machine Sequencing Problem," *Management Science*, vol. 16, no. 10, pp. 630–637.

Ciaramello, Michael [1992], "Lessons in Plastic: Scheduling Tools Make All the Difference," *APICS*, June, pp. 47–49.

Cox, James F., John H. Blackstone, and Michael S. Spencer (eds.) [1992], *APICS Dictionary*, 7th ed., American Production and Control Society, Falls Church, Va.

Fry, Timothy D., James F. Cox, and John H. Blackstone, Jr. [1992], "An Analysis and Discussion of the Optimized Production Technology Software and Its Use," *Production and Operations Management*, vol. 1, no. 2, pp. 229–242.

Goldratt, E. M., and R. E. Fox [1986], *The Race,* North River Press, Croton-on-Hudson, N.Y.

Hakanson, W. P. [1993], "MES: Taking the Kinks out of Managing Manufacturing Operations," *APICS,* October, pp. 43–47.

Huettel, J. [1993], "Finite Capacity Scheduling: Just a Luxury, Right?" *APICS,* June, pp. 37–39.

Jacobs, F. Robert [1984], "OPT Uncovered: Many Production Planning and Scheduling Concepts Can Be Applied with or without the Software," *Industrial Engineering,* October, pp. 32–41.

Johnson, M. [1954], "Optimal Two Stage and Three Stage Production with Setup Times Included," *Naval Research Logistics Quarterly,* vol. 1, no. 1, pp. 61–68.

Melnyk, Steven A. [1988], "Production Control: Issues and Challenges," in M. Oliff (ed.), *Intelligent Manufacturing: Proceedings from the First International Conference on Expert Systems and the Leading Edge in Production Planning and Control,* Benjamin/Cummings, Menlo Park, Calif., pp. 199–232.

Martin, John [1992], "Expert Systems Solve a Scheduling Problem for Carpenter Technology," *APICS,* November, pp. 37–39.

Mondon, Yasuhiro [1983], *Toyota Production System: Practical Approach to Production Management,* Industrial Engineering and Management Press, Atlanta, Ga.

Noori, H. [1984], "Scheduling a High Contact Service Organization," *Simulations & Games,* vol. 15, no. 3, pp. 315–327.

Oliff, M. (ed.) [1988], *Intelligent Manufacturing: Proceedings from the First International Conference on Expert Systems and the Leading Edge in Production Planning and Control,* Benjamin/Cummings, Menlo Park, Calif.

Roder, P. I. [1993], "Finite Scheduling Systems," *APICS,* August, pp. 40–42.

Rogers, Paul, and Maureen T. Flanagan [1991], "On-Line Simulation for Real-Time Scheduling of Manufacturing Systems," *Industrial Engineering,* December, pp. 37–40.

Spearman, Mark L., David L. Woodruff, and Wallace J. Hopp [1990], "CONWIP: A Pull Alternative to Kanban," *International Journal of Production Research,* vol. 28, no. 5, pp. 879–894.

Taylor, Sam G., and Steven F. Bolander [1990], "Process Flow Scheduling: Mixed-Flow Cases," *Production and Inventory Management Journal,* fourth quarter, pp. 1–5.

—— and —— [1991], "Process Flow Scheduling Principles," *Production and Inventory Management Journal,* first quarter, pp. 67–71.

Thompson, Michael B. [1993], "Computer Simulation Drives Innovation in Scheduling," *APICS,* February, pp. 31–34.

Vollman, T. E., W. L. Berry, and D. C. Whybark [1988], *Manufacturing Planning and Control Systems,* 2d ed., Irwin, Homewood, Ill.

White, Christopher, and Nicholas A. J. Hastings [1986], "Scheduling the Factory of the Future," a paper presented to the Twenty-Seventh International Meeting of the Institute of Management Sciences (TIMS), Gold Coast, Australia, July 20–23.

Whybark, D. Clay [1984], "Production Planning and Control at Kumera Oy," *Production and Inventory Management,* first quarter, pp. 71–81.

CHAPTER 18

UPSTREAM-DOWNSTREAM MATERIALS MANAGEMENT

Minimizing the time "distance" between recognition and satisfaction of customer demand is a necessity for a firm that wishes to remain responsive in a competitive environment. Demand management and internal control of operations first establish the demand to be met and then determine how to satisfy it in the most effective and efficient manner. Internal conditions are only one part of the process, though, and most operations managers ask the following questions:

- How should the firm manage its relationships with its suppliers?
- How can the firm influence the passage of its product between its production facility and the consumer's hands?

Both questions acknowledge the tight interdependence of all the links in the value chain and the need for effective management of the entire process. Fast-response organizations cannot coexist with slow suppliers and a tortuous distribution system.

This chapter examines a system for coordinating distribution by employing MRP principles. It also looks at a model for stronger supplier-user relationships. By the end of this chapter you will understand and be able to prescribe effective supplier and distribution networks that improve quality and reduce response times.

EXHIBIT 18.1 FRO MANUFACTURING PROFILE

Each year Procter & Gamble (P&G) buys close to $50 million worth of packaging and introduces about 60 new products. Sixteen companies used to supply P&G with boxes, and on average, the turnaround time for a new design was 20 weeks.

After studying the performance of the 16 suppliers, the purchasing department discovered that only 3 could be classified as superior. P&G decided to place all its business with those three; in return, the suppliers reduced their prices by 9 percent. Even more important was the tenfold reduction in turnaround time for newly designed boxes. This drastic reduction enabled P&G to beat its competitors to market by two months with a new product line. P&G estimates that this has translated into a 27 percent increase in market share and $80 million in additional sales.

EXHIBIT 18.2 FRO SERVICE PROFILE

Fed up with shopping at electronics stores where he knew more than the salespeople, Michael Dell decided to sell PCs himself. With $1,000 in savings, Dell launched a mail-order business housed in his college apartment in Austin, Texas. Nine years later Dell Computer's fiscal sales reached $2 billion, making it the fourth largest PC maker in the United States, behind IBM, Apple, and Compaq. In 1992 Dell Computer led Dataquest's customer satisfaction survey.

Unlike its competitors, Dell bypasses dealers and distributors and sells directly to customers who read about the products in newspaper ads and catalogs. Dell owns no plants but leases two small factories to assemble computers to customer's specifications. Customers can choose a color Mitsubishi monitor, an extra-powerful Intel microprocessor, or a host of other options. Dell also offers a wide range of software and accessories but neither makes nor stocks the products. It simply orders them from Merisel, a large distribution company. Merisel often delivers directly to the customer.

Dell is an excellent example of a modular company. It focuses on a few core activities—marketing and service—and outsources the rest to outside specialists. This keeps costs low and avoids the huge investments and inflexibility associated with building parts in-house.

Source: Adapted from Forest and associates (1993), pp. 82–88; Sellers (1993), p. 79; and Tully (1993), pp. 106–114.

18.1 MANAGERIAL ORIENTATION

Sole sourcing. Supplier certification. Reverse marketing. Electronic data exchange. Distribution requirements planning. These are some of the ways in which firms are improving their management of materials coming in (**upstream material flows**) from suppliers and finished products moving out (**downstream material flows**) to customers.

The movement of goods and services through the value chain is sometimes as simple as the chain depicted in Exhibit 18.3A. In practice, however, value chains tend to be much more complex (see Exhibit 18.3B).

Part of the success of Dell Computer (see Exhibit 18.2) can be traced to its decision to simplify its distribution system and sell directly to consumers. Outsourcing all but core activities is another component of Dell's strategy.

Dell is not the only company to realize the strategic importance of upstream-downstream material management. Think back to the discussion of Wal-Mart in Exhibit 3.2. By investing heavily in the management of its supply chain, Wal-Mart can respond quickly to customers' needs and consistently offer high-quality products at everyday low prices. Aggressive supplier management has given Procter & Gamble (see Exhibit 18.1) a competitive edge by drastically reducing the time to market for some of its new products. General Electric's Direct Connect system (see Exhibit 13.1) has reduced a complex and expensive distribution system to 10 strategically located warehouses that can deliver appliances to 90 percent of the United States within 24 hours.

An entire chapter on upstream-downstream material flows appears in this book on operations management because operations management is not limited to the production of goods and services. In conjunction with other functional areas, operations managers are also concerned with the management of resources and the distribution of finished goods and services to customers.

18.2 UPSTREAM MATERIALS MANAGEMENT

Most North American firms spend 20 to 30 percent of their total expenditures acquiring goods and services[1] from outside suppliers; manufacturers tend to spend more than twice that amount. The trend is toward outsourcing more goods and services while focusing on a few core activities.

Chrysler, for example, purchases 70 percent of its parts from outside suppliers, but rather than buying thousands of separate items, it designs its cars to be built in modules and purchases complete modules from individual suppliers. In many cases the suppliers are intimately involved in designing the modules. Nike and Reebok concentrate on their strengths—designing and marketing high-tech fashionable athletic footware—and contract out virtually all footwear production to suppliers in Taiwan, South Korea, and other Asian countries.

As firms increase the number of goods and services they outsource, the importance of effective and efficient supply line management also increases. In the last decade fast-response organizations (FROs) have actively improved their supply line management. The huge gap between world-class procurement practices and those of ordinary companies has been recognized (see Exhibit 18.4).

---

[1] Services that are often outsourced include security, cleaning and maintenance, data processing, and the design of parts and services.

EXHIBIT 18.3 UPSTREAM-DOWNSTREAM VALUE CHAIN SYSTEMS

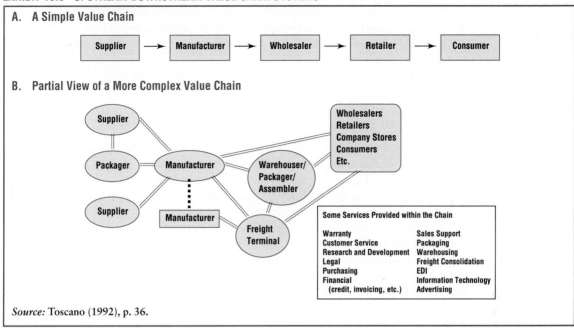

A. A Simple Value Chain

Supplier → Manufacturer → Wholesaler → Retailer → Consumer

B. Partial View of a More Complex Value Chain

Supplier

Packager — Manufacturer — Warehouser/Packager/Assembler

Supplier — Manufacturer — Freight Terminal

Wholesalers
Retailers
Company Stores
Consumers
Etc.

Some Services Provided within the Chain

Warranty	Sales Support
Customer Service	Packaging
Research and Development	Warehousing
Legal	Freight Consolidation
Purchasing	EDI
Financial	Information Technology
(credit, invoicing, etc.)	Advertising

Source: Toscano (1992), p. 36.

EXHIBIT 18.4 WORLD-CLASS PROCUREMENT

A recent study by McKinsey & Co. has uncovered incredible gaps between the procurement practices of world-class firms and those of typical companies.

	Typical Performance	World-Class Performance
Cost factors		
Suppliers per purchasing agent	3.4	5
Agents per $100 million of purchases	5.4	2.2
Purchasing costs as a percentage of purchases made	3.3	0.8
Time factors (weeks)		
Supplier evaluations	3	0.4
Time spent placing an order	6	0.001
Quality of deliveries		
Late (%)	33	2
Rejected (%)	1.5	0.0001
Materials shortages (number of instances per year)	400	4

Source: Adapted from Port, Carey, and Kelly (1992), p. 72.

The following sections will discuss some of these world-class procurement practices.

The Outsourcing (Make versus Buy) Decision

It was mentioned earlier that firms are increasing the number of goods and services they purchase from outside suppliers. How does a firm decide which goods and services to produce internally and which to **outsource?** Factors that should be considered in making **make versus buy decisions** include the following:

- Strategic importance of making the item in-house
- Nature of demand for the item (high? low? steady? wide fluctuations?)
- Technical expertise of the firm versus that of outside suppliers
- Potential contribution of suppliers to the firm's product development and improvement efforts
- Ability of the firm and potential suppliers to produce the item when required in the quantity required
- Quality of internally produced versus purchased items
- Cost of producing the item in-house versus purchasing it, and future price trends

Typically, a large company can potentially outsource thousands of goods and services, and evaluating the desirability of outsourcing each one can be difficult and time-consuming. The process proposed by Venkatesan (1992) and depicted in Exhibit 18.5 is one way in which sourcing decisions can be brought under control and linked to a firm's competitive strategy.

Venkatesan suggests that a firm focus on the production of components that are critical to the firm's products and that the company is good at making. All other components should be purchased from suppliers with which the firm has developed technical and commercial partnerships. Even though a component is outsourced, the firm still must understand the relationship between that component and customer requirements. It should also be able to develop detailed specifications for each component on the basis of this relationship.

EXHIBIT 18.5 A FRAMEWORK FOR SOURCING DECISIONS

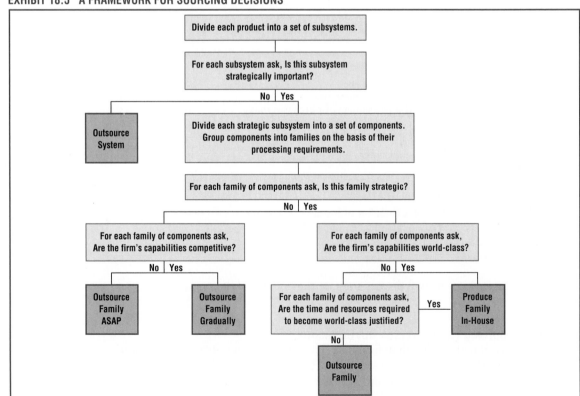

Should a firm routinely purchase an outsourced item from a single supplier or from a variety of suppliers? The next section will show that both strategies have advantages but that the trend is toward sole sourcing.

Multiple versus Sole Sourcing Policies

Traditionally, purchasers have followed a **multiple sourcing** policy.

> **DEFINITION:** Multiple sourcing refers to the practice of having more than one independent supplier for each product purchased by a firm.

Multiple sources provide a hedge against supplier problems such as strikes, equipment breakdowns, and bankruptcy, making it relatively easy to find emergency supplies. Having many suppliers allows a buyer to identify the lowest-cost supplier each time a purchase is required and to trade suppliers off against each other.

> **DEFINITION:** *Sole sourcing* refers to the practice of having a single independent supplier for each product purchased by a firm.

Many firms are moving toward sole sourcing. Look back at the factors that affect the outsourcing decision. Firms are interested in more than low unit costs; quality, flexibility, reliability, and design support are also important.

Meeting these increased expectations may be difficult or impossible for suppliers who receive only small, sporadic orders and have an arm's-length relationship with the firm. But suppliers that receive a long-term commitment[2] are more willing and able to do this. Suppliers are looking for the following:

- Insight into the purchaser's plans. This includes sharing information on the firm's short-, intermediate-, and long-term production plans. It may even entail supplier involvement in design decisions.
- Demand stability for the items purchased. Purchases should be as regular as possible.
- Support in meeting mutually agreed on objectives. For example, the purchasing firm may provide engineering and management support in redesigning processes to reduce costs and increase quality. The supplier may need help in applying just-in-time (JIT) concepts to its operations.

Working with fewer, more dependable suppliers benefits both the firm and its suppliers (see Exhibit 18.6).

In some cases, firms simply "prune" the current list of suppliers to move to sole sourcing, but in other cases firms have to search aggressively for suppliers willing to *become* sole suppliers. Supplier certification is becoming a popular way of handling the first situation; reverse marketing is a good option for the second.

Supplier Certification and ISO 9000

How can a firm separate the wheat from the chaff and identify suppliers worthy of sole supplier status? One way is to set performance standards for suppliers and grant **certified supplier status** to those which meet the standards.

> **DEFINITION:** Certified supplier status is awarded to suppliers that consistently meet predetermined quality, cost, delivery, and financial standards.

---

[2] This commitment may take the form of a blanket order that commits the firm to purchase a minimum quantity of specified goods over a stated time period.

EXHIBIT 18.6   SOLE SOURCING: BUYERS AND SELLERS BENEFIT

A long-term relationship with a single supplier of a specific product or group of products results in benefits to both the supplier and the firm.

BUYER BENEFITS OF SOLE SOURCING

Administrative efficiency

- There is no need to solicit and review bids from a variety of suppliers.
- There are fewer contracts to negotiate, and these contracts must be renegotiated less often.
- Blanket purchase orders reduce paperwork.
- There are fewer telephone calls to make and suppliers to visit.
- It is easier to streamline accounting and identification systems.

Lower inventory costs

- Since the supplier makes frequent deliveries of small lots, the average inventory level is much lower.
- Need for incoming quality inspections can be minimized.

Improved product quality

- The short time span between the delivery of items and their use within the firm means that defective items are discovered quickly.*
- The firm can work with the supplier to improve the quality of the supplier's (and firm's) products.

Access to new technology

- The supplier may be willing to share its technology and contribute to the design of new products.

SUPPLIER BENEFITS OF SOLE SOURCING

Administrative efficiency

- Large volumes are sold to relatively few customers.
- Paperwork is reduced.

Lower production costs

- Production planning is easier when the customer provides insights into its production plans.
- Production capacity can be better utilized.
- Finished goods inventories can be reduced.

Improved product quality

- Working closely with the customer makes it easier to produce items that meet the customer's needs.

Access to new technology

* As was discussed earlier, the sooner a quality problem is discovered, the faster it can be solved. This means that fewer units will be defective and that the production process will be disrupted for a shorter period.

Once certified, suppliers for the communications giant Northern Telecom can supply any of the company's divisions worldwide. To become certified, however, suppliers must pass Northern Telecom's rigorous certification program (see Exhibit 18.7). The company feels that its certification program has been instrumental in fostering a sense of JIT partnerships with its suppliers. The program also reduces to a minimum all activities that do not add value to the company's goods and services. The ultimate goal is zero defects, on-time delivery, and superior service.

Northern Telecom also asks its suppliers to register for **ISO 9000** certification.

DEFINITION: ISO 9000 is a series of quality assurance standards developed by the International Standards Organization.

The ISO 9000 series consists of five standards: ISO 9000, ISO 9001, ISO 9002, ISO 9003, and ISO 9004. Since their publication in 1987 these standards have

EXHIBIT 18.7   VENDOR CERTIFICATION AT NORTHERN TELECOM

Northern Telecom Ltd. manufactures and markets electronic telecommunications equipment around the world. It has five subsidiaries that operate as autonomous profit centers.

By establishing a comprehensive value management program, Northern Telecom has been able to reduce its supply base and establish closer long-term relationships with its remaining suppliers.

Once a supplier's products have passed Northern Telecom's qualification tests, that supplier is added to the approved vendor list and is eligible for the company's certification process. Each of Northern Telecom's divisions can select and sponsor suppliers on this list. The sponsoring division, corporate engineering, and subsidiary headquarters all work with the supplier throughout the certification process.

A detailed and mutually agreed on implementation plan is created. The supplier's sponsoring division then reviews Northern Telecom's product requirements to ensure that they are clear and unambiguous. Inspection and testing procedures are developed, and the supplier demonstrates its control over its production processes and shows how it will continually improve these processes.

The supplier's performance is monitored and evaluated. When performance standards have been met or exceeded, the firm recommends that the supplier be awarded certified supplier status. At this time a complete report evaluating the supplier is sent to the corporate contract manager, who then invites comments from other divisions. Final approval is given by a group of senior managers called the Certification Council.

SUPPLIER CERTIFICATION PROCESS

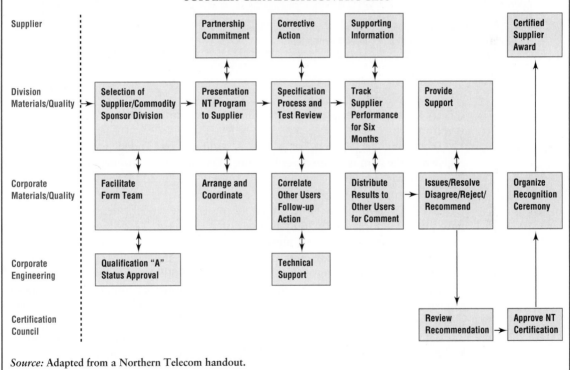

Source: Adapted from a Northern Telecom handout.

become the accepted basis for quality systems requirements for product conformity and assessment in the global marketplace [see Durand and associates (1993)]. Exhibit 18.8 provides more detail on the contents of each standard.

The primary intent is to use these standards to provide guidance for quality management and a justification for contractual agreements between first and second parties. The ISO 9000 standards are also used as benchmarks for second-party

EXHIBIT 18.8 ISO 9000 SERIES OF QUALITY STANDARDS

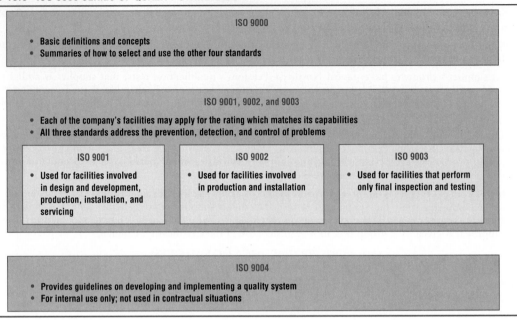

quality approval or registration and third-party quality system certification or registration.

To become an ISO supplier, a firm is audited by an independent agency. Once registered, the firm is audited periodically to confirm its continued adherence to the ISO standards. This process reduces or eliminates the need for the firm to be audited by every company it supplies.

ISO 9000 compliance is becoming an imperative worldwide; over 89 countries have already adopted ISO 9000 as a national standard. To do business in Europe, ISO registration has become a must. In the United States many companies, government agencies (e.g., Department of Defense, Food and Drug Administration, and NASA), and industry associations have made ISO 9000 compliance a requirement.[3]

The International Organization for Standardization is committed to continuous improvement. All standards are under constant review and are subject to revision every five years.[4] The implications for certified and yet to be certified organizations are significant, for the audits will be increasingly stringent. This means that organizations cannot rest on their laurels, as the status quo is not acceptable.

Supply Keiretsu

Even if a firm sole sources all its purchases, a large number of suppliers will be used. How can a firm effectively manage hundreds or even thousands of suppliers?

One option is to have several tiers of suppliers (see Exhibit 18.9). The primary manufacturer or retailer deals directly with a relatively small set of tier 1 suppliers.

---

[3] The American National Standards Institute, with the endorsement of the American Society for Quality Control, has Americanized the wording of ISO 9000 and relabeled it the *ANSI/ASQC Q90-1987 series*.

[4] The technical committees' recommendations require the endorsement by the full council of ISO before a revision can take effect.

EXHIBIT 18.9 SUPPLY KEIRETSU RELATIONSHIPS

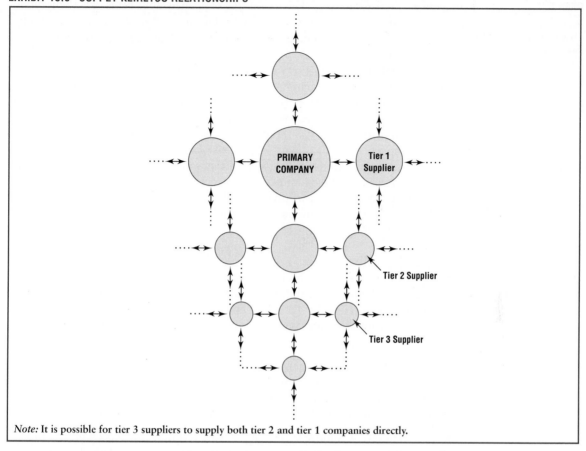

PRIMARY COMPANY

Tier 1 Supplier

Tier 2 Supplier

Tier 3 Supplier

Note: It is possible for tier 3 suppliers to supply both tier 2 and tier 1 companies directly.

Each tier 1 supplier deals directly with its own set of tier 2 suppliers, each tier 2 supplier is the center of a set of tier 3 suppliers, and so on.

The Japanese have used this structure to create **supply (vertical) keiretsu.**[5]

> **DEFINITION:** Supply keiretsu are groups of companies integrated along a supplier chain dominated by a major manufacturer.

Although the major manufacturer in a supply keiretsu may have extremely close relationships with only the first one or two tiers of suppliers, its influence is felt all the way down the supply network to the point of dictating profit margins and determining to whom each supplier may sell. These interlocking webs of share ownership and corporate board membership give a handful of Japanese corporations control over vast networks of suppliers and workers.

Japanese firms such as Honda, Mitsubishi, and Toyota have extended their supply keiretsu to North America.[6] Some American firms are beginning to adapt

---

[5] Supply keiretsu is one of two forms of keiretsu in Japan. A *bank-centered keiretsu* is a set of diversified businesses centered on a bank which offers loans to the members. As in supply keiretsu, the business network is characterized by interlocking directorates and mutual shareholding. Members often buy from each other, work jointly on R&D projects, and coordinate their operations.

[6] Keiretsu practices that exclude American firms from competition may violate U.S. antitrust laws. These practices are under government examination.

keiretsulike practices as well. This book has explained how firms are abandoning multiple sourcing for sole sourcing and working more closely with the remaining suppliers. Suppliers are becoming involved in product design and continuous improvement efforts.

The financial relationship between firms and their suppliers is also changing. Companies such as Ford and Digital Equipment are taking equity positions in their strategic suppliers. Ford owns 40 percent of Excel Industries U.S., for example, and purchases the majority of Excel's windows. Ford owns 25 percent of Mazda, which sells vehicles to it for sale in Japan (and vice versa) and has engineered Ford's latest Escort subcompact. Ford also owns 49 percent of Hertz and supplies the rental car agency with its vehicles. Nouvellus Systems Inc. and other firms lend money to suppliers to purchase capital equipment and sometimes even buy equipment for them. IBM has advanced money to troubled suppliers and researchers. These and other North American companies are finding that adapting keiretsu to their own circumstances helps level the playing field.

Reverse Marketing

What if a firm wants to purchase a good or service it currently produces but suppliers are not lining up at the door? A proactive approach to vendor relations dubbed **reverse marketing** by Leenders and Blenkhorn (1988) may be needed to identify potential suppliers and persuade them to enter into a long-term relationship with the firm.

> **DEFINITION:** In reverse marketing the initiative comes from the purchaser, not the seller. Instead of the supplier attempting to persuade the purchaser to buy, the purchaser tries to persuade the supplier to provide exactly what the purchaser needs.

Reverse marketing is more than a purchasing technique. It represents the proactive, future-oriented stance that purchasing managers in an FRO must take. Because the purchaser takes the initiative, the purchaser's needs drive the relationship.

Reverse marketing makes sense in a wide variety of situations. Exhibit 18.1 demonstrates how P&G used reverse marketing techniques to prune its list of suppliers and reduce the turnaround time for new products. Reverse marketing can be used to persuade a supplier or potential supplier to become a firm's sole source for a group of items. A supplier may be unaware that it currently produces or has the potential to produce a product that the firm needs. It also may be unaware of how the firm's needs will change in the future. Foreign exchange limitations and local unemployment conditions may encourage the firm to develop local sources of supply. A new source of supply may have to be created for environmental reasons.

18.3 DOWNSTREAM MATERIALS MANAGEMENT AND DISTRIBUTION SYSTEMS

To whom does a firm supply its goods and services? Some manufacturers (e.g., Avon) and most service sector firms (e.g., accounting firms, hairstylists, and repair shops) sell products directly to consumers. Alternatively, goods and services can be sold to intermediaries such as retailers, wholesalers, and industrial distributors.

> **DEFINITION:** A *distribution channel* consists of a series of organizations that take title, or assist in transferring title, to a product as it moves from its producer to its consumer.

The design and management of a distribution channel suitable for a firm's products are extremely important because they affect the firm's ability to compete on time, service, cost, quality, flexibility, and dependability.

Firms such as Frito-Lay and the hardware giant Canadian Tire use their **physical distribution** systems as a competitive weapon. Within two days of receiving an order, Canadian Tire can ship any one of its 25,000 auto parts to any one of its 400 stores. Frito-Lay dominates the market for salted snacks by providing unmatched service to smaller stores. Frito-Lay equips its salespeople with hand-held computers; each night the data collected are analyzed for sales trends and relayed back to the sales force. The analysis is used to advise retailers about what to put on their shelves and how much to order.

> **DEFINITION:** Physical distribution refers to the range of activities involved in the handling, storage, and movement of products from a firm to its customers.

The firm may deliver all its goods and services directly from its facility to the next link in the distribution channel or, like Wal-Mart (see Exhibit 3.2), may use a distribution network that consists of a set of geographically dispersed warehouses.

A simple multiechelon distribution system similar to that used in retail stores such as Sears and K-Mart is illustrated in Exhibit 18.10. The top echelon (or level) is composed of retail stores throughout Florida. These stores submit replenishment orders to the next echelon, the regional distribution centers. The regional distribution centers are supplied by the Tallahassee distribution center, where the manufacturing facility is located.

Once the firm has decided how many warehouses it should have and where they should be located, it is left with a wide range of materials management issues. How much inventory should it store at each facility or stock-keeping point? How frequently should these inventories be replenished? What transportation modes should be used? Should the firm store inventories of finished products or assemble to order? How will demand requirements be communicated to the operations? What will the relationship between the master production schedule and these demand requirements be? If demand exceeds the firm's capacity in the short run, how should inventories be allocated? Let us now examine the physical distribution issue that is most closely related to operations: how to respond quickly and cost-effectively to customer demand.

The distribution system described earlier and illustrated in Exhibit 18.10 is a

EXHIBIT 18.10 A MULTIECHELON DISTRIBUTION NETWORK

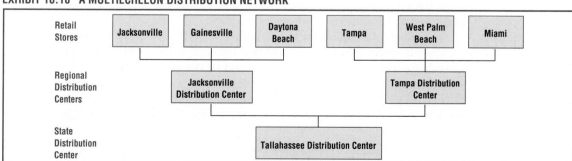

pull system.[7] Each retailer and regional distribution center orders independently, that is, without considering inventory located at or required by other retailers or warehouses. Each level does its own planning and maintains an individual safety stock. Alternatively, the firm may choose a *push* distribution system in which a central distribution facility forecasts the needs of each warehouse or retailer on the basis of market information and supplies it accordingly.

In both push and pull replenishment systems the firm must know how much inventory to transfer to each stock-keeping point, when it should be transferred, and how much safety stock should be maintained.

The reorder point, economic order quantity (EOQ), and base stock models discussed in Chapter 13 are often used for warehouse replenishment systems. There are, however, weaknesses in these systems. First, these models are designed for independent demand situations, but demand is independent only at the last link in the distribution channel. Demand for regional or national warehouses is derived from this demand and is a function of the firm's decisions regarding shipment sizes and timing. Second, these systems rely on historical demand, not forecast demand. Third, there is a definite risk of a stockout if a number of branch warehouses reach their reorder points at the same time. Large quantities of safety stock must be held to avoid stockouts.

Fortunately, alternatives to these traditional replenishment systems exist. One is distribution requirements planning.

Distribution Requirements Planning

Just as material requirements planning (MRP)[8] can reduce inventory levels and lead times for items that display dependent demand within a firm, **distribution requirements planning (DRP)** can reduce inventory levels and lead times through the firm's distribution channels.

> **DEFINITION:** Distribution requirements planning is a computerized technique that calculates the time-phased inventory requirements at various levels of a distribution network by working backward from the requirements specified by each independent demand center.

DRP follows the same logic as MRP and can use the same database as a firm's MRP system. Each product has a bill of distribution (BOD) that indicates the structure of its distribution network: the components of each distribution echelon.

A standard lead time is calculated for each link in the BOD. For example, it may take one week for an order to be received from the Tallahassee distribution center in Exhibit 18.10 once the Jacksonville distribution center has released its order.

The net requirements for each period are converted into planned order receipts, using the same lot sizing techniques as in MRP. Planned order receipts are offset by lead times and become planned order releases.

The master distribution schedule is developed by exploding the BOD and using the planned order releases in each period for each independent demand center. This extends from the current period to the end of the planning horizon. The planning horizon must be at least as long as the cumulative lead time in the BOD.

In Exhibit 18.11 the requirements for each retail store are converted into planned order releases. The order releases for the stores in Jacksonville, Gainesville, and

---

[7] Pull and push systems are discussed in Chapter 16.

[8] Chapter 15 describes MRP in detail.

EXHIBIT 18.11   TOOLBOX: DISTRIBUTION REQUIREMENTS PLANNING

The Jacksonville store orders every other week; the other stores order every week. As with MRP records, the projected inventory refers to the inventory level at the end of the period. Scheduled receipts are existing replenishment orders that are due at the beginning of each period, while planned order receipts have not yet been released.

	Quantity of Table X31 in Week								
	1	2	3	4	5	6	7	8	9
Jacksonville Store **Lead time: 1 week**									
Gross requirements	20	20	30	30	40	40	50	30	30
Scheduled receipts	20	—	—	—	—	—	—	—	—
Projected inventory |0	—	30	—	40	—	50	—	30	—
Net requirements	—	20	—	30	—	40	—	30	—
Planned order receipts	—	50	—	70	—	90	—	60	—
Planned order releases	50	—	70	—	90	—	60	—	—
Gainesville Store **Lead time: 1 week**									
Gross requirements	40	40	70	70	95	95	80	80	70
Scheduled receipts	40	—	—	—	—	—	—	—	—
Projected inventory |0	—	—	—	—	—	—	—	—	—
Net requirements	—	40	70	70	95	95	80	80	70
Planned order receipts	—	40	70	70	95	95	80	80	70
Planned order releases	40	70	70	95	95	80	80	70	—
Daytona Beach Store **Lead time: 2 weeks**									
Gross requirements	20	25	35	30	45	40	40	35	30
Scheduled receipts	20	—	—	—	—	—	—	—	—
Projected inventory |0	—	—	—	—	—	—	—	—	—
Net requirements	—	25	35	30	45	40	40	35	30
Planned order receipts	—	25	35	30	45	40	40	35	30
Planned order releases	35	30	45	40	40	35	30	—	—

The gross requirements for the Jacksonville distribution center are found by summing the planned order releases for the Jacksonville, Gainesville, and Daytona Beach stores.

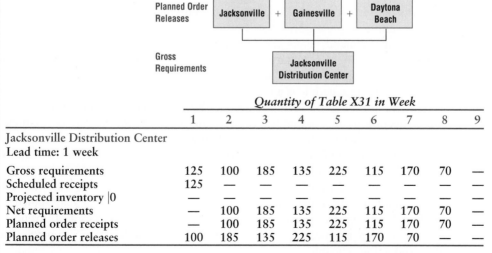

	Quantity of Table X31 in Week								
	1	2	3	4	5	6	7	8	9
Jacksonville Distribution Center **Lead time: 1 week**									
Gross requirements	125	100	185	135	225	115	170	70	—
Scheduled receipts	125	—	—	—	—	—	—	—	—
Projected inventory |0	—	—	—	—	—	—	—	—	—
Net requirements	—	100	185	135	225	115	170	70	—
Planned order receipts	—	100	185	135	225	115	170	70	—
Planned order releases	100	185	135	225	115	170	70	—	—

The gross requirements for the Tallahassee distribution center are found by combining the planned order releases for the Jacksonville and Tampa distribution centers.

(Exhibit 18.11 continues on next page)

EXHIBIT 18.11 *(continued)*

Planned Order Releases	Jacksonville Distribution Center					Tampa Distribution Center			

Gross Requirements				Tallahassee Distribution Center					

	Quantity of Table X31 in Week								
	1	2	3	4	5	6	7	8	9
Tallahassee Distribution Center									
Lead time: 1 week									
Gross requirements	250	225	350	175	450	200	340	125	—
Scheduled receipts	250	—	—	—	—	—	—	—	—
Projected inventory |0	—	—	—	—	—	—	—	—	—
Net requirements	—	225	350	175	450	200	340	125	—
Planned order receipts	—	225	350	175	450	200	340	125	—
Planned order releases	225	350	175	450	200	340	125	—	—

Daytona Beach are aggregated and form the gross requirements for the Jacksonville regional warehouse. These requirements are converted into planned order releases and combined with those of the Tampa regional warehouse. The planned order releases for the Tallahassee distribution center constitute an important input to the firm's demand management activities and have a significant impact on the plant's master production schedule. Thus, DRP facilitates the integration of marketing and replenishment information into the overall management control process.

Safety stocks at each echelon of the distribution network can be eliminated because the firm can more accurately predict when and where its products will have to be available. DRP safety stocks need be carried only by the lowest echelon (the retail store level in this example) to protect it against fluctuations in customer demand.

Since aggregated demand expectations rather than historical data are used to develop the master production schedule, it should be more accurate. Customer service levels should improve, and distribution costs should decrease. Special orders and anticipated demand peaks can be built into the schedule. Surprises that can disrupt operations can be eliminated. If local demand cannot be met, the DRP system can help managers make realistic delivery promises.

A more accurate schedule is a more stable schedule that results in smoother and more efficient production. Savings also can be generated through more efficient logistical operations. For example, better transportation routes can be planned. Higher vehicle capacity utilization can be obtained through more effective decisions about vehicle dispatching. Distribution centers can ensure that they have scheduled an appropriate number of workers for loading and unloading operations.

The data captured by DRP systems can benefit the firm in other ways as well. Constant communication throughout the distribution network can be maintained by using the DRP computer system. Modifications to demand forecasts and inventory levels can be used to update the master distribution schedule and ultimately the master production schedule.

As with MRP, the scope of DRP systems is expanding. Ross (1993) refers to these expanded systems as *distribution resource planning (DRPII)*. These systems provide another example of the trend toward integrating the entire value chain and creating enterprise logistic planning (ELP) systems (see Exhibit 15.19).

Improving Distribution Systems with Just-in-Time Concepts

Just-in-time (JIT) concepts can improve the effectiveness of distribution systems and improve upstream and internal operations. For example, reducing lead times, switching from weekly to daily time buckets, and utilizing small batch sizes can lower the costs of a DRP system and increase its responsiveness to market demand.

In practice, small lot-for-lot deliveries are uneconomical for many companies. However, current innovations in distribution are lowering transportation costs. For example, consider the two scenarios illustrated in Exhibit 18.12. In the first scenario 12 companies supply products to the same plant three times a day. In the second scenario companies that are close to each other take turns transporting all their products to the plant together. Each company may make one delivery per day or three deliveries every third day. The delivery truck can be divided into several sections, one for each company.

The transfer of certain final assembly and/or packaging operations to warehouses also can reduce inventory levels within the distribution system. For example, consider a firm that produces a wide variety of products from a relatively small set of components. The variability of demand for the firm's end products is wider than that for the components that constitute those products. Therefore, if final assembly is performed at the warehouse in response to actual demand, the level of safety stock can be reduced. Transferring the packaging operation to the firm's warehouse may be worth the cost of duplicated equipment if the same product is sold under different brand names or in different quantities.

As demonstrated by Wal-Mart (see Exhibit 3.2), **cross-docking** is another way in which low inventory holding costs and fast, frequent delivery can be supported.

> **DEFINITION:** Cross-docking is a logistics technique in which goods arrive at a warehouse, are repacked, and cross to a loading dock from which they are shipped out.

Cross-docking requires close, frequent communication among the vendors that supply the warehouse, the warehouse, and the retailers the warehouse serves. Electronic data interchange facilitates this communication.

Electronic Data Interchange

Electronic data interchange (EDI) is becoming a popular mode of communication between firms and the organizations they supply. The Big Three American automobile manufacturers and many major retailers are forcing their suppliers to exchange business data through EDI. Pharmaceutical manufacturers are using EDI to tie directly into major health care providers and business groups.

> **DEFINITION:** Electronic data interchange is the computer-to-computer exchange of business information in a standard data format.

What is EDI, and how does it differ from electronic mail and fax? This is best answered with a simple example. Suppose the Koontz Company supplies the Little Rock Furniture Company with leather. Whenever Little Rock needs more leather, its purchasing department uses its computer system to prepare a paper purchase order. The purchase order is mailed or faxed to Koontz, which enters the information on its own computer system; obviously this is a time-consuming and error-prone

EXHIBIT 18.12 JIT DELIVERY

Scenario 1. Each supplier delivers its own products to the plant

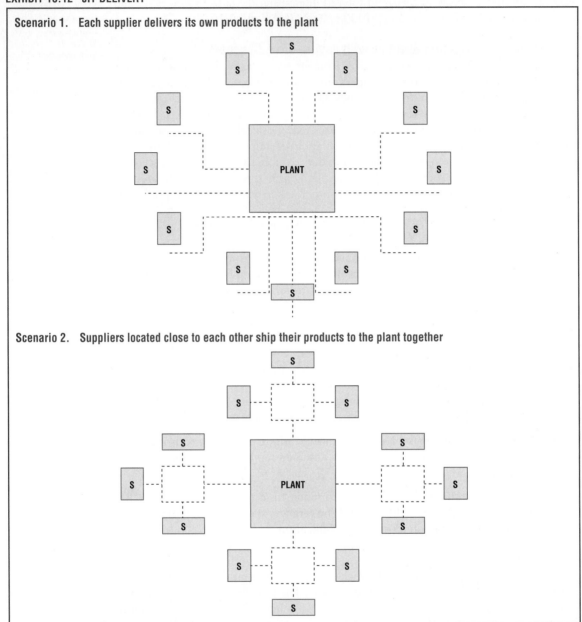

Scenario 2. Suppliers located close to each other ship their products to the plant together

process. With EDI, however, data are sent electronically (either directly or via a third-party network service) from Koontz's computer to Little Rock's computer and vice versa.

EDI does not necessarily require firms to purchase compatible hardware and software. EDI translation software can be used to translate data from the source computer into a standardized format. Once translated, the data are transferred to

EXHIBIT 18.13 AN EDI-LINKED CUSTOMER-SUPPLIER CHAIN

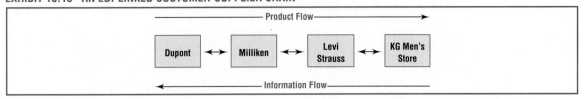

the destination computer, which then uses the translation software to convert the data into a format suitable for its own systems. Since standardized formats for many common transactions have been developed by the Accredited Standards Committee, a group chartered by the American National Standards Institute, standardized formats do not vary from one company to the next.

Purchase orders, advance shipping notices, and invoices are common EDI transactions. Since data are not entered twice (by the sender and by the receiver) and do not have to travel by mail or courier, time and money are saved. EDI can save 10 to 20 percent a year of the cost of sending documents—Canadian Customs expects that EDI will reduce its annual paper flow by 100 million pieces—and reduce order cycle times by as much as 40 percent. The quality of information transfer is improved because fewer clerical errors can be made. EDI is playing a key role in some firms as they switch to JIT deliveries.

The real benefits of EDI are realized when firms go a step further and use this technology to change the way they share information and work together. For example, rather than using demand forecasts, a manufacturer can employ actual point-of-sale data to drive its production planning. Not only will the manufacturer be more responsive to its customers, this also will lower production costs through lower buffer inventories and more efficient scheduling. By increasing the speed with which information about the sale of the firm's products travels, the firm can determine the success of new and improved products more quickly.

Whole chains of suppliers and customers can be linked with EDI (see Exhibit 18.13). Whenever customers buy a pair of jeans at the KG Men's Store in Dallas, for example, the clerk scans the bar code label. The inventory level on the database is reduced by one, and Levi Strauss automatically provides a replacement pair. Levi Strauss is connected via EDI with Milliken, its fabric supplier, which is connected with Dupont, the firm that makes the fiber for Milliken. Levi Strauss reports that EDI has enabled it to reduce its replenishment cycle time from 9 weeks to 4 days and its total cycle time from 66 weeks to 11 weeks. Inventory levels and costs have fallen drastically for all the firms in the chain.

EDI is an excellent example of how external integration can help firms become FROs. The EDI concept also can be used internally to link the firm's functional areas or business units. In fact, the companies that have been most successful with EDI have used it not only to meet their customers' needs but also to improve their internal operations.

Integration and responsiveness must extend throughout the value chain if a firm expects to become a fast-response organization. What most needs to be integrated is information. From a physical distribution standpoint, goods should be constantly in motion until they reach the ultimate customer, and this movement should be swift and direct. The shorter the time between the start of the journey (as a component or raw material) and the time when the complete product is in the customer's hands, the less uncertainty can enter the internal and external environments.

Integration is knowledge-intensive, and computers will be increasingly relied on to achieve it. Managers need to remember, though, that critical flexibility and responsiveness can be achieved only through people and nonprogrammed activity. While the communication links make accurate and fast information transfer possible, people make the critical decisions. This applies particularly to strategic decisions involving the design of products and processes and the timing of product introduction. System architecture cannot take into account hesitant decision making or a poorly implemented concurrent engineering philosophy.

Invariably, the value chain cycle time is longer than the time a customer is prepared to wait for a product; this is particularly true of items expected to be on the shelf. Inventory has to be carried in the value chain, and logic dictates that location be as close as possible in time to the customer. The shorter the physical resupply time, the more product mix risk the retailer can take and the less inventory is needed on display. Time *is* money for *everyone* in the value chain. Because travel time is only a small fraction of total cycle time, managers should look for time savings through improvement in internal procedures and elimination of unnecessary storage points rather than through faster and more costly means of physical transport.

CHAPTER SUMMARY

The management of upstream (suppliers to firm) and downstream (firm to customers) material flows is strategically important because these flows affect a firm's ability to compete on cost, quality, flexibility, dependability, and time. This chapter discussed several ways in which upstream and downstream flows can be improved. Important points to remember include the following:

- Traditionally, firms have followed a multiple sourcing policy (i.e., having several potential suppliers for each item purchased). The competitive pressures faced by firms today, however, are increasing the demands placed on suppliers and making this policy unattractive. Instead, many firms are actively reducing the number of suppliers with which they deal and establishing a much closer and longer-term relationship with the remaining suppliers.
- Vendor certification programs can help firms identify and develop superior suppliers.
- ISO 9000 is a series of quality assurance standards developed by the International Standards Organization and adopted by over 89 countries.
- When suitable suppliers do not approach a firm, reverse marketing can identify potential suppliers and persuade them to enter into a long-term relationship with that firm.
- Even if a firm has reduced the number of its suppliers to sole sourcing levels, hundreds of suppliers may still be needed. One option for dealing with a large number of suppliers is the supply keiretsu structure, in which suppliers are arranged in tiers.
- Distribution channels can be short (firm to final customer) or can involve several layers of intermediaries, such as retailers, wholesalers, and industrial distributors.

- Inventory levels and lead times throughout a firm's distribution channels can be reduced by distribution requirements planning (DRP). DRP follows the same logic as materials planning requirements, which can be used within the firm itself.
- Applying just-in-time (JIT) concepts to the distribution system can improve its effectiveness. For example, reducing lead times, switching from weekly to daily time buckets, and utilizing small batch sizes can lower the costs of a DRP system.
- Cross-docking and electronic data interchange are other ways in which costs can be lowered and lead times reduced.

KEY TERMS

Upstream material flows
Downstream material flows
Outsource
Make versus buy decision

Multiple sourcing
Sole sourcing
Certified supplier status
ISO 9000

Supply (vertical) keiretsu
Reverse marketing
Distribution channel
Physical distribution

Distribution requirements planning (DRP)
Cross-docking
Electronic data interchange (EDI)

DISCUSSION QUESTIONS

1. What are the benefits to a firm of reducing the number of suppliers? What are the potential dangers?

2. How would you identify a likely candidate for long-term sole supplier status?

3. Under what conditions would a firm be likely to outsource? What would a firm be *unlikely* to outsource?

4. What are the following organizations *least likely* to outsource?
   a. A university
   b. An airline
   c. A plastic injection molder
   d. An automobile manufacturer
   e. A national fast-food chain

5. People tend to think of outsourcing as a purchasing or supply issue. Is it possible to outsource downstream? Can you think of any examples?

6. What is the principal basis on which to make an outsourcing decision? What other bases can you think of?

7. Are there inherent risks in becoming a sole source supplier to a large company? How might these risks be offset?

8. What impact is the ISO 9000 series of standards likely to have on supplier certification? Is this good or bad?

9. What *are* supply keiretsu? Who is the power in the chain? How do they differ from other forms of keiretsu?

10. What is reverse marketing? What are its implications for purchasing organizations?

11. What is distribution requirements planning? How does it differ from material requirements planning?

12. How could just-in-time be useful in distribution? What disadvantages does the concept have?

13. Can a service organization use DRP? How?

14. What advantages does electronic data interchange have for manufacturing firms? What, if anything, will be integrated?

15. How does upstream-downstream materials management help a firm become more responsive?

PROBLEMS

1. A local store has given its regional distribution center a requirement plan for item A over the next five weeks. It takes the regional distribution center one week to obtain item A from the national distribution center and one week to deliver it to the local store. Assume that the store orders the EOQ of item A (500 units) each time. Also assume that the regional distribution center has 500 units of item A on hand now and expects to receive 200 more at the beginning of week 2. Develop a DRP schedule

for the regional center by using the lot-for-lot method.

	Week				
	1	2	3	4	5
Net requirement for item A	—	400	300	550	480

2. Using the lot-for-lot technique, develop a DRP schedule for the Toronto distribution center. Assume that none of the distribution centers have any inventory on hand and that the lead time for all products between each two levels is one week.

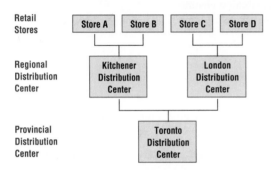

The net requirements by store are shown in the table below.

Net Requirements by Store	Item	Week					
		1	2	3	4	5	6
Store A	×11	—	—	200	350	280	320
	×12	—	—	300	325	310	320
Store B	×11	—	—	100	115	125	95
	×12	—	—	500	520	510	515
Store C	×11	—	—	300	310	305	300
	×12	—	—	320	310	325	320
Store D	×11	—	—	450	550	500	480
	×12	—	—	220	210	190	200

3. Develop another DRP schedule for the Toronto distribution center, using the information provided in problem 2. This time use the EOQ lot size method. Assume that the EOQ is 50 for item ×11 and 75 for item ×12. What is the effect of changing the lot sizing technique?

4. Given the following bill of distribution and net requirements schedule, develop a DRP schedule for the producer. Assume that each regional distribution center has 100 units of each item on hand and that the lead time between each two levels is one week. Use the lot-for-lot technique.

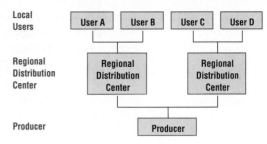

Net requirements by user:

Net Requirements by User	Item	Week					
		1	2	3	4	5	6
User A	×11	—	—	150	250	250	310
	×12	—	—	350	340	360	370
	×13	—	—	225	260	280	295
User B	×11	—	—	200	215	225	195
	×12	—	—	400	420	410	415
	×13	—	—	300	330	320	295
User C	×11	—	—	320	330	325	320
	×12	—	—	340	330	345	340
	×13	—	—	350	350	365	260
User D	×11	—	—	450	575	575	495
	×12	—	—	220	235	145	225
	×13	—	—	310	305	340	335

5. In problem 4, assume that item ×11 is produced in lots of 100, item ×12 in lots of 150, and item ×13 in lots of 50. Develop DRP schedules using these lot sizes.

6. In problem 4, user A has just reported a quality problem with item ×11 that will require a recall of the product for replacement of a part. All four users have a current stock of 196 units each, and a lot of ×11 has just been completed in the plant. It will take 15 minutes for one worker to replace the part in each unit; the new part will not be available for a week. The work can be done by newly hired workers, and there is room in the plant for six workers. The plant is currently working at single-shift capacity. What are you going to do, and how long will it take?

7. Conway Containers, a manufacturer of plastic containers, has recently installed a DRP system to manage the movement of products between its sole manufacturing plant, its three distribution centers, and its retailers. The firm's most popular product is a five-liter plastic pail which is shipped in pallets of 60 pails. The pail is made on a dedicated injection molding machine, but a color change is made each hour, so that the effective batch size is 300 units. The plant works a 16-hour (two-shift) day in a five-

day workweek. The consolidated demand projections for the white pail for the three distribution centers for the next 10 days have just landed on your desk; you are the distribution planner. You allow a two-working-day lead time from the time of placing a manufacturing order to shipment. Prepare the distribution plan, given that you have 20 pallets of white five-liter pails in the plant's finished goods area.

Number of Pallets Required per Day

Day:	1	2	3	4	5	6	7	8	9	10
Pal:	8	6	9	8	8	7	7	10	8	7

8. Refer to problem 7. As the distribution manager, you have asked the distribution centers to give you their demand projections every 5 days for a 10-day period. You have just received the next projections, and the consolidation shows that day 14's projection is 21 pallets and day 15's projection is 24 pallets. What should you do? Keep in mind that each distribution center has a two-day lead time of its own.

9. Burger Express, an American fast-food chain has five major distribution centers across the nation and distributes product to its outlets on a four-day cycle. Having just launched a new product that was expected to increase sales volumes by 2 percent, the chain took the precaution of placing in each outlet enough raw materials to produce twice the first week's anticipated sales of the new product. The distribution managers have just received the first week's sales data, and the trends are disturbing. Sales volume overall is running ahead of target: For distribution center A, which serves the East Coast, actual volume is 33 percent of that planned, while for distribution centers D and E, which serve the West Coast, actual volume is 135 percent of that planned for each. Centers B and C, serving the rest of the country, are running about 5 percent ahead of planned volume. Each distribution center has approximately the same throughput. Indications are that these trends will continue and that the expected sales decay after the launch will be more gradual than anticipated. Another problem is that the major ingredients are purchased from plants in the central part of the country, which are operating at capacity. These plants ship to distribution center B, which then transships to the other centers. The average time stock sits in center B waiting for transshipment is two days. How should this situation be managed?

10. You are the purchasing manager for a firm with one manufacturing plant on the East Coast. Traditionally, you have arranged for goods to be moved to the plant by rail, and you have tracks into your warehouse. Each of your suppliers ships in full boxcars, and you consume about one boxcar per supplier per week. The railroad schedules your cars to arrive at the plant at midnight, but your records indicate that the cars are an average of three hours late, with a standard deviation of 0.5 day. How much safety stock would you like to have on hand, and what additional policies might you explore?

11. You are the purchasing manager in problem 10. One of your suppliers has suggested that it can supply you daily by road and will use a freight company that guarantees delivery within one hour of the planned arrival. The planned arrival will not be until 9 a.m., two hours after work starts each day. How much safety stock of this item do you plan to hold, and what else might you suggest to the supplier?

12. You are the purchasing manager in problem 10. All your suppliers now intend to supply you daily by road. Eight of the suppliers are in the same city, and they all promise delivery as in problem 11. How much safety stock of each item do you plan to hold, and what else might you suggest to the suppliers?

13. Your company currently manufactures a bracket for motors you build. Each bracket has material costs of $3.50 and takes one minute to machine on each of three machines (at a combined operator-machine rate of $25 per hour); overhead is allocated at a rate of 90 percent of material cost. Setup takes one hour per machine at $25 per hour, and the carrying cost of inventory is 12 percent per year. Demand for the bracket is currently 2,400 per month. A supplier has offered to produce the bracket at a cost of $5 per bracket plus an order cost of $100. Do you continue to make the bracket?

14. The company in problem 13 has decided to make a new bracket to take the place of 15 old brackets. Average demand for the old brackets was 2,400 per month. The new bracket has a material cost of $5 and requires 1.2 minutes of machining on each of three machines. Rates are the same as in problem 13, and there are enough machines available to make twice the demand of the new bracket. The outside supplier offers to make the new bracket at a cost of $7 with no order cost provided that a

blanket order is given at the beginning of the year for 400,000 brackets. Do you purchase the bracket? In either event, how do you want delivery to the assembly area?

15. What other factors would you consider in deciding whether to outsource in problems 13 and 14, and how might you quantify or qualify these factors?

GROUP EXERCISES

Many of the tools and concepts discussed in this chapter are meant to be used in a team setting. The following problem is best solved by small groups of students. Ideally, each group should be composed of people with different backgrounds, interests, or areas of expertise.

As a group, develop two alternative methods of integrating the whole value chain to provide fast-response service to customers. You may want to revisit Exhibits 3.2 and 13.1. In developing the two means of managing external materials flows, identify the circumstances in which each is appropriate. What allows you to decide which system is better? Is the means of integrating suppliers into the system independent of the downstream stakeholders? What do you need to put in place besides the structure? If you were looking to improve the system, against what would you benchmark, and why?

REFERENCES AND SELECTED BIBLIOGRAPHY

Arai, E. [1989], "JIT in Purchasing: A Progress Report," *Purchasing,* Sept. 14, pp. 58–75.

Barber, Norman F. [1991], "EDI: Making It Finally Happen," *P&IM Review,* June, pp. 35–40.

Blenkhorn, David L., and Peter M. Banting [1991], "How Reverse Marketing Changes Buyer-Seller Roles," *Industrial Marketing Management,* vol. 20, no. 3, pp. 185–191.

—— and Hamid Noori [1990], "What It Takes to Supply Japanese OEMs," *Industrial Marketing Management,* vol. 19, pp. 21–30.

Bookbinder, James H., and Timothy D. Locke [1986], "Simulation Analysis of Just-in-Time Distribution," *International Journal of Physical Distribution and Materials Management,* vol. 16, no. 7, pp. 31–45.

Burr, John T. [1990], "The Future Necessity," *Quality Progress,* June, pp. 19–23.

Craighead, Thomas G. [1989], "EDI Impact Grows for Cost Efficient Manufacturing," *P&IM Review,* July, pp. 32–33.

Davidow, William H., and Bro Uttal [1989], *Total Customer Service: The Ultimate Weapon,* Harper & Row, New York.

Durand, I. G., D. W. Marquardt, R. W. Peach, and J. C. Pyle [1993], "Updating the ISO-9000 Quality Standards: Responding to Marketplace Needs," *Quality Progress,* July, pp. 23–28.

Ferreira, John A. [1993], "Re-Engineering the Materials and Production Function," *APICS,* October, pp. 48–51.

Forest, Stephanie Anderson, Catherine Arnst, Kathy Rebello, and Peter Burrows [1993], "The Education of Michael Dell," *Business Week,* Mar. 22, pp. 82–88.

Freeman, Virginia T., and Joseph L. Cavinato [1990], "Fitting Purchasing to the Strategic Firm: Frameworks, Processes, and Values," *Journal of Purchasing and Materials Management,* January, pp. 6–10.

"How to Build Quality" [1989], *The Economist,* Sept. 23, pp. 91–93.

Kelly, Kevin, Otis Port, James Treece, Gail DeGeorge, and Zachary Schiller [1992], "Learning from Japan," *Business Week,* Jan. 27, pp. 52–60.

Krupp. J. A. G. [1991], "JIT in Distribution and Warehousing," *Production and Inventory Management Journal,* second quarter, pp. 18–21.

Leenders, M. R., and D. L. Blenkhorn [1988], *Reverse Marketing: The New Buyer-Supplier Relationship,* Free Press and Collier Macmillan, New York.

Oldland, John [1989], "Distribution: The Key to Innovative Marketing," *Marketing,* Oct. 23, p. 13.

O'Neal, Charles R. [1989], "The Buyer-Seller Linkage in a Just-in-Time Environment," *Journal of Purchasing and Materials Management,* pp. 34–40.

Port, Otis, John Carey, and Kevin Kelly [1992], "Quality: Small and Midsize Companies Seize the Challenge—Not a Moment Too Soon," *Business Week,* Nov. 30, pp. 66–72.

Ramsey, J. [1990], "The Myth of the Cooperative Single Source," *Journal of Purchasing and Materials Management,* Winter, pp. 2–5.

Ross, David F. [1993], "DRPII: The Answer to Connecting the Distribution Enterprise," *APICS,* March, pp. 59–62.

Schonberger, Richard J., and Abdolhossein Ansari [1984], "Just-in-Time Purchasing Can Improve Quality," *Journal of Purchasing and Materials Management,* Spring, pp. 2–7.

Sellers, Patricia [1993], "Companies That Serve You Best," *Fortune,* May 31, pp. 75–88.

Stenger, Alan J., and Joseph L. Cavinato [1979], "Adapting MRP to the Outbound Side-Distribution Requirements Planning," *Production and Inventory Management,* fourth quarter, pp. 1–13.

Toscano, Diane M. [1992], "A Tip for Survival: Manage the Supply Chain," *APICS,* October, pp. 34–36.

Tully, Shawn [1993], "The Modular Corporation," *Fortune,* Feb. 8, pp. 106–114.

Venkatesan, Ravi [1992], "Strategic Sourcing: To Make or Not to Make," *Harvard Business Review,* November–December, pp. 98–107.

Vollman, T. E., W. L. Berry, and D. C. Whybark [1992], *Manufacturing Planning and Control Systems,* 3d ed., Irwin, Homewood, Ill.

CHAPTER 19

PERFORMANCE
MEASUREMENT

The link between a firm's performance-measuring system and its actual performance is strong. In a fast-response organization managers should ask the following questions:

- How can ongoing efforts to meet the firm's goals and objectives be evaluated?
- How can people be encouraged to improve the firm's performance?

These two questions are related in a fundamental way. If individual or group performance that improves the firm's performance is to be rewarded, appropriate measures for individual and group performance must be established. This raises questions such as, How often and when should those measurements be made? and How aggregate should those measures be?

By the end of this chapter you will have been exposed to several different types of performance measures. You will be familiar with the essential characteristics of an effective performance-measuring system and the fundamental factors that should be considered in designing reward systems.

EXHIBIT 19.1   FRO MANUFACTURING PROFILE

Faced with increased competition, explosive growth in the product mix, shortening product life cycles, and increased pressure to reduce product costs, managers at Wang Laboratories Inc. knew they had to implement major changes in the firm's manufacturing operations. Wang, which produces and markets computer systems, had suffered marked decreases in overall profitability for several years as the computer market shifted from a seller's to a buyer's market.

As an experiment, Wang launched an improvement program called EPIC (Experimental Process Improvement Challenge) for its circuit board assembly operation. Without being allowed to purchase new equipment, the EPIC team was asked to reduce throughput time from 20 to 3 days, improve quality, and increase process flexibility. Using JIT and OPT principles, the team was able to meet those challenging goals.

The EPIC experiment was a success, but 90 percent of the manufacturing managers believed that widespread adoption of the concepts employed by EPIC was not possible because Wang's existing performance-measuring systems would inhibit such changes. Performance measures focused solely on financial goals, favoring high rates of resource utilization that led to large work-in-process inventories, poor quality, and long throughput times.

Source: Adapted from Dixon, Nanni, and Vollman (1990), pp. 48–52.

EXHIBIT 19.2   FRO SERVICE PROFILE

USAA, an insurance and investment company, used to measure productivity by using a very simple measure: the total number of policies on the books was divided by the number of people who wrote, sold, and maintained them.

When productivity began to slip in the early 1980s, USAA's managers became alarmed. They concluded, however, that the problem was not the performance of USAA employees but the way in which it was measured. Excellent customer service is one of the keys to success in the industry, but attempts to improve service by hiring more people resulted in productivity losses at USAA.

A revolutionary evaluation system called the family of measures (FOM) was developed to put the customer into the productivity equation. Every month USAA's 14,000 employees are scored on quality, timeliness, quantity, and customer service. In the telephone sales department, for example, people are rated on the number of policies sold, the accuracy of price quotes, the amount of time spent on postcall paperwork, and the pleasantness of

Exhibit 19.2 continues on next page

EXHIBIT 19.2 *(continued)*

> their telephone manners. Bonuses and promotions are based on FOM scores, and teams with the best monthly scores are singled out for public praise.
>
> Nearly 99 percent of USAA's policyholders renew their policies every year; the company ranked second in the prompt and satisfactory settlement of claims in a recent *Consumer Reports* survey of automobile insurers.
>
> *Source:* Adapted from Henkoff (1992), pp. 78 and 82.

19.1 MANAGERIAL ORIENTATION

Wang's problem (see Exhibit 19.1) is typical of firms that are struggling to shed their focus on cost and compete simultaneously along all six dimensions of competition. Although their strategic goals and objectives have been altered, their performance-measuring and appraisal systems have not been changed at all. As a result, these firms face two major problems.

First, the firm's **performance-measuring systems** are not measuring the degree to which its strategic goals and objectives are being met. But research shows that performance can be improved *only when specific goals are combined with feedback* [Locke and associates (1981)]. Without the feedback provided by **performance measures,** employees do not know if their efforts are helping the firm meet its goals or are even being noticed.

The second problem relates to the powerful effect performance measurement and appraisal systems have on the behavior of people within a firm. By measuring one set of factors but not another, a firm sends strong signals to its employees about what is and what is not important. Since people tend to work toward measures, it is difficult for a firm to achieve its goals if its performance-measuring systems are not strategically aligned with its goals. USAA (see Exhibit 19.2) is a good example: measures had to change before performance could change.

This look at enhancing and improving operations therefore would not be complete without an investigation of performance measurement. Let us begin by examining a well-established and deceptively simple performance measure: productivity. When used improperly or in isolation, this measure may reinforce inappropriate behavior. A framework for measuring performance in nonfinancial as well as financial terms will then be presented. The discussion concludes by examining reward systems and their impact on a firm.

19.2 PRODUCTIVITY AS A MEASURE OF PERFORMANCE

Chapter 1 discussed **productivity** from the viewpoint of the national economy and in terms of gross domestic product. Productivity is, however, also a measure of operational performance. This chapter will focus on productivity measures at the level of the firm.

Productivity

$$\text{Productivity} = \frac{\text{Total outputs}}{\text{Total inputs}} \qquad (19.1)$$

EXHIBIT 19.3 PRODUCTIVITY AND ITS RELATIONSHIP TO PROFITABILITY

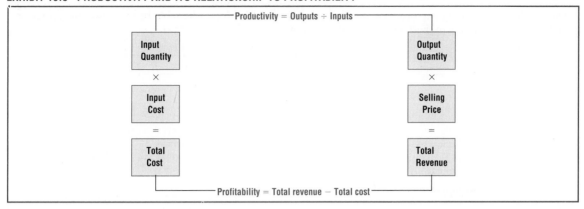

Productivity's popularity as a measure of performance stems from its apparent simplicity and the ease with which it can be used throughout a firm. It is often employed to compare the performance of different departments or firms. Stockholders, investors, and managers commonly believe that high rates of productivity [equation (19.1)] are an indicator of high profitability and good shareholder returns. In many cases profitability does improve when productivity improves (see Exhibit 19.3).

Productivity is essentially an efficiency measure that shows how well a firm consumed resources in a given time period. Outputs are typically equal to the total value of goods and services produced during that period, while inputs are equal to the cost of the resources required to produce that output. Productivity gain is the rate of change in output with respect to input.

Productivity can be expressed in many ways. **Partial-factor productivity (PFP)** measures productivity with respect to a specific resource [equation (19.2)].[1]

Partial-Factor Productivity (PFP)

$$\text{PFP} = \frac{\text{Total outputs}}{\text{Input of a specific resource}} \qquad (19.2)$$

Productivity can be expressed in other forms as well. **Single-factor productivity (SFP)** measures the ratio of a specific output to a single input [equation (19.3)]. For example, a firm can measure the number of hamburgers produced per hour by a specific employee or the quantity of leather used to produce a batch of running shoes.

Single-Factor Productivity (SFP)

$$\text{SFP} = \frac{\text{Output of a specific product}}{\text{Input of a specific resource}} \qquad (19.3)$$

Calculating an SFP measure is often simple and can be done for each resource used to produce a good or service. Several SFP measures have been calculated for a manufacturer of water bed sheets in Exhibit 19.4.

[1] When economists talk about productivity, more often than not they mean *labor* productivity, which is really a measure of partial-factor productivity. The U.S. Government Bureau of Labor Statistics calculates national productivity by dividing the total economic output for the country by the total number of worker-hours expended.

EXHIBIT 19.4 TOOLBOX: SINGLE-FACTOR PRODUCTIVITY MEASURES

The Coldratt Sheet Company produces three sizes of water bed sheets. The table below shows the resources used to produce queen-size sheets over the last two months.

	January		February	
	Quantity	Cost, $	Quantity	Cost, $
Output	2,000 sets		2,200 sets	
Inputs				
Material				
Cloth	200,000 feet^2	600,000	200,000 feet^2	600,000
Thread	100,000 feet	1,000	110,000 feet	1,100
Labor	500 hours	5,000	579 hours	5,790
Equipment	1,000 hours	7,500	1,158 hours	8,565
Total Inputs		613,500		615,455

The single-factor productivity (SFP) associated with each process input can be calculated each month. The SFP for cloth, for example, is shown below.

$$SPF_{Jan} = \frac{2,000 \text{ sets}}{200,000 \text{ feet}^2 \text{ of cloth}} = 0.01 \text{ sets/feet}^2 \text{ of cloth}$$

The SFP for cloth increased to 0.011 set per square foot in February; this was the only SFP measure to increase from January to February.

	SFP Ratios	
Input	January	February
Cloth	0.01 sets/feet^2 of cloth	0.011 sets/feet^2 of cloth
Thread	0.02 sets/feet of thread	0.02 sets/feet of thread
Labor	4 sets/direct labor hour	3.8 sets/direct labor hour
Equipment	2 sets/equipment hour	1.9 sets/equipment hour

The net effect on total productivity (TP), however, is positive:

$$TP_{Jan} = \frac{2,000 \text{ sets}}{\$613,500} = 0.0033 \text{ sets/input dollar}$$

$$TP_{Feb} = \frac{2,200 \text{ sets}}{\$615,455} = 0.0036 \text{ sets/input dollar}$$

Complications arise when there is a significant time gap between inputs and their corresponding outputs (e.g., R&D and new products). Because their output is intangible, some service-oriented operations have problems determining what value to use as the numerator in the SFP ratio.

Once they have been calculated, interpreting the resultant set of SFP ratios can be difficult. If labor productivity goes up from 5 to 6 units per labor hour while material productivity goes down from 20 to 18 units per yard, what is the overall impact? Is the firm better off? The answer is not clear.

If only a few inputs or resources account for the majority of input costs, **multifactor productivity (MFP)** can be used. MFP measures the ratio of output to a set of key resources [equation (19.4)]. If some resources have a greater impact on productivity than do others, the resources can be weighted differently [equation (19.5)].

Multifactor Productivity (MFP)

$$MFP = \frac{\text{Total output}}{\text{Input of key resources}} \qquad (19.4)$$

$$\text{or} \qquad MFP = \frac{\text{Total output}}{\sum_{i=1}^{n} w_i R_i} \qquad (19.5)$$

where R_i = consumption of key resource i $i = 1$ to n
      w_i = weight assigned to resource i

$$0 \le w_i \le 1 \qquad \sum_{i=1}^{n} w_i = 1$$

Since the values in the denominator are added together, the resource quantities used in the PFP measures must all be expressed in the same units, that is, in dollar amounts. In some cases this may be difficult. Another problem with PFP is its often invalid assumption that the consumption values are independent and additive.

Every activity in the firm consumes resources, contributes to the output of the firm, and is a candidate for productivity improvements. **Total factor productivity (TFP)** reflects the use of a firm's total resources to produce its outputs.

As with all productivity measures, TFP should be used with care. As was mentioned earlier, productivity is a measure of **efficiency;** an FRO needs to measure both efficiency and **effectiveness.**

> **DEFINITION:** A measure of efficiency shows how well a firm consumed resources in order to produce output during a given time period. The efficiency of a process or activity can be equated to its output.

> **DEFINITION:** A measure of effectiveness indicates how well a firm has been able to produce goods and supply services during a given time period. The effectiveness of a process or activity can be equated to its outcome.

Productivity and other common performance measures (labor cost variances, return on investment, equipment utilization) tend to focus on costs. These measures often lead to practices that actually hurt the firm's long-term competitiveness. Managers begin to strive for short-term improvements in costs at the expense of quality, flexibility, and other competitive dimensions. The firm's products become less attractive to the consumer, product costs fall marginally (if at all),[2] and the firm's competitive position weakens rather than strengthens. Instead of a single measure of efficiency, the firm needs a *set of measures* that can provide an accurate picture of how well it is meeting all its goals.

Monitoring current performance and comparing it with operational goals is not the only function of performance measures. They are also used by a firm to compare itself with its competitors and develop benchmarks for improvement, for example, during competitive benchmarking.[3] Predicting the success of alternative strategies is another function of performance measures.

19.3 PERFORMANCE-MEASURING SYSTEMS

Wang was introduced at the beginning of this chapter as a firm that made a set of dramatic changes that far outpaced its performance-measuring system. How did

---

[2] As was discussed in Chapter 6, the cost of a product is determined largely by its design. Quality plays an important role as well; improving product and process quality often decreases costs.

[3] Refer to the Chapter 3 Supplement for a review of competitive benchmarking.

Wang deal with the problem? After reviewing its system, Wang discarded approximately 40 percent of its existing measures, redefined many of the remaining measures, and added many new ones. These performance measures form the basis of its new system, SMART (Strategic Measurement Analysis and Reporting Technique). SMART's constantly evolving measures cross functional boundaries, focus on horizontal work flows, and reflect Wang's operating objectives (see Exhibit 19.5).

Like Wang, many firms are replacing their performance-measuring systems with a radically different system. The next section will look at the qualities these systems should exhibit.

Essential Characteristics of an Effective Performance-Measuring System

An essential characteristic of a performance-measuring system is its ability to indicate the effectiveness as well as efficiency of efforts within the firm to accomplish specific goals. Let us look at the other characteristics of a good performance-measuring system.

- Nonfinancial performance measures must be included in the system because many of the firm's goals are not cost-based.

   Throughput time, equipment availability, schedule attainment, and percentage of defect-free products are nonfinancial performance measurements. Performance measures that correspond to each of the six dimensions of competition are listed in Exhibit 19.6.

   Note that financial measures such as return on investment, market share, and earnings per share are still required because the firm needs to know how well it is translating its ability to compete along the six competitive dimensions into bottom-line results.[4]

---

[4] Suppose the firm's efforts to eliminate waste from its production process have cut the amount of factory space in half. Unless the firm finds alternative uses for this space, it has not fully capitalized on its improvement.

EXHIBIT 19.5   PERFORMANCE MEASUREMENT AT WANG

Its corporate vision dictates which products Wang will produce and in which markets it will compete. Strategic business objectives (i.e., market and financial goals) are based on the corporate vision and lead to customer satisfaction, flexibility, and productivity operating objectives. These operating objectives are the basis for quality, delivery, process time, and waste criteria at the department and work center levels.

HIERARCHY OF OBJECTIVES AND MEASURES

At least one performance measure is used to reflect each goal, objective, or criterion.

Source: Adapted from Dixon, Nanni, and Vollman (1990), p. 53.

EXHIBIT 19.6   PERFORMANCE MEASURES FOR THE SIX DIMENSIONS OF COMPETITION

Quality
- Percentage of defect-free products
- Number and type of warranty claims
- Internal and external customer satisfaction rates
- Number of employee suggestions generated and implemented

Cost
- Product cost
- Inventory level (in days on hand)
- Total cost of ownership for purchased parts and/or materials (purchase price + ordering cost + inspection cost + receiving cost + scheduling delivery cost, etc.)

Dependability
- Percentage of delivery promises met
- Equipment availability (ratio of hours required to hours available)
- Number and/or frequency of changes to schedule given to suppliers

Service
- Response time to customers' inquiries
- Type and number of services offered
- Number of customer complaints
- Ease of contacting firm

Timeliness
- Throughput time (processing time + inspection time + movement time + waiting and/or storage time)
- Ratio of processing time to throughput time
- Equipment setup times
- Length of new product development cycle

Flexibility
- Economic batch size
- Setup downtime, batch run time
- Ratio of customer demand lead time to the combined supplier, in-house, and distribution lead time.

- Performance measures must be complementary rather than conflicting.
- Performance measures must motivate employees to help the firm achieve its long-term as well as short-term goals and objectives. Experience shows that performance measures that are set participatively, stated in positive terms, and easy to understand are more successful.
- Performance measures should be able to move across functional boundaries and encourage horizontal integration. The time interval between a customer preparing an order and the delivery of the product to the customer is a measure that spans several functional areas.
- The information provided by the measures must be capable of being aggregated as well as disaggregated. This allows the information to be useful at different levels of the firm. Aggregate data are generally more suitable for strategic planning, while more detailed data are needed to guide and monitor tactical decisions. By disaggregating a measure, managers can discover how performance can be improved.
- The data needed for the measures selected must be available, timely, and cost-effective to collect. Choosing performance measures that limit the data collected helps focus attention and reduce collection, collation, and dissemination costs.
- When performance measures are not equally important, they should be weighted differently. The weight reflects the relationship between the performance being measured and the organizational goals to which it contributes. The stronger the

relationship and the more important the goal, the larger the weight. These weights change as the firm's strategy changes and the firm learns more about these complicated cause-and-effect relationships.

- Flexibility is essential to a performance-measuring system. Over time, some performance measures may be dropped from the system and others may be added. Like Wang, Northern Telecom has found that carefully monitoring the value of each performance measure has improved the effectiveness of its performance-measuring system. Employees at Northern Telecom regularly complete questionnaires that encourage them to comment on the system.

After one reads through the list, it becomes clear that establishing and maintaining an effective performance-measuring system are challenging tasks. One of the major difficulties is developing an accurate, responsive information system to support performance measurement. An unresponsive information system can be the "Achilles' heel of performance measurement" [Kaplan and Norton (1992), p. 75].

In the past firms relied on information derived from their cost accounting systems, but as is discussed in the supplement to this chapter, the original intent of these systems was to provide information for external reporting purposes. Today FROs need more and better information more often. Activity-based costing (see the supplement to this chapter) is one way to obtain this information.

Another challenge in performance measurement is to interpret and integrate the results of individual performance measures. The next section will present a tool that can help a firm address this problem.

The Performance-Measuring Matrix

The **performance-measuring matrix** can be used to monitor a firm's performance along each of the six dimensions of competition as well as its overall performance over time.[5]

The actual performance-measuring matrix is the last of a series of matrices developed during a seven-step procedure. This procedure can best be understood through a simple illustration.

Suppose the Willkins Insurance Company has just updated its corporate strategy. For each of its product lines, the company has developed aggressive goals and objectives along each of the six dimensions of competition: cost, quality, dependability, flexibility, time, and service. Note that the emphasis placed on each dimension reflects its importance to the consumer and thus varies from one product line to the next. For example, service is much more important to the company's commercial automobile policyholders than to its household insurance policyholders.[6]

Let us develop a performance-measuring matrix for Willkins' line of household insurance.

> **Step 1.** Assign a weight between 0 and 100 percent to each dimension of competition. The weight should reflect the competitive emphasis the firm wishes to place on that dimension. The sum of the weights must equal 100 percent.

---

[5] The performance-measuring matrix can also be employed to help the firm predict and monitor the impact of an existing or proposed program on its performance. See Noori and Gillen (1994).

[6] Although the proposed performance-measuring matrix is straightforward and easy to understand, the actual implementation is a time-consuming and delicate process. Experience has shown that a cross-functional team approach should be taken and that the team must be provided with clear goals and up-to-date accurate information.

As illustrated in Exhibit 19.7, product quality is the most important competitive dimension for Willkins' household insurance policyholders; it has been assigned a weight of 25 percent. Product cost is the next important dimension and has been assigned a weight of 20 percent. Time, service, dependability, and flexibility have been assigned weights of 15 percent, 15 percent, 15 percent, and 10 percent, respectively.

Step 2. For each dimension of competition, examine the firm's corresponding goals and objectives and translate them into a set of performance measures.

Although one or more performance measures are needed for each of the six competitive dimensions, let us focus on quality. Over the next two years Willkins wants to cut its product defect rate tenfold and better match the coverage its policies provide with the coverage demanded by consumers. These goals have been translated into three performance measures: the transaction error ratio, the average number of underwriting errors, and the customer survey index (see Exhibit 19.8).

Step 3. On the basis of its relative importance, assign a weight between 0 and 100 percent to each performance measure. The sum of the weights for the performance measures relating to each dimension of competition must equal 100 percent.

Not all performance measures are equally important. Willkins, for example, feels that the customer survey index is the best indicator of product quality; this measure has been assigned a weight of 50 percent. The transaction error ratio and the average number of underwriting errors have been assigned weights of 30 percent and 20 percent, respectively. Similarly, Willkins must assign weights to the performance measures corresponding to the other five dimensions of competition.

EXHIBIT 19.7   TOOLBOX: ILLUSTRATING THE FIRM'S COMPETITIVE EMPHASIS

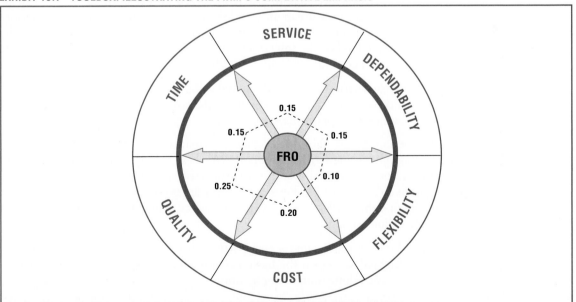

Note that the emphasis Willkins places on each competitive dimension is different for each of its five product lines.

EXHIBIT 19.8   TOOLBOX: QUALITY-RELATED PERFORMANCE MEASURES

The Willkins Insurance Company has chosen two performance measures to track its defect rate. The transaction ratio reflects the number of policy transactions (new business, amendment, and renewal) issued with errors that have been caught by the company, the agent, or the policyholder.

$$\text{Transaction error ratio} = \frac{\text{Number of new or revised policies that must be reissued}}{\text{Number of new or revised policies issued}}$$

Each month senior underwriters randomly select and review a sample of 50 policies. The number and type of errors are recorded. The results are shared at the monthly underwriting meeting, and the underwriters discuss ways in which these errors can be prevented.

$$\text{Average number of underwriting errors per 100 policies} = \frac{\text{Number of underwriting errors found}}{\text{Number of policies investigated}} \times 100$$

Another important aspect of product quality relates to the coverage provided by the policy. Periodically, Willkins revises its coverages to reflect changing market needs.

Each month an independent consulting firm conducts a survey of a sample of Willkins's clients. Among other things, the survey evaluates the quality of the coverage Willkins provides, and the quality of the service provided by its agents and customer service representatives. The quality index values range from 0 to 100 percent; the higher the index value, the better the perceived quality.

Note that since performance-measuring values are eventually added together, they should be statistically independent and not highly correlated.

Step 4. Develop the *scoring key matrix,* which will be used to convert performance measure values to scores between 0 and 10.

Subsequent steps require the firm to multiply the weights developed in step 3 by the actual performance measure values achieved and then sum the weighted values. Before this can be done, however, the firm must convert the performance-measuring values into common units. This can be done by using the scoring key in Exhibit 19.9A.

For each performance measure, a score of 10 corresponds to the desired or expected value of the measure in an established time frame (e.g., two years). A score of 3 corresponds to the current level of performance, while a score of zero is the lowest acceptable level or the lowest level recorded in the recent past. Intermediate scores can then be derived (see Exhibit 19.9B).

Step 5. In each period calculate the actual value of each performance measure. Convert these values into scores by using the scoring key matrix. Record the scores on the *basic performance matrix.*

Each period, the actual value of the performance measures must be calculated. Then, using the scoring key in Exhibit 19.9A, these values are translated into common units. For example, in month 6 the transaction error ratio was 0.035, which corresponds to a score of 7. This score is recorded on the basic performance matrix for quality in Exhibit 19.10A. A basic performance matrix will be required for each competitive dimension.

Step 6. Multiply the weight for each performance measure by its score. Record these weighted scores on the basic performance matrix. Sum the weighted scores for each dimension of competition.

The weighted score for the transaction error ratio is 2.1, and the sum of the weighted scores for quality is 5.4.

EXHIBIT 19.9 THE SCORING KEY

A. The Scoring Key Matrix

Performance Measure	Value of Measure That Corresponds to Score										
	0	1	2	3	4	5	6	7	8	9	10
Transaction error ratio	0.10	0.09	0.08	0.07	0.061	0.052	0.043	0.034	0.025	0.016	0.007
Customer survey index (%)	65	69	73	77	80	83	86	89	92	95	98
Average number of underwriting errors per 100 policies	20	16	12	8	6.97	5.94	4.91	3.89	2.86	1.83	0.8

B. How to Calculate Intermediate Score Values

The scale is anchored at three values: 0, 3, and 10. Consider, for example, the customer survey index. This measure is anchored at 65 percent (score 0), 77 percent (score 3), and 98 percent (score 10).

Score	Meaning
0	Lowest acceptable level or lowest level recorded in the past
3	Current level of performance
10	Desired level to be obtained within a predetermined time frame (e.g., two years)

The values between score 3 and score 10 are determined as follows. The value of the score 3 anchor is subtracted from that of the score 10 anchor. The result is divided by seven.

Continuing on with the example, 98 percent − 77 percent = 21 percent; 21 percent ÷ 7 scores = 3 percent per score. Therefore, each score between 3 and 10 corresponds to an improvement of 3 percent in the customer survey index. For example, a customer survey index value of 80 percent corresponds to a score of 4, an index of 83 percent corresponds to a score of 5, and so on.

There is a 12 percent difference between the current customer survey index value of 77 percent (score 3) and the poorest recent performance of 65 percent (score 0). Thus, 12 percent ÷ 3 scores = 4 percent per score. Therefore, a customer survey index value of 69 percent corresponds to a score of 1 and an index value of 72 percent corresponds to a score of 2.

EXHIBIT 19.10 TOOLBOX: PERFORMANCE MATRICES

A. The Basic Performance Matrix for Quality in Month 6

Performance Measure	Actual Value for Month 6	Score	Weight	Weighted Score
Transaction error ratio	0.035	7	30%	2.1
Customer survey	82%	5	50%	2.5
Average number of underwriting errors per 100 policies	6.8	4	20%	0.8
			Total quality score	5.4

B. The Aggregate Performance Matrix in Month 6

Dimension of Competition	Total Score	Weight, %	Weighted Score
Quality	5.4	25	1.35
Cost	5.2	20	1.04
Flexibility	4.2	10	0.42
Dependability	4.6	15	0.69
Service	5.6	15	0.84
Time	6.2	15	0.93
Performance index			5.27

Step 7. Multiply the score for each competitive dimension by its weight. Record these weighted scores on the *aggregate performance matrix*. Sum the weighted scores; this sum is equal to the *performance index*.

The quality score of 5.4 is carried over from the basic performance matrix to the aggregate performance matrix in Exhibit 19.10B. Similarly, the scores for the other five competitive dimensions are also carried over to this matrix.

The sum of the weighted scores—the performance index—is 5.27. What does this mean? In isolation, a performance index of 5.27 means little, but it does have meaning when it is compared with other performance indexes over time.

The graphs in Exhibit 19.11 illustrate the firm's performance over a six-month period. The first graph plots the monthly performance index, the second plots the quality scores, and the third plots the transaction error ratio. By monitoring the details, the firm can gain insight into the causes of poor (or better than expected) performance.

The CCAF Effectiveness Model

Another way to measure longer-term performance is to use the **CCAF effectiveness model** developed by the Canadian Comprehensive Auditing Foundation. This model has been proposed for use in the public sector, principally because of the inappropriate nature of the financial measures used in the business sector. The model consists of 12 attributes of effectiveness and assumes that senior executives can and want to develop information systems that allow managers and other stakeholders to make reasoned judgments about each attribute.

The 12 attributes are as follows:

Soundness
- Monitoring and reporting
- Protection of assets
- Working environment

Operations
- Financial results
- Responsiveness
- Costs and productivity

Results
- Secondary impacts
- Acceptance
- Achievement of intended results

Intentions
- Appropriateness
- Relevance
- Management direction

Two types of information are required for each attribute: "qualitative" descriptions of the strategic choices that affect each attribute and "quantitative" information explaining performance pertaining to each attribute. Further descriptions of the 12 attributes are provided below.[7]

1. *Monitoring and reporting* refers to the extent to which key matters pertaining to performance and organizational strength are identified, reported, and monitored. A qualitative assessment focuses on the information considered most important by senior managers. Quantitative information deals with the manner in which information is developed and made available.

2. *Protection of assets* is the extent to which important assets are safeguarded. Key assets include sources of supply, valuable property, key personnel, agreements, and important records and information. Qualitative assessments center on assessment of risk; quantitative assessments focus on levels of investment in security and backup.

[7] All 12 definitions are adapted from pages 22 and 23 of the CCAF (1987) book.

EXHIBIT 19.11   TOOLBOX: MONITORING PROGRESS WITH THE PERFORMANCE MATRICES

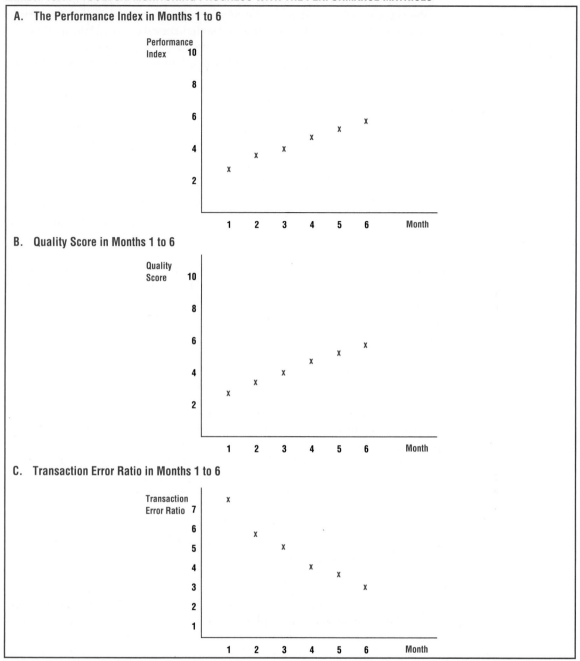

A.   The Performance Index in Months 1 to 6

B.   Quality Score in Months 1 to 6

C.   Transaction Error Ratio in Months 1 to 6

3. *Working environment* is the extent to which the organization provides appropriate developmental work and promotes commitment, initiative, and safety. The qualitative assessment is concerned with clarifying the characteristics of the appropriate work environment, and the quantitative perspective includes looking at the variables that together indicate the extent to which employees are motivated to work together.

4. *Financial results* refers to the matching of and accounting for revenues and costs and the accounting for and valuation of assets, liabilities, and equity. Quantitative measures include traditional ratios and statement values, while the qualitative focus is on comparisons with other organizations' principles and practices.

5. *Responsiveness* is the organization's ability to adapt to strategic changes. Quantitative measures include the investment in environmental scanning and the speed with which a response occurs. Qualitative measures focus principally on the confidence managers have in the ability to respond.

6. *Costs and productivity* deals with the relationships among costs, inputs, and outputs. Quantitative measures focus on the resources consumed per unit of output. Qualitative measures focus on longer-term issues and relationships, such as investments in knowledge or equipment and their impact on productivity.

7. *Secondary impacts* refers to the extent to which other significant consequences have occurred. Quantitative perspectives include the impact on health and the environment as well as factors such as community development. The qualitative perspective also looks at these factors, but more from the point of view of dependency.

8. *Acceptance* is the extent to which constituencies to whom a program or line of business is directed judge it to be satisfactory. The qualitative perspective includes elements such as name recognition by the public and trust and public confidence. Quantitative measures include market share, penetration rates, and repeat business.

9. *Achievement of intended results* refers to the extent to which goals and objectives have been realized. Quantitatively, the measures include performance measured against a plan, goals, and objectives that stretch individuals and the organization.

10. *Appropriateness* is the extent to which the design of a program or its major components and the level of effort being made are logical in light of specific objectives. A qualitative perspective involves choices about the existence, priority, and design of things such as service delivery methods, production facilities, and administrative support procedures. The quantitative perspective involves indicators of the time, costs, and other resources devoted to an activity.

11. *Relevance* is the extent to which a line of business or a program continues to make sense in regard to the problems or conditions to which it is intended to respond. Qualitatively, reviewers look for logical links between the strategies being pursued and the needs and expectations of the customers. The quantitative focus is on the volumes and margins obtained, adjusted for factors such as uniqueness.

12. *Management direction* refers to the extent to which an organization's objectives, component programs, and employees are clear, well integrated and understood, and appropriately reflected in its plans, structures, and decision-making process. Quantitative measures include elements such as the number of levels of management and the extent to which values are shared. Qualitative measures include leadership and the ability to inculcate vision and culture.

The CCAF model does not specify the exact measures to use in each case; these should be determined by management. Nor does the model indicate a time horizon; the appropriate times also are management-determined. To this end, it is much less prescriptive than the performance-measuring matrix discussed in the previous section. This makes the CCAF model much more difficult to operationalize than is the performance-measuring matrix.

Both are, however, aimed at effective performance measurement, including assessment of quantitative and qualitative factors within the strategic context of the firm. This implies a long-term outlook—not next week, next month, or even next year. As in all things, managers must be committed to the long haul.

MANAGERIAL IMPLICATIONS

A firm is what it measures. Therefore, if a firm wants to be an integrated, flexible, responsive organization that provides value to the customer, it must design measures and measurement systems that give it the feedback on performance it needs. First, though, the firm must decide exactly what performance is. The general rule should be as general as necessary and as specific as possible. When there is only one unit to measure, the firm can design specific measures and a unique measurement system. When there is more than one unit and the firm operates at more than one level, it needs to worry about the transitivity of its measurements so that it can compare different units. If any trade-off has to be made, it should be in favor of specificity, for the firm wants to be able to identify changes over time in any unit.

Continuous improvement and increasing the satisfaction of the customers will be recognized ultimately as an improvement in the firm's efficiency or productivity. Effectiveness should therefore be translated into efficiency. The question then arises, how should the firm distribute the increased revenues increasing efficiency brings? If a decision is made to have employees share in the increased profits, a mechanism for allocating the surplus needs to be developed. Regardless of the mechanisms chosen, the reward and incentive systems must be set so that individuals are encouraged to work in the firm's interests while furthering their self-interests.

This means that the reward system should be tied to the performance-measuring system. Taking this to its logical conclusion, the measurement-reward system should be tied to the strategic drivers the firm has chosen to work with and feedback should be frequent enough to allow necessary changes to be made within the strategic cycle times established for each market.

CHAPTER SUMMARY

As firms modify their strategic goals and objectives to match the new competitive environment, they must also modify their performance-measuring and appraisal systems. Key points to remember from this chapter include the following:

- It is difficult to improve a firm's performance unless feedback with respect to specific goals is provided.
- People tend to work toward measures. Therefore, performance measures must be strategically aligned with the firm's goals.
- Productivity is a widely used performance measure. Partial-factor productivity, single-factor productivity, multifactor productivity, and total factor productivity are productivity measures.
- Productivity indicates the efficiency with which a firm has consumed resources in order to produce output.
- A performance-measuring system should include measures that enable a firm to evaluate its effectiveness as well as its efficiency.
- Other essential characteristics of a good performance-measuring system include the following:
  1. Composed of financial and nonfinancial measures.
  2. Measures are complementary.
  3. Measures motivate employees to help the firm achieve its long-term as well as short-term goals and objectives.

4. Measures cross-functional boundaries and encourages horizontal integration.
5. Information provided by the measures can be aggregated and disaggregated.
6. Data required for the measures must be available, timely, and cost-effective to collect.
7. Measures are weighted to reflect their relative importance.
8. Measures should be modified over time to match changes in the firm's strategic goals and objectives.

- A responsive information system that provides timely and accurate data must be in place to support the firm's performance-measuring systems. In most cases a traditional accounting information system is insufficient.
- The performance-measuring matrix can be used to monitor the firm's performance along all six dimensions of competition. Its ability to integrate the results of individual performance measures into a single index is one of its major strengths.

KEY TERMS

Performance-measuring system	Single-factor productivity (SFP)	Efficiency	Basic performance matrix
Performance measure	Multifactor productivity (MFP)	Effectiveness	Aggregate performance matrix
Productivity		Performance-measuring matrix	Performance index
Partial-factor productivity (PFP)	Total factor productivity (TFP)	Scoring key matrix	CCAF effectiveness model

DISCUSSION QUESTIONS

1. In an operations sense, what is meant by performance? Does one's understanding of the term vary from firm to firm? Why or why not?

2. What is productivity? How does it differ from performance?

3. What is partial-factor productivity? Why would a firm use partial measures?

4. What are the relationships among labor, capital, and material partial productivity measures?

5. What is total factor productivity? What advantages does it have over PFP?

6. What is the relationship between TFP and PFP? Why might a firm use both?

7. At what level of aggregation would a firm use TFP? Why?

8. What are the essential characteristics of an effective performance-measuring system? What are the essential characteristics of effective performance measurement?

9. What does a single-factor measure of performance mean? How should a firm use one?

10. What are the steps in developing a useful performance-measuring matrix? How important are the weighting systems?

11. To what uses can a firm put the results of a performance-measuring matrix?

12. What is activity-based costing? Under what conditions does this concept work? What do cost drivers drive? (Refer to the supplement to this chapter to answer these questions.)

13. When should a firm use product life cycle costing? Can this concept be extended to product families? Why or why not? (Refer to the supplement to this chapter to answer these questions.)

14. What is the CCAF effectiveness model? How would you use it? What disadvantages do you see in the model?

15. Given the various measures and models of measurement in this chapter, what model would be most appropriate in your college or university? Which would be most appropriate for a multinational consumer electronics manufacturing company? For a farm? Which would be least appropriate in each setting? Why?

PROBLEMS

1. Blue Parrot, a small but distinguished restaurant has two waiters. Waiter A serves four tables, each with four seats. In the course of an evening the waiter's detached but clinical service encourages people to eat and leave, and today each table has been used twice. The checks for each meal (including wine) were $125.15, $118.20, $112.00, $127.30, $118.75, $126.60, $145.50, and $117.20. The average wine sales were $30 per meal, and the waiter received a 10 percent tip on average.

   Waiter B also serves four tables; this waiter has a more outgoing personality and spends more time with the customers. Tonight two tables have been used twice, but at the others the dinner parties have stayed longer. The checks for the meals (including wine) were $107.50, $87.75, $190.30, $189.65, $230.90, and $176.50. Wine bills were $35.00, $24.50, $100.30, $95.00, $140.00, and $75.50. The average tip received by the waiter was 20 percent, of which $80 came from the table with the largest check.

   The margin for food is 35 percent, and that for drinks is 50 percent. Which waiter has the highest productivity? Which is the more productive? What other information would you like to have?

2. Blank and Blank Engineering makes doorknobs by turning brass rods on a lathe. Given the likely increase in the cost of electricity, the firm has investigated producing the knobs from brass strip that is formed by a three-stage stamping process. The characteristics of each process are as follows:

   Current: Four automatic lathes, each producing one knob every two minutes. Two machine operators tending the lathes, one material handler and forklift employed for one hour per day to move brass rods to and finished knobs from the department. Each knob uses three inches of brass rod at $1 per inch; swarf (the material removed by the tool) weighs 0.8 pound and sells for $0.03 per pound. Each lathe uses 80 kwh of electricity each eight-hour day, at $0.045 per kwh. Other costs of lathe operation are figured at $2 per hour. Machine operators are paid $17.50 per hour, including benefits; the cost charged to the department for the materials handler and forklift is $35 per hour. A lathe costs $20,000, and setting up a lathe takes 30 minutes for one setup technician paid $20 per hour, including benefits.

   Proposed: One stamping press with one progressive die capable of producing one knob every 10 seconds. One machine operator and one material handler and forklift for one hour per day. Each knob uses six inches of brass strip at $6.50 per foot; stamping waste is 0.2 pound and will sell for $0.05 per pound. The press will use 200 kwh of electricity per eight-hour day. Other costs of press operation are figured at $2.50 per hour. The stamping press costs $180,000, and a die (good for 200,000 pieces) costs $25,000. Setting up the press takes three setup technicians four hours.

   Both processes will operate no more than 40 hours per week. What are the productivity differences between the two processes? Which would you recommend? Why?

3. Englebert Engineering, a contract engineering design company, has had the following results over the last six months:

Month 1	New contracts $100,000 Billed contracts $87,000 Beginning WIP $243,000
Month 2	New contracts $124,000 Billed contracts $132,000
Month 3	New contracts $112,000 Billed contracts $107,000
Month 4	New contracts $133,000 Billed contracts $178,000
Month 5	New contracts $127,000 Billed contracts $143,000
Month 6	New contracts $115,000 Billed contracts $200,000

What does the monthly productivity look like if Englebert has the following information about resources:

Office costs and all indirect personnel costs are $27,000 per month. Three engineers are 100 percent on design in months 1 to 4, with a fourth on staff in month 5 (60 percent billable) and month 6 (100 percent billable). Each engineer costs $12,000 per month. CAD equipment rental is $5,000 per month. The proportions of overhead, direct labor, and equipment use are constant for all jobs.

Note that WIP is held at contract price, not at cost, and is really just a summary of incomplete projects.

4. General Grinder, a manufacturer of automotive parts, has had the following results for six months: **623**

Month	Materials Purchased, $	Materials Used, $	Work Completed, $	Parts Billed, $
1	60,000	48,000	100,000	122,000
2	56,000	61,000	121,000	118,000
3	62,000	55,000	123,000	102,000
4	60,000	60,000	110,000	110,000
5	48,000	66,000	118,000	125,000
6	58,000	62,000	115,000	110,000

The firm employs three direct workers at $5,000 per month each; total overhead amounts to $10,000 per month. Material is a constant 70 percent of planned product cost. WIP at the beginning of month 1 is $237,000; the finished goods inventory is $102,000. Total costs are forecast to be 82 percent of the sales price. What does the productivity of the firm look like?

5. Two sculptors buy three blocks of stone each at $5,000 per block. Sculptor A turns out three individual pieces in six months, with the works selling for $26,000, $18,000, and $22,000. Sculptor B turns out one work consisting of two blocks in four months, with the work selling for $82,000; the third block was damaged beyond repair when a flaw was found in the stone. Which sculptor has the greater productivity?

6. Baby-Protect, a manufacturer of private-label disposable diapers measures the performance of the plants solely on the basis of an internal quality check: the ratio of acceptable-quality batches to total batches. Material PFP is planned to be 2.33. Over a six-month period the quality ratio or factor is 0.98, 0.97, 0.98, 0.97, 0.99, and 0.98; in the same period the material PFP is 1.88, 1.95, 1.45, 1.65, 1.99, and 1.70. The customer service department says that consumers are complaining about product quality. You work for the manufacturer, and your boss has asked you to investigate this issue. What is your initial hypothesis?

7. Deli Horton, a quick-service food restaurant had sales of $173,000 last week. The restaurant has a manager who is paid $45,000 per year, four shift managers paid $25,000 per year, and 42 shift workers paid $5.50 per hour. Each worker worked the full 35-hour shift during the week, and 10 worked 6 hours overtime at time and a half.

The restaurant purchased $120,000 of materials last week, $102,000 of which was delivered. The restaurant drew down its inventory of consumable and other supplies by $12,000. Utility costs (including garbage and lot maintenance) were $21,000, and building maintenance costs were $7,000. Some new dining tables costing $10,000 were received and installed, as was a new range hood at $21,000. Depreciation of equipment was $3,000, and franchise costs and royalties totaled $8,000.

What was the productivity of the restaurant?

8. TJ Enterprises, a lawn-mowing and landscape service operated by two students in your hometown, recently won a contract to mow the lawns at several senior citizens' condominium complexes. The owners know that their average rate of mowing is 1,000 square yards per mower per hour. The operating expenses per hour for their mowers are $2.56, which includes normal maintenance costs, and they pay themselves as employees $7.50 per hour.

The firm dumps the grass clippings in the local civic compost bins; it costs nothing to dump in the bins, but it costs approximately $1.50 in vehicle operating expenses to drive the clippings to the bins. The truck holds the clippings from 15 average homes, the lawns of which are around 600 square yards. The firm operates on a 100 percent variable cost contribution to cover future capital costs and provide profits for the owners. What is the target productivity figure, which measure would be most appropriate, and what is the minimum contract price they should have sought?

9. Bastani, an ice cream manufacturer, has traditionally manufactured ice cream for a retail chain's private label. Three flavors are manufactured: vanilla, chocolate, and strawberry. The single plant has operated at single-shift capacity for the last three years and for at least three months each year has operated overtime or with a second shift.

The productivity ratio of sales dollars to input cost dollars has been around 1.25, within the limits of 1.45 and 1.10. Now management is toying with the idea of becoming a local branded product, adding several more flavors, and becoming more responsive to local tastes.

What do you expect will happen to the productivity figure? What will influence any movement in it?

10. In keeping with its practice of continuous improvement, the Willkins Insurance Company has decided to upgrade the scoring key matrix in Exhibit 19.9A. It is month 8, and the current level of performance for the transaction error ratio and the number of underwriting errors are 0.06 and 6, respectively;

desired targets are 0.003 and 0.5. The lowest levels remain the same. Recalculate the two scales.

11. Although the measures in problem 10 have improved, the customer survey index has dropped from 77 percent to 73 percent. What may be some reasons for this, and what should be done?

12. Before the scoring key matrix was adjusted in problem 10, the total quality score for month 8 was calculated. What is the total quality score for the month? Use the matrix in Exhibit 19.10A.

13. Using Exhibit 19.10, what is the performance index for Willkins in month 8? How does this compare with the performance in month 6? The total scores for all dimensions except quality have remained the same since month 6.

14. How will your answers for problem 13 change if you learn that the weights for quality, cost, and flexibility in month 8 have changed to 26 percent, 15 percent, and 14 percent, respectively?

15. The Willkins Insurance Company maintains a simple productivity measure in addition to the performance index. Over the past two years the productivity number has changed steadily from 1.14 to 1.28. In that time total cost, as measured by the performance matrix, has remained constant. The three components of cost have changed, however. Two years ago labor, materials, and equipment were 60, 22, and 18 percent, respectively, of total costs; now the figures are 48, 20, and 32 percent. The equipment cost reflects the energy costs and maintenance costs of buildings and equipment; one branch office closed two months ago. What do these figures and others you have tell you? If you were the CEO of Willkins, on what would you concentrate in the immediate future?

16. Simeons Inc. bakes and decorates wedding cakes. Each cake is unique. With the help of Renee, Simeons' designer, customers determine the general design of the cake (i.e., icing flavor and color, cake flavor, number of tiers, and size of each tier). The details of the design are usually left to Renee. One person bakes all the cakes; two others decorate them under Renee's supervision. Renee spends about 60 percent of his time in the kitchen. Simeons Inc.'s general manager takes care of all purchases, scheduling, and deliveries; this takes about half her time. What cost driver or drivers would you suggest for each of the following production resources?

- Cake and icing ingredients
- Equipment leases
- Salaries (Renee, general manager, baker, cake decorators, delivery person)
- Rent

(Refer to the supplement to this chapter to solve this problem.)

17. Von Richtofen Manufacturing makes four products. A review of the firm's records reveals the following information about each product. Material overhead is 10 percent of material dollars, direct labor overhead is $10 per hour, and machine overhead is $15 per hour. Other overhead costs include setups ($960), orders ($1,500), material handling ($200), and engineering ($2,000).

	Product A	Product B	Product C	Product D
Production volume last year (units)	10	100	10	100
Production details (per unit basis)				
Material ($)	6	6	18	18
Direct labor hours	0.5	0.5	1.5	1.5
Machine hours	0.5	0.5	1.5	1.5
Number of setups	1	3	1	3
Number of orders	3	3	3	1
Number of times handled	1	1	1	1
Number of parts	3	3	3	1

What is the overhead cost per unit based on direct labor hours? On a cost driver of your choosing? Which one makes more sense? Why? (Refer to the supplement to this chapter to solve this problem.)

GROUP EXERCISES

Many tools and techniques discussed in this chapter are meant to be used in a team setting. The following problems are best solved by small groups of students. Ideally, each group should be composed of people with different backgrounds, interests, or areas of expertise.

1. The performance-measuring matrix is a detailed method of analyzing and improving performance. As a group, identify a company to which you have access and develop and use the performance-measuring matrix for one plant or operation of the company. You should do this in stages, developing each matrix in sequence with your instructor and the management of the firm. At the end ask yourself what the exercise and its results have taught you about performance measurement, evaluation, and

improvement and about operations management in general.

2. The CCAF effectiveness model depends on an organization's management to design the measures to be used. Apply the CCAF model to your faculty or school. As a group, choose two of the attributes (from different sections), decide what quantitative and qualitative variables you want to measure, and decide how you will measure them. You might want to discuss this with members of your administration as you conduct the exercise. Note particularly the areas in which you have difficulty applying the model; why is this?

REFERENCES AND SELECTED BIBLIOGRAPHY

CCAF [1987], *Reporting and Auditing Effectiveness in the Public Sector*, Ottawa, CCAF.

Cross, K. F. [1988], "Wang Scores EPIC Success with Circuit Board Assembly Redesign," *Industrial Engineering*, January.

Dixon, R. J., A. J. Nanni, and T. E. Vollman [1990], *The New Performance Challenge: Measuring Operations for World Class Competition*, Dow Jones–Irwin, Homewood, Ill.

Evans, James R., and William M. Lindsay [1993], *The Management and Control of Quality*, 2d ed., West, St. Paul, Minn.

Kaplan, Robert S., and David P. Norton [1992], "The Balanced Scorecard: Measures That Drive Performance," *Harvard Business Review*, January–February, pp. 71–79.

Locke, E. A., L. M. Saari, K. N. Shaw, and G. P. Latham [1981], "Goal Setting and Task Performance: 1969–1980," *Psychological Bulletin*, vol. 90, pp. 125–152.

Noori, H., and D. Gillen [1994], "A Performance Measuring Matrix for Capturing the Impact of Advanced Manufacturing Technology," working paper series, Research Center for Management of Advanced Technology/Operations (REMAT), Wilfrid Laurier University, Waterloo, Ontario. To appear in *International Journal of Production Research*.

SUPPLEMENT TO

CHAPTER 19

AN OPERATIONS PERSPECTIVE ON COST ACCOUNTING

S19.1 MANAGERIAL ORIENTATION

Chapters 1 and 2 discussed the myriad changes that have taken place in the North American marketplace in the last few decades. Product life cycles are shortening, customers are becoming more discriminating, and global competition is intensifying. Companies are moving away from a mass-production strategy and toward economies of integration. Quality, service, time, dependability, and flexibility are increasing in importance.

These trends have changed the way in which companies do business and the type of information managers need to make decisions. Consider the following examples:

- Since a company must be able to compete on quality, service, dependability, time, and flexibility, feedback regarding its performance on these competitive dimensions is essential.
- Capital investment decisions, especially those involving advanced operations technologies, must take into consideration intangible benefits such as improved flexibility. In many cases these benefits exceed those which are tangible.
- Direct labor costs no longer account for the lion's share or product costs. Overhead costs such as R&D, design, computer programming, training, marketing, and sales are becoming more significant.[1]

     To make informative decisions, therefore, managers need to be able to accurately trace overhead costs to products, understand what drives overhead costs, and isolate the costs of unnecessary activities.
- Emphasis is being placed on designing the right product the first time. This means that designers need to know how their design decisions will affect manufacturing and support costs.

Although their information needs have changed substantially, managers typically rely on cost accounting information systems that have not kept pace with these changing needs. The goal of this supplement is to highlight the major weaknesses of using a traditional cost accounting system to make operational decisions

in an FRO. The supplement will also present alternative approaches to cost accounting—activity-based accounting and life cycle costing—that can overcome many of these weaknesses.

S19.2 THE WEAKNESSES OF TRADITIONAL COST ACCOUNTING SYSTEMS

Six major weaknesses associated with traditional cost accounting systems have been identified. Note that each one relates to the changing informational needs presented in the last section.

- The focus of these systems is on the costs of *physically producing the product.* Significant product costs, such as those resulting from R&D, design, and support activities, are not accurately traced back to individual products.[2] Complex products tend to be undercosted, while simple products are overcosted.
- These systems are unable to support managers as they gauge the firm's success in meeting goals that are not cost-based. They also cannot help managers fully evaluate alternative investments or courses of action.
- In some cases the financial measures commonly derived from these systems are at odds with the firm's strategic goals. For example, to maintain high equipment utilization, an operations manager may produce more than what is necessary at the current time.
- The reports generated detail how much money was spent during the reporting period, by which departments, and on what items. They say nothing, however, about the causes of resource consumption that prompted the spending in the first place.
- The information provided is often presented along functional lines. Many activities in which a firm must excel, however, cross functional boundaries.[3] Actions that improve the performance of one functional area may be detrimental to the performance of the firm as a whole.

---

[1] In many industries direct labor now accounts for only 10 to 15 percent of total product costs and is continuing to decrease. Overhead constitutes about 35 percent of total product costs, while material costs account for the remaining 50 percent.

[2] There are two reasons for this. First, these product costs are generated to value the firm's inventory for external reporting purposes. Only the costs that can be capitalized and assigned to inventory are normally included. Other costs, such as selling, administrative, and warranty costs, are considered period expenses and are omitted. Second, overhead expenses are often collected and then allocated to products by using a **cost driver** such as direct labor hours. In practice, the causal relationship between direct labor hours and actual overhead consumed is very weak. Products with high direct labor costs may not have high overhead costs, and vice versa. As overhead expenses increase, the resultant cost distortions are magnified.

[3] Examples include new product development and filling customers' orders.

- The information provided is often too aggregated to provide real insights at the operating level. Reports are not generated as frequently as needed by managers to make daily operating decisions.

What happens when traditional cost accounting systems are used for internal purposes? Often managers unknowingly make inappropriate decisions or work around the system, even to the point of developing private accounting systems (see Exhibit 19S.1). In both cases the competitiveness of the firm as a whole suffers.

S19.3 ALTERNATIVE COST INFORMATION SYSTEMS

In response to the problems discussed in Section S19.2, the Consortium for Advanced Manufacturing-International, Inc. (CAM-I), has formed a consortium of industrial organizations, accounting firms, and government agencies to define the role of cost management in today's environment. CAM-I is proposing a number of modifications to current cost systems, including activity-based costing and life cycle costing.

Activity-Based Costing

Products do not consume resources directly. Activities consume resources, and products consume those activities. This observation forms the basis of **activity-based costing (ABC)**.

> **DEFINITION:** Activity-based costing attempts to trace the costs of all significant activities back to the products, projects, or processes that consume them. Both value-added and non-value-added activities are included.

Typically, ABC divides costs into four general categories: (1) unit level (e.g., direct labor and materials), (2) batch level (e.g., equipment setups and purchase orders), (3) product-sustaining (e.g., product and process design), and (4) facility-sustaining (e.g., plant maintenance and heating).[4]

As many unit, batch, and product-sustaining costs are directly assigned to products as possible. By first separating these costs into their different levels, managers gain insight into how they can be reduced.

When the direct assignment of costs to products is not possible or economical, cost drivers that best reflect the cause-and-effect relationship between the product characteristic and the activity costs incurred are used. Exhibit 19S.2 shows how cost drivers are identified.

Tektronix, IBM, Weyerhaeuser, Northern Telecom, and dozens of other companies are using activity-based costing to find the real costs of their products and processes. Northern Telecom estimates that the vast majority of its products had been undercosted by more than 20 percent, while several high-volume products had been overcosted by as much as eight times.

Isolating costs incurred by non-value-added activities is another benefit of ABC. Lucas Industries, for example, was shocked to discover that a component worth less than $1 traveled an unnecessary 20,000

---

[4] See Cooper and Kaplan (1991), p. 132.

EXHIBIT 19S.1 ACTIVITY-BASED ACCOUNTING AT HEWLETT-PACKARD

When private accounting systems were uncovered at Hewlett-Packard's Roseville Networks Division (RND), the firm realized that its internal cost accounting system was not giving managers the information they needed. Marketing managers, operations managers, and product designers all collected their own cost data in an effort to generate more accurate product costs.

RND's internal accounting system carefully tracked direct labor costs and allocated overhead to products on the basis of their direct labor content. However, by the early 1980s direct labor accounted for only 2 percent of total production costs; some products carried overhead allocations well over 400 percent. Distorted product cost data resulted in pricing errors, improper design initiatives, and poor capacity decisions.

Today, however, the internal accounting system is no longer viewed as a necessary evil but seen as an ally. Together, the people using the system have applied the principles of activity-based costing to overhaul the system.

The revised system allocates overhead by using cost drivers that reflect the underlying causes of overhead expenses. Product costs are becoming more accurate as RND continually improves its selection of cost drivers.

The activity-based system at RND has been so successful that Hewlett-Packard has made activity-based costing mandatory for all its computer-manufacturing divisions.

Source: Adapted from Berlant, Browning, and Foster (1990), pp. 178–183.

Hewlett-Packard found that cost drivers were obvious to the people on its shop floor. If they are not obvious, a close examination of activity costs is in order. A combination of cost drivers may be needed if several key factors seem to drive costs. In this situation multiple regression analysis can be a useful tool for uncovering cause-and-effect relationships.

Some costs are volume-related, while others correspond more closely to the characteristics of the product being produced. In some cases cost drivers such as machine hours and direct labor hours are still valid. In other cases cost drivers such as the number of batches made, the number of times an item is handled or ordered, and the number of parts maintained are more appropriate.

Often the characteristics of a product influence costs much more than does the volume produced. The number of moving parts or the product's shape, for example, may be the overriding influence. Product complexity frequently drives costs. Consider a tax return. The more complex the investment portfolio, the more time it takes an accountant to prepare the return.

The higher the relative cost of an activity, the more accurate the cost driver should be because the higher the relative cost, the greater the distortion caused by inaccurately tracing the cost. The reverse is true as well.

The cost of tracking and measuring the cost driver in relation to its accuracy should also be considered. The increased accuracy corresponding to a cost driver that is very expensive to measure may not be justified. The behavioral effect the cost driver has on individuals within the firm and the decisions they make must be considered as well.

miles, including several trips to and from California, before it had any value added to it.

Because ABC systems are such a departure from traditional accounting systems, they can be difficult and time-consuming to implement. A phased approach to implementation, such as the one taken by Hewlett-Packard, seems to be the most appropriate. Information from ABC systems was first used to supplement information from existing systems. The existing systems were gradually changed on the basis of input from people in a variety of functional areas. ABC systems then spread to other areas of the company.

While ABC reduces many of the problems associated with traditional cost accounting systems, it does not solve all of them. The next section will review a concept that addresses another aspect of the product costing problem.

Life Cycle Costing

As was mentioned earlier, traditional cost systems focus on recurring manufacturing costs. However, a significant portion of a product's costs are incurred during the design and development phases of its life cycle. Other nonrecurring costs include logistical support and marketing costs, the purchase price of special equipment, and training costs. Costs normally excluded for external reporting purposes must be considered as well.

DEFINITION: *Life cycle costing* refers to the accumulation of actual costs for each product from its initial research and development through final customer servicing and support in the marketplace.

By tracing all of a product's costs throughout its life cycle, a firm can obtain a better picture of its profitability. Products currently being produced are no longer expected to absorb overheads that include R&D and design costs for future products.

Life cycle costing enables a firm to focus on minimizing a product's cost over its entire life cycle, not just over several time periods during the production stage.

The cost impact of product design and process technology decisions becomes clearer.

KEY TERMS

Cost driver
Activity-based costing (ABC)
Life cycle costing

REFERENCES AND SELECTED BIBLIOGRAPHY

Berlant, D., R. Browning, and G. Foster [1990], "How Hewlett-Packard Gets Numbers It Can Trust," *Harvard Business Review*, January–February, pp. 178–183.

Berlinger, C., and J. A. Brimson (eds.) [1988], *Cost Management for Today's Advanced Manufacturing: The CAM-I Conceptual Design*, Harvard Business School Press, Boston.

Cooper, R. [1988], "The Rise of Activity-Based Costing: Part 1: What Is an Activity-Based Cost System?" *Journal of Cost Management,* Summer, pp. 45–54.

—— [1988], "The Rise of Activity-Based Costing: Part 2: When Do I Need an Activity-Based Cost System?" *Journal of Cost Management,* Fall, pp. 41–48.

—— [1989], "The Rise of Activity-Based Costing: Part 3: How Mnay Cost Drivers Do You Need, and How Do You Select Them?" *Journal of Cost Management,* Winter, pp. 34–46.

—— and Robert S. Kaplan [1991], "Profit Priorities from Activity-Based Costing," *Harvard Business Review,* May–June, pp. 130–135.

Henkoff, K. [1992], "Make Your Office More Productive," *Fortune,* Feb. 25, pp. 72–84.

Kelley, Kevin [1991], "A Bean-Counter's Best Friend," *Business Week,* Oct. 25, p. 42.

Parker, Thornton, and Theodore Lettes [1991], "Is Accounting Standing in the Way of Flexible Computer-Integrated Manufacturing?" *Management Accounting,* January, pp. 34–38.

Udo, G. J. [1993], "A Modified Cost-Accounting System Can Generate Valid Product Costs," *Production and Inventory Management Journal,* vol. 34, no. 2, pp. 28–31.

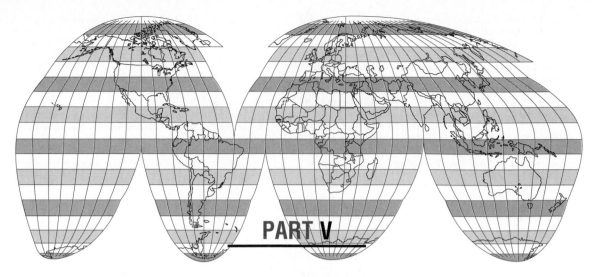

PART V

A LOOK BACK AND
A LOOK FORWARD

**Setting
the Stage**

It is time to complete this book with an important chapter. Every closure must achieve two objectives: It must draw together the disparate threads that have been spun earlier, and it must provide a platform for new departures.

The model described in Chapter 2 is an integrative model. Integration has been stressed throughout this book, but a question that must be addressed squarely is, How do firms realize the potential synergies available to them? The answer is that the use of multifunctional teams composed of qualified, dedicated people who are uncomfortable with maintaining the status quo greatly increases the chances of achieving synergy. This works best when the synergy is focused on achieving on behalf of the customers. When these conditions exist, it is reasonable to assume that the firm actively espouses the total quality management philosophy; when the firm has a sustainable competitive advantage that is based on fast, focused response, it is evident that the firm actively practices TQM.

Chapter 20 looks at how those synergies can be materialized. In an operations management book, though, it is also important to think about how to integrate the various sets of activities that make up the practice of operations management across the firm and across time. In looking at this, one finds that the elements of the integrative framework are important. It can be concluded from this that no firm can truly be an FRO or effectively practice TQM if any of its elements fail to meet these expectations and standards.

This is the big challenge to operations managers, but not because operations management is more important than the other elements of a firm. It is a challenge because operations managers *must* be proactive in ensuring that they have an effective and appreciated voice in all strategic decision making and must accept the fact that others play a role in operations decision making. This is the secret of true integration: actively committed and mutually respecting individuals are at the core of integration.

In looking forward, it is clear that integration is also a key ingredient. Integration of the whole value chain and across value chains is the logical direction in which firms should go. But what will the firm of the future look like? One can be certain that the environment will have a great impact on its structure and processes. Once the environment's impact has been pared away, though, one sees at the heart of the future competitiveness a management philosophy that is based on responsiveness and total quality.

How long will that last? Again, it is impossible to tell. One can take comfort from the fact that the leading firms will adapt and change to fit the competitive environment, always focusing on effectively supporting the customer. One can also expect others to learn from and profit by the experiences of the leaders.

CHAPTER 20

GLOBAL ENTERPRISE INTEGRATION

Now that you have looked at the elements of operations, it is important to collect your thoughts. In effect, you need to integrate everything that has been discussed concerning integration. Managers, especially generalist managers, cannot afford to think in terms of separate and separable business functions. They must be able to visualize and manage an enterprise as a single coherent, cohesive unit. Unless that is achieved, there is a great risk that the full synergies of the aggregation of people and nonhuman resources called the firm will not be achieved.

As stressed throughout the book, operating managers need to think about these questions:

- What are the relationships among business functions, and how are synergies derived?
- What are the relationships among the elements of operations, and how can they be dynamically strengthened?

By the end of this chapter you will have been presented with a final look at the theme and scope of this book. Central to this is the significance of total quality management and how it relates to the descriptive model of fast-response organizations.

EXHIBIT 20.1 FRO MANUFACTURING PROFILE

Despite a growing market share, Motorola Inc. discovered that some of its customers were dissatisfied with the quality of its products. To combat this trend, Motorola adopted total customer satisfaction as its number one priority.

Over the last 10 years Motorola has implemented a wide range of programs that have revolutionized the way in which products are designed and produced.

- Product designers now focus on fulfilling customers' needs, minimizing the total number of parts used, and ensuring that parts are easy to manufacture.
- Shop floor employees can now perform all the jobs on the production line and are able to stop the line whenever a quality problem surfaces.
- Statistical process control is used to identify, control, and eliminate sources of variation in the production process.
- Competitive benchmarking is used to set goals and measure performance.
- The number of suppliers has been reduced; remaining suppliers have passed the firm's Certified Supplier Program. Motorola's goal is to eliminate all incoming quality testing.

By setting high standards and ensuring that everyone works together to meet them, Motorola has been very successful in its improvement efforts. In 1988 Motorola won the first Malcolm Baldrige National Quality Award, and it is now the envy of U.S. Industry.

Source: Adapted from Denton (1991), pp. 22–25.

EXHIBIT 20.2 FRO SERVICE PROFILE

In 1989 Florida Power and Light (FPL) became the first non-Japanese company to win the prestigious Deming Prize for quality. To win the prize, FPL implemented a rigorous, highly statistical quality review system. Nineteen hundred quality teams were assembled throughout the firm, involving three-quarters of FPL's employees. A quality department with a staff of 85 was created. Hundreds of pages of analysis required by the contest judges were compiled. The instant bureaucracy and long workdays led to plummeting morale.

Despite the winning of the prize, the resulting improvements in customer service were insignificant compared to FPL's massive quality efforts.

Today the quality department has been reduced to only six employees, and most of the quality teams have been disbanded. Employees are encouraged to apply their training within their own departments, and the quality review system is a lot less rigid. Customers now count for everything.

Source: Adapted from "The Cracks in Quality," (1992), p. 67.

20.1 RETRACING OUR STEPS

This book has introduced a number of issues and concerns that influence or are influenced by operations. It began with a walk through several progressive and proactive companies that have established themselves as world-class competitors. Then, after examining the extremely competitive and dynamic global marketplace, the book introduced a descriptive framework that brings together the key characteristics of firms that have succeeded and continue to succeed in this harsh environment. These firms were called fast-response organizations (FROs), and some time was spent discussing their foundations.

Structurally, an FRO has relatively few layers of management. A well-integrated, lean organization can react quickly, and individuals within the firm can work together easily. Transforming a multilevel firm with clearly delineated functional areas and responsibilities into such an organization is challenging. However, firms as large as Chrysler, General Electric, and Procter & Gamble have begun to make this transformation.

Do you remember the Viper example in Chapter 5 and the Neon example in Chapter 6? Chrysler is now developing new cars in record time and under budget by tearing down the walls between functional areas, working with customers and suppliers, and delegating authority to development teams. Design integration has worked so well that Chrysler is applying the concept to all of its programs.

This book has discussed from an operations perspective the myriad challenges faced by FROs over the entire planning horizon. The book started with the long-term structural strategic issues—product, process, and facility design—and then addressed aggregate planning, inventory management, project management, and other medium-term planning concerns. The day-to-day aspects of operations, such as shop floor control and scheduling, were discussed next. The analysis ended with a look at how FROs can control and enhance their capabilities.

The topics reviewed can also be grouped into four major categories: customers and products, production processes, logistics, and support functions. The close relationships among these categories become clear when one takes a closer look at the activities within each category. As demonstrated by the dynamic diamond in Exhibit 20.3, this reinforces the need for internal and external integration.

The book has also reviewed a variety of tools, techniques, and management concepts that help managers address the challenges faced by their firms (see Exhibit 20.4). Some of these tools, techniques, and concepts date back to the nineteenth century, while others, such as knowledge-based expert systems and virtual plants and companies, are relatively new. Motorola (Exhibit 20.1), for example, has revolutionized the way in which its products are designed and produced by implementing several new management concepts and utilizing many new tools. The same can be said about Florida Power and Light (Exhibit 20.2).

Naturally, as the issues and concerns facing the firm evolve, the tools and techniques used in—in fact, the entire process of—evaluating alternative courses of action may have to be reexamined.

20.2 REAFFIRMING THE IMPORTANCE OF OPERATIONS MANAGEMENT

This text has been written for an introductory course in operations management; you are not expected to be an operations management expert after working through the book or to be able to apply every operations management tool flawlessly. It is

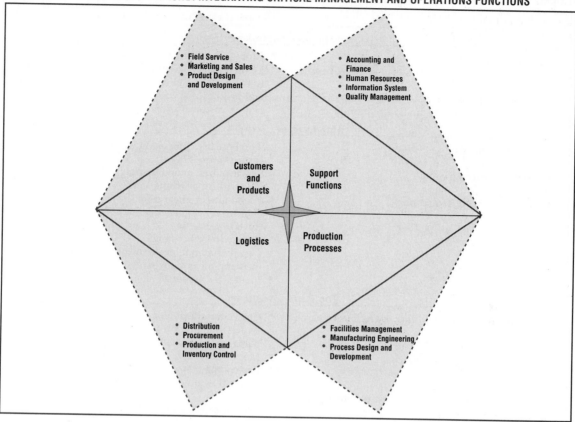

important, though, that you have a good working knowledge of operations management and realize its strategic importance. Even if your career will not be in operations management, this understanding is extremely important.

FROs are composed of closely coupled functional areas. Almost every activity in which a functional area is involved influences and is influenced by other functional areas. As the firm becomes more integrated and the boundaries between functional areas become hazy, the ability of managers in other functions to communicate and work closely with operations managers becomes more important.

Accountants, for example, need to understand the processes by which goods and services are produced to keep the firm's internal cost accounting systems timely and informative. Marketers need to be able to work with engineers as they design product families and exploit the potential of the firm's manufacturing resources. Human resources professionals need to help develop the technical and problem-solving capabilities required by the people on the shop floor. Purchasers need to coordinate deliveries more closely with the firm's production schedule. And everyone needs to be actively involved in the firm's quest for total quality.

20.3   TOTAL QUALITY MANAGEMENT REVISITED

The elements of total quality management (TQM) have been examined throughout this book, which has discussed how quality can be built into a firm's products and the processes by which they are made (see Chapters 5, 6, 9, 10, and 11). Building

EXHIBIT 20.4   OPERATIONS MANAGEMENT TOOLS, TECHNIQUES, AND CONCEPTS

Mass-Production Era (1890–1975)	Flexible (Lean) Production (1975 on)
Competitive Environment	
• Expanding markets • Improved transportation, access to seemingly un-limited resources • Few foreign competitors • Customer acceptance of standardized products	• Global competition • Limited market growth • Rapid advances in technology, shortening product and process life cycles • Higher customer expectations
Management Concepts	
• Shop floor control • Product life cycle • Experience/learning curve • Process life cycle • Economies of scale and scope	• Total quality control (TQC) • Just-in-time (JIT) • Synchronized manufacturing • Competitive benchmarking • Economies of integration • Concurrent engineering • Reverse marketing • Activity-based costing • Quality function deployment • Information as a corporate resource • Virtual (or modular) plants and companies
Tools and Techniques	
• Linear programming and other operations research tools • Gantt charts, PERT, and CPM • Quantitative forecasting models • Acceptance sampling • Statistical process control (SPC) • Return on investment, internal rate of return, payback period • Economic order quantity (EOQ) • Master production schedules • Material requirements planning (MRP)	• Computer-aided design tools • Expert system tools for facility design, aggregate planning, and scheduling • Manufacturing resource planning (MRPII) • Bar coding • Taguchi methods • Kanban • Vendor certification

quality into products and processes, however, constitutes only part of a firm's **total quality management (TQM)** system. Let us revisit the definition of TQM in the Startup Chapter.

DEFINITION: Total quality management is a philosophy which advocates four basic principles: (1) intense focus on customer satisfaction, (2) accurate measurement of activities, (3) continuous improvement of products and processes, and (4) empowerment of people.

This definition is based on the management philosophy of the late W. Edwards Deming, a major influence on international quality leadership since the 1940s.

Only since the 1980s have North American companies begun to realize the potential of Deming's philosophy. The similarity between Deming's 14 points (see Exhibit 20.5) and the practices of companies described by the FRO model attests to the value of Deming's work and the concept of TQM. Today, prestigious awards such as the Deming Prize, the Malcolm Baldrige National Quality Award, and the Canada Awards for Business Excellence[1]—all anchored in Deming's philosophy—are encouraging firms to pursue TQM.

[1] Refer to the Startup Chapter for an overview of these awards.

EXHIBIT 20.5   DEMING'S 14 QUALITY POINTS

Deming (1985) deems that the following 14 points are essential to quality transformation within any organization, whether it is in the service or manufacturing sector, regardless of its size.

1. Create constancy of purpose toward improvement of the product and service, with the aim of staying in business and providing jobs.

2. Adopt the new philosophy. This is a new economic age created by Japan. Transformation of the western style of management is necessary to halt the continued decline of industry.

3. Cease depending on inspection to achieve quality. Eliminate the need for inspection on a mass basis by building quality into the product in the first place.

4. End the practice of awarding business on the basis of the price tag. Purchasing must be combined with design of the product, manufacturing, and sales to work with the chosen supplier, with the aim of minimizing total cost, not merely initial cost.

5. Improve constantly and forever every activity in the company to improve quality and productivity and thus constantly decreases costs.

6. Institute training and education on the job, including management.

7. Institute supervision. The aim of supervision should be to help people and machines do a better job.

8. Drive out fear so that everyone can work effectively for the company.

9. Break down barriers between departments. People in research, design, sales, and production must work as a team to foresee problems of production and use that may be encountered with a product or service.

10. Eliminate slogans, exhortations, and targets for the workforce asking for zero defects and new levels of productivity. Such exhortations only create adversarial relationships, as most of the causes of low quality and low productivity belong to the system and thus lie beyond the power of the workforce.

11. Eliminate work standards that prescribe numerical quotas for the day. Substitute aids and helpful supervision.

12a. Remove barriers that rob the hourly worker of his or her pride of workmanship. The responsibility of supervisors must be changed from sheer numbers to quality.

  b. Remove the barriers that rob people in management and engineering of pride of workmanship. This means abolishing the annual or merit rating of management by objectives and management by numbers.

13. Institute a vigorous program of education and retraining. New skills are required for changes in techniques, materials, and service.

14. Put everyone in the company to work in teams to accomplish the transformation.

About three-quarters of American firms claim that they have some form of quality improvement program. Less than a third of these companies, however, have reported significant quality and productivity improvements. Why has TQM worked so well for companies such as Motorola and Xerox but not for others?

Exhibit 20.1 outlined some of the programs implemented by Motorola as part of its quality improvement efforts. These and other tools and concepts that can significantly improve process and product quality have been discussed throughout the book. Unfortunately, there is no one right way of using these tools and concepts, no TQM recipe that guarantees success for any firm that follows it. A TQM program must be an integral part of the firm's basic business strategy: quality is simply a way of doing business. Deming put this into perspective when he said that a company does not have to implement a quality program because a company's survival is not compulsory.

Recent studies suggest that lack of top management support is a major contributor to the failure of many TQM efforts. Managers create a firm's corporate mission by choosing the markets in which the firm will compete and the emphasis that will be placed on each competitive dimension. Responsibility for general resource allocations, performance-measuring and compensation systems, and organizational structure is in their hands.

Impatience is often a problem. Truly embedding quality into the organizational culture has taken Toyota, Nippondenso, and Japan's other success stories decades. Many TQM programs in North America fizzle after just a few years because they fail to produce impressive results. But perhaps the most significant cause of TQM failure is losing sight of the customer. Even Florida Power and Light (see Exhibit 20.2), the first non-Japanese winner of the Deming Prize, found itself just going through the motions of TQM. Today customers count for everything at Florida Power and Light.

If you reread the definition of total quality management at the beginning of this section, you will notice that a customer orientation is mentioned first. If you look carefully at the Malcolm Baldrige National Quality Award examination categories, for example, the award's underlying philosophy becomes evident: Implementing ongoing quality improvement programs increases productivity, customer satisfaction, and ultimately a firm's market success. Succeeding by delighting the customer is both the goal of TQM and the apex of the FRO framework (see Exhibit 20.6).

Remember that *the FRO framework is a road map* that describes how successful companies are achieving long-run profitability by competing along the six dimensions of competition. The four structural prerequisites—continuous improvements, research and development, the adoption of advanced technology, and the integration of people and systems—enable a firm to compete simultaneously along all these dimensions. It is the firm's strategy that coordinates its efforts and drives the firm toward its goals.

Of the four structural prerequisites, the integration of people and systems along the value chain is regarded as the most challenging task faced by managers today.

Let us take a quick look at the components of **enterprise integration** discussed in Chapter 2.

- **Internal integration.** Activities and decisions made within the firm must be coordinated across functional areas (horizontal integration) as well as up and down the hierarchy (hierarchical integration).
- **External, or vertical, integration.** Upstream and downstream linkages must be close and strong. Upstream integration allows the firm to respond quickly to real market needs. Downstream integration ensures that the goods and services the firm purchases are provided at the right time and in the right quantities.

Achieving internal and external integration requires an information infrastructure that encourages frequent exchanges of information, knowledge, experiences, and goals. If decisions regarding product and process design, production capacity, scheduling, and inventory control are to be integrated, the computerized tools that support these decisions must also be integrated. This leads to a new paradigm of operations, the integration of information, and the emerging field of **computer integrated enterprises.**

> **DEFINITION:** Computer-integrated enterprises are business practices and technologies that result in a business infrastructure that allows the dissemination of information, coordination of decisions, and management of actions by and among people and systems both within the organization and outside it, resulting in the efficient, coordinated achievement of the enterprise's goals.[2]

[2] This definition is based on Fox (1993).

EXHIBIT 20.6   THE FRO DESCRIPTIVE FRAMEWORK

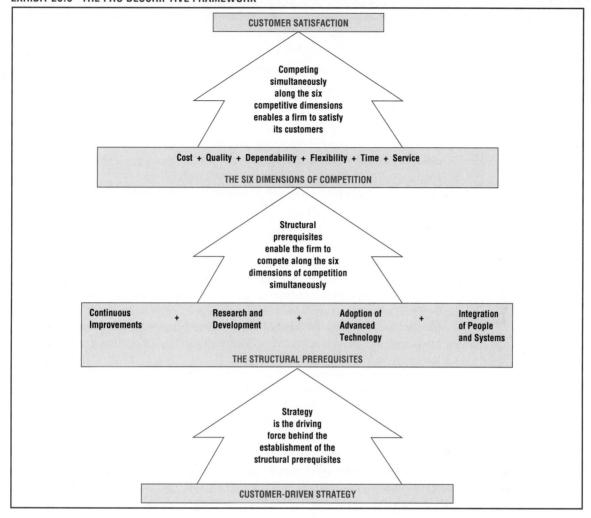

20.4 A LOOK INTO THE FUTURE

The fast-response organization is the paradigm for the successful organization of the present and the near future. Nothing is permanent, though, and managers need to think about what the longer-term paradigm is likely to be. If history is any guide, the future can be dimly glimpsed by extrapolating the trends examined throughout this book. The most significant of these trends are outlined below:

- An increase in the number of companies competing internationally and locating facilities around the globe
- A trend toward project-specific organizations, alliances formed within organizations and across organizations to achieve time- and scope-limited objectives
- The development of global netware, or software designed to integrate activities across the organization and the whole value chain. The information superhighway is a precursor of the structure required to support this netware.

- The use of knowledge as a fundamental competitive weapon and the development of computer-based intelligence to determine *what* knowledge will be required to compete effectively against other global competitors
- An increase in the strategic use of time-based competition

The competitive firm of the future will therefore still need to be agile. **Agility** implies the ability to do the following:

- Continuously monitor market conditions and market demand
- Quickly respond to demand conditions by providing new goods, services, and information as the need is recognized by the market
- Quickly introduce new technologies
- Quickly modify the way in which the firm does business
- Quickly use the abilities of all the people in the firm's value chain

How this will be achieved is conceptually straight-forward: the senior management of the organization will develop an organic approach to competitive structure, using the information "spine" of the organization to link together focused networks of organic elements along the complete value chain. These networks will consist of units from within and outside the parent organization, cooperatively rather than legally integrated through the pursuit of mutually beneficial market objectives. These limited-duration organizations will be developed in response to market need and disbanded when the need is satisfied. It is these firms which will use enterprise integration and will need integrative software that allows planning and integration at the global rather than local level.

What form this integration will take is not clear. However, its implementation will be fraught with challenge and difficulty because even the best firms still cannot effectively manage existing "local" integrative mechanisms such as computer-integrated manufacturing, computer-assisted product planning, electronically integrated design, and distributed inventory management.

These integrative technologies are global only in the geographic sense, allowing managers to coordinate limited activities at different places. As everyone knows, though, "global" also means across *all* elements and *all* activities. MRPII, for example, is evolving into enterprise logistic planning (ELP), allowing firms to globally integrate in all three strategic senses of the term.

The closer one gets to enterprise organization, the closer one gets to the operationalization of economies of integration. That means, as was discussed in earlier chapters, the potential to eliminate niche competitors by allowing global competitors to battle over very small markets as well as very large ones. This will require changes in the nature of industry organization, the nature of competition, and the nature of the firm. How these forces will evolve is difficult to predict, but thinking managers must prepare themselves and their companies for the new forms of competition that will inevitably occur. These managers will not develop the newer and more powerful technologies that will allow true global integration of the enterprise or be able to dictate the nature of market demand or industry dynamics. They will, though, need to be able to respond to the challenges presented by these changes so that their firms can evolve to meet the new competition. Strategic responsiveness and agility are, and will remain, dependent on the abilities, imagination, and inclinations of company managers.

The complex interactions afforded by the forces underpinning the fast-response organization are difficult to master. As the nature of competition continues to evolve, though, it becomes difficult to comprehend the implications for the enterprise and impossible to predict the actual nature of the more complex organization.

It is the responsibility of thinking managers to anticipate what those changes will be and encourage developments that take advantage of the evolutionary path. By understanding the leading firms of today and what makes them outstanding and by understanding the evolutionary forces at work in the global environment, managers will be able to establish the boundaries within which effective development should take place. Focused development will then create the ability to take advantage of the opportunities that become available.

Luck is an essential and inevitable element in business, but managers can create their own luck by preparing to take advantage of opportunities. In the increasingly competitive world of global business the opportunities will continue to exist, but they will exist for shorter periods and will be more difficult to identify. That is the challenge managers must accept if they expect their firms to survive and prosper in the future.

KEY TERMS

Total quality management (TQM)
Enterprise integration

Computer-integrated enterprises
Agility

DISCUSSION QUESTIONS

1. What is meant by the term *total integration?* What examples can you think of to illustrate this concept?

2. How does a firm achieve total integration? Is integration easier or harder to achieve in a service firm compared with a manufacturing firm? Why?

3. This book has stressed the fact that every business function is as important as every other. Why, then, has the importance of operations been stressed in this chapter?

4. Apply the dynamic diamond in Exhibit 20.3 to an accounting practice. To a bank. To a fast-food restaurant. Which of these operations best suits the model? Which seems least suited? Why?

5. In Exhibit 20.4, what essential differences are there between the tools and techniques of the mass-production era and those of the flexible-production era? How significant are these differences?

6. Which are the 3 most important of Deming's 14 points? Which one is the most important? Why?

7. How does a firm "drive out fear"? What "fear" does it want to drive out?

8. What do you think the next competitive focus will be? Why?

9. What relationship does Deming's list of points have to the concept of total integration? What other elements are required?

10. How does the concept of delighting the customer relate to the concept of total integration? Why is delighting the customer important?

GROUP EXERCISES

Many of the tools and concepts discussed in this chapter are meant to be used in a team setting. The following problem is best solved by small groups of students, each group ideally composed of people with different backgrounds, interests, or areas of expertise.

Find a service or manufacturing company close to you (including companies in databases you have available, such as PIMS or COMPUSTAT, and companies in teaching cases you have read).

Using the data available to you, try to work out the impact on costs of the following:

- Reducing cycle times by 10 percent
- Reducing employee turnover by 50 percent
- Eliminating 50 percent of work in process

- Improving reliability by 50 percent
- Reducing defects by 90 percent

Try to work out what the impact on market share and profits would be.

This will probably involve some detective work and require some major assumptions. You will need to justify your assumptions quite rigorously. Also, you will probably have to analyze the major competitors and the industry.

REFERENCES AND SELECTED BIBLIOGRAPHY

Bounds, G., L. Yorks, M. Adams, and G. Ranney [1994], *Beyond Total Quality Management,* McGraw-Hill, Inc., New York.

"The Cracks in Quality" [1992], *The Economist,* Apr. 18, pp. 67–68.

Deming, W. Edwards [1985], "Transformation of Western Style of Management," *Interfaces,* May–June, pp. 6–11.

Denton, D. Keith [1991], "Lessons on Competitiveness: Motorola's Approach," *Production and Inventory Management Journal,* third quarter, pp. 22–25.

Feigenbaum, A. V. [1983], *Total Quality Control,* 3d ed. McGraw-Hill, New York.

Fox, Mark [1993], National Research Council of Canada, Enterprise International Workshops, Ottawa, Ontario, June 2–3.

Loring, John [1990], "Dr. Deming's Traveling Quality Show," *Canadian Business,* September, pp. 38–42.

Sullivan, L. P. [1986], "The Seven Stages in Company-Wide Quality Control," *Quality Progress,* May, pp. 77–83.

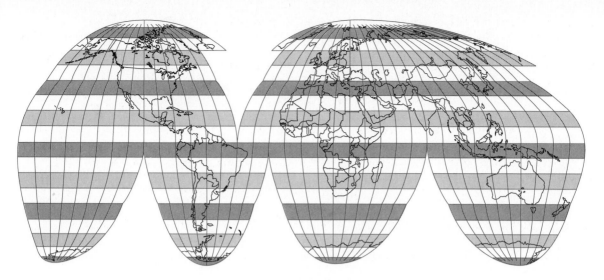

APPENDIXES

LEARNING CURVE:
TABLES OF UNIT AND
CUMULATIVE VALUES

APPENDIX A

TABLE OF UNIT VALUES

Learning Curve Equation

$$Y_x = ax^b = ax^{\frac{\log \rho}{\log 2}}$$

where Y_x = number of hours required to produce xth unit
a = number of hours required to produce first unit
b = coefficient related to slope of curve
ρ = improvement ratio or learning percentage

The table on page 648 gives the value x^b for various improvement ratios (ρ) when the first unit takes one labor-hour.

TABLE OF CUMULATIVE VALUES

Cumulative Learning Curve Equation

$$\sum_{x=1}^{n} Y_x = a \sum_{x=1}^{n} x^b = a \sum_{x=1}^{n} x^{\frac{\log \rho}{\log 2}}$$

n = total number of units produced
Y_x = number of hours required to produce xth unit
a = number of hours required to produce first unit
b = coefficient related to slope of curve
ρ = improvement ratio or learning percentage

The table on page 649 gives the value Σx^b for various improvement ratios (ρ) when the first unit takes one labor-hour.

TABLE OF UNIT VALUES

Unit Number (x)	Improvement Ratios (ρ)							
	60%	65%	70%	75%	80%	85%	90%	95%
1	1.0000	1.0000	1.0000	1.0000	1.0000	1.0000	1.0000	1.0000
2	0.6000	0.6500	0.7000	0.7500	0.8000	0.8500	0.9000	0.9500
3	0.4450	0.5052	0.5682	0.6338	0.7021	0.7729	0.8462	0.9219
4	0.3600	0.4225	0.4900	0.5625	0.6400	0.7225	0.8100	0.9025
5	0.3054	0.3678	0.4368	0.5127	0.5956	0.6857	0.7830	0.8877
6	0.2670	0.3284	0.3977	0.4754	0.5617	0.6570	0.7616	0.8758
7	0.2383	0.2984	0.3674	0.4459	0.5345	0.6337	0.7439	0.8659
8	0.2160	0.2746	0.3430	0.4219	0.5120	0.6141	0.7290	0.8574
9	0.1980	0.2552	0.3228	0.4017	0.4930	0.5974	0.7161	0.8499
10	0.1832	0.2391	0.3058	0.3846	0.4765	0.5828	0.7047	0.8433
12	0.1602	0.2135	0.2784	0.3565	0.4493	0.5584	0.6854	0.8320
14	0.1430	0.1940	0.2572	0.3344	0.4276	0.5386	0.6696	0.8226
16	0.1296	0.1785	0.2401	0.3164	0.4096	0.5220	0.6561	0.8145
18	0.1188	0.1659	0.2260	0.3013	0.3944	0.5078	0.6445	0.8074
20	0.1099	0.1554	0.2141	0.2884	0.3812	0.4954	0.6342	0.8012
25	0.0933	0.1353	0.1908	0.2629	0.3548	0.4701	0.6131	0.7880
30	0.0815	0.1203	0.1737	0.2437	0.3346	0.4505	0.5963	0.7775
35	0.0728	0.1097	0.1605	0.2286	0.3184	0.4345	0.5825	0.7687
40	0.0660	0.1010	0.1498	0.2163	0.3050	0.4211	0.5708	0.7611
45	0.0605	0.0939	0.1410	0.2060	0.2936	0.4096	0.5607	0.7545
50	0.0560	0.0879	0.1336	0.1972	0.2838	0.3996	0.5518	0.7486
60	0.0489	0.0785	0.1216	0.1828	0.2676	0.3829	0.5367	0.7386
70	0.0437	0.0713	0.1123	0.1715	0.2547	0.3693	0.5243	0.7302
80	0.0396	0.0657	0.1049	0.1622	0.2440	0.3579	0.5137	0.7231
90	0.0363	0.0610	0.0987	0.1545	0.2349	0.3482	0.5046	0.7168
100	0.0336	0.0572	0.0935	0.1479	0.2271	0.3397	0.4966	0.7112
120	0.0294	0.0510	0.0851	0.1371	0.2141	0.3255	0.4830	0.7017
140	0.0262	0.0464	0.0786	0.1287	0.2038	0.3139	0.4718	0.6937
160	0.0237	0.0427	0.0734	0.1217	0.1952	0.3042	0.4623	0.6869
180	0.0218	0.0397	0.0691	0.1159	0.1879	0.2959	0.4541	0.6809
200	0.0201	0.0371	0.0655	0.1109	0.1816	0.2887	0.4469	0.6757
250	0.0171	0.0323	0.0584	0.1011	0.1691	0.2740	0.4320	0.6646
300	0.0149	0.0289	0.0531	0.0937	0.1594	0.2625	0.4202	0.6557
350	0.0133	0.0262	0.0491	0.0879	0.1517	0.2532	0.4105	0.6482
400	0.0121	0.0241	0.0458	0.0832	0.1453	0.2454	0.4022	0.6419
450	0.0111	0.0224	0.0431	0.0792	0.1399	0.2387	0.3951	0.6363
500	0.0103	0.0210	0.0408	0.0758	0.1352	0.2329	0.3888	0.6314
600	0.0090	0.0188	0.0372	0.0703	0.1275	0.2232	0.3782	0.6229
700	0.0080	0.0171	0.0344	0.0659	0.1214	0.2152	0.3694	0.6158
800	0.0073	0.0157	0.0321	0.0624	0.1163	0.2086	0.3620	0.6098
900	0.0067	0.0146	0.0302	0.0594	0.1119	0.2029	0.3556	0.6045
1,000	0.0062	0.0137	0.0286	0.0569	0.1082	0.1980	0.3499	0.5998
1,200	0.0054	0.0122	0.0260	0.0527	0.1020	0.1897	0.3404	0.5918
1,400	0.0048	0.0111	0.0240	0.0495	0.0971	0.1830	0.3325	0.5850
1,600	0.0044	0.0102	0.0225	0.0468	0.0930	0.1773	0.3258	0.5793
1,800	0.0040	0.0095	0.0211	0.0446	0.0895	0.1725	0.3200	0.5743
2,000	0.0037	0.0089	0.0200	0.0427	0.0866	0.1683	0.3149	0.5698

TABLE OF CUMULATIVE VALUES

Total Number of Units (n)	\multicolumn{8}{c}{*Improvement Ratios (ρ)*}
	60%	65%	70%	75%	80%	85%	90%	95%
1	1.000	1.000	1.000	1.000	1.000	1.000	1.000	1.000
2	1.600	1.650	1.700	1.750	1.800	1.850	1.900	1.950
3	2.045	2.155	2.268	2.384	2.502	2.623	2.746	2.872
4	2.405	2.578	2.758	2.946	3.142	3.345	3.556	3.774
5	2.710	2.946	3.195	3.459	3.738	4.031	4.339	4.662
6	2.977	3.274	3.593	3.934	4.299	4.688	5.101	5.538
7	3.216	3.572	3.960	4.380	4.834	5.322	5.845	6.404
8	3.432	3.847	4.303	4.802	5.346	5.936	6.574	7.261
9	3.630	4.102	4.626	5.204	5.839	6.533	7.290	8.111
10	3.813	4.341	4.931	5.589	6.315	7.116	7.994	8.955
12	4.144	4.780	5.501	6.315	7.227	8.244	9.374	10.62
14	4.438	5.177	6.026	6.994	8.092	9.331	10.72	12.27
16	4.704	5.541	6.514	7.635	8.920	10.38	12.04	13.91
18	4.946	5.879	6.972	8.245	9.716	11.41	13.33	15.52
20	5.171	6.195	7.407	8.828	10.48	12.40	14.61	17.13
25	5.668	6.909	8.404	10.19	12.31	14.80	17.71	21.10
30	6.097	7.540	9.305	11.45	14.02	17.09	20.73	25.00
35	6.478	8.109	10.13	12.72	15.64	19.29	23.67	28.86
40	6.821	8.631	10.90	13.72	17.19	21.43	26.54	32.68
45	7.134	9.114	11.62	14.77	18.68	23.50	29.37	36.47
50	7.422	9.565	12.31	15.78	20.12	25.51	32.14	40.22
60	7.941	10.39	13.57	17.67	22.87	29.41	37.57	47.65
70	8.401	11.13	14.74	19.43	25.47	33.17	42.87	54.99
80	8.814	11.82	15.82	21.09	27.96	36.80	48.05	62.25
90	9.191	12.45	16.83	22.67	30.35	40.32	53.14	69.45
100	9.539	13.03	17.79	24.18	32.65	43.75	58.14	76.59
120	10.16	14.11	19.57	27.02	37.05	50.39	67.93	90.71
140	10.72	15.08	21.20	29.67	41.22	56.78	77.46	104.7
160	11.21	15.97	22.72	32.17	45.20	62.95	86.80	118.5
180	11.67	16.79	24.14	34.54	49.03	68.95	95.96	132.1
200	12.09	17.55	25.48	36.80	52.72	74.79	105.0	145.7
250	13.01	19.28	28.56	42.08	61.47	88.83	126.9	179.2
300	13.81	20.81	31.34	46.94	69.66	102.2	148.2	212.2
350	14.51	22.18	33.89	51.48	77.43	115.1	169.0	244.8
400	15.14	23.44	36.26	55.75	84.85	127.6	189.3	277.0
450	15.72	24.60	38.48	59.80	91.97	139.7	209.2	309.0
500	16.26	25.68	40.58	63.68	98.85	151.5	228.8	340.6
600	17.21	27.67	44.47	70.97	112.0	174.2	267.1	403.3
700	18.06	29.45	48.04	77.77	124.4	196.1	304.5	465.3
800	18.82	31.09	51.36	84.18	136.3	217.3	341.0	526.5
900	19.51	32.60	54.46	90.26	147.7	237.9	376.9	587.2
1,000	20.15	34.01	57.40	96.07	158.7	257.9	412.2	647.4
1,200	21.30	36.59	62.85	107.0	179.7	296.6	481.2	766.6
1,400	22.32	38.92	67.85	117.2	199.6	333.9	548.4	884.2
1,600	23.23	41.04	72.49	126.8	218.6	369.9	614.2	1001.0
1,800	24.06	43.00	76.85	135.9	236.8	404.9	678.8	1116.0
2,000	24.83	44.84	80.96	144.7	254.4	438.9	742.3	1230.0

AREAS UNDER THE
STANDARD NORMAL CURVE

FROM −∞ TO −z

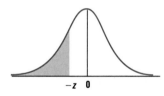

.09	.08	.07	.06	.05	.04	.03	.02	.01	.00	z
.0002	.0003	.0003	.0003	.0003	.0003	.0003	.0003	.0003	.0003	−3.4
.0003	.0004	.0004	.0004	.0004	.0004	.0004	.0005	.0005	.0005	−3.3
.0005	.0005	.0005	.0006	.0006	.0006	.0006	.0006	.0007	.0007	−3.2
.0007	.0007	.0008	.0008	.0008	.0008	.0009	.0009	.0009	.0010	−3.1
.0010	.0010	.0011	.0011	.0011	.0012	.0012	.0013	.0013	.0013	−3.0
.0014	.0014	.0015	.0015	.0016	.0016	.0017	.0018	.0018	.0019	−2.9
.0019	.0020	.0021	.0021	.0022	.0023	.0023	.0024	.0025	.0026	−2.8
.0026	.0027	.0028	.0029	.0030	.0031	.0032	.0033	.0034	.0035	−2.7
.0036	.0037	.0038	.0039	.0040	.0041	.0043	.0044	.0045	.0047	−2.6
.0048	.0049	.0051	.0052	.0054	.0055	.0057	.0059	.0060	.0062	−2.5
.0064	.0066	.0068	.0069	.0071	.0073	.0075	.0078	.0080	.0082	−2.4
.0084	.0087	.0089	.0091	.0094	.0096	.0099	.0102	.0104	.0107	−2.3
.0110	.0113	.0116	.0119	.0122	.0125	.0129	.0132	.0136	.0139	−2.2
.0143	.0146	.0150	.0154	.0158	.0162	.0166	.0170	.0174	.0179	−2.1
.0183	.0188	.0192	.0197	.0202	.0207	.0212	.0217	.0222	.0228	−2.0
.0233	.0239	.0244	.0250	.0256	.0262	.0268	.0274	.0281	.0287	−1.9
.0294	.0301	.0307	.0314	.0322	.0329	.0336	.0344	.0351	.0359	−1.8
.0367	.0375	.0384	.0392	.0401	.0409	.0418	.0427	.0436	.0446	−1.7
.0455	.0465	.0475	.0485	.0495	.0505	.0516	.0526	.0537	.0548	−1.6
.0559	.0571	.0582	.0594	.0606	.0618	.0630	.0643	.0655	.0668	−1.5
.0681	.0694	.0708	.0721	.0735	.0749	.0764	.0778	.0793	.0808	−1.4
.0823	.0838	.0853	.0869	.0885	.0901	.0918	.0934	.0951	.0968	−1.3
.0985	.1003	.1020	.1038	.1056	.1075	.1093	.1112	.1131	.1151	−1.2
.1170	.1190	.1210	.1230	.1251	.1271	.1292	.1314	.1335	.1357	−1.1
.1379	.1401	.1423	.1446	.1469	.1492	.1515	.1539	.1562	.1587	−1.0
.1611	.1635	.1660	.1685	.1711	.1736	.1762	.1788	.1814	.1841	−0.9
.1867	.1894	.1922	.1949	.1977	.2005	.2033	.2061	.2090	.2119	−0.8
.2148	.2177	.2206	.2236	.2266	.2296	.2327	.2358	.2389	.2420	−0.7
.2451	.2483	.2514	.2546	.2578	.2611	.2643	.2676	.2709	.2743	−0.6
.2776	.2810	.2843	.2877	.2912	.2946	.2981	.3015	.3050	.3085	−0.5
.3121	.3156	.3192	.3228	.3264	.3300	.3336	.3372	.3409	.3446	−0.4
.3483	.3520	.3557	.3594	.3632	.3669	.3707	.3745	.3783	.3821	−0.3
.3859	.3897	.3936	.3974	.4013	.4052	.4090	.4129	.4168	.4207	−0.2
.4247	.4286	.4325	.4364	.4404	.4443	.4483	.4522	.4562	.4602	−0.1
.4641	.4681	.4721	.4761	.4801	.4840	.4880	.4920	.4960	.5000	−0.0

FROM −∞ TO +z

z	.00	.01	.02	.03	.04	.05	.06	.07	.08	.09
.0	.5000	.5040	.5080	.5120	.5160	.5199	.5239	.5279	.5319	.5359
.1	.5398	.5438	.5478	.5517	.5557	.5596	.5636	.5675	.5714	.5753
.2	.5793	.5832	.5871	.5910	.5948	.5987	.6026	.6064	.6103	.6141
.3	.6179	.6217	.6255	.6293	.6331	.6368	.6406	.6443	.6480	.6517
.4	.6554	.6591	.6628	.6664	.6700	.6736	.6772	.6808	.6844	.6879
.5	.6915	.6950	.6985	.7019	.7054	.7088	.7123	.7157	.7190	.7224
.6	.7257	.7291	.7324	.7357	.7389	.7422	.7454	.7486	.7517	.7549
.7	.7580	.7611	.7642	.7673	.7703	.7734	.7764	.7794	.7823	.7852
.8	.7881	.7910	.7939	.7967	.7995	.8023	.8051	.8078	.8106	.8133
.9	.8159	.8186	.8212	.8238	.8264	.8289	.8315	.8340	.8365	.8389
1.0	.8413	.8438	.8461	.8485	.8508	.8531	.8554	.8577	.8599	.8621
1.2	.8643	.8665	.8686	.8708	.8729	.8749	.8770	.8790	.8810	.8830
1.2	.8849	.8869	.8888	.8907	.8925	.8944	.8962	.8980	.8997	.9015
1.3	.9032	.9049	.9066	.9082	.9099	.9115	.9131	.9147	.9162	.9177
1.4	.9192	.9207	.9222	.9236	.9251	.9265	.9279	.9292	.9306	.9319
1.5	.9332	.9345	.9357	.9370	.9382	.9394	.9406	.9418	.9429	.9441
1.6	.9452	.9463	.9474	.9484	.9495	.9505	.9515	.9525	.9535	.9545
1.7	.9554	.9564	.9573	.9582	.9591	.9599	.9608	.9616	.9625	.9633
1.8	.9641	.9649	.9656	.9664	.9671	.9678	.9686	.9693	.9699	.9706
1.9	.9713	.9719	.9726	.9732	.9738	.9744	.9750	.9756	.9761	.9767
2.0	.9772	.9778	.9783	.9788	.9793	.9798	.9803	.9808	.9812	.9817
2.1	.9821	.9826	.9830	.9834	.9838	.9842	.9846	.9850	.9854	.9857
2.2	.9861	.9864	.9868	.9871	.9875	.9878	.9881	.9884	.9887	.9890
2.3	.9893	.9896	.9898	.9901	.9904	.9906	.9909	.9911	.9913	.9916
2.4	.9918	.9920	.9922	.9925	.9927	.9929	.9931	.9932	.9934	.9936
2.5	.9938	.9940	.9941	.9943	.9945	.9946	.9948	.9949	.9951	.9952
2.6	.9953	.9955	.9956	.9957	.9959	.9960	.9961	.9962	.9963	.9964
2.7	.9965	.9966	.9967	.9968	.9969	.9970	.9971	.9972	.9973	.9974
2.8	.9974	.9975	.9976	.9977	.9977	.9978	.9979	.9979	.9980	.9981
2.9	.9981	.9982	.9982	.9983	.9984	.9984	.9985	.9985	.9986	.9986
3.0	.9987	.9987	.9987	.9988	.9988	.9989	.9989	.9989	.9990	.9990
3.1	.9990	.9991	.9991	.9991	.9991	.9992	.9992	.9992	.9993	.9993
3.2	.9993	.9993	.9994	.9994	.9994	.9994	.9994	.9995	.9995	.9995
3.3	.9995	.9995	.9995	.9996	.9996	.9996	.9996	.9996	.9996	.9997
3.4	.9997	.9997	.9997	.9997	.9997	.9997	.9997	.9997	.9997	.9998

PRESENT-VALUE
INTEREST FACTORS
OF AN ANNUITY

PRESENT-VALUE INTEREST FACTOR OF AN ANNUITY EQUATION

$$\text{PVIFA}_{i,n} = \sum_{j=1}^{n} \frac{1}{(1+i)^j}$$

where $\text{PVIFA}_{i,n}$ = present-value interest factor for an annuity of \$1
for n periods at i percent

Year	1%	2%	3%	4%	5%	6%	7%	8%	9%	10%
1	.990	.980	.971	.962	.952	.943	.935	.926	.917	.909
2	1.970	1.942	1.913	1.886	1.859	1.833	1.808	1.783	1.759	1.736
3	2.941	2.884	2.829	2.775	2.723	2.673	2.624	2.577	2.531	2.487
4	3.902	3.808	3.717	3.630	3.546	3.465	3.387	3.312	3.240	3.170
5	4.853	4.713	4.580	4.452	4.329	4.212	4.100	3.993	3.890	3.791
6	5.795	5,601	5.417	5.242	5.076	4.917	4.767	4.623	4.486	4.355
7	6.728	6.472	6.230	6.002	5.786	5.582	5.389	5.206	5.033	4.868
8	7.652	7.326	7.020	6.733	6.463	6.210	5.971	5.747	5.535	5.335
9	8.566	8.162	7.786	7.435	7.108	6.802	6.515	6.247	5.995	5.759
10	9.471	8.983	8.530	8.111	7.722	7.360	7.024	6.710	6.418	6.145
11	10.368	9.787	9.253	8.760	8.306	7.887	7.499	7.139	6.805	6.495
12	11.255	10.575	9.954	9.385	8.863	8.384	7.943	7.536	7.161	6.814
13	12.134	11.348	10.635	9.986	9.394	8.853	8.358	7.904	7.487	7.103
14	13.004	12.106	11.296	10.563	9.899	9.295	8.746	8.244	7.786	7.367
15	13.865	12.849	11.938	11.118	10.380	9.712	9.108	8.560	8.061	7.606
16	14.718	13.578	12.561	11.652	10.838	10.106	9.447	8.851	8.313	7.824
17	15.562	14.292	13.166	12.166	11.274	10.477	9.763	9.122	8.544	8.022
18	16.398	14.992	13.754	12.659	11.690	10.828	10.059	9.372	8.756	8.201
19	17.226	15.679	14.324	13.134	12.085	11.158	10.336	9.604	8.950	8.365
20	18.046	16.352	14.878	13.590	12.462	11.470	10.594	9.818	9.129	8.514
21	18.857	17.011	15.415	14.029	12.821	11.764	10.836	10.017	9.292	8.649
22	19.661	17.658	15.937	14.451	13.163	12.042	11.061	10.201	9.442	8.772
23	20.456	18.292	16.444	14.857	13.489	12.303	11.272	10.371	9.580	8.883
24	21.244	18.914	16.936	15.247	13.799	12.550	11.469	10.529	9.707	8.985
25	22.023	19.524	17.413	15.622	14.094	12.783	11.654	10.675	9.823	9.077
30	25.808	22.397	19.601	17.292	15.373	13.765	12.409	11.258	10.274	9.427
35	29.409	24.999	21.487	18.665	16.374	14.498	12.948	11.655	10.567	9.644
40	32.835	27.356	23.115	19.793	17.159	15.046	13.332	11.925	10.757	9.779
45	36.095	29.490	24.519	20.720	17.774	15.456	13.606	12.108	10.881	9.863
50	39.197	31.424	25.730	21.482	18.256	15.762	13.801	12.234	10.962	9.915

PRESENT-VALUE INTEREST FACTORS FOR A ONE-DOLLAR ANNUTITY, PVIFA *(continued)*

Year	11%	12%	13%	14%	15%	16%	17%	18%	19%	20%
1	.901	.893	.885	.877	.870	.862	.855	.847	.840	.833
2	1.713	1.690	1.668	1.647	1.626	1.605	1.585	1.566	1.547	1.528
2	2.444	2.402	2.361	2.322	2.283	2.246	2.210	2.174	2.140	2.106
4	3.102	3.037	2.974	2.914	2.855	2.798	2.743	2.690	2.639	2.589
5	3.696	3.605	3.517	3.433	3.352	3.274	3.199	3.127	3.058	2.991
6	4.231	4.111	3.998	3.889	3.784	3.685	3.589	3.498	3.410	3.326
7	4.712	4.564	4.423	4.288	4.160	4.039	3.922	3.812	3.706	3.605
8	5.146	4.968	4.799	4.639	4.487	4.344	4.207	4.078	3.954	3.837
9	5.537	5.328	5.132	4.946	4.772	4.607	4.451	4,303	4.163	4.031
10	5.889	5.650	5.426	5.216	5.019	4.833	4.659	4.494	4.339	4.192
11	6.207	5.938	5.687	5.453	5.234	5.029	4.836	4.656	4.487	4.327
12	6.492	6.194	5.918	5.660	5.421	5.197	4.988	4.793	4.611	4.439
13	6.750	6.424	6.122	5.842	5.583	5.342	5.118	4.910	4.715	4.533
14	6.982	6.628	6.303	6.002	5.724	5.468	5.229	5.008	4.802	4.611
15	7.191	6.811	6.462	6.142	5.847	5.575	5.324	5.092	4.876	4.675
16	7.379	6.974	6.604	6.265	5.954	5.669	5.405	5.162	4.938	4.730
17	7.549	7.120	6.729	6.373	6.047	5.749	5.475	5.222	4.990	4.775
18	7.702	7.250	6.840	6.467	6.128	5.818	5.534	5.273	5.033	4.812
19	7.839	7.366	6.938	6.550	6.198	5.877	5.585	5.316	5.070	4.843
20	7.963	7.469	7.025	6.623	6.259	5.929	5.628	5.353	5.101	4.870
21	8.075	7.562	7.102	6.687	6.312	5.973	5.665	5.384	5.127	4.891
22	8.176	7.645	7.170	6.743	6.359	6.011	5.696	5.410	5.149	4.909
23	8.266	7.718	7.230	6.792	6.399	6.044	5.723	5.432	5.167	4.925
24	8.348	7.784	7.283	6.835	6.434	6.073	5.747	5.251	5.182	4.937
25	8.422	7.843	7.330	6.873	6.464	6.097	5.766	5.467	5.195	4.948
30	8.694	8.055	7.496	7.003	6.566	6.177	5.829	5.517	5.235	4.979
35	8.855	8.176	7.586	7.070	6.617	6.215	5.858	5.539	5.251	4.992
40	8.951	8.244	7.634	7.105	6.642	6.233	5.871	5.548	5.258	4.997
45	9.008	8.283	7.661	7.123	6.654	6.242	5.877	5.552	5.261	4.999
50	9.042	8.305	7.675	7.133	6.661	6.246	5.880	5.554	5.262	4.999

CUMULATIVE POISSON PROBABILITIES

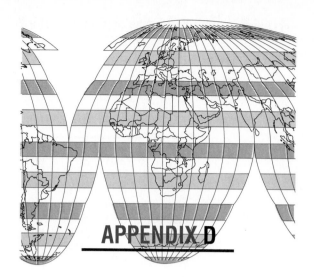

CUMULATIVE POISSON PROBABILITY EQUATION

$$P(x \le c) = \sum_{x=0}^{c} \frac{\mu^x e^{-\mu}}{x!}$$

The following table gives the value of $P(x \le c)$ for various values of μ.

CUMULATIVE POISSON PROBABILITIES

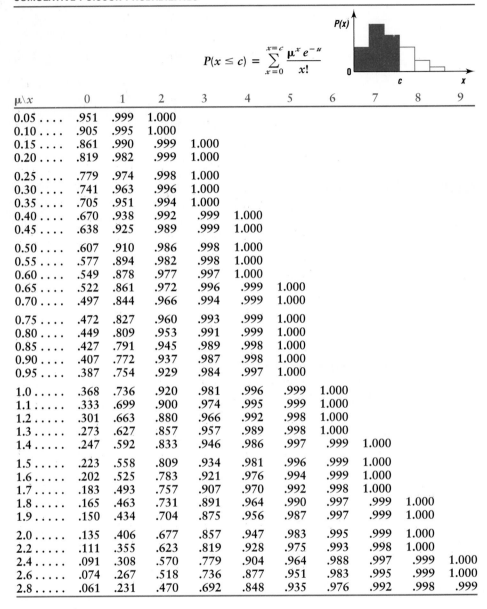

$$P(x \le c) = \sum_{x=0}^{x=c} \frac{\mu^x e^{-\mu}}{x!}$$

μ\x	0	1	2	3	4	5	6	7	8	9
0.05	.951	.999	1.000							
0.10	.905	.995	1.000							
0.15	.861	.990	.999	1.000						
0.20	.819	.982	.999	1.000						
0.25	.779	.974	.998	1.000						
0.30	.741	.963	.996	1.000						
0.35	.705	.951	.994	1.000						
0.40	.670	.938	.992	.999	1.000					
0.45	.638	.925	.989	.999	1.000					
0.50	.607	.910	.986	.998	1.000					
0.55	.577	.894	.982	.998	1.000					
0.60	.549	.878	.977	.997	1.000					
0.65	.522	.861	.972	.996	.999	1.000				
0.70	.497	.844	.966	.994	.999	1.000				
0.75	.472	.827	.960	.993	.999	1.000				
0.80	.449	.809	.953	.991	.999	1.000				
0.85	.427	.791	.945	.989	.998	1.000				
0.90	.407	.772	.937	.987	.998	1.000				
0.95	.387	.754	.929	.984	.997	1.000				
1.0	.368	.736	.920	.981	.996	.999	1.000			
1.1	.333	.699	.900	.974	.995	.999	1.000			
1.2	.301	.663	.880	.966	.992	.998	1.000			
1.3	.273	.627	.857	.957	.989	.998	1.000			
1.4	.247	.592	.833	.946	.986	.997	.999	1.000		
1.5	.223	.558	.809	.934	.981	.996	.999	1.000		
1.6	.202	.525	.783	.921	.976	.994	.999	1.000		
1.7	.183	.493	.757	.907	.970	.992	.998	1.000		
1.8	.165	.463	.731	.891	.964	.990	.997	.999	1.000	
1.9	.150	.434	.704	.875	.956	.987	.997	.999	1.000	
2.0	.135	.406	.677	.857	.947	.983	.995	.999	1.000	
2.2	.111	.355	.623	.819	.928	.975	.993	.998	1.000	
2.4	.091	.308	.570	.779	.904	.964	.988	.997	.999	1.000
2.6	.074	.267	.518	.736	.877	.951	.983	.995	.999	1.000
2.8	.061	.231	.470	.692	.848	.935	.976	.992	.998	.999

CUMULATIVE POISSON PROBABILITIES (*continued*)

μ\x	0	1	2	3	4	5	6	7	8	9	10	11	12	13	14	15	16	17	18	19	20
3.0	.050	.199	.423	.647	.815	.916	.966	.988	.996	.999	1.000										
3.2	.041	.171	.380	.603	.781	.895	.955	.983	.994	.998	1.000										
3.4	.033	.147	.340	.558	.744	.871	.942	.977	.992	.997	.999	1.000									
3.6	.027	.126	.303	.515	.706	.844	.927	.969	.988	.996	.999	1.000									
3.8	.022	.107	.269	.474	.668	.816	.909	.960	.984	.994	.998	.999	1.000								
4.0	.018	.092	.238	.433	.629	.785	.889	.949	.979	.992	.997	.999	1.000								
4.2	.015	.078	.210	.395	.590	.753	.868	.936	.972	.989	.996	.999	1.000								
4.4	.012	.066	.185	.359	.551	.720	.844	.921	.964	.985	.994	.998	.999	1.000							
4.6	.010	.056	.163	.326	.513	.686	.818	.905	.955	.980	.992	.997	.999	1.000							
4.8	.008	.048	.143	.294	.476	.651	.791	.887	.944	.975	.990	.996	.999	1.000							
5.0	.007	.040	.125	.265	.441	.616	.762	.867	.932	.968	.986	.995	.998	.999	1.000						
5.2	.006	.034	.109	.238	.406	.581	.732	.845	.918	.960	.982	.993	.997	.999	1.000						
5.4	.005	.029	.095	.213	.373	.546	.702	.822	.903	.951	.978	.990	.996	.999	1.000						
5.6	.004	.024	.082	.191	.342	.512	.670	.797	.886	.941	.972	.988	.995	.998	.999	1.000					
5.8	.003	.021	.072	.170	.313	.478	.638	.771	.867	.929	.965	.984	.993	.997	.999	1.000					
6.0	.003	.017	.062	.151	.285	.446	.606	.744	.847	.916	.957	.980	.991	.996	.999	.999	1.000				
6.2	.002	.015	.054	.134	.259	.414	.574	.716	.826	.902	.949	.975	.989	.995	.998	.999	1.000				
6.4	.002	.012	.046	.119	.235	.384	.542	.687	.803	.886	.939	.969	.986	.994	.997	.999	1.000				
6.6	.001	.010	.040	.105	.213	.355	.511	.658	.780	.869	.927	.963	.982	.992	.997	.999	.999	1.000			
6.8	.001	.007	.030	.082	.173	.301	.450	.599	.729	.830	.915	.955	.978	.990	.996	.998	.999	1.000			
7.0	.001	.007	.030	.082	.173	.301	.450	.599	.729	.830	.901	.947	.973	.987	.994	.998	.999	1.000			
7.2	.001	.006	.025	.072	.156	.276	.420	.569	.703	.810	.887	.937	.967	.984	.993	.997	.999	.999			
7.4	.001	.005	.022	.063	.140	.253	.392	.539	.676	.788	.871	.926	.961	.980	.991	.996	.998	.999	1.000		
7.6	.001	.004	.019	.055	.125	.231	.365	.510	.648	.765	.854	.915	.954	.976	.989	.995	.998	.999	1.000		
7.8	.000	.004	.016	.048	.112	.210	.338	.481	.620	.741	.835	.902	.945	.971	.986	.993	.997	.999	1.000		
8.0	.000	.003	.014	.042	.100	.191	.313	.453	.593	.717	.816	.888	.936	.966	.983	.992	.996	.998	.999	1.000	
8.2	.000	.003	.012	.037	.089	.174	.290	.425	.566	.692	.796	.873	.926	.960	.979	.990	.995	.998	.999	1.000	
8.4	.000	.002	.010	.032	.079	.157	.267	.400	.537	.666	.774	.857	.915	.952	.975	.987	.994	.997	.999	1.000	
8.6	.000	.002	.009	.030	.074	.150	.256	.386	.523	.653	.763	.849	.909	.949	.973	.986	.993	.997	.999	1.000	1.000
8.8	.000	.002	.007	.024	.062	.128	.226	.348	.482	.614	.729	.822	.889	.935	.964	.981	.990	.995	.998	.999	1.000
9.0	.000	.001	.006	.021	.055	.116	.207	.324	.456	.587	.706	.803	.876	.926	.959	.978	.989	.995	.998	.999	.999
9.5	.000	.001	.004	.015	.040	.089	.165	.269	.392	.522	.645	.752	.836	.898	.940	.967	.982	.991	.996	.998	.999

QUEUING MODELS: INFINITE-SOURCE VALUES FOR L_q AND P_0 GIVEN λ/μ AND M

APPENDIX E

INFINITE-SOURCE VALUES FOR L_q AND P_0 GIVEN λ/μ AND M

λ/μ	M	L_q	P_0	λ/μ	M	L_q	P_0	λ/μ	M	L_q	P_0
0.15	1	0.026	.850		3	0.019	.447	1.6	2	2.844	.111
	2	0.001	.860	0.85	1	4.817	.150		3	0.313	.187
0.20	1	0.050	.800		2	0.187	.404		4	0.060	.199
	2	0.002	.818		3	0.024	.425		5	0.012	.201
0.25	1	0.083	.750		4	0.003	.427	1.7	2	4.426	.081
	2	0.004	.778	0.90	1	8.100	.100		3	0.409	.166
0.30	1	0.129	.700		2	0.229	.379		4	0.080	.180
	2	0.007	.739		3	0.030	.403		5	0.017	.182
0.35	1	0.188	.650		4	0.004	.406	1.8	2	7.674	.053
	2	0.011	.702	0.95	1	18.050	.050		3	0.532	.146
0.40	1	0.267	.600		2	0.277	.356		4	0.105	.162
	2	0.017	.667		3	0.037	.383		5	0.023	.165
0.45	1	0.368	.550		4	0.005	.386	1.9	2	17.587	.026
	2	0.024	.633	1.0	2	0.333	.333		3	0.688	.128
	3	0.002	.637		3	0.045	.364		4	0.136	.145
0.50	1	0.500	.500		4	0.007	.367		5	0.030	.149
	2	0.033	.600	1.1	2	0.477	.290		6	0.007	.149
	3	0.003	.606		3	0.066	.327	2.0	3	0.889	.111
0.55	1	0.672	.450		4	0.011	.367		4	0.174	.130
	2	0.045	.569	1.2	2	0.675	.250		5	0.040	.134
	3	0.004	.576		3	0.094	.294		6	0.009	.135
0.60	1	0.900	.400		4	0.016	.300	2.1	3	1.149	.096
	2	0.059	.538		5	0.003	.301		4	0.220	.117
	3	0.006	.548	1.3	2	0.951	.212		5	0.052	.121
0.65	1	1.207	.350		3	0.130	.264		6	0.012	.122
	2	0.077	.509		4	0.023	.271	2.2	3	1.491	.081
	3	0.008	.521		5	0.004	.272		4	0.277	.105
0.70	1	1.633	.300	1.4	2	1.345	.176		5	0.066	.109
	2	0.098	.481		3	0.177	.236		6	0.016	.111
	3	0.011	.495		4	0.032	.245	2.3	3	1.951	.068
0.75	1	2.250	.250		5	0.006	.246		4	0.346	.093
	2	0.123	.455	1.5	2	1.929	.143		5	0.084	.099
	3	0.015	.471		3	0.237	.211		6	0.021	.100
0.80	1	3.200	.200		4	0.045	.221	2.4	3	2.589	.056
	2	0.152	.429		5	0.009	.223		4	0.431	.083

λ/μ	M	L_q	P_0	λ/μ	M	L_q	P_0	λ/μ	M	L_q	P_0
	5	0.105	.089		9	0.007	.030		10	0.015	.011
	6	0.027	.090	3.6	4	7.090	.011	4.6	5	9.289	.004
	7	0.007	.091		5	1.055	.023		6	1.487	.008
2.5	3	3.511	.045		6	0.295	.026		7	0.453	.009
	4	0.533	.074		7	0.091	.027		8	0.156	.010
	5	0.130	.080		8	0.028	.027		9	0.054	.010
	6	0.034	.082		9	0.008	.027		10	0.018	.010
	7	0.009	.082	3.7	4	10.347	.008	4.7	5	13.382	.003
2.6	3	4.933	.035		5	1.265	.020		6	1.752	.007
	4	0.658	.065		6	0.349	.023		7	0.525	.008
	5	0.161	.072		7	0.109	.024		8	0.181	.008
	6	0.043	.074		8	0.034	.025		9	0.064	.009
	7	0.011	.074		9	0.010	.025		10	0.022	.009
2.7	3	7.354	.025	3.8	4	16.947	.005	4.8	5	21.641	.002
	4	0.811	.057		5	1.519	.017		6	2.071	.006
	5	0.198	.065		6	0.412	.021		7	0.607	.008
	6	0.053	.067		7	0.129	.022		8	0.209	.008
	7	0.014	.067		8	0.041	.022		9	0.074	.008
2.8	3	12.273	.016		9	0.013	.022		10	0.026	.008
	4	1.000	.050	3.9	4	36.859	.002	4.9	5	46.566	.001
	5	0.241	.058		5	1.830	.015		6	2.459	.005
	6	0.066	.060		6	0.485	.019		7	0.702	.007
	7	0.018	.061		7	0.153	.020		8	0.242	.007
2.9	3	27.193	.008		8	0.050	.020		9	0.087	.007
	4	1.234	.044		9	0.016	.020		10	0.031	.007
	5	0.293	.052	4.0	5	2.216	.013		11	0.011	.007
	6	0.081	.054		6	0.570	.017	5.0	6	2.938	.005
	7	0.023	.055		7	0.180	.018		7	0.810	.006
3.0	4	1.528	.038		8	0.059	.018		8	0.279	.006
	5	0.354	.047		9	0.019	.018		9	0.101	.007
	6	0.099	.049	4.1	5	2.703	.011		10	0.036	.007
	7	0.028	.050		6	0.668	.015		11	0.013	.007
	8	0.008	.050		7	0.212	.016	5.1	6	3.536	.004
3.1	4	1.902	.032		8	0.070	.016		7	0.936	.005
	5	0.427	.042		9	0.023	.017		8	0.321	.006
	6	0.120	.044	4.2	5	3.327	.009		9	0.117	.006
	7	0.035	.045		6	0.784	.013		10	0.042	.006
	8	0.010	.045		7	0.248	.014		11	0.015	.006
3.2	4	2.386	.027		8	0.083	.015	5.2	6	4.301	.003
	5	0.513	.037		9	0.027	.015		7	1.081	.005
	6	0.145	.040		10	0.009	.015		8	0.368	.005
	7	0.043	.040	4.3	5	4.149	.008		9	0.135	.005
	8	0.012	.041		6	0.919	.012		10	0.049	.005
3.3	4	3.027	.023		7	0.289	.130		11	0.017	.006
	5	0.615	.033		8	0.097	.013	5.3	6	5.303	.003
	6	0.174	.036		9	0.033	.014		7	1.249	.004
	7	0.052	.037		10	0.011	.014		8	0.422	.005
	8	0.015	.037	4.4	5	5.268	.006		9	0.155	.005
3.4	4	3.906	.019		6	1.078	.010		10	0.057	.005
	5	0.737	.029		7	0.337	.012		11	0.021	.005
	6	0.209	.032		8	0.114	.012		12	0.007	.005
	7	0.063	.033		9	0.039	.012	5.4	6	6.661	.002
	8	0.019	.033		10	0.013	.012		7	1.444	.004
3.5	4	5.165	.015	4.5	5	6.862	.005		8	0.483	.004
	5	0.882	.026		6	1.265	.009		9	0.178	.004
	6	0.248	.029		7	0.391	.010		10	0.066	.004
	7	0.076	.030		8	0.133	.011		11	0.024	.005
	8	0.023	.030		9	0.046	.011		12	0.009	.005

λ/μ	M	L_q	P_0
5.5	6	8.590	.002
	7	1.674	.003
	8	0.553	.004
	9	0.204	.004
	10	0.077	.004
	11	0.028	.004
	12	0.010	.004
5.6	6	11.519	.001
	7	1.944	.003
	8	0.631	.003
	9	0.233	.004
	10	0.088	.004
	11	0.033	.004
	12	0.012	.004
5.7	6	16.446	.001
	7	2.264	.002
	8	0.721	.003
	9	0.266	.003
	10	0.102	.003
	11	0.038	.003
	12	0.014	.003
5.8	6	26.373	.001
	7	2.648	.002
	8	0.823	.003
	9	0.303	.003
	10	0.116	.003
	11	0.044	.003
	12	0.017	.003
5.9	6	56.300	.000
	7	3.113	.002
	8	0.939	.002
	9	0.345	.003
	10	0.133	.003
	11	0.051	.003
	12	0.019	.003
6.0	7	3.683	.001
	8	1.071	.002
	9	0.392	.002
	10	0.152	.002
	11	0.059	.002
	12	0.022	.002
6.1	7	4.394	.001
	8	1.222	.002
	9	0.445	.002
	10	0.173	.002
	11	0.068	.002
	12	0.026	.002
6.2	7	5.298	.001
	8	1.397	.002
	9	0.504	.002
	10	0.197	.002
	11	0.078	.002
	12	0.030	.002
6.3	7	6.480	.001
	8	1.598	.001
	9	0.571	.002
	10	0.223	.002
	11	0.089	.002
	12	0.035	.002
6.4	7	8.007	.001
	8	1.831	.001
	9	0.645	.002
	10	0.253	.002
	11	0.101	.002
	12	0.040	.002
6.5	7	10.341	.001
	8	2.102	.001
	9	0.730	.001
	10	0.285	.001
	11	0.115	.001
	12	0.046	.001
6.6	7	13.770	.000
	8	2.420	.001
	9	0.825	.001
	10	0.285	.001
	11	0.130	.001
	12	0.052	.001
6.7	7	19.532	.000
	8	2.796	.001
	9	0.932	.001
	10	0.363	.001
	11	0.147	.001
	12	0.060	.001
6.8	7	31.127	.000
	8	3.245	.001
	9	1.054	.001
	10	0.409	.001
	11	0.167	.001
	12	0.068	.001
6.9	7	66.055	.000
	8	3.786	.001
	9	1.191	.001
	10	0.460	.001
	11	0.188	.001
	12	0.077	.001
7.0	8	4.447	.001
	9	1.347	.001
	10	0.517	.001
	11	0.212	.001
	12	0.088	.001
7.1	8	5.270	.000
	9	1.525	.001
	10	0.581	.001
	11	0.238	.001
	12	0.099	.001
7.2	8	6.314	.000
	9	1.729	.001
	10	0.652	.001
	11	0.268	.001
	12	0.112	.001
7.3	8	7.675	.0003
	9	1.963	.0005
	10	0.732	.0006
	11	0.300	.0007
	12	0.126	.0007
7.4	8	9.511	.0003
	9	2.233	.0005
	10	0.820	.0006
	11	0.337	.0006
	12	0.142	.0006
7.5	8	12.109	.0002
	9	2.546	.0004
	10	0.920	.0005
	11	0.377	.0005
	12	0.160	.0005
7.6	8	16.039	.0002
	9	2.912	.0004
	10	1.031	.0004
	11	0.421	.0005
	12	0.179	.0005
7.7	8	22.636	.0001
	9	3.343	.0003
	10	1.157	.0004
	11	0.471	.0004
	12	0.201	.0004
7.8	8	35.898	.0001
	9	3.856	.0002
	10	1.298	.0004
	11	0.525	.0004
	12	0.224	.0004
7.9	8	75.827	.00003
	9	4.474	.00023
	10	1.457	.00031
	11	0.586	.00035
	12	0.251	.00036
8.0	9	5.227	.00020
	10	1.637	.00028
	11	0.653	.00031
	12	0.280	.00033
8.1	9	6.161	.00017
	10	1.841	.00025
	11	0.728	.00028
	12	0.312	.00029
8.2	9	7.344	.00014
	10	2.074	.00022
	11	0.811	.00025
	12	0.347	.00026
8.3	9	8.884	.00011
	10	2.341	.00019
	11	0.903	.00022
	12	0.386	.00024
8.4	9	10.960	.00009
	10	2.647	.00017
	11	1.006	.00020
	12	0.429	.00021
8.5	9	13.891	.00007
	10	3.003	.00015
	11	1.121	.00018
	12	0.476	.00019

TABLE OF
RANDOM NUMBERS

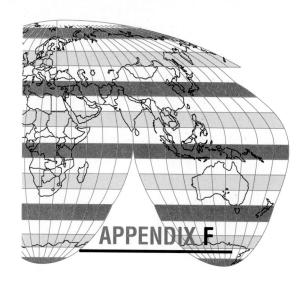

63271	59986	71744	51102	15141	80714	58683	93108	13554	79945
88547	09896	95436	79115	08303	01041	20030	63754	08459	28364
55957	57243	83865	09911	19761	66535	40102	26646	60147	15702
46276	87453	44790	67122	45573	84358	21625	16999	13385	22782
55363	07449	34835	15290	76616	67191	12777	21861	68689	03263
69393	92785	49902	58447	42048	30378	87618	26933	40640	16281
13186	29431	88190	04588	38733	81290	89541	70290	40113	08243
17726	28652	56836	78351	47327	18518	92222	55201	27340	10493
36520	64465	05550	30157	82242	29520	69753	72602	23756	54935
81628	36100	39254	56835	37636	02421	98063	89641	64953	99337
84649	48968	75215	75498	49539	74240	03466	49292	36401	45525
63291	11618	12613	75055	43915	26488	41116	64531	56827	30825
70502	53225	03655	05915	37140	57051	48393	91322	25653	06543
06426	24771	59935	49801	11082	66762	94477	02494	88215	27191
20711	55609	29430	70165	45406	78484	31639	52009	18873	96927
41990	70538	77191	25860	55204	73417	83920	69468	74972	38712
72452	36618	76298	26678	89334	33938	95567	29380	75906	91807
37042	40318	57099	10528	09925	89773	41335	96244	29002	46453
53766	52875	15987	46962	67342	77592	57651	95508	80033	69828
90585	58955	53122	16025	84299	53310	67380	84249	25348	04332
32001	96293	37203	64516	51530	37069	40261	61374	05815	06714
62606	64324	46354	72157	67248	20135	49804	09226	64419	29457
10078	28073	85389	50324	14500	15562	64165	06125	71353	77669
91561	46145	24177	15294	10061	98124	75732	00815	83452	97355
13091	98112	53959	79607	52244	63303	10413	63839	74762	50289
73864	83014	72457	22682	03033	61714	88173	90835	00634	85169
66668	25467	48894	51043	02365	91726	09365	63167	95264	45643
84745	41042	29493	01836	09044	51926	43630	63470	76508	14194
48068	26805	94595	47907	13357	38412	33318	26098	82782	42851
54310	96175	97594	88616	42035	38093	36745	56702	40644	83514
14877	33095	10924	58013	61439	21882	42059	24177	58739	60170
78295	23179	02771	43464	59061	71411	05697	67194	30495	21157
67524	02865	39593	54278	04237	92441	26602	63835	38032	94770
58268	57219	68124	73455	83236	08710	04284	55005	84171	42596
97158	28672	50685	01181	24262	19427	52106	34308	73685	74246
04230	16831	69085	30802	65559	09205	71829	06489	85650	38707
94879	56606	30401	02602	57658	70091	54986	41394	60437	03195
71446	15232	66715	26385	91518	70566	02888	79941	39684	54315
32886	05644	79316	09819	00813	88407	17461	73925	53037	91904
62048	33711	25290	21526	02223	75947	66466	06232	10913	75336

This table is reproduced with permission from The Rand Corporation, *A Million Random Digits*, The Free Press, New York, 1955.

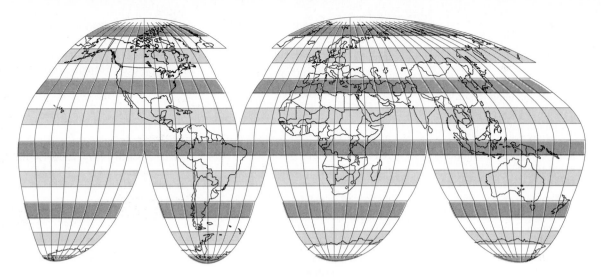

INDEX